Cadventure
The Building C....,
26 Store Street, London WC1E 7BT
Tel: 020 7436 9004
Fax: 020 7323 9764
Web: www.cadventure.co.uk
Email: sales@cadventure.co.uk

MicroStation 2D By Examples

2nd Edition

Noel Addison

First Edition September 1996

Second Edition April 1999

Copyright © 1996, 1999 Pen and Brush Publishers

Published by:

Pen and Brush Publishers.

P.O. Box 808,

Hawthorn, Victoria 3122.

Australia.

Fax: (03) 9818 3704. International 61 3 9818 3704.

E-mail: penbrush@ozemail.com.au

ISBN 0-646-37095-2

Published & printed in Australia.

For Marijke

Acknowledgments

This is book number four for Khoi Dinh-Vu and Pen & Brush Publishers. While this is a second edition of an established title, in practice only the outline and the example models remain intact from the first. New functionality has been added to the software since the first edition was written, so this book is larger. In short, the publisher had to accept a new book when only an update was expected. Thanks, Khoi, for the commitment of the extra time to allow for this project.

Producing a technical book on new software is always a daunting task, one I could not have even considered without the backing of my wife. Marijke has accepted very graciously the down side of living with an author. My extreme degree of focus, the long hours at the computer, the scattered books and paper were all accepted with very little complaint.

Many thanks Andrew Novinc of Reality Bytes for his imaginative work of art on the cover. He based this on my Alloy wheel model created as an example in the companion to this book, *"MicroStation 3D by Examples"* (Now also in its second edition).

Finally, my thanks to Bentley Systems, especially to the staff at the Asia Pacific headquarters. Their support and encouragement has made my task much easier.

Noel Addison

About the Author

Noel lives in Hobart, Australia. He has many years of experience as a professional trainer, training administrator and technical author. In recent years he has concentrated solely on the application of Bentley's MicroStation based products. He provides documentation, training consultation and conducts courses at all levels. His leisure interests include racing and cruising the family yacht (which he designed himself and built with his family's help), listening to jazz and classical music, walking and mountain bike riding.

Introduction

The computer power available on the desktop continues to increase, almost by the day. Software developers continue to develop their applications to keep pace with the hardware. One of the effects of this spiral is the availability of very sophisticated Computer Aided Design software to the design industry as a whole, not just the "high tech" end.

MicroStation is a prime example of software that has increased its capability and speed over the years, while every version becomes easier to learn and to use. The user interface is improved with every version of MicroStation, with "J" having the best one so far.

Bentley's policy of continuous improvement to the software means that there are no huge steps to take when an update occurs. Since this is combined with a stability in file format and basic operation, this book will still be relevant after many updates.

Little prior knowledge is required to understand the terms and techniques used in this book. It is assumed that you have know enough about your computer and operating system to start a program, but little more is demanded. No prior Computer Aided Design experience is necessary.

MicroStation 2D By Examples is written specifically for MicroStation J and its successors, running on any platform. Much of the content also applies to MicroStation PowerDraft.

After studying this book and completing the exercises, the next step is into the "Real world" of 3D CAD. *MicroStation 3D By Examples* (by the same author) will take you there.

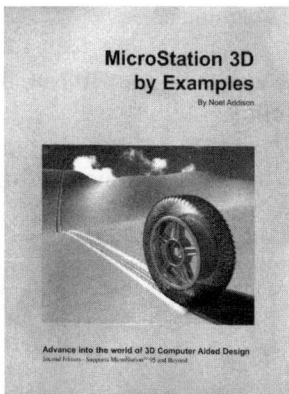

How to Use This Book

It is written primarily as a self-teaching tool and as a training course resource text book. When used as a student resource in training courses, the book provides a set of fully documented practical examples as well as the background theory. It can be used for self-paced instruction and private study, or in structured training activities.

For those readers starting out with MicroStation, it is suggested that you work through the book from front to back. Each chapter builds on the previous one, with practical exercises designed to complement and reinforce new concepts as they are introduced. For more experienced readers, each chapter can stand alone to complement any previous experience or knowledge you may already have. A comprehensive cross referenced Index is available at the back of the book.

The exercises are structured introductions to the available tools and features. Each one is designed to be as specific as practicable to the subject being introduced. The reader is encouraged to go beyond these exercises and invent some of their own, perhaps related to a particular work area or project. This will especially be the case later on in the book, where the skills and knowledge gained earlier can be related to the outside world.

Remember, with every step of the exercises, **Read The Prompts in the Status bar!**

Note: Work created in early exercises is frequently built upon in later chapters, thus it is necessary to retain your designs in the condition they are in after the last exercise step.

Terminology and Formats Used

Terminology used in this book is consistent with that generally used in computer software documentation. A couple of conventions to keep in mind are:

Keyboard keys, key combinations and key-mouse button combinations will be **bold** and in angle brackets, e.g. **<Enter>**, **<Ctrl+E>**, **<Ctrl+click>**.

Settings>Level>Display means "choose *Display* from the *Level* sub-menu of the *Settings* menu.

Exercises

Wherever possible, diagrams are used to enhance textural information. Where possible, diagrams will be numbered. This will provide a second source of information and a means of checking your progressive results while you are working at your computer. It will also allow some study away from the computer, following the exercise graphically without the benefit of a screen.

Where the numbers relate to steps of an exercise, they are shown in **bold**, followed by a dot; e.g. **1.**, **2.**, **3.**

Where a sequence of actions are indicated in an illustration that do not relate to exercise steps, they will be **bold** and sometimes in parenthesis, but without the dot; e.g. **1**, **2**, **3** or **(1)**, **(2)**, **(3)**.

User Interface

We have assumed your graphical input device to be a mouse and that tool selection etc. will be from the screen. A digitizer cursor may substitute for a mouse, but no digitizer "paper" menus are referred to. Icon "tools" and menu selections have been used in all examples. Key-in commands are introduced, but seldom needed in any of the examples.

Pen and Brush Publishers.

P.O. Box 808,

Hawthorn, Victoria 3122.

Australia.

Fax: (03) 9818 3704. International 61 3 9818 3704.

E-mail: penbrush@ozemail.com.au

\<This page has been intentionally left blank\>

Table of Contents

1 : MicroStation J Environment

2 : MicroStation Basics

3 : Creating a Design

4 : Manipulation and Grouping

5 : Beyond The Basics

6 : Cells

7 : Areas

8 : Adding Text

9 : Dimensioning a Design

10 : Reference Files

11 : Increasing Efficiency

12 : From Design Files to Documents

12 : From Design Files to Documents

1 : MicroStation J Environment

MicroStation J and PowerDraft have a similar look and feel to "Microsoft Office", sharing a similar set of operation standards with many Windows based applications. MicroStation retains this same look and feel even when it is operating on a system other than Windows, thus ensuring standardization. The two MicroStation products are very similar, thus most of this chapter (and this book) applies to both. The start-up procedure is a little different, as would be expected, so there will be a couple of pages that only apply to MicroStation J.

We will refer to the Graphical User Interface for both products as "the MicroStation J Interface", as it is essentially the same for both. You will be familiar with the basic concepts of this User Interface by the time you have completed this chapter. We will be using only one example design throughout the chapter, one supplied with MicroStation as a *"Design File"*. You will be helped to *Open* this file the first time it is used, from then on it is assumed to have already been opened for each exercise.

Only the primary mouse button will be used in this chapter, where it will be referred to as the *Data Button,* the MicroStation terminology.

When you have completed this chapter, you will be able to:

- Start MicroStation;
- Identify the components of the *MicroStation Application Window*;
- Use the windowing controls to view a design;
- Open, close and arrange view windows.
- Identify and Manipulate Tool boxes, Tool Frames and Tool bars.

Starting MicroStation

For the purposes of this book, we have assumed that MicroStation is already installed on your system. The *tutorial* Workspace option needs to be available for the first exercises. This requires the *Visualization and Learning Tutorials* box to be checked (in the Workspace Options dialog) when MicroStation J is installed.

◆ **To start MicroStation**

   1. For the Windows version, double-click the **MicroStation** icon, or click **MicroStation J** via the **Start** button and the **MicroStation_J** program group.
   The *MicroStation Manager* dialog box opens (See Figure 1.1).

The MicroStation Manager Dialog Box

The MicroStation Manager dialog box provides file management tools, disk and directory navigation facilities, including very useful history facilities for both files and directories. It allows us to configure the way MicroStation "looks and acts" with the selection of particular "Workspace" components.

We can open a file as "Read Only", thus we can be certain we will not make any unintended permanent changes to the file. Most importantly, it is where we select the existing *design file* we intend to work with, or create a new one.

Changing Workspaces

We will work through the large range of facilities offered by the MicroStation Manager dialog box as we progress through the book, but for now we will use a couple of basic choices only. We will start as a "Tutorials User", using the "Newuser" Interface, the most basic of the user interfaces. We will study *workspaces* in more detail later, see chapter 10. The Style option menu does not need to be changed from the default *Status Bar*, this is the standard Microsoft Office® style.

◆ **Change Workspaces**

   1. Click the User option menu.

   2. Click the *tutorials* option.

   3. Click the Interface option menu.

   4. Click the *newuser* option.

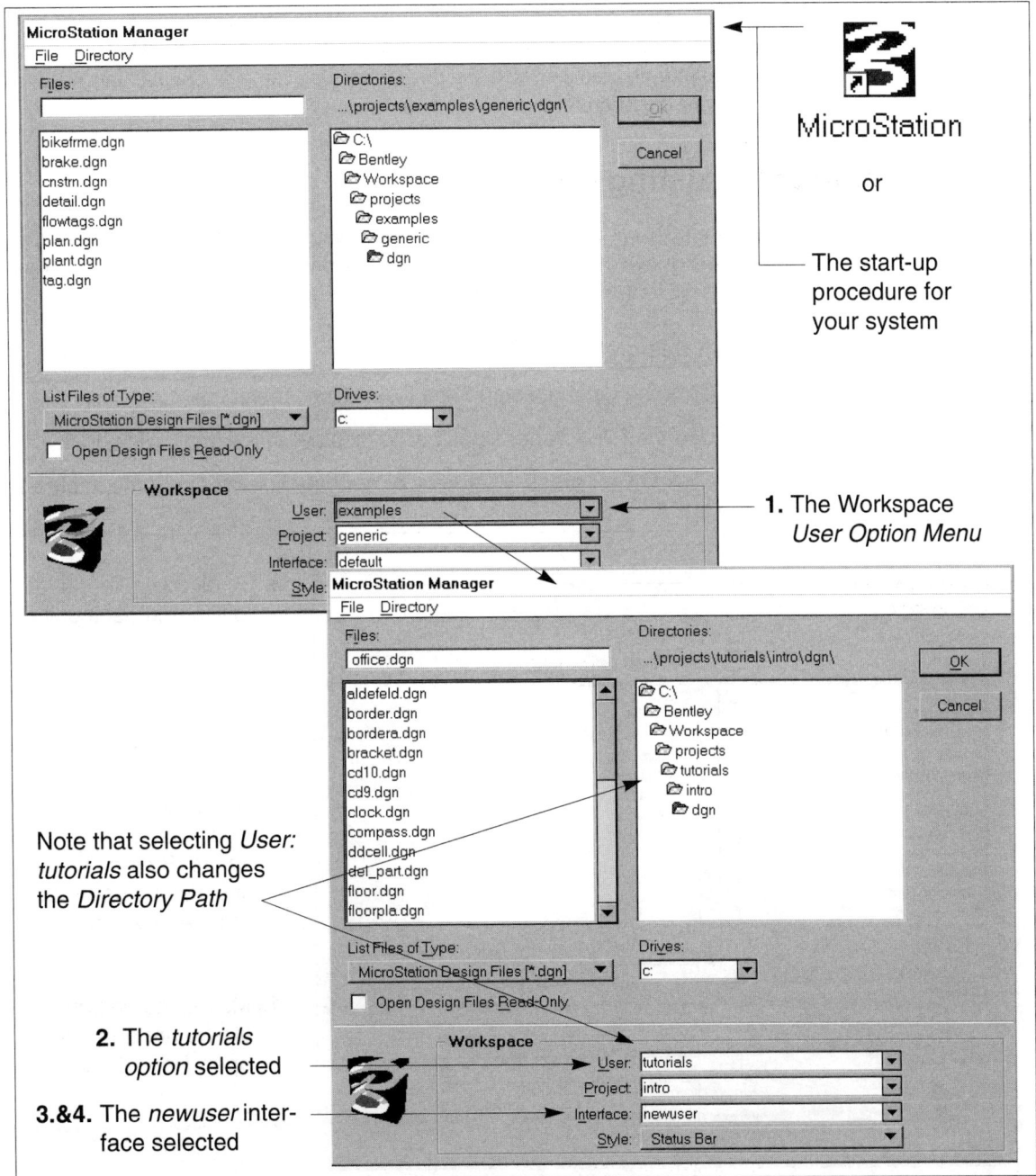

Figure 1.1 *MicroStation Manager - selecting a Workspace*

Choosing the "tutorials" User workspace component option automatically selects the "intro" Project component. This means we will be "pointed to" a directory to find (and create) our Design Files. The directory now displayed in the Directories panel of MicroStation Manager will be the ...projects\examples\tutorials\intro\dgn sub-directory of the MicroStation Workspace directory.

Opening an Existing Design File

The design file we are about to open is an example file provided with the software called "office.dgn". We will be viewing the file only at this stage. We do not want to add anything to it, so we will open it as *Read-Only*.

◆ **Open Design File "office.dgn"**

1. Click the Open Design Files Read-Only check box.

2. Use the Files Panel scroll bar to display "office.dgn", click on it.

3. Click OK, or press <Return>, or double-click the file name in step **2**

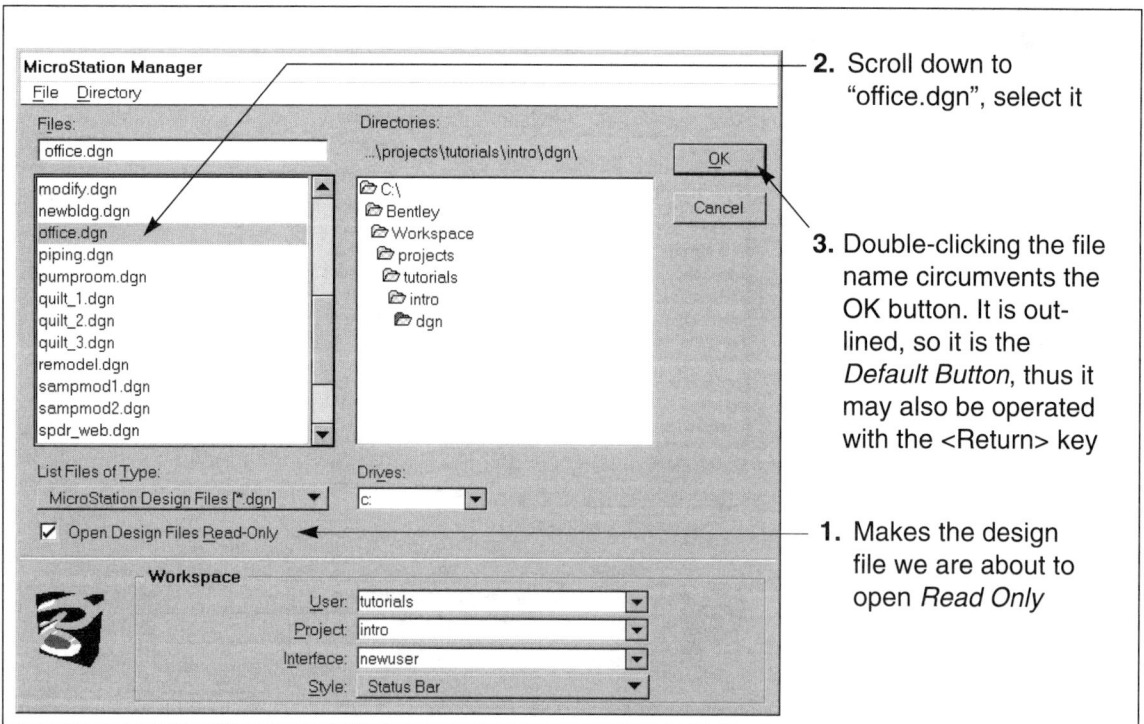

MicroStation Manager

File   Directory

Files:
office.dgn

modify.dgn
newbldg.dgn
office.dgn
piping.dgn
pumproom.dgn
quilt_1.dgn
quilt_2.dgn
quilt_3.dgn
remodel.dgn
sampmod1.dgn
sampmod2.dgn
spdr_web.dgn

Directories:
...\projects\tutorials\intro\dgn\

C:\
Bentley
Workspace
projects
tutorials
intro
dgn

[OK]
[Cancel]

List Files of Type:
MicroStation Design Files [*.dgn]

Drives:
c:

☑ Open Design Files Read-Only

Workspace

User: tutorials
Project: intro
Interface: newuser
Style: Status Bar

2. Scroll down to "office.dgn", select it

3. Double-clicking the file name circumvents the OK button. It is out-lined, so it is the *Default Button*, thus it may also be operated with the <Return> key

1. Makes the design file we are about to open *Read Only*

Figure 1.2 MicroStation Manager - selecting the example file "office.dgn"

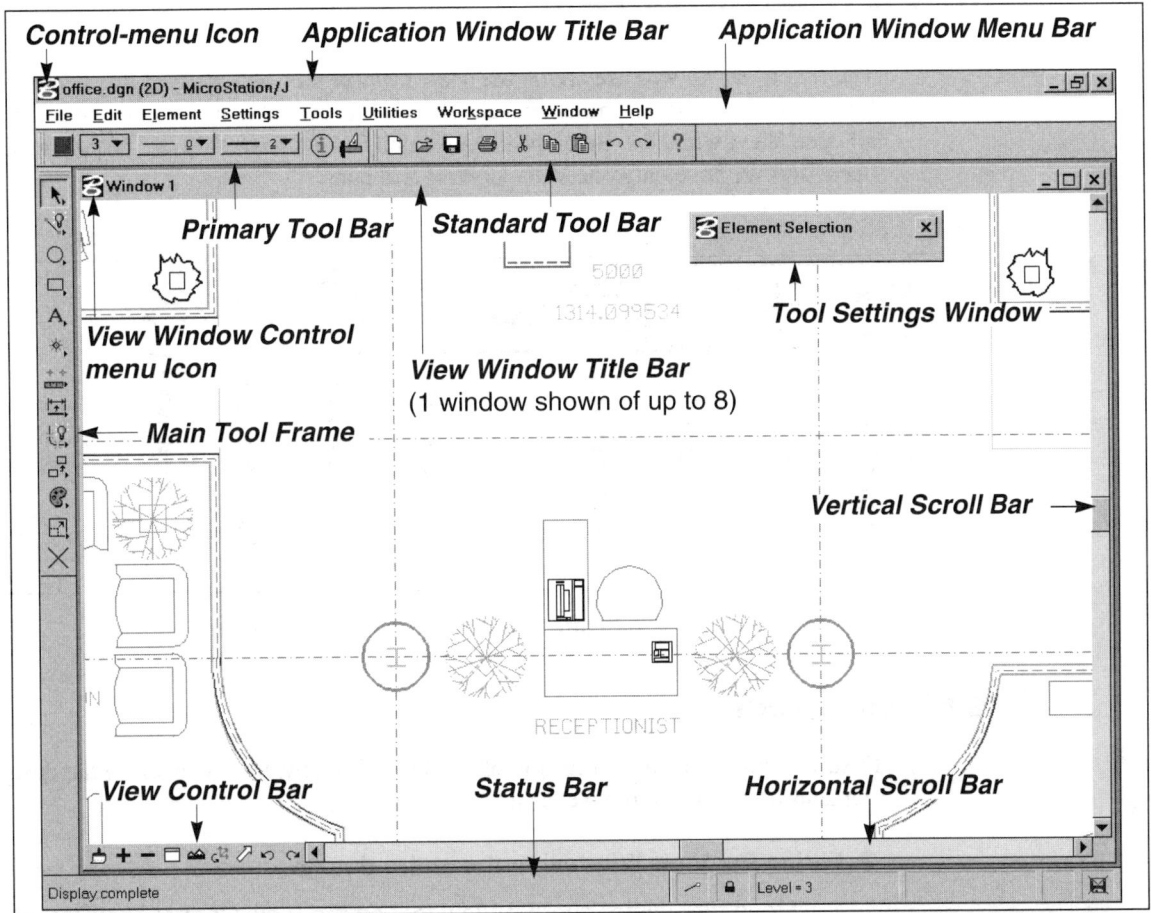

Figure 1.3 The MicroStation Application Window, displaying "office.dgn"

The MicroStation J Application Window

Figure 1.3 illustrates the *Application Window* with a part of "office.dgn" displayed in the single *View Window*. The various *Tool Bars*, the *Menu Bar*, the *Status Bar* and the *Tool Settings Window* are identified. This is the default arrangement only, we will be continually optimizing this to suit each task we undertake. Note the "crossed out disk" icon at the right end of the Status bar, indicating that the file is Read-Only.

We can have up to eight *View Windows* within the one *Application Window*. Each *View Window* has its own *Title Bar*, *Scroll Bar* and *View Control Bar*.

The View Control Bar

The first tools we will use are on the *View Control* tool bar. We find this bar on the left of the View window horizontal Scroll bar. It is available in the same position on all open View windows. In the following examples we have only one View window open, thus we have only one View Control tool bar.

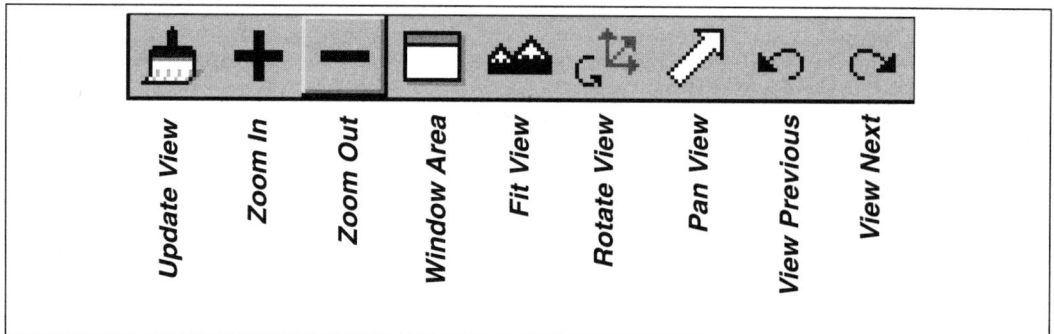

Figure 1.4   The View Control Tool Bar

The Fit View Tool

First, we will set the magnification of the View Window, to display all of the design elements of the design file we have just opened.

◆ **Fitting the View Window to the entire design**

1. Move the pointer over Fit View tool on the View Control Tool Bar.
    Read the description of the tool function in the Status Bar, it will be as shown in the inset of figure 1.5.

2. Click on the *Fit View* tool to choose it (activate the command).
    The View Window contents will change to display the entire design.

We have used the first of the huge numbers of tools that are available within MicroStation. We will continue to work through this particular tool bar and experiment with each of the tools, continuing to use "office.dgn" as the example file.

We will view the entire design as a whole and examine it in fine detail by magnifying sections, just as we would to obtain information from an existing design. As you will find as we work through the examples in this book, being able to control the viewing of our design files is critically important in the design creation process.

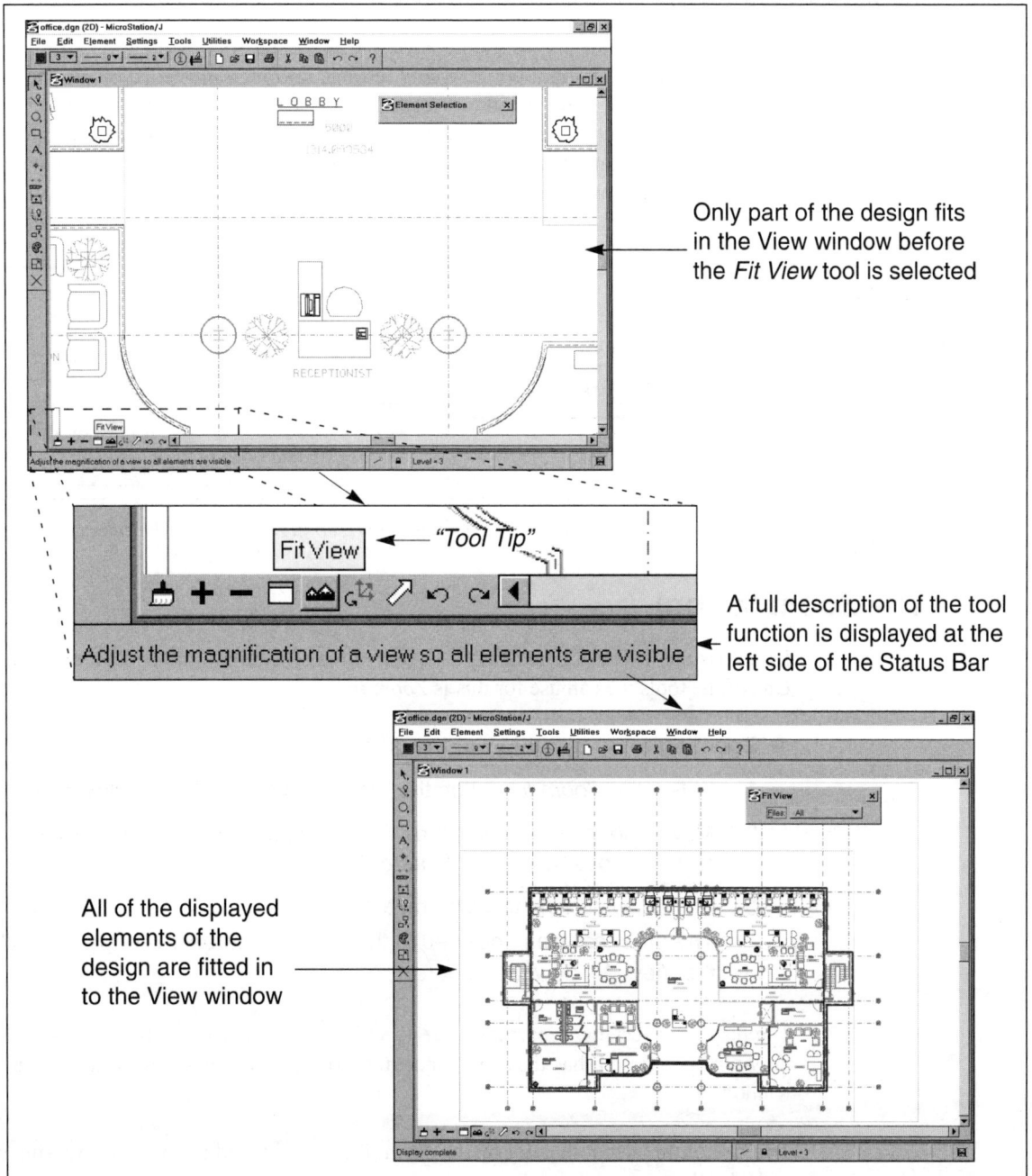

Only part of the design fits in the View window before the *Fit View* tool is selected

"Tool Tip"

A full description of the tool function is displayed at the left side of the Status Bar

All of the displayed elements of the design are fitted in to the View window

Figure 1.5   Fitting the View Window to all of "office.dgn"

The Tool Settings Window

Before we go any further, we should have a word on the Tool Settings Window. This window is used as an input point for any settings information needed by the tool we are about to use. The window reconfigures to suit the tool selected. The configuration for a tool may provide an input field for a dimension, a menu choice, or any combination of many types of settings. We will be using this window extensively from now on.

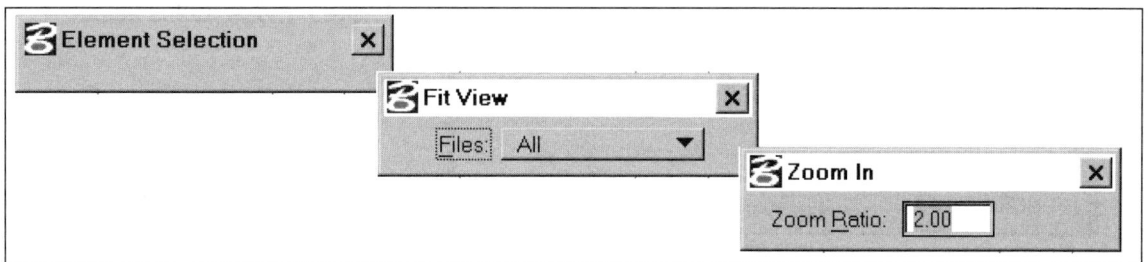

Figure 1.6   The Tool Settings window re-configures to suit the selected tool

The Zoom In Tool

Let us assume we need to magnify a section of the office to examine it in more detail. One of the tools we can use for this is *Zoom In*.

◆ Zooming In on a section of the Office.dgn

1. Select the *Zoom In* tool on the View Control Tool Bar by clicking on it.

2. Move the pointer over the View Window, position the displayed rectangle over an *Area of Interest*.

3. *Accept* by clicking the data button.
    The area that was enclosed in the *Area of Interest* rectangle now fills the View Window. See figure 1.7.

The displayed rectangle represents the *View window* boundary of the view after the *Zoom In* operation. It has the same aspect ratio (ratio of width to height) as the View window.

The size of this window is set by the Zoom Ratio setting, which we will experiment with shortly.

The *Area of Interest* rectangle can be moved over any part of the View window, with the mouse pointer at its center

Increase a view window's magnification, making elements appear larger

The elements that were enclosed by the *Area of Interest* rectangle are magnified to fill the entire View window

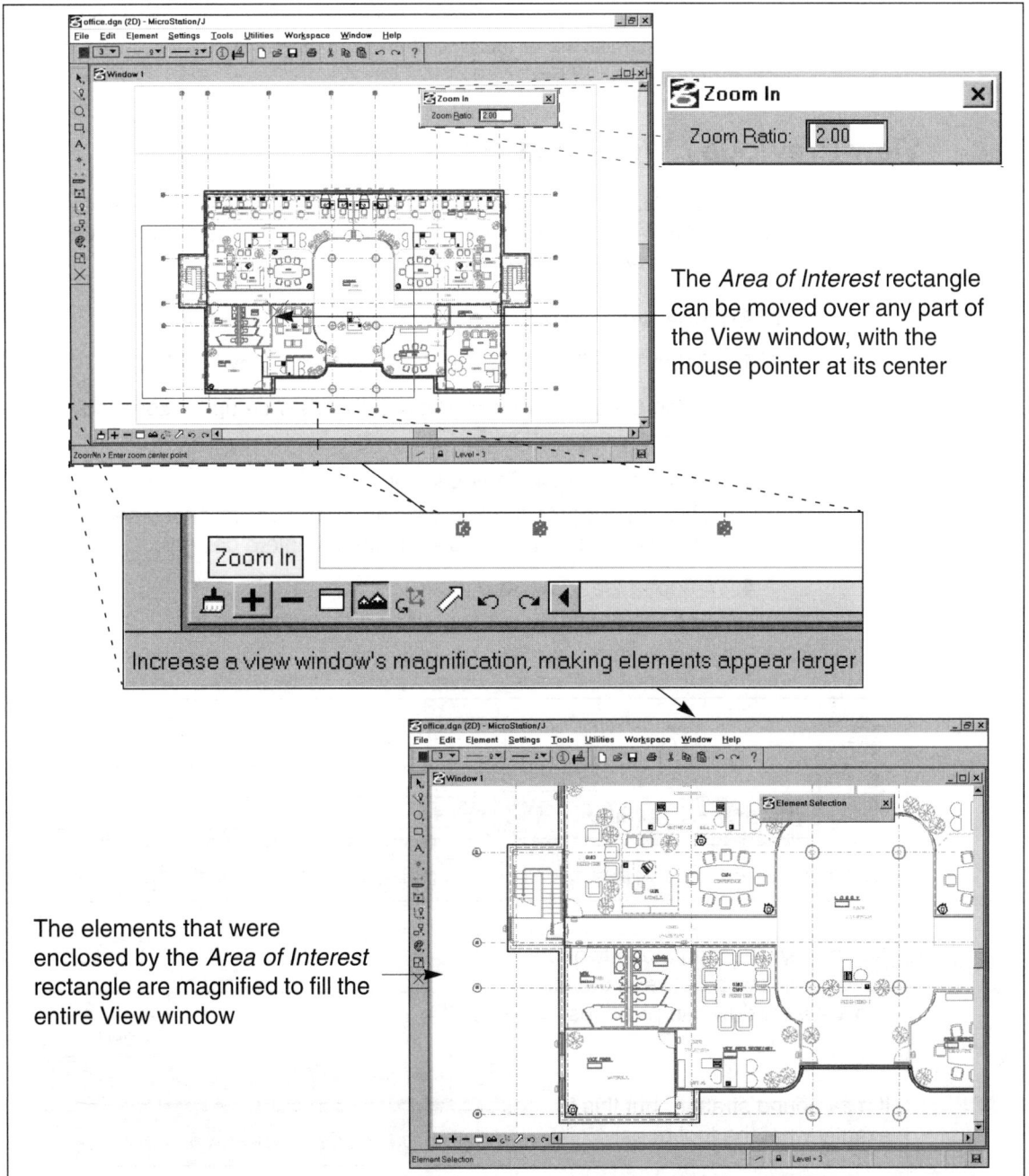

Figure 1.7   Defining the Area of Interest and Zooming In on it

It is often necessary to revert back to the previous viewing arrangement after we have zoomed in, or changed the area of the design in the View window by any other means. We will make use of the *View Previous and View Next* tools, then experiment with different *Zoom Ratios*.

View Previous / View Next Tools

In this example, we will arrange one of the View windows to display the overall view (e.g. FIT VIEW) and the other a ZOOMED IN VIEW. We can swap between the two *views by using the View Previous* and the *View Next* tools.

◆ **Arrange two viewing setups and swap between them**

1. Select the *Fit View* tool and click onto the View window 1.

2. Using the *Zoom In* tool, change the view setup by zooming in on an area of View window 1.

3. Choose the *View Previous* tool.
   This will "Negate the last viewing operation" and resume the viewing arrangement created in step **1** (the complete design).

4. Choose the *View Next* tool.
   The View window will appear as it did after step **2**.

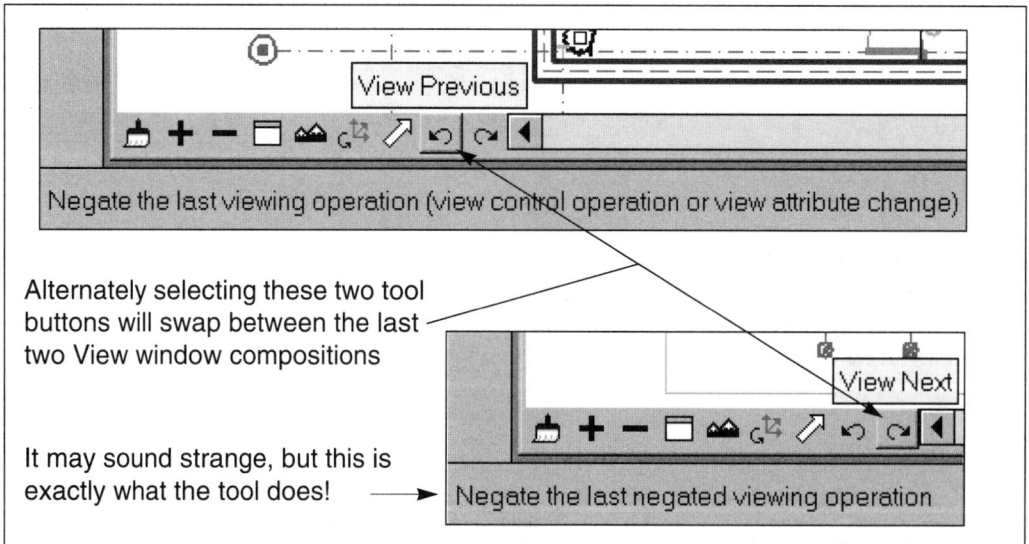

Figure 1.8   Swapping between arrangements within the View window

Changing the Zoom Ratio

The default *Zoom Ratio* setting of **2.00** was used in the previous *Zoom In* exercise. This is the ratio of the new "zoomed in" on-screen size (of a particular part of the design) to the original. The "Area of Interest" rectangle appears to be half the height and half the width of the View window in figure 1.7, illustrating the 2 : 1 ratio.

You may have noticed that the *Tool Settings* window was highlighted (its Title bar colored) when we selected the *Zoom In* tool. Highlighting indicates that the window has *Input Focus*, in other words, any keyboard input will be directed to the *Data Entry Field(s)* within it. The ratio setting in the only *Data Entry Field* of the *Tool Settings* window is also highlighted, indicating that any keyboard input will overwrite the current setting.

◆ **Zoom In using a Zoom Ratio of 4**

   1.   Select the *Zoom In* tool, by clicking on it as before.

   2.   Press <4> on the keyboard, enter the number by pressing <**Return**>.

   3.   Position the displayed rectangle over an *Area of Interest*.

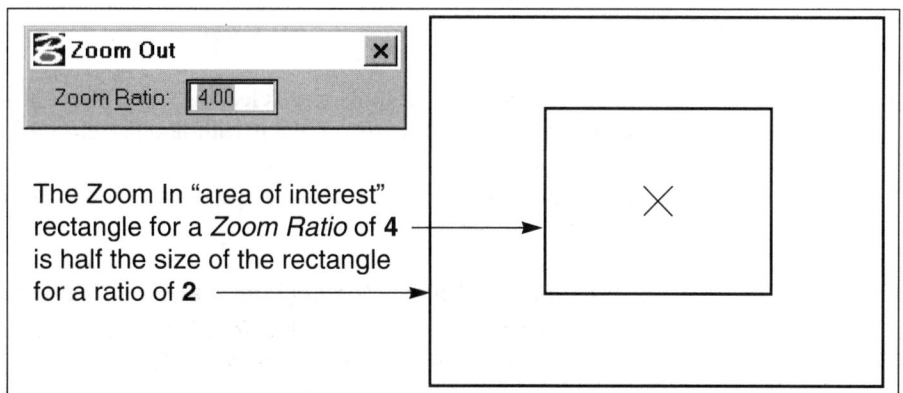

Figure 1.9   Zoom ratio settings

   4.   *Accept* by clicking the Data button.

The detail of the office design now appears four times the size, or more correctly, all *Linear* dimensions of the displayed components have been increased by a factor of four.

The Zoom Out Tool

This tool is the complement to Zoom In, but there can not be an "Area of Interest" rectangle, as it would need to be bigger than the screen. The first Zoom Out operation will reduce the magnification by the *Zoom Ratio* as it remains set from the previous Zoom operation. The part of the design that was currently at the center of the screen will stay there and all of the surrounding features will get closer to it.

◆ **Sequential Zoom Out operations**

1. Select the *Zoom Out* tool from the *View Control* tool bar.

   The design elements will "shrink" by the ratio last set in the Tool Settings window for a zoom (*In* or *Out*) operation.

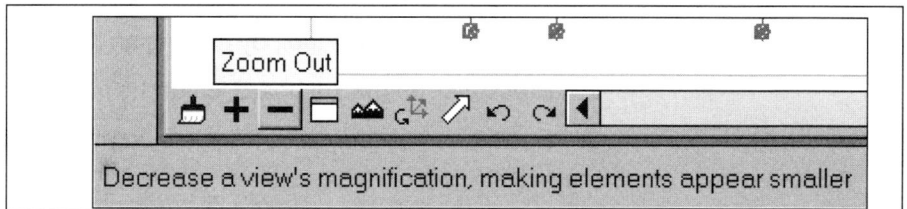

Figure 1.10 Location of the Zoom Out tool

Do not select any other tool, or re-select the *Zoom Out* tool for now. The tool remains *Active*, that is it will perform again with another click of the Data button without pointing to the tool itself. We can tell it is still *Active*, it still appears to be pressed in and is highlighted with a color. It performs slightly differently the second time around, however.

2. Enter <**1.5**> via the keyboard, apply it by pressing <**Enter**>.

   Input Focus was on the Tool Settings window and the number just keyed in will define a new *Zoom Ratio*.

3. Move the pointer on to the View window area, pointing to a recognizable feature of the design.

   Note that the tool description at the left of the status bar is now replaced by the tool name, followed by a *Prompt* "Enter zoom center point".

4. Still pointing to the same recognizable feature, click the Data button.

   The elements reduce in size again, but the features that were situated under the pointer are now in the center of the View window.

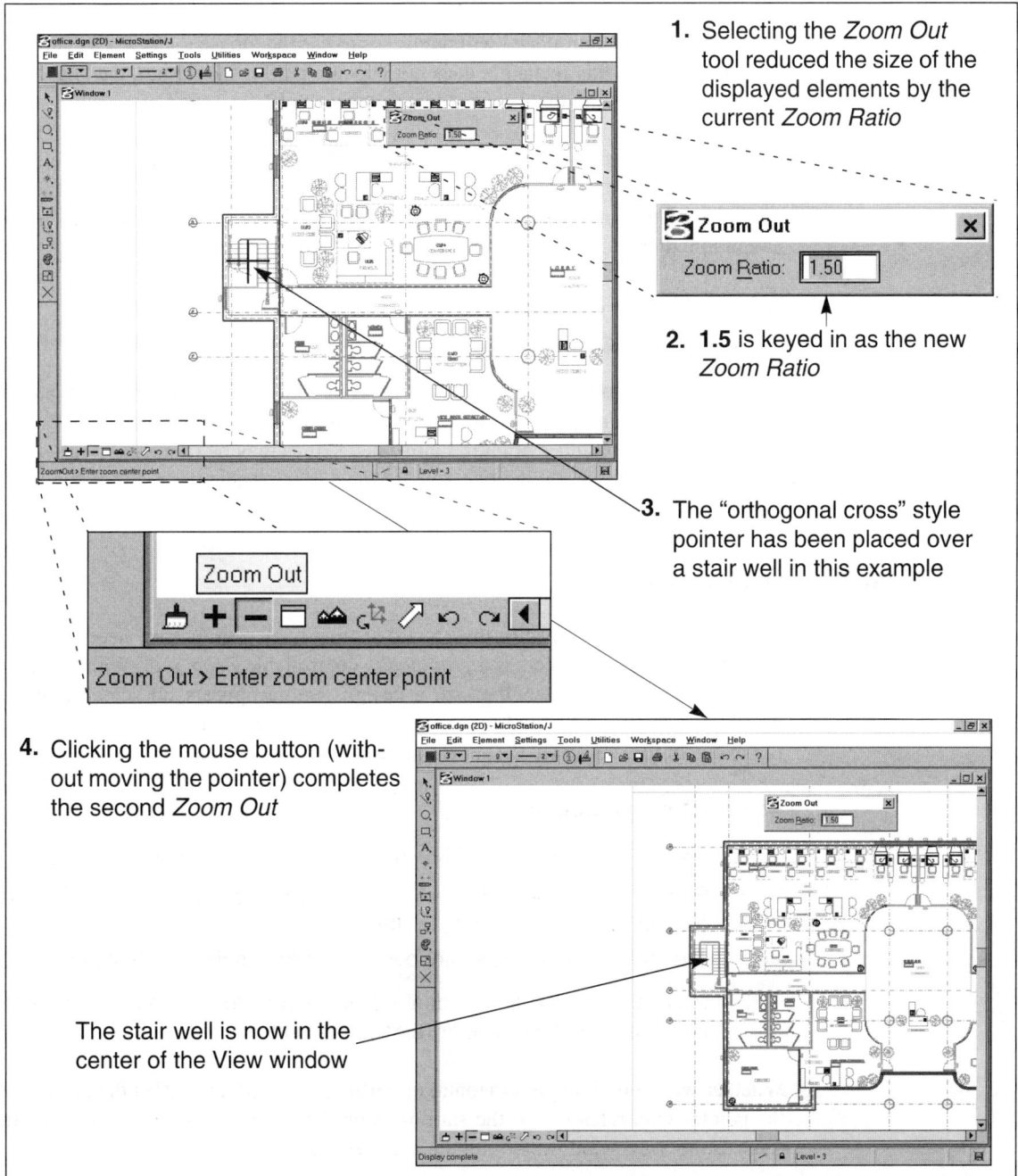

1. Selecting the *Zoom Out* tool reduced the size of the displayed elements by the current *Zoom Ratio*

2. **1.5** is keyed in as the new *Zoom Ratio*

3. The "orthogonal cross" style pointer has been placed over a stair well in this example

4. Clicking the mouse button (without moving the pointer) completes the second *Zoom Out*

The stair well is now in the center of the View window

Figure 1.11   Zooming Out about a defined point

Using the Mouse as a Drawing Tool

The next tool to be introduced will require us to use the mouse to draw a rectangle on the screen. While this rectangle does not become part of the design, the "freehand" drawing principles involved are the same as those used for design elements.

At this stage we are still only using the "main" mouse button, usually the left one. This button (referred to as the "Data" button in MicroStation) controls the start and the finish of the line or shape we are creating. There are two ways we can use the button to indicate the start and finish points on the screen:

1. *Click - Move - Click*

2. *Press - Move - Release*

The former method does not require pressure on the button while we are re-positioning the mouse, thus it may improve control. The latter is the most economical in the number of button movements, thus may be fractionally faster. The technique you use will be the one you are most comfortable with, either one is OK for use in the next example.

The Window Area Tool

This tool allows us to specify the precise section of design that we need to fill the window. It can be described as a *graphically* controllable *Zoom* tool. With the Zoom tools we have used so far, the size a design feature appears on screen after the operation depends on a keyed-in *Zoom Ratio*. The *Window Area* tool sets this ratio to fit an area of the design we define with a rectangle drawn using the mouse.

◆ Windowing a Defined Area

1. Select the *Window Area* tool from the *View Control* tool bar.

2. Position one side of the new View window boundary with the mouse, click or press-and-hold-down the button.
   The pointer is full View window size while defining the first side.

3. Move the mouse to the desired position of the opposite side of the new View window, click or release the button.

Whether we are defining a horizontal or vertical side will depend on the position of the pointer with reference to the starting point. The aspect ratio will always be the same as the View window, as with the *Zoom In* tool.

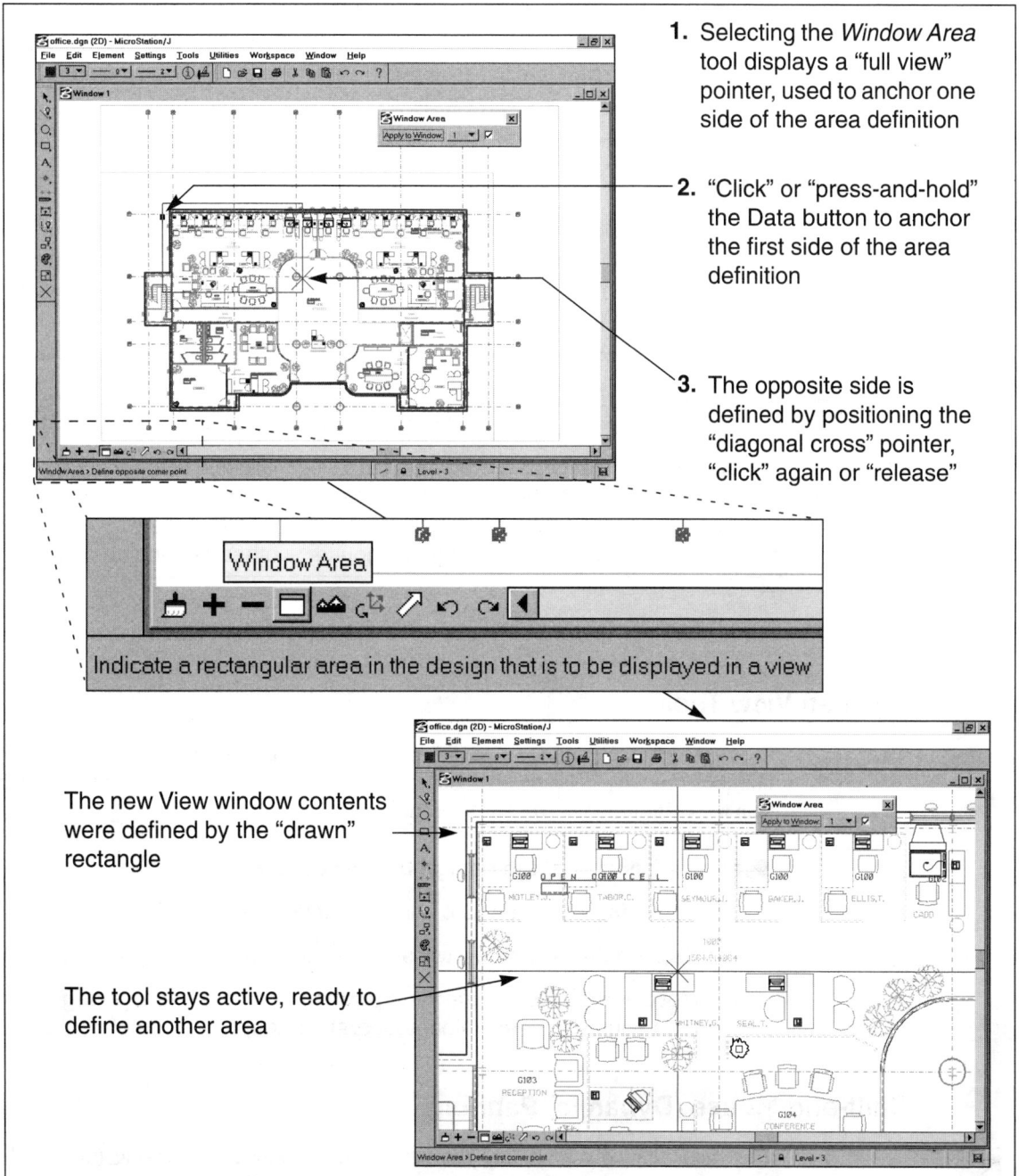

1. Selecting the *Window Area* tool displays a "full view" pointer, used to anchor one side of the area definition

2. "Click" or "press-and-hold" the Data button to anchor the first side of the area definition

3. The opposite side is defined by positioning the "diagonal cross" pointer, "click" again or "release"

Indicate a rectangular area in the design that is to be displayed in a view

The new View window contents were defined by the "drawn" rectangle

The tool stays active, ready to define another area

Figure 1.12   Using the Window Area tool

Moving the Design in the View Window

It is constantly necessary to change the area of the design that is displayed at any one time. We have already tried changing the magnification of various areas, now we will see how to move the display without changing magnification.

Using the Scroll Bars

The default configuration of MicroStation features *Scroll Bars* on the View windows. We use these separately to provide horizontal and vertical movements in three different ways. Figure 1.13 illustrates a Horizontal bar, but the vertical controls work in the same way.

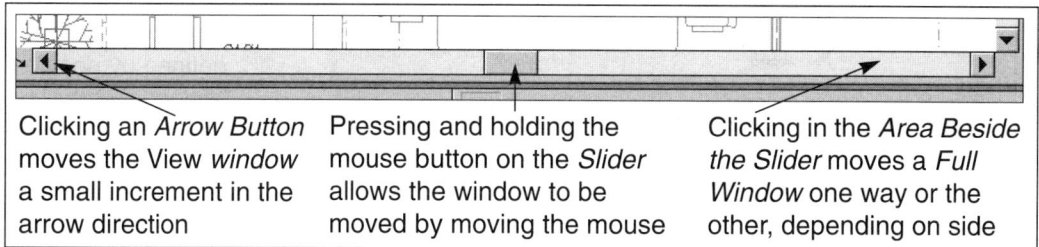

Clicking an *Arrow Button* moves the View *window* a small increment in the arrow direction

Pressing and holding the mouse button on the *Slider* allows the window to be moved by moving the mouse

Clicking in the *Area Beside the Slider* moves a *Full Window* one way or the other, depending on side

Figure 1.13   Using the Scroll Bar controls

The Pan View Tool

In this context the term *Pan* is used for both horizontal and vertical movement. Using this tool *Panning* conceptually moves the *Design* within the *View window*, rather than re-positioning the *Window* over the *Design*.

◆ **Move a section of the design to view center**

1.   Select the *Pan View* tool from the *View Control* tool bar (Figure 1.14).

2.   Click on the feature we will use to re-position the design in the View.

3.   Move the pointer to the new position on the screen (a large arrow from source to destination appears), click again to complete the *Pan*.

Shift-and-Mouse (Dynamic) Panning

This method involves holding down the <**Shift**> key then pressing (and holding down) the data button. The shift key may then be released and the mouse moved a small distance in the direction that we want to move the *Window* over the *Design*.

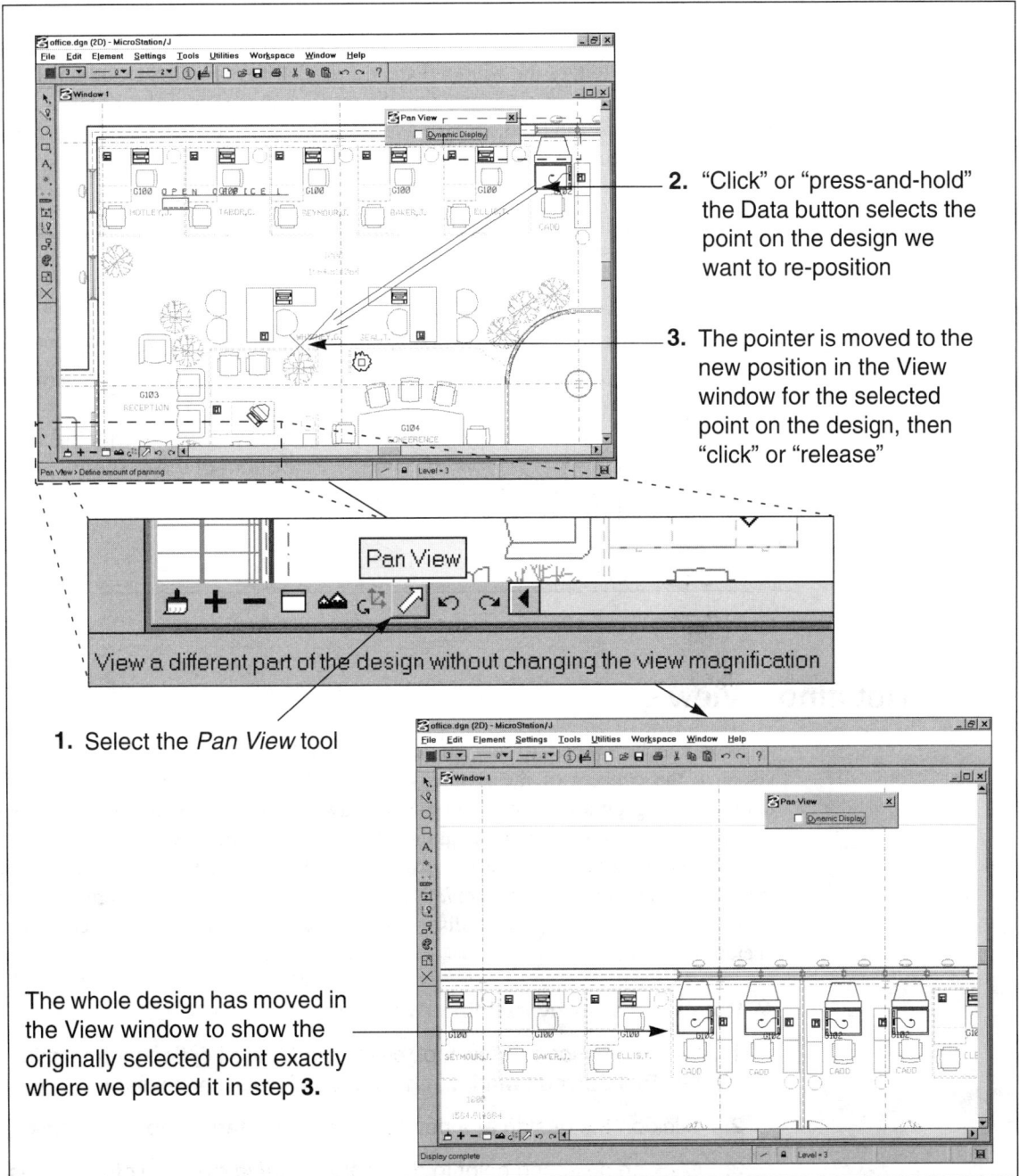

2. "Click" or "press-and-hold" the Data button selects the point on the design we want to re-position

3. The pointer is moved to the new position in the View window for the selected point on the design, then "click" or "release"

View a different part of the design without changing the view magnification

1. Select the *Pan View* tool

The whole design has moved in the View window to show the originally selected point exactly where we placed it in step **3.**

Figure 1.14   Moving the display with the Pan View tool

The View Axes

Complying to the normal convention, the View window has an *x axis* (always parallel to the bottom of the window) and a *y axis* (always parallel to the sides of the window). Convention also dictates that the positive direction of the *x* axis is *Left to Right*, or *Bottom to Top* for the *y* axis. We will introduce the *View Coordinate System* in more detail shortly.

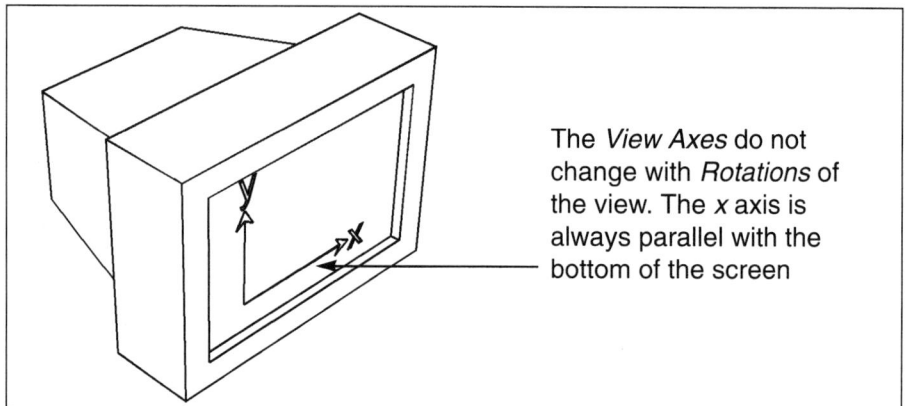

The *View Axes* do not change with *Rotations* of the view. The *x* axis is always parallel with the bottom of the screen

Figure 1.15   The View axes

Rotating a View

A View can be rotated to any angle. We can use a "paper" analogy to help us visualize the concept of the *Rotate View* tool. Imagine "office.dgn" was a paper drawing laying on a table or a horizontal drawing board. The "unrotated" view of this would be seen when standing at the bottom of the sheet. If we walked around the table we would see a variety of *Rotated Views*. When we rotate a view, keep in mind that we are rotating the *View window* around the *Design*, not the design within the window. This is an important distinction, as it affects the way we control the operation.

◆ **Rotating a view by defining two points**

1. Select the *Rotate View* tool, check the Method option menu setting in the Tool Settings window, change to *2 Points* if necessary.

2. Click on the design at a point to define the start of the new *x axis*.

3. Click on a second point to define the *positive direction* of the *x axis*.

4. Undo the rotation by choosing *Unrotated* in the Tool Settings window.

1. Select *2 points* from the options menu as the *Method* of rotation

2. Select a point on the design as the origin of the *x axis* direction after rotation

This rectangle represents the view outline after rotation

3. Select a point on the design defining the *positive x axis* direction after rotation

Point 2.

Point 3.

x Axis of View

4. Restore original rotation with *View Previous* (if no subsequent viewing changes made) or select the *Unrotated* option

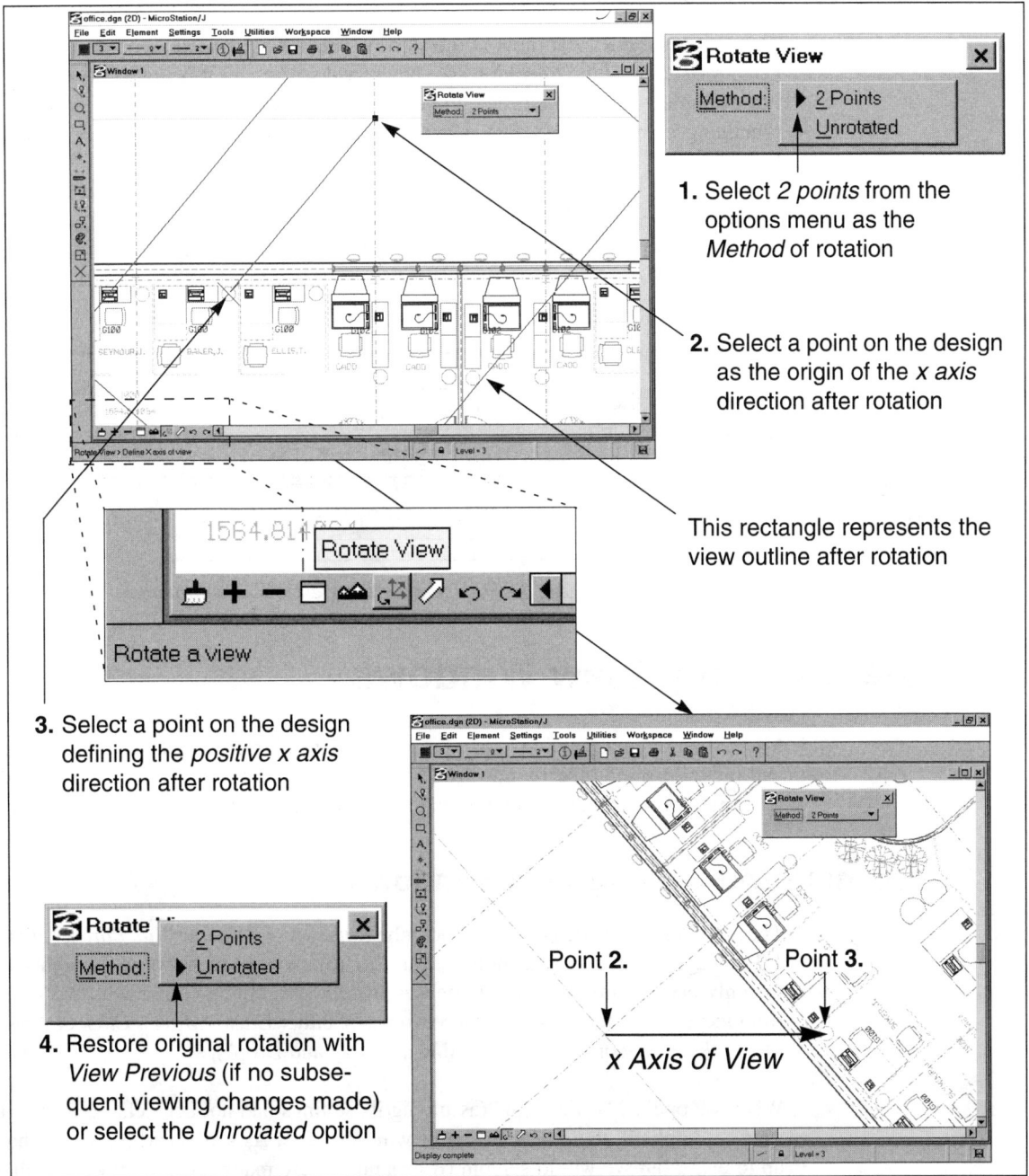

Figure 1.16   Rotating a View

The Update View tool

This tool "redraws" the view on the screen. This has happened automatically as we performed each of the operations we have tried so far, but it is not always the case. For example, when we start deleting elements of a design, there may be gaps left in remaining elements. This may occur where the deleted lines originally obscured them.

In complex designs a redraw can use up a noticeable amount of time, thus it is left up to the operator to decide when the task is to be performed. By clicking the update view tool, the View window automatically refreshes or updates.

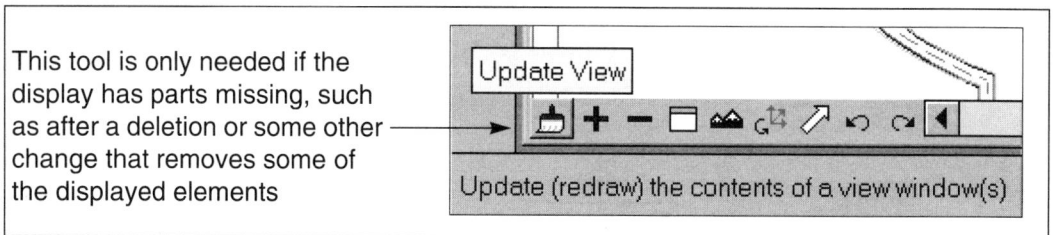

This tool is only needed if the display has parts missing, such as after a deletion or some other change that removes some of the displayed elements

Update View

Update (redraw) the contents of a view window(s)

Figure 1.17   Updating the View window contents

Manipulating View Windows

MicroStation View windows may be opened, closed, rearranged, reshaped, resized and hidden behind other windows. They are manipulated in the same way that the windows are manipulated in other graphically interfaced applications.

Opening and Closing View Windows

The *Menu* bar is situated directly below the *Application Window Title Bar*, see Figure 1.3 on page 1-5. It contains choices from *File* (on the left) to *Help* (on the right), but the only one we are interested in now is *Window*. Making a choice with the mouse from these menu items can the done two ways, either *Click - Move - Click* or *Press - Move - Release* (sometimes referred to as "Drag and Drop").

When we opened "office.dgn" (assuming its settings had not been changed from its state as supplied), there was one View window open. As stated earlier, we can have up to eight, but we would seldom (if ever) use these many, especially with a single screen installation. In the following exercises we will open another View window and manipulate it in various ways.

◆ **Open the View Window Open/Close Dialog Box**

1. Select *Window* from the *Application Window Menu Bar* (see Figure 1.18).

    The "*Drop Down*" panel now displayed has more options displayed in the top section, with a list of windows currently open in the lower section.

2. Select *Open/Close* from the drop down panel.

    The next drop down lists all of the available View windows, with a tick beside those open, only **1** in this case. Above the list is a choice of *Dialog.*

3. Select *Dialog.*

    The *Open/Close* dialog window opens, with settings buttons for each View window.

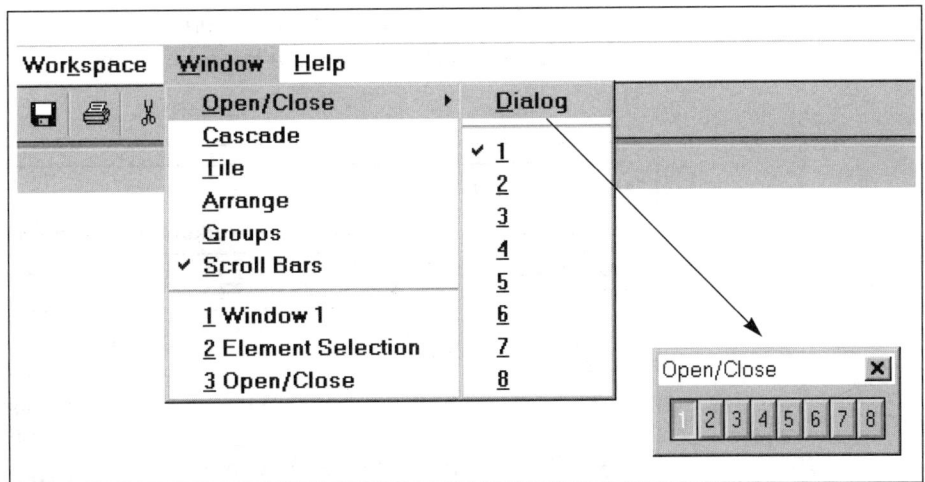

Figure 1.18   Window>Open/Close>Dialog

In the next step, we will open a second View window. Open View windows are represented by the crosses in the Open/Close dialog.

◆ **Open View window 2 and exchange windows front-to-back**

1. Click setting button **2** on the Open/Close Dialog.

    View window **2** will appear in the view window area of the Application window, hiding part of View window **1**. Its position and size will depend on previous view manipulations in the file.

We need not have selected *Window>Open/Close/Dialog* to open (or close) another view. We could have gone as far as *Window>Open/Close,* then chosen the view directly by number (see Figure 1.18). If the view was already open (represented by the tick), it would close, or if it was closed it would open.

In either case, the menu options would disappear immediately after making the choice. Choosing *Dialog* leaves this window open and available for opening and closing the View windows without "working down" through the menu options each time.

◆ **Moving hidden View windows to front for manipulation**

1. Choose *Window>Window 1.*

    Window 1 will now be in front of window 2, in this case completely covering it.

2. Choose *Window>Window 2.*

    Window 2 will re-appear in front of window 1, but window 1 is still partially visible as it is the larger of the two.

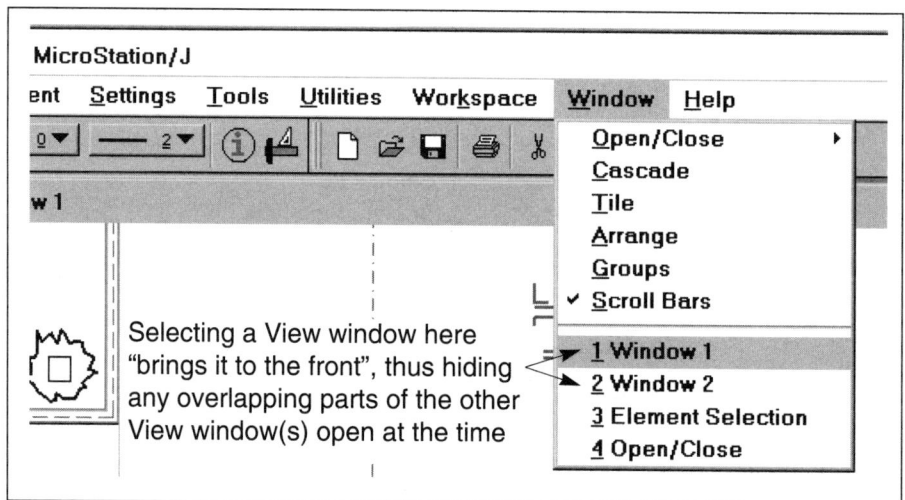

Figure 1.19   Window Menu "top level" options

3. Click on the *Title bar* or a *Border* of View window **1**.

    This will also bring window 1 to the front. We cannot use this technique to bring window 2 to the in front this case, as it does not have any Title bar or border visible.

Moving and Re-sizing View Windows

If you are already familiar with other applications running under Windows (or another similar operating system), the above manipulations may not have introduced anything particularly new. In the following exercises we experiment with moving, changing size and changing the proportions of the View windows. The procedures may again look familiar, but the subtle differences make it advisable to practice on this particular application.

◆ **Re-position View window 2**

1. Move the pointer into the Title bar of window **2**, press (and hold down) the data button.

2. Move the window with the mouse (still holding the button pressed) until the top-left corners of the two views coincide, release the button.

3. Point precisely to the lower border of window **2**, press the Data button when the pointer becomes a double-headed arrow.

4. "Drag" the bottom of the view down to window **1**'s Scroll or View Control bar, release the button.

5. Point to the right side border of window **2**, again press the Data button when the pointer becomes a double-headed arrow.

6. Reduce the width of window **2** to about half its height by "dragging" the right side border, release the button.

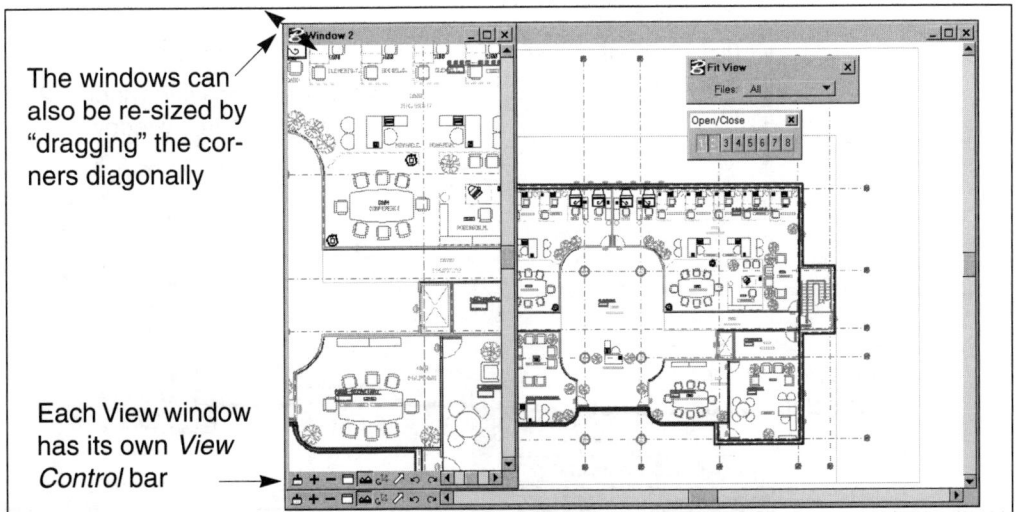

The windows can also be re-sized by "dragging" the corners diagonally

Each View window has its own *View Control* bar

Figure 1.20   View window 2 reconfigured

View window 2 has been re-configured to a new size and shape. In the next exercise we will experiment with the use of the *Window Area* tool (introduced on page 1-14), in conjunction with multiple views. We will define the area of interest in window 1 and it will be automatically shown in window 2.

◆ Window an area defined in a different View window

1. Select the *Window Area* tool from the **View window 2** *View Control* tool bar.

    This tool is specific to each individual View window.

2. Position one side of the new View window boundary at the top-left inside the right side stair well, click or press (and hold down) the Data button.

    The full View window size pointer is useful for judging the position of the new view in relation to design features.

3. Move the mouse to the bottom-right of the stair well, click or release the button.

    Note the rectangle changed to the same aspect ratio (height to width) as View window 2, while the new area of interest was being defined.

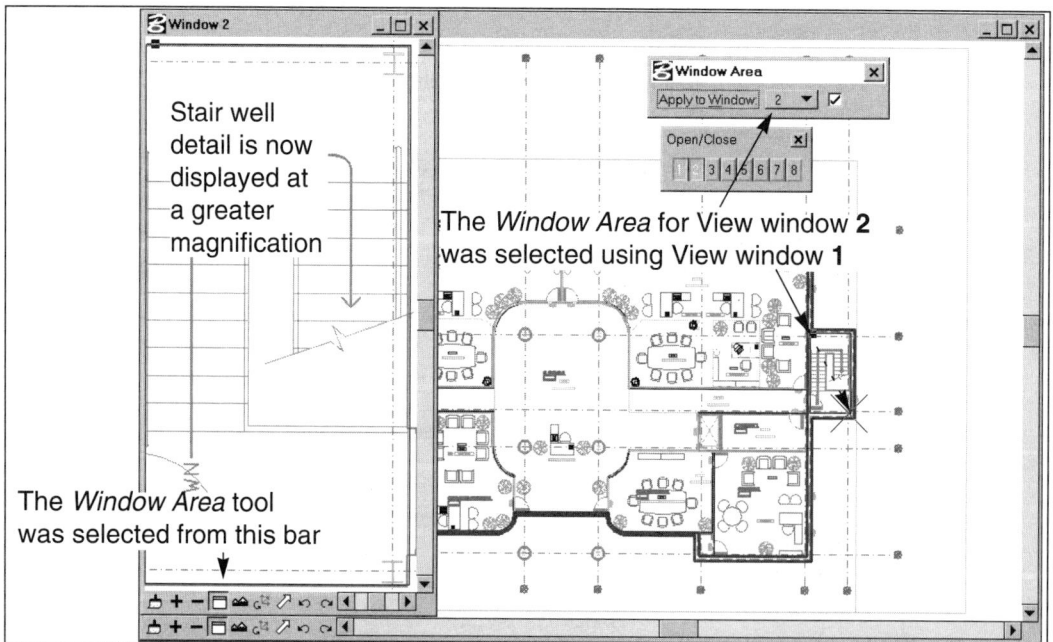

Figure 1.21   Using the Window Area tool in View window 2

Standard View Window Arrangements

In the preceding exercises we arranged the View windows in a "customized" layout, to suit a specific viewing need. There are *Standard* layouts available as well, *Tile* and *Cascade*.

◆ **Cascading and Tiling open View windows**

1. Using the View window *Open/Close* dialog box, open View windows **3** and **4** (leave View windows 1 and 2 open).

2. Choose *Window>Cascade.*

3. Choose *Window>Tile.*
   Figure 1.22 illustrates the resulting View window areas.

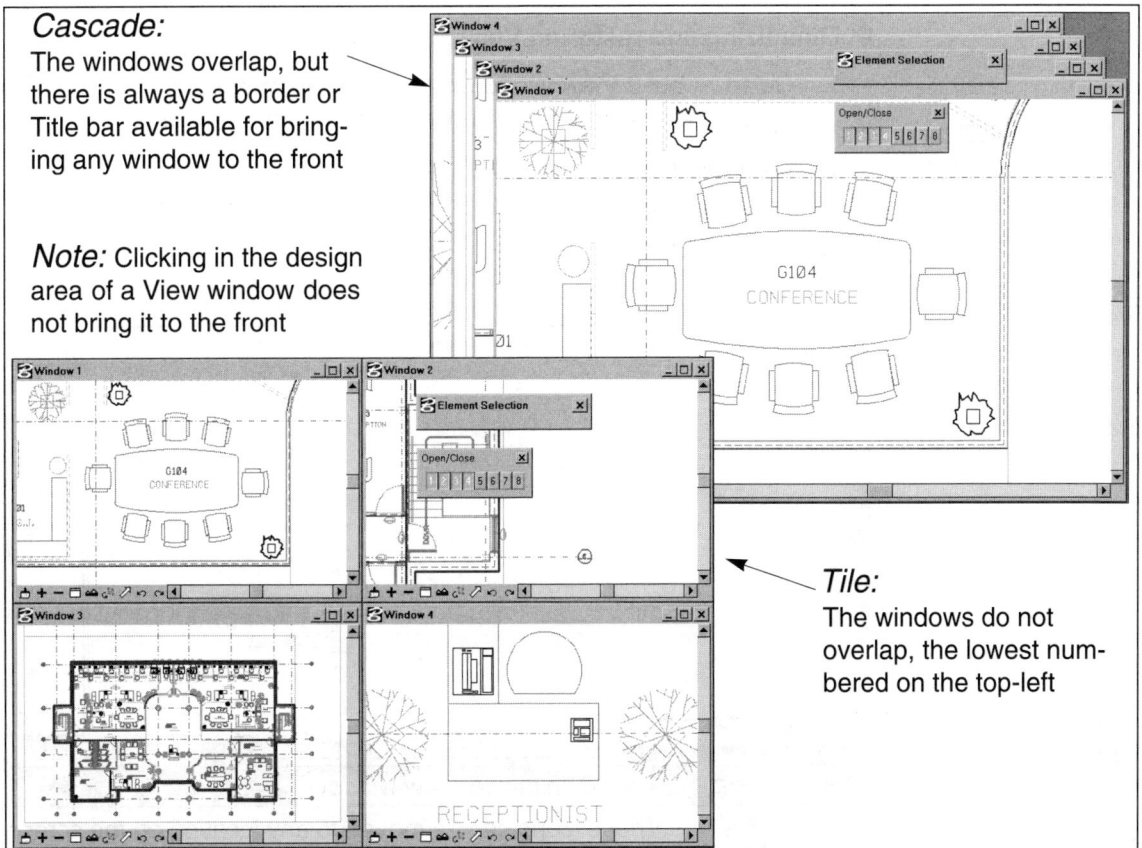

Cascade:
The windows overlap, but there is always a border or Title bar available for bringing any window to the front

Note: Clicking in the design area of a View window does not bring it to the front

Tile:
The windows do not overlap, the lowest numbered on the top-left

Figure 1.22   Cascading and Tiling View windows

Maximized View Windows

Any View window can be maximized by clicking the *Maximize* button found at the top-right of all windows. Maximizing a window means it will occupy the entire View window area of the Application window, thus giving us the maximum "real estate" for creating design elements. Once a view is maximized the button used will be replaced by a *Restore* button.

Minimized View Windows

Minimizing a view reduces the view to an *Icon* occupying a minimal amount of screen space. This allows us to have a number of View windows open, each with an area of the design optimized for particular a particular drawing or information recovery task. The *Minimize* button is immediately to the left of the Maximize (or Restore) button for the window.

◆ Minimizing and restoring View windows

1. Close all but 2 View windows, click the *Minimize* button for one of the open windows (the minimized window will appear as an icon).

2. Click the minimized window icon's *Restore* button.
   The View window will re-appear at the location and size it was before minimization, but always at the front.

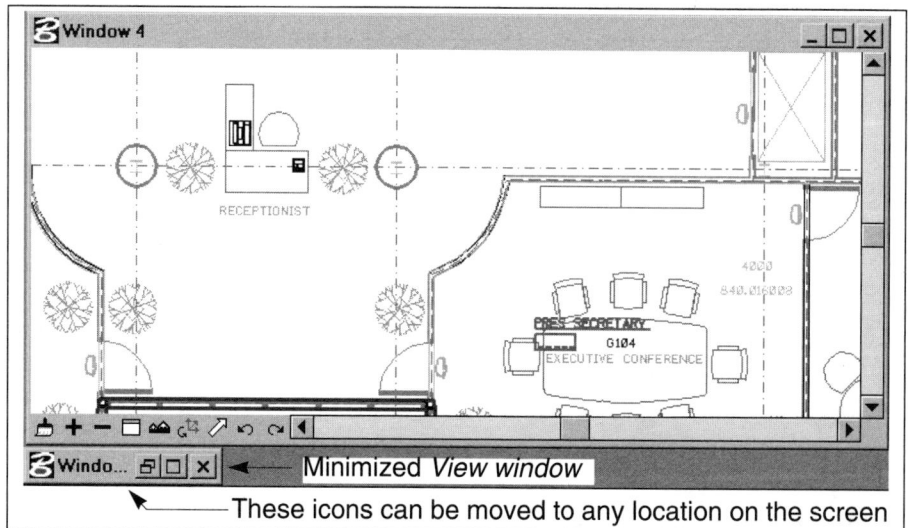

Figure 1.23   Two View windows, one Minimized to an icon

Saved Views

It is sometimes necessary to return to a particular area of interest or section of a design in a particular View window. To save the time involved with re-creating a defined view arrangement, we can *Save* the *Definition* of a View window for use as often as we like. View window definitions are saved to become part of the design file (unless it is "Read-Only") and remain there permanently, or until they are deleted.

Saving a View Definition

The view definition to be saved is set up in a View window, this is called the *Source View*. This definition does not only include the *Area* of the design displayed in the *Source View*, but also the *Level Display* and the *View Attributes* settings (to be introduced in chapters 2 and 3). The View window definition is then *Saved* (to the design file) with a *Name* and *Description* to allow recall in the future.

◆ **Save a View window Definition of a Conference Room**

1. *Close* "office.dgn", check the *Read-Only* box *Off* in the MicroStation Manager dialog box, re-open "office.dgn".

2. *Maximize* View window **1**, close any other View windows, *Fit View.*

3. *Window Area* about one of the Conference rooms (see Figure 1.24).

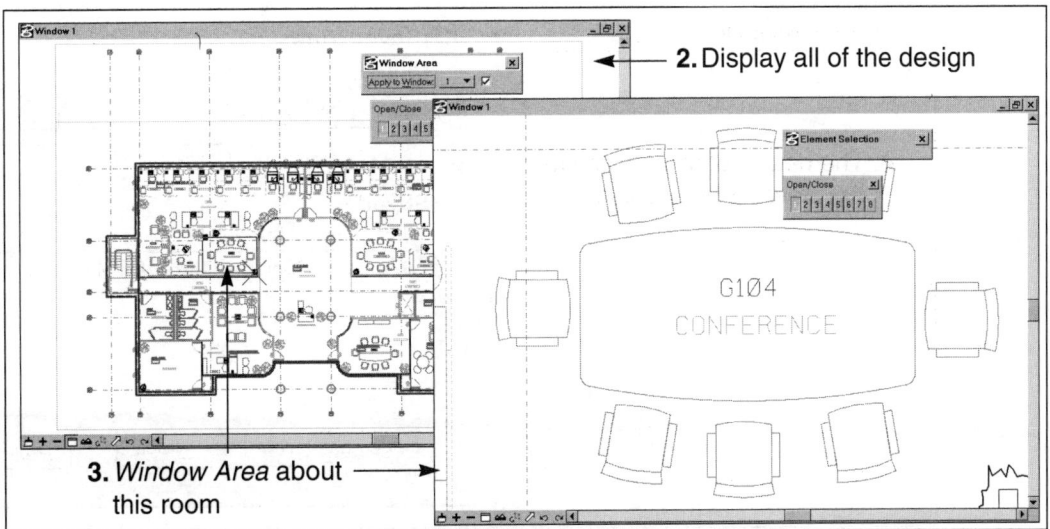

Figure 1.24   Preparing to Save a View Definition

4. **Either** Click (once only) the *View Control Menu Icon*, select **View Save/Recall** from the *View Control Menu*

   Or Select *Utilities>Saved Views* from the Application window menu.

5. Key in **G104** to the *Name:* field, press <**Tab**>, key in **Conference Room 1** to the *Description* field, click the *Save* button.

   The *View* option menu shows **1** as the *Source* View window, since this is the only one open. We can select *Source Views* from here if we using more than one.

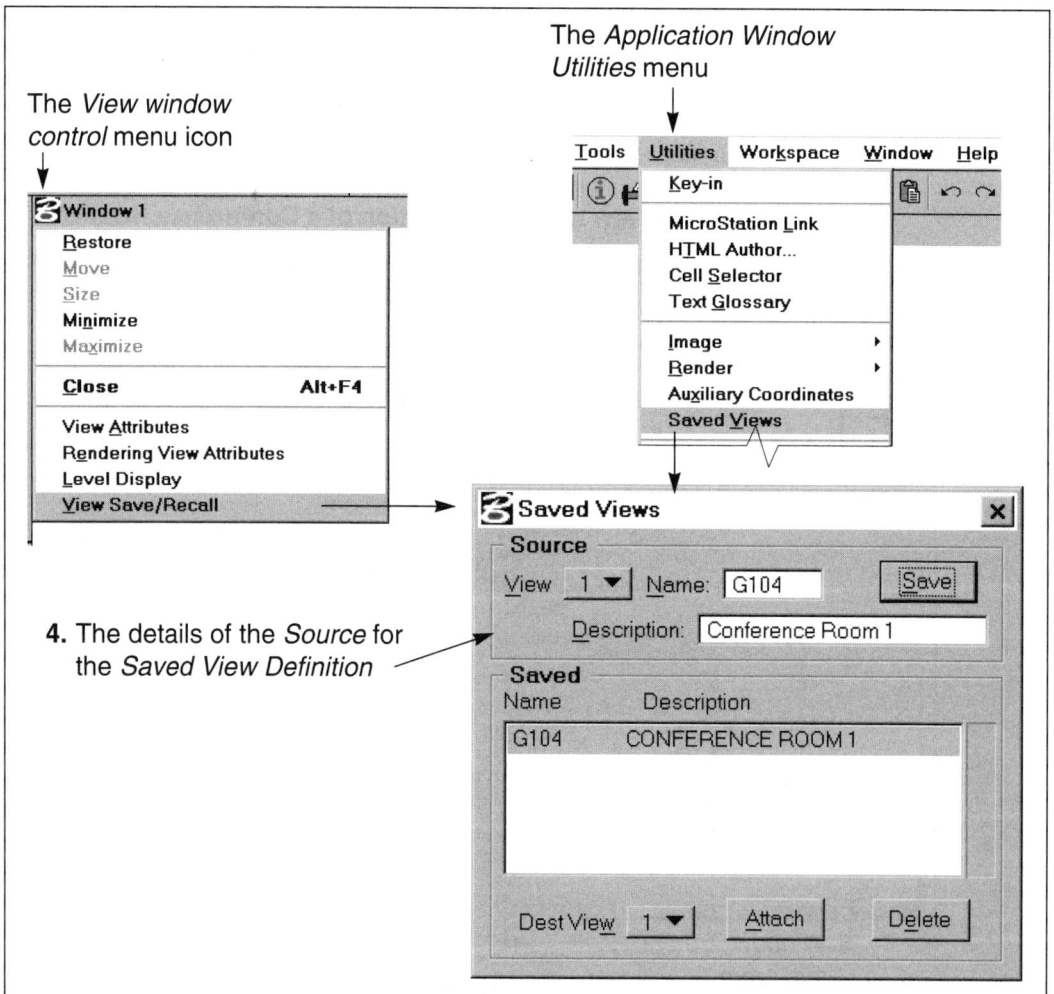

The *Application Window Utilities* menu

The *View window control* menu icon

4. The details of the *Source* for the *Saved View Definition*

Figure 1.25   Saving a View definition

Recalling a Saved View Definition

When the definition is recalled, a View window, called the *Destination View window,* is designated to display the saved definition. We highlight the named view in the *Saved Views* settings box, then *Attach* its definition to the *Destination* view. The *Name* of the *Saved View* will now be displayed in the View window title bar.

◆ Attaching Saved Views

1. Change the view contents (using any of the *View Control* tools) from those *Saved* in the last exercise.

2. Re-open the *Saved Views* settings box (if necessary), using either of the techniques described in the last exercise.

3. Highlight the desired *Saved View* in the *Saved* panel.

4. Select a *Destination View* (not necessary if only one View window is open), click the *Attach* button and the view contents will match those *Saved.*

5. Save some other view arrangements, try *Attaching* each one.

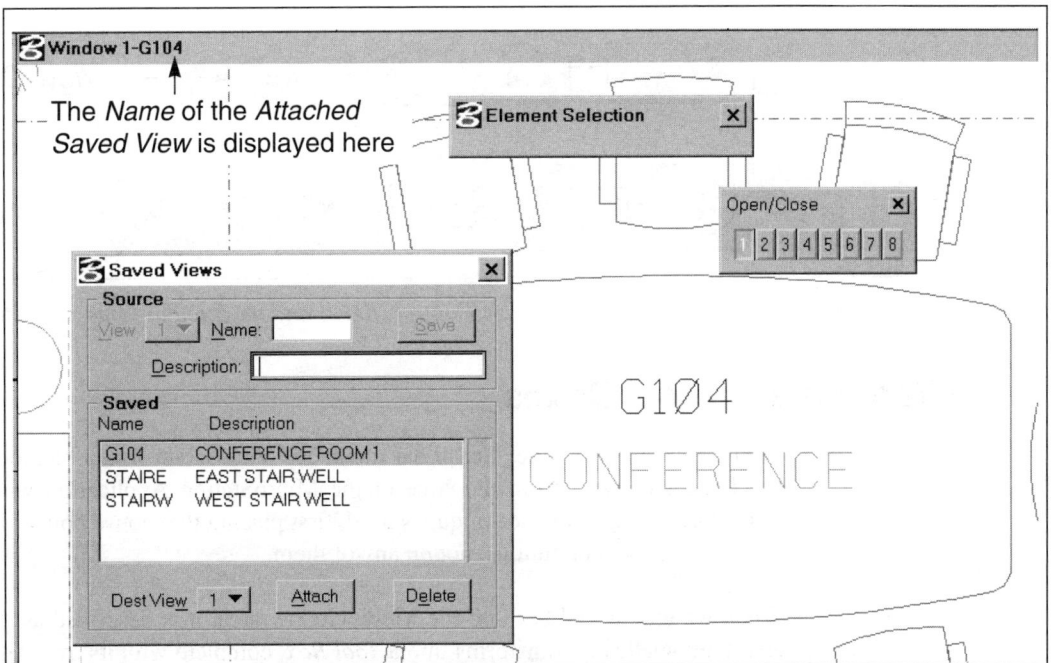

Figure 1.26   Attaching a Saved View definition

Tool Bars, Boxes and Frames

We have been making good use of one type of tool bar already, the *View Control Tool Bar*. There are many more groups of tools that may be described as tool bars, or tool boxes, or tool frames. We will soon be *Creating* our own designs and we will need to access some of these other tools, thus we will examine the conventions used and "learn the language" used to identify them.

Fixed vs. Movable Tool Bars

The *View Control* tool bars are fixed in place on the left of the horizontal Scroll bar for each of the open View windows. We can opt to remove them altogether, but not move them about the screen. Removal is only to be contemplated if there is a very severe lack of screen "real estate", such as with small, low resolution screens.

You will see in Figure 1.27 that the tool buttons in the View Control bar have no spaces between or around them. If a tool bar is to be moved, it needs to have a border or area of bar around the tools to "drag" it by. The View Control tool bars do not have such areas, but the Standard tool bar does.

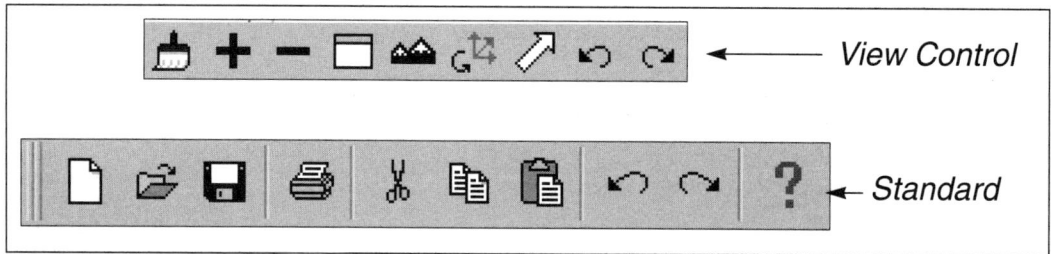

Figure 1.27   The View Control (fixed) and the Standard (movable) tool **bars**

Tool Bars vs. Tool Boxes

With the exception of the "Scroll bar mounted" View Control tool bar, tool bars can be "Dragged" away from the edge of the MicroStation Application window. The usual "press-drag-drop" technique is used, first placing the mouse pointer in the *area surrounding* the tool buttons, not *on* any of them.

When we drag a tool bar into the View window area, it is described as *"Floating"* and it automatically transforms into a *Tool Box*, complete with its own Title bar and Control Menu box.

◆ **Float and Dock the Standard Tool Bar/Box**

   1. Point to the border area of the Standard tool bar (it will be under the Application window Menu bar by default, see page 1-5).

   2. Drag it down into the View window area, drop it anywhere.
      Note that it changes to a *Tool Box*, as illustrated in figure 1.28.

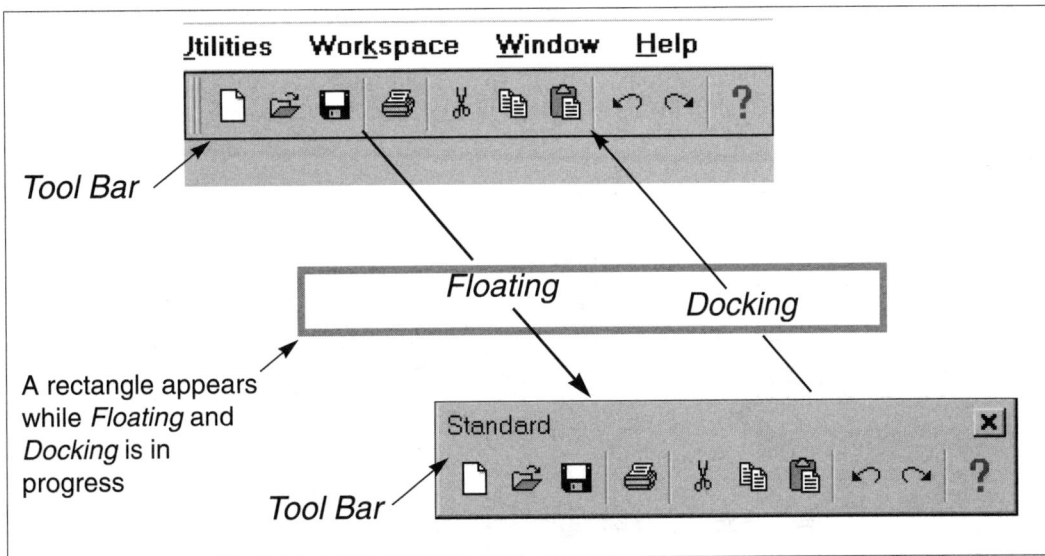

Figure 1.28   Floating and Docking a toolbar/toolbox

When a *tool box* is dragged to the area near the edge of the Application window, it is said to be *"Docked"* and it sheds its Title bar to become a *tool bar.*

◆ **Dock the Standard Tool Bar/Box**

   1. Drag it across as far as possible to one side, drop it there.
      It will change from a horizontal to a vertical format, changing back to a *bar*. The View window(s) will be reduced in size to accommodate it.

   2. Drag it back to the top edge of the Applications window, drop it.
      It will automatically sit beside any other tool bars without a gap, but it will not overlap them as it *Docks*.

Tool Frames

The most obvious example of a *Tool Frame* is the *Main*, by default docked as a tool bar. A *Tool Frame* can be likened to framework for the storage of *Tool Boxes*, or perhaps a "box of tool boxes". Each of the tool buttons displayed in the frame is the "top" tool (the last one to be selected) of a complete tool box. Sometimes these are called *"Child"* tool boxes, with the Frame as the *"Parent"*.

Figure 1.29 shows the Main tool frame of the *Default interface*, showing the large number of individual tools that can be accessed from a small area on the screen. The equivalent tool frame in specialized interfaces (for example our current *Newuser*) may differ from this. We will "graduate" to the *Default interface* in the next chapter.

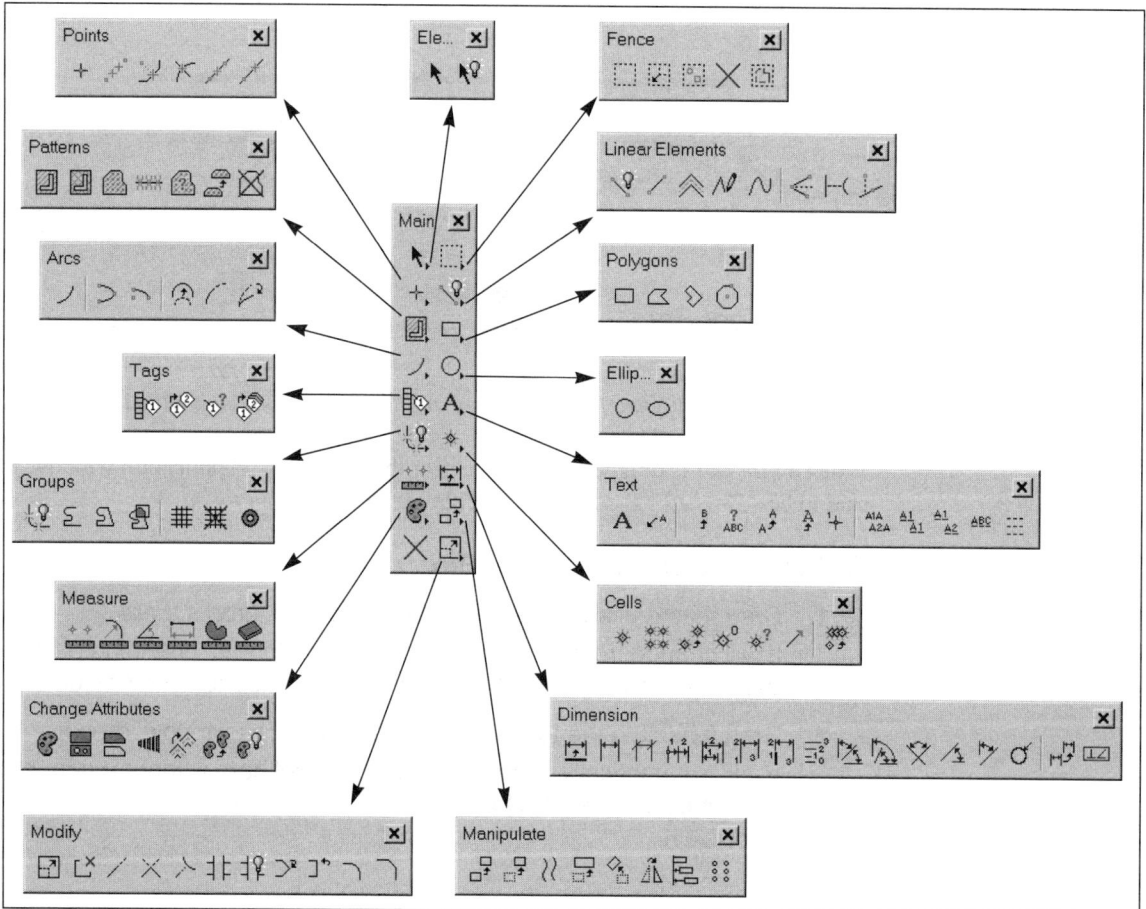

Figure 1.29   Main tool frame (Default) with its "Child" tool boxes

Accessing Tools

We can access the tools in a "Child" tool box two ways:

(a)   By pointing to the "top" tool, pressing the mouse button and moving the pointer along the tools that appear, releasing on the one we require (drag and drop tool selection);

(b)   By dragging the tool box away from the frame, the same action as in 1., but taking the pointer further to outside the tool box itself. The tool box will now be *"Torn off"* and *"Floating"* clear of the frame, with all of the tools permanently displayed for selection.

◆ Selecting a Measuring tool from the Main Tool Frame

1.   Move the mouse pointer to the "measure" tool (seventh tool down on the Main tool bar/frame (assuming the *Newuser* interface), see Figure 1.30 on page 1-34).

Note: All the measuring tools have a ruler represented across the bottom of the button.

2.   Select any of the tools with the "drag and drop" technique.
       Note the tool description in the Status bar at the bottom-left of the application window. This tool button will now be displayed "on top" in the frame, replacing the tool appearing there before.

3.   Repeat the "drag and drop" action as in **2.**, but this time drag the tool box clear of the frame before releasing the mouse button.
       This action is known as *Tearing off* and *Floating* a tool box.

4.   Place the tool box back on the frame by closing (dismissing) it with a double-click to its *Control Menu box*.
       Note that the tool last selected now displays in the frame position of the tool box.

Tip!   Select the leftmost tool on the tool box before closing it, this gives a consistent look to the frame, thus making tool box selection easier.

Window 1

These arrowheads indicate that there are more tools available from *Tool Boxes* accessible via the buttons.

The tool buttons displayed in the *Main Tool Frame* are those of the tools last selected from the *Tool Box* "under" the button.

Accessing "Child" Tool Boxes from the Main Tool Frame

A *Tool Box* may be dismissed (closed) by clicking its *Close* button

1.   **2.**   **3.**

Drag and drop tool selection

Measure

Floating tool box

Alternative method for accessing Tool boxes

Settings	Tools	Utilities	Workspace	Window

Tool Boxes...   Ctrl+T

✓ Tool Settings

✓ Primary
✓ Standard

Tool Boxes

Tool Boxes/Frames ▼

☐ Hatch
☐ Isometric
☐ Linear Elements
☒ **Main**
☐ Manipulate
☐ Match
☒ Measure
☐ Modify
☐ Modify Constraint
☐ Modify Curves

Tool Frames listed in BOLD text

☐ Large Buttons   ☑ Show Tool Tips

OK
Cancel
New...
Remove
Customize

Tool boxes may be opened (independently of the Main tool frame) from the Application window menu bar, by clicking their check box in the *Tool Boxes* settings box.

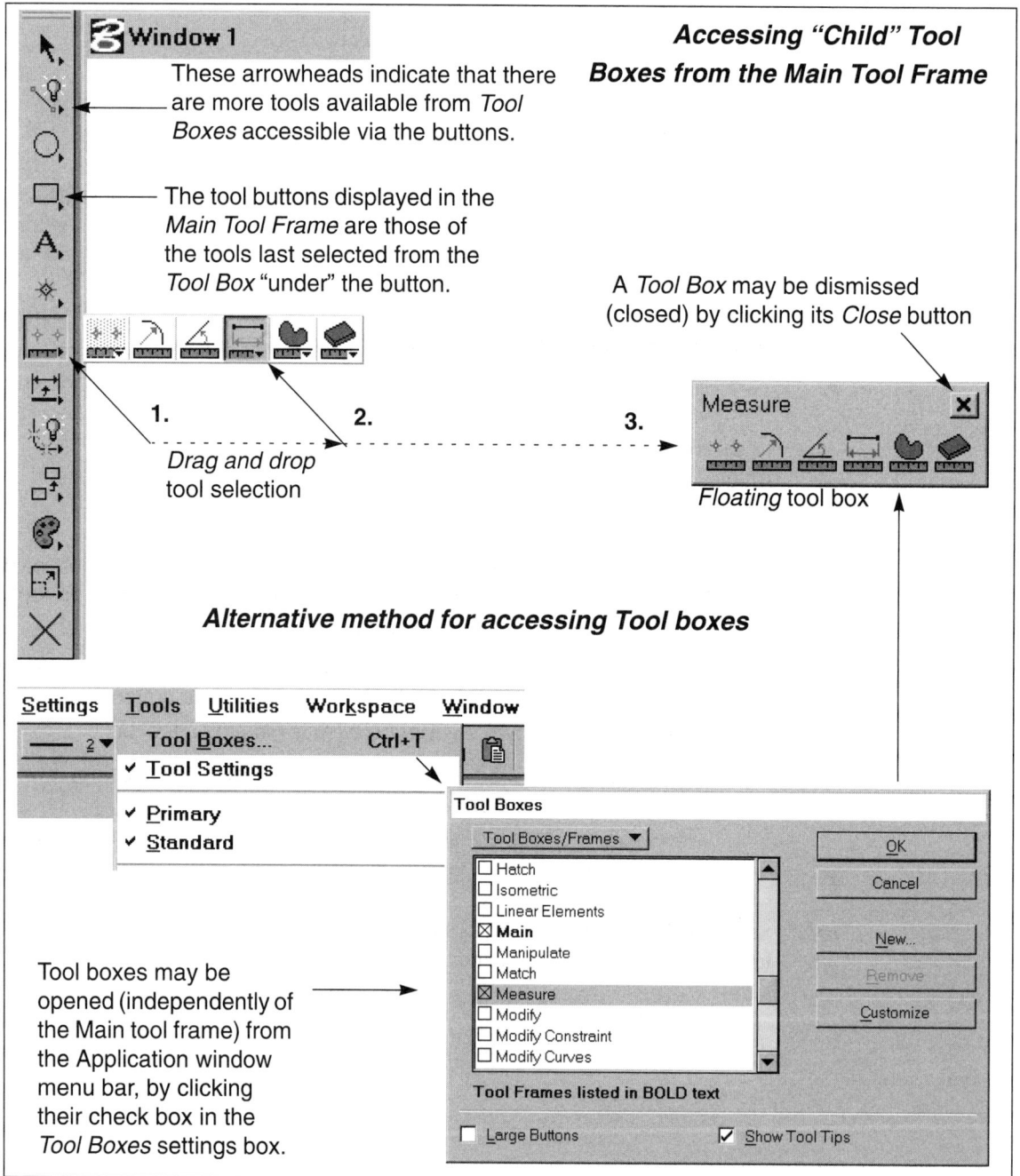

Figure 1.30   Tool Frame and Child Tool Box.

Resizing Tool Boxes

Floating tool boxes are windows in their own right, they have a Title bar, a Control-menu box and a border. They can be treated like any other window, in that they can be resized to suit their environment.

The limitation to the resizing of these particular windows is that all the buttons must show, so we may change their proportions but not their tool button area. To resize them we can "push or pull" on side borders, or use the window corners to change its width and height, just like most other windows.

◆ Float and Resize the Measure tool box

1. *Tear off* and *Float* the "Measure" tool box from the Main tool frame, as illustrated in the top part of Figure 1.30.

2. Move it about within the View window area by dragging it by its Title bar, or by the area between the buttons and the border.

3. Experiment with resizing, dragging corners and borders to achieve the combinations illustrated in figure 1.31.

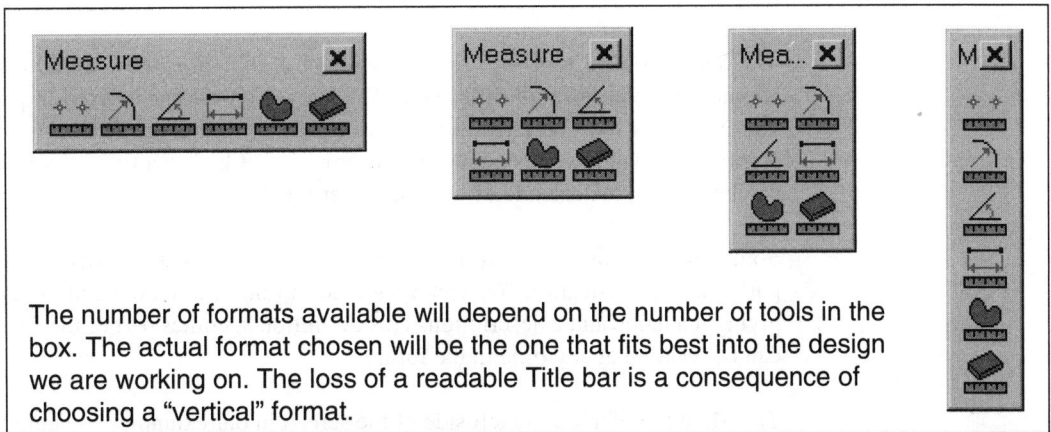

The number of formats available will depend on the number of tools in the box. The actual format chosen will be the one that fits best into the design we are working on. The loss of a readable Title bar is a consequence of choosing a "vertical" format.

Figure 1.31   Resizing a tool box - some options

These *Child* tool boxes may be *Docked* at the edge of the application window as a tool bar, as we did with the Standard tool box on page 1-31. An instance when this action may be worthwhile, could be when we have numerous measurements to make while checking a design. In that case, the tools from the "Measure" tool box could be made constantly visible on a *Tool Bar*.

Summary

MicroStation J (in the usual configuration) starts with the MicroStation Manager dialog box, which provides file, interface and directory management functions. MicroStation PowerDraft starts with a design file open, by default a blank file called "untitled.dgn". Once a design file is open in either version, there are *File* functions, such as *Open* another file, available from an *Application Window Option Menu*.

The *Application Window* has all the components we would expect in a Microsoft Office® compatible application. The standard window manipulation techniques apply, such as window resizing by "dragging" borders and corners, Minimize/Maximize/Restore etc.

An area where designs are viewed and created is known as a *View* window. There can be up to eight of these open at any one time, but there are usually less, often just one. When there are multiple View windows open, they can be individually sized and positioned, or automatically arranged in a *Tile* or a *Cascade* arrangement. Each View window has a *View Control Tool Bar* providing control of the contents displayed in the View window. In addition to this bar, there are horizontal and vertical *Scroll Bars* which can also be used to change the area of the design on display.

The View Control tools are one example of a *Tool Bar*, the *Standard Tool Bar* is another, but with a small difference. The View Control bar is fixed in place, but all the other bars may be moved. If a tool *bar* is moved away from the edges of the Application window it becomes a tool *box*. A tool box is a type of window, thus it can be moved, resized and closed like other windows.

Sometimes we need to return to a particular set of View window contents at a particular magnification. We can *Save* a definition of a View window arrangement, giving it a name and a description. This definition becomes part of the design file and can be recalled at any time in the future.

The Main tool bar, on the left side of the screen in our examples, is actually a type of *Tool Frame*. While it appears to have a fairly limited number of tool buttons, most of these represent a whole *tool box*, each with it own specialized range of tools. The individual tools may be accessed "in place" using "drag and drop" selection, or the entire tool box may be *torn off* and *floated* by dragging it away from the frame. Once floated clear of the frame, these tool boxes may be *docked* anywhere along the edges of the Application window, to become new *tool bars*.

2 : MicroStation Basics

In this chapter we start creating our own designs, making use of the competency we gained in chapter 1 in controlling the MicroStation J environment. In that chapter we found MicroStation to have very much in common with modern "GUI" based software. We used the view controls to display various parts of an existing design file and to rearrange the *Tool Boxes* and *Windows* within the *Applications Window.*

We will build on this competency with practice on the more MicroStation specific operations, actually creating a simple design. To do this, we will learn how to create and set up a new design file, making use of menu options. The first drawing tools will be introduced and the "other" mouse buttons will be found to have important functions.

When you have completed this chapter, you will be able to:

- Create a new *Design File*, based on an appropriate *Seed File*;
- Use the mouse (or tablet cursor) buttons to place *Data Points*, *Tentative Points* and *Reset*;
- Use the *Grid* and *Grid Lock* for precision design element creation;
- Set up *Working Units* and other design file settings to configure the *MicroStation Design Plane;*
- Use the *Place SmartLine* and *Place Block* tools with their default tool settings;
- Place elements on different *Levels* and control their display;
- Use the *Undo* and *Redo* facilities.

Creating New Drawings

In the first chapter we worked with an existing design, "office.dgn". Now we will create a design file of our own and place some design elements in it.

Creating a New Design File from MicroStation Manager

When we first start MicroStation J, or when we *Close* a design file when it is running, the *MicroStation Manager* dialog box appears. To create a new file from this dialog box, we use the *File* pull-down menu from the *menu* bar from below the *MicroStation Manager* dialog box *Title Bar,* choosing *New* (see Figure 2.1).

Creating a New Design File from Within Another Design

We will frequently need to create a new design file from within an open MicroStation design file. (this is the only option available in PowerDraft, as this application does not have an equivalent of the *MicroStation Manager* dialog box).

Within a design, we choose the *New* option from the *File* pull-down menu in the *Application window Menu Bar*, see Figure 1.3 on page 1-5. Either way (from within *MicroStation Manager* or an existing *Design File*), choosing *File>New* will open the *Create Design File* dialog box.

◆ **Create a new Design File**

1. Choose *File>New* from menu bar of either the MicroStation Manager or the Application window.
    The *Create Design File* dialog box opens.

The Seed File

When we create a *new* design file we always base it on an *existing* design file, which we call a *Seed File*. This file is rather like a template we may use when creating a word processing document. The Seed file has already been configured to have many of the appropriate settings made for us, thus we can start drawing immediately. One of these pre-sets is the *Dimensions* of the file, whether it is two-dimensional or three-dimensional (2D or 3D).

There are a variety of Seed files supplied with MicroStation, one of which we will use for the next exercise. Later on in the book we will create our own Seed file with settings to suit the example designs being created.

MicroStation Manager

File Directory

New...   Ctrl+N
Copy...
Rename...
Delete...
Info...   Ctrl+I
Merge...
Compress...

1 ...\intro\dgn\office.dgn
2 ...\intro\dgn\clock.dgn
3 ...\intro\dgn\border.dgn
4 ...\intro\dgn\pumproom.dgn

Exit
tagset.dgn

Directories:
...\projects\tutorials\intro\dgn\

C:\
Bentley
Workspace
projects
tutorials
intro
dgn

OK
Cancel

List Files of Type:
MicroStation Design Files [*.dgn]

Drives:
c:

☐ Open Design Files Read-Only

Workspace
User: tutorials
Project: intro
Interface: newuser
SMe   Status Bar

Either
Choose *File>New*
from the MicroStation
Manager dialog box

OR
Choose *File>New*
from the MicroStation
Application window
when we have a file
already open

office.dgn (2D) - MicroStation/J

File Edit Element Settings Tools

New...   Ctrl+N
Open...   Ctrl+O
Open URL...
Close   Ctrl+W
Save As...

Print/Plot   Ctrl+P
Page Setup
Send...

1 ...\intro\dgn\office.dgn
2 ...\intro\dgn\clock.dgn
3 ...\intro\dgn\border.dgn
4 ...\intro\dgn\pumproom.dgn

Exit

Create Design File

Directory

Files:

aldefeld.dgn
border.dgn
bordera.dgn
bracket.dgn
cd10.dgn
cd9.dgn
clock.dgn
compass.dgn
ddcell.dgn
del_part.dgn
floor.dgn
floorpla.dgn

Directories:
...\projects\tutorials\intro\dgn\

C:\
Bentley
Workspace
projects
tutorials
intro
dgn

OK
Cancel
Help

List Files of Type:
MicroStation Design Files [*.dgn]

Drives:
c:

Seed File
C:\Bentley\Workspace\system\seed\seed2d.dgn   Select...

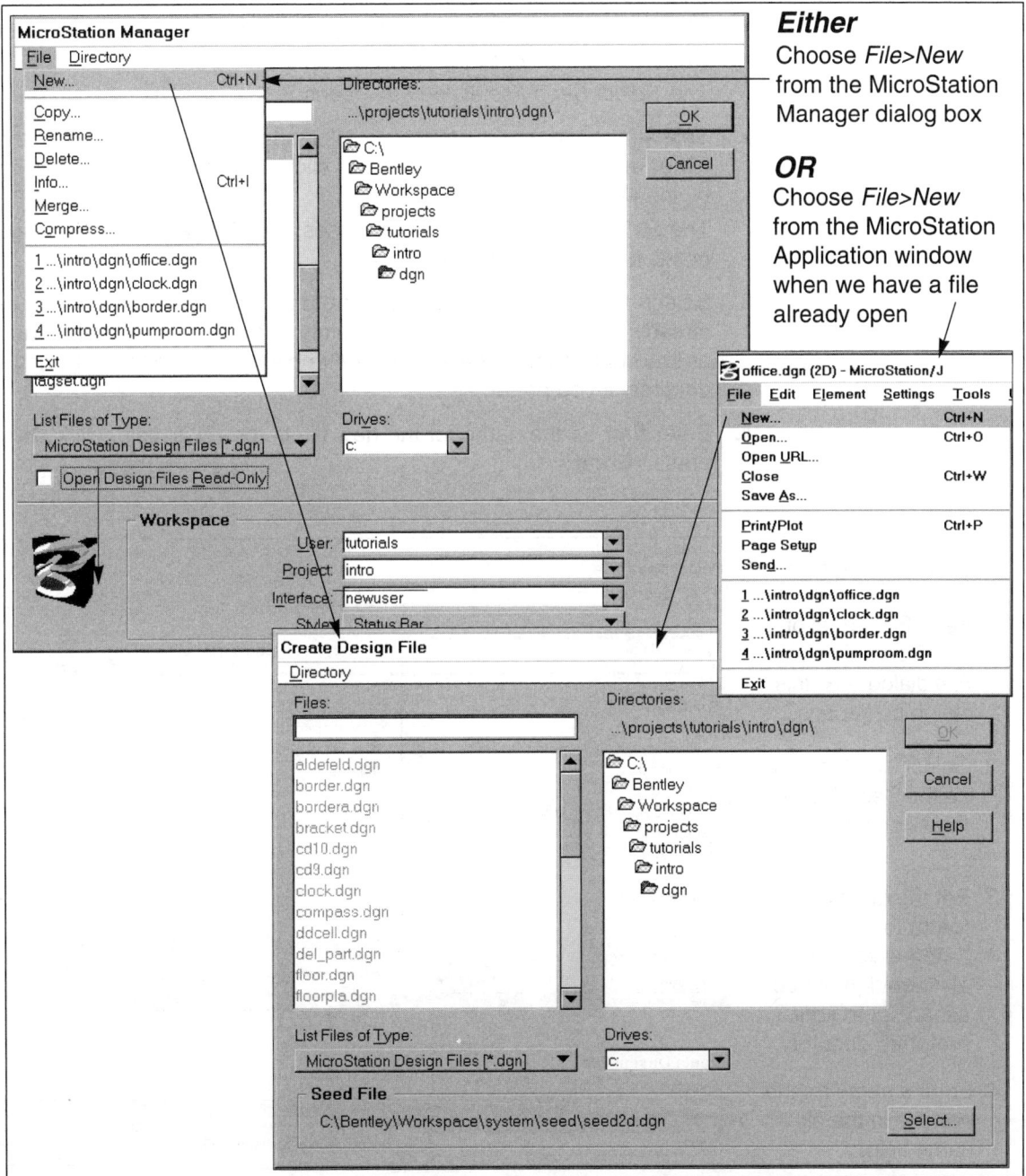

Figure 2.1   Opening the "Create Design File" dialog box

◆ **Selecting the Seed File**

1. Click the *Select* button in the Seed File panel (at the bottom of the *Create Design File* dialog box).

   The *Select Seed File* dialog box opens.

2. Select "seed2d.dgn" from the . . .Workspace\system\seed\ directory, either double-click the file name, or click the file name once followed by the **OK** button.

   The *Select Seed File* dialog box closes, the *Create Design File* dialog box is once more has *Input Focus*.

3. Select the "...\projects\tutorials\intro\dgn" directory (if it does not already appear as the current directory in the *Directories* information at the right of the *Create Design File* dialog box), or select another directory if you prefer.

4. Enter **first** as the name for the new file in the *Files:* field, click **OK** or press <**Enter**>.

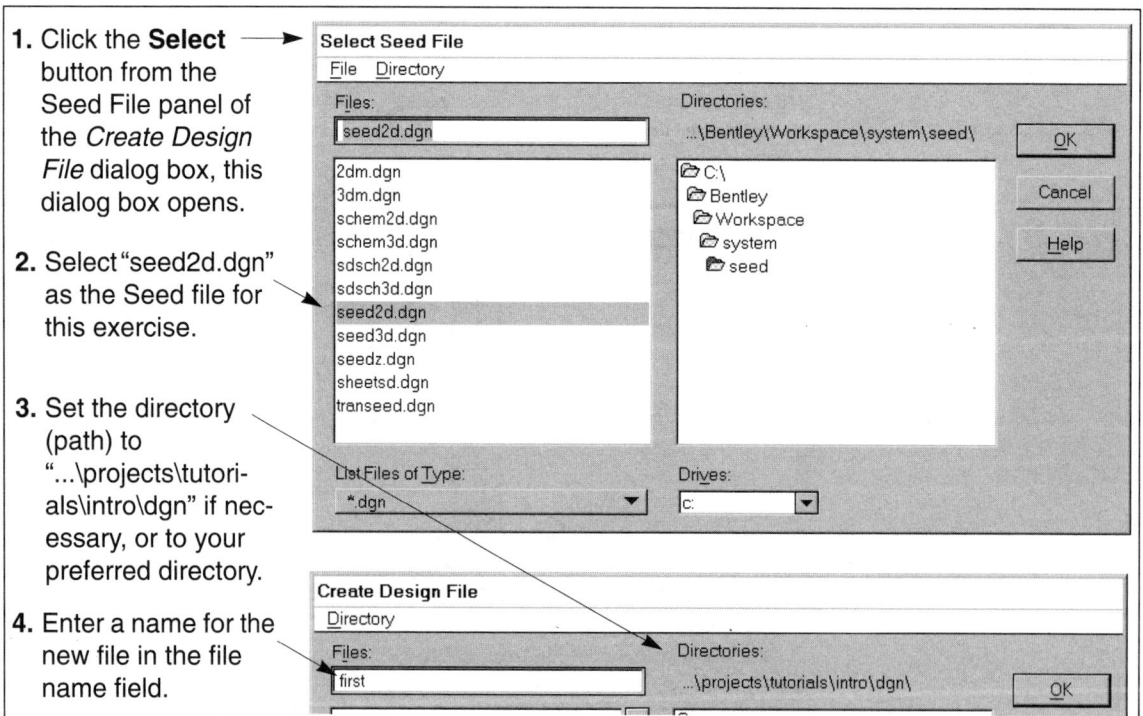

---

1. Click the **Select** button from the Seed File panel of the *Create Design File* dialog box, this dialog box opens.

2. Select "seed2d.dgn" as the Seed file for this exercise.

3. Set the directory (path) to "...\projects\tutorials\intro\dgn" if necessary, or to your preferred directory.

4. Enter a name for the new file in the file name field.

Select Seed File	
File Directory	

Files:
seed2d.dgn

2dm.dgn
3dm.dgn
schem2d.dgn
schem3d.dgn
sdsch2d.dgn
sdsch3d.dgn
seed2d.dgn
seed3d.dgn
seedz.dgn
sheetsd.dgn
transeed.dgn

Directories:
...\Bentley\Workspace\system\seed\

📂 C:\
📂 Bentley
📂 Workspace
📂 system
📂 seed

OK   Cancel   Help

List Files of Type:
*.dgn

Drives:
c:

Create Design File
Directory

Files:
first

Directories:
...\projects\tutorials\intro\dgn\

OK

Figure 2.2   Selecting a seed file and naming the new design file

The extension ".*dgn*" will automatically be appended to complete the file name. If we created the file from MicroStation Manager, this dialog box will again have input focus (with "first.dgn" highlighted). If we created the file from within another design, "first.dgn" will replace it as the *Active Design.*

5. Press **Enter** or click **OK** if the MicroStation Manager dialog box has input focus and "first.dgn" opens, as shown in Figure 2.3.

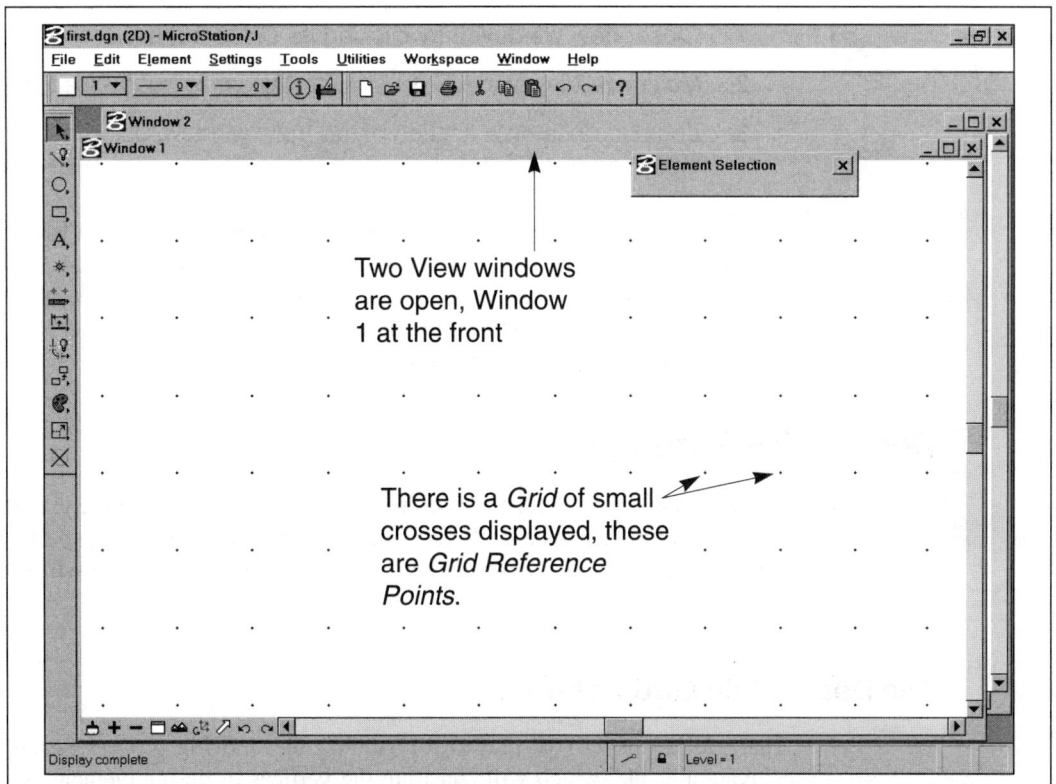

Figure 2.3   Applications window with the "seed2d.dgn" settings

Choice of Directory for your Design File

We used the "...\intro\dgn" directory for our new file, but another directory may have been selected. Using a "floppy" drive is not recommended, as it slows down the operation and can create some other difficulties. There are no other limitations on the path to the design files, but the choice of another directory may require some minor configuration changes for some exercises found later in the book.

Preparing the Design File for drawing

When we created 'first.dgn" we used a *Seed File* as a *template* to start from and the current View window arrangements are from that Seed File, "seed2d.dgn". We have two *View windows* open and there is a *Grid* displayed in View window 1, appearing as dots. We only need one View window open for our first project and we will be utilizing the Grid, so we will start by arranging the file accordingly.

◆ Prepare the View window

1. Close View window 2 by clicking its *Close* button.

2. Maximize View window 1 using its *Maximize* button (see page 1-26).

3. Zoom In once on a section of the View window, using a *Zoom Ratio* of **4.00** (see page 1-11).

If the View controls have not been used before in this new design file, a section of the View window will resemble the section illustrated in figure 2.4. It will display very small grid dots, with larger dots forming a *Reference Grid* every 10 grid dots. The grid can be likened to linear graph paper, where there are heavier *Reference* lines placed at intervals of several *Grid* lines.

Design File Settings

There are numerous design file settings we can optimize to suit the projects we have in hand. These settings can all be modified, in fact we will frequently be modifying various settings as we create designs. The first of the settings we will look at is the *Grid*.

The Design File Grid Settings

The grid is not only displayed for guiding the drawing process visually. We can activate a "lock" which will constrain the vertices of design elements such as lines and shapes to fall on the *Grid Unit Points*. This is one way of assuring the precision location and size of the design elements. Logically, these settings can be accessed from the *Settings* menu, by choosing *Settings>Design File>Grid*.

◆ Examine Grid settings, activate Grid Lock

1. From the Application window menu bar, choose *Settings>Design File*. The *Design File Settings* settings box opens.

2. Click on **(a)** *Grid* (the settings box displays the *Grid Parameters*), **(b)** click the *Grid Lock* button *On.*

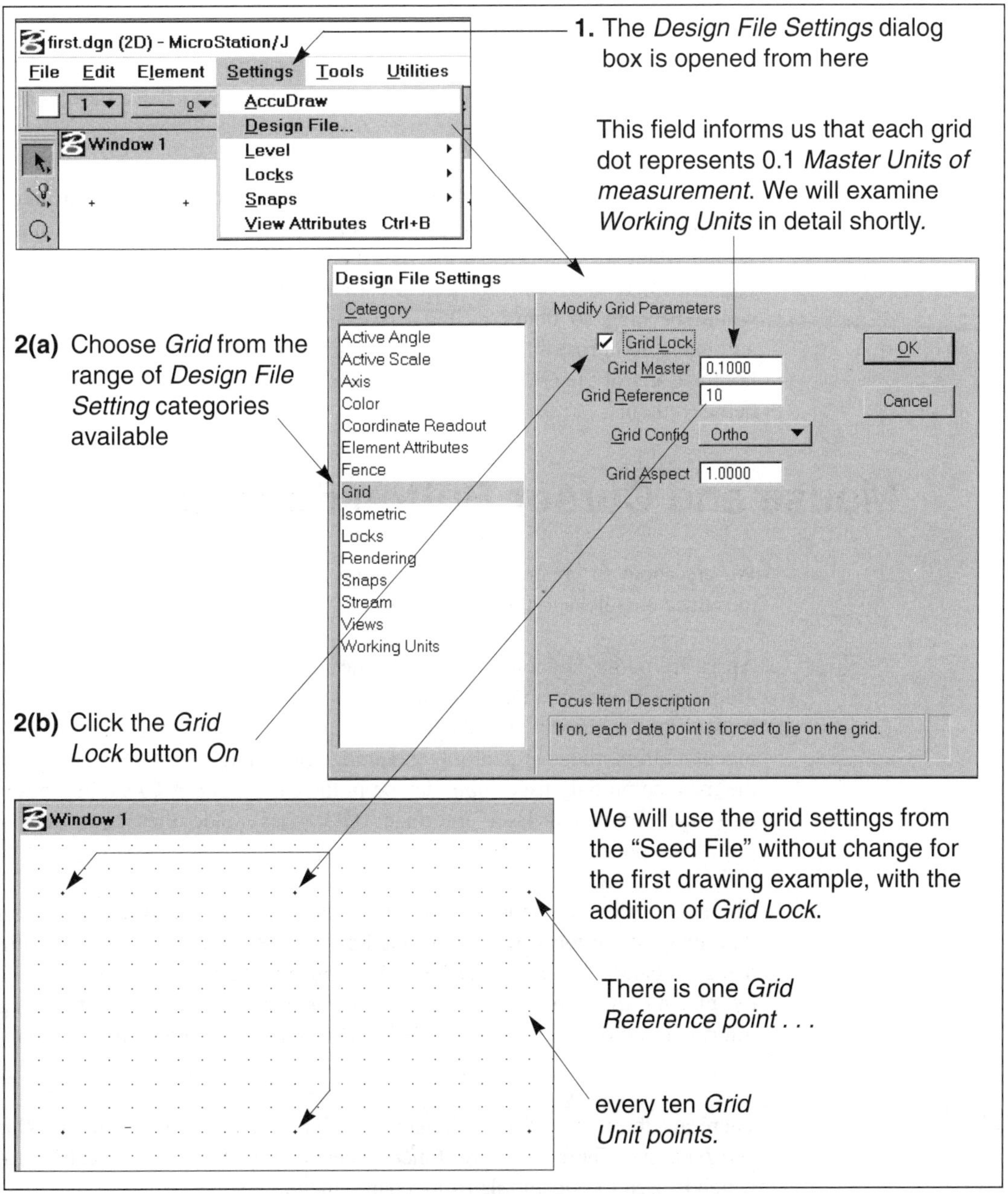
first.dgn (2D) - MicroStation/J
File Edit Element Settings Tools Utilities
AccuDraw
Design File...
Level
Locks
Snaps
View Attributes Ctrl+B
Window 1
1. The Design File Settings dialog box is opened from here
This field informs us that each grid dot represents 0.1 Master Units of measurement. We will examine Working Units in detail shortly.
Design File Settings
Category
Active Angle
Active Scale
Axis
Color
Coordinate Readout
Element Attributes
Fence
Grid
Isometric
Locks
Rendering
Snaps
Stream
Views
Working Units
Modify Grid Parameters
Grid Lock
Grid Master 0.1000
Grid Reference 10
Grid Config Ortho
Grid Aspect 1.0000
OK
Cancel
Focus Item Description
If on, each data point is forced to lie on the grid.
2(a) Choose Grid from the range of Design File Setting categories available
2(b) Click the Grid Lock button On
Window 1
We will use the grid settings from the "Seed File" without change for the first drawing example, with the addition of Grid Lock.
There is one Grid Reference point . . .
every ten Grid Unit points.

Figure 2.4 Grid settings for 'first.dgn"

3. Click **OK**, or press <**Enter**> to accept the *Grid Settings* and close the dialog box.

4. Use the *View Previous* tool to restore the magnification setting to the original, as illustrated in figure 2.3.

   It may be necessary to use other tools from the *View Control* tool bar if you have made more than one change to the magnification since opening the file.

You will notice a difference in the grid displays between the two magnification settings. Only the *Grid Reference Points* were displayed with the magnification setting when we first opened the file, the *Grid Unit Points* did not appear until we zoomed in. If we zoom out past a certain point, even the *Grid Reference Points* would become so dense as too make viewing the design difficult, so the grid automatically turns off. In the other direction, it is possible to zoom in so that we do not have any of the *Grid Unit Points* appearing on the screen, we would be "looking between them".

Mouse and Cursor Button Functions

We are about to create our first drawing, but before we start on this, we need to introduce ourselves to the other mouse button(s) and to the drawing tool we will use.

Apart from the keyboard, the input device for MicroStation can be either the ubiquitous Mouse or a Digitizer tablet cursor (sometimes called a "Puck"). The latter device varies greatly in shape and number of buttons between the various manufacturers, thus we can only generalize here. Digitizer tablets and cursors were the most commonly used input device in the early days of CAD, but these days the on-screen Graphical User Interface (GUI) has made the mouse the generally preferred option.

The main difference between using the mouse and the cursor/tablet combination is that many of the tools may be selected from a "Paper Menu" on the digitizer tablet using the cursor. It is also possible to input information from existing paper drawings by placing these on the tablet and identifying points etc. "Digitizing" paper information this way is generally less efficient than using a modern "Scanner" to do the job.

There are three main functions names assigned to the mouse buttons, *Data*, *Reset* and *Tentative*. There is a fourth function needed for a tablet cursor button, *Command*, which is used to select tools from a paper menu.

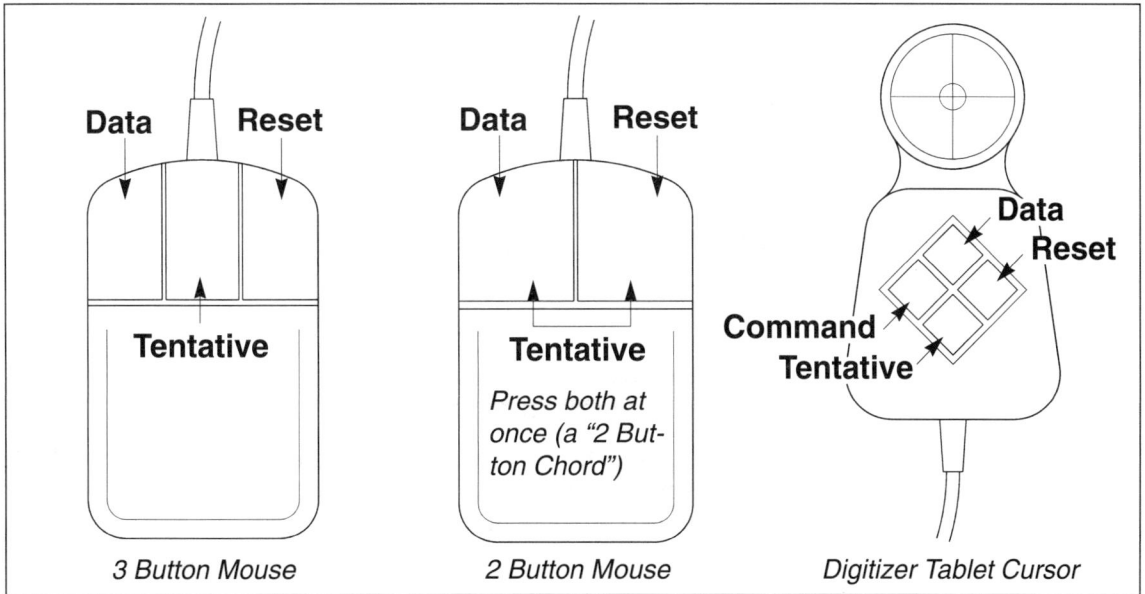

Figure 2.5 Typical Button Assignments

The Data Button

We must already be familiar with the *Data* button to have progressed this far, it is the primary mouse button used for selection. It is called the *Data* button in MicroStation because it is used to Place *Data Points* in a file. Data points define the location of certain points of a *Design Element*, such as the ends of a line or the center of a circle.

The Reset Button

The *Reset* button may be used to cancel an operation, reject an offered choice or signal the end of an operation (such as placing a "string" of lines).

The Tentative Button

The *Tentative* button is used to place a *Tentative Point*, a proposed location for a *Data* point. If we place a Tentative point and it falls in the wrong place, we can "Tentative" again, as often as we like. When we are satisfied with the position of the point, we *Accept* it by clicking the *Data* button. The position of the mouse pointer is irrelevant when we *Accept* a *Tentative* point. Tentative points are often placed by *Snapping* to existing elements, which will be covered in detail later.

Checking and Changing Button Assignments

It is possible that the default button assignments do not meet your needs for some reason. The default arrangement is for a two-button mouse, as illustrated at the top-center of figure 2.6, but a three-button mouse may be fitted for added convenience. Assuming the mouse hardware and software driver configurations (if any) are complete, re-assigning the buttons is simple.

◆ **Configure the button assignments**

1. Choose *Workspace>Button* Assignments.
   The Button Assignments dialog box opens.

2. Highlight the particular function you wish to re-assign by clicking on it with the current *Data* button.

3. Click the button, combination of buttons, or Alt-key-and-button combination you wish to use for the highlighted function in the *Button Definition Area* at the bottom of the dialog box.

4. Repeat as required for any other functions, Click **OK** to change the configuration, or **Cancel** to leave them as they were.

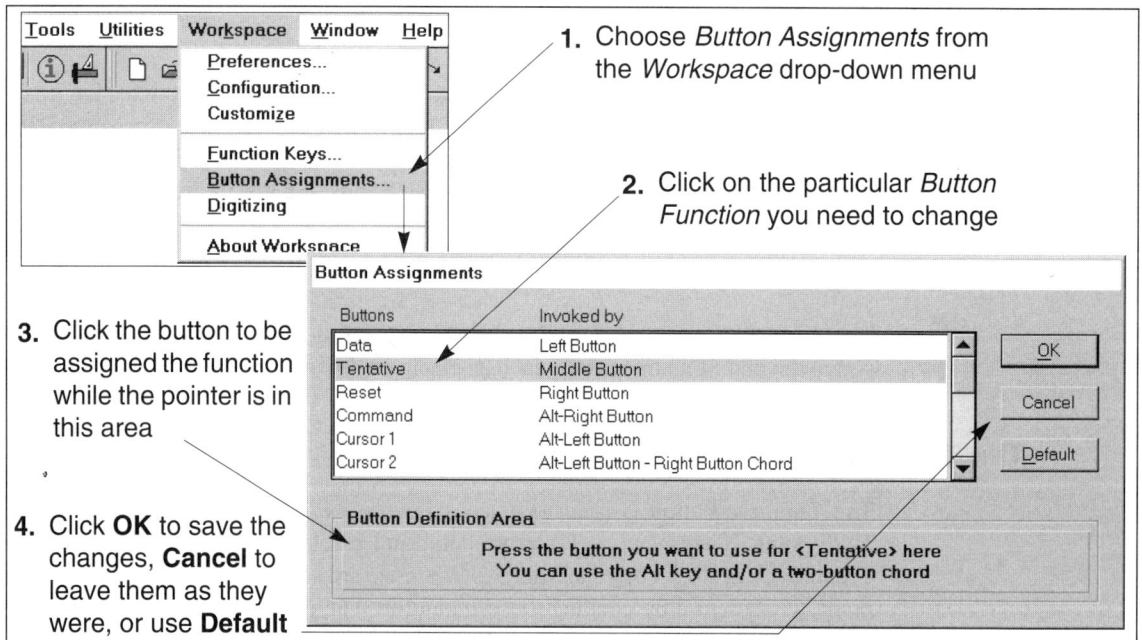

Figure 2.6   Button Assignments

Drawing Using the Grid Lock

We will now create our first drawing in "first.dgn". It will be a "Direction Arrow" similar to the one illustrated in figure 2.9, with each of its vertices on *Grid Reference Points*. If we have kept "first.dgn" open since the last exercise, the *Grid Lock* will still be *On*. With this lock on, each vertex will be constrained to fall precisely on either a *Unit* or a *Reference* grid point.

If we have closed the design since the grid setting was made, revise the exercise starting on page 2-6.

The Place SmartLine Tool

This is the tool, found on the *Main* tool frame, that we will use most frequently for line drawing. It will be used to create a simple shape in the next exercise, but it can also create other types of *Elements*, such as individual lines, line strings, arcs, even circles. We will introduce the features of SmartLine progressively, as we use it in different ways in various exercises.

When we select the *Place SmartLine* tool, its *Tool Settings* window offers a variety of menu choices and a data entry field. For this exercise we will use all the default settings, as shown in figure 2.7.

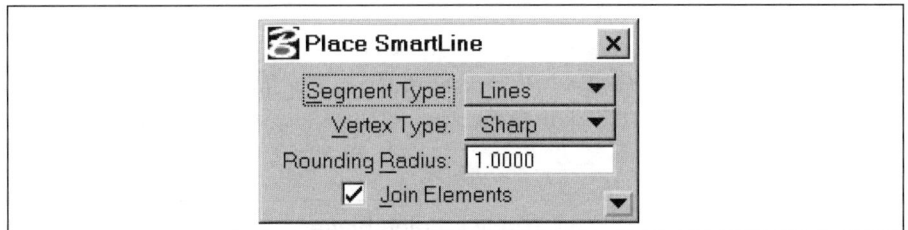

Figure 2.7   Default tool settings for the Place SmartLine tool

Using Tentative Points

We will use a *Tentative Point* (see "The Tentative Button" on page 2-9) to place the *final point only* to accurately close the arrow shape in the next exercise. With the default settings, clicking the Tentative button with the pointer on, (or very close to) an element will cause the pointer to *Snap* to the nearest *Keypoint* on that element. There will be more detail on *Keypoints* later, but one example of a *Keypoint* is the end of a line.

The pointer becomes a larger orthogonal cross when a tentative point is placed. If we decide the placement of the point is *Accept*able, we click the *Data* button to convert it to a *Data Point*. The location of this data point will form part of the definition of the element in the *Design File*.

If we have a problem during the process of creating the Arrow shape in the next exercise, choose *Edit>Undo* . . . from the Application window menu (or press **<Ctrl+Z>**, the equivalent *Keyboard Shortcut*). This will undo the last point placed.

◆ Draw the Direction Arrow

1. Check that the View window in "first.dgn" is displaying *Grid Reference Points* only, as it was when we first opened the design file. If not, adjust the magnification with the *View Control* tools to display **12** *Grid Reference Points* across the screen.

2. Select the *Place SmartLine* tool.

3. Position the Screen Pointer on the grid reference point corresponding with grid reference **B3** on Figure 2.9, click the *Data* button (do not use the *Tentative* button at this stage, it will override the grid lock).

   Move the pointer slightly, check that the new line starts from the required grid point. If it does not, click the *Reset* button and repeat.

4. Position the diagonal cross of the drawing pointer on the point corresponding with grid reference **G4** and place another *Data Point* as in step **3**.

Note that the pointer shape changes to indicate the stage we have reached in the *Element Placement* process. The line *Dynamically Updates* ("*rubber bands*") from the origin to the grid points as it is being placed.

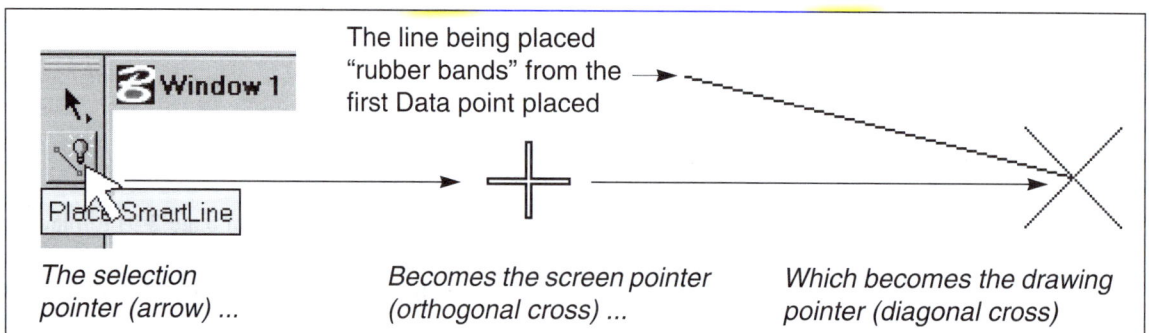

Figure 2.8 The different pointer shapes during line placement

5. Continue positioning the drawing pointer on each of the remaining vertices in turn, placing a *Data Point* on each one as shown in Figure 2.9, except when we return to the *Origin* (for now).

6. Position the pointer on the first line placed, near the origin of the first line segment placed (grid reference **B3**), click the *Tentative* button.

The pointer increases in size to become the *Tentative* pointer. This *Snaps* to the end of the first line, which highlights.

Note that the *Tool Settings* window expands to include choices for "Closed Element", which is *On* by default.

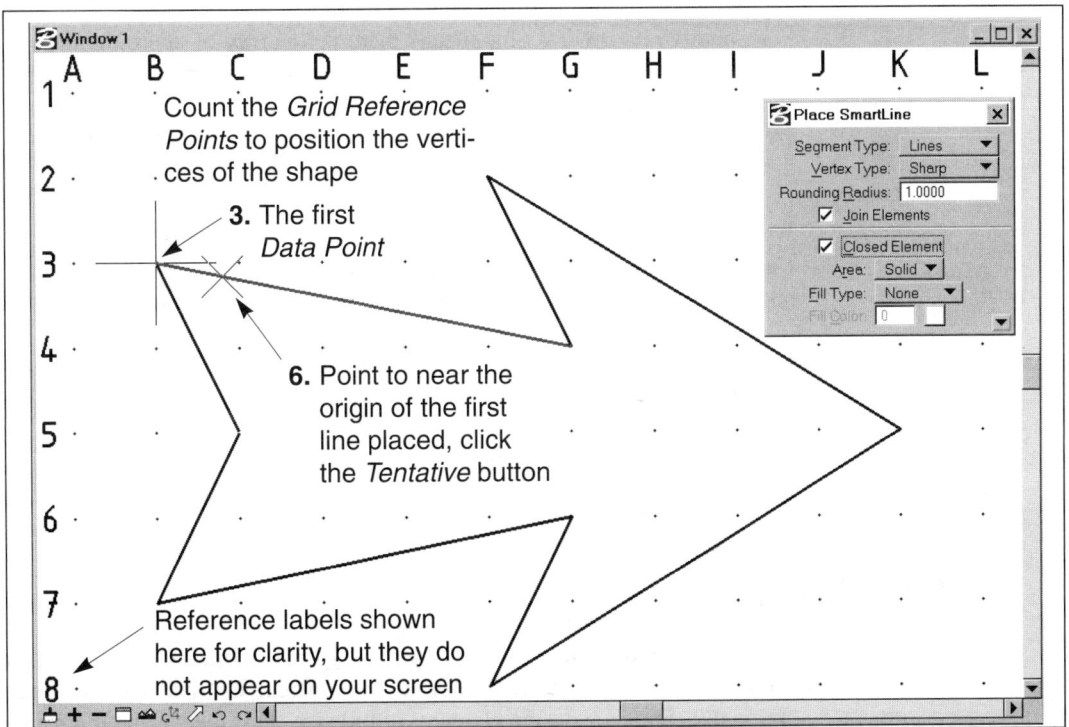

Figure 2.9 The Direction Arrow

7. *Accept* the *Tentative* point by clicking the Data button.

This completes the closed shape.

Closing the shape signals the end of the drawing operation in this case. If we had not created a closed shape, we would have needed to click the *Reset* button to signal the end of the operation.

We have created our first MicroStation *Element,* which will be used during several future exercises, so keep it. For now, we will look at the process we used to create it in some more detail. We used *Grid Reference Points* to control the dimensions of the *Shape* type element. This provided a simple method of producing a predictable outcome at this early stage, but it is by no means the only way to produce elements with precise dimensions.

The MicroStation 2D Design Plane

When we work in 2D, we have a planar area to operate within, with the positions of the elements on this plane defined by *x* and *y* coordinates. The 2 axes are split into approximately 4.29 billion Units Of Resolution (UOR's), sometimes called Positional Units (PU's). This means there is an array of approximately 4.29 billion by 4.29 billion finite positions available to start or finish a line on, place a vertex of a shape on, in fact to locate any part of any element. In practice, the *x* and *y* dimensions are each defined by a 32 bit integer, which means the actual number of finite points available is 2^{32} by 2^{32}.

We are free to allocate any number of these *Positional Units* to "real world" *Working Units,* such as millimeters, meters, feet, inches, nanometers or kilometers. There are no restrictions on the definition of our working units, we could even invent our own.

When allocating a number of *Positional Units* to a *Working Unit* we need to consider two main factors:

1.   The *Area* we need to be able to cover with our drawing;

2.   The *Resolution* required.

Full Size Vs. Scale

The scale of a drawing in CAD is normally only defined when we are producing a printout (sometimes called a plot) of the design. Until this stage is reached, we notionally create the design elements at full size. This means that if we are drawing a section of roadway one kilometer long, we do not "scale it down" to fit on a small drawing sheet as we would if we were using pen and paper. We therefore ignore scale when we are setting up our *Working Units* for a design.

We are about to change some settings in our file to allow us to use "real world" dimensions. Before we do, however, we need to be able to save these settings for later use and this is not permitted while we are using the *Newuser* interface. We will change to the *Default* interface and we will continue to use it from now on.

◆ **Select the Default Interface**

1. If we have "first.dgn" open, *Close* it using *File>Close.* Otherwise, start *MicroStation*, either way we need the *MicroStation Manager* dialog box open (See Figure 2.10).

2. Click the Interface option menu, choose the *Default* option.

3. Check that our directory is still the one containing "first.dgn". If not, click **Directory** from the MicroStation Manager dialog box menu and select the correct one from the "history" options, or select it using the *Directories* panel.

4. Find "first.dgn" and open it.

You will notice some small changes in the application window, including some more tools on the *Main* tool bar. *Grid Lock* will no longer be *On*, as any settings changes made in the *Learning* workspace session were not saved to the file.

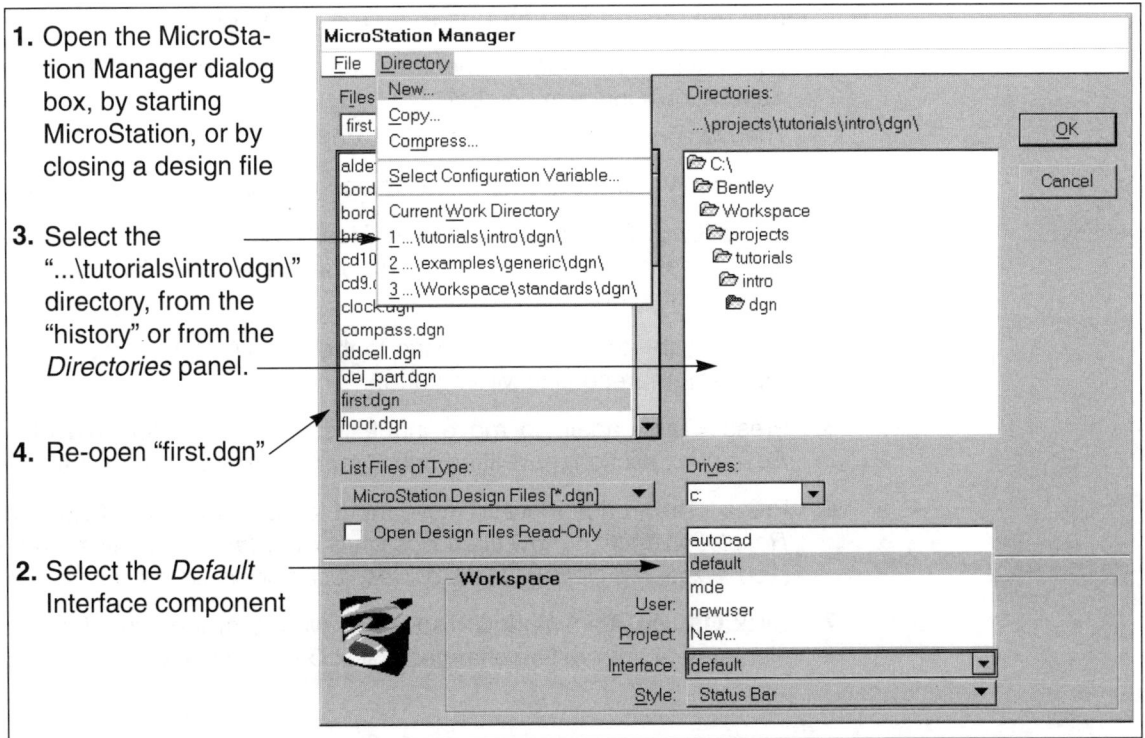

1. Open the MicroStation Manager dialog box, by starting MicroStation, or by closing a design file

3. Select the "...\tutorials\intro\dgn\" directory, from the "history" or from the *Directories* panel.

4. Re-open "first.dgn"

2. Select the *Default* Interface component

Figure 2.10   Changing to the Default Workspace Interface Component

Working Units Vs. Positional Units

The following exercise in setting working units will use the *Meter* as the *Master Unit*. *Sub Units* are also supported if we need them, so initially we will use the *Millimeter* as the *Sub Unit*. We will standardize on the internationally accepted metric units for all the examples used in this book. However, as suggested earlier, MicroStation will allow us to just as easily use the foot, the mile, the inch or any other units you may imagine.

The choice of working units, sub units and their relationship to positional units is made separately for each design file. As is the case for all of the choices from the *Settings* menu, the working unit settings can be "imported" with the *Seed File* used when the new design file was created.

The seed file we used, "seed2d.dgn", has working unit settings that are neither Metric or English (Imperial) units. We will set the *Working Units* for our *Design File* in the following exercise.

◆ **Change the design file settings to Metric Working Units**

1. With "first.dgn" open, choose *Settings>Design File* from the Application window menu bar.
   The *Design File Settings* settings box opens.

2. Choose *Working Units* from the *Category* panel.

3. In the *Unit Names* section of the *Modify Working Unit Parameters* panel, change the existing text ("mu") in the *Master Units* field to **m** (representing Meters).

4. Press <Tab> to move input focus to the *Sub Units* field, replace "su" with **mm** (representing Millimeters).

5. Press <**Tab**> again to move input focus to the upper field of the *Resolution* section (now titled *mm Per m*), make this read **1000**.

6. Press <Tab> once more to move input focus to the lower field of the *Resolution* section (now titled *Pos Units Per mm*), make this read **100** (100 *Positional Units* or *Units of Resolution* per millimeter).

7. Click **OK**, an *Alert* window displays to warn that the size of existing elements (if any) will be changed. Click **OK** in this box.

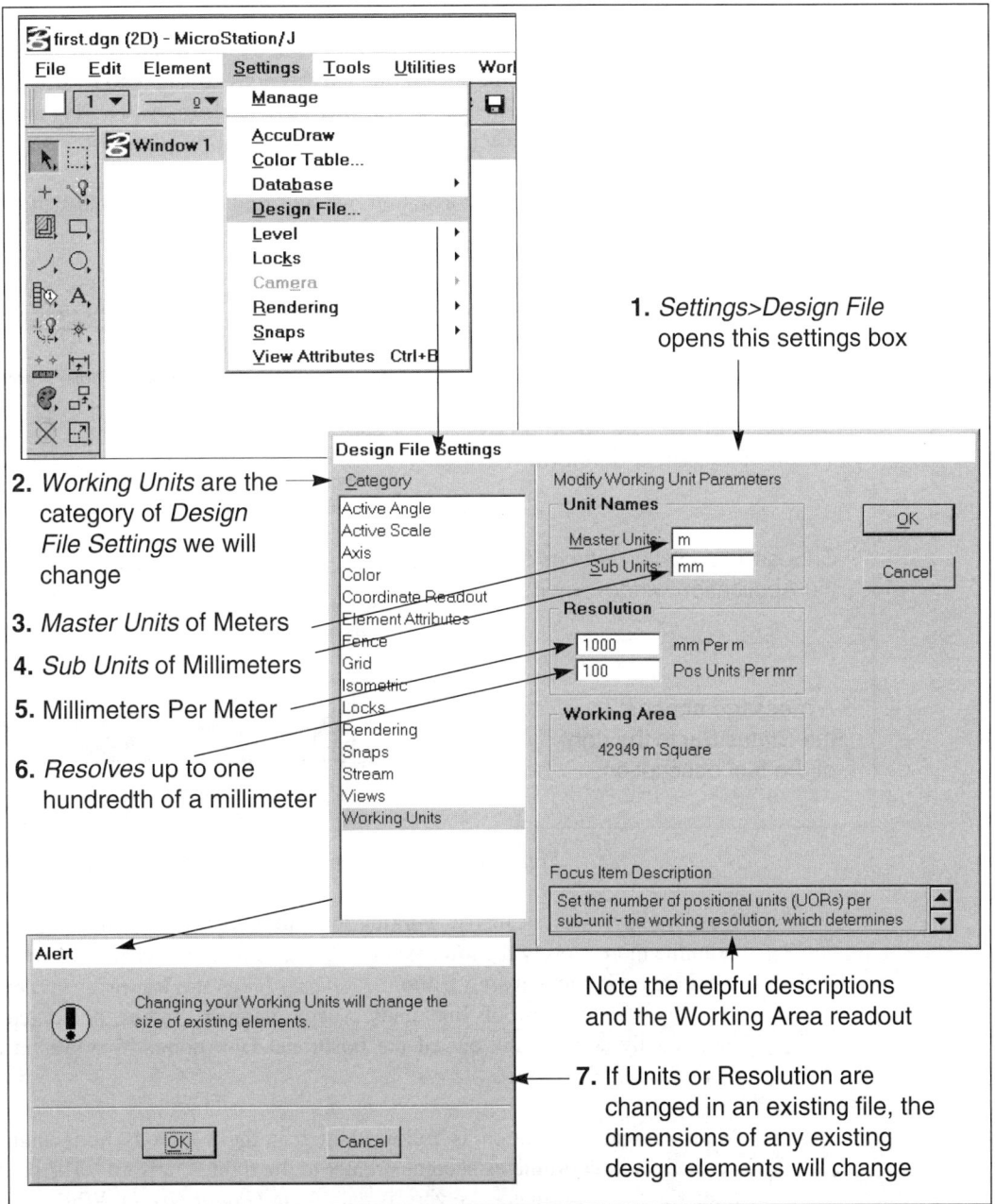

Figure 2.11 Changing the Working Units in "first.dgn"

Saving Design File Settings

In the default configuration of MicroStation J, changes to the design are automatically saved in the design file, but this does not apply to *Design File Settings*. In order to save the changes in settings we have made to the working units and to the resolution, it is necessary to *Save Settings* manually.

Since this is a *File* related operation, we will find the option under the Application window's *File* menu.

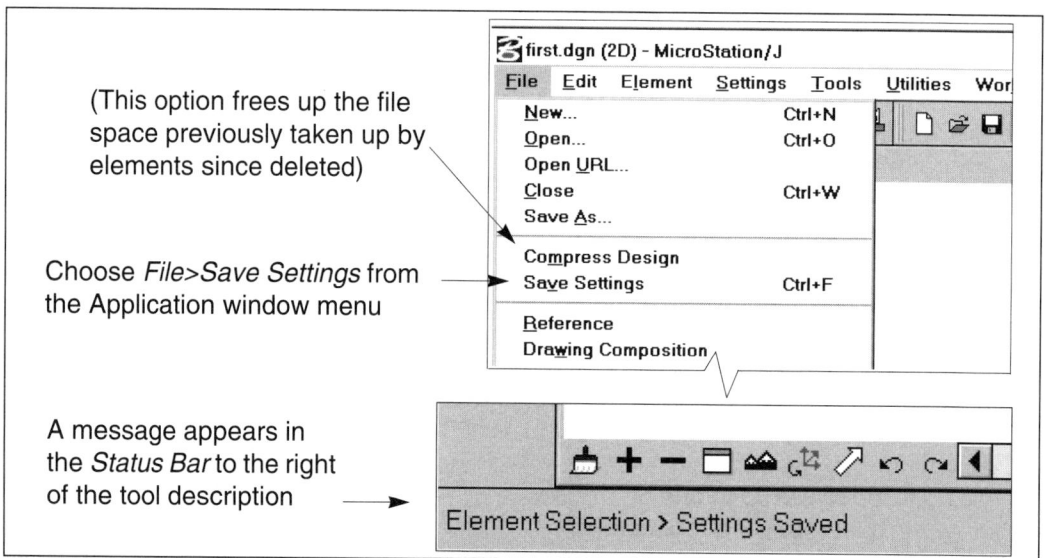

Figure 2.12   Saving changes to Design File Settings

Now we have a set of metric working units to work with in our design file, we will examine more closely the *MicroStation Design Plane*. On page 2-14 we learned that there are approximately 4.3 Billion^2 *Positional Units* (also known as *Units of Resolution*) to define the location of line ends, shape vertices, radius points etc. We can individually address any one of the Positional Unit points by a system of x and y *Coordinates*.

Mathematical convention is followed in that the x axis is horizontal and the y vertical, the x coordinates become greater to the right, y upwards. The point at which both x and y coordinates are zero is called the *Global Origin*. While we placed the vertices of our first drawing (the "Direction Arrow" visually with the help of the *Grid* and *Grid Lock*, we may alternatively have defined each one by its x and y Coordinates.

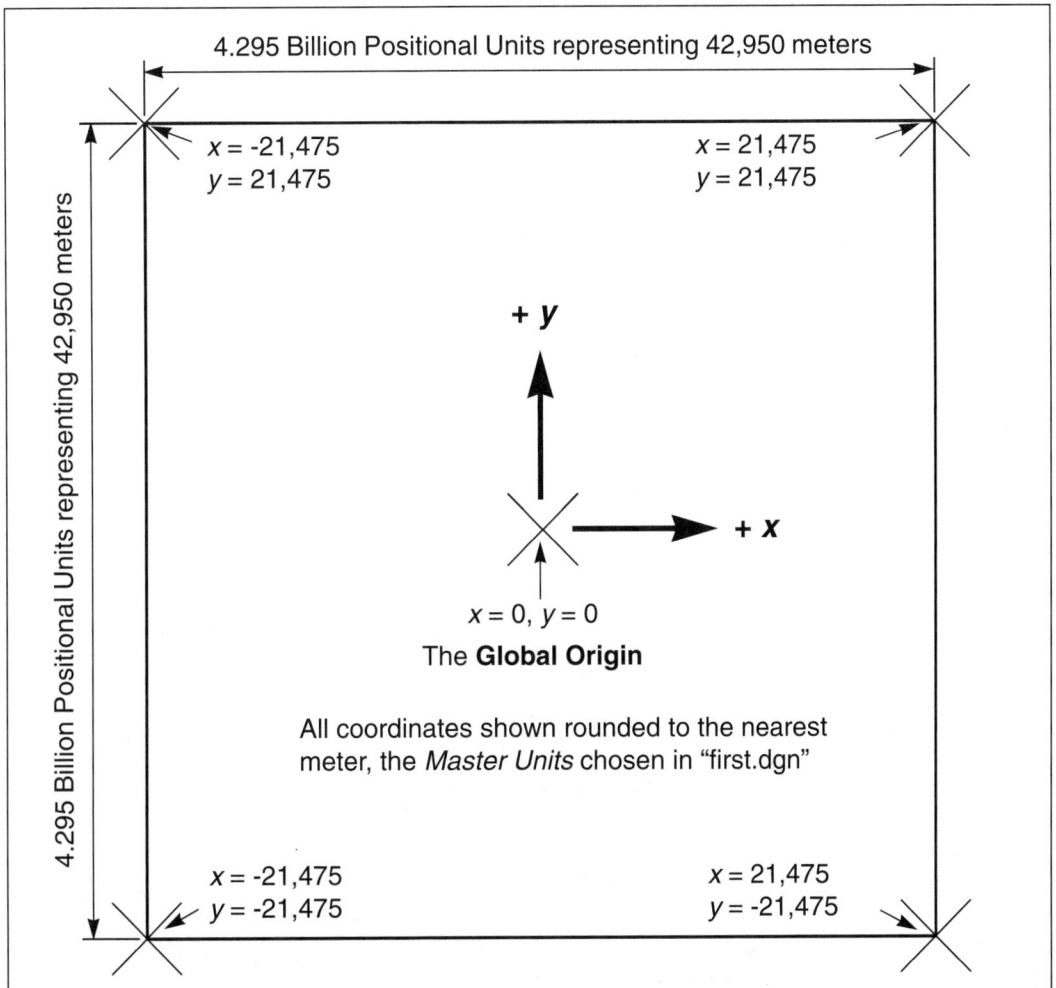

Figure 2.13 MicroStation Drawing Plane with "first.dgn" Working Units

So, what could we draw with the *Working Units* and the *Resolution* chosen? For a start the 42.9 by 42.9 kilometer area would allow us draw a map of a large city. The resolution of 100 positional units per millimeter would allow us to draw a fly on the roof of one of the city buildings in reasonable detail.

We can allocate more positional units for each sub unit if we need more precision, or less positional units for each sub unit if we need more area, such as for large area mapping.

Coordinate Readout

There are several methods of displaying the coordinates of a point on a design. The format for the readout may be configured as another *Design File Setting*, in a similar manner to the *Working Units* just set.

◆ **Change the design file Coordinate Readout settings**

1. With "first.dgn" open, choose *Settings>Design File* from the Application window menu bar, see figure 2.14.

2. Choose *Coordinate Readout* from the *Category* panel.

3. Change the *Format* to *Master Units* (the default setting may have been *Sub Units*).

4. Change the *Accuracy* to **0.123 (**3 decimal places).

5. Click **OK** to apply the changes and close the window, *Save Settings* (see "Saving Design File Settings" on page 2-18).

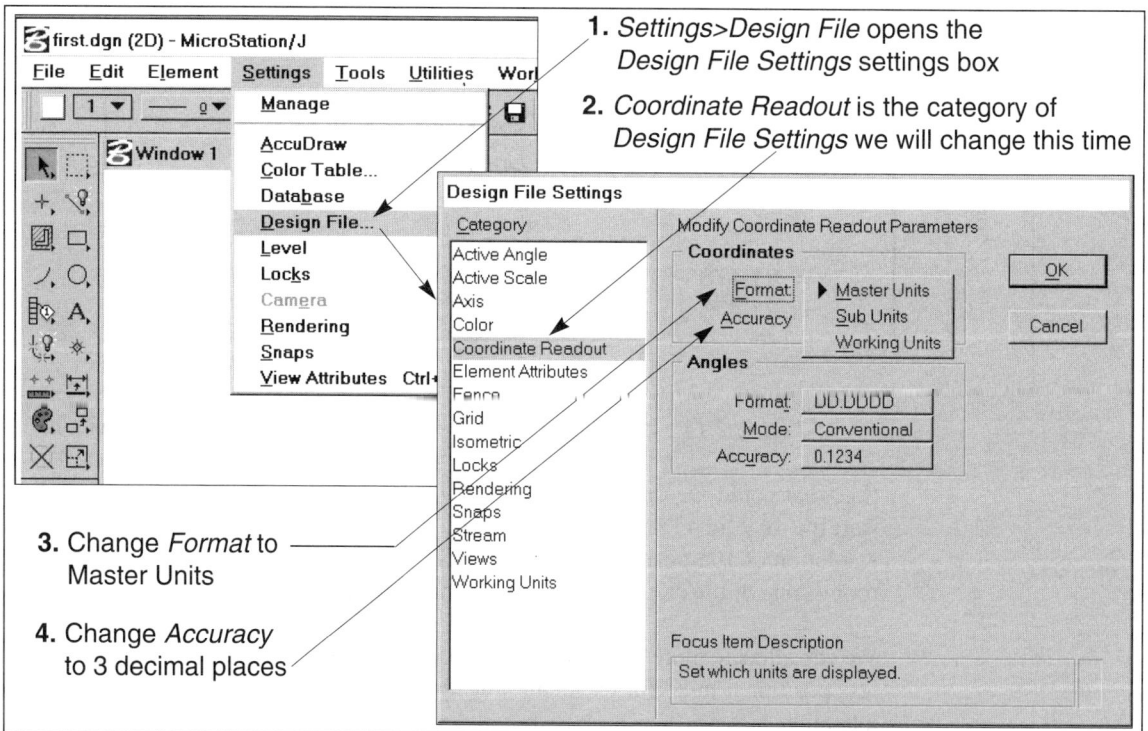

Figure 2.14 Changing the Coordinate Readout in "first.dgn"

Next, we will readout the coordinates of the vertices of the Arrow shape we created earlier. The method we will use is *Tentative Point Readout*, where the coordinates of a tentative point are displayed in the Status bar message area, near the right side.

◆ **Find the *x* and *y* coordinates of the arrow shape vertices**

   1. Position the pointer on a line near the vertex to be read, click the *Tentative* button.

   The shape will highlight and the *x* and *y* coordinates (*x* first) will be displayed in the Status bar Message area.

The coordinates shown in figure 2.15 may not agree with yours, it depends which reference grid points were chosen.

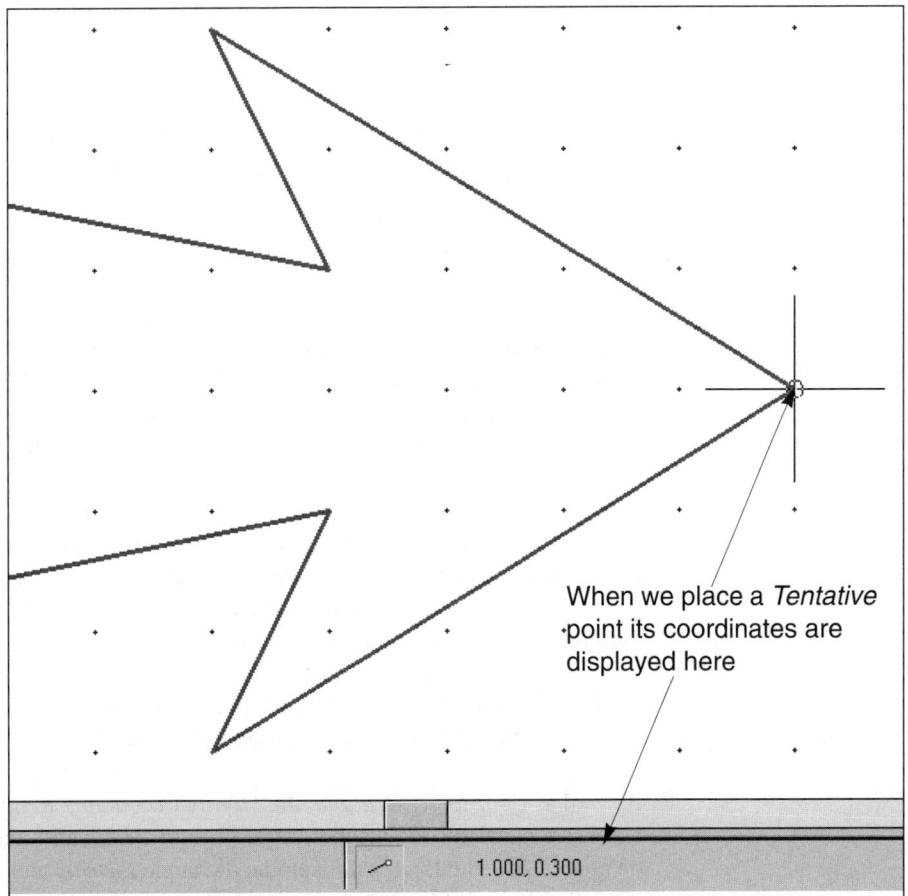

Figure 2.15   Reading the coordinates of the arrow vertices

2. Place tentative points at each of the other vertices, observing the coordinates to gain an impression of the size of the arrow.

We set the *Coordinate Readout* to display the coordinates in the form of *Master Units* (which we had previously set to be meters) to three decimal places. The readout we observe reflects this, with figures such as **1.000, 0.300**.

3. Change the *Coordinate Readout* format again, this time to *Sub Units* with an *Accuracy* of one decimal place (repeat the exercise on page 2-20).

4. Place some more tentative points, not necessarily on the arrow vertices, observe the coordinates.

This time we notice that the readout has a colon (**:**) between the *Master Units* and the *Sub Units*, with the sub units (millimeters) displayed with one decimal place, for example **1:0.0, 0:300.0**.

5. Change the *Coordinate Readout* once more, this time to *Working Units*, leaving the *Accuracy* at the previous setting.

6. Randomly place some more tentative points, observe the coordinates.

Now the coordinate readout does not display any decimal places, the *Accuracy* setting has no effect. The readout has colons separating *Master Units*, *Sub Units* and *Positional Units*. It will appear in the form **1:122:2, 0:756:89**. The format chosen will depend on the requirements of the design project. When Metric units are used, *Master Units* is commonly chosen and we will revert to this format.

In this example, the *Tentative Point Readout* has displayed the *Location* of the point on the design plane. In practice, the tentative point readout mode may be changed to display other information, but for now we will leave this mode as it is. As we progress, more coordinates readouts will appear, all of them affected by *Settings>Design File>Coordinate Readout*.

7. Change the *Coordinate Readout* back to *Master Units*, set the *Accuracy* to four decimal places (**0.1234**).

As well as *Coordinate Readout*, the *Modify Coordinate Readout Parameters* settings box has a panel for setting the Angle *Format, Mode* and *Accuracy* (see Figure 2.14 on page 2-20). Next, we will examine the angle *formats* and *modes* available and the interrelationship of the two.

Defining Angles

In MicroStation, angles are always defined with the degree as the base unit. We have a choice of *Angle Formats* and *Angle Modes* to comply with the needs of the various disciplines and standards that we may be working to. *Angle Format* only needs to be taken into account when we are entering other than whole degrees.

Angle Formats

We can choose to enter angles in *Degrees*, including decimals of a degree, or in *Degrees, Minutes* and *Seconds*. Either way we may use *Bearing* prefixes and suffixes (N, S, E & W). Independently of this, we can set the *Coordinate Readout* setting of our design file to display angles in either *Degrees* or *Degrees, Minutes* and *Seconds*. This means we may enter an angle in one format and read it out in another.

Angle Entry Formats

Entering an angle in *Degree* format is the same as entering any other decimal number. We enter the whole degrees first, the decimal point, then the decimal part of the angle. A format definition (to four decimal places) is abbreviated to DD.DDDD.

In *Degrees, Minutes and Seconds* we need to use specified separators between the three parts. We use the "^" (Carat, usually **<Shift 6>**) after the Degrees, then the usual symbology of " ' " (single quote) after the minutes and " " " (double quote) after the seconds. It is permissible, although seldom necessary, to use decimals in the *Seconds* part. This format definition is usually abbreviated to DD^MM'SS".

We can also enter angles in the *Bearing* format, for example *S30E*, indicating an angle 30° East of South on the compass. Angles can only be entered in this format if the *Coordinate Readout>Angle Mode* is set to *Bearing*. The numeric part of the angle must always be prefixed by **N** or **S** and suffixed by **E** or **W**. A totally numeric input is interpreted as being in *Conventional Mode*. The Angle Modes are described on page 2-24.

Angle Readout Formats

This is a *Design File Setting*, one of the *Coordinate Readout* options menu choices. We have already visited this settings box via *Settings>Design File>Coordinate Readout* when we set the coordinate readout to *Master Units* on page 2-20. It sets the angle readout format in various places, including the *AccuDraw Window* fields (to be introduced shortly) when *Polar* coordinates are in use.

Angle Modes

We can use *Conventional, Azimuth* or *Bearing* modes of angle definition within MicroStation. The *Angle Mode* chosen affects the angle readout in such places as the *AccuDraw Window* and, in some cases, how keyboard input is interpreted. The angle mode is set in the *Settings>Design File>Coordinate Readout* settings box.

Figure 2.16 illustrates the differences between the three modes, showing how an angle input will be interpreted in each mode. We will leave the *Angle Mode f*or the examples we are creating in "first.dgn" as *Conventional*.

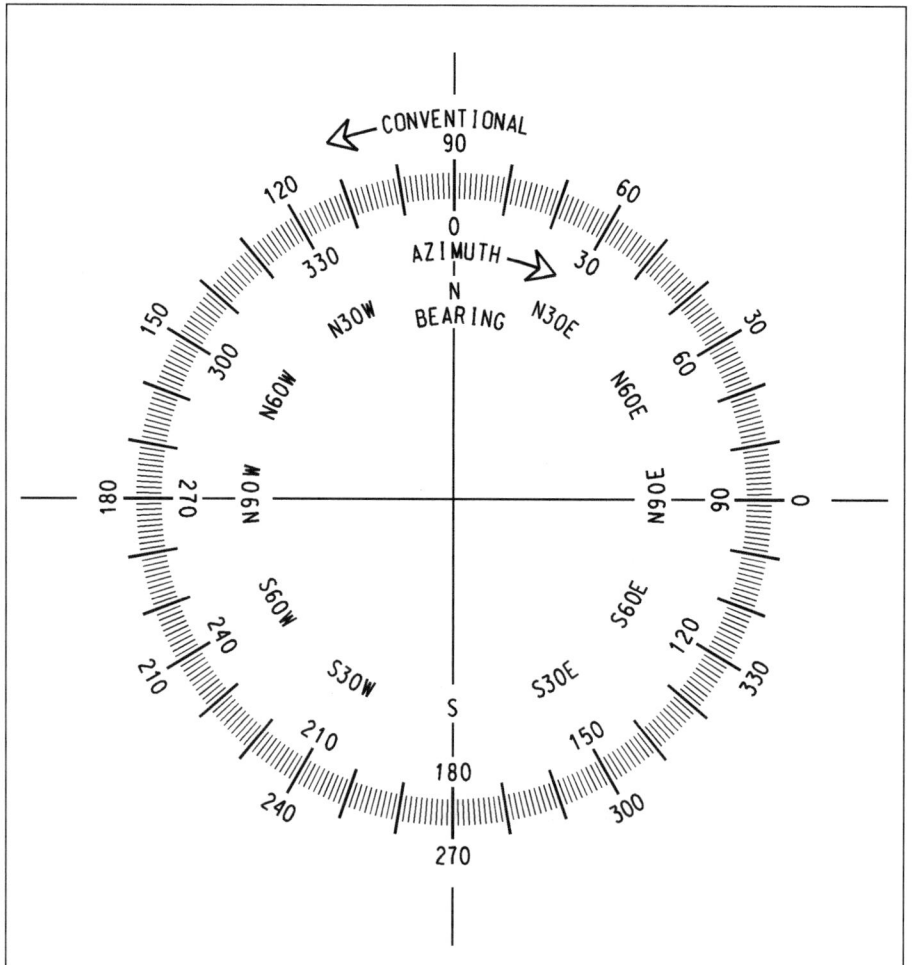

Figure 2.16 The three angle modes compared

Drawing Tools

The *Place Smartline* drawing tool used to create the Direction Arrow is just one of many drawing tools available in MicroStation. Before we look at some others in detail, we will take a preliminary look at the concepts used, including the use of the Tool Settings window.

Comparable types of tools are grouped together in various "Child" tool boxes of the *Main* tool frame. When the tool we require is appearing on the frame as the "top" tool, we only have to click on it to select it, just as we did with the Place Smartline tool. If it does not appear as the "top" tool, we have the option of *"tearing off"* the appropriate tool box from the frame and *"Floating"* it, or use *"drag and drop"* tool selection, as described under "Tool Frames" on page 1-32.

For an example, let us assume we need to place an ellipse. Circles are a form of ellipse, so it is logical that the tools for placing these two types of element are in the same tool box. The *Ellipses* "child" tool box is the fourth down on the right side of the Main tool frame. Selecting the tool will configure the Tool Settings window as shown in figure 2.17. Experiment with selecting a variety of tools, note how the Tool Settings window re-configures to accept different types of inputs.

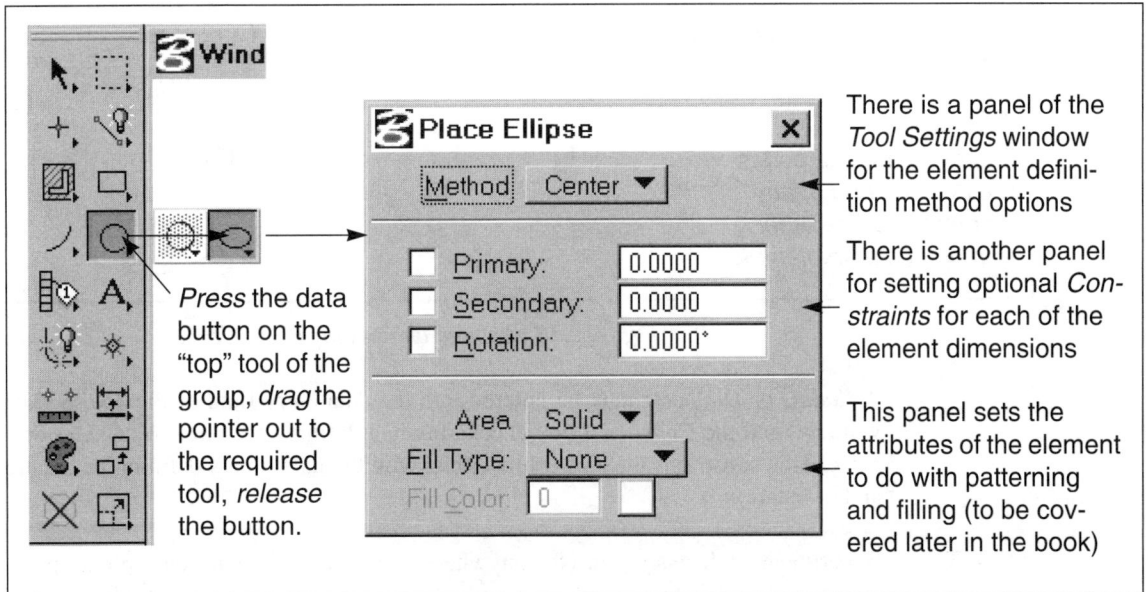

Figure 2.17 Selecting a tool not "on top", with Tool Settings window details

Tool Settings

We will use the *Place Circle* tool as a typical example of placing design elements. When we select a particular tool, the corresponding *Tool Settings window* provides us with a set of options to choose from. In this case, the options include a choice of the *Method* we need to use for placing the element and constraints on its dimension. Figure 2.18 shows the choices that affect the *Method* of placement of a *Circle*.

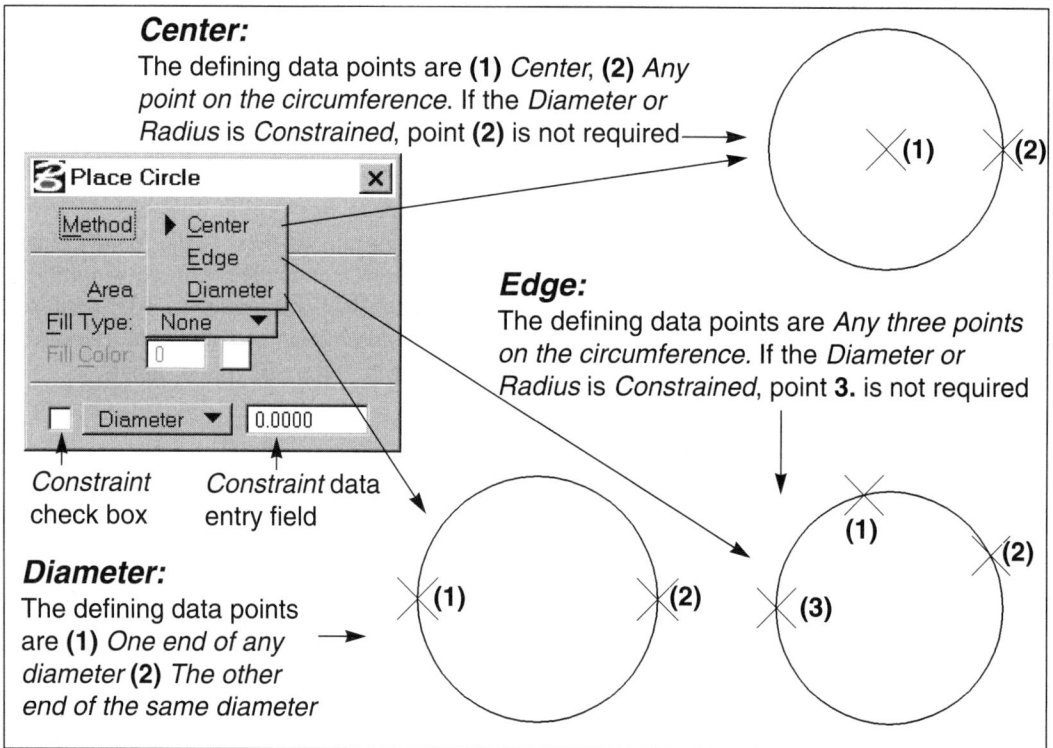

Center:
The defining data points are **(1)** *Center,* **(2)** *Any point on the circumference.* If the *Diameter or Radius* is *Constrained*, point **(2)** is not required⟶

Place Circle

Method ▶ Center
          Edge
Area   Diameter
Fill Type: None ▼
Fill Color: 0

☐ Diameter ▼ 0.0000

Constraint check box   *Constraint* data entry field

Edge:
The defining data points are *Any three points on the circumference.* If the *Diameter or Radius* is *Constrained*, point **3.** is not required

Diameter:
The defining data points are **(1)** *One end of any diameter* **(2)** *The other end of the same diameter*

Figure 2.18   Method choices for Place Circle

A *Radius* or *Diameter* may be entered into the data entry field of the *Tool Settings* window (and the *Constraint* box checked) when defining the circle by *Center* or by *Edge*. This constrains the size of the circle, with the data points defining its location and orientation.

Experiment with placing circles anywhere in the design, using data points placed "freehand" and with the aid of AccuDraw. When you are familiar with all three methods, remove the "experimental" circles using the *Delete* tool, found at the bottom-left of the Main tool frame. Select the tool, then click on the elements.

Precision Input using the AccuDraw Facility

The design process demands that we place design elements at precise positions and with precise dimensions. The AccuDraw facility provides us with an efficient means of numerically defining the placement of elements. AccuDraw can be used with most of the tools we are likely to use in MicroStation, but is not a drawing tool by itself.

The AccuDraw Window

The *AccuDraw Window* has *Data Input Fields* that are the usual input point for precision element placement data. These fields may accept *x* and *y* coordinate data if we are using the *Rectangular Coordinate System*, or *Distance* and *Angle* when the *Polar Coordinate System* is in use. It is normally left open during the design creation process and it can be positioned at any convenient place on the screen.

◆ Starting AccuDraw

1. Click the *Start AccuDraw* tool, which is found in the *Primary* tool bar. The AccuDraw window opens, either *Floating* or *Docked* (see page 1-31), depending on how it was last positioned.

Note that the data entry fields of the AccuDraw window are continually updating as the pointer is moved within the View window area. When there is no drawing tool active, they display the *Absolute* (relative to the *Global Origin*) coordinates of the pointer in the particular coordinate readout format selected.

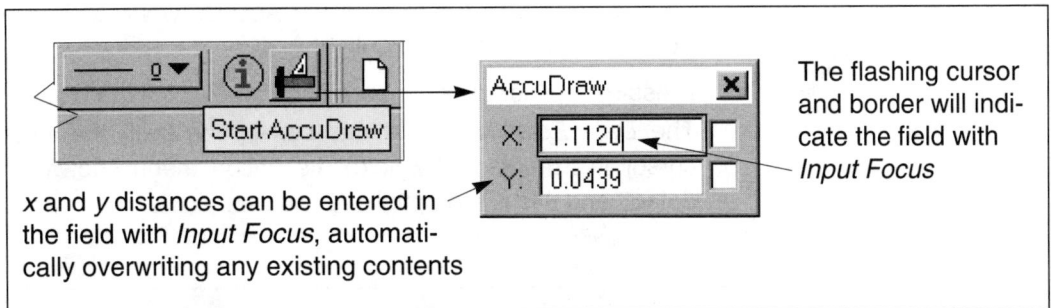

Figure 2.19   The AccuDraw Window

In the following example, we will use the *Place Block* tool in conjunction with AccuDraw to create a 1m X 0.7m rectangle with its bottom-left vertex at the *Global Origin* (*x* and *y* coordinates of **0,0**).

◆ **Place the first vertex of a block at *x*=0, *y*=0.**

1. Still using "first.dgn" with the *Default* interface, *Zoom out* to leave some space around the Arrow shape. Click the *Start AccuDraw* tool (if it is not already running).

2. Select the *Place Block* tool from the *Main* tool frame.
   The *Tool Settings* window for this tool displays the default settings, which are the settings we will use.

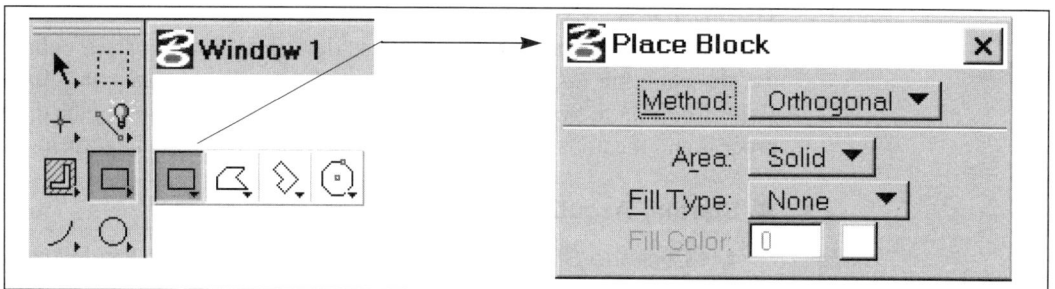

Figure 2.20   The Place Block tool

The *Place Block* tool creates a rectangle defined by two diagonally opposite points. In this case, the first of these two points will be defined by entering the *Absolute* coordinates of the *Global Origin*, *x*=0, *y*=0. The diagonally opposite vertex will be defined *Relative* to the first point, **1m** to the right (positive *x*) and **0.7m** up the screen (positive *y*).

3. Click the title bar or border of the AccuDraw window to direct *Input Focus* to it (The title bar highlights).

4. Press<**p**> (either case) to enter the first *Point* of the block.
   The *Data Point Keyin* settings box opens (with the insertion point cursor in its data entry field). Its option menu shows *Absolute* by default and this is the option we will use.

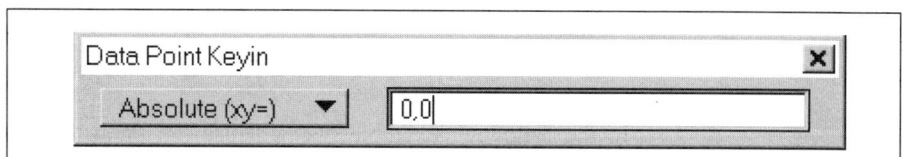

Figure 2.21   The Data Point Keyin settings box

5. Key in **0,0** as the *x* and *y* coordinates of the first point on the block, press <**Enter**>

    The Data Point Keyin settings box closes and the *AccuDraw Compass* appears with its center at the coordinates *x*=0, *y*=0.

6. Move the pointer to the right, the +*x* direction, key in **1**, do not press <Enter>, as the value is entered automatically.

The insertion point cursor will have automatically moved into the X: data entry field, as we have moved the drawing pointer predominantly in the *x* direction. We can manually change from one field to the other by pressing the <**Tab**> key. The coordinates in the X: and Y: fields are relative to the point just placed.

7. Move the pointer upwards (towards the diagonally opposite corner of the block). Key in **.7** to the Y: field. Again, do not press <Enter> after the data entry.

The current contents will always be overwritten, no need to highlight them or move the insertion point cursor. The check boxes to the right of the data entry fields are checked automatically when we enter data. This indicates the point is locked to the entered coordinate, regardless of movement of the pointer.

8. Click the *Data* button to *Accept* the placement of the block.

9. *Click the* Reset button to stop the *Place Block* operation.

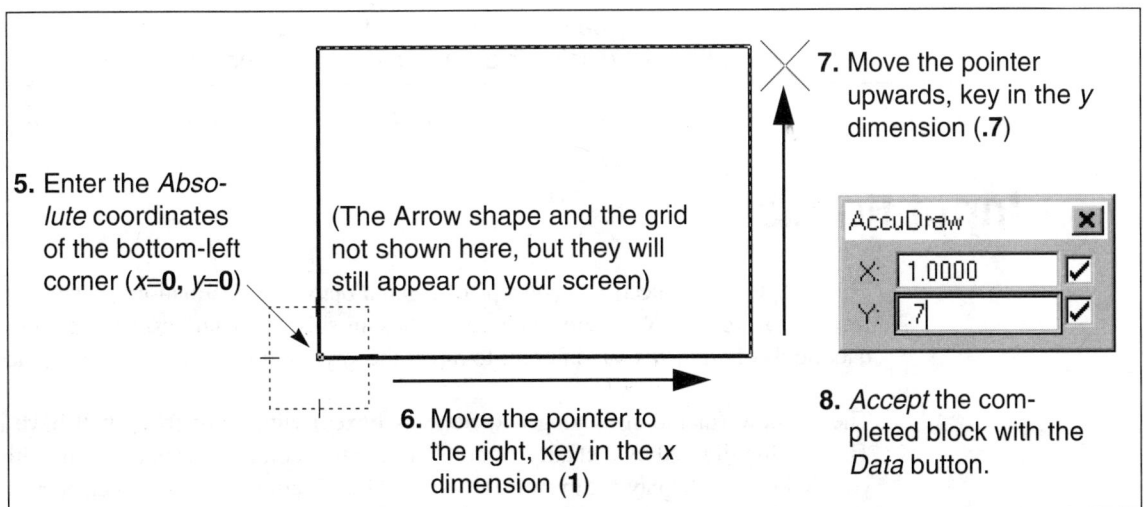

Figure 2.22   Placing a block using AccuDraw

The AccuDraw Compass

The AccuDraw *Compass* may be square, when it allows us to enter *Rectangular Coordinates* (*x* and *y* values). It may also be circular, when the inputs are interpreted as *Polar Coordinates* (*Distance* and *Angle*). To change from one coordinate system to the other, press **<Spacebar>**. The positive *x* and *y* axes of the compass have colored indicators, by default red and green respectivly. For this example, we are using *Rectangular Coordinates*, so if the AccuDraw Compass displays as a circle, press **<Spacebar>**. Each time press the spacebar a "Shortcut indicator" flashes over the AccuDraw window.

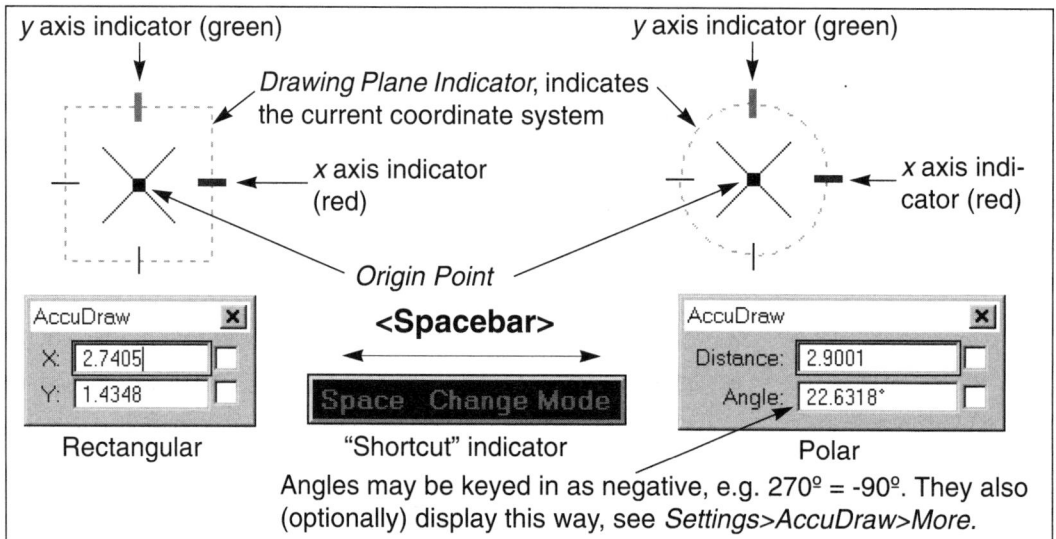

Figure 2.23   AccuDraw Compass' and windows

Input Focus

This chapter introduced the concept of *Input Focus*, the destination of data input from the keyboard. We were required to click in specific windows, settings boxes, data fields of windows etc. in order to direct the keyboard input to the correct place.

The window (including Dialog and Settings boxes) with input focus will have its Title bar highlighted by a change of color. The actual color is selectable from within your Windows Display setup or from within MicroStation itself for other operating systems. The illustrations in this book show the highlight as white, whereas a the title bar of a window without input focus appears the same grey as the window borders.

We can allocate *Input Focus* by clicking on the Title bar or the border of a widow. Input focus can also be cycled between the various open windows with the **<F6>** key, with the *Primary Tool Bar* having the top position in the hierarchy. **<Shift-F6>** will reverse the order of transfer of input focus.

Within particular windows the *Input Focus* can be further directed into a particular *Field* or *List box*. Again, we can do this by clicking in the field, or we can cycle through multiple fields and list boxes using the **<Tab>** key. Within a field we can highlight any existing contents for overwriting by double-clicking or "wiping over" with the data button pressed.

The *AccuDraw Window* data input fields are an exception to this, their contents will always be overwritten by new keyboard input when they have focus, the previous contents do not need to be highlighted.

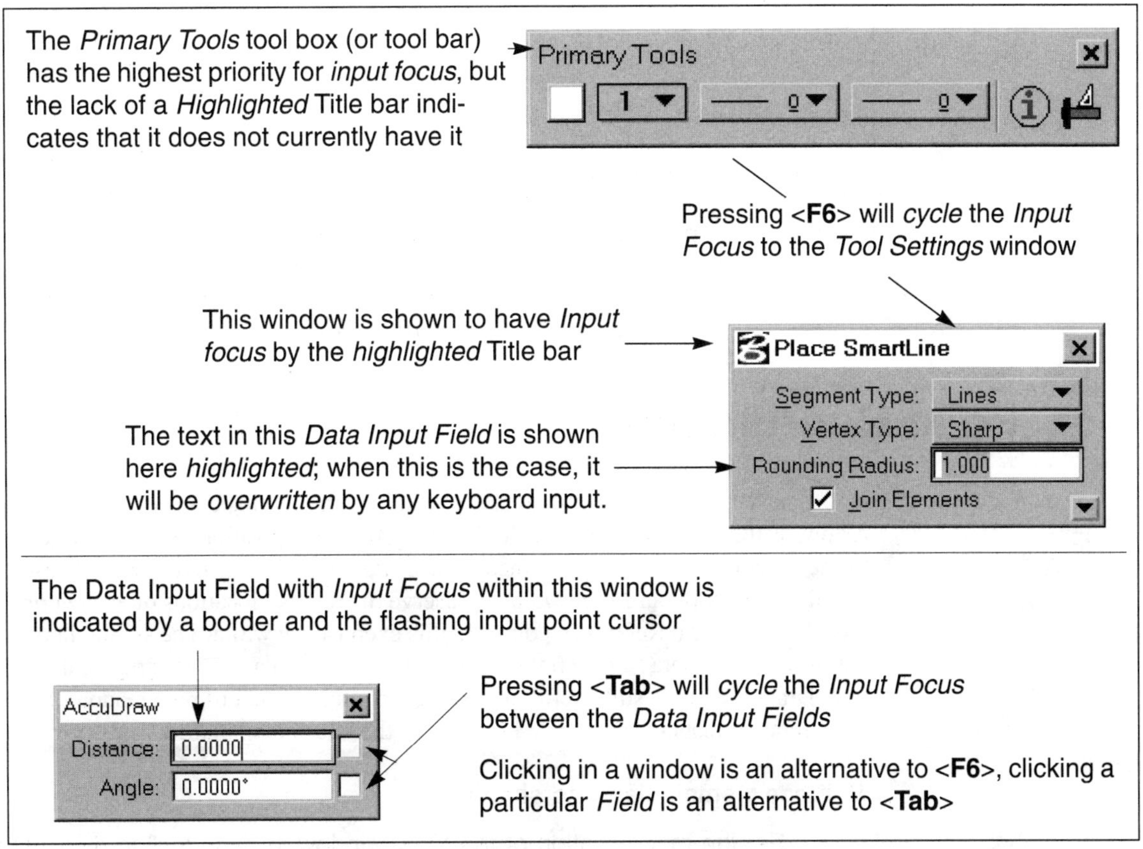

The *Primary Tools* tool box (or tool bar) has the highest priority for *input focus*, but the lack of a *Highlighted* Title bar indicates that it does not currently have it

Pressing **<F6>** will *cycle* the *Input Focus* to the *Tool Settings* window

This window is shown to have *Input focus* by the *highlighted* Title bar

The text in this *Data Input Field* is shown here *highlighted*; when this is the case, it will be *overwritten* by any keyboard input.

The Data Input Field with *Input Focus* within this window is indicated by a border and the flashing input point cursor

Pressing **<Tab>** will *cycle* the *Input Focus* between the *Data Input Fields*

Clicking in a window is an alternative to **<F6>**, clicking a particular *Field* is an alternative to **<Tab>**

Figure 2.24 Directing Input Focus

The Locks Settings Box

We need the *Grid Lock* **On** for our next exercise, just as we did when we placed the Direction Arrow shape. We have closed the design file (without saving the settings) since setting it *On* in that exercise, so it will have reverted to the default *Off* setting. We will set it in a different area this time, the *Locks settings box*.

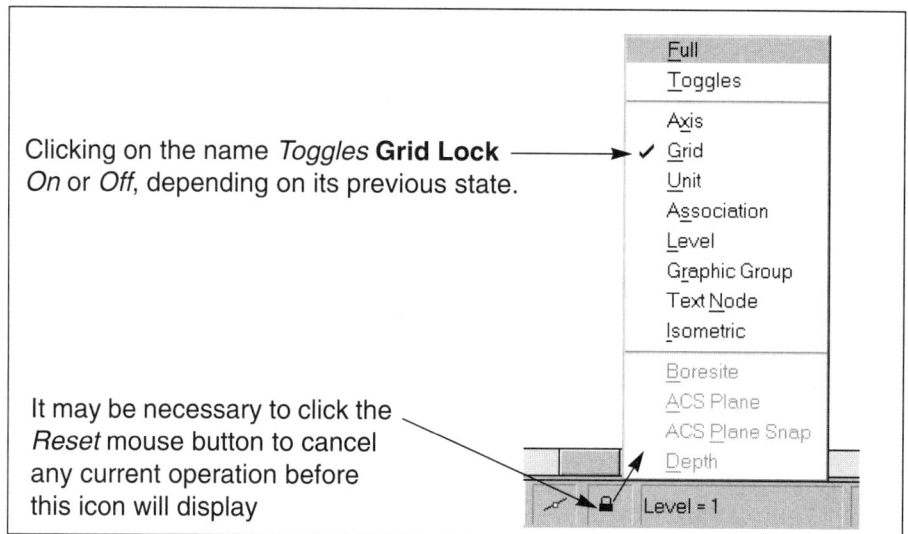

Clicking on the name *Toggles* **Grid Lock**
On or *Off*, depending on its previous state.

It may be necessary to click the
Reset mouse button to cancel
any current operation before
this icon will display

Figure 2.25   The Locks settings box - setting Grid Lock

Polar Coordinates

In the next example, we will place a small diamond shape inside the Direction Arrow, as illustrated in Figure 2.26. In *Polar Mode* the position of a point in relation to the AccuDraw *Origin* is defined as a *Distance* and an *Angle*. We will use the AccuDraw window in *Polar Mode* to observe the relative locations of each vertex as it is placed on Grid Reference points. In this exercise we will not be keying in data to the AccuDraw data input fields, but placing the data points graphically. The AccuDraw facility is still useful, providing a continuous coordinate readout, as well as facilitating distance and angle indexing of the lines being placed.

◆ **Place a small diamond shape**

1. Set the magnification of the View window in "first.dgn" to display the Arrow, set *Grid Lock On* (see Figure 2.25).

2. Select the *Place SmartLine* tool, place data points on each of the reference grid points as shown in Figure 2.26.

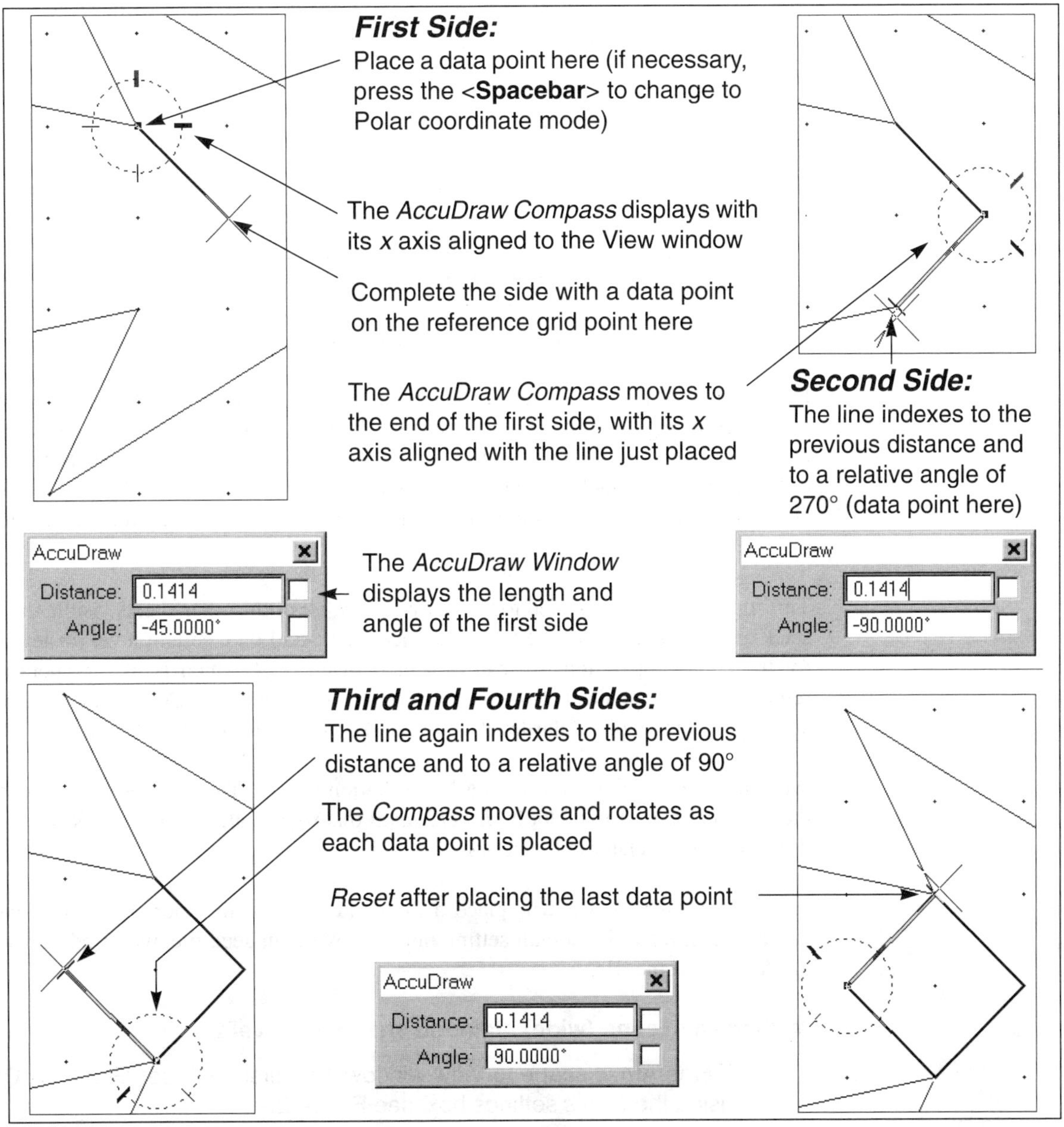

First Side:
Place a data point here (if necessary, press the <**Spacebar**> to change to Polar coordinate mode)

The *AccuDraw Compass* displays with its *x* axis aligned to the View window

Complete the side with a data point on the reference grid point here

The *AccuDraw Compass* moves to the end of the first side, with its *x* axis aligned with the line just placed

Second Side:
The line indexes to the previous distance and to a relative angle of 270° (data point here)

The *AccuDraw Window* displays the length and angle of the first side

AccuDraw	☒
Distance: 0.1414	☐
Angle: -45.0000°	☐

AccuDraw	☒
Distance: 0.1414	☐
Angle: -90.0000°	☐

Third and Fourth Sides:
The line again indexes to the previous distance and to a relative angle of 90°

The *Compass* moves and rotates as each data point is placed

Reset after placing the last data point

AccuDraw	☒
Distance: 0.1414	☐
Angle: 90.0000°	☐

Figure 2.26 Operation of AccuDraw with Polar coordinates

Levels

On the *Primary* tool bar or tool box the second button along allows us to choose the *Active Level*. This is nothing to do with a third dimension, it controls the *Level* (also called the *Layer* in some CAD applications) of the design file that we are placing elements on.

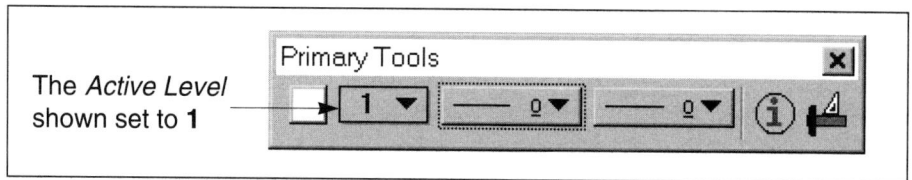

The *Active Level* shown set to **1**

Figure 2.27   The Active Level button

Levels are a means of controlling the amount of design information that we have on the screen at a given time. Using a manual drawing analogy, this is like creating a design on a number of transparent sheets, different details being drawn on each. If all of these sheets are stacked in alignment on the drawing board, we will be able to see all of the details in their relationship to one another, but we can only draw on the top one.

This top sheet can be likened to the *Active Level*, all of the other sheets visible in the stack are *Displayed levels*. If we do not need the detail on a certain level (or levels) for the current operation, we can turn their display *off*, which is like temporarily removing a sheet or sheets from the stack on the drawing board. Continuing the same analogy, making a particular level *Active* is like moving a sheet to the top.

We can utilize up to 63 levels in a MicroStation design. They can be identified by their number from 1 to 63, or by *Level Names* that we can allocate ourselves. We will use *Named* levels later in the book.

In the next exercise we will place a diamond shape within our Arrow on level number **2**. Level **1**, the default setting imported with our seed file, was used to place the Arrow and the Block.

◆ **Place a second (wide) diamond shape on Level 2**

1. Fit the Arrow shape to View window 1 in "first.dgn", set *Grid Lock* **Off** using the *Locks* settings box, see Figure 2.25.
    AccuDraw will not be needed for this exercise, but it may be left running, so its window may be left open.

2. Click the *Active level* button in the *Primary* tool bar, choose level **2**.
   Any new elements being placed will be on this level, regardless of the
   View window we happen to be using.

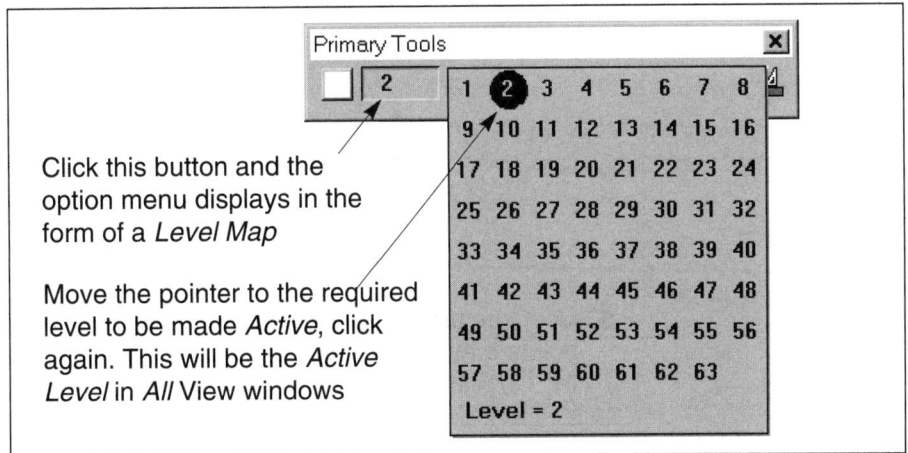

Click this button and the
option menu displays in the
form of a *Level Map*

Move the pointer to the required
level to be made *Active*, click
again. This will be the *Active
Level* in *All* View windows

Figure 2.28   Selecting a Level to be made Active

3. Select the *Place Smartline* tool, place a *Tentative point* on the vertex
   marked **(a)** in figure 2.29, *Accept* with the *Data* button when the Arrow
   shape highlights and the tentative pointer is in the right place.

4. Continue around vertices **(b)**, **(c)**, **(d)** and again to **(a)**, placing
   tentative points and *Accepting* them when they have *Snapped* to the
   desired vertex.

   The Data points have all been placed by accepting *Tentative* points.
   We will explore the *Snapping* abilities of Tentative points shortly.

Now we have elements placed on both level 1 and level 2, all of them displayed in
View window 1 at this stage. In the next exercise, we will switch the display of the
elements placed on the different levels off and on.

Our design so far is quite simple, so the need for this changing of the display is not as
necessary as it would be for more complex designs, for example a large building.
This feature allows us to produce a variety of specialized printouts from the one
design. We will be considering this feature when we are printing out (sometimes
referred to as "plotting") drawings in chapter 12.

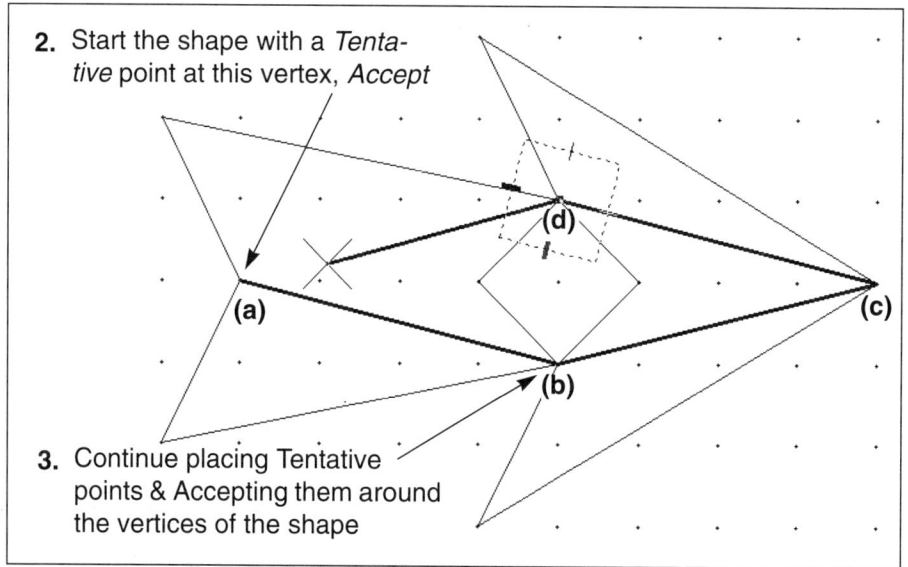

Figure 2.29   Placing the Diamond on Level 2

Switching the display of levels On and Off.

Choosing *Settings>Level>Manager* opens the *Level Manager* settings box. It can also be opened from the View window's *Control Menu*. This settings box is where we switch the display of design elements on various levels *On* and *Off*.

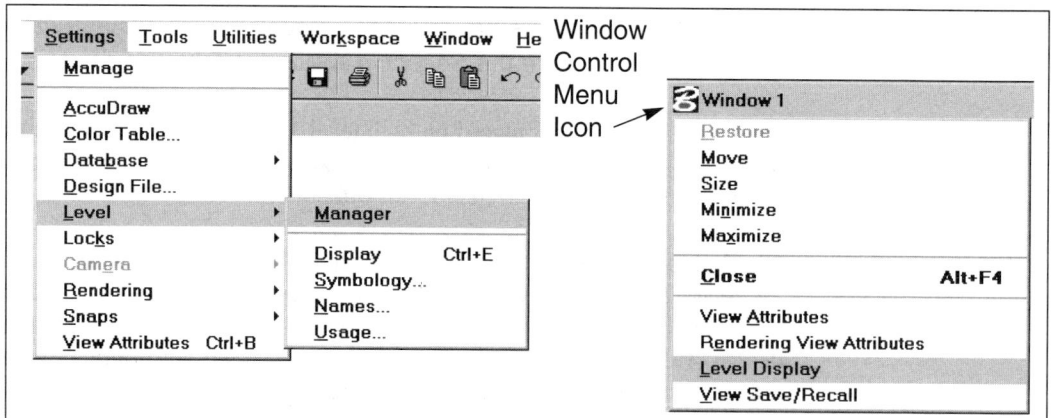

Figure 2.30   Choosing the Level Manager settings box

The *Level Manager* settings box is shown in figure 2.31 displaying the default *Level Numbers* tab. It shows all 63 levels, indicating if the display of elements is *On* or *Off* for each level. A level turned *On* is indicated by a square highlight, the *Active* level is indicated by a circular highlight. Vacant levels are indicated by a grey number.

The *View Number* button allows us to select any of the open View windows to check the level display status and change it if required. Each View window may be set up with different levels *On* and *Off*. Click the number to change any level from *On* to *Off* or vice-versa, this is a *Toggle* action. We have the option of setting the *Active* level in this box (as well as in the Primary tool bar and various other places) by double-clicking the number. The *Active Level* can not be turned *Off*.

Nothing actually happens in the View windows until we *Apply* any changes we have made to the status of levels in this window. There are two buttons at the bottom of the settings box we can use to apply changes:

1.   The *Apply* button applies the *On/Off* changes to the *View (window) Number* selected and any *Active Level* change to all open View windows;

2.   The *All* button applies all changes to all the open View windows.

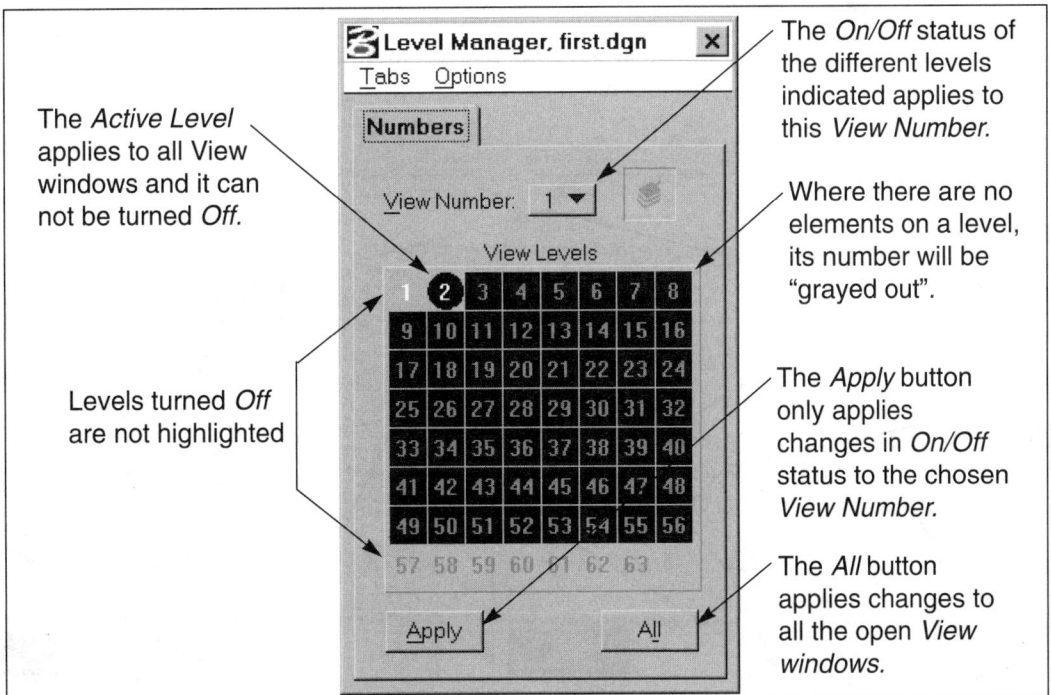

Figure 2.31   The Level Manager settings box

◆ Controlling level display

1. Make level **3** in "first.dgn" *Active*, using the *Active Level* button on the *Primary* tool bar.

This is a vacant level, now neither of the levels in use (**1** & **2**) are *Active*, therefore we are able to turn them *Off*.

2. Choose *Settings>Level>Manager*, position the *Level Manager* settings box at a convenient place on the screen, use the *View Control* tools to make the Arrow fully visible.

3. Click level **1** *Off*, *Apply* the change to View window 1, *Update* the View.

Note the change to the display. The *Update* of the view is often necessary to replace parts of the design removed along with the elements from the level that was turned off.

4. Click level **2** *Off* and **1** back *On*, *Apply* the change to View window 1, *Update* the View.

The original arrow and block will re-appear.

5. Make level **2** *Active*, by double-clicking it, or by using the *Active Level* button on the *Primary* tool bar.

Making level **2** active automatically turns it back *On* in all View windows.

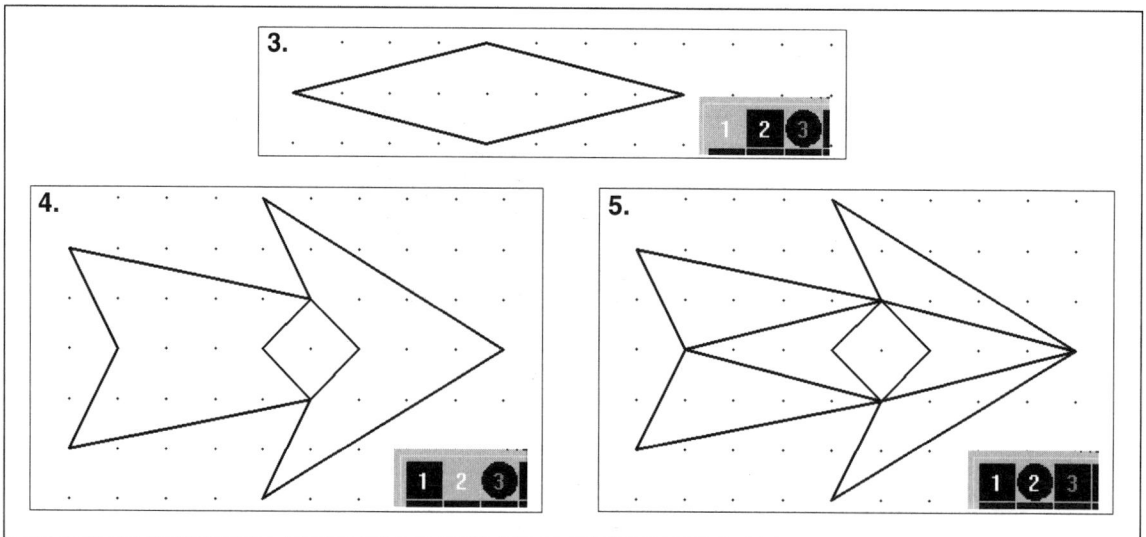

Figure 2.32   Switching displayed levels

Finding Which Levels are in Use

It is often desirable to know which levels have elements placed on them. We can find out using *Level Manager* (by noting the numbers that are not grayed out, see page 2-37).

For more detail, open the *Level Usage* settings box (illustrated in Figure 2.33) available under *Settings>Level>Usage*. This has a panel displaying the level numbers, with the numbers highlighted that contain geometry. There is a second panel with *Level Names* (to be introduced next). It also has information about the number of elements on each. We even have the facility to find out the total of each of the *Types* of element placed in the design.

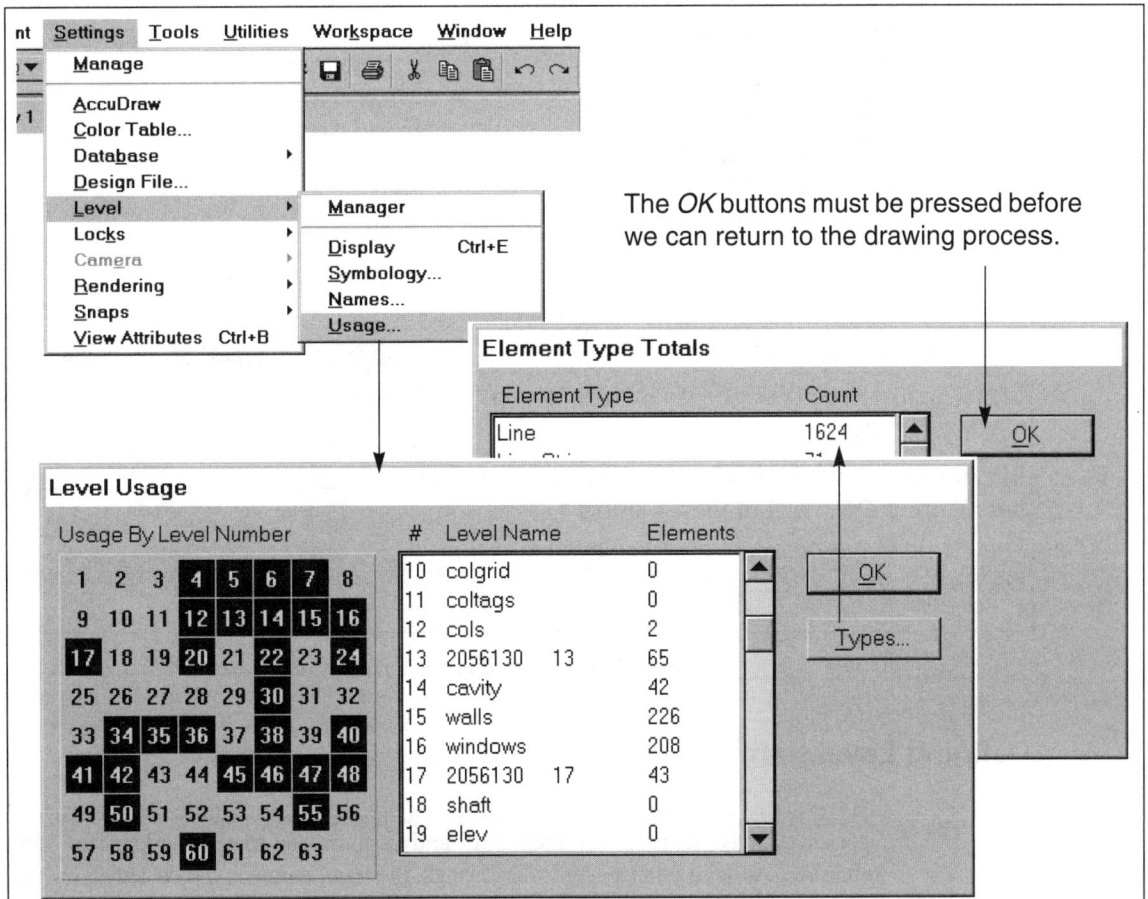

Figure 2.33   Level Usage display

Identifying Levels by Name

The *Level Manager* settings box illustrated in Figure 2.31 has a menu of *Tabs* options, which includes *Names*. When this tab is checked *On* and selected, levels are identified by their *Name* instead of their *Number*, as illustrated in Figure 2.34.

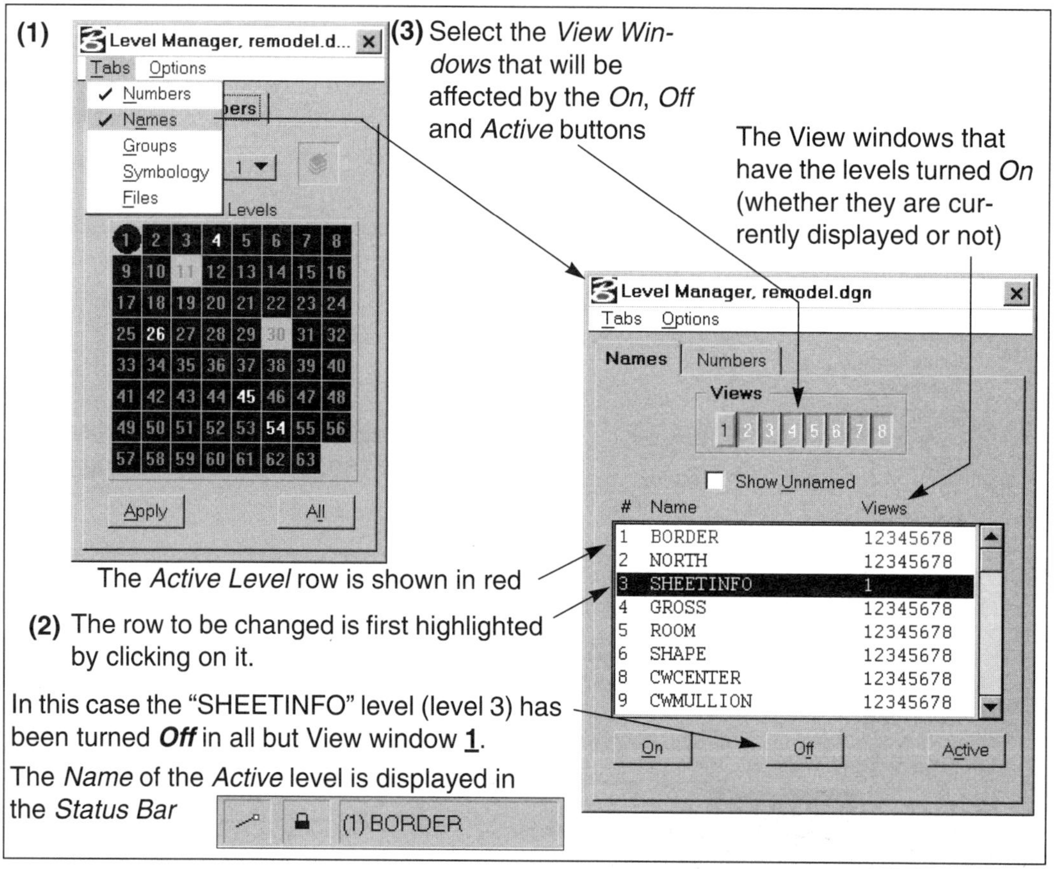

Figure 2.34   Controlling the display using level names

Defining Level Names

The process of adding names to levels is illustrated in Figure 2.35. Up to 16 characters may be used for the name and a comment may be added for future reference. As with other design file settings, the level names must be *Saved* for them to be available in later sessions, see "Saving Design File Settings" on page 2-18.

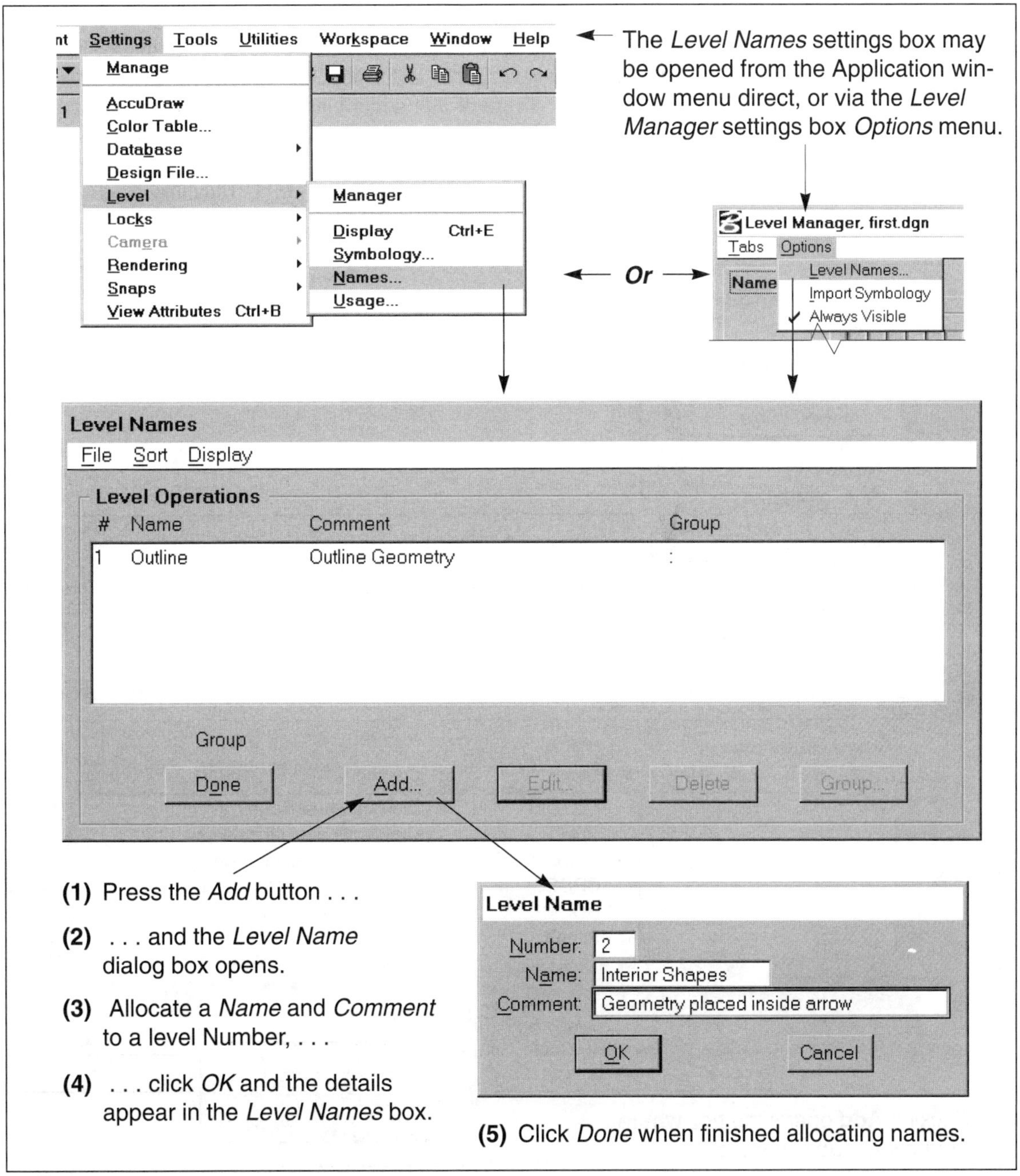

The *Level Names* settings box may be opened from the Application window menu direct, or via the *Level Manager* settings box *Options* menu.

Level Names

File   Sort   Display

Level Operations

#	Name	Comment	Group
1	Outline	Outline Geometry	:

Group

Done   Add...   Edit...   Delete   Group...

(1) Press the *Add* button . . .

(2) . . . and the *Level Name* dialog box opens.

(3) Allocate a *Name* and *Comment* to a level Number, . . .

(4) . . . click *OK* and the details appear in the *Level Names* box.

Level Name

Number: 2
Name: Interior Shapes
Comment: Geometry placed inside arrow

OK   Cancel

(5) Click *Done* when finished allocating names.

Figure 2.35 Naming levels

Level Groups

Levels may be grouped together to enable them to be displayed or hidden by a single action, as opposed to switching *On* and *Off* a number of levels individually. For example, let us consider a case of a building plan. Related components of the plan could be grouped, thus when we are working on say walls, we would display only the group of levels containing walls. The illustration in Figure 2.36 uses the design file *remodel.dgn* from the "...\projects\tutorials\intro\dgn" directory.

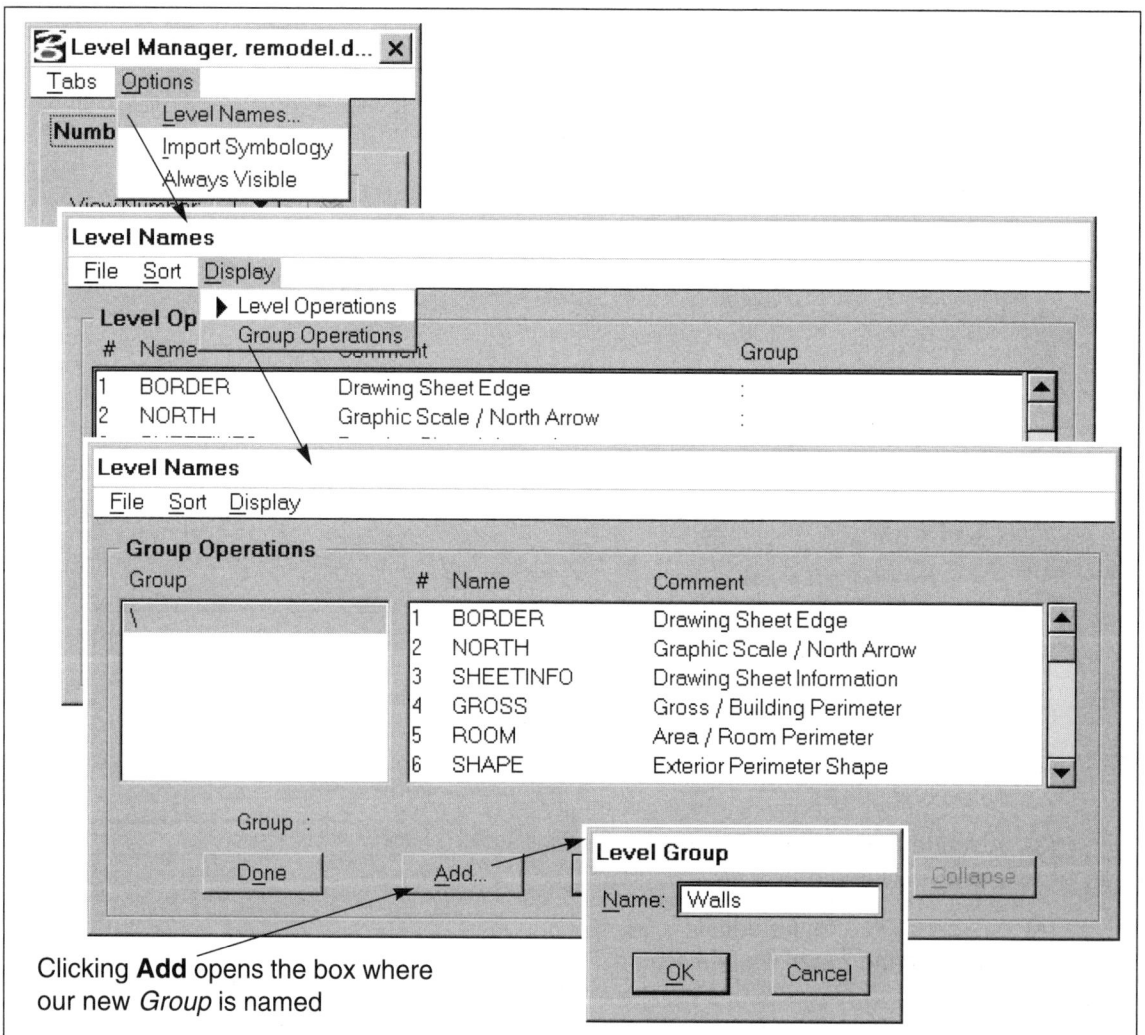

Figure 2.36   Level Operations Displays - Creating a new Group

Figure 2.36 shows the *Level Names* dialog box, first in the *Level Operations* display mode, then in the *Group Operations* mode. The latter display shows all the defined level names in the right side panel, with the left panel showing only a backslash (\). The backslash indicates the *Root* group, which is the group of all named levels.

We may now go ahead and create sub-group names under this root in a "tree" structure, just like directories. After the name(s) are created, a selection of named levels may be copied to it, or levels may be moved from another group into the new one.

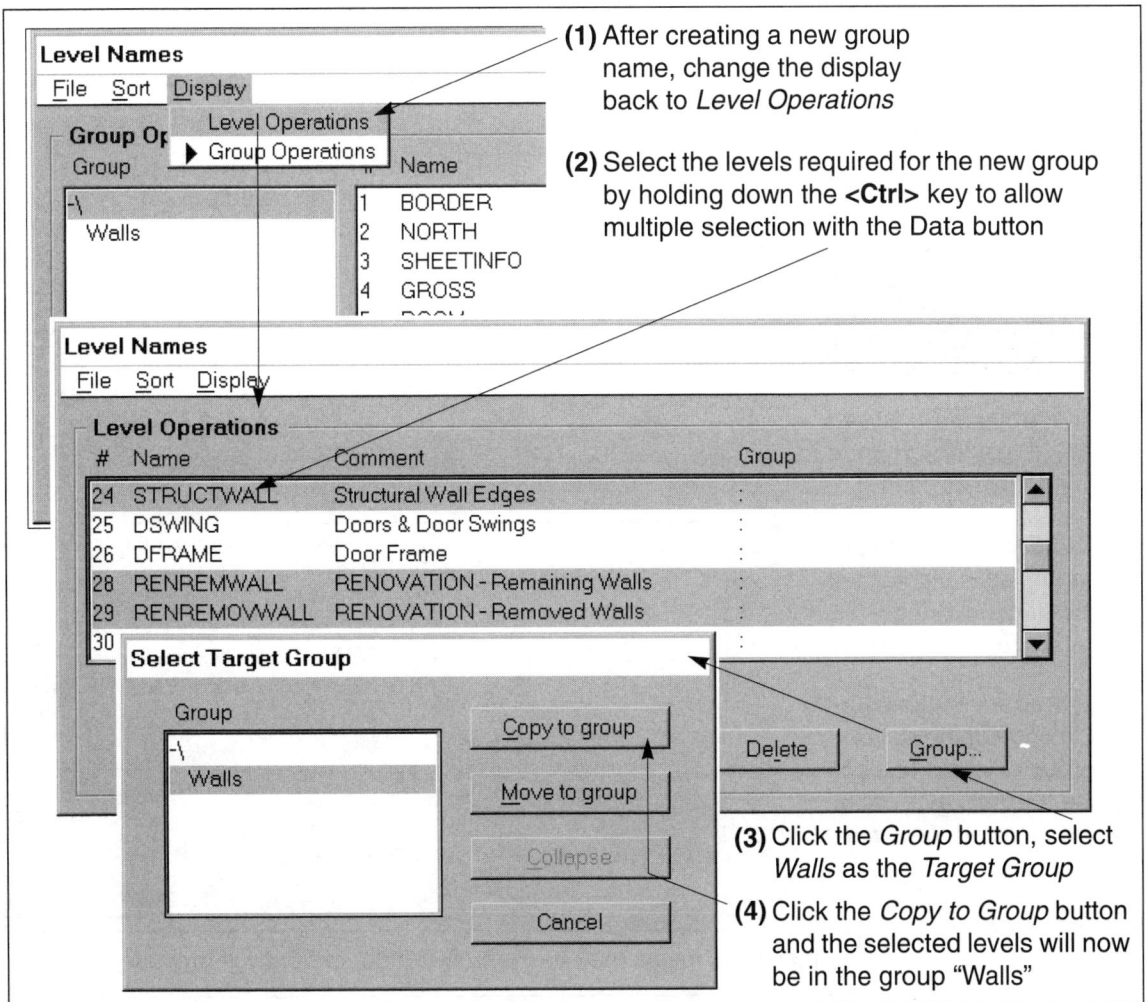

Level Names

File   Sort   Display

(1) After creating a new group name, change the display back to *Level Operations*

(2) Select the levels required for the new group by holding down the **<Ctrl>** key to allow multiple selection with the Data button

(3) Click the *Group* button, select *Walls* as the *Target Group*

(4) Click the *Copy to Group* button and the selected levels will now be in the group "Walls"

Figure 2.37   Selecting Levels to be Grouped

Controlling Levels in a Group

The group of levels shown being created in Figure 2.37 is a sub-group of the *Root*. We could create other groups as subgroups under this one, thus creating *Tree* structures. As with Directory structure, these may be expanded and collapsed, with a collapsed group structure indicated with a "+", an expanded one with "-". For example, the root group is shown expanded in Figure 2.38, thus it is shown "-\". It may be collapsed or expanded again by double-clicking it.

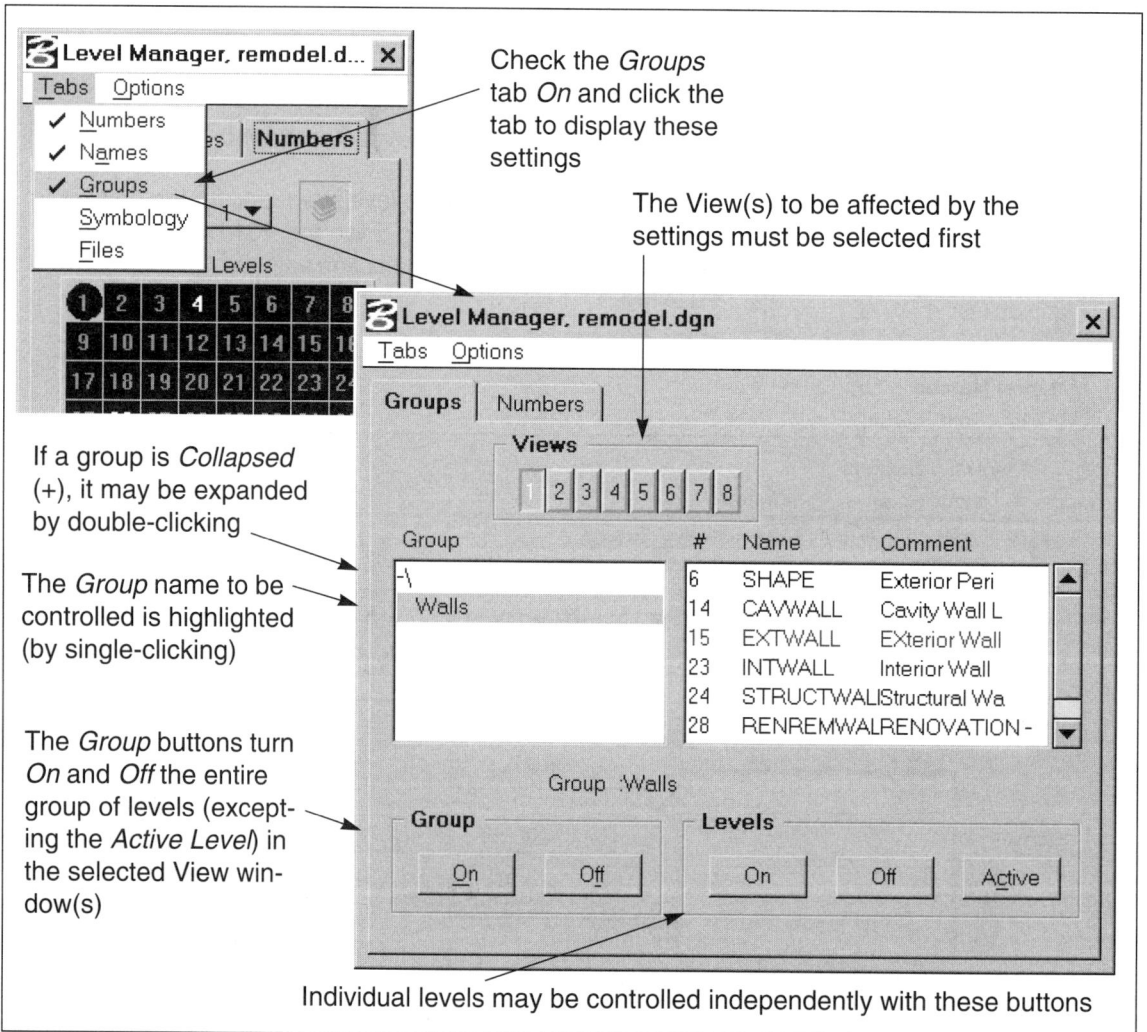

Figure 2.38   Control of Levels in a Group

Undoing an Operation

The *Undo* facility was first mentioned on page 2-12 while we were creating our "Direction Arrow". MicroStation records all operations in a set aside area of memory known as the *Undo Buffer*. This allows us to undo the last operation, then the operation just before it, then the one before that - and so on until the limit is reached. This limit is set firstly by the amount of memory (RAM) set aside for the Undo buffer, then by the last closing of the design file. Closing a design file empties the *Undo Buffer*, so a design file will always open without any operations "undoable".

The size of the Undo buffer can be changed under *Workspace>Preferences>Memory Usage from* the Application window menu. The larger the buffer, the more operations we can undo, but the less memory is available for the rest of MicroStation.

The complement to *Undo* is *Redo*, using this negates the last *Undo* operation. Both *Undo* and *Redo* are found in the *Edit* Application window menu, where they display the name of the operation that is affected.

Also found under *Edit* is *Set Mark*. This feature allows us to *Mark* our place in a series of operations, giving us the option of undoing all of the operations made since the position was *Marked*. We employ this multiple undo facility by choosing *Edit>Undo Other>To Mark*. When we undo to a mark, the mark is removed.

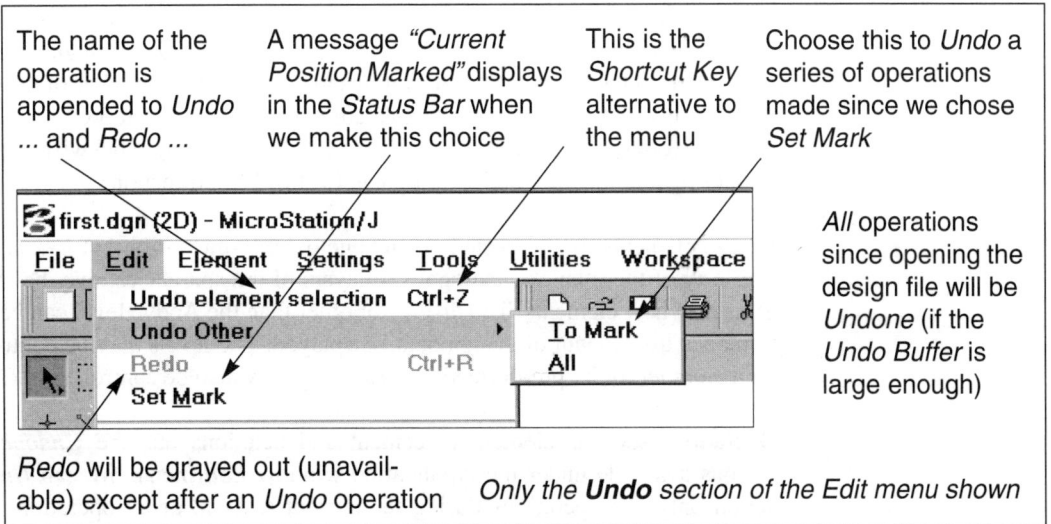

The name of the operation is appended to *Undo* ... and *Redo* ...

A message *"Current Position Marked"* displays in the *Status Bar* when we make this choice

This is the *Shortcut Key* alternative to the menu

Choose this to *Undo* a series of operations made since we chose *Set Mark*

first.dgn (2D) - MicroStation/J

File   Edit   Element   Settings   Tools   Utilities   Workspace

Undo element selection   Ctrl+Z

Undo Other

Redo   Ctrl+R

Set Mark

To Mark

All

All operations since opening the design file will be *Undone* (if the *Undo Buffer* is large enough)

Redo will be grayed out (unavailable) except after an *Undo* operation

*Only the **Undo** section of the Edit menu shown*

Figure 2.39   The Undo and Redo options

Summary

When we create a new design file, we use a *Seed File* to provide a basic set-up. Our new file is in effect a copy of this Seed file, which usually does not have any actual design elements placed in it. The new file can be created either from within the Application window when we have an existing design open, or from within the MicroStation Manager dialog box. The new file can be placed in any Directory.

The mouse or digitizer tablet cursor can have its buttons assigned to three main functions, *Data*, *Tentative* and *Reset*. We can assign any button to any function, but the standard arrangement has the *Data* (main) button as the left button.

The optionally displayed *Grid* was used to place our first *Design Element*, the Arrow shape. In this case we turned on *Grid Lock* to ensure the vertices of the element fell exactly on the *Grid Reference Points*. We used the *Place SmartLine* tool to create the shape, placing the final *Data Point* by *Snapping* a *Tentative Point*, then *Accepting* it.

The *MicroStation Design Plane* has a coordinate system with 4.29 billion *Positional Units* along both its x and y axes. These positional units are divided down into *Master Units* and *Sub Units* to form *Working Units*, used to define the position and size of elements. The master and sub units may be any measurement at all. We are free to choose the names, master unit to sub unit ratio and the number of positional units allocated to each one. The exact position of the Arrow shape vertices was found using tentative points and a *Coordinate Readout* provided in the Status bar.

Angles may be defined for element placement using *Decimal Degrees*, *Degrees, Minutes* and *Seconds* or *Bearing* format. The readout of angles can also be configured in these formats, with settings available for the number of decimal points displayed. The *Angle Modes* available are *Conventional* (0° at 3 O'clock, increasing counter-clockwise), *Azimuth* (0° at 12 O'clock, increasing clockwise) and *Bearing*, (angles related to North and South, in an East or West direction).

Design elements can be placed on any one of sixty-three different *Levels* in a design file. Any of these levels, analogous to layers of transparencies, may be made *Active* to receive new elements. The display of other than the Active level can be turned *Off* to reduce the amount of design detail displayed. The levels may be controlled using their *Number*, or by pre-defined *Names*. They may also be controlled in *Groups*.

Operations such as element placement and deletions may be *Undone* using the options available under the Application window *Edit* menu. We can *Undo* the last action only, *All* operations during the current session, or all operations performed since a *Mark* was set.

3 : Creating a Design

We have already placed some design elements in the previous chapter, now we will apply the knowledge and skills gained to more complex designs. In this chapter we will explore the Main tool frame further and use some more of the tools in exercises. While using these tools, we will be working with the facilities that enable us to place the elements precisely how and where they are required. The settings associated with the tools will be introduced where they are needed.

The control of the attributes of the view, just what is to be displayed and how, will be introduced. We will make use of some of the range of element attributes available to distinguish the components of a design.

When you have completed this chapter, you will be able to:

- Control the display of *Grid* and other optionally displayed items;
- Specify the *Symbology* used for particular elements;
- Perform simple *Modifications* to elements already placed;
- Change the *Active* and *Override Snap Modes*;
- Use the *Place SmartLine* tool with *AccuDraw* to produce composite design components;
- Place circles using three different methods;
- Display information about the *Attributes* and *Properties* of elements.

Basic Design File Settings

We are about to open another new design file. We will be using "first.dgn" again later on, so keep it intact. This design will be set up slightly differently, optimized for designing smaller objects. We will continue to work in the same Workspace.

In the last chapter we set up working units that gave our *Design Plane* an effective size of approximately forty-three kilometers by forty-three kilometers. We will use a smaller design plane in this design, with the millimeter (mm) as the *Master Unit* with a resolution of 1000 *Positional Units* per millimeter.

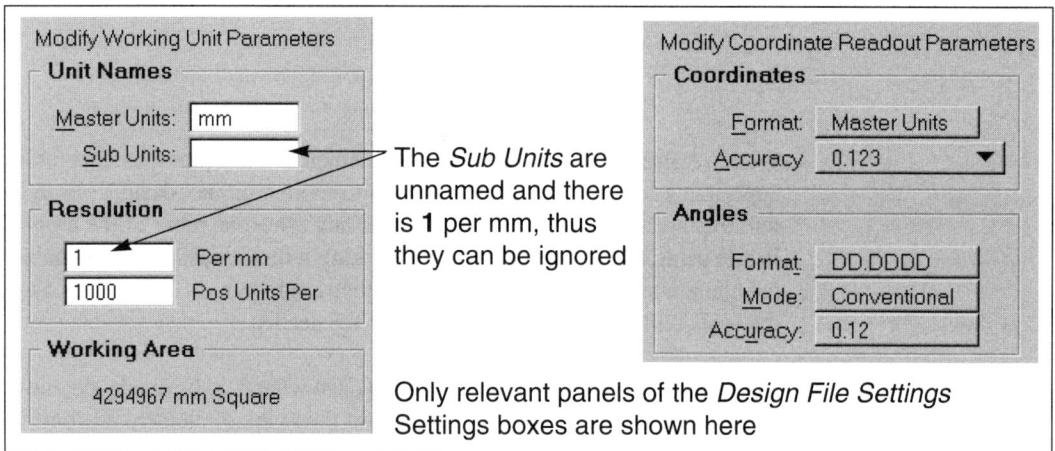

Modify Working Unit Parameters

Unit Names

Master Units: mm
Sub Units:

The *Sub Units* are unnamed and there is **1** per mm, thus they can be ignored

Resolution

1   Per mm
1000   Pos Units Per

Working Area

4294967 mm Square

Modify Coordinate Readout Parameters

Coordinates

Format: Master Units
Accuracy   0.123   ▼

Angles

Format: DD.DDDD
Mode: Conventional
Accuracy: 0.12

Only relevant panels of the *Design File Settings* Settings boxes are shown here

Figure 3.1   Settings for the new design file "second.dgn"

◆ **Create a new Design File named "second.dgn"**

1. Choose the *Default Workspace Interface Component* (see page 2-15). Choose *File>New* from menu bar of either MicroStation Manager or the MicroStation Application window.

2. Create the new file "second.dgn" based on "seed2d.dgn", in the same directory as "first.dgn" (see "Creating New Drawings" on page 2-2).

3. Open the file and select *Settings>Design File>Working Units*, set the working units as shown in Figure 3.1 (see "Working Units Vs. Positional Units" on page 2-16).

4. Choose *Settings>Design File>Coordinate Readout*, set the coordinate readout as shown above (see "Coordinate Readout" on page 2-20). From the *File* menu, choose *Save Settings*.

Attributes of the View Window

Before we place any elements in this new file, we will introduce ourselves to the *View Attributes* settings box. It has twenty-one check boxes, but only twenty apply to 2D designs and thus to this book. The *Camera* setting is grayed out, indicating that it does not apply to the open design file.

View Attributes are the settings that define basically *What* is displayed in a particular View window, and in some cases *How* it is displayed. These *Settings* are controlled from the *View Attributes* settings box. We can open this box from the application menu bar by selecting *Settings>View Attributes*, or from the View window's *Control Menu*.

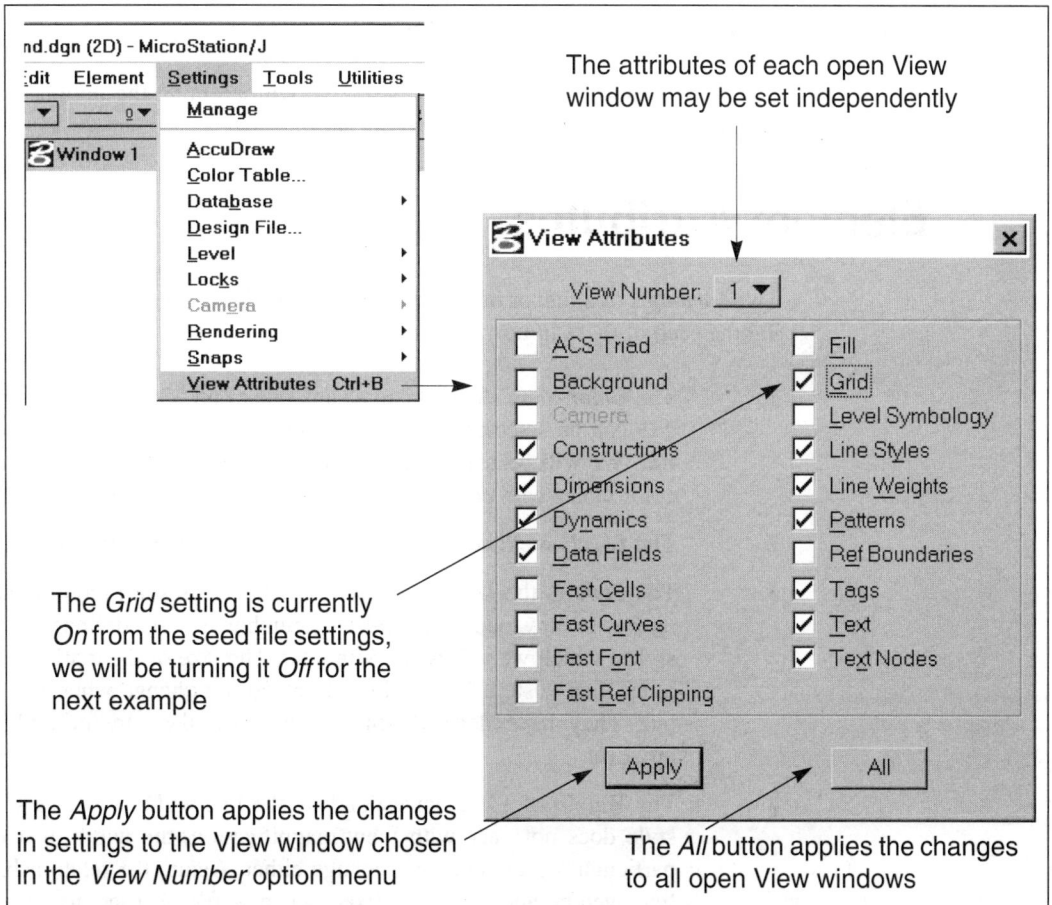

Figure 3.2   The View Attributes settings box

Setting View Attributes

The *Grid* displayed in our new file, part of the set-up inherited from "seed2d.dgn". We will not be using it in the next project, so we will set its display to *Off*. We will start by setting the grid off in the *View Attributes* settings box.

◆ Prepare the View window

1. Close View window 2, maximize View window 1.

2. Select *View Attributes* from the View window control menu (or *Settings>View Attributes* from the Application window menu).

3. Click the *Grid* check box *Off*, click the *Apply* or the *All* button (it does not matter which one in this case, as there is only one view open).

4. Close the *View Attributes* settings box.

The View window is now set up. Next, we will examine the options we have for defining the appearance of design elements.

Element Attributes

The *Attributes* of a line or other element are its *Color*, *Level*, *Style*, *Weight* and *Class*. Taking each of these in turn:

1. The **Color** of an element can be any one of 65,536 colors, but of these only 255 can be selected from the *Color Table* attached to a particular design file. We will be using the default color table, but we can create our own color tables with colors mixed to suit our particular needs.

2. The **Level** an element is placed on was covered earlier, refer to page 2-34.

3. The **Style** is the *Line Style* used, whether it is solid (continuous), dotted, dashes or any one of an infinite number of user-definable *Custom* line styles, which we will work with later. The size of the marks and spaces in other than custom broken line styles do not change when we zoom in or out. They have defined dimensions when they are printed or plotted, however.

4. The **Weight** of a line corresponds to the line width. Just as a standard line style does not vary with view magnification, the width of a line with a particular *Weight* does not change either. Again, the relationship between line weight and width is fixed when a file is used to create a paper document.

5.   The *Class* of a line can be either *Primary* or *Construction*. The display of elements with the latter *Class* may be turned *Off* and *On* within the *Settings>View Attributes* settings box. This allows elements placed purely as construction aids to be left as a part of the design, but not printed out.

Methods of Setting Element Attributes

The most convenient method of setting the element attributes, except for class, is via the *Primary Tool Bar*. Another method uses the *Element Attribute* settings box, which may be opened under the *Settings* menu. This settings box provides a *Class* option and supports the direct keying-in of the other attributes by number. It also allows us to select from the same graphical drop-down option menus as found on the Primary tool bar.

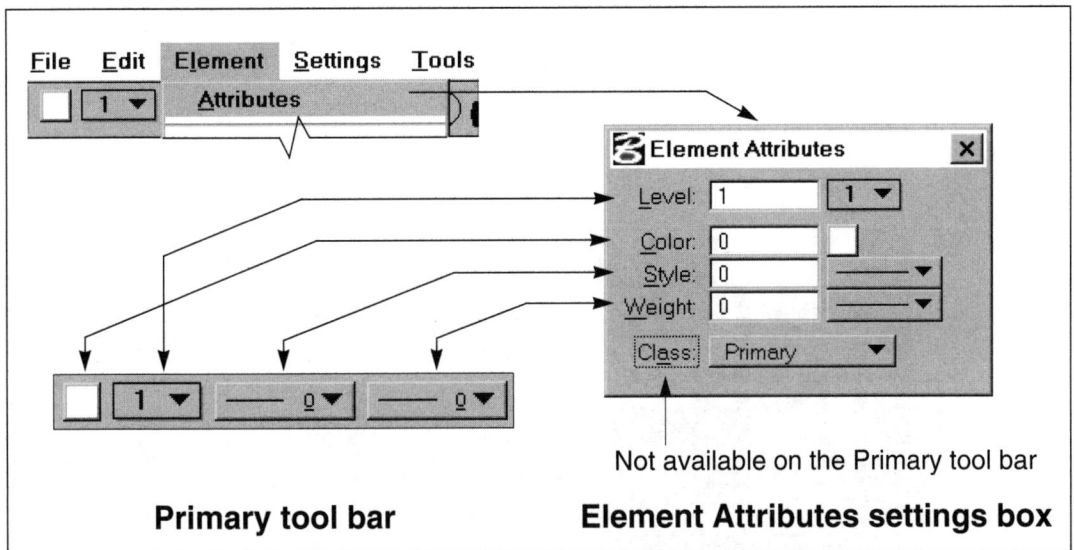

Figure 3.3   Settings>Element Attributes and Primary tool bar equivalents

The default (and generally preferred) View window background is black, with color **0** appearing as *white* on the screen.

As you will find when we put our designs to paper, the software is generally configured to convert color **0** to *print* as *black*. Exactly how the remaining colors appear on paper will depend on the type of printer or plotter, and on the configuration of printer driver software. For general appearance and printing considerations, this book uses black lines on a white background for all the illustrations of the screen.

Defining the initial Element Attributes

The **Visible** *Element Attributes*, (Color, Line Style and Line Weight) are referred to as the *Symbology. Level* and *Class* are *Display Control Attributes*. We will use the *Primary Tool Bar* to set all of the *Symbology* and the *Active Level* for the first elements placed in the next example drawing.

The *Color* will be number **2** from the default color table (green), the line style will be **0** (solid), the line weight **2** and the Active Level **10**. These settings are illustrated in Figure 3.4. Set up each of these initial element attributes by clicking on the appropriate tool, then on the required setting.

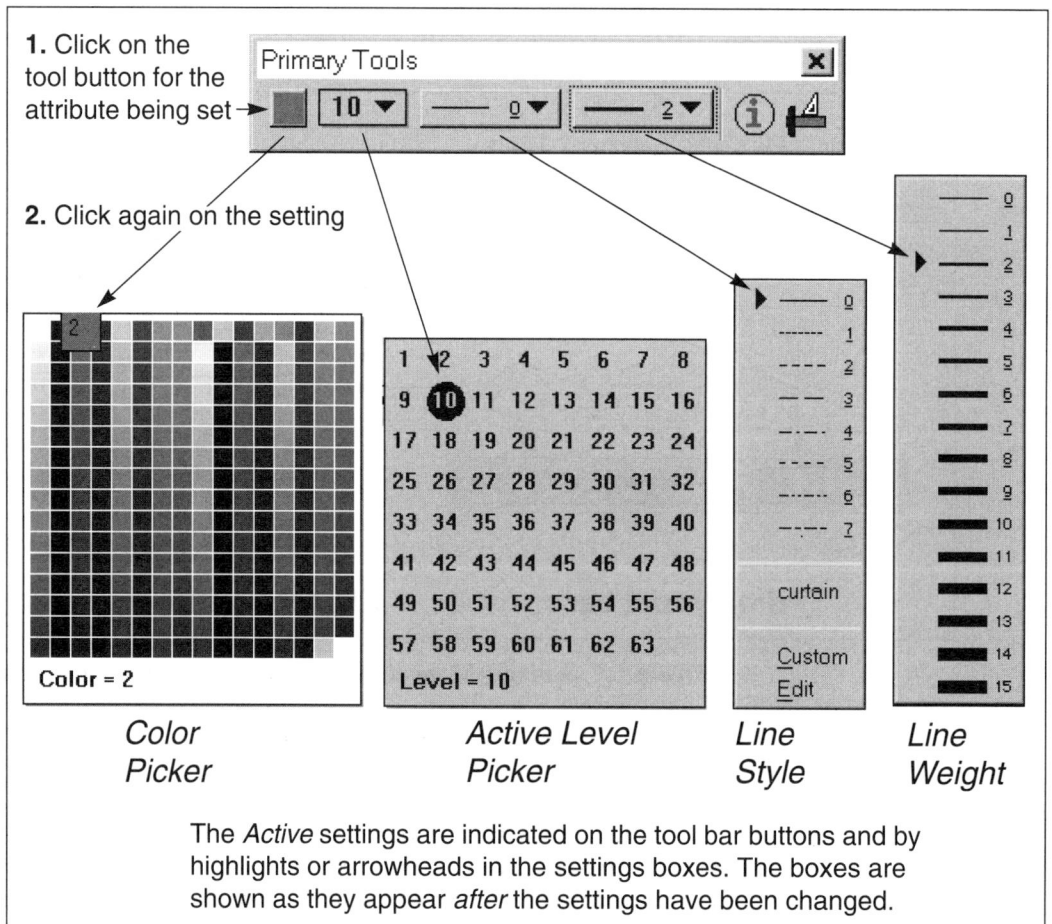

1. Click on the tool button for the attribute being set →

Primary Tools

10 ▼   —— 0 ▼   —— 2 ▼

2. Click again on the setting

Color = 2

Color Picker

```
 1  2  3  4  5  6  7  8
 9 10 11 12 13 14 15 16
17 18 19 20 21 22 23 24
25 26 27 28 29 30 31 32
33 34 35 36 37 38 39 40
41 42 43 44 45 46 47 48
49 50 51 52 53 54 55 56
57 58 59 60 61 62 63
```
Level = 10

Active Level Picker

—— 0
------ 1
---- 2
— — 3
--·-- 4
---- 5
--·--- 6
--·-- 7

curtain

Custom
Edit

Line Style

—— 0
—— 1
—— 2
—— 3
—— 4
—— 5
—— 6
—— 7
—— 8
—— 9
—— 10
—— 11
—— 12
—— 13
—— 14
—— 15

Line Weight

The *Active* settings are indicated on the tool bar buttons and by highlights or arrowheads in the settings boxes. The boxes are shown as they appear *after* the settings have been changed.

Figure 3.4   Element Attribute Settings Boxes

Slotted Stay Plate example (stage 1)

The next example is a stay plate with one mounting hole slotted for adjustment. The design is shown in Figure 3.5 with dimensions to help us create it for ourselves, but we will not be dimensioning our version for now. We will use the *Place SmartLine* and the *Place Circle* tool, both in conjunction with the *AccuDraw* facility.

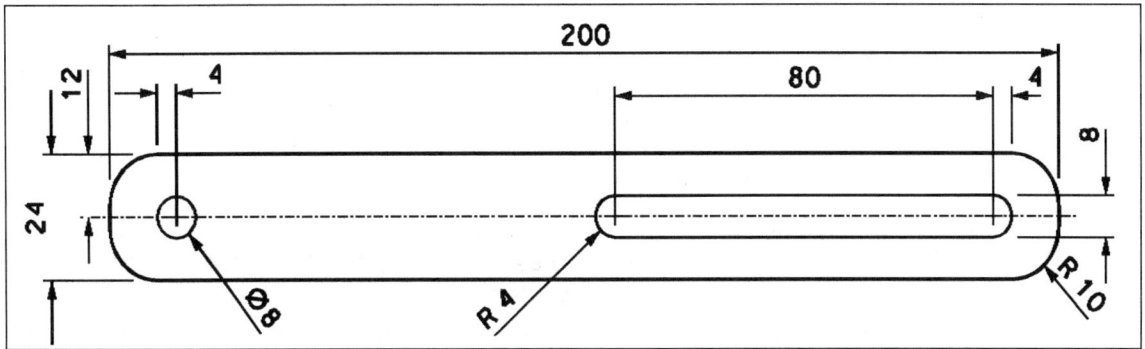

Figure 3.5   Slotted stay plate

We will arrange the magnification of the View window to suit our new design next, then complete its outline geometry.

◆ Prepare the view magnification & coordinates

1. With "second.dgn" open, *Start AccuDraw* (if it is not already running) by clicking the tool in the Primary tool bar. Check that the initial *Element Attributes* are set according to Figure 3.4.

2. Select the *Place SmartLine* tool, click in the *AccuDraw* window to direct *Input Focus* to it.

3. Press <P>, enter **0,0** in the *Data Point Keyin* settings box as an *Absolute* point, press <**Enter**>.

   This has placed the first point on the line at the *Global Origin*, which may not be within the view.

4. Enter **300** in the X: field of the *AccuDraw* window, press <**Tab**> to change to the Y: field, enter **0** (do not press <Enter> either time).

5. Click the Data button to place the other end of the line and *Reset* to complete the operation.

   The line may not be visible yet, it may be off the screen.

6. Click the *Fit Design* button.

The 300mm line will now be displayed across the center of the view, ensuring that the view will be wide enough for the 200mm long stay plate. The *Global Origin* is now on the screen, remember we defined the left end of the line at this point with the coordinates 0,0.

7. Select the *Delete* tool from the bottom-left of the *Main* tool frame, data point on the line to select it for deletion, *Accept* its deletion data point.

It may seem strange to place a line just to delete it. However, this is a quick and easy method of ensuring that the first element placed for the actual design is placed in full view and well within the limits of the design plane.

◆ Create the stay plate outline

1. Select the *Place SmartLine* tool, in its *Tool Settings* window set the *Segment Type* to **Lines**, *Vertex Type* to **Rounded**, *Rounding Radius* to **10** and *Join Elements* checked **On**.

Note: We instructed the *Place SmartLine* tool to automatically place arcs at each vertex when we set the Vertex Type to *Rounded* and specified a radius. With Join Elements *On* the arcs and lines will be joined together to form a *Complex Shape* when the outline is completed.

2. Click in the *AccuDraw* window to direct *Input Focus* to it, place the first vertex of the outline shape with a Data point near the left of the View window. The *Absolute* position of the outline is not critical.

3. Move the pointer directly to the right, change to *Rectangular* coordinates with the <**Spacebar**> if necessary.

Note that the dynamic element *Indexes* itself to the *x* axis when the pointer is within a pre-set distance from that axis.

4. The X: field will have *Input Focus*, Key in **200** to this field, the Y: field will be zero when the line is indexed to the *x* axis.

5. Click the Data button to *Accept* the first side (the AccuDraw compass moves to the new vertex).

6. Move the pointer directly up the screen so that the line *Indexes* to the *y* axis.

7. The Y: field will have *Input Focus*, Key in **24**.

This time the X: field will be zero while the line is indexed to the *y* axis.

8. *Accept* with the Data button.

The compass moves to the next vertex, this time the AccuDraw Drawing Plane rotates in anticipation of the move back to the left. The last used axis of the compass, the *y*, retains input focus, thus we do not need to change to another data entry field.

9. Move the pointer back to the left so that it indexes to the AccuDraw plane *y* axis, key in **200**, *Accept.*

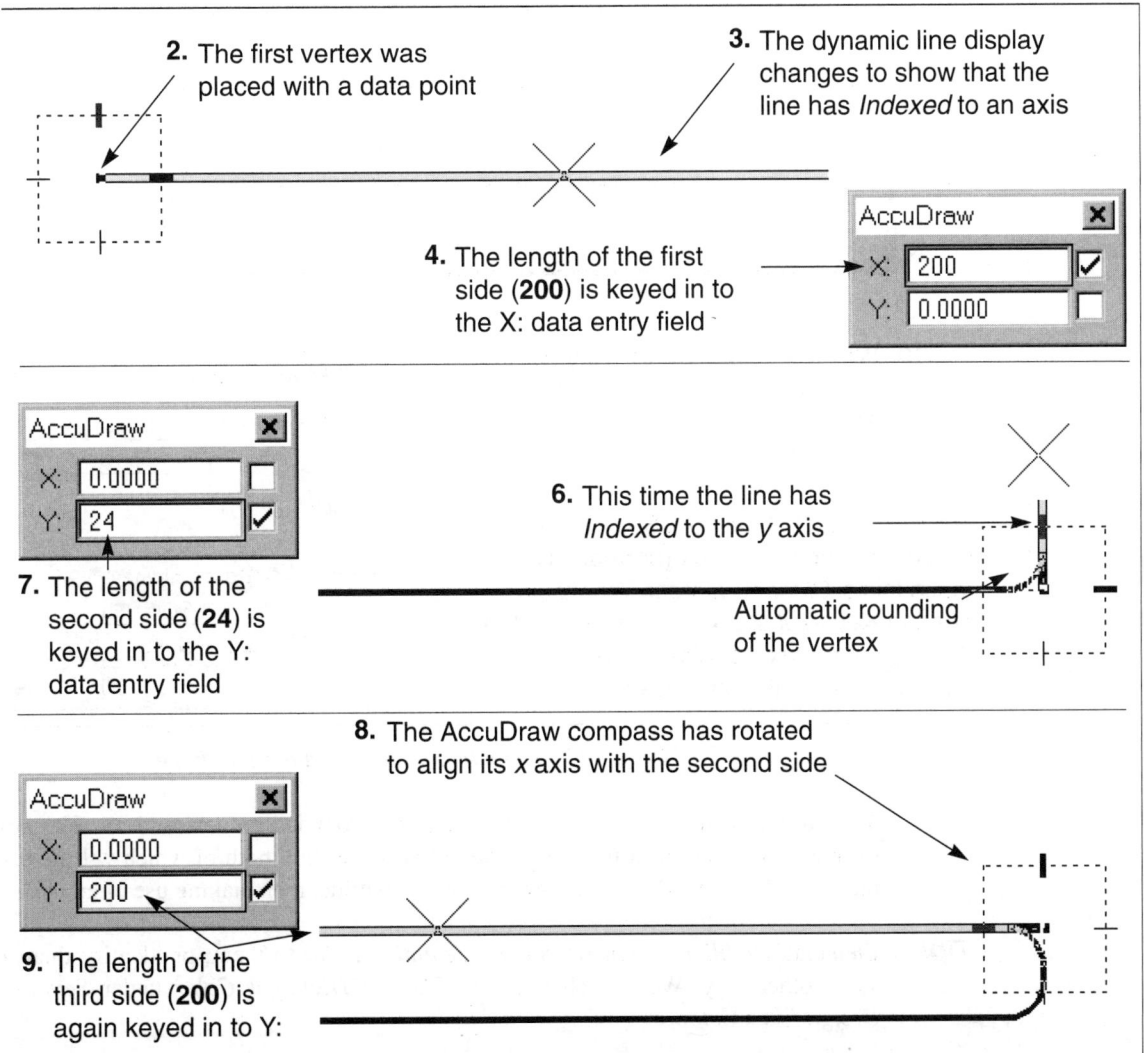

2. The first vertex was placed with a data point

3. The dynamic line display changes to show that the line has *Indexed* to an axis

4. The length of the first side (**200**) is keyed in to the X: data entry field

AccuDraw
X: 200
Y: 0.0000

AccuDraw
X: 0.0000
Y: 24

7. The length of the second side (**24**) is keyed in to the Y: data entry field

6. This time the line has *Indexed* to the *y* axis

Automatic rounding of the vertex

8. The AccuDraw compass has rotated to align its *x* axis with the second side

AccuDraw
X: 0.0000
Y: 200

9. The length of the third side (**200**) is again keyed in to Y:

Figure 3.6   Placing the first three sides of the Stay Plate

10. Move the pointer over the first vertex placed.

When the pointer is within a pre-set distance from the original vertex, the line indexes to it.

Note: The Tool Settings window displays some extra options, including a check box for *Closed Element*. It will show *Closed* by default, which is what we want. If we needed to change this, we can "mark our place" while doing so with a *Tentative* point.

11. *Accept* with the Data button, taking care not to move the pointer.

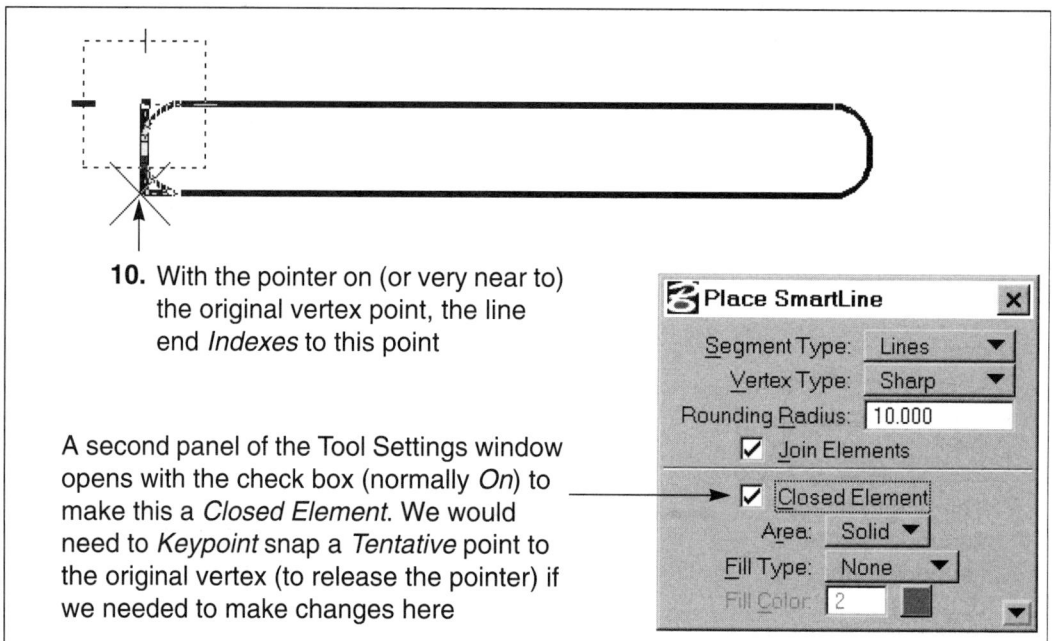

10. With the pointer on (or very near to) the original vertex point, the line end *Indexes* to this point

A second panel of the Tool Settings window opens with the check box (normally *On*) to make this a *Closed Element*. We would need to *Keypoint* snap a *Tentative* point to the original vertex (to release the pointer) if we needed to make changes here

Figure 3.7   Completing the closed outline shape

The outline of the stay plate is now complete, rounded corners and all. The next exercises in this project is to place the hole and the slot, both of which will involve placing a *Tentative Point* to a *Keypoint* on the outline, then making use of an *Offset*.

Tip! Elements *Highlight* when we *Snap* a *Tentative Point* to them, or identify them in some other way. We can change this *Element Highlight Color* under *Settings> Design File>Color*.

Snapping Tentative Points

We have already used the facility of *Snapping* Tentative points, now we will examine **Snaps** in some more detail. There are up to fourteen *Snap Modes*, which will be introduced progressively as we apply them.

Selecting a Snap Mode

We can set the snap mode by:

- Clicking the *Snap Mode* icon in the *Status* bar, or
- choosing *Settings>Snaps>* followed by the snap mode required, or
- choosing *Settings>Snaps>Button Bar*, which opens the bar, or
- click the *Tentative* mouse button while the **<Shift>** key is pressed.

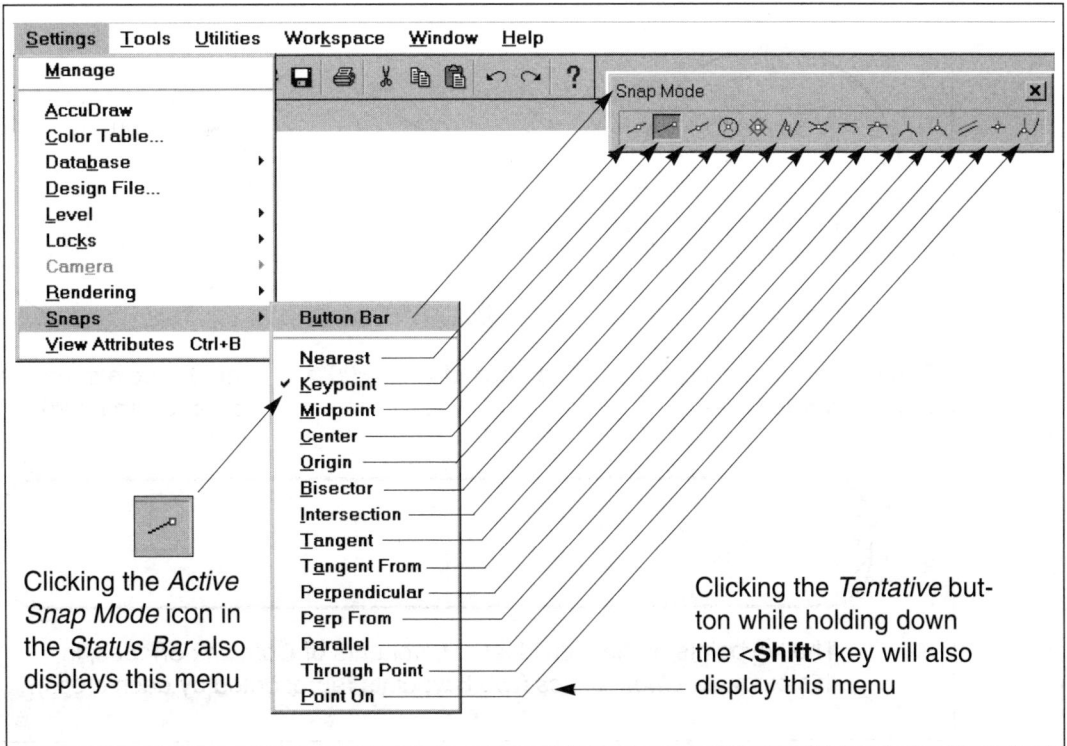

Figure 3.8   The complete range of Snap modes available for the Place Line tool

Keypoint Snap

The *Keypoint Snap Mode*, which is *Active* from the seed file set-up, is the mode most frequently used. When we place tentative points on, or very near elements, the tentative point will *Snap* to a *Keypoint*. All types of elements have *Keypoints*. The keypoint positions for some typical element types are illustrated in figure 3.9.

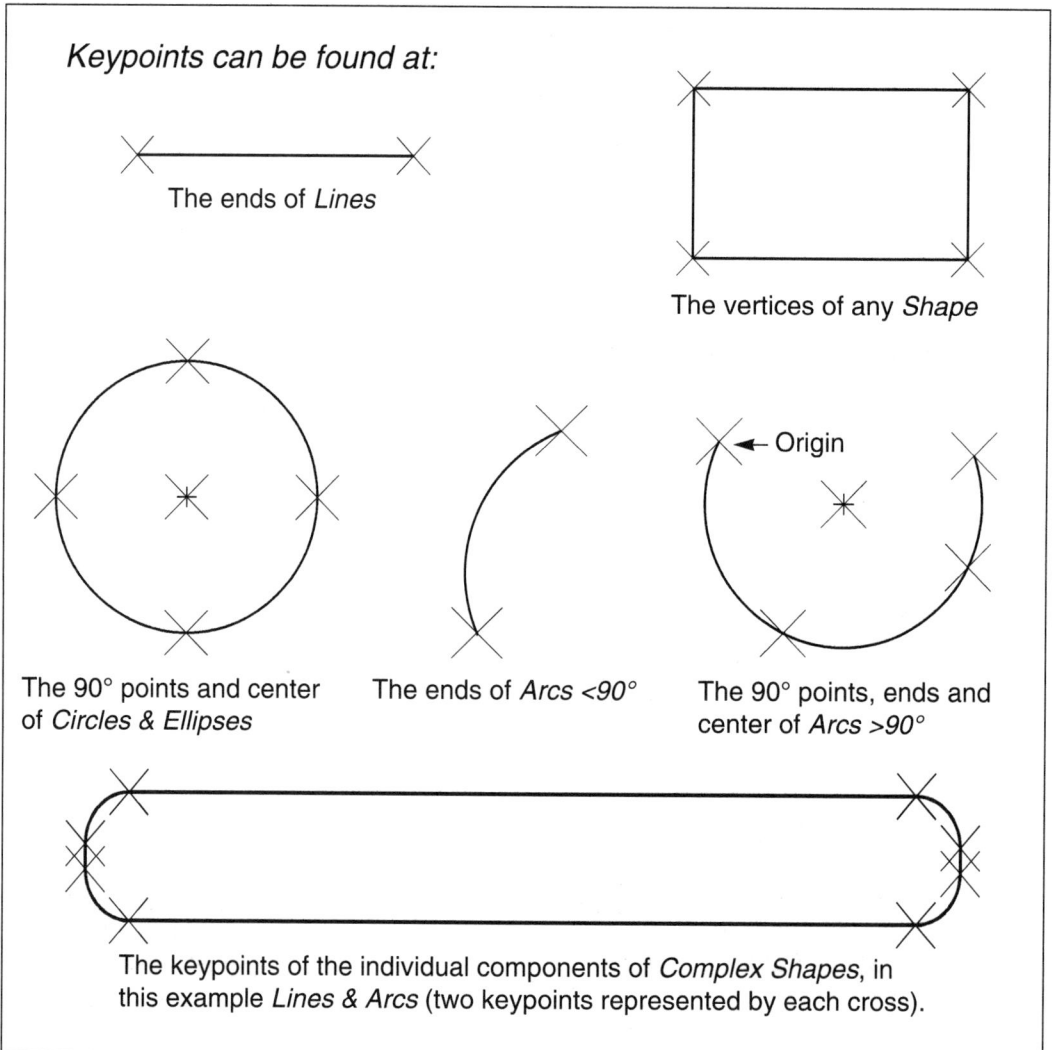

Keypoints can be found at:

The ends of *Lines*

The vertices of any *Shape*

← Origin

The 90° points and center of *Circles & Ellipses*

The ends of *Arcs <90°*

The 90° points, ends and center of *Arcs >90°*

The keypoints of the individual components of *Complex Shapes*, in this example *Lines & Arcs* (two keypoints represented by each cross).

Figure 3.9 Keypoints of typical elements

Keypoint Snap Divisor

It is also possible to *Snap* to a number of equally spaced points *Between Keypoints*, still using *Keypoint Snap.* We do this by dividing the distance along the element into a number of distances between snap points with a *Snap Divisor.*

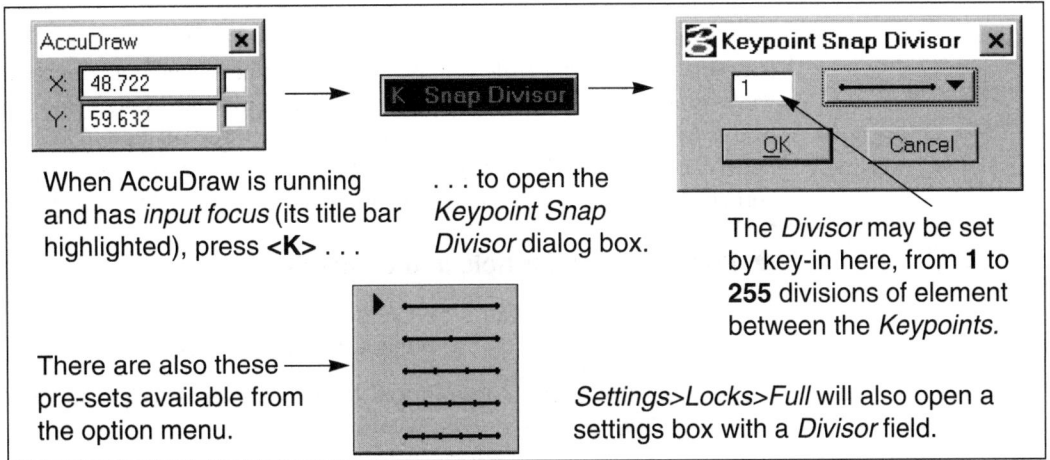

When AccuDraw is running and has *input focus* (its title bar highlighted), press **<K>** . . .

. . . to open the *Keypoint Snap Divisor* dialog box.

The *Divisor* may be set by key-in here, from **1** to **255** divisions of element between the *Keypoints.*

There are also these pre-sets available from the option menu.

Settings>Locks>Full will also open a settings box with a *Divisor* field.

Figure 3.10   Setting the Snap divisor

The usual method of setting the *Snap Divisor* is via the AccuDraw *Shortcut* **<K>** (for **K**eypoint), or it may be set in the *Snap* panel of the *Locks* settings box. This settings box may be opened from the Application menu bar by choosing *Locks>Full* from the *Settings* menu, or from the Status bar *Locks* icon.

For general use, the setting of **1** is the most convenient. However, setting the *Snap Divisor* to a number greater than 1 is useful for locating a number of equally spaced elements along another element, usually a line. Extra snap points are added between the usual *keypoints* equalling the [*Snap Divisor*]-**1**.

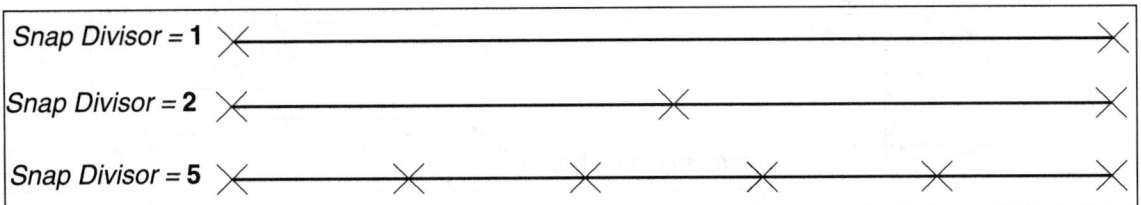

Figure 3.11   Keypoint Snap points, the effect of varying the Snap Divisor

Experiment with different *Snap Divisor* settings, snapping tentative points to your Stay Plate outline, where the *Complex Shape* has the keypoints of the individual line and arc components. When you have finished experimenting, leave *Keypoint* as the *Active Snap Mode* and the *Snap Divisor* set to 1 for the next exercise.

Slotted Stay Plate Example (stage 2)

We will now place the circular hole in the left end of the Stay Plate. The difference between a *Solid* and a *Hole* is that a hole cannot be hatched or patterned, we will be working with this subject in detail later. We will place the hole using a combination of a *Keypoint Snap* and an *Offset* in AccuDraw. We will first *Tentatively* place an 8mm diameter circle by *Snapping* it to the end of the top outline where it joins to the corner rounding. We will then *Offset* it down by 12mm and to the right by 4mm.

◆ **Place the circular hole in the Stay Plate**

1. Choose an *Active Line Weight* of **1** for the holes (leave the color and level the same as the outline, see page 3-6).

2. Use the *View Control* tools to fit the View window to the Stay Plate outline, start *AccuDraw* if necessary.

3. Select the *Place Circle* tool, in the *Tool Settings* window choose **By Center** (the default *Method*), *Area* **Hole**, as shown in figure 3.12.

4. Choose **Diameter** from the bottom panel of the Tool Settings window, click the diameter constraint check box **On**. Enter **8** to the data entry field, press <**Enter**>.

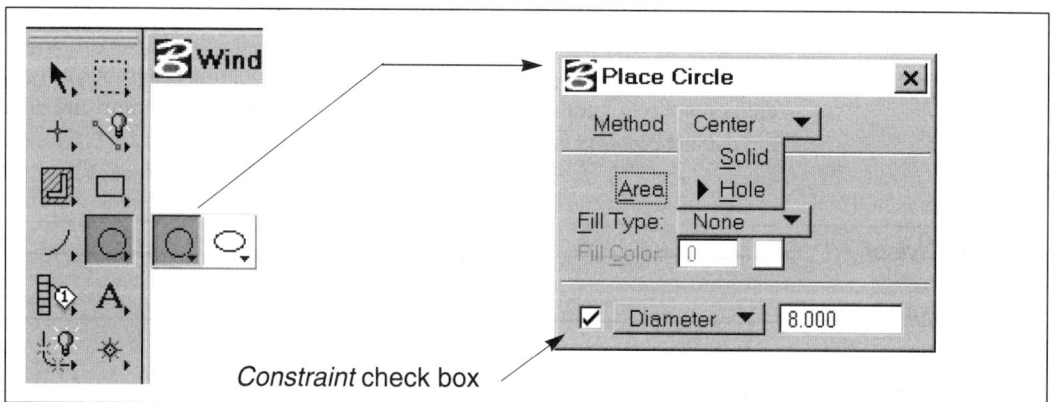

Figure 3.12   The Place Circle tool settings

5. Place a *Tentative* point using *Keypoint Snap* on the left end of the upper outline (see "Snapping Tentative Points" on page 3-11). Do not click the data button yet.

The upper line will highlight.

6. Press <**O**> (for **O**ffset the AccuDraw Drawing Plane), Move the pointer down and to the right to the approximate position for the hole, as illustrated on page 3-7.

We have probably moved further in the *-y* direction than in the *+x*, thus *Input Focus* will be in the Y: data input field.

7. Key **12** in to the Y: field, **4** in to the X:, using <**Tab**> to change between the fields.

8. *Accept* the placement of the circle with a Data point, then click *Reset* to indicate that we have finished with the Place Circle tool.

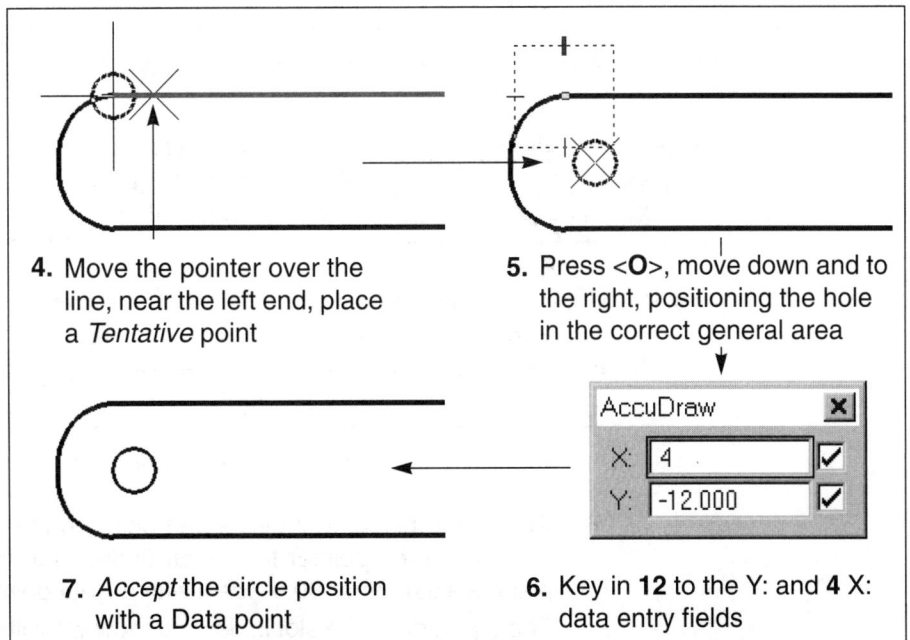

4. Move the pointer over the line, near the left end, place a *Tentative* point

5. Press <**O**>, move down and to the right, positioning the hole in the correct general area

6. Key in **12** to the Y: and **4** X: data entry fields

7. *Accept* the circle position with a Data point

Figure 3.13   Placing the round hole in the Stay Plate

Next, we will place the slot in the other end of the plate. This is constructed from lines and arcs placed using the *Place SmartLine* tool. It will be *Offset* from an initial *Tentative* point, in a similar way to the round hole.

◆ **Place the slot in the Stay Plate**

1. Keep the *Element Attributes* the same as for the circular hole, Select the *Place SmartLine* tool, set the *Segment Type* to **Lines**, *Join Elements **On***, the *Vertex Type* does not matter.

2. Direct *Input Focus* to the AccuDraw window (Click on it, press **<Esc>**, or press <**F6**> until its title bar highlights).

3. Place a *Tentative* point (only) using *Keypoint Snap* on the right end of the upper outline.

4. Press <**O**> (for **O**ffset the AccuDraw Drawing Plane), Move the pointer down and to the left to the approximate position for the start of the top side of the slot, as it appears on page 3-7.

5. Key **4** in to the X: field, **8** in to the Y:, using <**Tab**> to change between the fields.

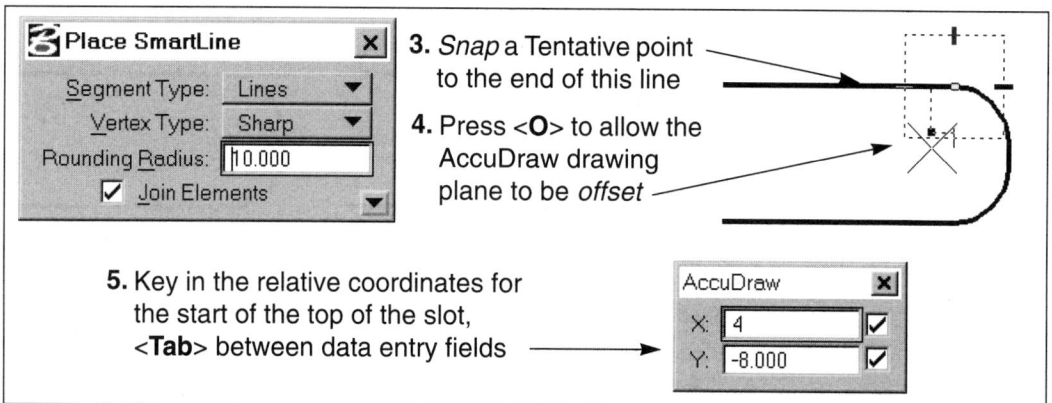

Figure 3.14   Placing the start of the slot

6. *Accept* the placement of the first point on the line with a Data point, (**6a**), move the pointer to the left (indexed to the AccuDraw drawing plane *x* axis), enter **80**, *Accept* with a Data point (**6b**).

   The top edge of the slot is defined, now we will use an *Arc* to form the left end. A line will "rubber band" as you make the change.

7. Change the *Segment Type* to **Arcs**, move the pointer directly down (indexed to 90°), key in **4** to the *Distance* field to define the arc center, *Accept* with a Data point.

   The AccuDraw Compass shows that changing *Segment Type* to *Arcs* caused the coordinate system to change to *Polar*.

7. Move the pointer down
(indexed to the *y* axis), key
in **4** to the *Distance* field,
Accept the arc center

Place SmartLine

Segment Type: Arcs
Vertex Type: Sharp
Rounding Radius: 10.000
☑ Join Elements

(6b) **(6a)**

7.

AccuDraw
Distance 4
Angle: 90.00°

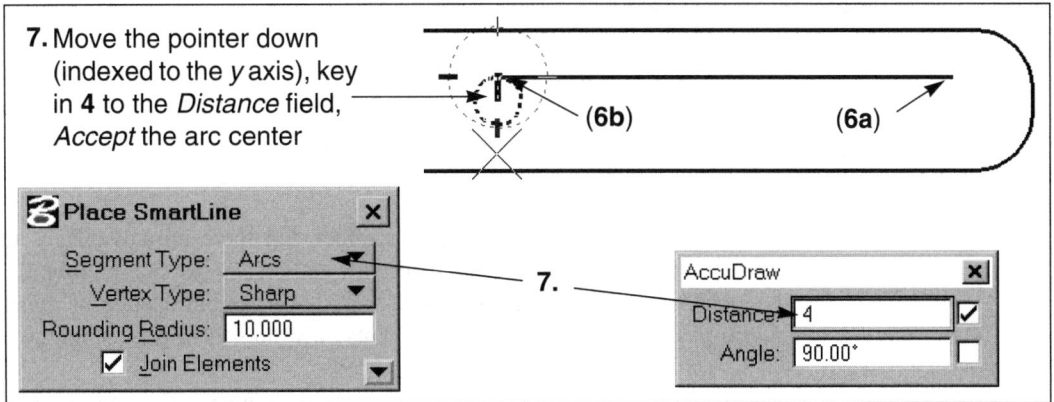

Figure 3.15   Placing a SmartLine arc

8. Move the pointer directly below the center of the arc just defined (the AccuDraw *Angle* field will show 180°), *Accept* the arc.

Note: The Accudraw Drawing Plane (as indicated by the Compass) rotates to anticipate our likely next move, the +*x* axis will generally be in the direction of the last element placed.

9. Change the *Segment Type* back to **Lines**, move the pointer directly to the right, enter **80** again, this time in to the *Distance* field, *Accept.*
The coordinate system remains *Polar* since we have included an arc.

10. Change the *Segment Type* back to **Arcs**, move the pointer directly upward (past the center), enter **4**, *Accept* the center then *Accept* the end of the arc at 180°.

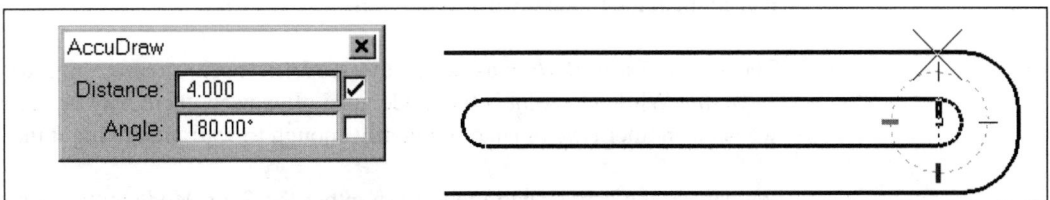

AccuDraw
Distance: 4.000
Angle: 180.00°

Figure 3.16   Completing the slot

That completes the geometry of the Stay plate itself, it only remains to place a centerline on it. This will involve changing most of the *Element Attributes* and the *Snap Mode*.

Midpoint Snap

The name of this snap mode tells us where the *Tentative* point will be placed when we click the button on an element. *Midpoint* is not to be confused with *Center*, which refers to arcs and ellipses. As you will recall, if we set the Snap Divisor to 2 we can snap to midpoints using keypoint snap.

In practice, many operators use this effect, but there are advantages to using the *Midpoint* mode. A *Midpoint* snap will only snap to the midpoint, not to the keypoints. Maintaining a Snap Divisor of 1 for general operations means *Keypoint Snaps* place tentative points on keypoints only, thus there is no ambiguity.

The *Midpoints* of the Stay plate component elements are shown in figure 3.17.

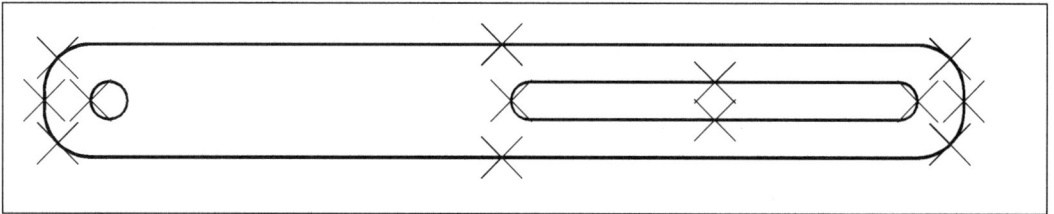

Figure 3.17   Midpoint Snap Points

Setting the Active Snap Mode

MicroStation permits us to set an *Active Snap Mode* and a *Snap Mode Override* or *One-shot Snap Mode*. The *One-shot* mode remains active only until a data point is placed, then the mode reverts to the *Active*.

The *Active Snap Mode* was set in the seed file used to create this design file as *Keypoint.* While keypoint is the mode most often used, there may be occasions when we need another type of snap frequently enough to warrant making it the *Active*.

We can set the active snap mode from either the *Snap Mode* button bar, or from the <**Shift**> plus **Tentative** pop-up menu. If we have the *Snaps* button bar floating or docked, we can make a snap mode *Active* by *Double-clicking* the relevant button, instead of the usual single-click selection method. Figure 3.18 shows the button bar with *Keypoint* as the *Active Mode*, with *Midpoint* the *Snap Mode Override*.

Snap modes not valid for the selected tool are grayed out.

Snap Mode

The *Keypoint* button is shaded, this has previously been made the *Active Snap Mode* by *Double-clicking*

The *Midpoint* button is *On*. It was clicked once only, making it the *Snap Mode Override* or *One-shot Snap Mode.*

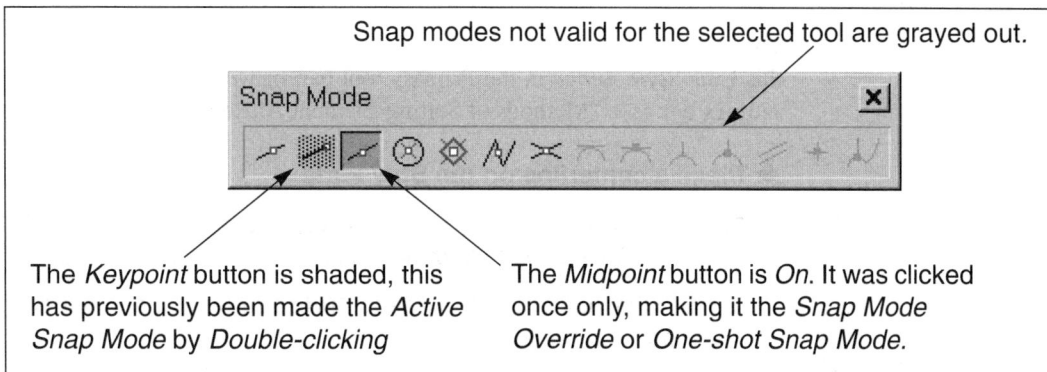

Figure 3.18   Snap Mode buttons with Keypoint as the Active mode

When we are using the pop-up menu, we make a selection *Active* by selecting it while the <**Shift**> key is held down. For a *One-shot* selection (the *Snap Mode Override*) with the menu, we make the snap mode selection without the <**Shift**> key held down.

The snap mode that will apply to the next Tentative point is indicated by a *Radio* button (a grey diamond in this case). If this is an *Override* there will be a white diamond button indicating the *Active* snap mode.

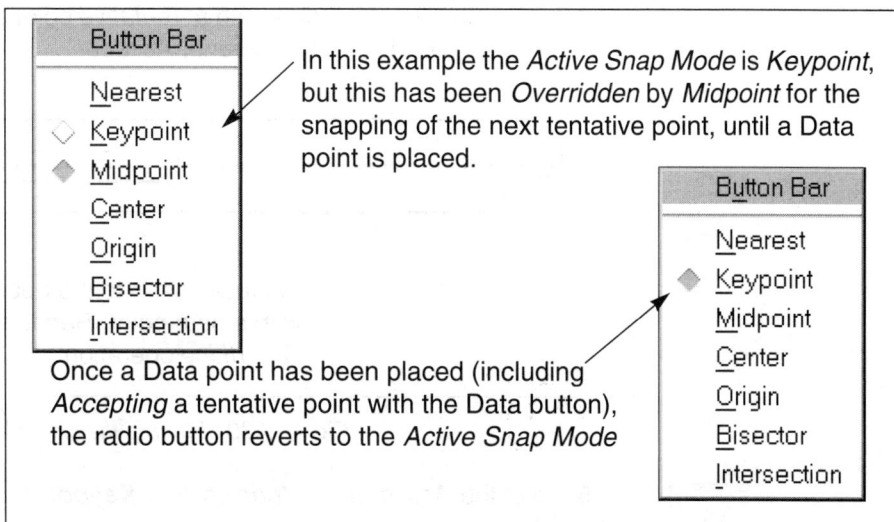

Button Bar

Nearest
◇ Keypoint
◆ Midpoint
Center
Origin
Bisector
Intersection

In this example the *Active Snap Mode* is *Keypoint*, but this has been *Overridden* by *Midpoint* for the snapping of the next tentative point, until a Data point is placed.

Button Bar

Nearest
◆ Keypoint
Midpoint
Center
Origin
Bisector
Intersection

Once a Data point has been placed (including *Accepting* a tentative point with the Data button), the radio button reverts to the *Active Snap Mode*

Figure 3.19   Active Snap Mode and Snap Mode Override in the pop-up menu

Slotted Stay Plate Example (stage 3)

The element we are about to place will be a dot-dash style centerline. We can make this Line Style *Active* in the Primary tool bar, or we can use the Element Attributes settings box (see "Methods of Setting Element Attributes" on page 3-5).

◆ Place a centerline on the Stay Plate

1. Set the *Active Color* to **Yellow** (**4**), the *Active Level* to **11**, the *Active Line Style* to **Dot-Dash** (**4**), the *Active Line Weight* to **0**.

2. Set the *Active Snap Mode* to **Midpoint** (see "Setting the Active Snap Mode" on page 3-18).

3. Select the *Place SmartLine* tool (set *Segment Type* to **Lines**), place a *Tentative* point on the section of line on one end of the outline, *Accept* (with the Data button).

   An alternative to setting the *Active* snap mode to *Midpoint* would have been to choose this mode as the *Snap Mode Override* twice, before both steps **3.** and **4.**

4. Place a *Tentative* point on the equivalent section of line at the opposite end of the outline, *Accept*, *Reset* to terminate the Place SmartLine operation.

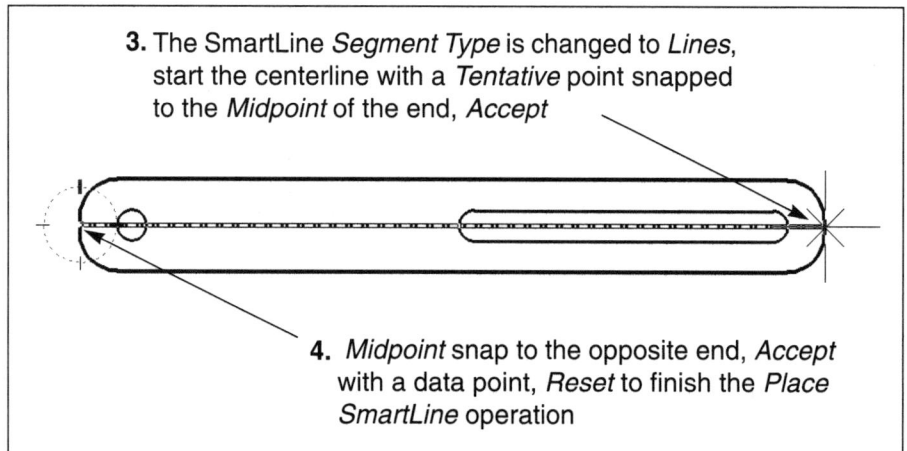

3. The SmartLine *Segment Type* is changed to *Lines*, start the centerline with a *Tentative* point snapped to the *Midpoint* of the end, *Accept*

4. *Midpoint* snap to the opposite end, *Accept* with a data point, *Reset* to finish the *Place SmartLine* operation

Figure 3.20   Placing the centerline

5. Set the *Active Snap Mode* back to **Keypoint**.

   Keypoint is the snap mode usually left *Active*, as it is the most commonly used.

You may have noticed in Figure 3.5 on page 3-7 that the centerline extended past the outline. We will introduce a new tool called *Extend Line* (see "The Extend Line Tool" on page 5-20 if you would like more details). It is used to *Modify* an existing element, thus it is found on the *Modify* child tool box from the *Main* tool frame. With this tool we can constrain the amount of the extension to a keyed-in value, or control the extension graphically. We nominate the end of the line to be extended by selecting it at the required end with a Data point.

◆ **Extend the centerline**

1. Select the *Extend Line* tool from the *Modify* tool box (bottom-right of the *Main* tool frame), using *press-move-release* selection, as shown in Figure 3.21.

2. Click the *Distance* constraint check box **On** in the Tool Settings window, key in **4** to the data entry field, press <**Enter**>.

3. Data point (move the pointer over the line and click the Data button) near one end of the line, *Accept* the proposed extension (displayed as a highlight).

4. Repeat step **3.** to extend the opposite end.

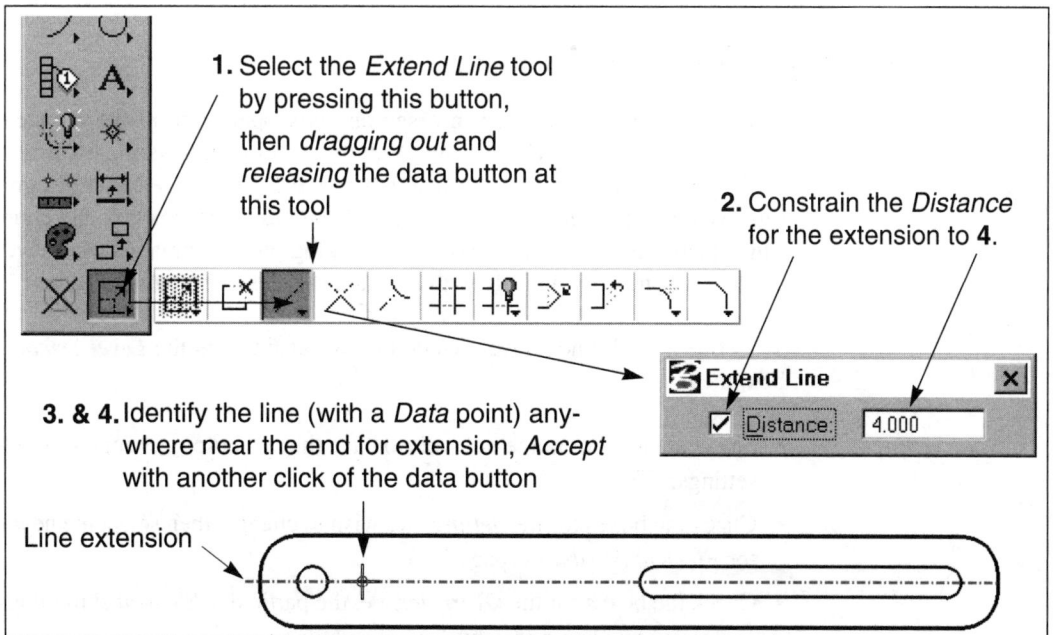

Figure 3.21   Extending the centerline

Level Symbology

We were introduced to the *Symbology* attributes when we set the *Element Attributes* for the first stage of the Stay Plate design (see "Defining the initial Element Attributes" on page 3-6). This element related symbology is generally what we see on the screen and on paper, but we also have the option of using symbology dependent on the *Level* the element is placed on. We can either display (and print) the design with *Element Symbology,* with *Level Symbology*, or with a combination of both.

Switching to *Level* symbology makes it possible to observe the level an element is on by its appearance. It also makes it possible to display a particular element with different symbology for different drawings. For example, one printout of a design file may show an element with solid, heavy linework, whereas on another it could be dotted and light.

The *Symbology* attributes are *Color*, *Line Style* and *Line Weight*. The symbology settings can each be defined as being an attribute of the *Level*, as well as of the *Element*. We can change between *Element* and *Level* symbology at any time, using a check box in the *View Attributes* settings box (see "Attributes of the View Window" on page 3-3).

Defining Level Symbology

Level symbology is defined in a settings box opened from the Application menu under *Settings>Level>Symbology*. With this box open, the simplest way of defining level symbology is by copying an existing definition from another design file. To do this, we click the *File* menu of the *Level Symbology* settings box and choose *Import*. This opens the *Import Level Symbology* dialog (not illustrated), where we can select an existing directory and file with a suitable level symbology definition.

To define a totally new level symbology we again open the *Level Symbology* dialog box, then:

- Select the level or range of levels to have the symbology changed from the default settings;
- Check the boxes for the *Settings* we wish to change, then select the new settings as for *Element Attributes* (page 3-5);
- Check the boxes for the *Overrides,* i.e. the particular *Element* symbology attribute settings to be *Overridden* by *Level Symbology*.

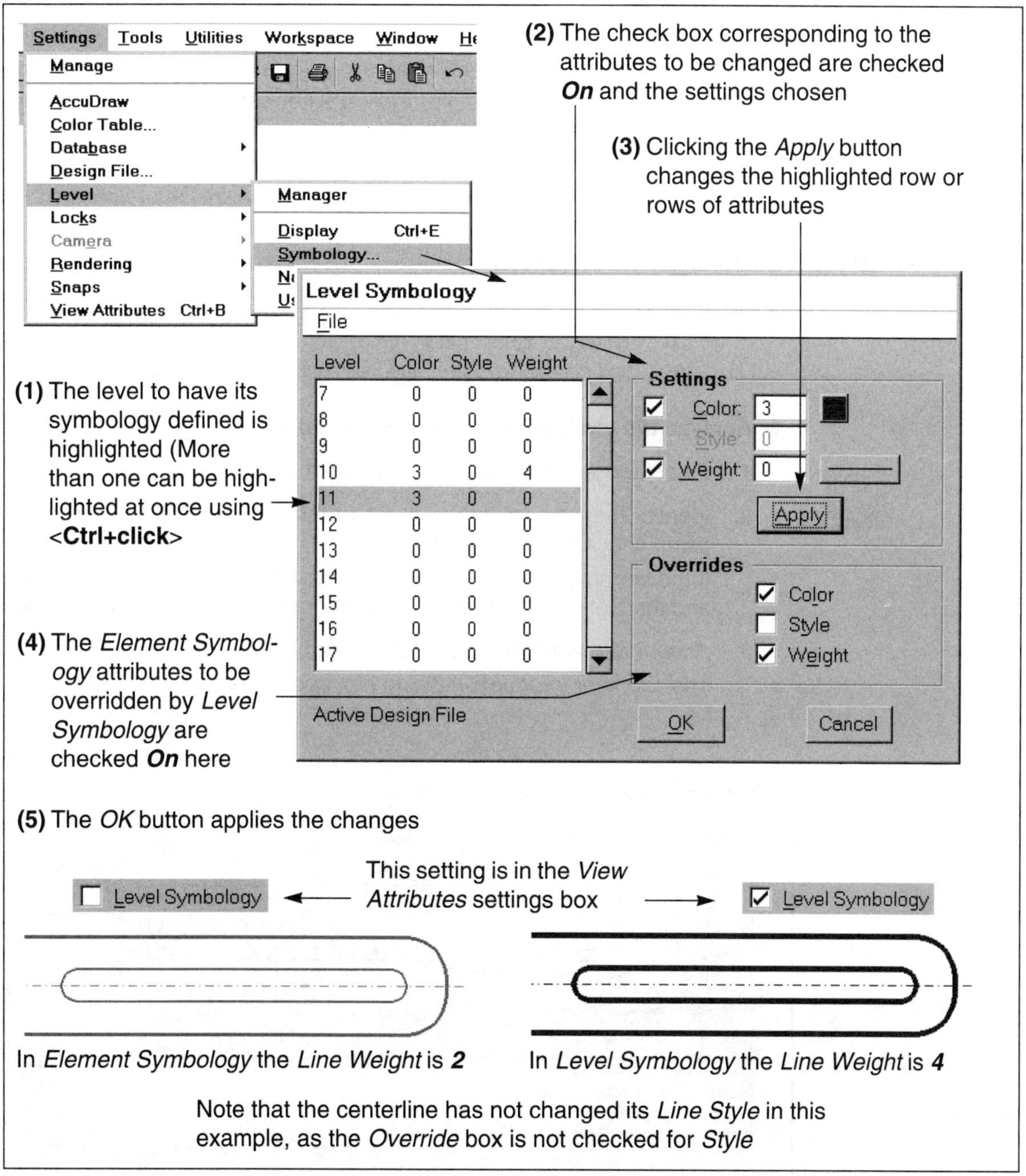

Settings	Tools	Utilities	Workspace	Window	He
Manage					
AccuDraw					
Color Table...					
Database ▶					
Design File...					
Level ▶		Manager			
Locks ▶		Display	Ctrl+E		
Camera ▶		Symbology...			
Rendering ▶					
Snaps ▶					
View Attributes Ctrl+B					

(2) The check box corresponding to the attributes to be changed are checked *On* and the settings chosen

(3) Clicking the *Apply* button changes the highlighted row or rows of attributes

Level Symbology

File

Level	Color	Style	Weight
7	0	0	0
8	0	0	0
9	0	0	0
10	3	0	4
11	3	0	0
12	0	0	0
13	0	0	0
14	0	0	0
15	0	0	0
16	0	0	0
17	0	0	0

Settings
- ☑ Color: 3
- ☐ Style: 0
- ☑ Weight: 0

Apply

Overrides
- ☑ Color
- ☐ Style
- ☑ Weight

Active Design File   OK   Cancel

(1) The level to have its symbology defined is highlighted (More than one can be highlighted at once using <**Ctrl+click**>

(4) The *Element Symbology* attributes to be overridden by *Level Symbology* are checked *On* here

(5) The *OK* button applies the changes

☐ Level Symbology ◄—— This setting is in the *View Attributes* settings box ——► ☑ Level Symbology

In *Element Symbology* the *Line Weight* is **2**

In *Level Symbology* the *Line Weight* is **4**

Note that the centerline has not changed its *Line Style* in this example, as the *Override* box is not checked for *Style*

Figure 3.22   Element Vs. Level Symbology

Element Information

We have placed various types of elements, each with its own set of *Element Attributes*. We can analyze these elements visually and recognize some of these attributes, but not all of them. The *Analyze Element* tool, found on the *Primary* tool bar is used to provide us with all the information about any element that we are likely to need.

Analyzing Design Elements

In the next exercises we will be investigating the Stay Plate to find out the *Element Types* we have created, as compared to the actual tools we used to create them. We will also check the *Element Attributes* and learn one method of changing these.

◆ **Analyze the circle placed in the Stay Plate**

1. Select the *Analyze Element* tool from the *Primary* tool bar.

2. Identify the 8mm diameter circle at the left of the plate with a Data point, check that it highlights.
   If the wrong element highlights (perhaps the centerline), press *Reset* and the Data point will cycle to another element close to the pointer.

3. *Accept* with another press of the Data button.
   The *Element Information* dialog box opens, as shown in Figure 3.23.

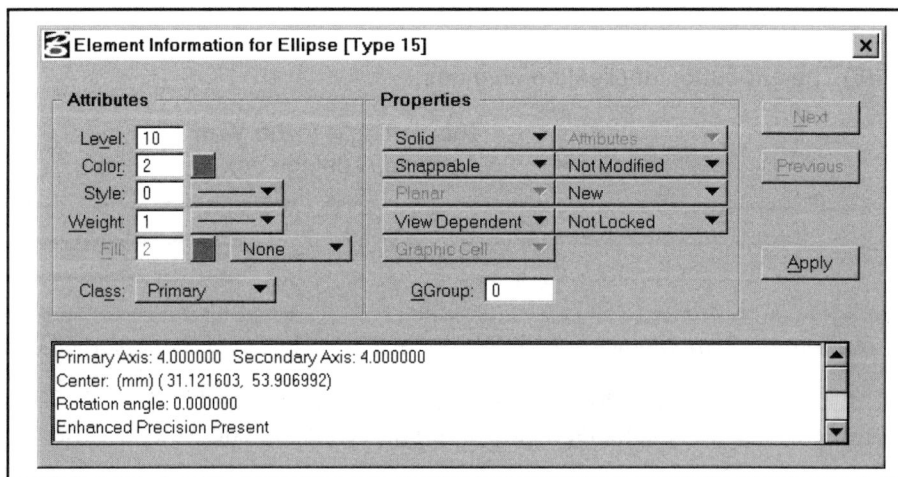

Figure 3.23   Information about the Circle in the Stay Plate

The amount of information offered may seem overwhelming at first, but much of it is relevant and understandable, even at this early stage. For a start, the *Attributes* panel can be compared with the exercise instructions on page 3-6 and page 3-14, where these attributes were selected.

Changing Elements from inside the Information dialog box

The *Attributes* panel of the *Element Information* dialog box is almost identical to the *Element Attributes* settings box. It not only displays information, but allows settings to be changed. If we use these menus to change settings, we must use the *Apply* button (on the right of the dialog box) for the changes to be applied to the element under analysis. Clicking the *Apply* button does not immediately make any changes to the element, an *Alert* box opens first. The question "Apply the changes to the currently displayed element?" can be answered either way with the *Yes/No* buttons.

The bottom panel displays much more information about the element, so much that the vertical scroll bar is often needed. For example you may have noticed that the title bar described the circle selected as an "Ellipse". This is normal within MicroStation, circles are defined as ellipses with equal radii on both their primary and secondary axes. This fact is apparent from the top line of information in the bottom panel, the 8mm diameter circle has a radius of 4 on both its primary and a secondary axes.

The next two lines in this panel give the coordinates of the center and the rotation of the primary axis with respect to the x axis of the drawing plane. The remaining information is mainly to do with the element data in the design file, thus it is not required for ordinary operation.

Analyzing Complex Shapes

When we used the *Place SmartLine* tool to create the outline of the Stay Plate, we actually placed a series of *Lines* and *Arcs* that combined into a *Complex Shape* when the last Data point was placed. When we *Analyze* the element the *Element Information* dialog box has this fact in its title bar. Just below the title bar is the label "1 of 9", which indicates there are another 8 boxes associated with this element. The circle we analyzed before only had one box, thus a comparable label did not display.

◆ **Analyze the outline shape of the Stay Plate**

1. If the *Element Information* dialog box is still open from the last exercise, move it if necessary to expose part of the Plate outline.

    If the box was closed, select the *Analyze Element* tool once more.

2. Data point anywhere on the outline of the plate, *Accept.*

Another *Element Information* dialog box opens, this time for a *Complex Shape,* as shown in Figure 3.24.

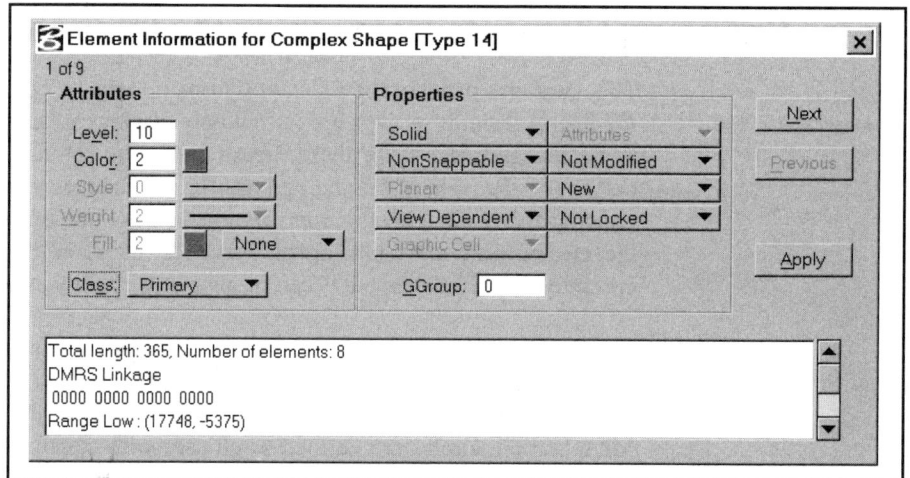

Figure 3.24   First box of Information about the Outline Shape

MicroStation has a defined set of *Element Types*, displayed in the Title bar of the Information dialog box. Each type is allocated a number, but these numbers are mainly of interest in programming and troubleshooting.

The Stay Plate outline *Complex Shape* has eight component elements, four *Lines* and four *Arcs.* Each of these component elements has its own *Element Information* dialog box, hence the total of nine. A (simple) *Shape*, such as a *Block* consists of only one element, the shape itself.

The first information dialog box displays the *Element Attributes* just as before. A *Complex Shape* has only one set of attributes, like any other element. All of the component elements will have the same attributes. We can prove this by clicking the *Next* button and examining the boxes. Each time we click *Next* the details of the next component element are displayed in the box, until all of them have been displayed.

Analyzing elements is an essential part of the process of creating and checking designs. We can use the tool check on our own work and to extract information from existing design files.

AccuDraw's Keyboard Shortcuts

AccuDraw accepts a large number of single and double character command directives, generally called *Shortcut Keys*. We have used a couple of these already, such as **<P>** to enter a **P**oint, **<Spacebar>** to change coordinate systems. The shortcut will not be interpreted as data input, as the shortcut characters are not numeric. The first character of a double-character input will open a dialog box with a scroll panel, with the first of the related shortcuts highlighted.

In the early stages of working with AccuDraw, the most useful key may be the one that displays the scroll list of all shortcuts, the **<?>** key. We will find that the shortcut key assignments have been chosen to be easily remembered. Shortcuts that are unavailable for 2D designs are grayed out.

We can invoke a *Shortcut* from the scroll list shown in Figure 3.25 by clicking on the required shortcut in the list box and then clicking *Run*. However, the most frequently used shortcuts are invoked by single keystrokes and the list will seldom be needed once these are committed to memory. As you become more familiar with MicroStation, re-examine this list from time to time to discover more time-savers.

Shortcuts will be introduced as we create the drawing examples throughout this book. The first one, *Set Origin* (also called *Offset*), has already been used when we placed the holes in the stay plate. We will now examine this vital facility in more detail, then we will introduce our second shortcut key, *Smart Lock*.

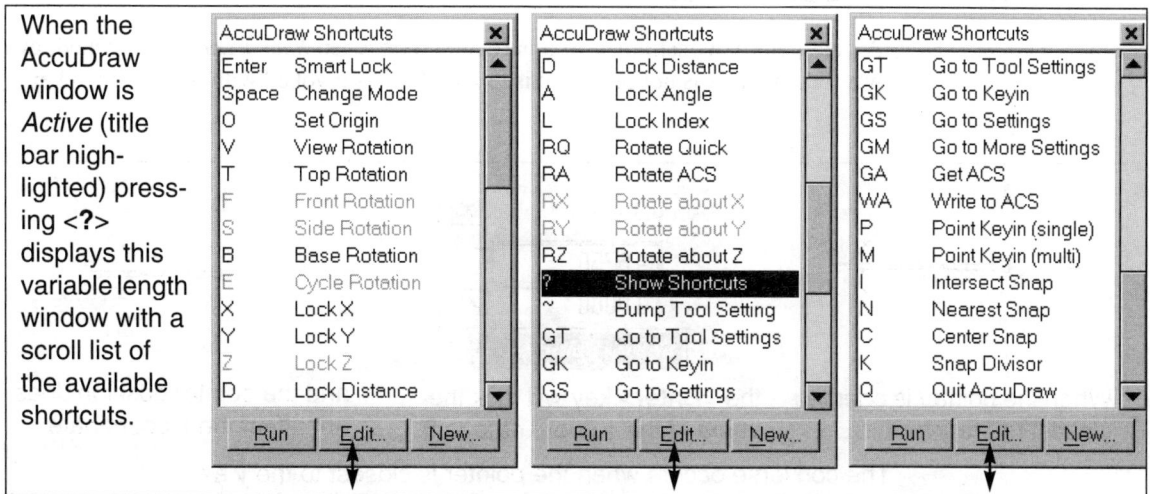

When the AccuDraw window is *Active* (title bar high-lighted) pressing **<?>** displays this variable length window with a scroll list of the available shortcuts.

AccuDraw Shortcuts	✕
Enter	Smart Lock
Space	Change Mode
O	Set Origin
V	View Rotation
T	Top Rotation
F	Front Rotation
S	Side Rotation
B	Base Rotation
E	Cycle Rotation
X	Lock X
Y	Lock Y
Z	Lock Z
D	Lock Distance

Run   Edit...   New...

AccuDraw Shortcuts	✕
D	Lock Distance
A	Lock Angle
L	Lock Index
RQ	Rotate Quick
RA	Rotate ACS
RX	Rotate about X
RY	Rotate about Y
RZ	Rotate about Z
?	Show Shortcuts
~	Bump Tool Setting
GT	Go to Tool Settings
GK	Go to Keyin
GS	Go to Settings

Run   Edit...   New...

AccuDraw Shortcuts	✕
GT	Go to Tool Settings
GK	Go to Keyin
GS	Go to Settings
GM	Go to More Settings
GA	Get ACS
WA	Write to ACS
P	Point Keyin (single)
M	Point Keyin (multi)
I	Intersect Snap
N	Nearest Snap
C	Center Snap
K	Snap Divisor
Q	Quit AccuDraw

Run   Edit...   New...

Figure 3.25   AccuDraw shortcut key listing

The Set Origin or Offset Shortcut

In 3.26, let us assume that we need to place a second block inside another. Its first vertex is to be Offset from the top-left vertex of the existing element, down by 0.25 and to the right by the same distance. There is another example of this on page 3-15.

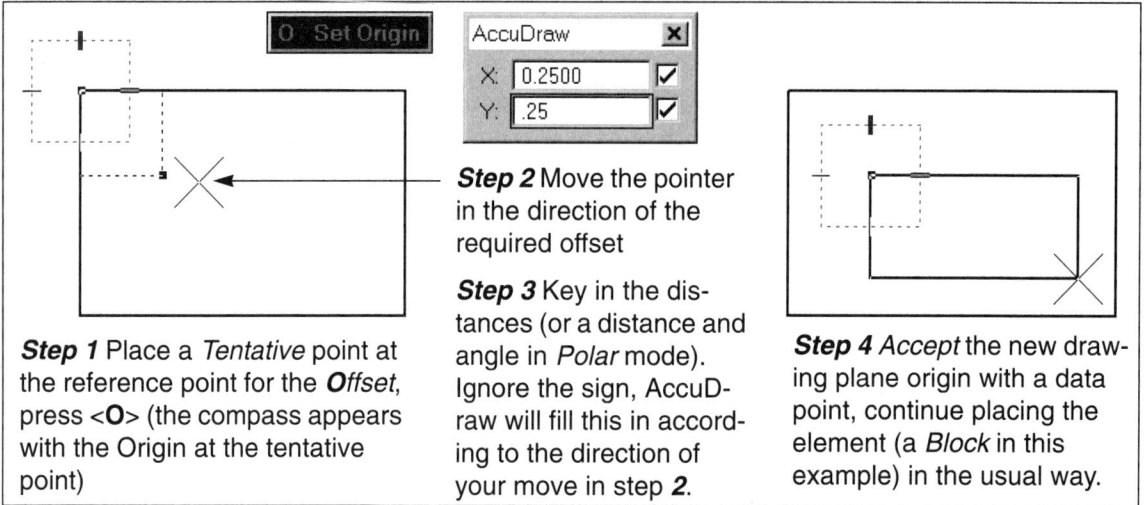

Step 1 Place a *Tentative* point at the reference point for the *Offset*, press <**O**> (the compass appears with the Origin at the tentative point)

Step 2 Move the pointer in the direction of the required offset

Step 3 Key in the distances (or a distance and angle in *Polar* mode). Ignore the sign, AccuDraw will fill this in according to the direction of your move in step **2**.

Step 4 *Accept* the new drawing plane origin with a data point, continue placing the element (a *Block* in this example) in the usual way.

Figure 3.26 Moving the AccuDraw Origin

The Smart Lock Shortcut

A data point is constrained to a particular axis when *Smart Lock* is activated, even when the pointer is not on that axis. *Smart Lock* is invoked with the <**Enter**> key.

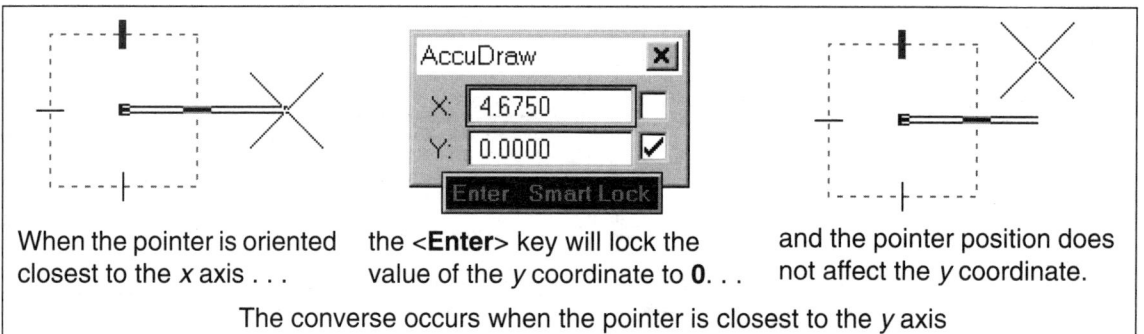

When the pointer is oriented closest to the *x* axis . . .

the <**Enter**> key will lock the value of the *y* coordinate to **0**. . .

and the pointer position does not affect the *y* coordinate.

The converse occurs when the pointer is closest to the *y* axis

Figure 3.27 Invoking Smart Lock with the Enter key

Pivot Pin Example (stage 1)

The next example is a drawing showing two views of a small pivot pin, as illustrated by Figure 3.28. As was the case with the "Stay Plate" example, we will not dimension the drawing or place the centerline yet. We will return to the drawing later in the book as an example for dimensioning exercises.

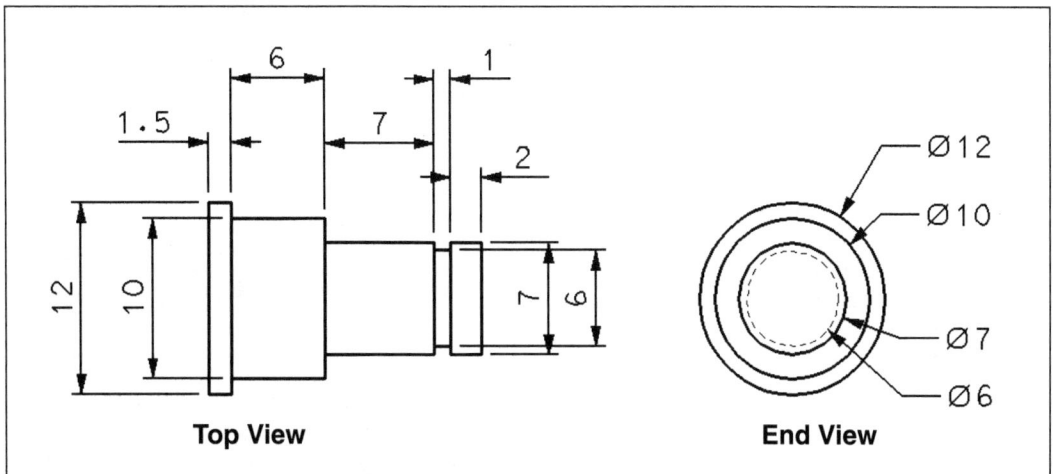

Figure 3.28   Pivot pin, two views

This pin can be taken as part of the same drawing as the Stay Plate, so we will create it in the same design file, "second.dgn". It will be spaced away from the Stay and created on a separate level. We will start the next exercise, practicing the use of the *Place Block* and *Place SmartLine* tools, with "second.dgn" assumed to be already open. This exercise will make use of the *Offset* and *Smart Lock* AccuDraw shortcuts.

◆ **Create the head and large bearing surface of the Pivot Pin**

1. Choose **0** as the *Active Color*, level **20** as the *Active Level,* **0** as the *Active Linestyle* and an *Active Line Weight* of **2**, all from the *Primary Tool Bar.*

2. With AccuDraw running, select the *Place Block* tool (as used in the exercise on page 2-28), data point 40mm or so below the left end of the plate to enter the *First Point*, as prompted.

   The exact position does not matter at this stage, we can easily re-arrange this later, as you will see.

3. Complete the head of the pin by placing the *Opposite Corner* down **12** and **1.5** to the right (remember that <**Tab**> changes data input fields). Use *Window Area* to fit the block to the left of the view.

4. Select *Place SmartLine, Keypoint Snap* a *Tentative Point* to the top right vertex of the "head" block, do not Accept the Tentative.

5. Press <**O**> (the *AccuDraw Shortcut Key* for *Set **O**rigin* or *Offset*), offset the start of the large diameter section down by **1**.

6. Move the pointer to the right (indexed to the *x* axis) and place a vertex **6** from the head, move the pointer directly down and place a vertex **10** below the last one.

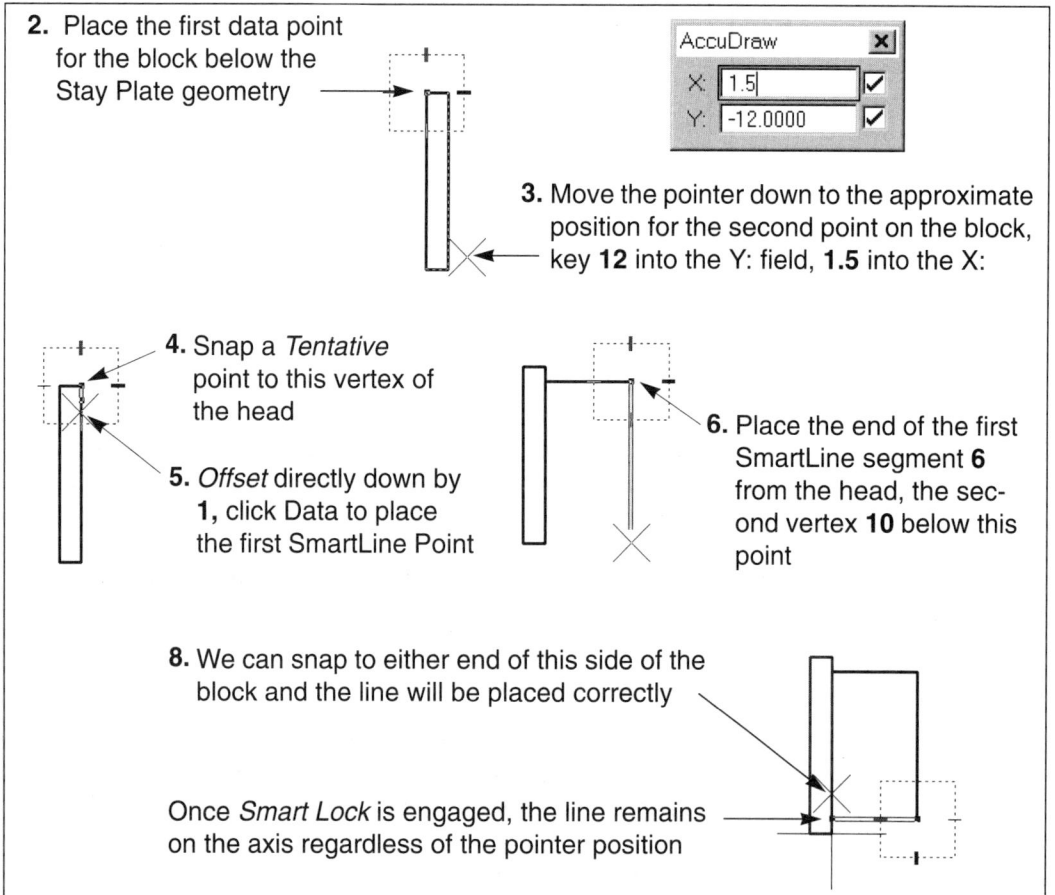

---

2. Place the first data point for the block below the Stay Plate geometry

AccuDraw	✕
X: 1.5	✓
Y: -12.0000	✓

3. Move the pointer down to the approximate position for the second point on the block, key **12** into the Y: field, **1.5** into the X:

4. Snap a *Tentative* point to this vertex of the head

5. *Offset* directly down by **1**, click Data to place the first SmartLine Point

6. Place the end of the first SmartLine segment **6** from the head, the second vertex **10** below this point

8. We can snap to either end of this side of the block and the line will be placed correctly

Once *Smart Lock* is engaged, the line remains on the axis regardless of the pointer position

Figure 3.29   Stage 1 of the Pivot Pin

7. Move the pointer back to the left, while it is indexed press <**Enter**> to engage *Smart Lock.*

Once *Smart Lock* is engaged, only the horizontal movement of the pointer affects the length of the line.

8. *Keypoint* snap a *Tentative* point with the pointer anywhere on the right side of the head block, *Accept*, *Reset.*

The end of the "U" shaped *Linestring* will abut precisely to the block, without any need to key in a dimension.

The AccuDraw Previous Distance Feature

This feature is useful when we are entering several points the same distance apart. It operates at any angle in the *Polar* coordinate mode, or when the line is indexed to either *Drawing Plane Axis* when AccuDraw is in the *Rectangular* coordinate mode. When we move the cursor near the previous distance, a small bar appears across the end of the line being dynamically displayed and the line is detained at this point until we move further away.

Pivot Pin Example (stage 2)

We will continue with the Pivot Pin example, this time drawing the smaller of the two bearing surfaces. We will apply the *Previous Distance* feature of AccuDraw in this stage.

◆ **Place the small bearing surface**

1. Select the *Place SmartLine* tool, *Keypoint Snap* a *Tentative Point* to the top right vertex of the large diameter bearing surface (do not Accept the Tentative).

2. Press <**O**> and offset the start of the small diameter section down **1.5**.

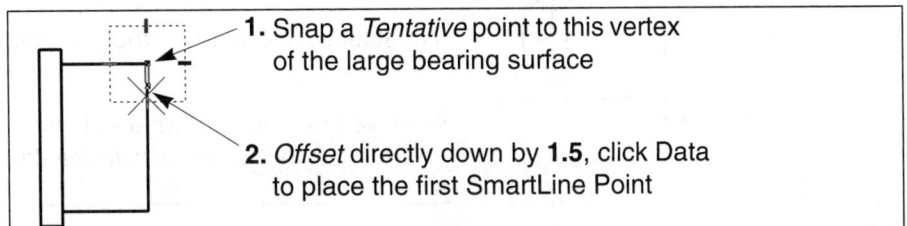

1. Snap a *Tentative* point to this vertex of the large bearing surface

2. *Offset* directly down by **1.5**, click Data to place the first SmartLine Point

Figure 3.30   Placing the first point on the small bearing surface

3. Move the pointer to the right along the *x* axis and place a vertex **7** from the start.

4. Move the pointer directly down, taking note of the readings in the AccuDraw window, until the reading temporarily holds at **7**, the *Previous Distance, Accept.*

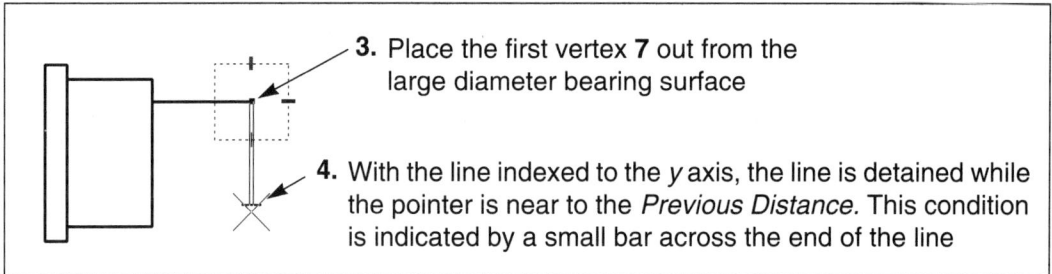

3. Place the first vertex **7** out from the large diameter bearing surface

4. With the line indexed to the *y* axis, the line is detained while the pointer is near to the *Previous Distance.* This condition is indicated by a small bar across the end of the line

Figure 3.31   Using the Previous Distance feature of AccuDraw

5. Move the pointer back to the left, (indexed to the *x* axis) until the reading temporarily holds at **7**, *Accept*, then *Reset* to complete this linestring.

6. Select the *Place Block* tool, *Keypoint Snap* a *Tentative Point* to the top right vertex of the small diameter bearing surface.

7. Press <**O**> and offset the first point of the end block by **1** mm to the right, *Accept* to enter the *First Point.*

8. Complete the tip of the pin by placing the *Opposite Corner* **7** down and **2** to the right, *Accept, Reset.*

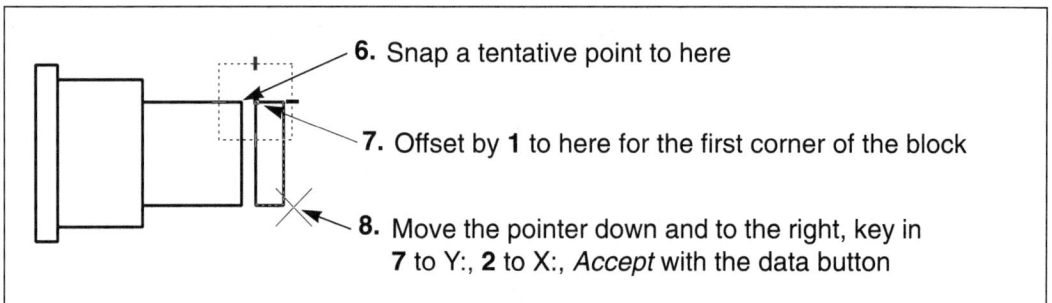

6. Snap a tentative point to here

7. Offset by **1** to here for the first corner of the block

8. Move the pointer down and to the right, key in **7** to Y:, **2** to X:, *Accept* with the data button

Figure 3.32   Placing the tip section

Recalling Previous AccuDraw Values

As well as the graphical *Previous Distance* feature that we applied in the last exercise, there is another feature available that can save us the time and effort of re-keying the same number more than once. The *Recall Value* facility can still be used when there has been different values keyed in since the one we wish to recall.

When *Input Focus* is in a data input field of AccuDraw, pressing <**Page Up**> will recall the last value, regardless of the *distance* field that this value was entered in to. Pressing <**Page Up**> again will recall the next to last entry, and so on. There are separate *AccuDraw Key-in Buffers* for *distances* and *angles*, thus *x* data can be recalled to a *y* field, but in polar mode only angle data can be recalled into the angle field. The *Key-in Buffers* are emptied when we exit MicroStation.

Pivot Pin Example (stage 3)

The side view of the Pivot Pin is nearing completion. We will now use the "previous values" facility described above to place the lines at the circlip groove base.

◆ **Draw the circlip groove lines**

1. Select *Place SmartLine,* start the first line from an offset (<**O**>) **.5** down from a *Tentative* point the top of the small diameter section.

    The dimension of **.5** has automatically been "recorded" in the *AccuDraw Key-in Buffer* for later use.

2. Move the pointer to the right, while it is indexed press <**Enter**> to engage *Smart Lock, Keypoint* snap a *Tentative* point to the other side of the groove, *Accept* then *Reset* to complete the line.

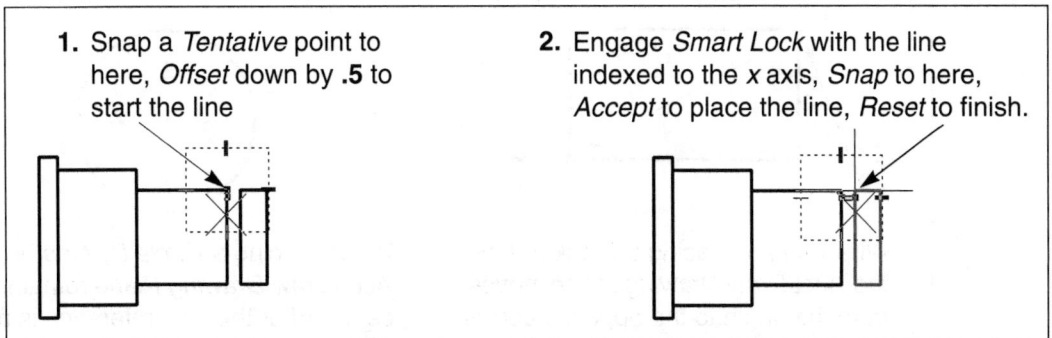

1. Snap a *Tentative* point to here, *Offset* down by **.5** to start the line

2. Engage *Smart Lock* with the line indexed to the *x* axis, *Snap* to here, *Accept* to place the line, *Reset* to finish.

Figure 3.33 Placing the first circlip groove base line

3. Snap a *Tentative* point to the bottom-left of the small diameter section, Press <**O**>, move the pointer up, indexed to the *y* axis.

4. Press <**Page Up**> twice (the distance of **.5** will be recalled), *Accept* the offset, repeat step **2.**

Note: The distance of 1mm that was entered graphically (using the *Smart Lock* and *Tentative Point*) was recalled, as well as the keyed-in values.

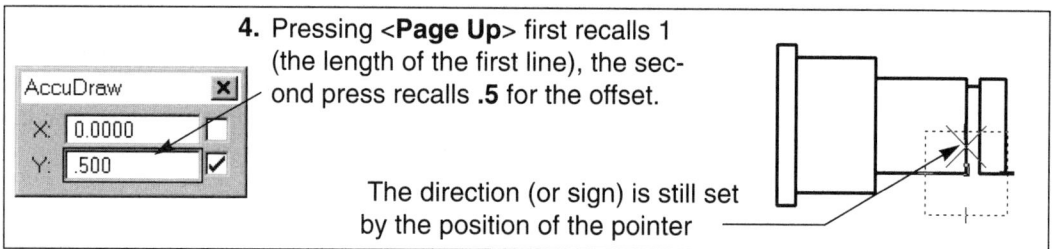

4. Pressing <**Page Up**> first recalls 1 (the length of the first line), the second press recalls **.5** for the offset.

The direction (or sign) is still set by the position of the pointer

Figure 3.34   Placing the tip section

Placing Circles with AccuDraw

AccuDraw changes its behavior to suit the type of element being placed. We have already observed the *Drawing Plane* relocating itself to the ends of lines and to the opposite corners of blocks, but this is not appropriate when we are placing *Circles*.

The drawing plane origin remains at the center of a circle when the circumference is placed, it does not move as it did when we placed lines and blocks. We will make use of this feature when we create the end view of the Pivot Pin in the next exercise.

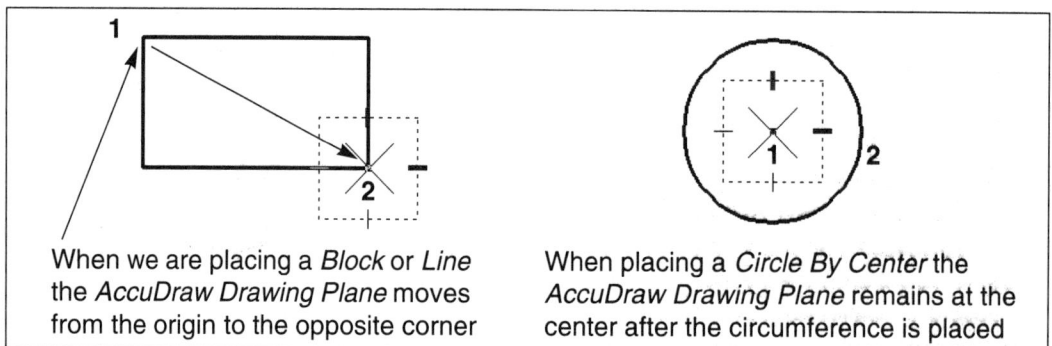

When we are placing a *Block* or *Line* the *AccuDraw Drawing Plane* moves from the origin to the opposite corner

When placing a *Circle By Center* the *AccuDraw Drawing Plane* remains at the center after the circumference is placed

Figure 3.35   Changes in AccuDraw behavior when circles are placed

If you make any mistakes during the next exercise, *Edit>Undo* back to step **1.** The techniques we would need to "recover" from missing a step will soon be introduced, but for now it will only take a few seconds if we need to re-do some of the circles.

◆ **Draw the end view of the Pivot Pin**

1. Select the *Place Circle* tool, *By Center*, diameter unconstrained.

2. Set the *Snap Mode Override* to **Midpoint** (see page 3-19), snap a *Tentative* point to the midpoint of the right side of the tip.

3. *Offset* the circle *Center Point* **20** to the right, with the offset indexed to the *x* axis, *Accept* to place the center of the circle.

    The perimeter of the circle will now be under the control of AccuDraw, which will automatically change to *Polar* coordinates with *input focus* on the *Distance* field.

4. Key in **6**, *Accept*, (*Pan* the View window if necessary, *Reset* to return to the drawing tool), move the pointer over the center of the Accudraw Compass, place a data point to *Identify the Center Point* of the next circle when it *Indexes* to the origin.

5. Repeat step **4.**, except key in **5**, the large bearing surface radius.

6. Repeat step **4.** again, this time key in **3.5**, the radius of the small bearing surface.

7. Change the *Active Line Style* to **2**, (medium dashed) and the *Active Line Weight* to **0**.

8. Click in the AccuDraw window to restore *Input Focus* to it, key in **3**, *Accept* with the pointer outside the AccuDraw window, *Reset*.

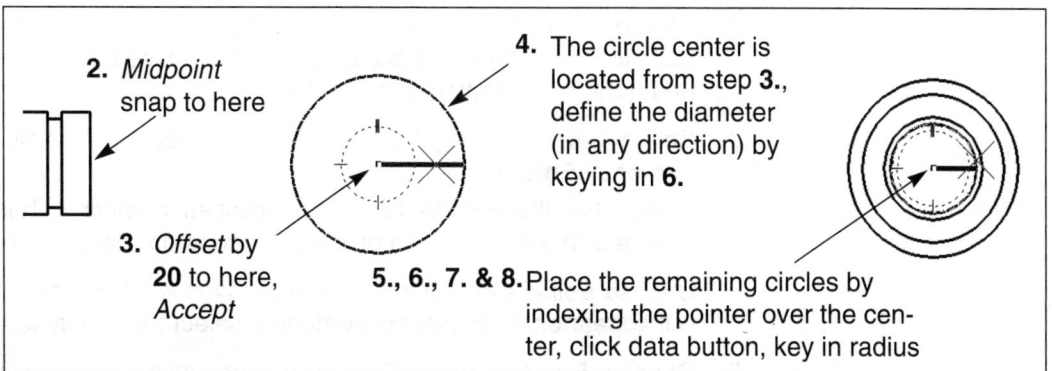

2. *Midpoint* snap to here

3. *Offset* by **20** to here, *Accept*

4. The circle center is located from step **3.**, define the diameter (in any direction) by keying in **6**.

5., 6., 7. & 8. Place the remaining circles by indexing the pointer over the center, click data button, key in radius

Figure 3.36 Placing the End view circles

Creating a New Seed File

We will create our own *Seed File* to speed up simplify the process of setting up our future example design files. The *Seed File* concept was introduced on page 2-2. We can use any existing design file as a *Seed File*, but for convenience we usually keep a set of design files especially for this purpose. These files are normally placed in a common folder, for example in "...Workspace\system\seed\", the folder where we found our seed files earlier. It is possible to have another path to the seed files, but we will assume an "as delivered" directory/folder structure for all our examples.

The initial settings for most of the design files used in this book will be the same as those already applied to "second.dgn". When we first created this file, we used an existing *Seed File* which did *not* have all the settings as we required them, for example the *Working Units*. To meet our requirements for the new design, we changed the *Working Units* and the *Coordinate Readout* (see "Basic Design File Settings" on page 3-2). We will apply the same settings as "second.dgn" in future design files by making it the basis of our own customized design file.

To achieve this we will first make a copy of "second.dgn" in the default folder for seed files, naming the copy "seed2dmm.dgn". This will give us a file with the required settings already saved, but it will have the "Stay Plate" and "Pivot Pin" geometry. The geometry will not be needed in a seed file, so we will remove it.

◆ **Create a metric Seed File from "second.dgn"**

  1. Open the design file "second.dgn".

Tip! If you have another design file open, "second.dgn" may appear in the "History" at the bottom of the Application window *File* menu. If that is the case, click on it and it will open, closing the previous one.

  2. Choose *File>Save As* from the Application window menu, set the path in the *Directories* panel to "...Workspace\system\seed\" from under the MicroStation root directory.

  3. Key in "seed2dmm.dgn" to the *Files:* name data entry field, click **OK** or press <**Enter**>.
      Check that the *File Name* in the Application window Title bar has changed. We are now in a new file, "second.dgn" was closed intact.

  4. Choose *Edit>Select All* from the Application window menu ("handles" will appear on all displayed elements), select the *Delete* tool.

  5. Choose *File>Compress Design* (to free up the file space formerly occupied by the elements), then *File>Close*.

Summary

There are a large range of *Settings* that affect a *Design File*. When we open a newly created design file the settings are "inherited" from the *Seed File* used in its creation. In this chapter we changed the *Working Units* from the generic units of the seed file to *millimeters* as the base unit. We also set the *Coordinate Readout* to appropriately display these units.

The *Attributes* of View windows are the definitions of *What* is displayed and *How* it is displayed within a particular View window. Included are such items as the *Grid* and *Construction* class elements. View Attributes are *Settings*, therefore the settings box is accessed via the Application window menu bar under *Settings*.

The *Attributes* of a particular *Element* are the *Symbology* attributes of *Color, Line Style* and *Line Weight*, along with the *Display Control* attributes of *Level* and *Class*. The latter two attributes allow the display of the element to be turned on and off. The settings can be made in a settings box accessible under *Settings*, or (more conveniently) from the *Primary* tool bar.

Tentative points allow us to preview where a data point is about to be placed. They give us the ability to precisely define the position of a particular point on a new element in relation to existing elements. This is called *Snapping* and there are a variety of *Snap Modes* to choose from. The most commonly used is *Keypoint*, where the *Tentative* point *Snaps* to one of a finite number of predictable *Key Points* on an element. The number of *Snap Modes* available varies with the tool being used.

The first of the very useful *Modify* tools was introduced, where the *Extend Line* tool was used to extend the Stay Plate centerline past its original defining points. In the example it was used to extend the line by a keyed-in distance, but it can also be used with "freehand" data points and points *Snapped* to other elements.

The *Symbology* attributes of elements (Color, Line Style and Line Weight) usually define the appearance of the element in the View windows and on paper. This symbology may optionally be overridden by another set of symbology, this time defined in relation to the *Levels* elements are placed on.

One form of symbology definition does not exclude the other. Elements may appear with *Level Symbology* if this is switched **On** in the *View Attributes* settings box, or with their *Element Symbology* if it is **Off**. There are also separate check boxes in the *Level Symbology* settings box to control which of the element symbology attributes are to be *Overridden*. For example, we may choose to override *Color* and *Weight*, but retain the *Element* setting for *Style*.

Very complete *Information* about individual design elements can be gained by using the *Analyze Element* tool, from the *Primary* tool bar. Once the information is displayed in the *Element Information* dialog box, changes can be made to the various element attributes and properties in this dialog. These changes can then be applied to the element under analysis. In the case of *Complex* elements there will be several dialog boxes needed to display the information for all of its components.

AccuDraw has the facility to accept a range of *Keyboard Shortcuts*. The range available can be displayed by pressing the **<?>** key (which is a keyboard shortcut itself) and selections may be made from the menu displayed. The most commonly used shortcuts, such as the use of the **<Enter>** key to invoke *Smart Lock*, will soon be committed to memory. *Smart Lock* constrains the data point about to be placed to fall on the *x* or *y* axis of the AccuDraw drawing plane.

Circles may be defined by *Center, Edge Points* on its circumference, or by points defining a *Diameter*. The *Radius* or the *Diameter* may be constrained, or the circle fully defined by the placement of data points.

Having *Seed Files* available with *Design File Settings* appropriate for specific projects and design types increases the efficiency of the design process. Creating new design files from customized Seed files does away with the need to make major changes to settings before the design creation begins.

4 : Manipulation and Grouping

We now have two design files, one with the Arrow and other associated shapes, another with the Stay plate and pivot pin. The Stay Plate example will be used again later in the book, the Arrow and shapes will be used in this chapter. We will be *Manipulating* its elements individually and in groups, retaining some of the modifications, *Undo*ing others.

In Computer Aided Design, manipulations are not only used to edit and update existing drawings, they are an integral part of the creative process. Elements may be created in one part of the design plane, then moved to another. Copies of geometry can be made and re-used elsewhere in the design, either "as is" or with modifications. Geometry can be mirror imaged, re-sized, even have its shape changed, all under precise control.

When you have completed this chapter, you will be able to:

- *Move* design elements to different design file coordinates;
- *Copy* design elements, with the copy positioned to specification;
- Create new geometry *Parallel* to existing elements;
- *Rotate* existing elements to a new orientation;
- Make *Mirror Images* of elements
- Construct multiple copies of elements in the form of *Arrays*;
- Pre-select elements individually and in groups for manipulation;
- Use the *Fence* to temporarily group elements for any form of manipulation.

Manipulating Existing Elements

In MicroStation, the words *Modify*, *Change* and *Manipulate* are used as names for three separate "boxes" of tools. While these three words are generally regarded as having similar meanings, the tool boxes so named each provide different classes of alterations to existing elements.

The first tools we will use to alter our existing designs will be from the *Manipulate* tool box, illustrated in Figure 4.1.

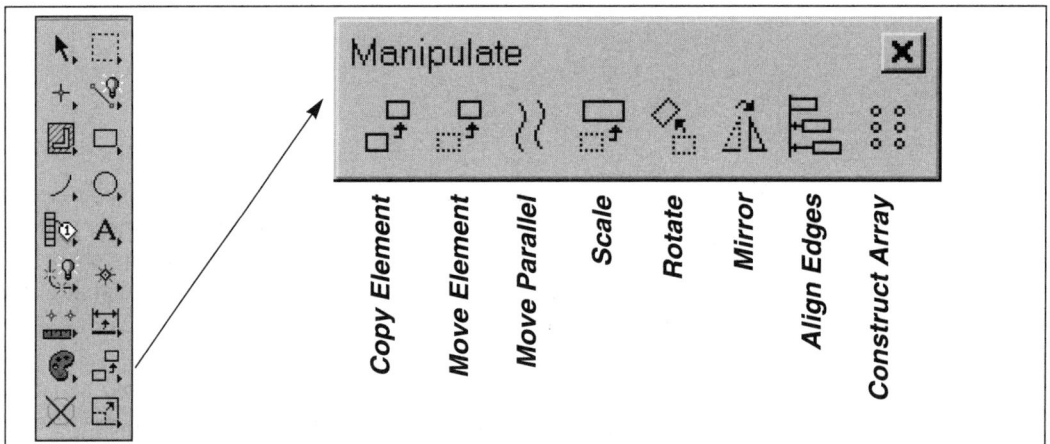

Figure 4.1   The Manipulate Tool Box

The Move Element Tool

This tool is used to move elements on the design plane, by altering the coordinates of a particular point on the element. It may be used in conjunction with the various snap options and with AccuDraw to control the move operations. When we select this tool, the *Tool Settings* window displays a *Copy* check box (*Off* by default), which allows the *Move* tool to "double" as a *Copy* tool. The other check box, *Use Fence*, will be grayed out unless a *Fence* is in place, a concept we will explore shortly. We will be working on individual elements initially, we simply need to identify the element, then define its new position in the design.

There are many methods available to us to define the new position. We can position the element with respect to its previous position, with respect to a feature on another element, or a keyed-in set of design file coordinates.

If the *Make Copy* box is
checked *On*, this tool will ⎯⎯⎯⎯⎯→
act as a *Copy* tool

Move Element   ☒

☐ Make Copy
☐ Use Fence   Inside   ▼

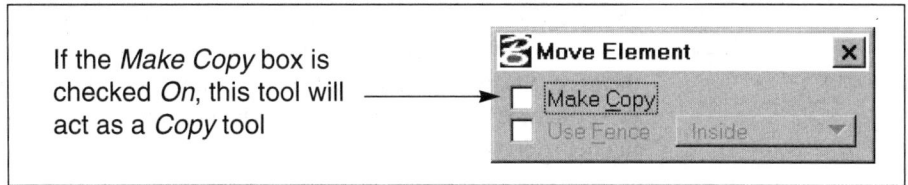

Figure 4.2   The Move Element Tool Settings window

Moving Individual Elements Using AccuDraw

In this example, we will use AccuDraw for the precision *Manipulation* of an existing
element, rather than for the *Creation* of one, as in previous exercises. We will *Move*
the Arrow shape created earlier by a precise *Distance* at a specified *Angle*, thus we
will be using *Polar* coordinates.

◆ **Move the Arrow shape 70mm at an angle of 130°**

1. With "first.dgn" open, all levels turned *On* and the *Grid Off*, use the
   view control tools as necessary to fit View window 1 to the arrow.

2. Start *AccuDraw (*if it not already running).

3. Select the *Move* tool, the second one from the left in the *Manipulate*
   child tool box from the Main tool frame.

4. When prompted (in the Status bar) to "Identify element", Data point to
   any part of the linework defining the Arrow shape.
   The Arrow shape (only) highlights, the AccuDraw Compass displays
   with the data point just placed at its *Origin*.

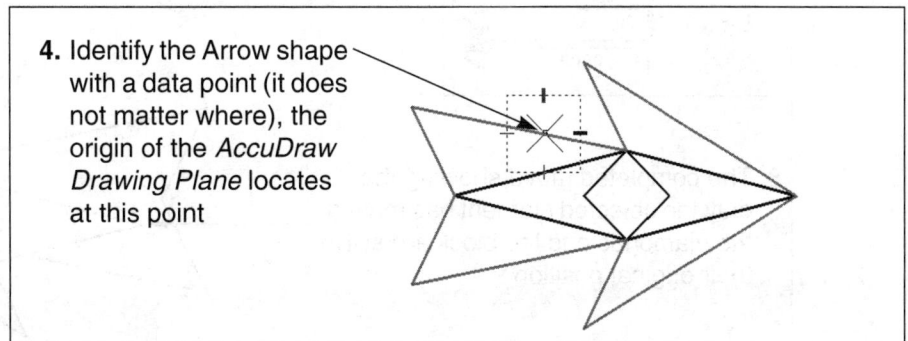

4. Identify the Arrow shape
with a data point (it does
not matter where), the
origin of the *AccuDraw
Drawing Plane* locates
at this point

Figure 4.3   Identifying the element for moving

At this stage the block placed in chapter 2 can be removed, retain only the Arrow shape and the two diamonds. Use the *Delete* tool from the bottom-left of the Main tool frame. We are going to move the Arrow in a defined direction for a defined distance, therefore it does not matter where we "grab" it for the move. However, there are times when the position we identify the element *does* matter, as you will see in later exercises.

5. Press <**Spacebar**>, the "shortcut" to change the AccuDraw coordinate system to *Polar* (if necessary).

6. Move the pointer up and to the left, the general direction we are to move the Arrow.

7. Key in **:70** to the *Distance* field, **130** to the *Angle* field.

    We set the *Working Units* for this file with *Master Units* as *Meters* and *Sub Units* as *Millimeters*. Since the distance is to be defined in millimeters, the "**:**" was used to indicate the number is in *Sub Units*.

8. Click the Data button to *Accept* the new position for the Arrow, the *Reset* button to cancel any further moves.

5. *Polar* coordinates indicated by the circular drawing plane indicator

6. The pointer is moved in the required general direction

7. *Distance* and *Angle* are keyed in, <**Tab**> between

AccuDraw
Distance: :70
Angle: 130.0000°

8. The completed move showing that only the selected element has moved, the diamonds and the block are still in their original position

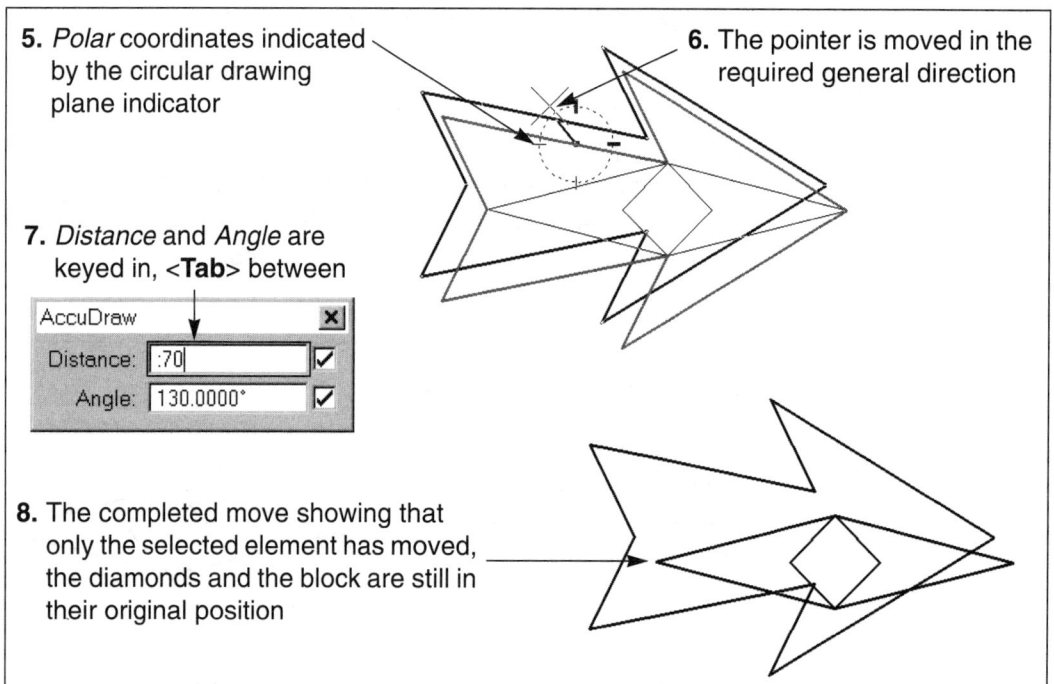

Figure 4.4 Moving the Arrow shape

Moving Individual Elements Using Snaps

When we moved the Arrow shape in the last exercise, the diamonds "stayed put". Next, we will move the larger diamond shape back into its original position in relation to the Arrow. We could do this using exactly the same process as we used for the Arrow, but we will introduce another technique instead. This technique involves using *Tentative* points *Snapped* to each of the two vertices that we wish to join.

◆ **Move the wide diamond back into the Arrow shape**

1. Select the *Move* tool, *Keypoint Snap* a *Tentative point* to the top vertex of the wide diamond as shown in Figure 4.5.

Tip! Position the pointer slightly away from the vertex, but exactly on the element we are trying to *Snap* to. If the wrong diamond highlights, click the Tentative button again.

2. Click the data button to *Accept* the tentative position for a data point. Since AccuDraw is running its compass will display at the position of each data point, but it is not serving any purpose when we are using this technique.

3. *Snap* a tentative point to the closest vertex of the Arrow shape.

4. *Accept* the second tentative, *Reset* to terminate the operation.

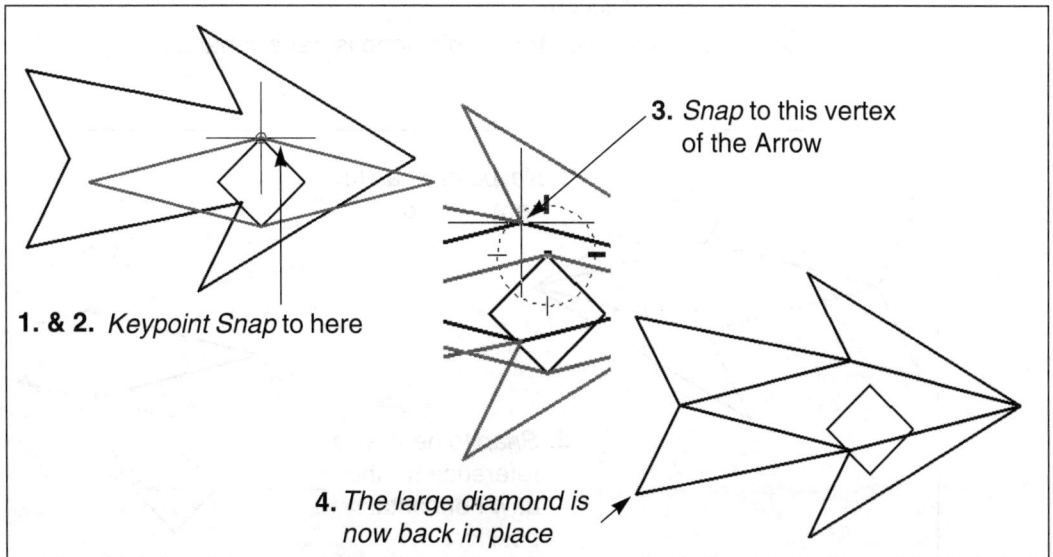

Figure 4.5 Moving the large diamond using Tentative points

We were able to move the large diamond precisely back into place by simply snapping tentative points and accepting them. We will move the small diamond next, but not aligning it *vertex to vertex* as we did with the large one. This shape will now take a new position in relation to the Arrow, as shown in Figure 4.6.

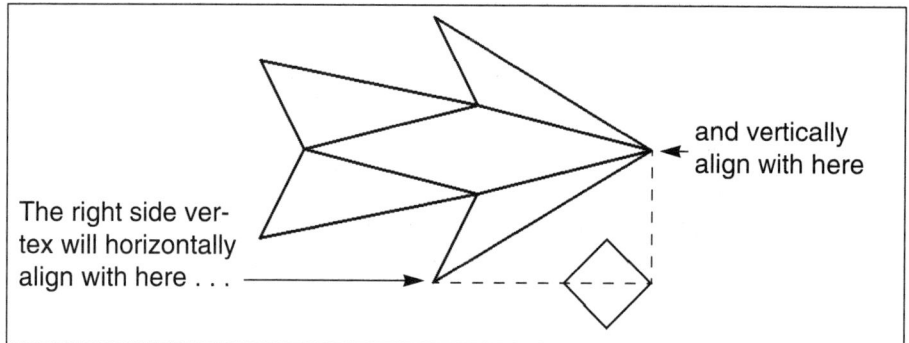

Figure 4.6   New position for the small diamond

◆ **Offset the small diamond from the Arrow shape**

   1. Select the *Move* tool, identify the small diamond by snapping a tentative point to its rightmost vertex, *Accept* with the data button.

   2. Snap another tentative point to the lowest vertex on the Arrow shape, *do not* accept.

   This position for the diamond is transitional only.

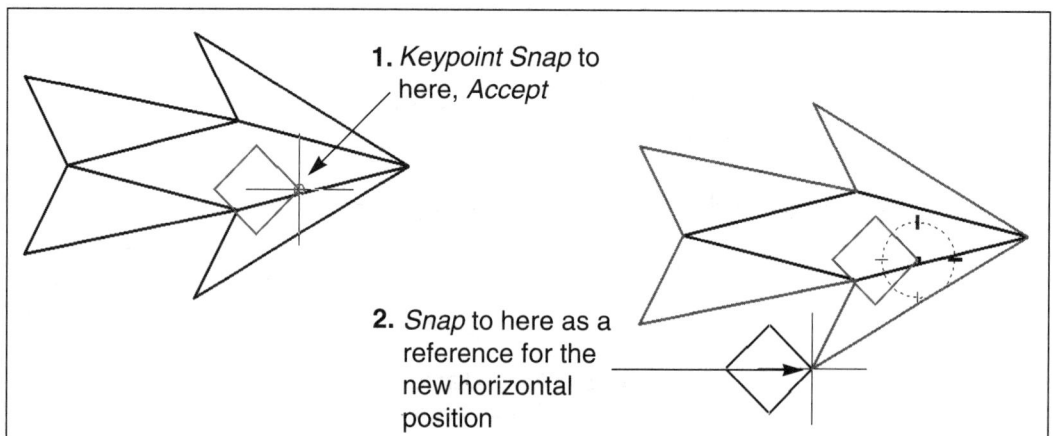

Figure 4.7   First part of the move process

3. Press **<O>**, move the pointer to the right indexed to the *x* axis, press **<Enter>** to engage *Smart Lock*.

4. Snap a tentative point to the rightmost vertex of the Arrow, *Accept*, *Reset*.

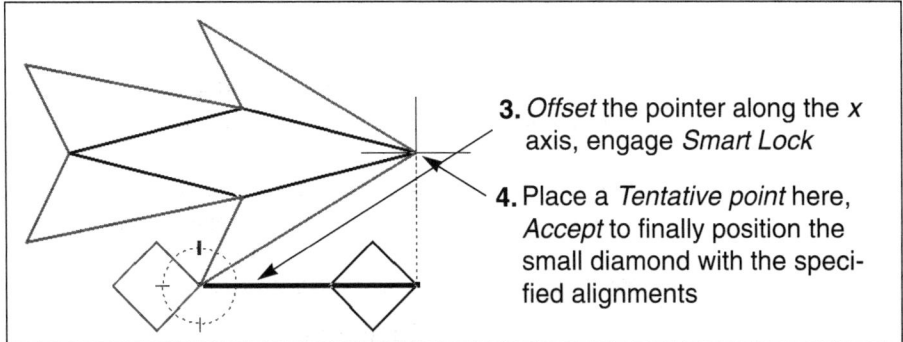

Figure 4.8   Moving the small diamond to its final position

The transitional position for the move process could just as well have been at the right side vertex of the arrow. The *Smart Lock* controlled move would then have been made downwards along the *y* axis.

The illustrations show a circular AccuDraw drawing plane indicator, indicating a polar coordinate system. We did not need to key in data, so the coordinate system in use does not affect this operation.

Levels and Manipulations

You may recall that we originally placed the large diamond on level 2 (see "Place a second (wide) diamond shape on Level 2" on page 2-34). We have since manipulated it without regard to level settings. If we *Analyze* the diamond after the move (using the *Analyze Element* tool, see page 3-24) we will find it has not changed Under the usual circumstances any manipulations (such as *Move* and *Copy* operations) can be made without regard to the level that is *Active* at the time of the operation.

There is an exception, however. If we have the *Level* lock *On*, only elements on the currently *Active* level may be altered or analyzed. This lock setting can be found on the *Locks* settings box from the Status bar (see page 2-32), the same settings box as the *Grid* lock setting we used when placing the Arrow and small diamond shapes. With Level lock *On*, any attempt to identify an element on other than the active level will return a message "*Element not found*" in the Status bar message area.

The Copy Element Tool

There is very little difference between the operation of this tool and that of the *Move* tool we have just applied. The only noticeable difference between the tools is that *Copy* retains the original element in its original position. The *Tool Settings* window for *Copy* differs only in title from the *Move* equivalent, except that the *Make Copy* check box is *On* by default.

The *Copy* tool may be used in conjunction with the snap options and with AccuDraw to position the copied element, in exactly the same way as we used them with *Move*.

In the next exercise we will place a *Copy* of the small diamond shape back into the Arrow, thus fully restoring the three shapes to their original relative positions.

◆ **Copy the small diamond shape**

1. Select the *Copy Element* tool.

2. *Keypoint* Snap a tentative point to the top vertex of the shape, *Accept* to identify the element to be copied.

3. Snap another tentative point to the vertex of the Arrow (or of the large diamond shape) as shown in Figure 4.9, *Accept*, *Reset*.

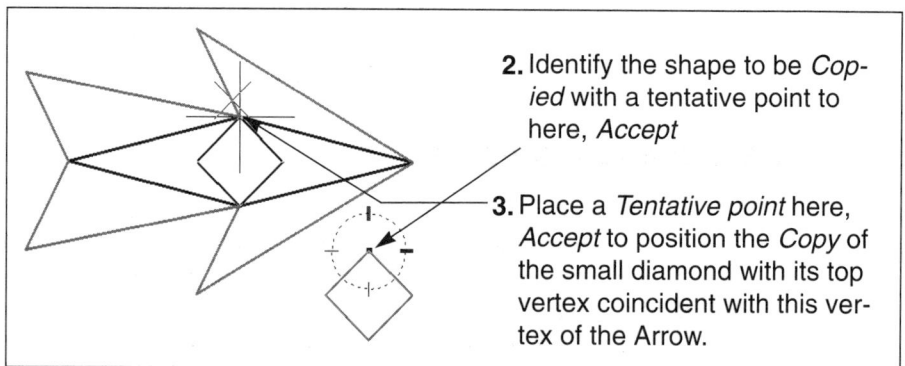

2. Identify the shape to be *Copied* with a tentative point to here, *Accept*

3. Place a *Tentative point* here, *Accept* to position the *Copy* of the small diamond with its top vertex coincident with this vertex of the Arrow.

Figure 4.9 Copying the small diamond back into the Arrow

The Move Parallel Tool

All the geometry associated with an element is moved or copied parallel to itself with this tool. We use two data points, the first one identifying the element to be moved or copied. The second data point defines the side of the original that the moved or copied version of the element is placed.

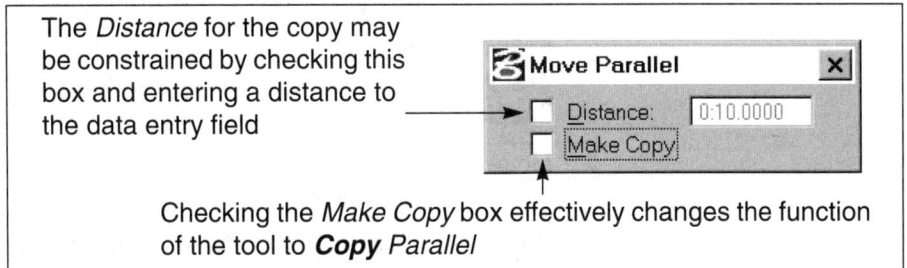

Figure 4.10   Move Parallel Tool Settings window

The *Distance* for the move may be constrained from within the Tool Settings window. It may also set using AccuDraw or tentative points. If the *Make Copy* box is checked, the original geometry remains and a *Copy* is moved. Figure 4.11 shows the effect of the tool on lines, arcs and circles.

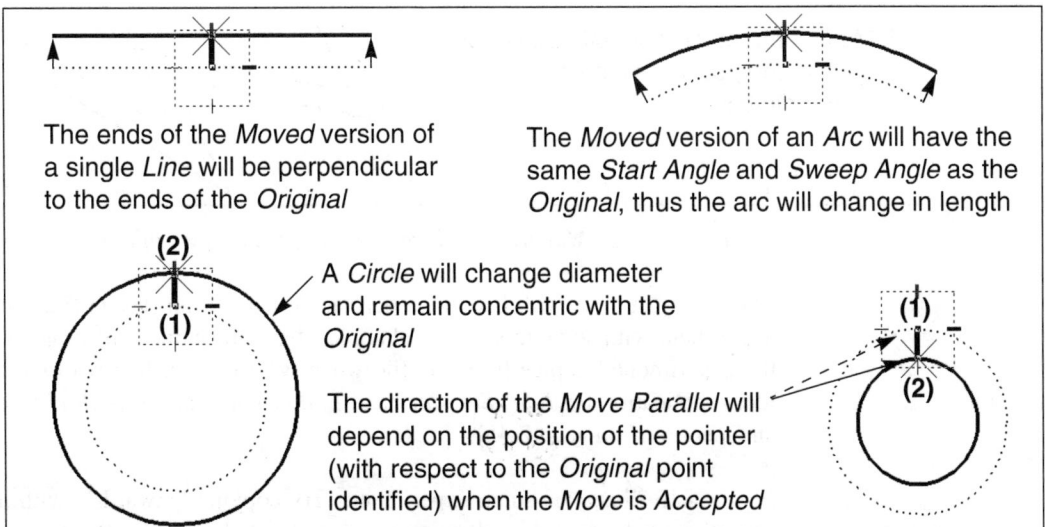

Figure 4.11   Some examples of the operation of the Move Parallel Tool

In the next exercise, we will *Copy* the Arrow shape outwards by 50mm, using the *Move Parallel* tool (with *Make Copy* ***On***). We could define the distance using the constraint button and data input field in the *Tool Settings* window (see Figure 4.10). However, this time AccuDraw is to be used to control the operation. Note that AccuDraw is "smart" enough to align its drawing plane *x* axis with the section of the element identified.

◆ **Make a larger copy of the Arrow shape**

   1. Select the *Move Parallel* tool, click *Make Copy* ***On***, identify the Arrow shape with a *Data* point near the midpoint of any perimeter segment.

   The AccuDraw compass displays with its *x* axis rotated to align with the element where the identifying data point was placed.

   2. Move the pointer outwards from the shape, indexed to the *y* axis of the AccuDraw drawing plane.

   3. Key in **:50** (millimeters) or **.05** (meters), *Accept, Reset.*

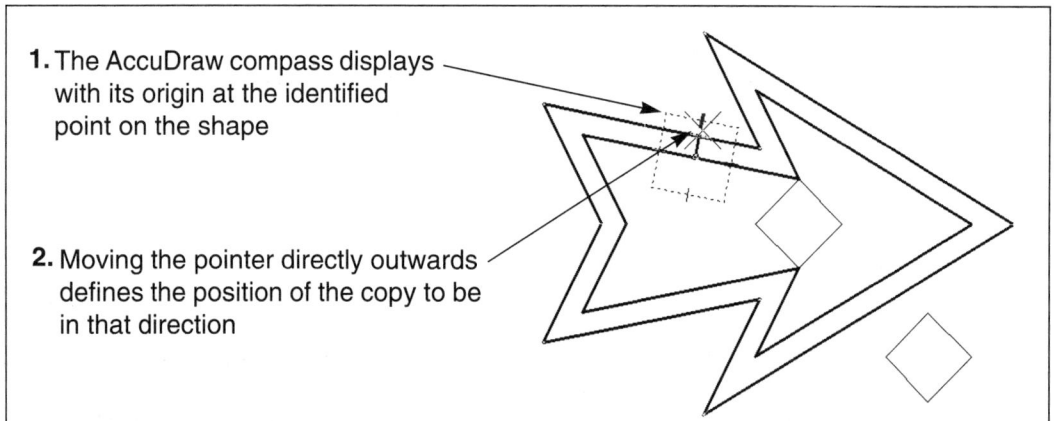

1. The AccuDraw compass displays with its origin at the identified point on the shape

2. Moving the pointer directly outwards defines the position of the copy to be in that direction

Figure 4.12   Making an enlarged copy of the Arrow with Move (Copy) Parallel

The copy just made will become a permanent part of our design file. Next, we will experiment with some more parallel copies, temporary ones this time. We will clear the experimental copies from the file when we have finished with them. This is a ideal application for *Edit>Set Mark* and *Edit>Undo Other>To Mark* (see "Undoing an Operation" on page 2-45).

Figure 4.13 illustrates some experiments. Try copying "inwards", with its potential distortion problems. As well, try operating the tool with the *Distance* constrained, where the *Direction* only is controlled by the pointer position.

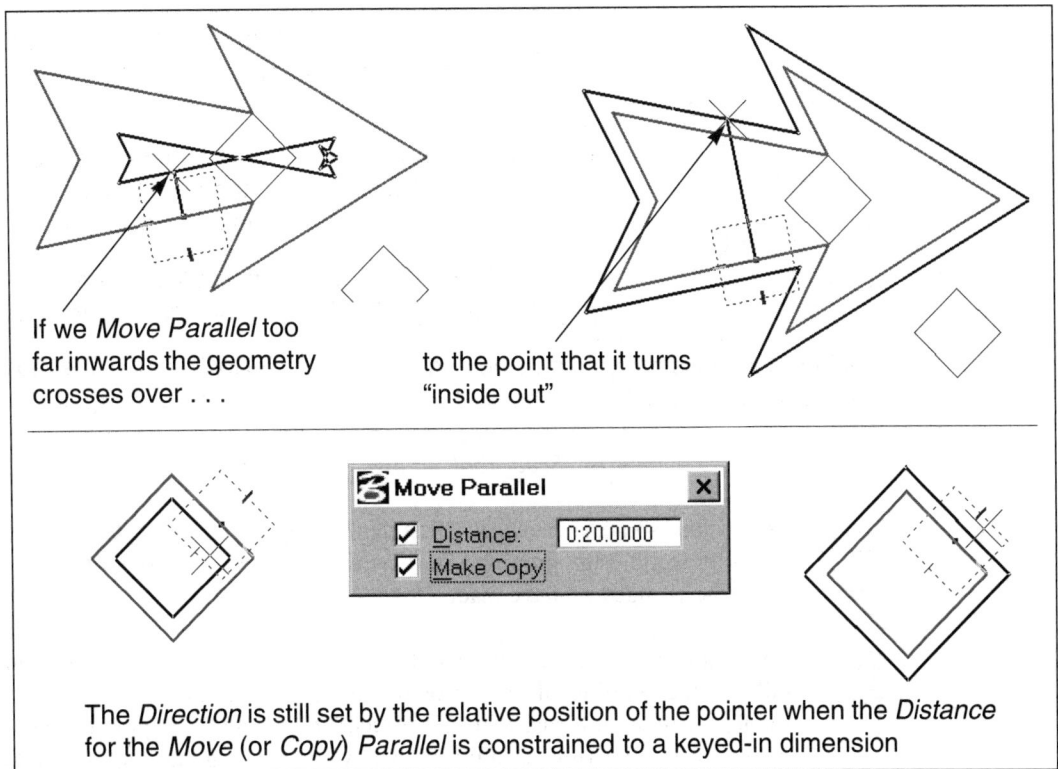

Figure 4.13   Using the Move Parallel tool

The Scale Tool

This tool is used to change the size of elements after they have been placed. This is not to be confused with "drawing to scale", we will continue to work at "full size". We can choose to change the proportions of elements as well, by using the *Scale* tool with a different scale on each axis.

Active Scale Method

There are two basic methods of setting the scale (or scales) for resizing elements in the Tool Settings window. The first method we will work with is *Active Scale*. Active Scale is a *Design File Setting* used in conjunction with some other tools, as well as *Scale*. The *Active Scale* may be set under *Settings>Design File> Active Scale*, but with this tool it is more convenient to set it in the *Tool Settings* window.

The *Active Scale* may be set here separately for *x* and *y* (normally restored to **1** after use)

Changing the scale of one axis automatically changes the other with the lock closed

With the lock open the two scales may be changed individually

The original element is not manipulated and a *Copy* resized when this box is checked

The lock can be opened and closed by clicking on it

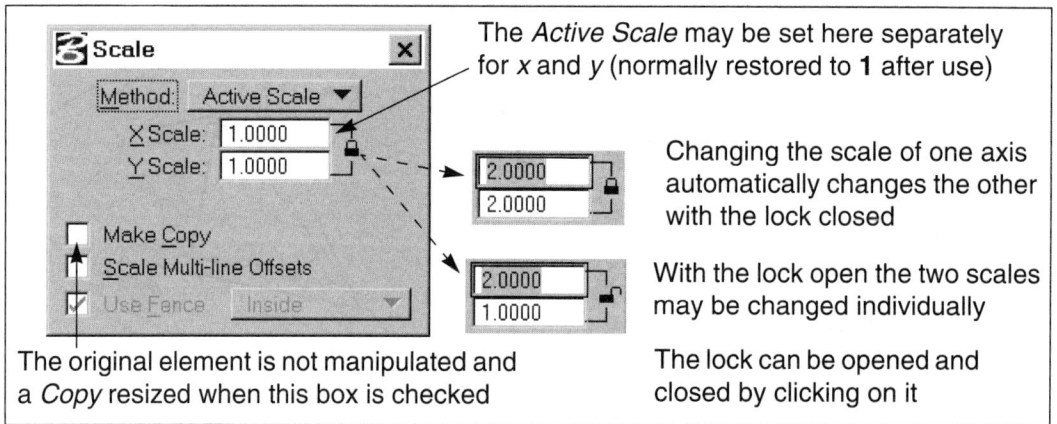

Figure 4.14   Scale Tool Settings window, Method choice of Active Scale

Try scaling some elements in "first.dgn" using a variety of *Active Scale* settings, carefully reading the prompts. Start by using *Edit>Set Mark* so that we can easily *Undo* the changes we have made.

This is a good opportunity to try out the *Center* snap mode, where the tentative point falls on the centroid of shapes or the center of arcs and circles. If AccuDraw is running with input focus, we can "shortcut" to this mode by pressing <**C**>. Have the pointer over the perimeter of the element when clicking the *Tentative* button.

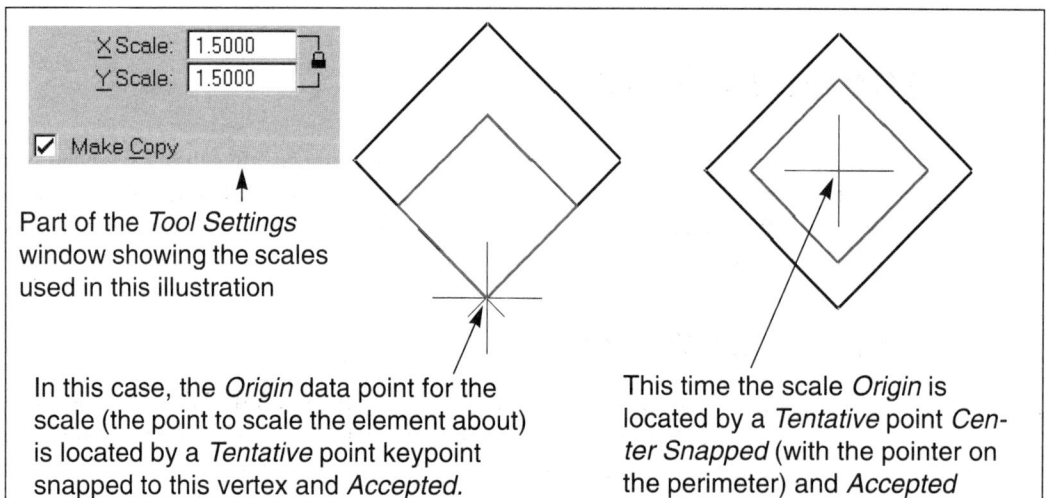

Part of the *Tool Settings* window showing the scales used in this illustration

In this case, the *Origin* data point for the scale (the point to scale the element about) is located by a *Tentative* point keypoint snapped to this vertex and *Accepted*.

This time the scale *Origin* is located by a *Tentative* point *Center Snapped* (with the pointer on the perimeter) and *Accepted*

Figure 4.15   Scaling an element using Active Scale settings

3 Points Method

This is a *Graphical* method for resizing elements, where the scale is set by the relative placement of three data points.

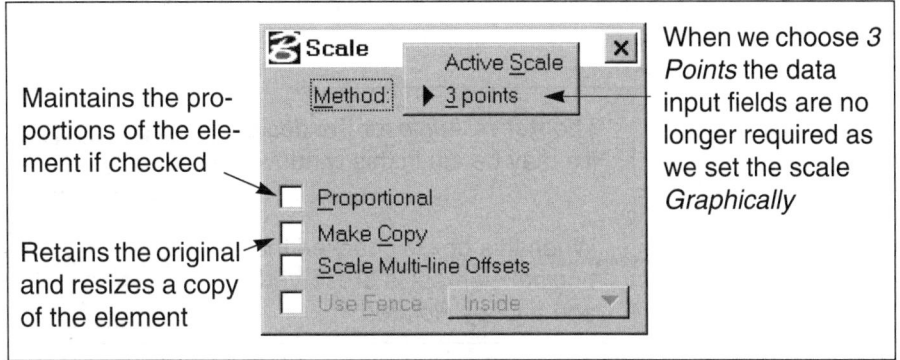

Maintains the proportions of the element if checked

Retains the original and resizes a copy of the element

When we choose *3 Points* the data input fields are no longer required as we set the scale *Graphically*

Figure 4.16   Scale Tool Settings window, Method choice of Active Scale

As shown in Figure 4.17, MicroStation set the required scale factors by dividing the distance between point **1** and **3** by the distance between points **1** and **2**. Point **2** does not have to fall on a line between point **1** and point **3**. The points may be placed anywhere in the design, not only on the element being scaled.

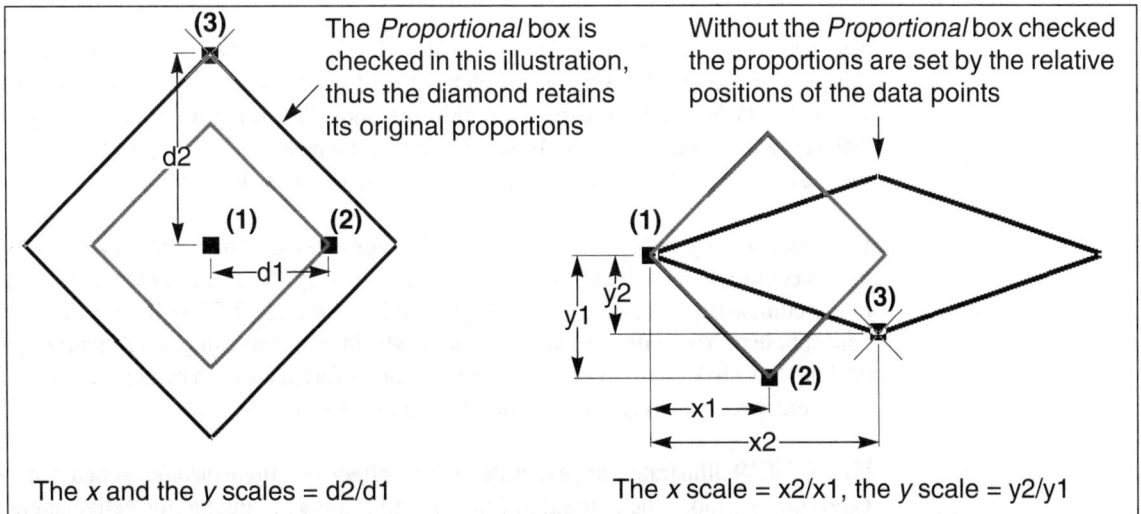

The *Proportional* box is checked in this illustration, thus the diamond retains its original proportions

Without the *Proportional* box checked the proportions are set by the relative positions of the data points

The *x* and the *y* scales = d2/d1

The *x* scale = x2/x1, the *y* scale = y2/y1

Figure 4.17   Scaling an element by three points

The Rotate Tool

We use this tool to rotate existing elements in the design. One method for defining the rotation is by using the current *Active Angle* setting for the design file, which we will investigate next. There are also two *Graphical* methods for defining the angle of rotation, one using two data points, the other three.

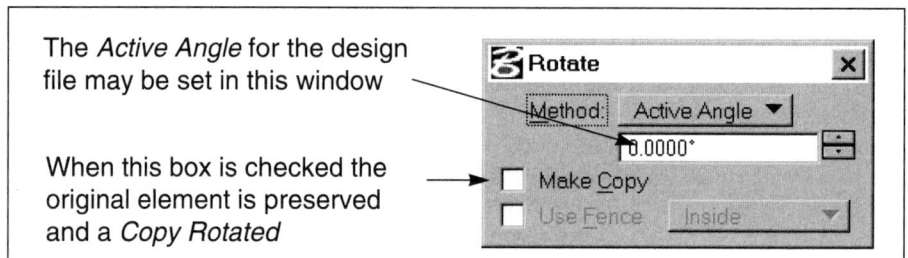

The *Active Angle* for the design file may be set in this window

When this box is checked the original element is preserved and a *Copy Rotated*

Figure 4.18   The Rotate Tool Settings window

Active Angle Method

Active Angle is a *Design File Setting* in a similar way to *Active Scale*. It too is used in conjunction with several tools to be introduced later in the book and it may be set under *Settings>Design File> Active Angle*. Again, we will set it in the *Tool Settings* window for the *Rotate* tool rather than using the slower method.

The *Active Angle* is an angle in degrees stored as a *Design File Setting*. It is used in this case to define the amount an element will rotate from its current orientation when the *Rotate* tool is used with this method. The rotation is defined by the difference between the *Active Angle* setting and the positive direction of the *x* axis of the view, measured in the conventional counter-clockwise direction.

It is occasionally necessary to take the *Settings>Design File>Angle Mode* setting into account when deciding on an *Active Angle* setting. An examination of the angle mode comparison diagram under"Angle Modes" on page 2-24 will help make this concept clear. You will see that an angle of **90°** input when using the *Azimuth* mode is along the *x* axis in the positive direction. The difference would be zero, therefore if this were the *Active Angle* no rotation would take place.

Figure 4.19 illustrates an example of the effect of *Angle Mode*. When we use *Conventional* mode the amount of rotation will always be equal to the active angle as it is keyed in. We are using this mode in both the design files we created so far.

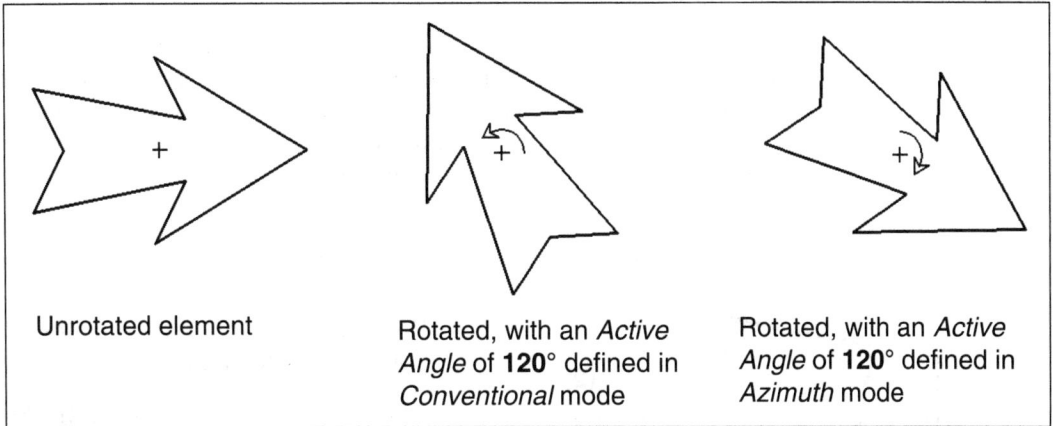

Unrotated element

Rotated, with an *Active Angle* of **120°** defined in *Conventional* mode

Rotated, with an *Active Angle* of **120°** defined in *Azimuth* mode

Figure 4.19   Effect of Angle Mode on Rotate (by Active Angle)

◆ **Rotate the small diamond shape by 45°**

1. Select the *Rotate* tool, choose the *Active Angle* method, set the *Active Angle* to **45°**, leave the check boxes *Off*.

2. Identify the small diamond shape *outside* the Arrow with a data point. You will now be prompted to "Enter pivot point (point to rotate about)".

3. Snap (tentative) to the rightmost vertex, *Accept*, *Reset* to terminate the operation (note that the result resembles Figure 4.20).

4. *Undo* the rotation, set the *Active Angle* back to **0°**
   If the *Active Angle* is left set away from the positive *x* axis, it can affect various other operations.

2. The first data point can be placed anywhere on the element to *Identify* it for *Rotation*

3. The pivot data point is defined by first snapping a tentative point here, then *Accepting*

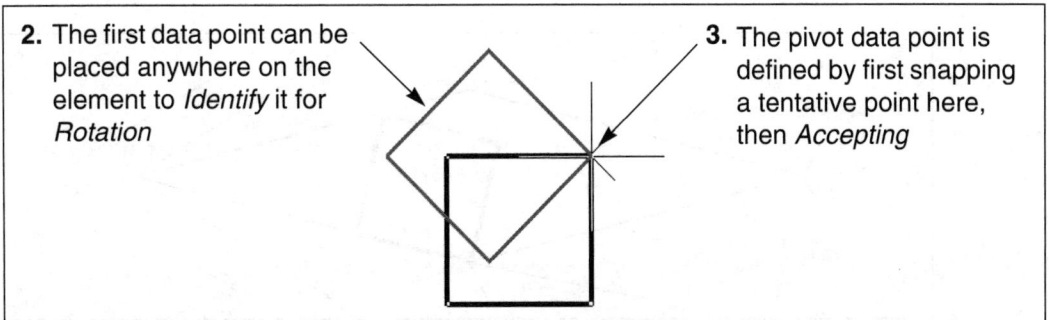

Figure 4.20   Rotating the small "diamond" by 45° to a "square"

Two Points Method

This method is used mostly for "freehand spinning" elements to orient them visually, rather than by precision manipulation. The rotation is defined by the relative positions of the *Pivot* data point and the data point placed to complete the rotation. The *Starting Angle* (or zero rotation position) for the second point is anywhere on a line in the positive *x* direction from the pivot point.

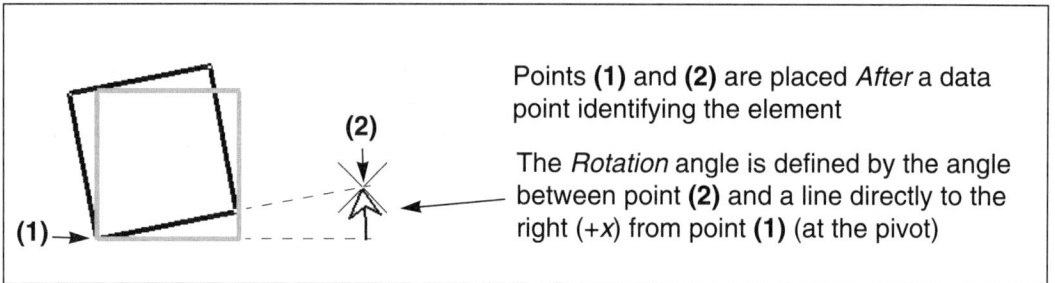

Points **(1)** and **(2)** are placed *After* a data point identifying the element

The *Rotation* angle is defined by the angle between point **(2)** and a line directly to the right (+*x*) from point **(1)** (at the pivot)

Figure 4.21   Operation of the Rotate tool with the 2 Points method

The pivot point for any rotation does not have to be placed on the element, but a distant pivot point will cause the element to move away from its nominal location. Try some two point rotations on any elements, but restore the file to its original state when you have finished.

Three Points Method

This method differs from *Two Points* in that the starting angle is definable, not fixed to the *x* axis. We will use this technique to rotate the small diamond inside the Arrow shape to have one of its sides aligned with a side of the large diamond (Figure 4.22).

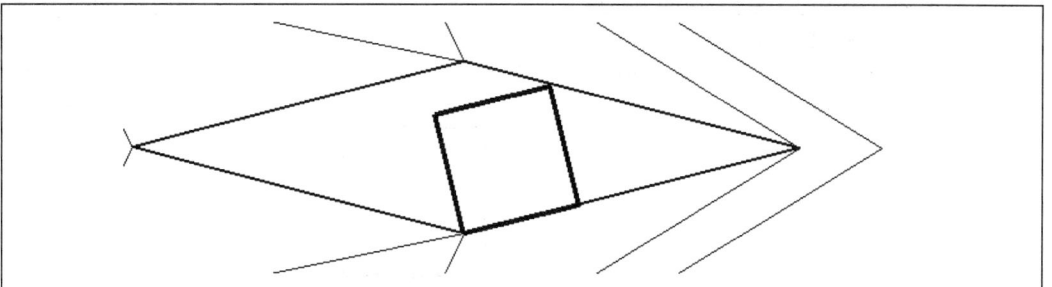

Figure 4.22   The small diamond rotated into alignment

◆ Align the small diamond

1. Select the *Rotate* tool, choose *3 Points* from the *Method* options, identify the small diamond inside the Arrow with a data point.

2. Keypoint snap to the lower vertex, *Accept* as the **Pivot** Point.

3. Keypoint snap to the rightmost vertex, *Accept* as the *Point to define* **Start** *of rotation.*

4. Keypoint snap to the rightmost vertex of the **large** diamond, *Accept* as the *Point to define* **Amount** *of rotation, Reset.*

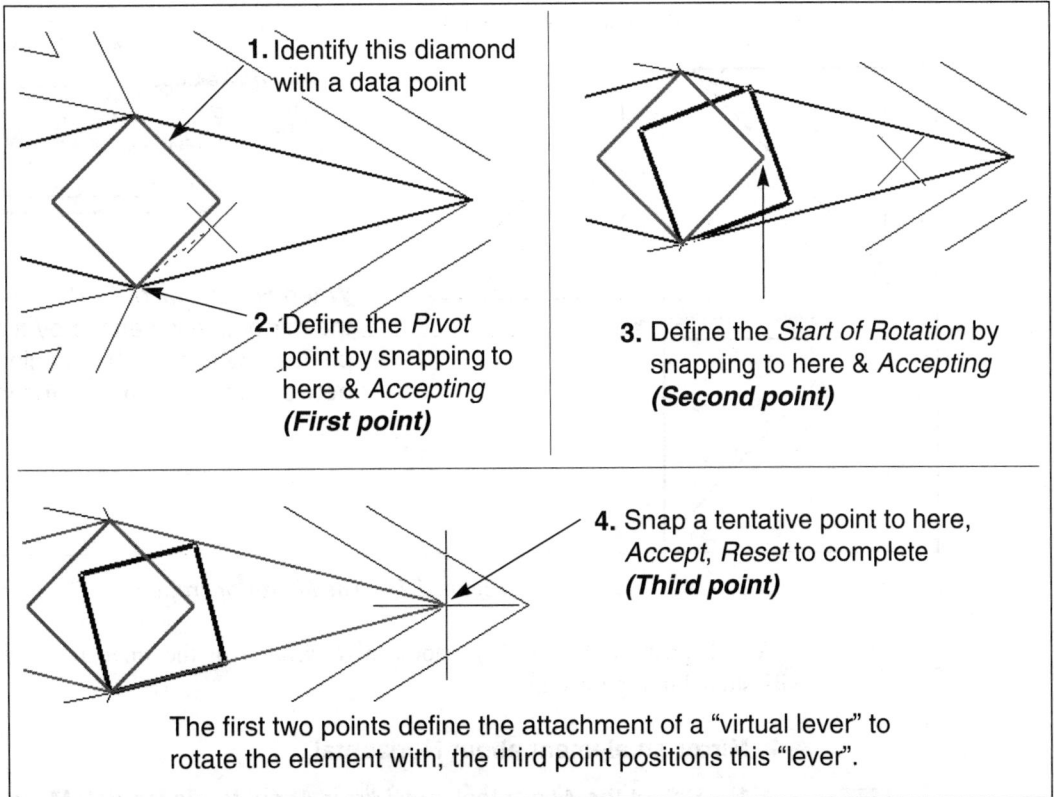

1. Identify this diamond with a data point

2. Define the *Pivot* point by snapping to here & *Accepting* **(First point)**

3. Define the *Start of Rotation* by snapping to here & *Accepting* **(Second point)**

4. Snap a tentative point to here, *Accept, Reset* to complete **(Third point)**

The first two points define the attachment of a "virtual lever" to rotate the element with, the third point positions this "lever".

Figure 4.23   Rotating an element using the Three Points method

The Mirror Tool

Mirror images of elements are created using this tool. It has the *Make Copy* option available in common with the other tools in this section of the tool box. The image element is created symmetrically about a defined line. The line may be horizontal, vertical or have an angle defined by two data points, which may be any distance apart and be placed away from the element. The mirroring of text and multi-line elements (to be introduced later) is optional.

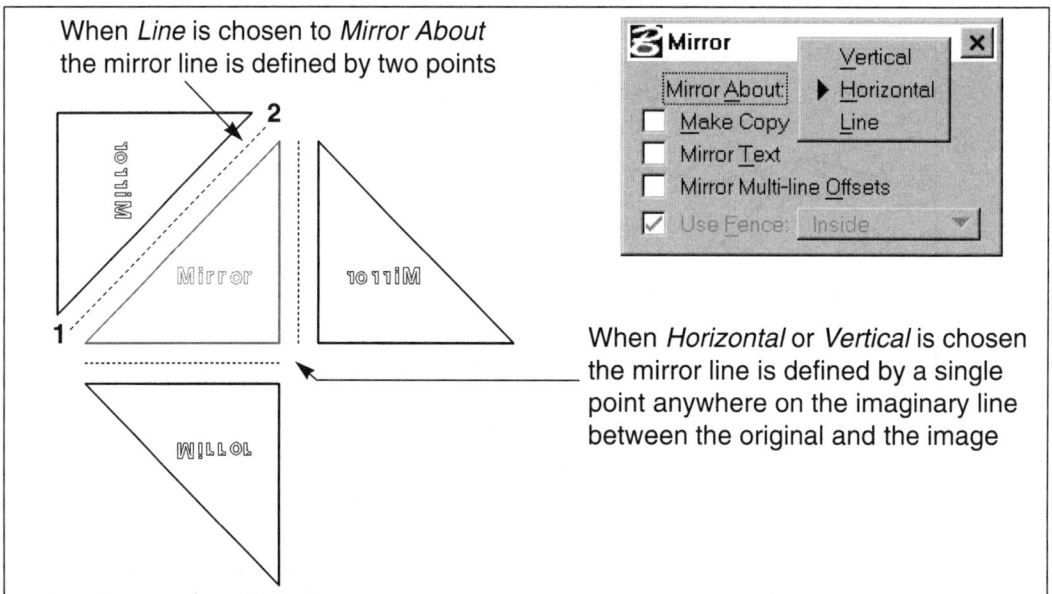

When *Line* is chosen to *Mirror About* the mirror line is defined by two points

When *Horizontal* or *Vertical* is chosen the mirror line is defined by a single point anywhere on the imaginary line between the original and the image

Figure 4.24   The Mirror operation

We will create a *Mirror Copy* about a *Horizontal* of the small rectangle next, as illustrated in Figure 4.25.

◆ **Mirror an element about Horizontal**

1.   Select the *Mirror* tool, set *Mirror About* to *Horizontal*, *Make Copy On* (checked), the remaining settings *Off*.

2.   Identify the rotated rectangle with a data point.
     The mirror image of the element will dynamically display, positioned symmetrically about the pointer with the original element.

3.   Snap to the right end vertex of an Arrow, *Accept*, *Reset*.

A *Copy* of the rectangle has been
Mirrored about a *Horizontal* (mirror
line) on the centerline of the Arrow

The *Mirror Line* is shown here for the illustration, but it does not appear on the screen

Original rectangle

2. Identify the element to be
Mirrored with a data point
anywhere on its geometry

3. The single data point to position the horizontal mirror line is
first located with a *Tentative
point* snapped to here

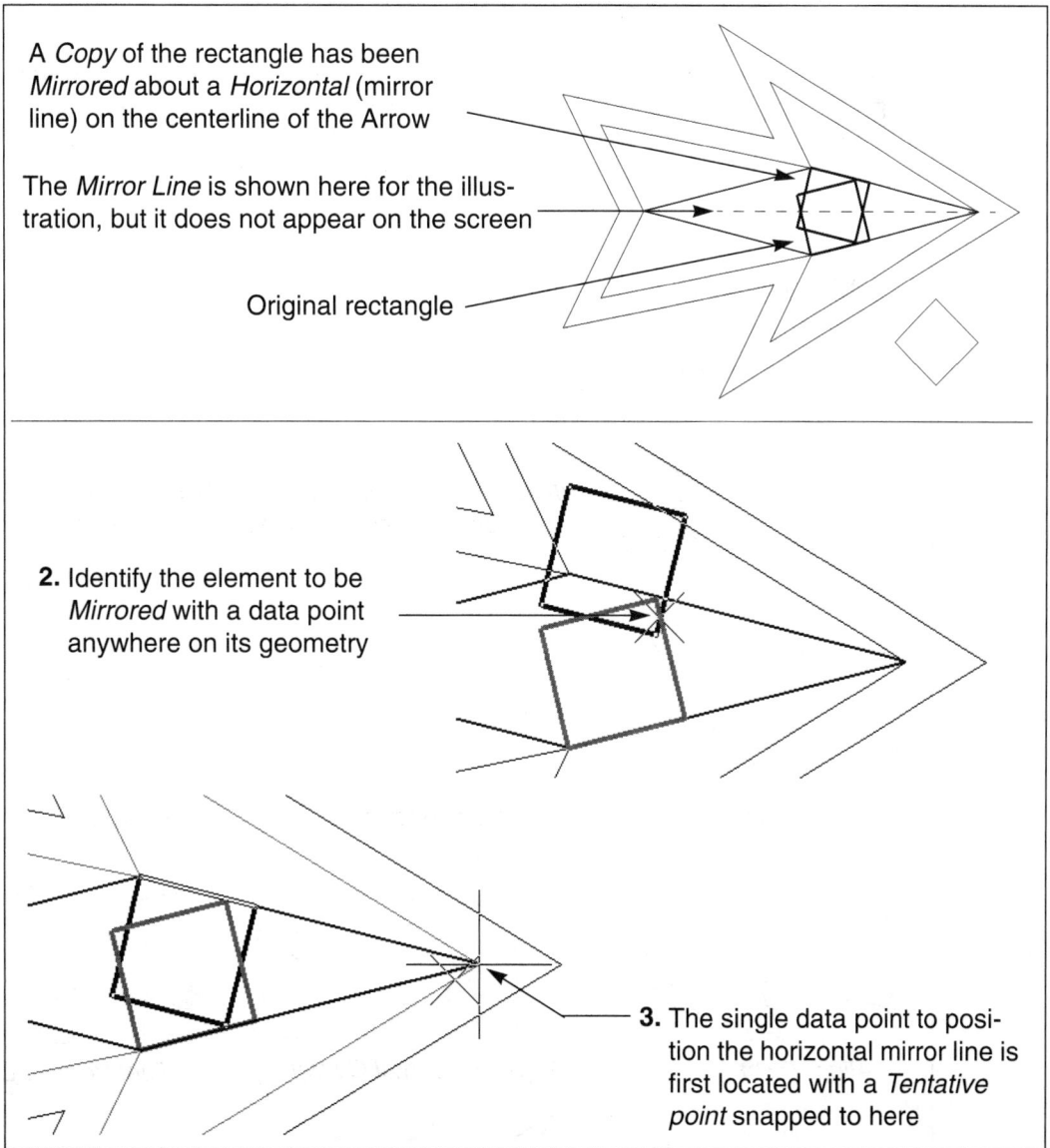

Figure 4.25   Mirroring about a Horizontal

That is the only Mirror operation to remain in "first.dgn", but set a *Mark* (with
Edit>Set Mark) and practice the other *Mirror About* options. *Undo>Other>To Mark*
when you are familiar with operation of the tool and are ready to proceed with more
Manipulations.

The Align Edges Tool

This tool instantly aligns edges or centers of elements. Alignment options are shown in Figure 4.26. The element being moved into alignment will move along one axis (only) to align its edge or center with the *base element*. The exception to this occurs when we choose the *Both Centers* option from the tool settings window *Align* menu.

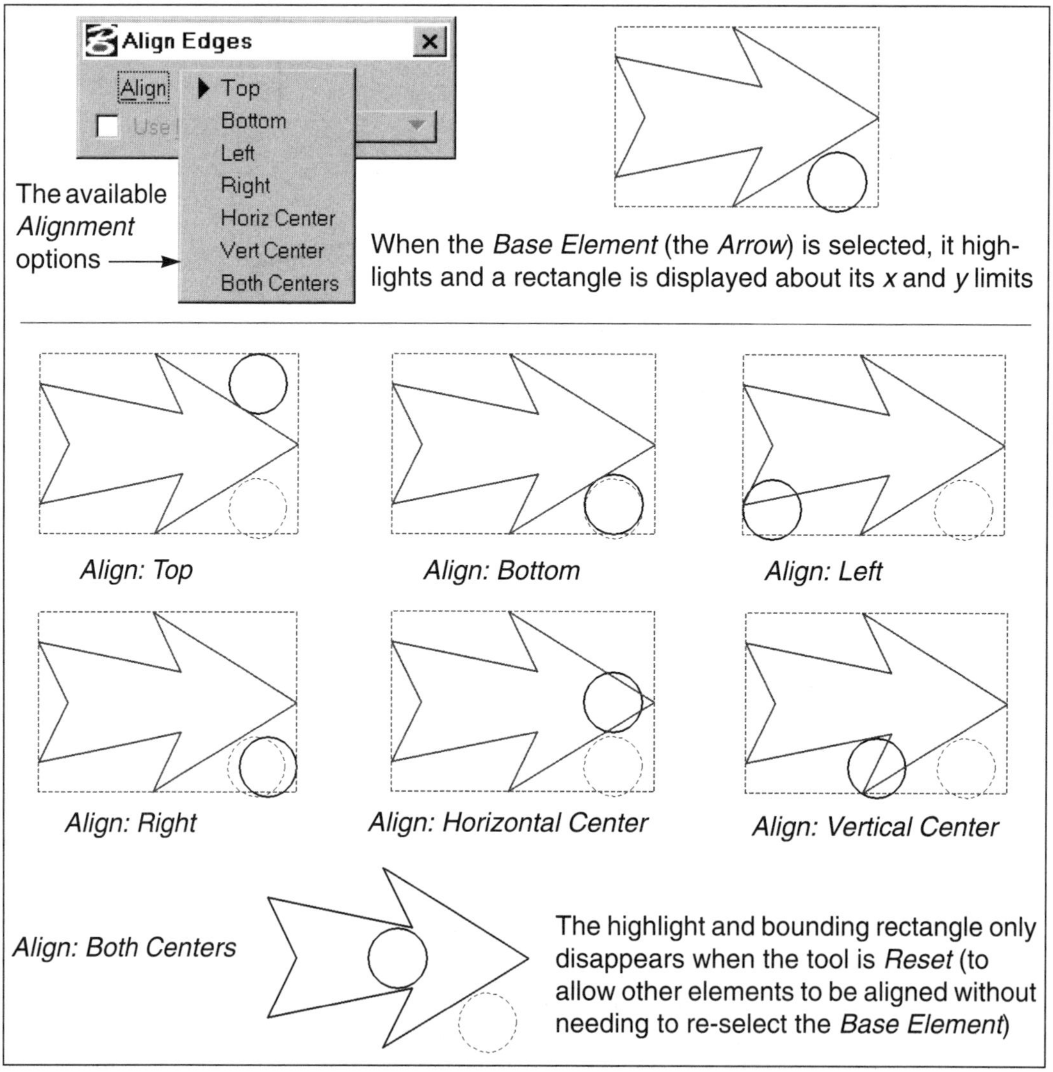

Figure 4.26   Aligning Elements

The Construct Array Tool

This tool makes multiple copies of elements. The copies may be arranged in columns and rows as *Rectangular Arrays*, or on an imaginary circle as *Polar Arrays*. In the latter type, the copies may retain the orientation of the original or be *Rotated* to maintain their angle with respect to the defining circle of the array.

Rectangular Array Type

The *Columns* and *Rows* of *Rectangular* arrays will always be orthogonal, but they may be rotated together under the control of the design file *Active Angle* setting. The *Row Spacing* and *Column Spacing* are distances between equivalent points on adjacent items, dimensioned in the working units of the design file.

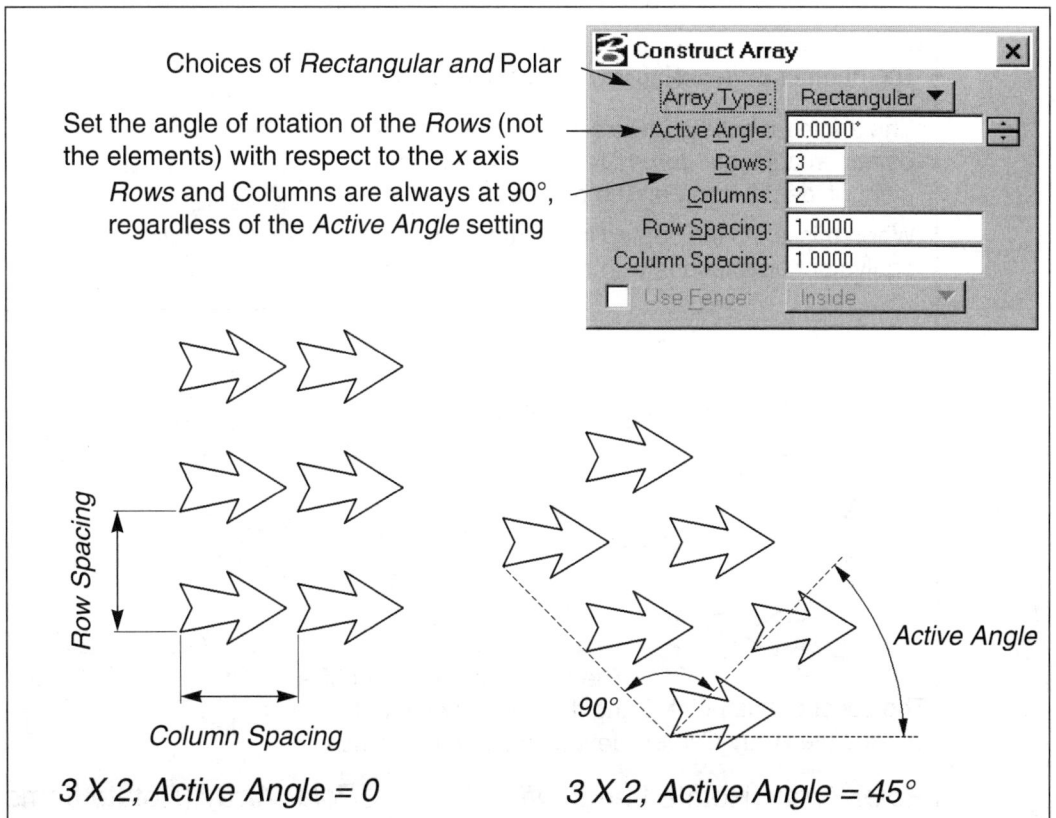

Figure 4.27   Rectangular Arrays

Try constructing some temporary *Rectangular Arrays* using one of the elements in "first.dgn", interpreting the prompts as instructions. The row and column spacing used in Figure 4.27 are both 1 meter. *Undo* the arrays when the experiment is complete.

Polar Array Type

The identified element in a *Polar* array is copied a defined number of times, each copied *Item* distributed around an imaginary circle. The items are separated by a defined *Delta Angle*. The center of this circle is defined by the second data point, its radius being the distance from the center to the identified point on the original.

A *Polar Array* does not always have items distributed around a full circle. The copied items may be optionally be *Rotated* by the *Delta Angle* to maintain the same orientation with respect to the circle center.

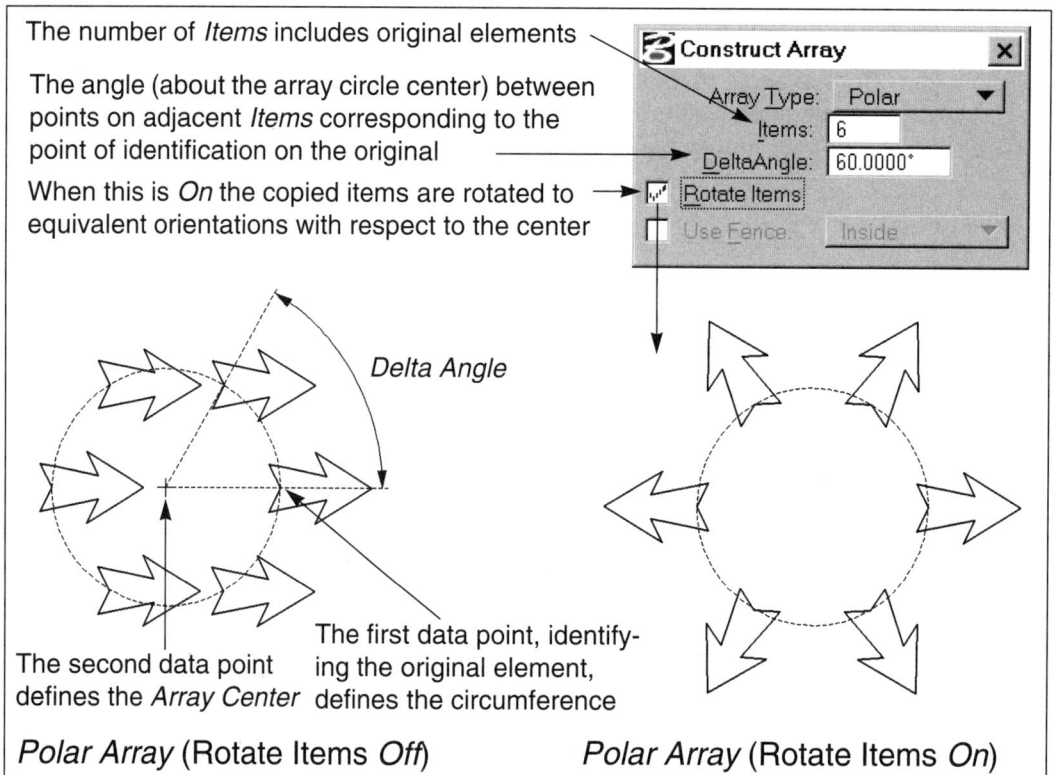

Figure 4.28   Polar Arrays, both 6 Items at 60°

Creating a Polar Array

We will use the Arrow shape to construct *Polar Arrays* as illustrated in Figure 4.28 as our next example. This will involve the definition of the array center with respect to a point on the original element. We will use the defining of this center to demonstrate another facility within AccuDraw.

The View Delta Data Point Keyin

We used a *Data Point Keyin* the first time we placed a block (see page 2-28). In that case, we used the *Absolute* keyin mode, where the actual design plane coordinates for the data point were defined. This time we will use a *View Delta* keyin, where our keyed in dimension is interpreted to be a *Change In* coordinates along the *View* axes.

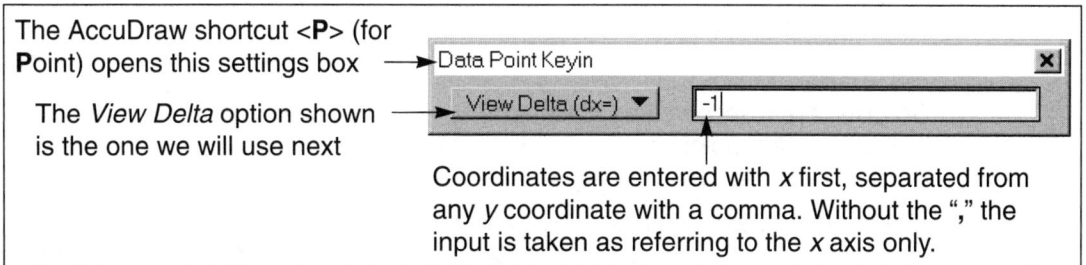

The AccuDraw shortcut <**P**> (for **P**oint) opens this settings box ——►

The *View Delta* option shown ——► is the one we will use next

Data Point Keyin [×]

View Delta (dx=) ▼ | -1|

Coordinates are entered with *x* first, separated from any *y* coordinate with a comma. Without the "**,**" the input is taken as referring to the *x* axis only.

Figure 4.29   The Data Point Keyin settings box, View Delta option

◆ Construct a Polar Array of Arrow shapes

1. Select the *Construct Array* tool, arrange the *Tool Settings* to *Array Type: **Polar**, Items* **6**, *Delta Angle* **60°**, *Rotate Items* check box **Off**.

2. *Keypoint* Snap a *Tentative* point to the middle of the back (left) of the original Arrow shape, *Accept* to identify the element.

    Make sure that the correct element highlights. Remember to snap *on* the original arrow, but a little away from the "target" vertex, or we may identify the large diamond shape.

3. *Snap* again to the same point as in **2.**, but *Do Not Accept* as yet.

    This Tentative point will be the reference position used to position the *Center* of the array.

4. With *Input Focus* in the *AccuDraw* window, press <**P**> (the *Shortcut* for *Point*).

    The *Data Point Keyin* window opens to accept the offset distance of the *Array Center* from the *Tentative Point* just placed.

5. Choose the *View Delta* option (for defining a *Change In* position using the *View window axes*), key in **-1**.

6. Press <**Enter**> to set the center 1 meter to the left of the *Tentative* point.

Pressing <**Enter**> places the data point that *Accepts* the array.

7. Select *Edit>Undo polar array* from the Application window menu, repeat steps **1.** to **6.**, this time with the *Rotate Items* box **On** (checked).

Do not *Undo* or *Delete* this one, we need it for the next exercises.

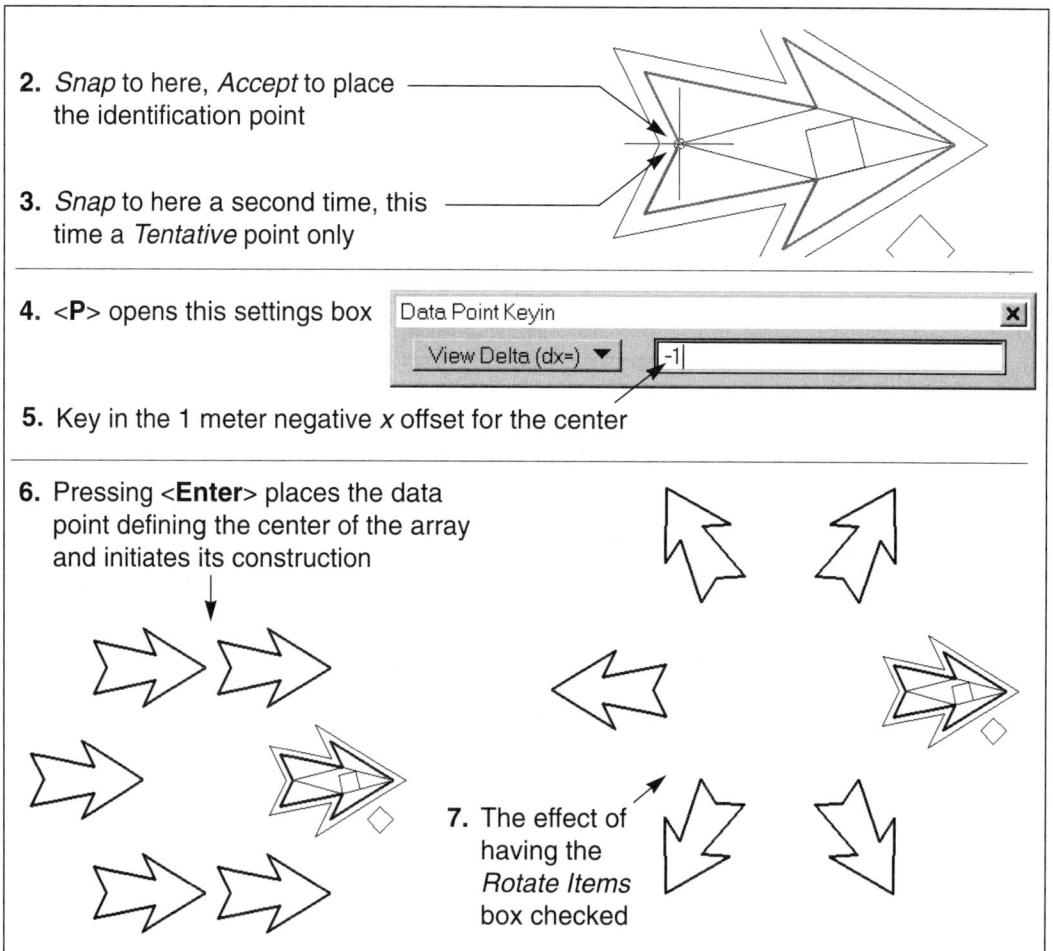

2. *Snap* to here, *Accept* to place the identification point

3. *Snap* to here a second time, this time a *Tentative* point only

4. <**P**> opens this settings box

Data Point Keyin

View Delta (dx=) ▼ | -1

5. Key in the 1 meter negative *x* offset for the center

6. Pressing <**Enter**> places the data point defining the center of the array and initiates its construction

7. The effect of having the *Rotate Items* box checked

Figure 4.30 Constructing Polar Arrays

Element Selection

We have *Manipulated* elements in this chapter by selecting the appropriate tool, for example *Move*, then identifying the element we intend to move. This is known as *Verb-Noun Selection*, as we are first defining the *action*, then identifying the element. There is an alternative to this order of operations.

These tools (available from the *Element Selection* tool box) enable us to *Select* an element (or elements) before we select the tool we intend to manipulate them with. This is referred to as *Noun-Verb Selection*, as we "name" the element(s) first, then define the *action* by selecting a tool such as *Move*.

With this method, more than one element can be selected at a time. By default, the *Selected* elements will have a number of small square "handles" displayed around them. When the *Workspace>Preferences>Input> Highlight Selected Elements* check box is ticked *On*, the selection is highlighted.

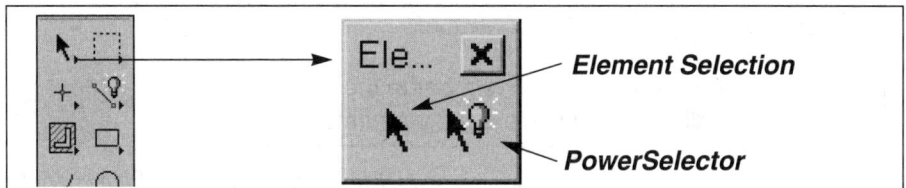

Figure 4.31   The Element Selection Tool Box

The Element Selection Tool

This is the more basic of the two tools in this tool box. If we use it to select elements with the <**Ctrl**> (Control) key held down, we can select any number of elements for simultaneous manipulation. Using the tool to identify elements *Without* the <**Ctrl**> key will result in the current selection cancelling the previous one.

When using *Noun-Verb Selection*, elements remain selected after the operation is complete, thus it can be used in other operations without the need to select it again. It follows that any element(s) left selected will be manipulated whenever an "action" tool is selected, even when the element is not displayed within the view boundaries.

"Action" tools include not only the *Manipulate* tools, but also the *Modify* and *Change* tools (to be introduced later), the *Delete* tool and even the <**Delete**> key on the keyboard. It is easy to imagine harm being done to an element that has accidentally been left selected.

Another technique for selecting a group of elements is to "drag" a rectangle around them. To do this we select the tool, move the pointer to one corner of an imaginary rectangle to enclose the elements. We then press and hold the Data button and drag the pointer to the diagonally opposite corner of the enclosing rectangle. When we release the Data button all of the elements fully within the rectangle will display selection "handles". Figure 4.32 illustrates this.

We *De-select* by *Selecting* individual elements a second time, or we can de-select the lot by placing a data point on a blank section of screen with the *Element Selection* tool selected. This is also known as *Selecting Off* or *Missing*.

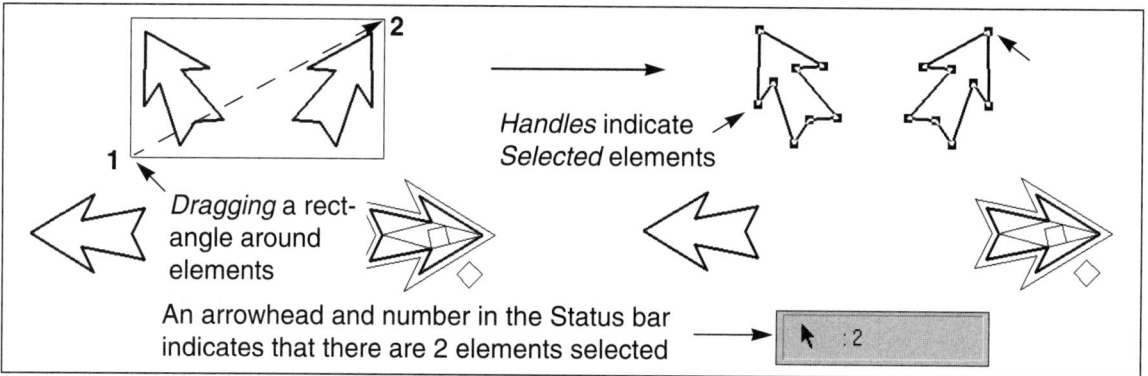

Figure 4.32   Multiple Element Selection

A *Selected* element may be modified by *Dragging* its handles with the *Element Selection* tool, or *Moved* by dragging on its geometry (away from handles). We only have visual control over these methods of modification and manipulation, so they may not be used for precision operations.

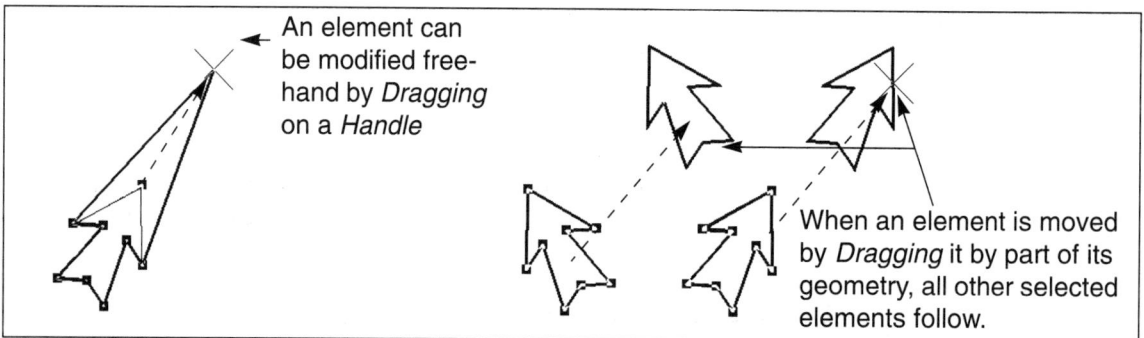

Figure 4.33   Modifying and Moving using the Element Selection tool

The PowerSelector Tool

This is the more powerful of the two *Selector* tools. With this tool we have a huge range of options for making a *Selection Set* of elements, including all of the options we had with the previously described *Element Selection* tool. It incorporates a set of keyboard shortcuts, which may be used as alternatives to the buttons in the tool's Settings window. These shortcuts (with Left and Right hand alternatives) are displayed in the Status Bar and in the *Tool Tip* associated with each of the icons.

The buttons are in two bars, *Method* and *Mode*. The buttons in the *Method* bar provide the options for making a selection, or for changing the members of an existing *Selection Set*. The *Mode* bar has the options for the *Action* we want to perform, for example Add elements to a selection set, or remove (de-select) items.

The tool also has the option of including *Element Attributes* in the criteria for selecting and de-selecting elements.

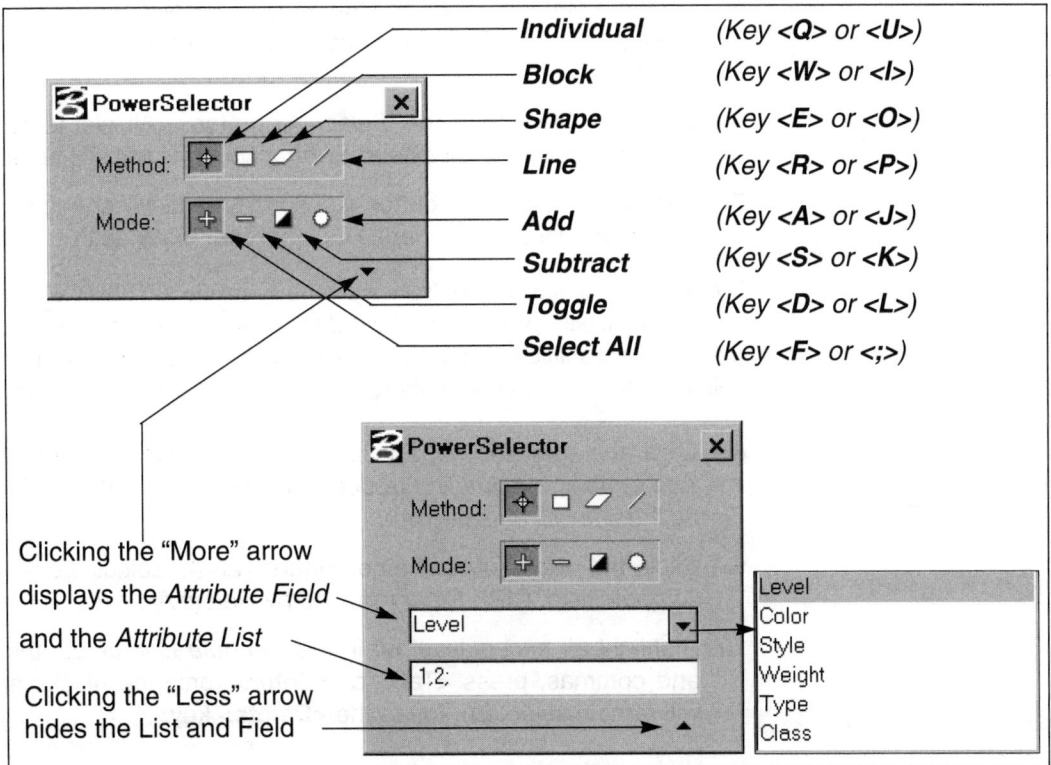

Figure 4.34 The PowerSelector Tool Settings

◆ **Experiment with the PowerSelector**

1. Open "second.dgn", place two circles and two blocks on **Level 60**, so that the view resembles Figure 4.35 (the exact dimensions do not matter).

2. Select the PowerSelector tool, with the *Method* set to *Individual* and the *Mode* to *Add*, select the left side circle and then the block
   Note that the second selection did not undo the first, we **Added** to the selection set each time we clicked on an element.

Note: The *Select All* mode button has changed since there are elements selected, it is now a *Clear* button.

3. Click the *Clear* button (the elements are de-selected and the button reverts to *Select All* mode).

4. Click the *Select All* button (all the elements in the design file will be selected).

5. Click the *Method: Block* and the *Mode: Subtract* buttons, draw a block closely about the Right side circle and block (These two elements will be de-selected).

6. Click the *Clear* then the *Select All* buttons (All elements will have handles again, the *Block* and *Subtract* buttons will still be active).

7. Click the *Mode: Block* button a second time (it will change from *Inside Selection Mode* to *Overlap*). Draw another block as in step **5.**

With *Inside Selection Mode*, only elements fully inside the block will be affected, whereas any element *Inside* or *Overlapped* by the block will be selected in *Overlap*. The block and the shape button icons change and the block itself appears as a broken line. Now all the elements except those on the Left side will have been de-selected.

8. *Clear* the selection set again, click the *Method: Line* and the *Mode: Add* buttons, draw a line through the two blocks (All the elements cut by the line will be selected).

9. Click the *More Arrow* (see Figure 4.34), select *Level* from the *Attribute* field. Click *Clear* followed by *Select All*.

10. Highlight all *except* level **60** in the *Attribute List*, delete the numbers and commas, press **<Tab>** or **<Enter>** (only the blocks and circles will remain selected), Press the **<Delete>** key.

1. These 2 circles and 2 blocks are temporarily placed in "second.dgn" for the PowerSelector tool experiments

2. Method: Mode:

3. Method: Mode:

4. Method: Mode:

5. Method: Mode:

7. Method: Mode:

8. Method: Mode:

10.

Level

10,11,20,60;

Pressing **<Delete>** will now remove all but the original geometry →

Delete these levels from the *Attribute List*, then press <**Tab**> (their elements will de-select).

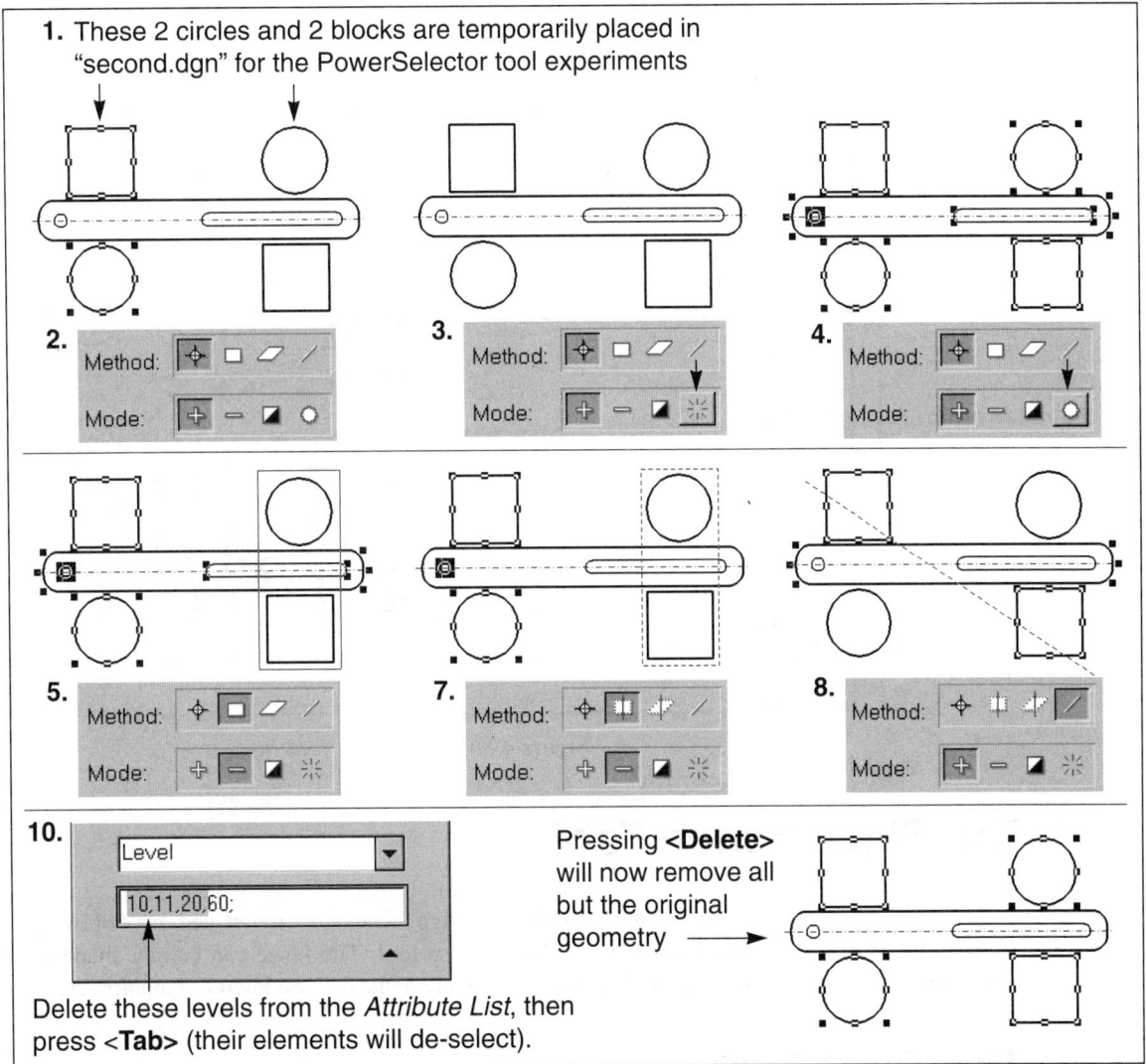

Figure 4.35   Some PowerSelector Options

Element Selection From the Edit Menu

There are also two *Element Selection* choices in the Application window *Edit* menu. We can choose *Edit>Select All* to select every element in the file, whether they are displayed or not. The other *Edit* method, *Select By Attributes*, allows logical selection of elements according to their *Element Attributes*.

Fence Operations

When we use the *Element Selection* tool to select more than one element at any one time, we are creating a *Temporary Group*. Grouped elements can be all be manipulated as one, which is an operation we frequently need to perform. Multiple selection is not the only way of creating a temporary group, there is another far more powerful facility, the *Fence*.

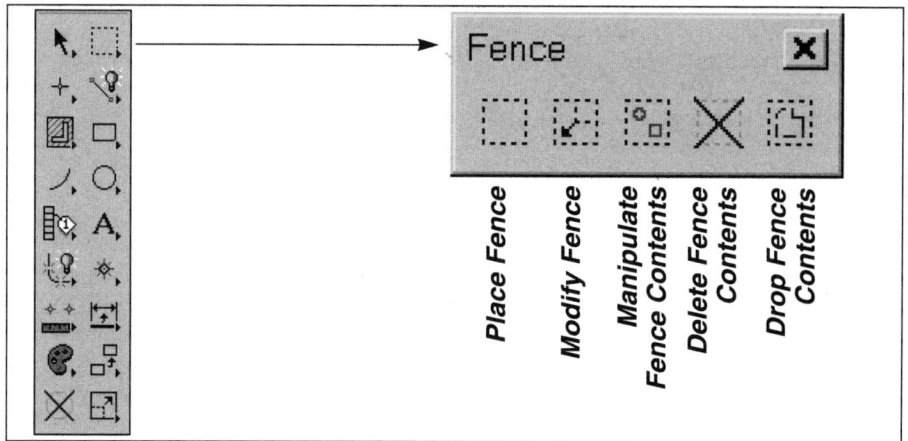

Figure 4.36   The Fence Tool Box

The Place Fence Tool

A *Fence* defines an area within a design. The area is defined by "drawing" a perimeter around it using the *Place Fence* tool. The fence can be any shape at all, thus we can define it to include only the elements that we intend to manipulate.

Place Fence Block

There are a number of choices available from the *Tool Settings* window to help us define the fence. We can draw it as a block, as a circle or as any shape enclosed by straight lines. We can also use a closed element within the design to define it, or use a View window border. Another choice is a rectangle placed automatically to fit around all displayed elements in the *Active Design*.

Note: To *Remove* a fence we select the *Place Fence* tool again, thus starting to place a new fence will remove any previous one.

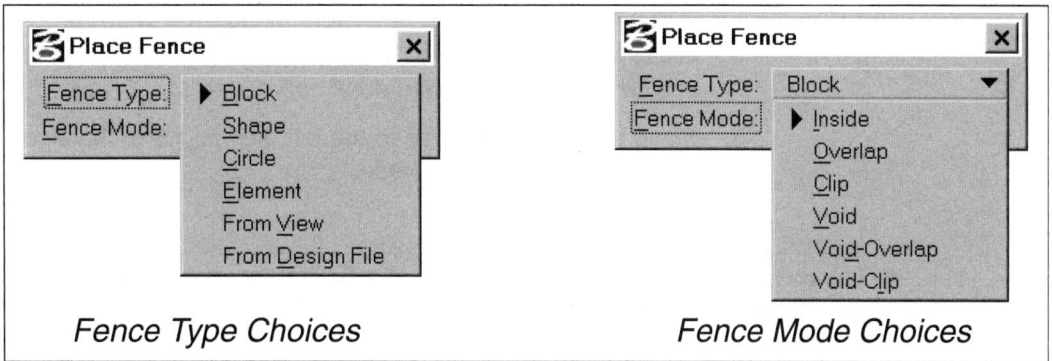

Figure 4.37   Place Fence Tool Settings options

◆ **Experiment with the Fence Mode**

1. Select the *Place Fence* tool, tool settings of *Fence Type* **Block**, *Fence Mode* **Inside**.

2. Place data points at two diagonally opposite corners of the *Fence Block* to fully enclose one Arrow and intersect with two, as shown in Figure 4.38.

3. Select *Either* **(a)** the *Manipulate Fence Contents* tool, choosing an *Operation* tool setting of **Move**, *Or* **(b)** the *Move* tool (from the *Manipulate* tool box) with the *Use Fence* check box **On**.

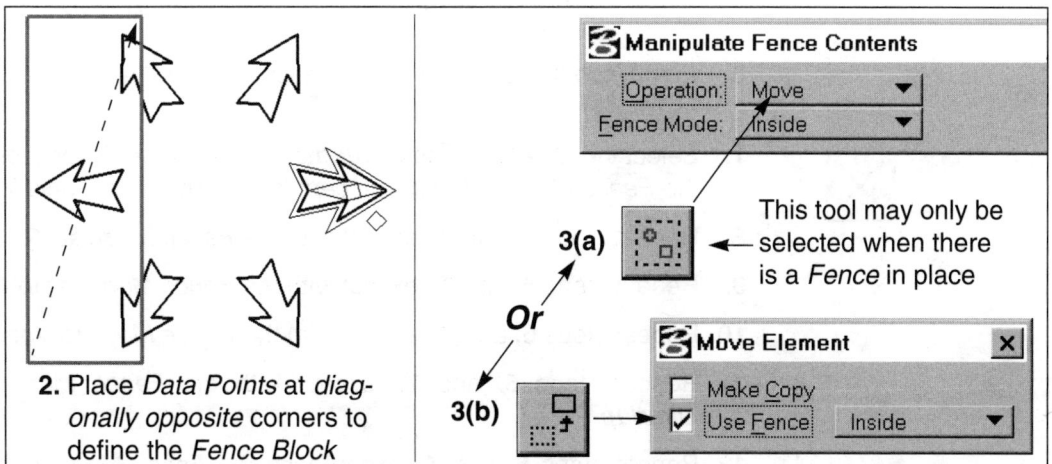

Figure 4.38   Preparing for a Fence Move Operation

4. With *AccuDraw* running, *Define* the *Origin* of the move (as prompted) with a data point placed anywhere in the View window.

We will move the *Fence Contents* a keyed-in distance, thus the actual position of the origin point does not matter.

5. Move the pointer directly to the left, key in **1.5** to the AccuDraw data input field, *Accept* then *Reset.*

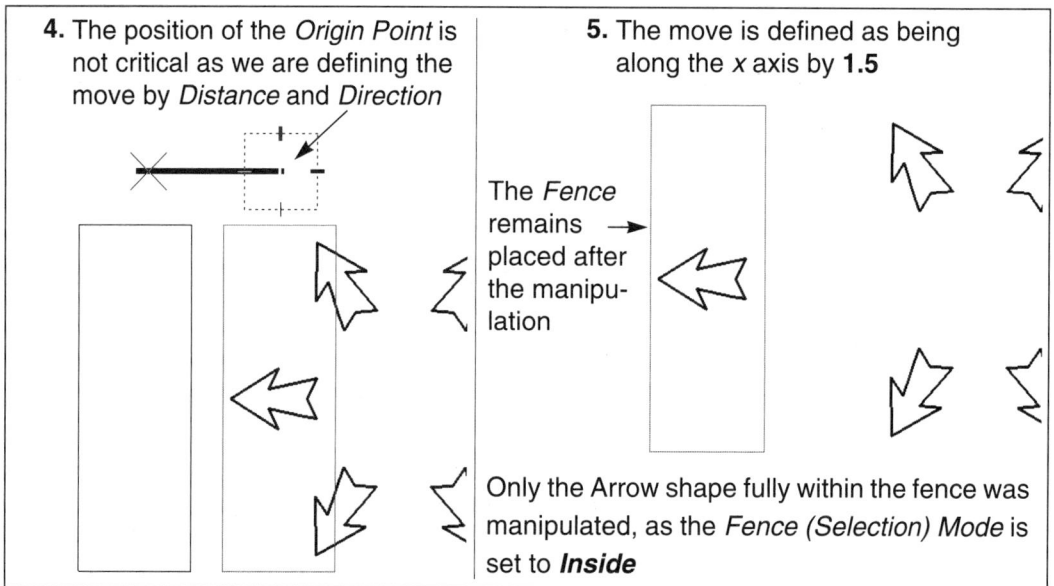

Figure 4.39   Fence Move, Inside selection mode

6. *Edit>Undo* the previous manipulation (or use the *Keyboard Shortcut* **<Ctrl+Z>**).

7. Select the *Delete* **Fence Contents** tool (from the *Fence* tool box), set the *Fence Mode* to **Inside**, *Accept* fence contents for deletion.

8. Repeat steps **6.** and **7.**, except with the *Fence Mode* set to **Overlap**

9. Repeat steps **6.** and **7.**, except with the *Fence Mode* set to **Clip**.

10. Repeat steps **6.** and **7.**, except with the *Fence Mode* to **Void**.

11. Repeat steps **6.** and **7.**, except with the *Fence Mode* to **Void-Overlap**.

12. Repeat steps **6.** and **7.**, except with the *Fence Mode* to **Void-Clip**, then *Undo* the deletion after noting the effect.

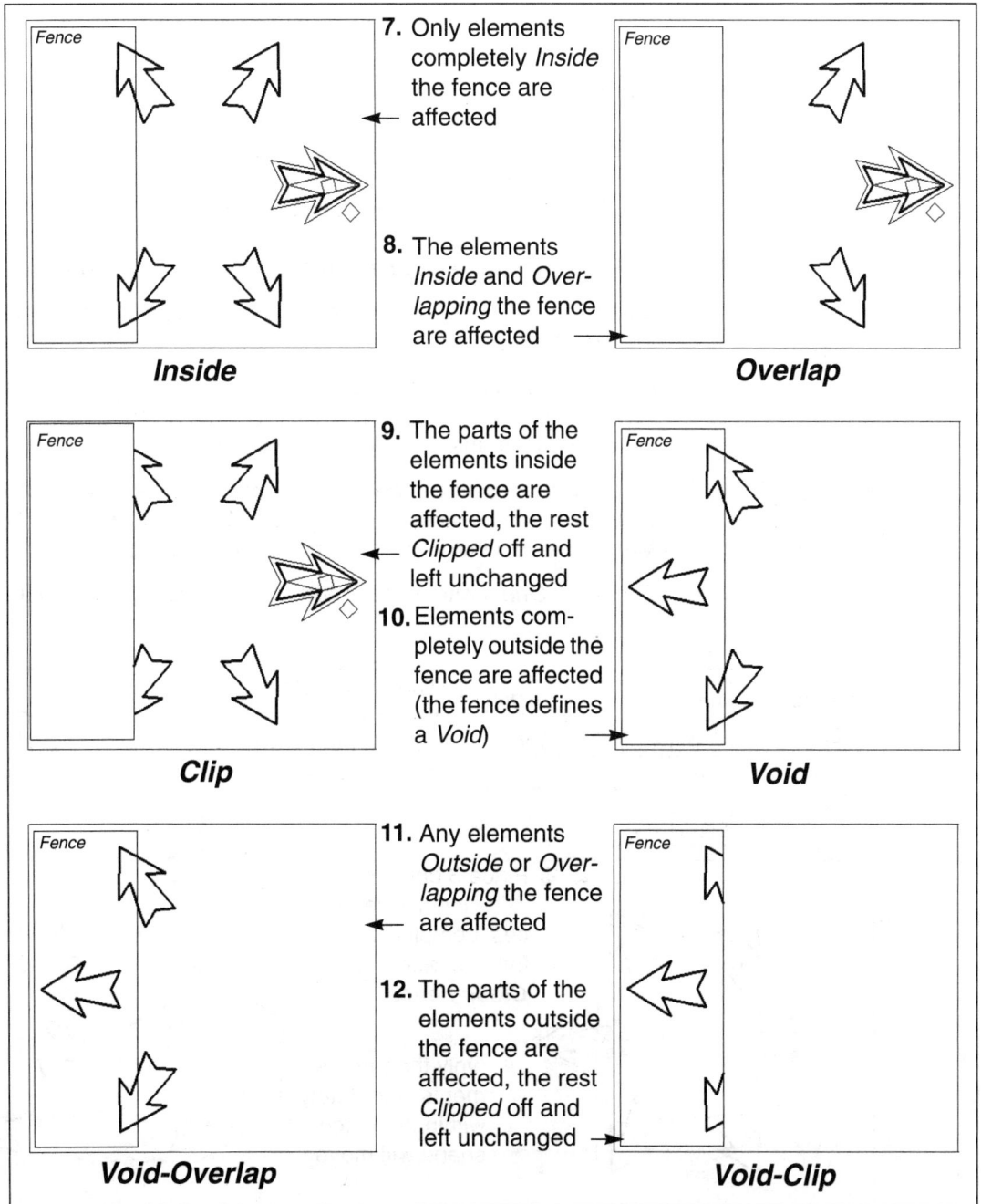

7. Only elements completely *Inside* the fence are affected

8. The elements *Inside* and *Over-lapping* the fence are affected

Inside

Overlap

9. The parts of the elements inside the fence are affected, the rest *Clipped* off and left unchanged

10. Elements com-pletely outside the fence are affected (the fence defines a *Void*)

Clip

Void

11. Any elements *Outside* or *Over-lapping* the fence are affected

12. The parts of the elements outside the fence are affected, the rest *Clipped* off and left unchanged

Void-Overlap

Void-Clip

Figure 4.40   Fence Modes, using Fence Delete to demonstrate the effects

Tip!   It is good practice to re-set the *Fence Mode* to **Inside** after we have finished fence manipulations. This is the most commonly used and the "safest" mode.

Place Fence Shape

The last exercise has given us an insight into the effects of the various *Fence Modes*. The next one will demonstrate alternatives to the block shaped *Fence Type*, the **Shape**. The *Fence Type* options are illustrated in Figure 4.37.

◆ **Use a Fence Shape to copy a selected group of elements**

1. Select the *Place Fence* tool, set the *Fence Type* to **Shape**, the *Fence Mode* to **Inside**.

2. Place a triangle shaped fence with freehand data points at the vertices as illustrated in Figure 4.41, finish the shape by clicking **Close Fence** in the *Tool Settings* window.

3. Select *Either* **(a)** the *Manipulate Fence Contents* tool, choosing an *Operation* tool setting of **Copy**, *Or* **(b)** the *Copy* tool (from the *Manipulate* tool box) with the *Use Fence* check box **On**.

4. Define an *Origin* with a data point, the *Distance* with another, *Reset*

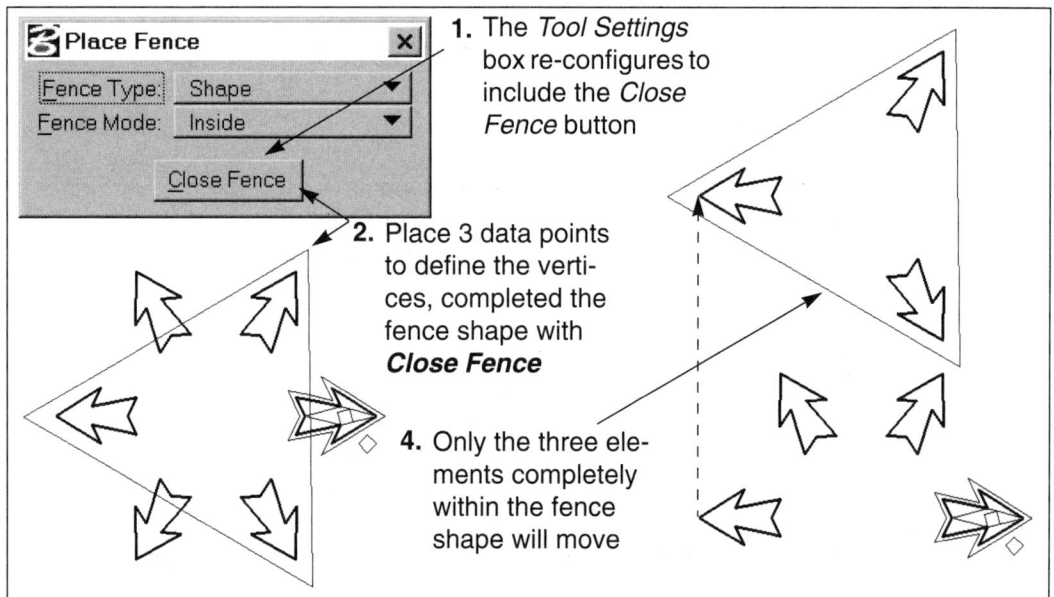

Figure 4.41 Using a Fence Shape

Place Fence Circle

The *Circle* is the other fence outline that we can "draw". There are situations where a circular fence outline will more conveniently define the desired group than a block, without the need to place multiple vertices for a shape.

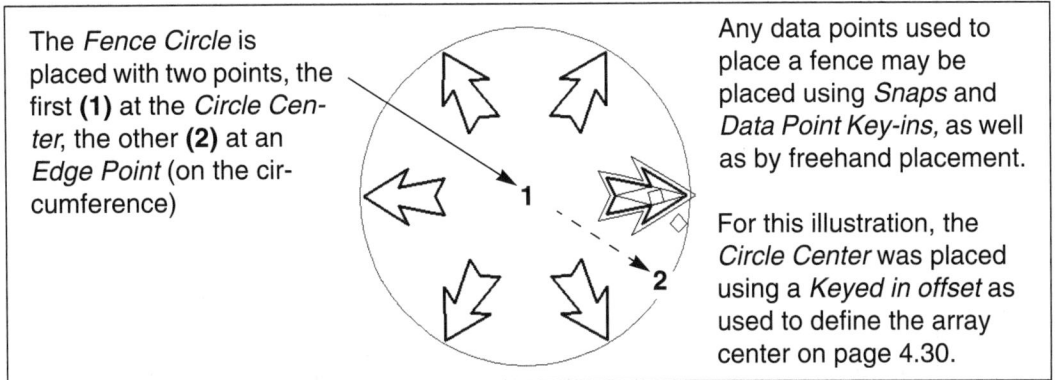

The *Fence Circle* is placed with two points, the first **(1)** at the *Circle Center*, the other **(2)** at an *Edge Point* (on the circumference)

Any data points used to place a fence may be placed using *Snaps* and *Data Point Key-ins,* as well as by freehand placement.

For this illustration, the *Circle Center* was placed using a *Keyed in offset* as used to define the array center on page 4.30.

Figure 4.42   Placing a Fence Circle

Place Fence Element

This fence outline is generated from an existing closed element, such as a complex shape, a shape, an ellipse etc. It is generated coincident with the identified element, therefore this element is only manipulated in the *Overlap* modes.

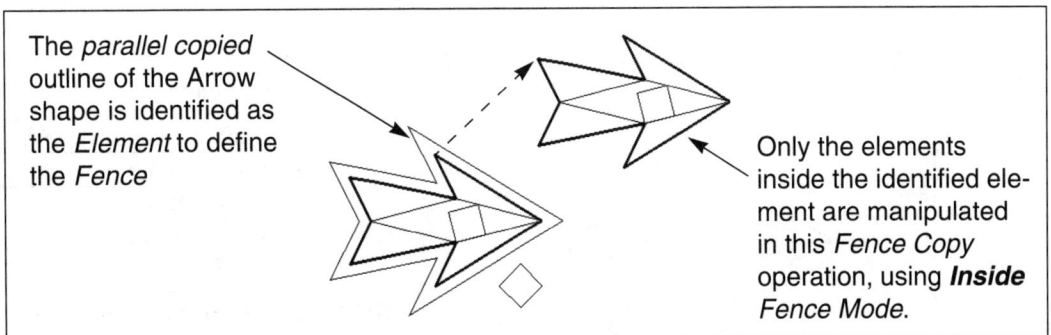

The *parallel copied* outline of the Arrow shape is identified as the *Element* to define the *Fence*

Only the elements inside the identified element are manipulated in this *Fence Copy* operation, using **Inside** *Fence Mode.*

Figure 4.43   Using an existing closed element to define a fence

Place Fence From View

The border of a *View window* defines the fence in this placement method. It is a quick method of temporarily grouping all the currently visible elements for manipulations.

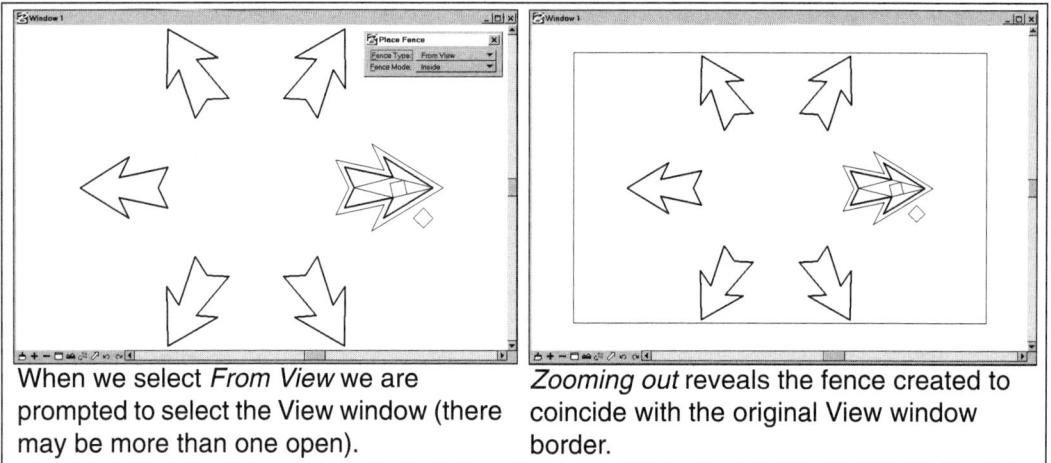

When we select *From View* we are prompted to select the View window (there may be more than one open).

Zooming out reveals the fence created to coincide with the original View window border.

Figure 4.44   Using a View window border to define a fence

Place Fence From Design File

This type of fence is defined as a block automatically placed to surround all the displayed elements (generally those placed on levels currently displayed).

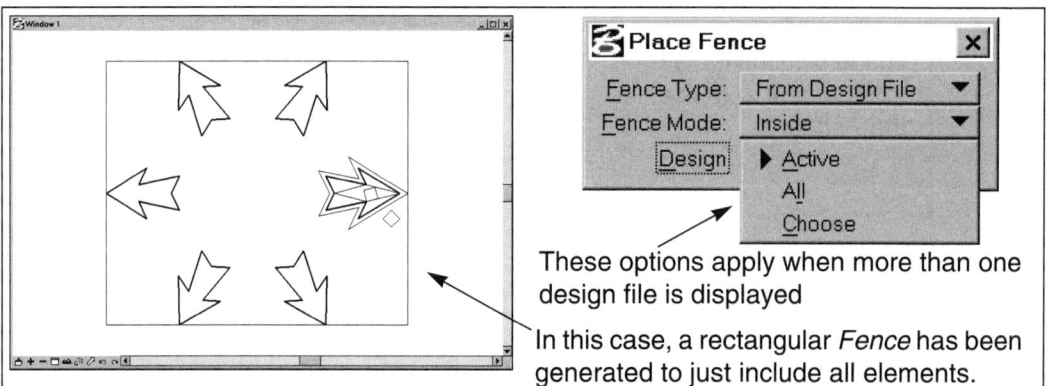

These options apply when more than one design file is displayed

In this case, a rectangular *Fence* has been generated to just include all elements.

Figure 4.45   A fence placed From Design File

The *Tool Settings* window changes to provide a choice of *Design*. This applies when we have *Reference* files displayed, additional files that may be displayed for reference and printing. When we have these files displayed (they will be introduced later in this book) we can have the fence surrounding *All* elements, or only the elements in a design file that we *Choose*. This choice is made by identifying any element in a particular file.

Stretching Elements Within a Fence

The *Fence* can be used to stretch elements in any direction. The technique involves placing a fence around certain defining points (usually vertices) of an element or elements and moving these defining points with respect to points outside the fence.

The Manipulate Fence Contents tool Stretch operation

All except one of the *Operation* Tool Setting choices for the *Manipulate Fence Contents* tool is also available from the *Manipulate* tool box. *Stretch* is this unique tool. With this operation the *Fence (Selection) Mode* is ignored, it will be *Inside* regardless of the setting chosen. AccuDraw can be used in conjunction with a fence stretch operation to control the distance and direction of the manipulation.

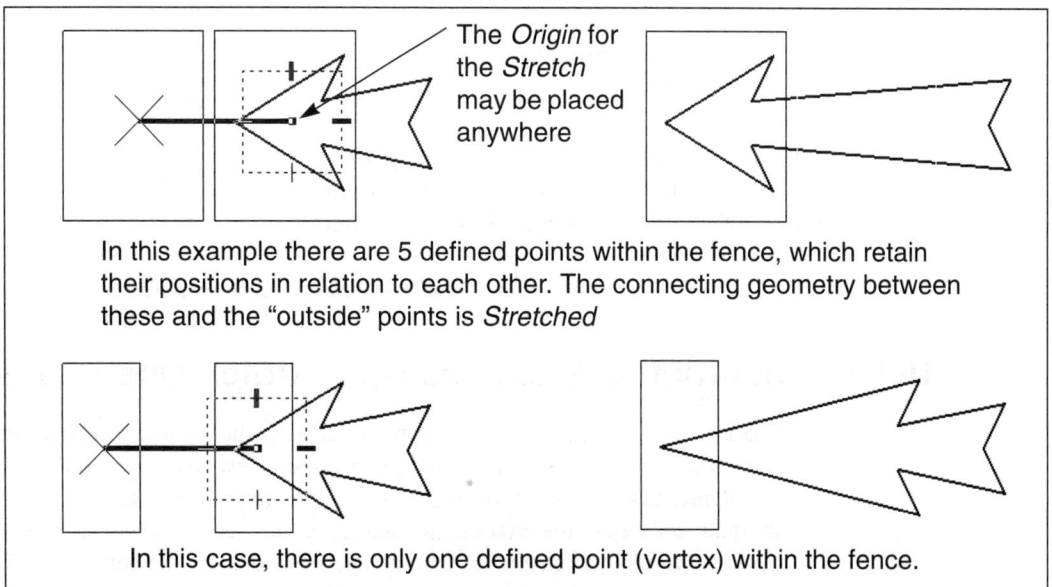

Figure 4.46   The Fence Stretch operation

In the following exercises we will stretch two of the Arrow shapes from the *Polar Array* created earlier in the design file "first.dgn". The first one will be stretched along the *x* axis of the View window as illustrated in Figure 4.46.

◆ **Stretch the left-pointing Arrow shape by .7**

1. Select the *Place Fence* tool, set the *Fence Type* to **Block**, the *Fence Mode* setting has no effect.

2. Place a fence around the 5 vertices defining the "head" of the arrow.

3. Select the *Manipulate Fence Contents* tool, set the *Operation* to **Stretch**.

4. Start *AccuDraw* (if necessary), define the *Origin* of the stretch with a data point.

    It is usual to place the *Origin* inside the fence as it is easier to visualize the result, but in practice it may be place anywhere.

5. Move the pointer to the left, keeping it indexed to the *x* axis, key in **.7**, *Accept*, *Reset*.

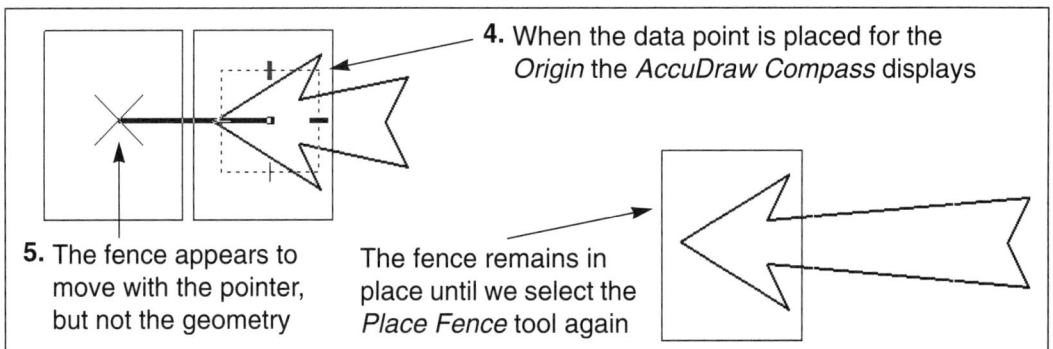

Figure 4.47 The Fence Stretch operation

Using Construction Elements with Stretch Operations

The next stretch operation will be performed on the slanted top-right arrow of the array, thus the stretch will not be along either view axis. We could do this using AccuDraw in the Polar coordinate mode with Smart Lock, or by using the **<RQ>** shortcut to rotate the AccuDraw axes. In this case, however, we will use a *Construction* line to ensure the stretch takes place along the centerline of the shape. We will apply the last of the *Element Attributes* at this stage, the *Class* attribute (see "Methods of Setting Element Attributes" on page 3-5).

Elements of this class normally do not appear on the final document printed out from the design file. They can be any type of element, like construction lines on a paper drawing, used while creating the final geometry, then "rubbed out".

In MicroStation, we can leave these lines in the file in case they are needed again, but only display them when they are needed. The display of *Construction* class elements is controlled from within the *Settings>View Attributes* settings box (see "Attributes of the View Window" on page 3-3).

We will also introduce the *Place Line* tool and the *Through Point* snap mode in this example. *Place line* differs from the *Place Smartline* tool in the following ways:

1.   It places individual lines only, it does not place arcs, rounded vertices or automatically create line strings and shapes;

2.   It may be *Constrained* to place lines of pre-defined length and/or angle;

3.   It has more *Snap Modes* available, including *Through Point*.

Tentative points placed with the *Through Point* snap mode will snap to key points and divisions between key points in a similar way to *Keypoint* snap (see page 3-12 and page 3-13). The difference is that a line or its extension passes *Through* this point, not necessarily *To* it.

◆ **Place a construction line for a Fence Stretch Operation**

1.   *Window Area* about the top-right Arrow shape of the array in "first.dgn", leaving some room for the extension.

2.   Set the *Element>Attributes>Class* to **Construction**.

3.   Select the *Place Line* tool from the *Lines* tool box (next to the *Place Smartline* tool). Leave the *Length* and the *Angle* check boxes **Off**.

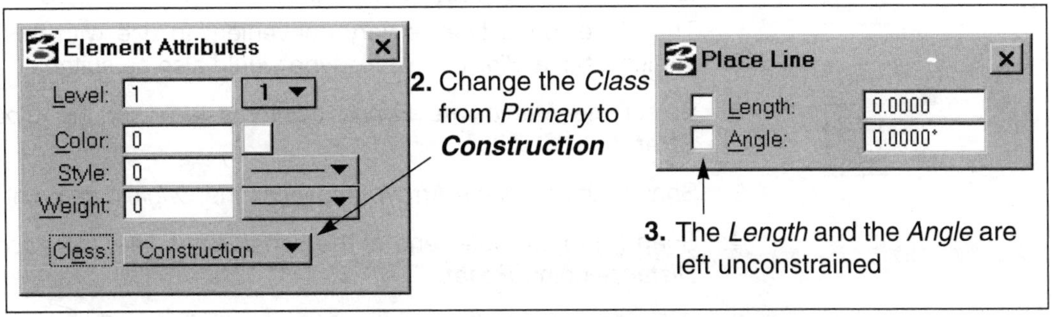

Figure 4.48   Settings for the construction line

4. *Keypoint* snap to the centre of the "tail" of the Arrow, *Accept* to place the first point on the line.

5. Change the *Snap Mode Override* to *Through Point* (see "Setting the Active Snap Mode" on page 3-18), Snap a *Tentative* point to the tip of the Arrow as shown in Figure 4.49, *Accept.*

6. Place the end of the line approximately an arrow length further on.

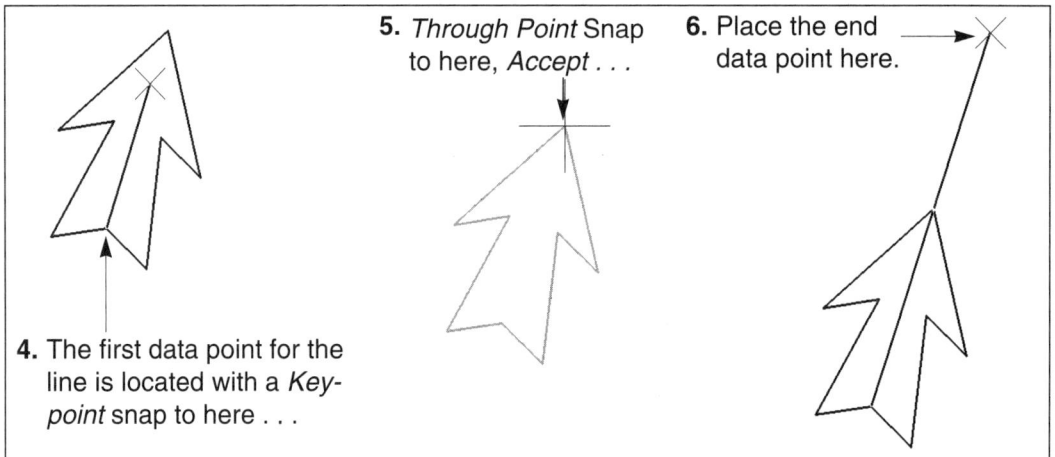

Figure 4.49   Placing the construction line

The *Fence Stretch* was defined with the help of *AccuDraw* in the last example, but this time we will use keypoint snaps to define both the *Origin* and the *Distance*.

◆ **Stretch the Arrow along the construction line**

1. Select the *Place Fence* tool, set the *Fence Type* to **Circle**, place the fence around the arrowhead vertices as shown in Figure 4.50.

    The circle fence type is very convenient to use with this group of vertices, but a *Block* or *Shape* type would also be suitable.

2. Select the *Manipulate Fence Contents* tool, set the *Operation* to **Stretch**.

3. Snap to the tip of the Arrow, *Accept* as the *Origin* data point.

4. Snap **(a)** to the outer end of the construction line, **(b)** *Accept* as the *Distance* point, *Reset.*

5. Press the data button on the *Manipulate Fence Contents* tool, drag back and release on the *Place Fence* tool to remove the fence.

6. Select *Settings>View Attributes* from the Application window menu (see page 3-3).

7. Click *Off* the *Constructions* check box (four down on the left column), click the *Apply* button.

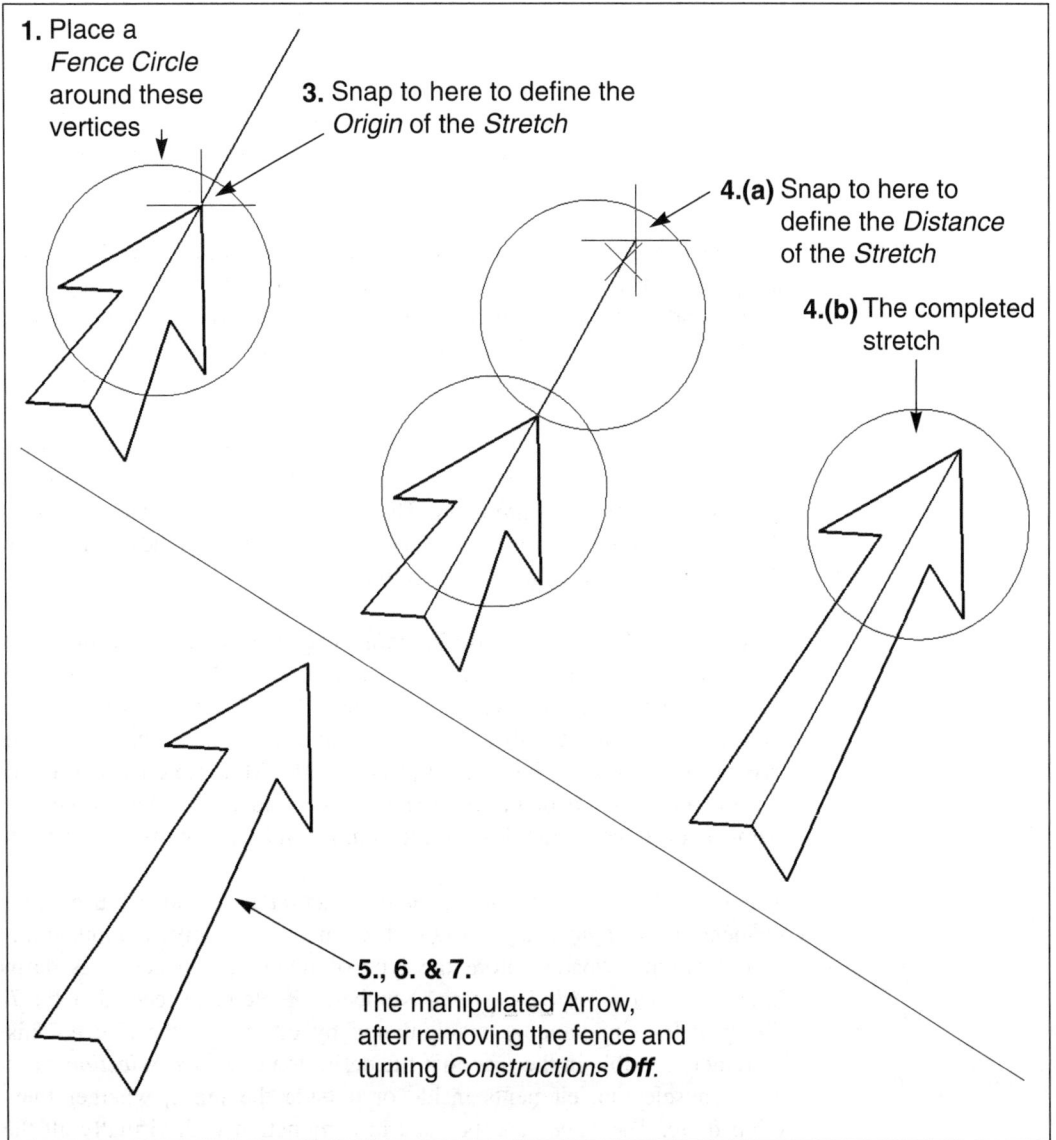

1. Place a *Fence Circle* around these vertices

3. Snap to here to define the *Origin* of the *Stretch*

4.(a) Snap to here to define the *Distance* of the *Stretch*

4.(b) The completed stretch

5., 6. & 7.
The manipulated Arrow, after removing the fence and turning *Constructions Off*.

Figure 4.50   Stretching fence contents using a construction line

Summary

Moving and *Copying* elements are very similar operations, the only noticeable difference is that with a *Copy* operation the original element is left intact. With either operation, the *Distance* and *Direction* for the move or copy is the relative distance and direction of two data points. The first data point *Identifies* the element, the second defines the new position for the original or copy. The new position can be defined with AccuDraw key-in, graphically, or with the help of *Tentative* points.

It is normally possible to manipulate elements on any *Level*, regardless of the level currently *Active*. We can choose to restrict our ability to manipulate to *only those elements on the Active Level* by setting *Level Lock On* in one of the *Locks* boxes.

Geometry can be moved or copied *Parallel* to itself, the distance defined either graphically or by keyboard entry. With this form of move or copy, a line between corresponding points on the manipulated element and the original will always be a perpendicular to both. This may cause radical changes in shape if "concave" geometry is copied too far.

The *Scale* tool changes the dimensions of elements, either in proportion or with different factors applied to the x and y axes. The scaling factors may be defined graphically or by keyboard entry. They are applied to the element with respect to a data point defining the *point to scale about*. This leads to the element moving on the design plane if this point is away from its center.

Rotations of elements can also be defined by angles entered from the keyboard, or graphically by placement of data points. The active *Angle Mode* must be taken into account when defining keyed-in rotations. The *Mirror* tool is used to make mirror images of an element, either of the *Original* or as a *Copy*. The images can be placed symmetrically about line defined at any angle. Multiple copies of elements in the form of *Rectangular* or *Polar Arrays* can be made. With *Arrays* we can define the numbers of items, the angles and the number and spacing of rows and columns.

The *PowerSelector* and the *Element Selection* tools can be used to identify an element, or a *Temporary Group* of elements, for any manipulation. Since the identification is made before the type of manipulation action is defined, this is known as *Noun-Verb Selection*. Numbers of elements can also be *Temporarily Grouped* for simultaneous manipulation by the use of the *Fence*. This facility is extremely flexible in the way that the definition of *Fence Selection* can be changed between selecting elements inside or outside the fence, whether they are to be clipped etc. The *Fence* can be used in conjunction with virtually all the tools that alter existing elements.

5 : Beyond The Basics

This chapter will introduce a large range of new tools, some to place new types of elements, others to modify elements already placed. Some of the new tools will be applied to a design we are to complete for use in following chapters, a top view of a typical "ergonomic" office chair.

While only *some* of the tools are to be applied immediately to the fully specified design exercises, it is recommended that *all* of the tools be experimented with, preferably as they are introduced. We can do this by placing temporary elements and modifying them, then *Undoing* the changes to the design file when we are satisfied with each particular operation. Take care to keep each stage of this chapter's main design project (the office chair) intact for continuing use.

When you have completed this chapter, you will be able to:

- Place reference points in a design using the *Place Active Points* tools;
- Place *Arcs* and *Ellipses* using a variety of methods;
- Combine a number of element types into one outline;
- Use the *Modify* tools on various types of existing elements as part of the design process;
- Place, modify and blend curved elements, including B-spline curves;
- Use the *Key-in window* utility to enter special commands.

Active Points

An *Active Point* has *Position*, but *No Dimension*. Its main use is as a reference point or monument point, defining a location on the design plane. It may or may not print out to a paper document, depending on the type chosen and the configuration of your printing/plotting equipment.

The Active Points Tool Box

The tools in this box place Active Points either singly or in multiples, standing alone or on existing elements. The *Point Type* is chosen and, where necessary, the character or cell selected in the Tool Settings window. When the particular tool constructs multiple points, the number of points is input to a Tool Settings field.

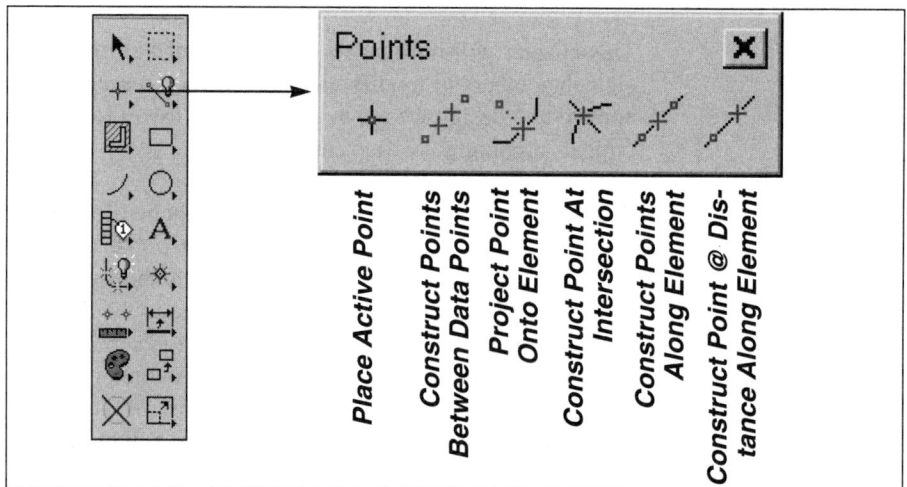

Figure 5.1   The Points Tool Box

On the screen, *Active Points* appear as one of three *Point Types*:

1.   An *Element*, actually a *Line* with *Zero Length*;

2.   A *Character* selected from the keyboard, its size, font etc. will depend on the currently active settings for the placement of text;

3.   A *Cell* (Cells are to be introduced later), typically a symbol drawing.

When we snap to an *Active Point* placed as an *Element* or *Character*, we snap to its true *Position* on the *Design Plane*. This will generally be at or near its center. Where a *Cell* indicates the point, we can snap to any of its elements in the usual way.

Place Active Point

A single *Active Point* is placed with a *Data Point*

(1)

Construct Active Points Between Data Points

A specified number of equally spaced *Active Points* are constructed between two *Data Points*

(1)   **(2)**

Project Active Point Onto Element

An *Element* is identified with *Data Point* **1**, then a single *Active Point* will be placed on the element at the point closest to *Data Point* **2**

(1)   **(2)**

Construct Active Point At Intersection

An *Element* is identified for *Intersection* with *Data Point* **1**, then the *Active Point* will be placed on the element identified with *Data Point* **2** at the point of intersection with the first element, or its extension

(2)

(1)

Construct Active Points Along Element

A specified number of equally spaced *Active Points* are constructed along an *Element* between two *Data Points*

(1)   **(2)**

Construct Active Points at Distance Along Element

A single *Active Point* is placed at a specified *Distance* (d) along an *Element* from the point at which it was identified with *Data Point* **1**. *Data Point* **2** defines the *Direction* along the element

(1)   --d---▸   **(2)**

As can be seen from the illustrations on page 5-2, the names given to each of the tools provide a good indication of how to place *Active Points* for particular applications. Our first application will be in the design of an office chair.

Office Chair Example (Stage 1)

After creating a new design file for the next group of example designs, we will start on the chair by placing a single *Active Point*, which will define its center. A circle indicating the floor area occupied by the chair will also be placed at this stage.

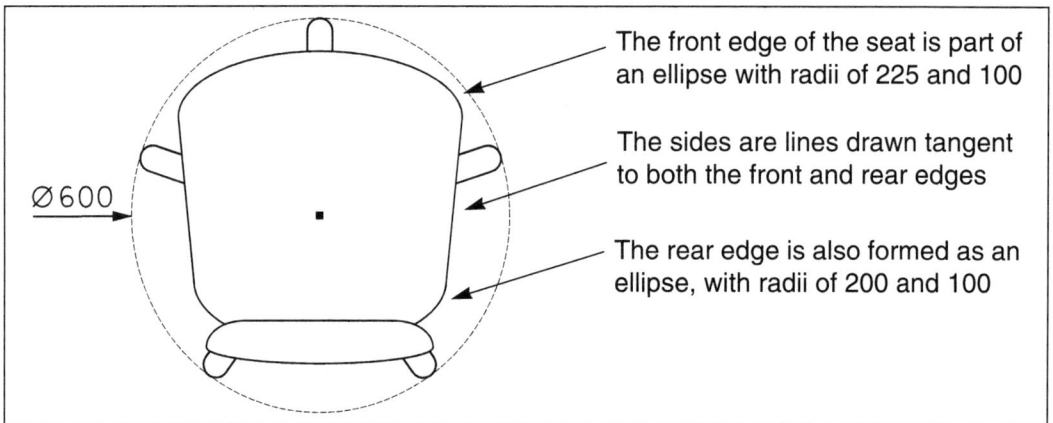

The front edge of the seat is part of an ellipse with radii of 225 and 100

The sides are lines drawn tangent to both the front and rear edges

The rear edge is also formed as an ellipse, with radii of 200 and 100

Ø600

Figure 5.2   The complete Office Chair

◆ **Place the center point and outer circle**

1. Create and open a new design file named "cells.dgn" in the same folder as "first.dgn" and "second.dgn". Use our own *Seed File* "seed2dmm.dgn" created in Chapter 3.

2. Set the *Active Level* to **20**, the *Color* and *Line Style* to **0**, the *Line Weight* to **10**, the *Class* to **Primary**.
   A heavy line weight (10) makes *Active Points* more visible.

3. *Start AccuDraw* (if it is not already running), select the *Place Active Point* tool, set *Point Type:* **Element**).

4. Click the *AccuDraw* window (or press **<F6>**) to direct *Input Focus* to it, Press **<P>**, enter **0,0** in the *Data Point Keyin* settings box as an *Absolute* point, press **<Enter>**, *Fit View*.
   The *Point* was placed at the *Global Origin*, which may not have been within the view until the *Fit View* operation.

Tip!   The comma and the second zero may be omitted when keying in to the *Data Point Keyin* settings box. Pressing <**Enter**> with a single zero (or a <**Space**>) in the field enters zeros as both the *x* and the *y* coordinates.

5.   Change the *Line Style* to **3** the and *Weight* to **0**.

6.   Select the *Place Circle* tool, choose *Method:***Center** and *constrain* (the constraint box checked **On**) the **Diameter** to **600** in the *Tool Settings* window.

7.   Move the pointer over the *AccuDraw Origin* (it will index to it), *Accept, Reset, Fit View.*

If the AccuDraw Compass has moved away from the center point for any reason since step **5.**, *Keypoint Snap* to the *Active Point.*

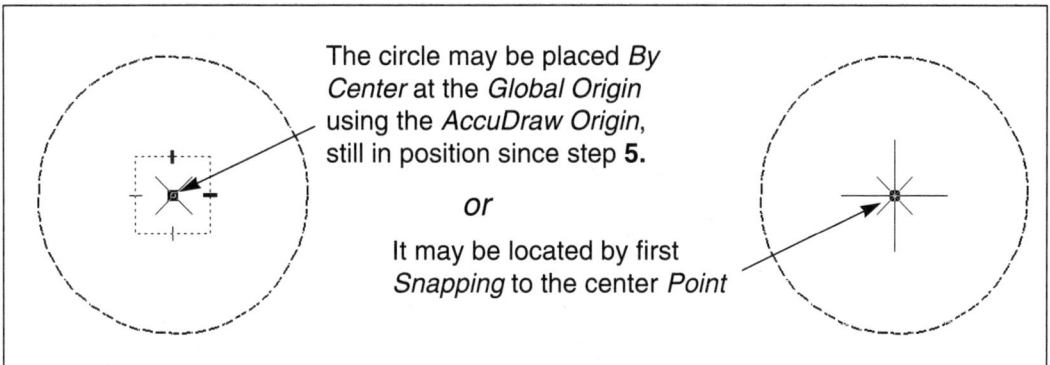

The circle may be placed *By Center* at the *Global Origin* using the *AccuDraw Origin*, still in position since step **5.**

or

It may be located by first *Snapping* to the center *Point*

Figure 5.3   Placing the 600mm diameter dashed circle

Before we proceed with the rest of the chair, we will examine some more of the tools that we are about to use. The chair outlines will consist of a combination of two *Ellipses*, a *Half Ellipse,* two *Quarter Ellipses* and two straight *Lines*.

Ellipses

An *Ellipse* has two radii, designated as *Primary* and *Secondary.* When the two are equal, the *Ellipse* is a *Circle.* The *Primary Radius* is measured along the *Primary Axis*, the axis defining the *Rotation* or orientation of the element with respect to the design plane axes.

The Ellipses Tool Box

The *Ellipses* tool box has already been accessed when we placed *Circles*. The *Place Ellipse* tool was used as an illustration of "Drawing Tools" on page 2-25, with only the *Place Circle* and *Place Ellipse* tools in the box. We will only describe the *Place Ellipse* tool now, since we have had some experience already with the *Place Circle* tool. The *Place Ellipse* tool places complete ellipses only, partial ellipses are *Arcs*. We will find them in the *Arcs Tool Box*, the next one to be introduced.

The Place Ellipse Tool

Figure 5.4 illustrates *Ellipses* placed using four different combinations of *Method* and *Constraint* choices. There are other combinations available, our choice will depend on the particular requirements we need to meet at the time.

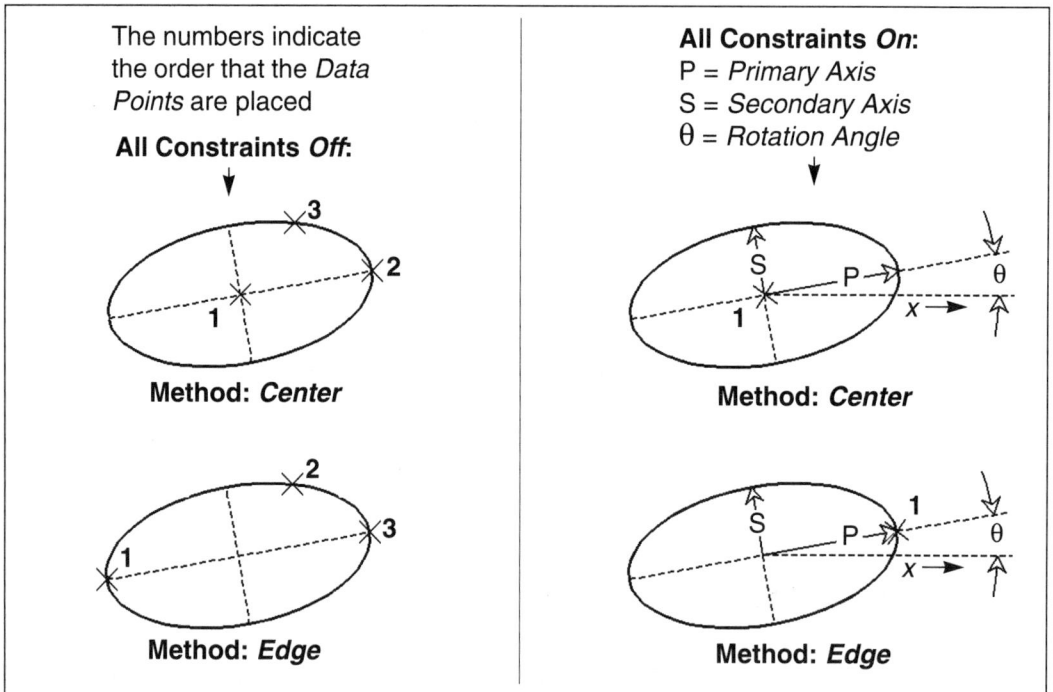

Figure 5.4   Placing Ellipses

We will proceed with stage 2 of the chair, which will be placed on another level. Figure 5.2 shows the completed chair with the remaining parts of the *Ellipses*.

Office Chair Example (Stage 2)

We will use the *Place Ellipse* tool in conjunction with AccuDraw to create the elliptical front and back edges for the seat. The full ellipses will be placed with their centers offset from the *Active Point* placed earlier. After these front and back edges are placed we will join them with lines forming the sides.

◆ **Place ellipses to form the front and back edges for the seat**

1. Set the *Active Level* to *10*, the *Line Style* to *0*, the *Weight to 1*, the *Color* and *Class* as before.

2. Select the *Place Ellipse* tool, the *Method:* to **By Center**, constrain the *Primary:* (radius) to **225**, the *Secondary:* to **100**, the *Rotation* (angle) to **0**.

   The ellipse is now fully defined, so it will appear on the screen with the pointer at its center.

3. Snap a *Tentative* point to the *Active Point* (do not accept), press <**O**>, move the pointer directly upward indexed to the *y* axis, key in **150**, *Accept.*

4. Click the *Primary:* and the *Rotation:* check boxes to turn those constraints **Off** (leave the *Secondary:* as **100**).

5. Snap to the *Active Point* again as in **3.** but this time **O**ffset down by **100**, *Accept.*

6. Move the pointer sideways, indexed to *x,* key in **200**, *Accept, Reset.*

   This demonstrates a method of defining an ellipse, *Partially Constrained.*

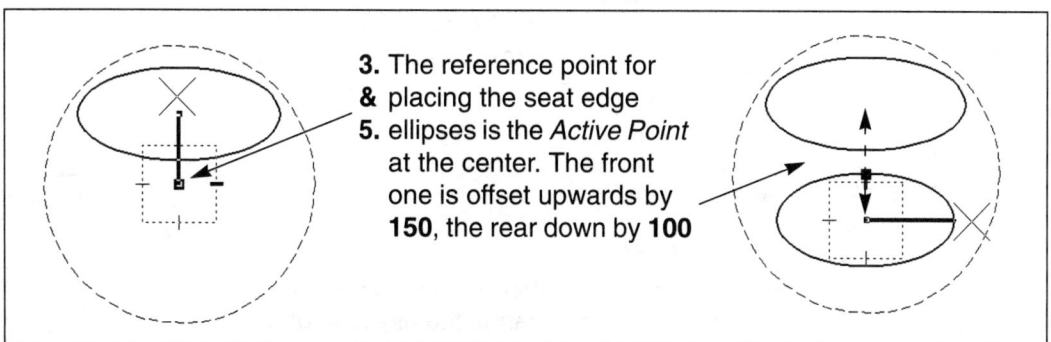

Figure 5.5   Placing the seat front and back ellipses for the Office Chair

Tangent Snap Mode

This snap mode is available for use with the *Place Line* tool, but not the *Place Smartline*. When we precede a data point for placing a line by a *Tangent* snap to an existing element, the line will be placed as a *Tangent* to that element. The point of tangency will move along the existing element depending on the direction of the line. This is where the *Tangent* mode differs from *Tangent From*, as in this mode the point of tangency is defined by the position of the tentative point on the existing element.

Both ends of a line may be entered as *Tangents*, in which case the line's position, length and direction will all be defined by the two tangencies. We will use this feature in the next exercise, which completes stage 2 of the drawing.

◆ **Place lines for the seat sides**

1. Select the *Place Line* tool, set the *Active Snap Mode* to *Tangent* (*Not* the *Snap Mode Override*, see page 3-18).

2. *Snap* and *Accept* the first point on one side of one ellipse, *Snap* and *Accept* the end point on the same side of the other ellipse, *Reset*.

3. Place the other side line in the same way as in step **2.**

4. Set the *Active Snap Mode back* to *Keypoint.*
   The snap setting is left in the most frequently used mode.

Tip!   If the tangental line dynamically displays in the wrong direction, spin the pointer around the outside of desired start point. Spin it so that it emerges in the required direction (for the tangent line) from the center of the element.

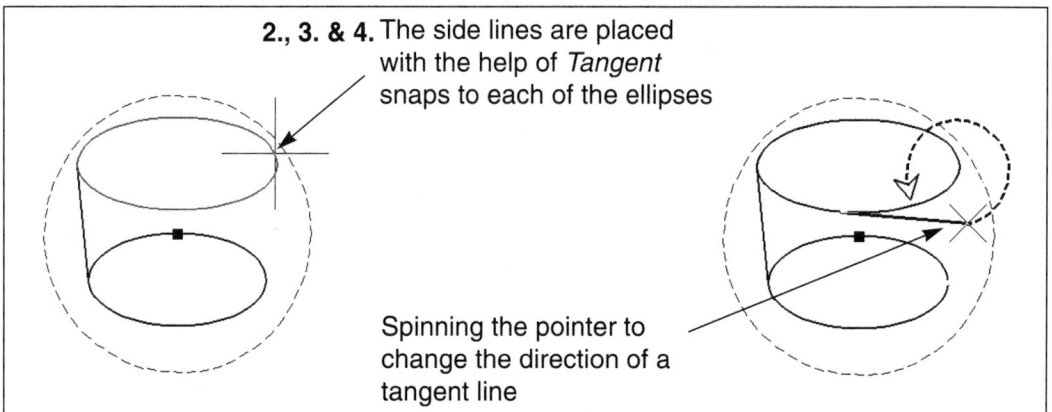

Figure 5.6 Placing the seat side lines for the Office Chair

Arcs

An *Arc* can either be a section of a circle or an ellipse. It has a *Center* and *End Points*, which together define its *Radius* (or *Radii*) and its *Sweep angle*. *Circular* arcs can also be placed using the *Place Smartline* tool, see "The Place SmartLine Tool" on page 2-11 and page 3-16.

The Arcs Tool Box

The tools in this box are in three sections, separated by boundary lines. The first tool is by itself, this one places *Circular* arcs. The next two place *Elliptical* arcs, then the remaining tools are there to *Modify* arcs already placed.

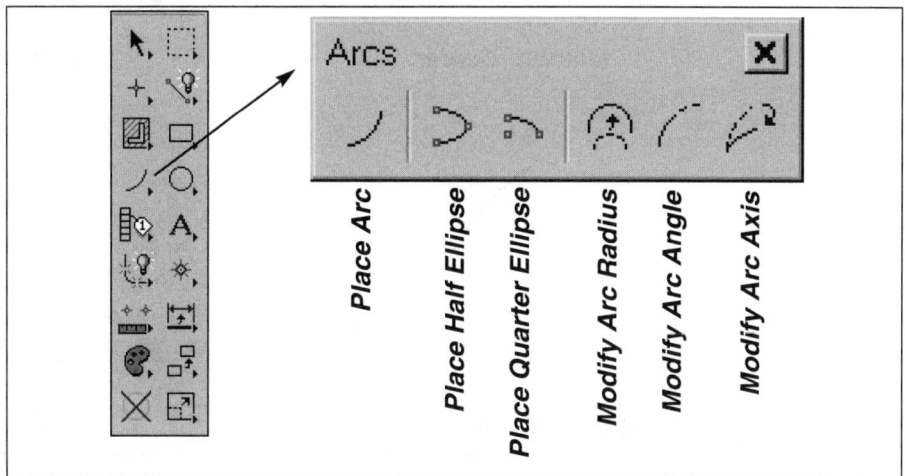

Figure 5.7   The Arcs Tool Box

The Place Arc Tool

Figure 5.8 illustrates *Circular Arcs* placed using four different combinations of tool settings *Method* and *Constraint* options. Circular arcs are placed in an *Anti-clockwise* direction with this tool, we do not have an option to place them either way as we do with *Place Smartline*. This tool, however, has the option of placing arcs by *Edge Points*, an option not offered when placing arc segments with *Place Smartline*.

The numbers indicate the order that the *Data Points* are placed

All Constraints *Off*:

All Constraints *On*:
R= *Radius*
θ_1 = *Start Angle*
θ_2 = *Rotation Angle*

Method: *Center*

Method: *Center*

Method: *Edge*

Method: *Edge*

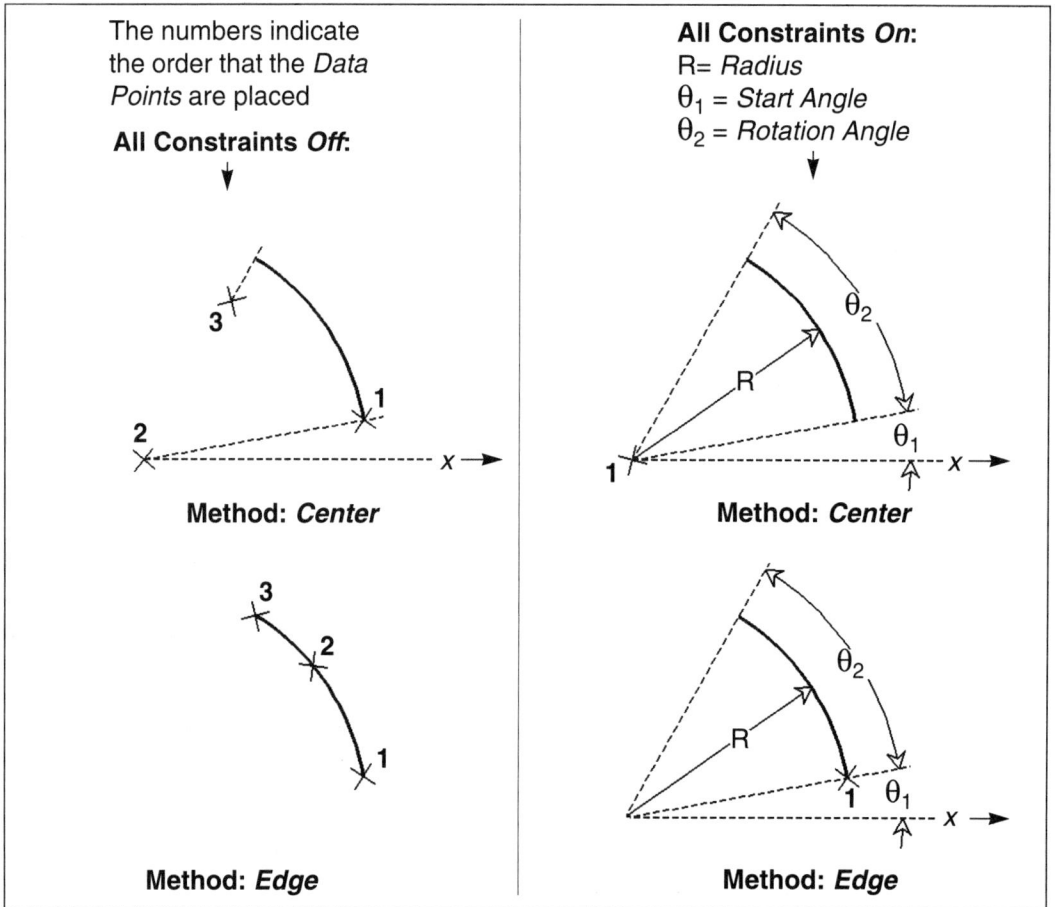

Figure 5.8   Placing Circular Arcs

The Place Half Ellipse Tool

A *Half Ellipse* is an *Elliptical Arc* with a *Sweep Angle* of **180°**. It is defined by three data points and cannot be constrained by tool settings. The first data point defines one end of the primary axis, the second can be anywhere on the ellipse, the third defines the other end of the primary axis.

The Place Quarter Ellipse Tool

A *Quarter Ellipse* is an *Elliptical Arc* with a *Sweep Angle* of **90°**. It is defined by three data points and cannot be constrained by tool settings. The first data point defines one *Endpoint*, the second can be anywhere on the *Primary Axis*, the third defines the *Other Endpoint*.

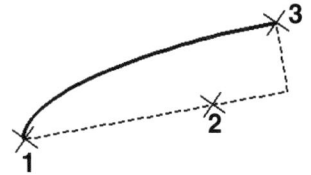

The Modify Arc Radius Tool

This tool simultaneously modifies the *Radius*, *Sweep Angle* and the *Center* position, with only the *Endpoints* maintained.

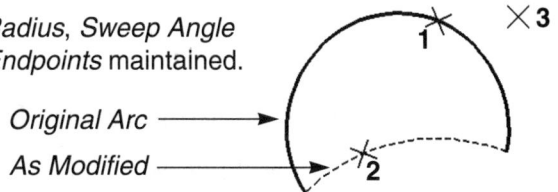

Original Arc

As Modified

The Modify Arc Angle Tool

The *Sweep Angle* (or *length* of the arc) is the only dimension changed. The arc is identified with a data point near the end to be modified, the new endpoint falls on an imaginary line passing through the *Arc Center* and the second *Data Point*. The change in *Sweep Angle* may be controlled using *AccuDraw*.

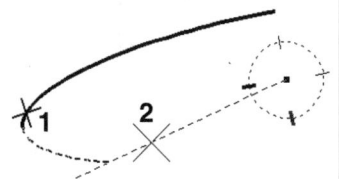

The Modify Arc Axis Tool

The length of either *Axis* of the arc can be changed, either lengthened or shortened. The position of the first *Data Point* identifying the arc (see diagrams **(a)** and **(b)**) defines the axis to be modified. Only one axis may be modified if the arc's *Sweep Angle* is less than **90°**

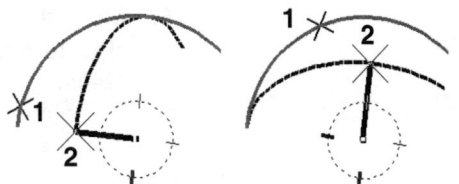

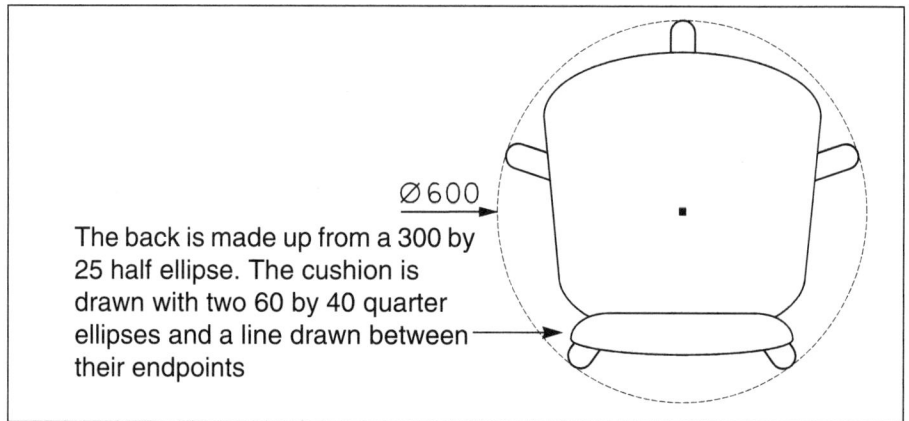

Ø 600

The back is made up from a 300 by 25 half ellipse. The cushion is drawn with two 60 by 40 quarter ellipses and a line drawn between their endpoints

Figure 5.9   The seatback section of the Office Chair

Office Chair Example (Stage 3)

Now the *Place Half Ellipse* and the *Place Quarter Ellipse* tools will be used to form the seatback section of the Office Chair. The cushion part of this section will be completed with a line placed using keypoint snaps to define its exact position.

◆ **Place the back curve for the seatback**

1. Select the *Place Half Ellipse* tool from the *Arcs* tool box, see Figure 5.7 for its location.

2. Snap to the *Active Point* (do not accept), press <**O**>, if necessary press <**Spacebar**> to change to *Rectangular Coordinates*.

3. Move the pointer down and to the left, key in **200** to each of the AccuDraw data entry fields, *Accept*.
    We have entered the point defining one end of the axis.

4. Move the pointer to the right and down the screen, key in **200** to the *x* field, **25** to the *y*, *Accept*.
    Now we have a point on the ellipse, the element dynamically displays.

5. Move the pointer to the right and up the screen, key in (or use <**Page Up**> to recall previous input) **200** to the *x* field, **25** to the *y*, *Accept, Reset*.

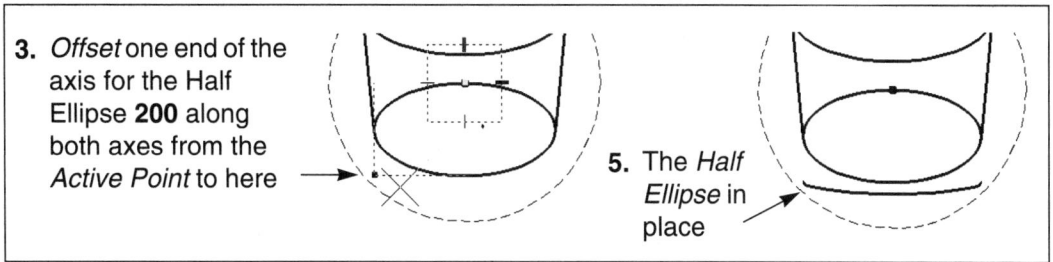

3. *Offset* one end of the axis for the Half Ellipse **200** along both axes from the *Active Point* to here ➞

5. The *Half Ellipse* in place

Figure 5.10   Placing the seatback line for the Chair

We will place a *Quarter Ellipse* to form one side of the seatback cushion.

◆ **Place one side of the seatback cushion**

1. Select the *Place Quarter Ellipse* tool from the *Arcs* tool box, found beside the *Place Half Ellipse* tool (see Figure 5.7).

2. Snap to the left end of the seatback line (half ellipse), *Accept* to enter one end of the ellipse quarter.

3. Move the pointer directly to the right, key in **60** to enter a point on the axis, *Accept.*

   We could have entered the point anywhere on the axis, but defining the position makes it easier to complete the element in this example.

4. Move the pointer directly up the screen, key in **40**, *Accept* to enter the endpoint, *Reset.*

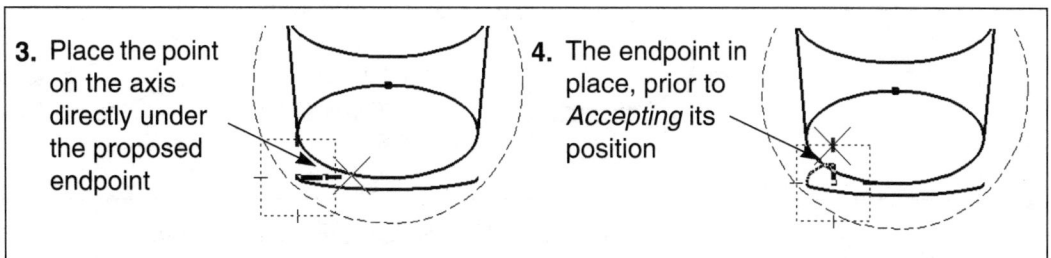

3. Place the point on the axis directly under the proposed endpoint

4. The endpoint in place, prior to *Accepting* its position

Figure 5.11   forming one side of the seatback cushion

A copy of this *Quarter Ellipse* will be *Mirrored* about a *Vertical* in the next exercise, to form the other side of the seatback cushion.

◆ **Complete the seatback cushion**

1. Select the *Mirror* tool from the *Manipulate* tool box (see page 4-18), set *Mirror About* to *Vertical*, *Make Copy On* (checked), the remaining settings *Off*.

2. Identify the *Quarter Ellipse* with a data point.
   The mirror image of the element will dynamically display.

3. Snap to the *Active Point* (or any other keypoint on the vertical centerline of the drawing), *Accept*, *Reset*.

4. Select the *Place Line* tool, enter the *First* point by snapping to the free end of one of the quarter ellipses, *Accept*.

5. Enter the *End* point by snapping to the free end of the other quarter ellipse, *Accept*, *Reset*.

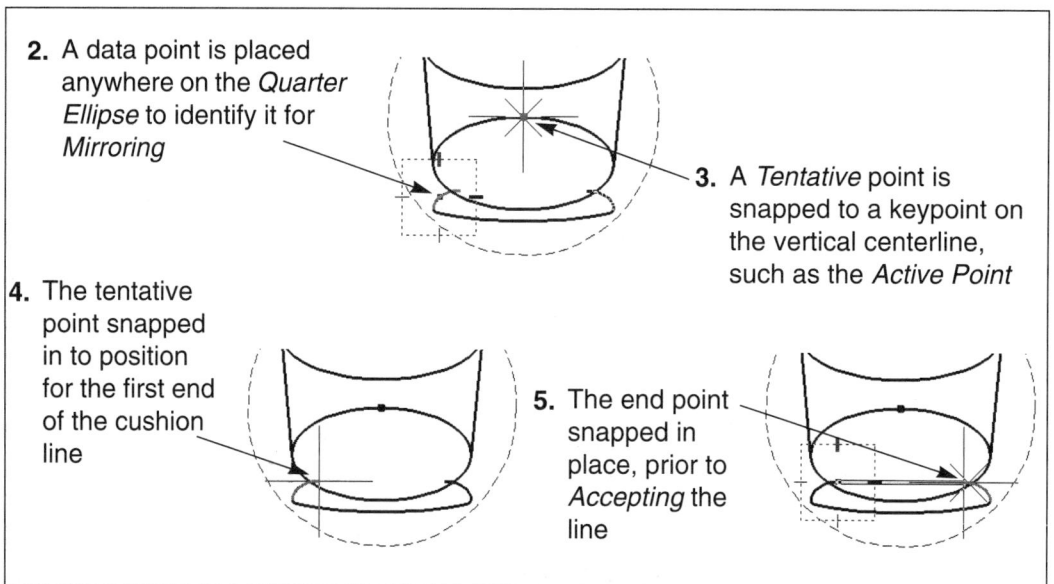

2. A data point is placed anywhere on the *Quarter Ellipse* to identify it for *Mirroring*

3. A *Tentative* point is snapped to a keypoint on the vertical centerline, such as the *Active Point*

4. The tentative point snapped in to position for the first end of the cushion line

5. The end point snapped in place, prior to *Accepting* the line

Figure 5.12   Completing the seatback cushion

The Accudraw Compass appearing in Figure 5.12 shows that the facility is still running, but it has no function to perform here. There is no need to stop it for these operations, it does not get in the way.

Modifying Existing Elements

The geometry of existing elements will often need to modified after they are placed. This may be part of the process of making changes to a previously completed design, but it is may also be part of the original design creation process. Elements may be placed in one form, then *Modified* to meet the exact requirements of the new design.

The Modify Tool Box

This is one of the larger tool boxes and one of the most frequently opened. The *Modify* tools all alter the geometry in some way. As a comparison, the *Manipulate* tools (introduced in chapter 4) generally left elements intact, but moved or replicated them.

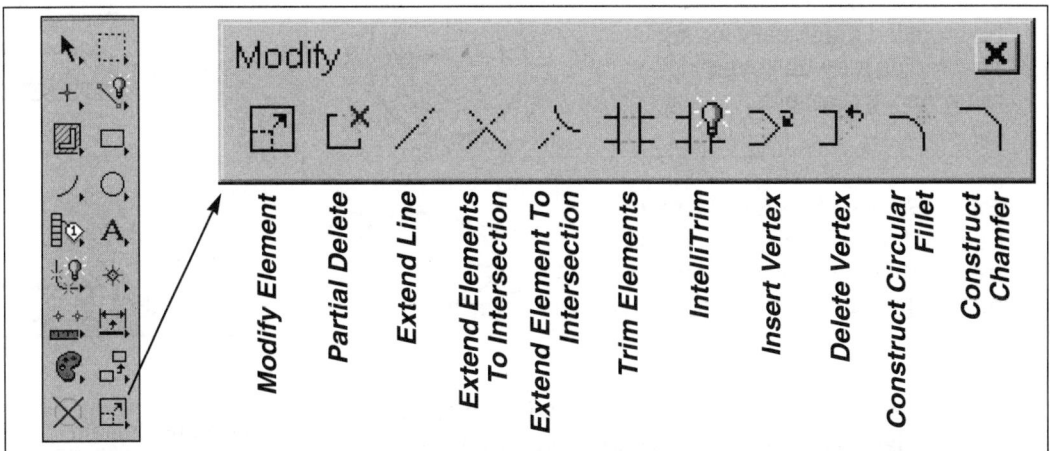

Figure 5.13   The Modify Tool Box

The Modify Element Tool

With this single tool we can modify elements in many ways. Its functionality changes initially with the type of element we identify for modification, then it changes again depending on the part of the element that is identified. Combining this one tool with the *AccuDraw* facility (for precision operations) we can:

- *Move* a vertex of a linear element such as a shape, line or line string;
- *Change* vertices of complex shapes and complex chains to rounded segments and vice-versa;

- *Modify* rounded segments of complex shapes and complex chains;
- *Scale* circular arcs (maintaining sweep angle) and blocks (about a vertex);
- *Change* the length of an axis of an ellipse or the radius of a circle;
- *Move* dimension text and change dimension extension line length.

The *Endpoint* of a *Line* can be modified by changing its length and/or angle. The identifying data point (**1**) is placed near the end to be modified

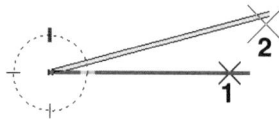

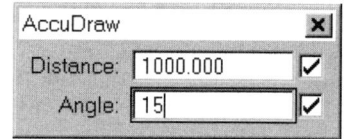

AccuDraw
Distance: 1000.000
Angle: 15

The *Radius* of a *Circle* may be modified graphically, or a new radius may be keyed in to an AccuDraw field.

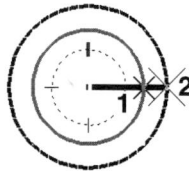

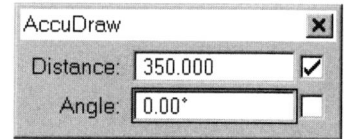

AccuDraw
Distance: 350.000
Angle: 0.00°

Either Radius of an *Ellipse* may be modified, the axis to be modified is chosen by placing data point (**1**) near to it.

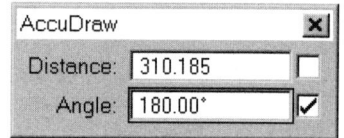

AccuDraw
Distance: 310.185
Angle: 180.00°

The *Sweep Angle* of an *Arc* may be modified by placing the identifying data point (**1**) near, but **not at** the end to be altered.

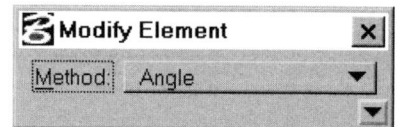

Modify Element
Method: Angle

The AccuDraw origin moves to the arc center with its *x* axis aligned with the fixed endpoint.

Choose *Method: Angle* in *Tool Settings*, the new sweep angle may now be set graphically or keyed in.

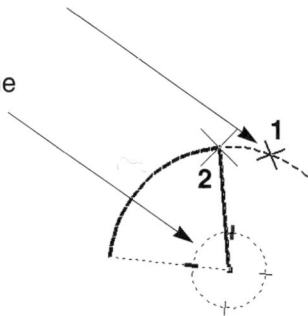

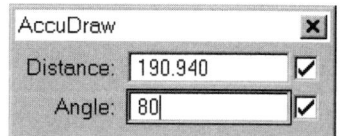

AccuDraw
Distance: 190.940
Angle: 80

Figure 5.14   Modify Element tool operations

The *Tool Settings* window changes with the element selected when we are using the *Modify Element* tool. When an arc is selected, the *Method* of modification becomes optional, whereas no options are offered when we select lines, circles and ellipses. Try placing some elements and modifying them, *Place Mark* before you start and *Undo Other>To Mark* when you have finished.

The *Radius* of an *Arc* may be modified *Without changing its center point* by placing the data point identifying the arc **away from** an endpoint.

The AccuDraw origin moves to the arc center with its *x* axis aligned with the View window axis.

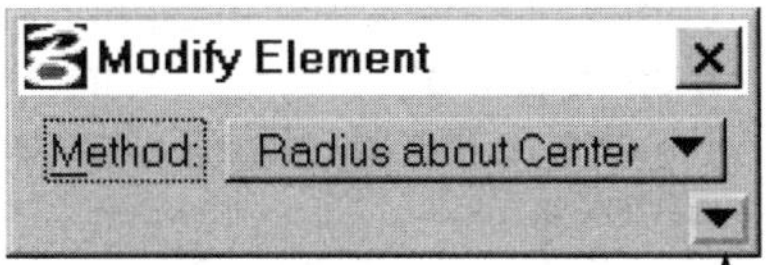

(This "More" arrow displays options for "SmartLine" modifications)

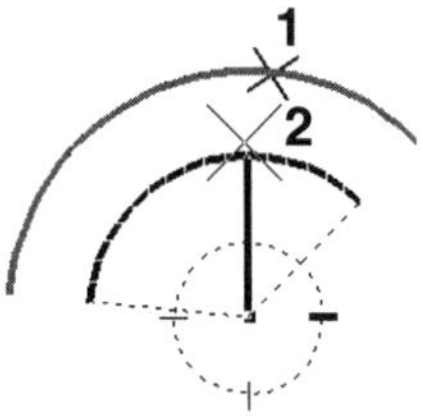

Choose *Method:* **Radius about Center** in *Tool Settings*, the new radius may now be set graphically or keyed in.

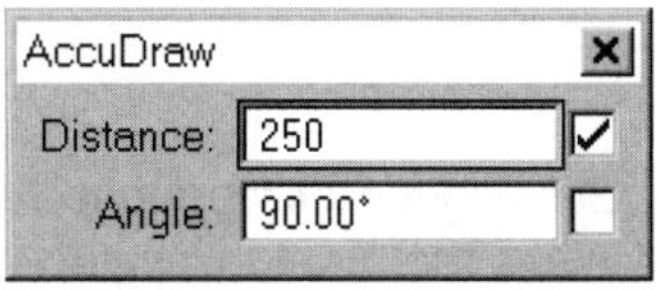

The *Radius* of an *Arc* may be modified *Without changing its endpoints* by placing the data point identifying the arc **away from** an endpoint.

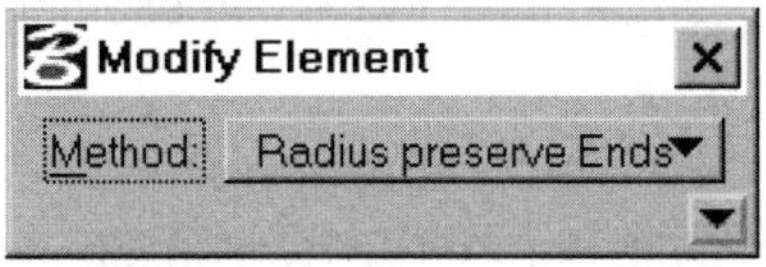

The AccuDraw origin moves to the arc center with its *x* axis aligned with the View window axis.

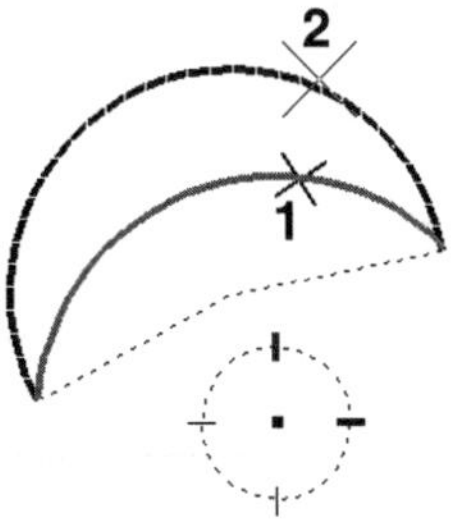

Choose *Method:* **Radius preserve Ends** in *Tool Settings*, the new radius may now be set graphically or a position of a point on the edge of the modified arc keyed in.

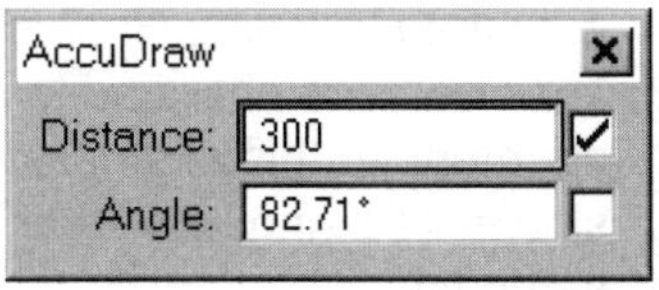

Figure 5.15   Modify Element tool operations

The illustrations in Figures 5.14 and 5.15 show examples of *single-segment* elements. The *Modify Element* tool will also alter *multi-segment* elements in a variety of ways. Multi-segment elements include shapes, line strings, complex chains and complex shapes. Figure 5.16 illustrates some modifications to these.

A *Vertex* can be moved under the control of Accudraw, while the tool settings for *Modify Element* provide options for changing *Vertex Type* and constraining the element to remain *Orthogonal*.

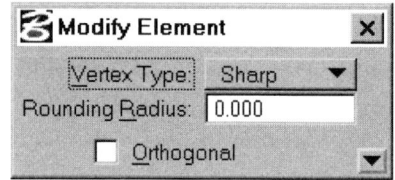

When the element is identified near a vertex **(1)** the drawing plane origin moves to that vertex, with its axes aligned to the identified segment if the vertex is 90°.

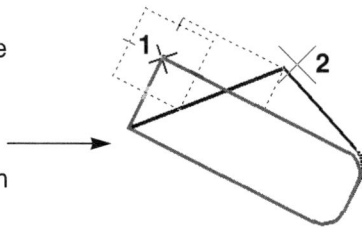

In this example the *Vertex Type* has been left as *Sharp* and it has not been constrained to remain orthogonal.

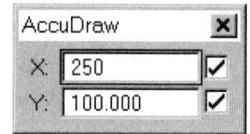

Clicking the *Orthogonal* check box in the Tool Settings window has this effect when the data points are both placed as in the above example.

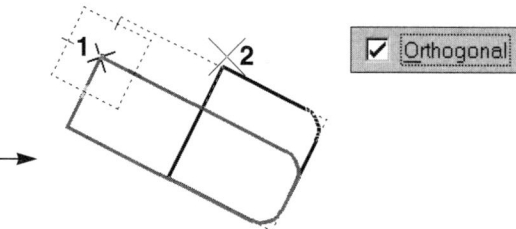

With the *Vertex Type* option set to **Rounded** and a radius keyed in to the *Rounding Radius* field a vertex can be changed to an arc segment. In this example it is shown as being moved at the same time.

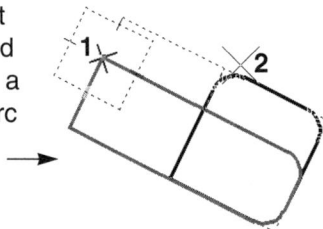

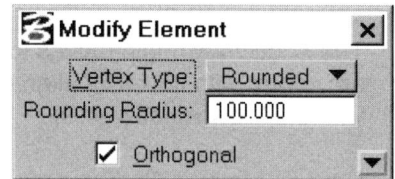

If we identify a segment at or near its midpoint **(1)**, the drawing plane moves to that point, with its *x* axis aligned to the identified segment. The segment will retain its rotation while the remainder of the element is being re-shaped.

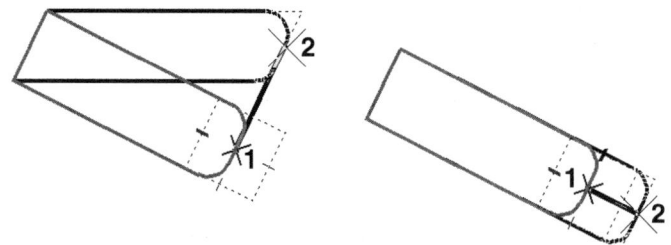

Figure 5.16   Modify Element tool operations

The Modify Element tool has been shown to combine a wide range of operations with the controllability offered by AccuDraw. Few tools can perform such a variety of functions, the examples shown in Figures 5.14, 5.15 and 5.16 do not illustrate all of the possibilities. Carry out your own experiments on a variety of temporary elements to gain more experience with the tool.

The Partial Delete Tool

This tool is used to delete part only of an element. In the case of open elements such as lines, we identify a *Start Point* and an *End Point* for the *Partial Delete* with data points. These points must both be in the interior of the element, there are other tools to reduce the length of open elements. Where we are deleting a part of a closed element, such as the full ellipse, we also need to indicate the *Direction of the Partial Delete*.

When an open element has a section removed by a *Partial Delete*, it becomes two elements of the same type. For example a line becomes two lines, an arc becomes two arcs etc. When we delete part of a closed element it becomes an open element, for example a shape will become a line string, an ellipse will become an elliptical arc.

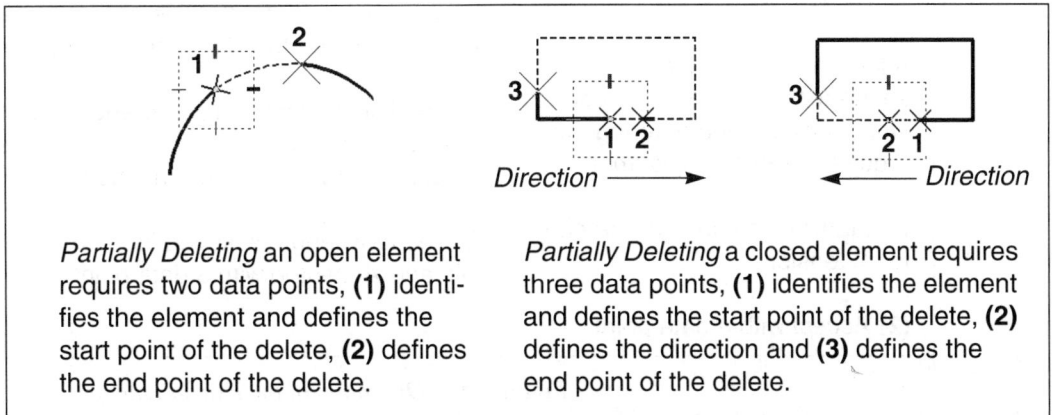

Partially Deleting an open element requires two data points, **(1)** identifies the element and defines the start point of the delete, **(2)** defines the end point of the delete.

Partially Deleting a closed element requires three data points, **(1)** identifies the element and defines the start point of the delete, **(2)** defines the direction and **(3)** defines the end point of the delete.

Figure 5.17   Partial Delete tool Operation

This tool can be controlled to make precise gaps in the elements using AccuDraw or points placed using snaps. It is also very common to use *Partial Delete* to break the element practically anywhere along its length, giving us two ends to modify later. The *Extend* tools we are about to introduce would most likely be used for these modifications.

The Extend Line Tool

Extend Line is an abbreviated name for this tool, as it can actually *Shorten* lines as well as *Extend* them. It operates on *Lines*, *Line Strings* and *Multi-Lines* (to be introduced later).

We have the choice of changing the length of the line graphically, or by keyboard entry. If we need to use a precision keyed in value, we again have two choices:

- The distance to extend (use minus for shorten) the line can be keyed in to the field in the Tool Settings window;

- We can key in a new total length for the line in the AccuDraw window.

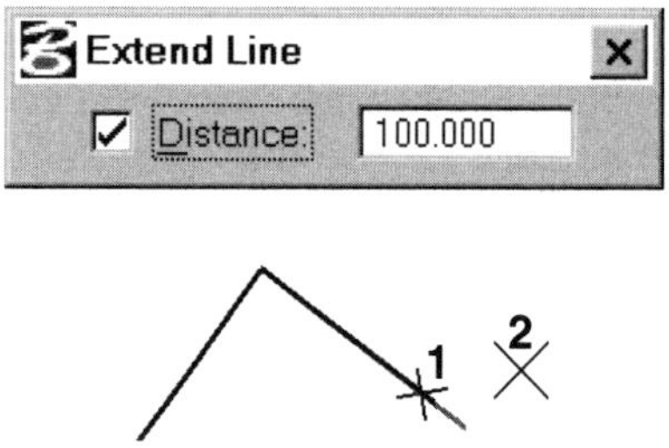

A line can be extended (or shortened) by clicking the constraint box *On* and entering the required extension *Distance*.

(1) Identify the line near the end for extension;

(2) *Accept* with a data point.

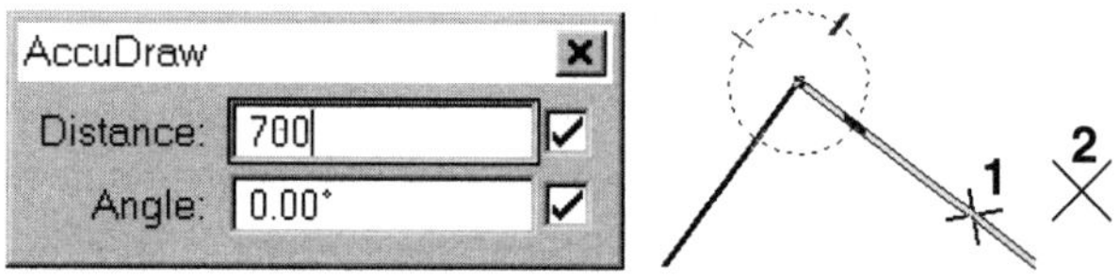

A new total length for the line can be keyed in via AccuDraw when the *Distance* constraint is *Off*.

(1) The line is identified at the end to be extended, the drawing plane origin locates at the opposite end with its *x* axis aligned to the line;

(2) The new length is keyed in to an Accudraw field and *Accepted* with a data point.

Figure 5.18   Operation of the Extend Line tool

The *Extend Line* tool is used to extend (or shorten) individual lines independently from other elements. There are other specialized extension tools for extending and shortening elements. The first of these tools to be introduced will simultaneously extend two elements to an intersection.

The Extend Two Elements To Intersection Tool

This tool affects two elements at once, each being extended or shortened to the point of intersection with the other. It will operate on arcs as well as the lines and line strings operated on by the *Extend Line* tool. There are no *Tool Settings* to make to *Extend Two Elements To Intersection*.

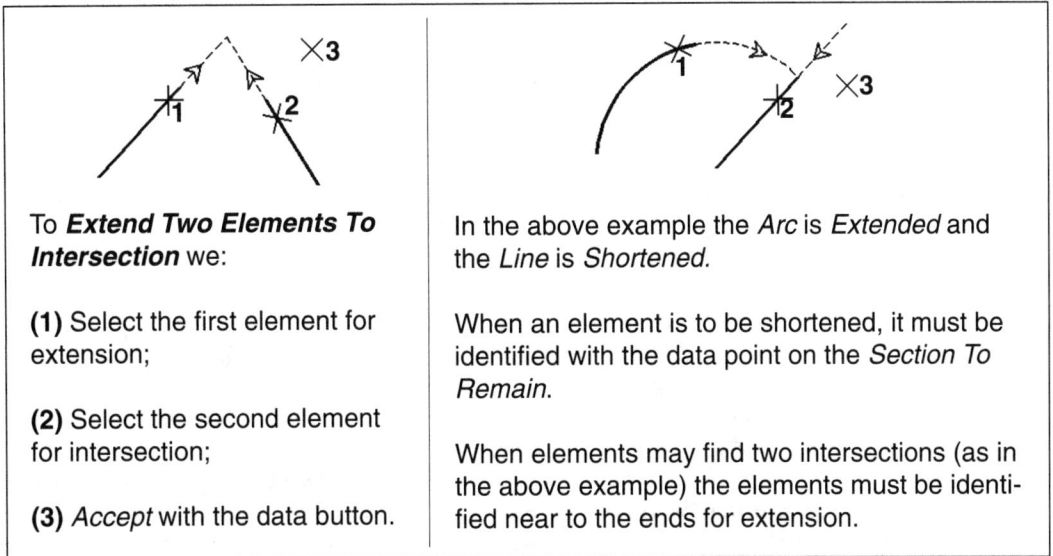

To **Extend Two Elements To Intersection** we:

(1) Select the first element for extension;

(2) Select the second element for intersection;

(3) *Accept* with the data button.

In the above example the *Arc* is *Extended* and the *Line* is *Shortened*.

When an element is to be shortened, it must be identified with the data point on the *Section To Remain*.

When elements may find two intersections (as in the above example) the elements must be identified near to the ends for extension.

Figure 5.19   Extending two elements to intersect

The Extend Element To Intersection Tool

This tool extends or shortens an arc, line or line string to the point of intersection with the another element, or its extension. The second element is not affected.

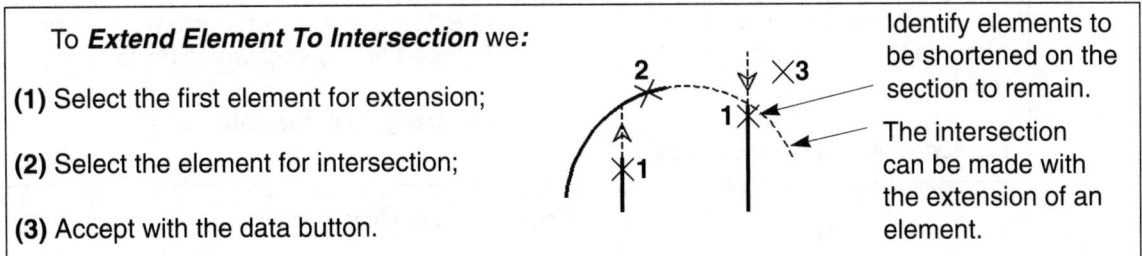

To **Extend Element To Intersection** we:

(1) Select the first element for extension;

(2) Select the element for intersection;

(3) Accept with the data button.

Identify elements to be shortened on the section to remain.

The intersection can be made with the extension of an element.

Figure 5.20   Extending an element to an intersection

The Trim Element Tool

This tool allows us to trim an element or a series of elements back to the point where they intersect with a *Cutting* element, or multiple cutting elements. The elements to be trimmed and the cutting elements can be lines, line strings, arcs, curves, shapes, ellipses, complex chains or complex shapes. The trimming can be back from the end of an element, or an internal section may be removed.

When we have more than one *Cutting Element* we need to make them into a temporary group by multiple selection (see "The PowerSelector Tool" on page 4-27 or "The Element Selection Tool" on page 4-25) before selecting the *Trim Element* tool.

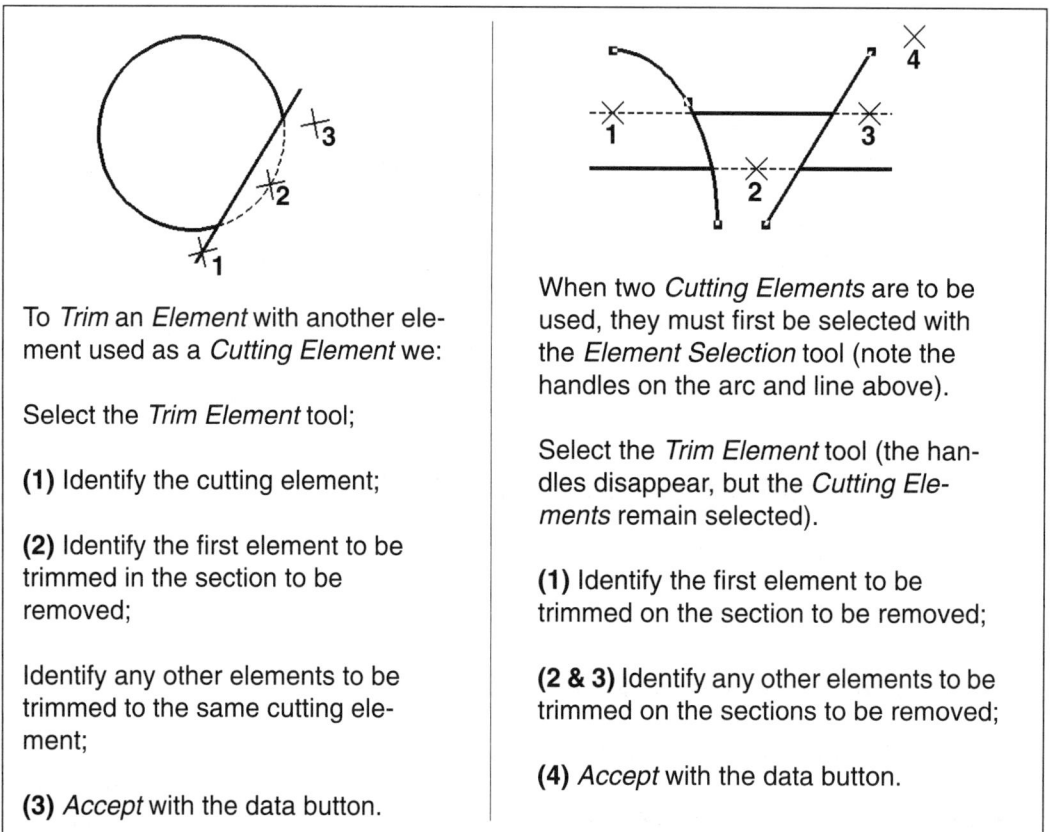

To *Trim* an *Element* with another element used as a *Cutting Element* we:

Select the *Trim Element* tool;

(1) Identify the cutting element;

(2) Identify the first element to be trimmed in the section to be removed;

Identify any other elements to be trimmed to the same cutting element;

(3) *Accept* with the data button.

When two *Cutting Elements* are to be used, they must first be selected with the *Element Selection* tool (note the handles on the arc and line above).

Select the *Trim Element* tool (the handles disappear, but the *Cutting Elements* remain selected).

(1) Identify the first element to be trimmed on the section to be removed;

(2 & 3) Identify any other elements to be trimmed on the sections to be removed;

(4) *Accept* with the data button.

Figure 5.21   Trimming elements

The IntelliTrim Tool

This tool will not only *Trim* elements, it will also *Extend* and *Cut* them as well. It will *Trim* or *Cut* most types of elements. However, only lines, line strings and complex open elements (called *Complex Chains*) that finish with a line or line string may be *Extended*. The tool has two modes of operation, selectable from its tool settings window, *Quick* and *Advanced*.

Quick Mode - Trim and Extend

In these operations the elements to be modified are identified by drawing an imaginary line through them. For *Trim* and *Extend*, the cutting element is selected before this line is drawn. The operations are illustrated in Figure 5.22.

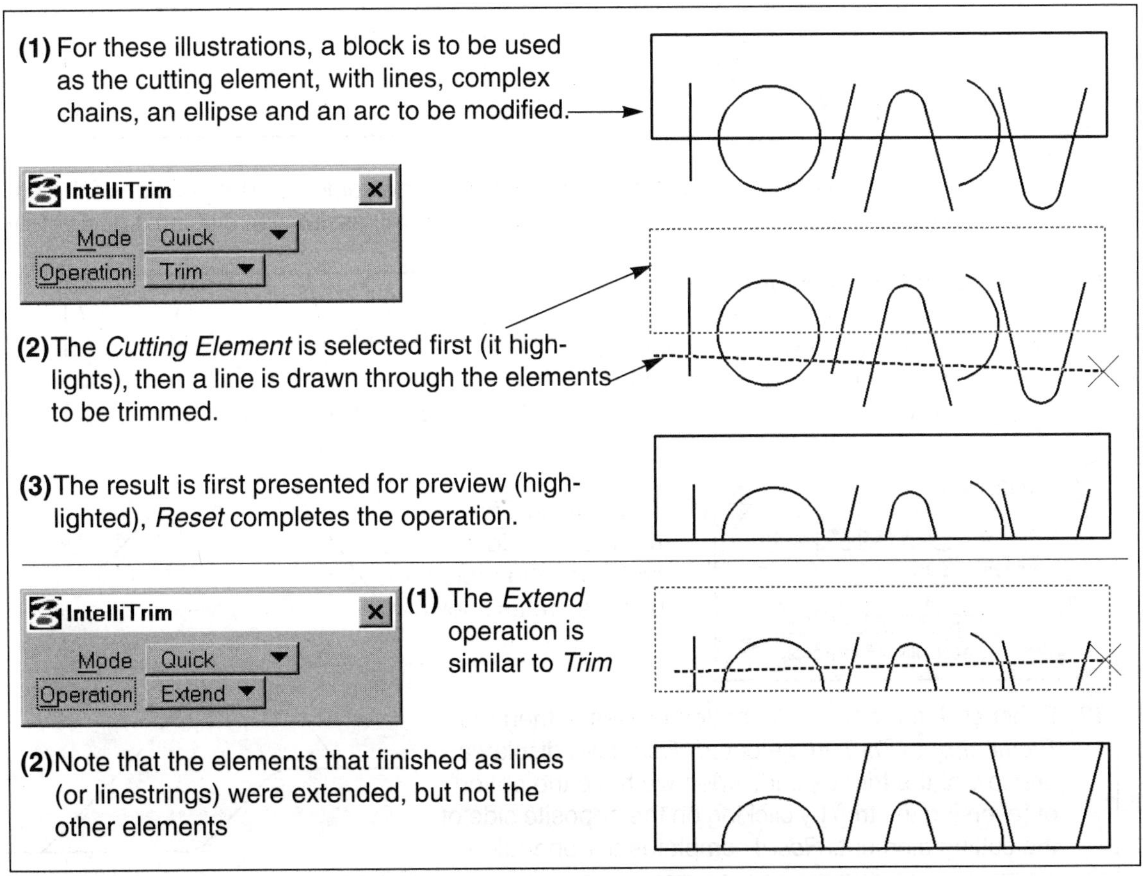

(1) For these illustrations, a block is to be used as the cutting element, with lines, complex chains, an ellipse and an arc to be modified.——→

IntelliTrim ✕

Mode   Quick ▼
Operation   Trim ▼

(2) The *Cutting Element* is selected first (it high-lights), then a line is drawn through the elements to be trimmed.

(3) The result is first presented for preview (high-lighted), *Reset* completes the operation.

IntelliTrim ✕

Mode   Quick ▼
Operation   Extend ▼

(1) The *Extend* operation is similar to *Trim*

(2) Note that the elements that finished as lines (or linestrings) were extended, but not the other elements

Figure 5.22   IntelliTrim - Quick mode

Quick Mode - Cut

Cut is used to split elements into two parts. As with Trim, lines, line strings, curves, arcs, ellipses, shapes, complex chains and shapes may all be Cut. The cut made has zero width, thus the result will not be apparent until the elements are selected for manipulation. The operation is illustrated at the top of figure 5.23.

Advanced Mode

Advanced mode only supports Trim and Extend, using Cutting Elements as with the Trim Element tool (page 5-22). In this mode, the tool is able to simultaneously Trim and Extend elements. Multiple cutting elements and elements to trim/extend may be selected to be operated on simultaneously. See the lower part of Figure 5.23.

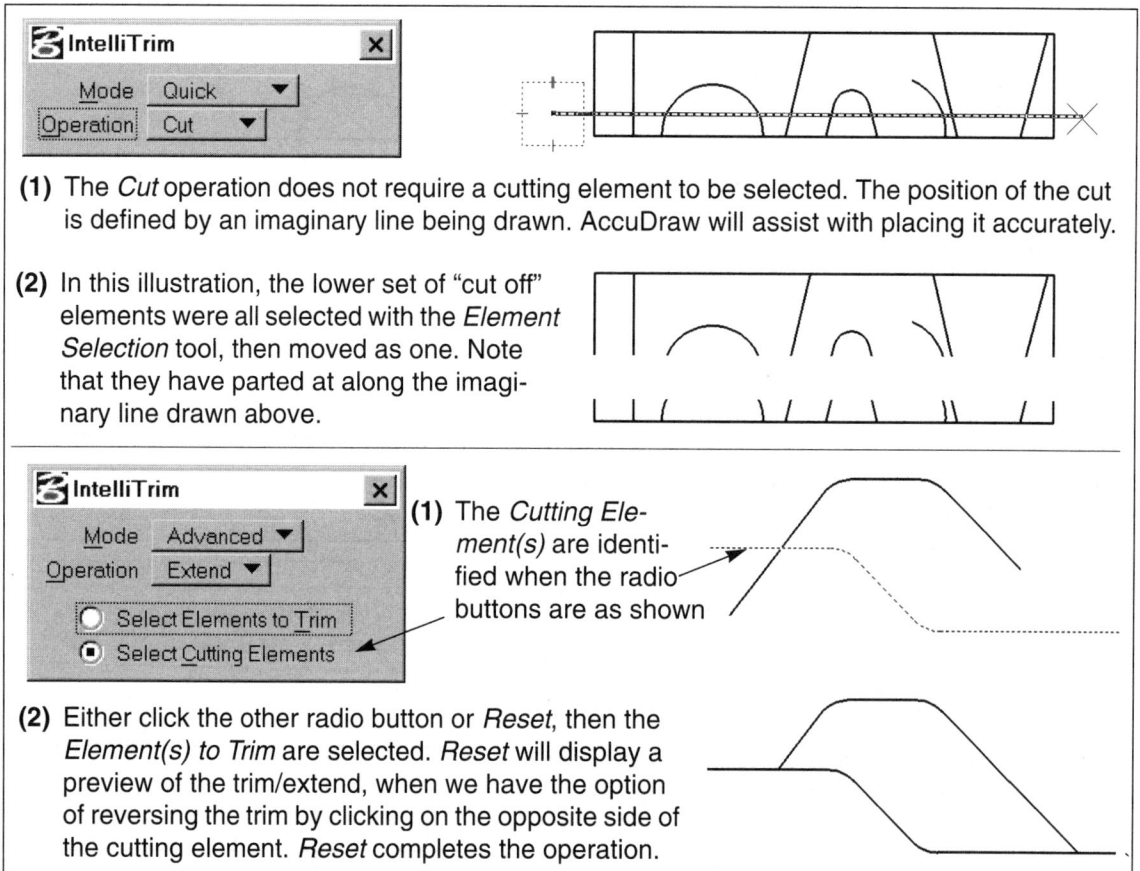

(1) The *Cut* operation does not require a cutting element to be selected. The position of the cut is defined by an imaginary line being drawn. AccuDraw will assist with placing it accurately.

(2) In this illustration, the lower set of "cut off" elements were all selected with the *Element Selection* tool, then moved as one. Note that they have parted at along the imaginary line drawn above.

(1) The *Cutting Element(s)* are identified when the radio buttons are as shown

(2) Either click the other radio button or *Reset*, then the *Element(s) to Trim* are selected. *Reset* will display a preview of the trim/extend, when we have the option of reversing the trim by clicking on the opposite side of the cutting element. *Reset* completes the operation.

Figure 5.23 More IntelliTrim options.

The Insert Vertex Tool

The *Insert Vertex* tool can be used to:

- Insert a vertex in a line, converting it to a *linestring*;
- Insert a vertex in a linestring or shape;
- Attach a line segment as an extension to a line or line string;
- Insert a vertex in a multi-line or in the control polygon of a B-spline curve (both of these elements are to be introduced later in the book);
- Extend a curve placed by points (to be introduced later);
- Add an extra extension line within an existing dimension element (to be introduced later).

To *Insert a Vertex* in a line or line segment of an element type we:

Select the *Insert Vertex* tool;

(1) Identify the line or line segment;

(2) Place the new vertex with a data point.

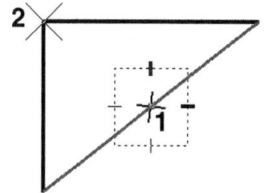

To *Attach a line segment* to an existing line or line string we:

Select the *Insert Vertex* tool;

(1) Identify the line or line segment at or near the end for the attachment;

(2) Place the new end point for the line string with a data point.

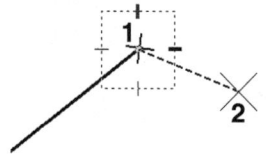

A *Shape* can have vertices inserted in the same way as a line or line string. The maximum number of vertices for a shape or line string is 101.

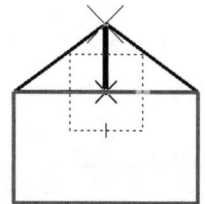

Figure 5.24   Inserting vertices

The Delete Vertex Tool

The *Delete Vertex* tool can be used to:

- Remove vertices from linestrings and shapes;
- Remove vertices from multi-line elements (to be introduced later);
- Remove an extension line within an existing dimension element (to be introduced later).

To *Delete a Vertex* in a line, line segment or shape we:

Select the *Delete Vertex* tool;

(1) Place a data point on or near to the vertex to be removed.

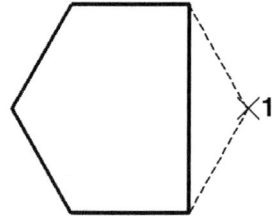

Figure 5.25   Deleting vertices

The last two tools in the *Modify* tool box modify vertices, making them into circular fillets or chamfers.

The Construct Circular Fillet Tool

This tool places circular fillets with a keyed-in radius at element vertices and between elements. The elements or segments of an element either side of the fillet may be:

- Left unchanged;
- The *First* side identified *Truncated* at the point of tangency to the fillet;
- *Both* sides *Truncated* at the point of tangency to the fillet.

The *Fillets* placed by this tool are new elements, placed with the currently active *Element Attributes*. They may have different symbology to the elements they are placed between, they may even be on a different level.

The controls for *Constructing Circular Fillets* are in the Tool Settings window, AccuDraw plays no part.

With the *Truncate* option set to **None** neither of the original elements or segments are modified.

To *Construct a Circular Fillet* we:

Select the tool and key in the *Radius* to the Tool Settings field;

(1) Identify the first element or segment;

(2) Identify the second element or segment;

(3) *Accept* with the data button.

Construct Circular Fillet ⊠
Radius: 400.0000
Truncate: None ▼

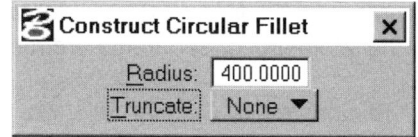

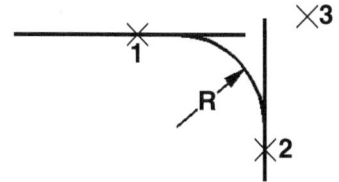

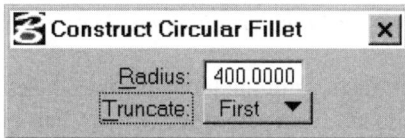

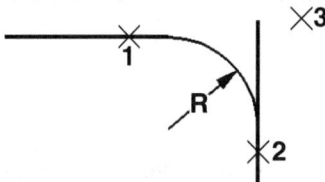

With the *Truncate* option set to **First** the first of the original elements or segments is *Truncated*, the other left unmodified.

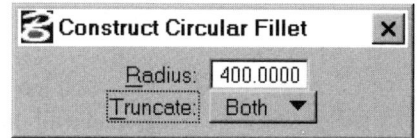

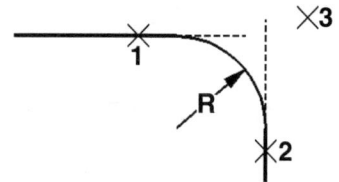

Construct Circular Fillet ⊠
Radius: 400.0000
Truncate: First ▼

With the *Truncate* option set to **Both** the original elements or segments are both *Truncated* to the point of tangency with the *Fillet*.

Construct Circular Fillet ⊠
Radius: 400.0000
Truncate: Both ▼

Figure 5.26   Construct Circular Fillet tool operations

The Construct Chamfer Tool

This tool constructs a chamfer at element vertices and between elements. The elements, or segments of an element either side of the chamfer are *Truncated* at their point of intersection with the *Chamfer* line.

The *Chamfer* line constructed by this tool is a new element, it is placed with the currently active *Element Attributes*, as is the case with *Circular Fillets*. The distances from the intersection of the original elements or segments *to the ends of the* Chamfer are keyed in to fields in the Tool Settings window.

With the *Truncate* option set to **None** neither of the original elements or segments are modified.

Construct Chamfer   [x]

Distance 1: 550.0000
Distance 2: 400.0000

To *Construct a Circular Fillet* we:

Select the tool and key in **D₁** to the Tool Settings *Distance 1* field, **D₂** to *Distance 2*;

(1) Identify the first element or segment;

(2) Identify the second element or segment;

(3) *Accept* with the data button.

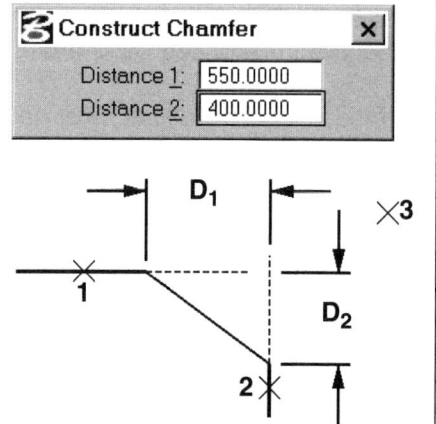

Figure 5.27   Construct Chamfer tool operation

When you have completed your experiments with the tools just introduced, undo or delete the all the elements placed that do not form part of the Office Chair example in "cells.dgn". Now we will complete this example, making use of some of the tools we have introduced from the *Modify* tool box.

Office Chair Example (Stage 4)

We will now use some of the tools just introduced to remove the unwanted sections of linework from the seat and seatback.

◆ **Trim the rear ellipse to the seatback cushion line**

1. Select the *Element Selection* tool, click on one of the quarter ellipses, then hold down the **<Ctrl>** key while clicking on the other.
    Handles will appear on both elements, but they will only stay there until we select the *Trim Element* tool.

2. Select the *Trim Element* tool, data point the part of the ellipse that we want to remove on the *Identify Trim Element* prompt.

We pre-selected a temporary group of two *Cutting Elements* in step **2.**, another example of *Noun-Verb Selection*. This tool can be used without pre-selection of the cutting element, but only one element can be identified this way.

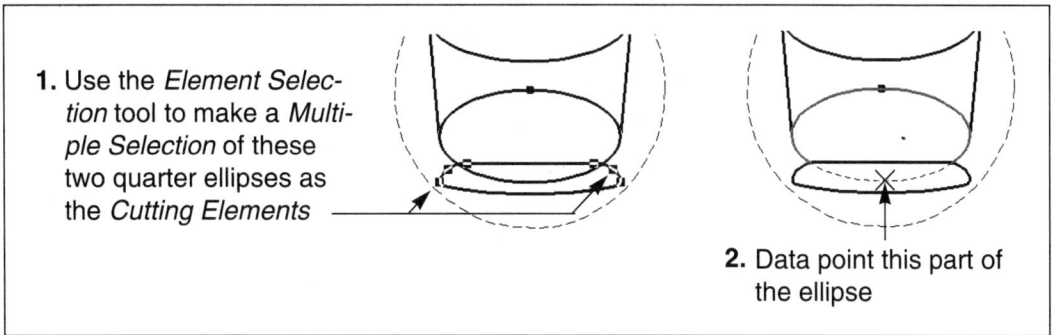

1. Use the *Element Selection* tool to make a *Multiple Selection* of these two quarter ellipses as the *Cutting Elements*

2. Data point this part of the ellipse

Figure 5.28   Trimming the rear Ellipse

The remaining full ellipse and the trimmed ellipse now must have a gap placed in them to allow us to continue with the process of removing unwanted linework.

◆ **Place a gap in the front and rear ellipses**

1. Select the *Partial Delete* tool, data point the lower edge of the full ellipse to select the *Start Point* for the next partial delete.

2. Move the pointer slightly to the left and place another data point to identify the *Direction* of the partial delete.

3. Move the pointer slightly further to the left and place another data point to identify the *End Point* of this partial delete.

4. Data point the top of the trimmed ellipse to select the *Start Point* for the partial delete.

5. Move the pointer slightly to the right and place another data point to identify the *End Point* for the partial delete.

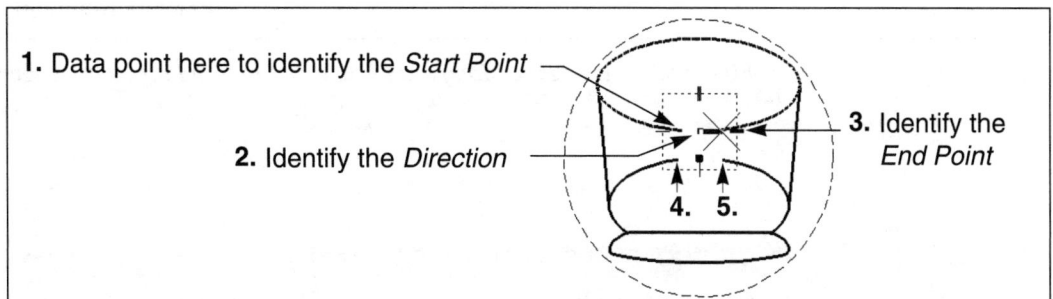

1. Data point here to identify the *Start Point*

2. Identify the *Direction*

3. Identify the *End Point*

4.   5.

Figure 5.29   Preparing the ellipses for final modification

◆ **Blend the front and rear seat edge ellipses to the sides**

1. Select the *Modify Arc Angle* tool (page 5-11).

2. Data point one of the partial ellipses near the end to be modified.
    The endpoint of the arc will now fall on a line passing through the
    center of the ellipse and the pointer.

3. Move the pointer over the side line, snap a *Tentative* point to the end
    to be blended to the arc, *Accept*, *Reset*.

4. Repeat step **3.** for the remaining three arcs.

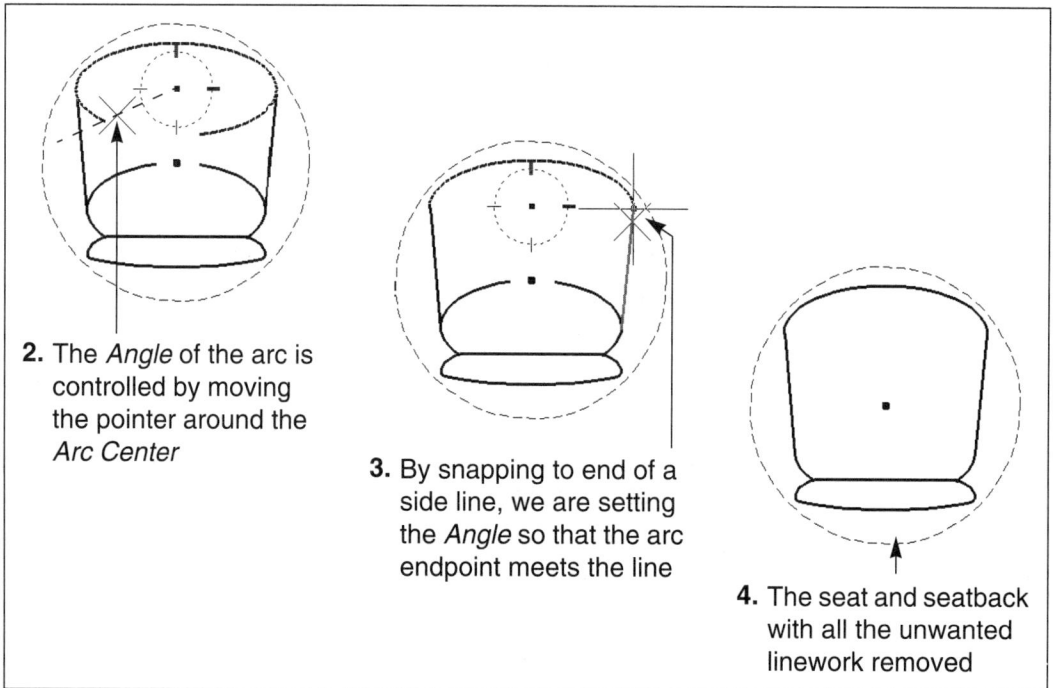

2. The *Angle* of the arc is
controlled by moving
the pointer around the
Arc Center

3. By snapping to end of a
side line, we are setting
the *Angle* so that the arc
endpoint meets the line

4. The seat and seatback
with all the unwanted
linework removed

Figure 5.30   Using the Modify Arc Angle tool to blend arcs with tangents

Office Chair Example (Stage 5)

This is the last stage of the Office Chair design, which we will retain complete to become part of other designs in following chapters. The final component to be created is the five leg swivel base. We do not need any new tools for this, *Place Smartline* will produce the first leg in the form of a *Complex Chain* composed of two line segments and an arc. This leg will be used to create a *Polar Array* of a total of five items, each rotated to radiate from the center of the chair.

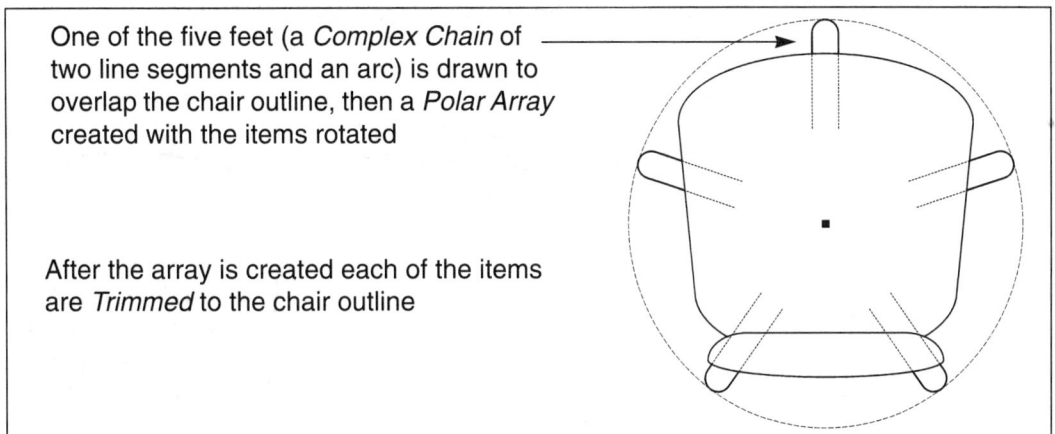

One of the five feet (a *Complex Chain* of two line segments and an arc) is drawn to overlap the chair outline, then a *Polar Array* created with the items rotated

After the array is created each of the items are *Trimmed* to the chair outline

Figure 5.31   The computer chair with the feet in position

We will start this stage by placing a "U" shaped *Complex Chain* to represent one of the feet. We will use *Place Smartline* to place the two line segments (Each **140** long) and the arc segment (**20** radius). The steps are illustrated in Figure 5.32.

◆ Place the first chair foot complex chain

1. Set the *Active Level* to **10**, *Line Style* and *Color* to **0**, *Line weight* to **2**. Start *AccuDraw* if necessary.

2. Select the *Place Smartline* tool, set the *Segment Type* to **Lines**, click *Join Elements On*, *Vertex Type* and *Rounding Radius* do not matter.

3. *Keypoint* snap a tentative point to the active point at the center, press <O> and *Offset* the first vertex up by **140**, to the left by **20**.

4. Move the pointer directly up until the line segment indexes to the previous *y* value (**140**), *Accept*.

5. With the next segment still rubberbanding from the pointer, change the *Segment Type* to **Arcs**.

6. Move the pointer directly to the right (indexed to the *x* axis), key in **20** for the position of the *Arc Center, Accept.*

7. Spin the pointer around the center in a clockwise direction to define the direction of the arc segment, *Accept* with the pointer on the +*x* drawing plane axis (3 O'clock).

8. With the next segment rubberbanding as before, change the *Segment Type back* to **Lines**.

9. Move the pointer directly down, press <**Enter**> (For *Smart Lock*), snap to the first vertex placed, *Accept, Reset*.

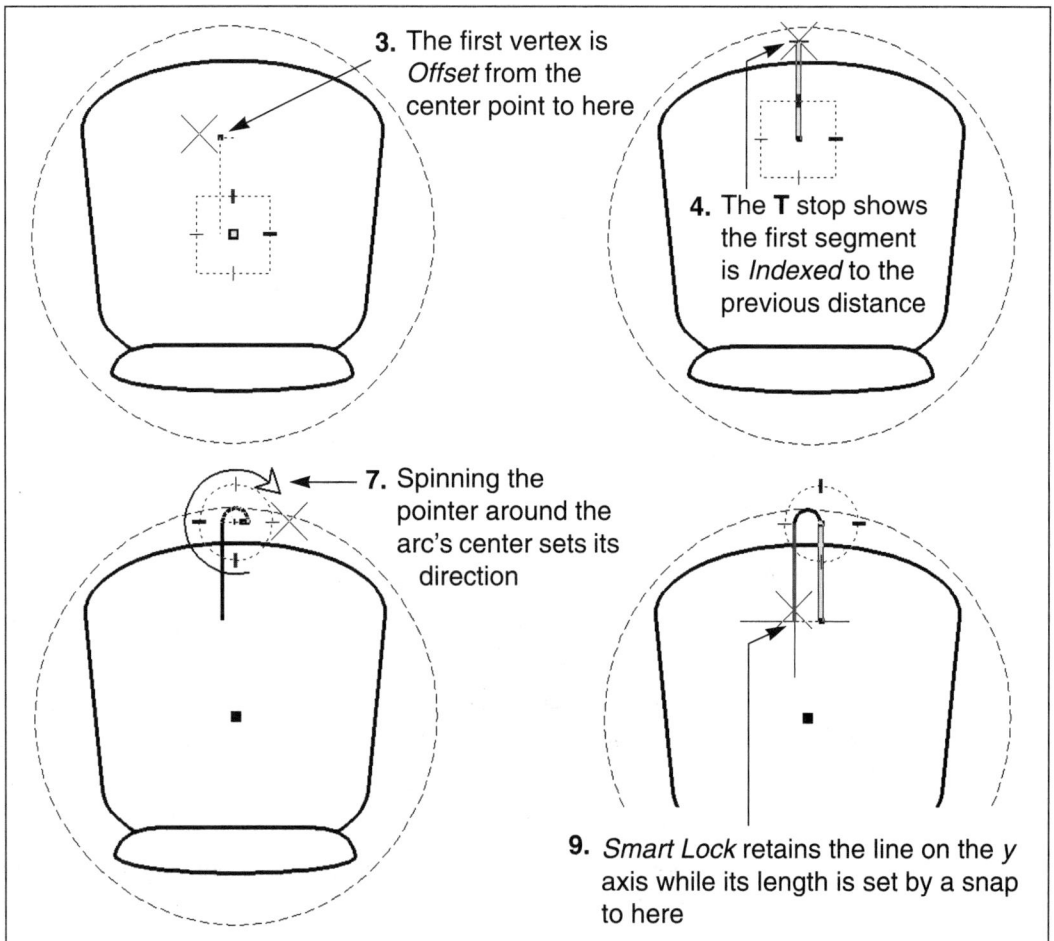

3. The first vertex is *Offset* from the center point to here

4. The **T** stop shows the first segment is *Indexed* to the previous distance

7. Spinning the pointer around the arc's center sets its direction

9. *Smart Lock* retains the line on the *y* axis while its length is set by a snap to here

Figure 5.32 Placing the first foot

◆ **Construct a Polar Array and Trim the chair feet**

1. Select the *Construct Array* tool, arrange the *Tool Settings* to *Array Type: **Polar**, Items **5**, Delta Angle **360/5**, Rotate Items* check box **On**.

2. Identify the foot original with a data point (anywhere on it will do, since *Rotate Items* is *On*).

3. Snap to the center point, *Accept.*

4. Select the *Element Selection* tool, *Select* the seat and seatback elements that cut the feet as *Cutting Elements.*
   Remember to hold down the <**Ctrl**> key *After* selecting the first one.

5. Select the *Trim Element* tool, click on the sections of the feet to be *Trimmed* off, *Accept* after the last one.

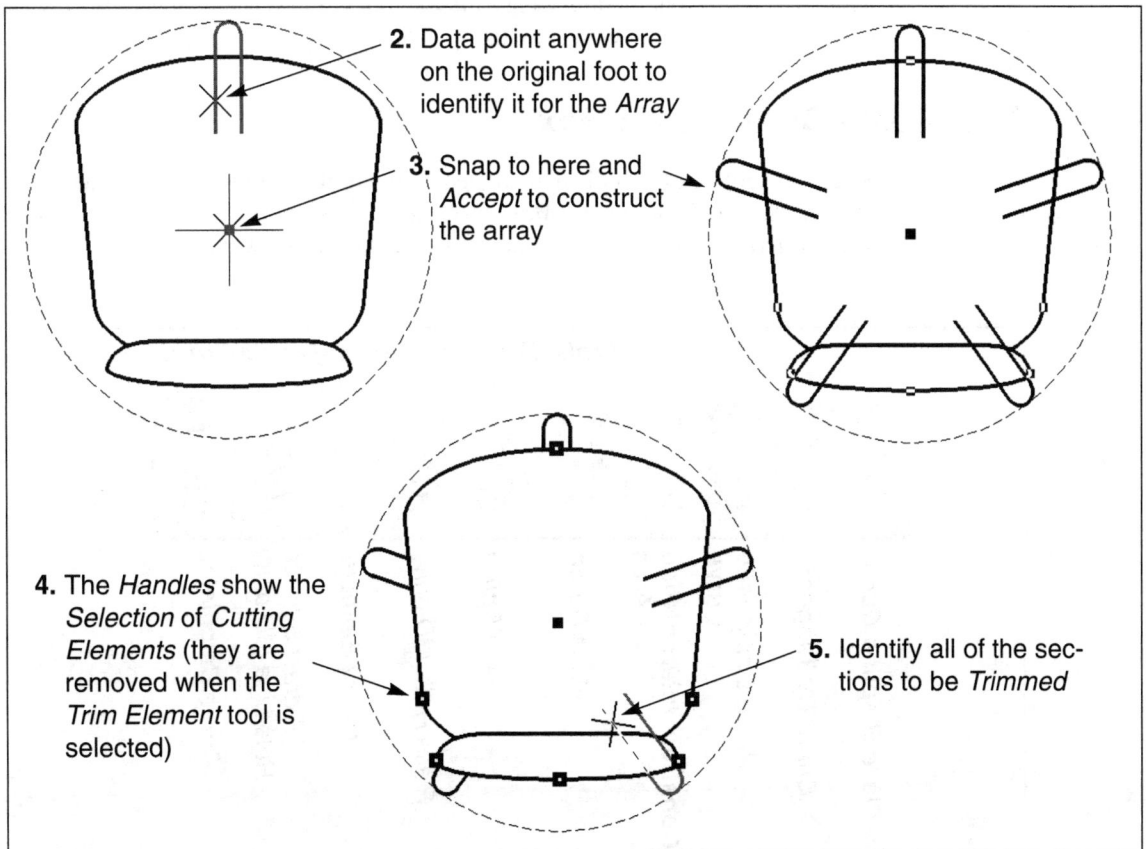

2. Data point anywhere on the original foot to identify it for the *Array*

3. Snap to here and *Accept* to construct the array

4. The *Handles* show the *Selection* of *Cutting Elements* (they are removed when the *Trim Element* tool is selected)

5. Identify all of the sections to be *Trimmed*

Figure 5.33   The final stage, Constructing and trimming the Array of chair feet

Curves

The number and variety of curve types available from within MicroStation is so great that it is not practicable to introduce them all with structured exercises. In any case, the names of the various tools and the tool settings available for each one tends to make them self-introducing. We will list the available tools here with basic illustrative examples.

Point Curves

These curves are the simplest mathematically. The curve generated passes through a set of defined points, dynamically displaying as the points are being placed. We place these using the *Place Point or Stream Curve* tool, found in the *Linear Elements* tool box, which is the same tool box as the *Place Smartline* tool. Its tool settings window gives the option of placing a *Stream* (continuous) curve, generally only used when manual digitizing with a digitizing tablet.

The Create Curves Tool Box

Since this tool box has tools that are generally not required for the usual day-to-day operations, thus is not in the *Main* tool frame. It is opened by choosing *Tools>B-spline Curves>Create Curves* from the Application window menus.

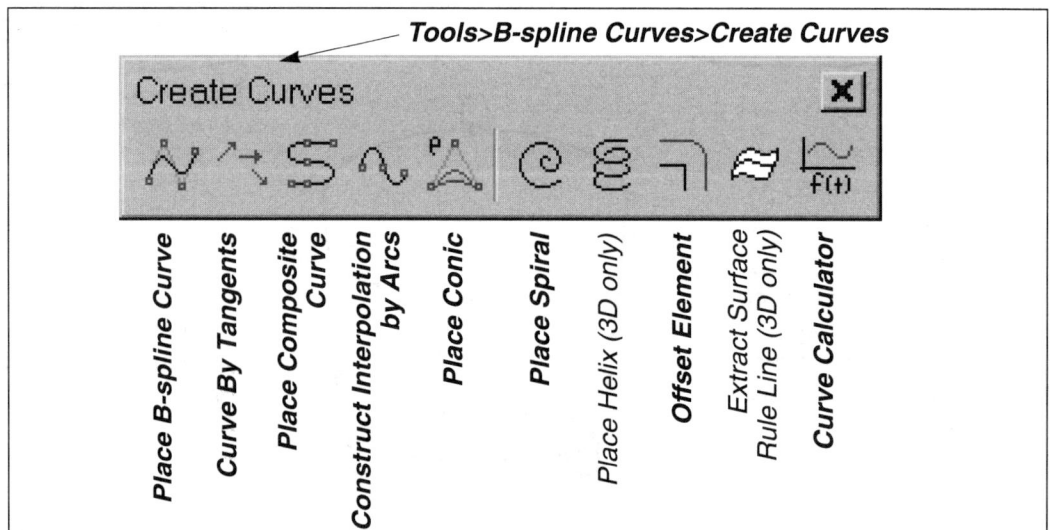

Figure 5.34 The Create Curves Tool Box

Place B-spline Curve

The shape of a B-spline curve is determined by the location of the *Poles* of the curve equation. These poles are represented by the vertices of a *Control Polygon* which may optionally be made visible. The curves shape may be "pulled and pushed" by the handles on this polygon, using the *Modify Element* tool(page 5-15).

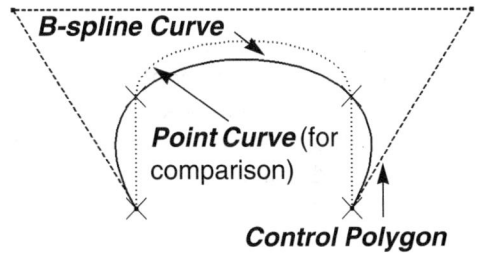

B-spline Curve

Point Curve (for comparison)

Control Polygon

Curve By Tangents

This tool is used to create a *Quadratic* or *Cubic* B-spline curve passing through a set of points. The curve takes its points and tangent directions from lines. This may be an invisible line between data points (*Input By: Enter Tangents*) or actual linear elements (*Input By: Pick Elements*).

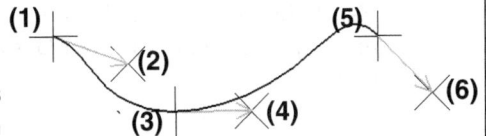

(1) **(2)** **(3)** **(4)** **(5)** **(6)**

Enter Tangents input: Data points are placed in pairs

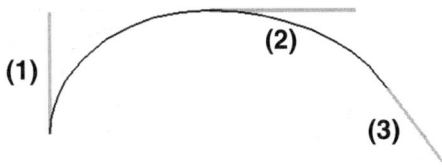

(1) **(2)** **(3)**

Pick Elements input: The curve passes through the *origins* (the start points) of the gray lines, at a tangent to these points.

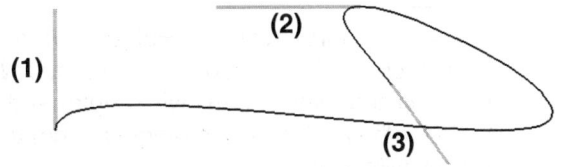

(1) **(2)** **(3)**

In this example the top (horizontal) line was placed right-to-left instead of left-to-right. The curve is tangent in this direction.

Place Composite Curve

This tool will place composites of *Arcs, Bézier Curves* (fourth order B-spline curves with four poles) and *Line* segments, optionally with smooth corners. The *Control Polygon* is visible here on the curve segment, but it would normally be made invisible in the final design.

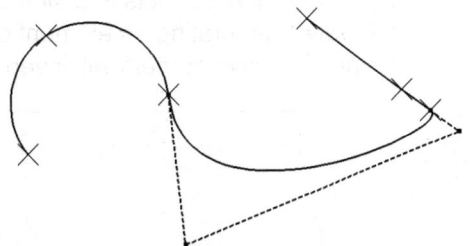

Construct Interpolation by Arcs

A *Complex Chain* of *Arcs* (eight in this example) is placed with smooth corners. When it is
defined by *Placement*, it passes through each
data points. It may also be defined by *Construction*, where it passes through the vertices
of an identified line string.

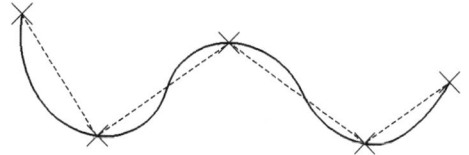

Place Conic

This tool places either a *Hyperbola* (**1**), a
Parabola (**2**) or a *Partial Ellipse* (**3**). They
are all placed as third-order B-spline
curves.

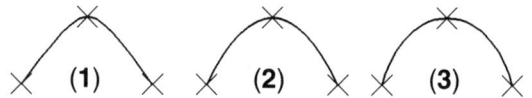

Place Spiral

There are three types available, *Clothoid*
(**1**, Arcs of different radii), *Archimedes* (**2**,
radius changing linearly with angle) and
Logarithmic (**3**, radius changing exponen-
tially with angle).

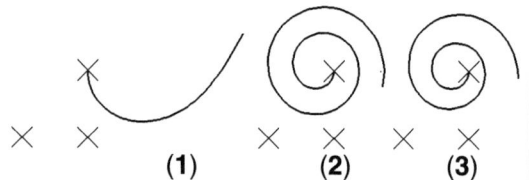

Offset Element

The *Cusp* setting for this tool can be *Round* (**1**,
where a B-spline curve is generated) or *Corner*
(**2**, where the tool acts in a similar way to *Copy
Parallel*, generating an element of the original
type. Concave corners will invert with (**1**).

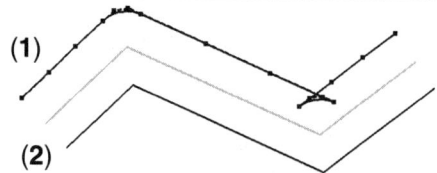

Curve Calculator

Using this tool, any conceivable curve can be placed as a *Non-Uniform Relational B-Spline* (**NURBS**) based on a mathematical formula. There is a supplied library of pre-defined curves, or we can define our own. Trigonometric, hyperbolic, exponential, Logarithmic and power functions may be used in formulae.

This is an example of one of the pre-defined curves, the parameters are set in the Tool Settings window.

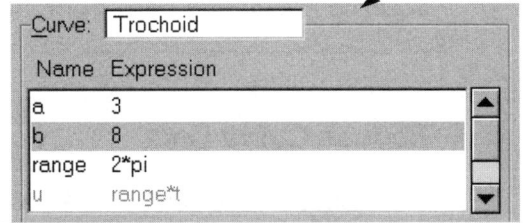

Curve: Trochoid

Name	Expression
a	3
b	8
range	2*pi
u	range*t

The Modify Curves Tool Box

Like *Create Curves*, this tool box is not in the *Main* tool frame. It is opened by choosing *Tools>B-spline>Curves>Modify Curves* from the Application window menus. One of the tools *Change Element Direction*, is also useful for re-defining the origin of elements other than curves, even individual lines.

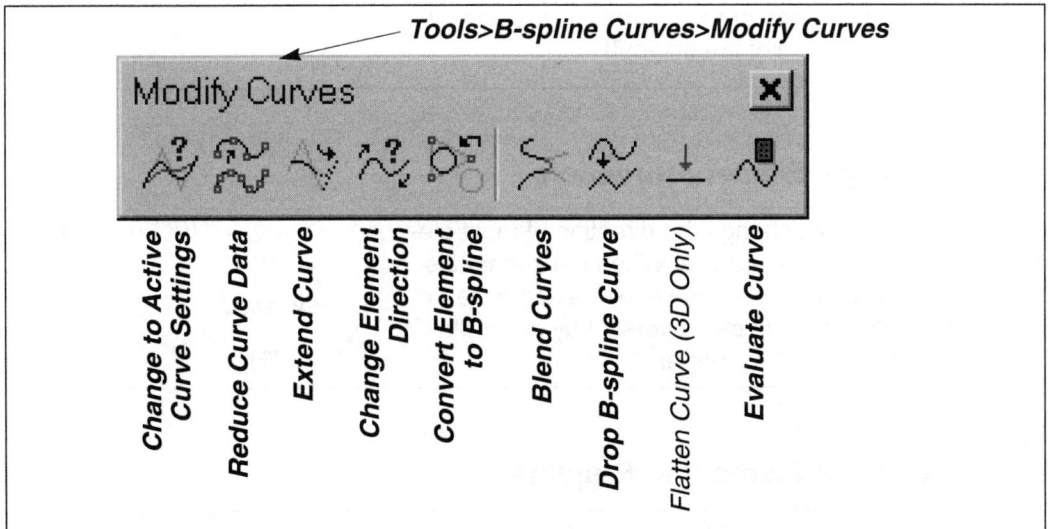

Tools>B-spline Curves>Modify Curves

Modify Curves

Change to Active Curve Settings
Reduce Curve Data
Extend Curve
Change Element Direction
Convert Element to B-spline
Blend Curves
Drop B-spline Curve
Flatten Curve (3D Only)
Evaluate Curve

Figure 5.35   The Modify Curves Tool Box

Change Curve to Active Settings

Used to change curve settings, including making the *Curve* and the *Polygon* visible or invisible, setting the *Order* of the curve equation and making it *Open* or *Closed*

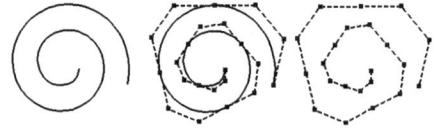

Reduce Curve Data

Used to reduce the number of *Poles* in a B-spline curve while maintaining its shape within a specified tolerance.

(1)

(2)

Extend Curve

Curves are extended by either *Position* (**1**, a straight line), *Tangent* (**2**, the extension is tangent continuous) or *Curvature* (**3**, the curvature at the end of the extension is relative to the curvature of the original).

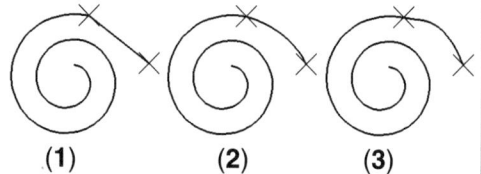

(1)   **(2)**   **(3)**

Change Element Direction

This tool will change the direction of most elements, not only curves. When the element is identified, a tangent line appears at the start of the element. We can reverse it by placing a data point at the other end

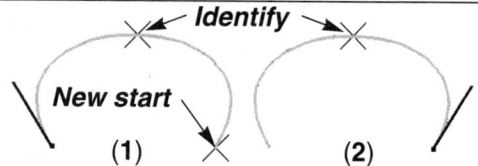

Identify

New start

(1)   **(2)**

Convert Element to B-spline

When any element (an *Arc* in this example) is converted to a B-spline, it initially retains its original shape. It gains a control polygon and can be modified like any other B-spline curve.

(1)   **(2)**

Blend Curves

In this example, two lower *Arcs* have been trimmed and blended into a single B-spline curve. The blend (trimming) points and the form of continuity is definable.

Drop B-spline Curve

This tool converts a B-spline curve to a line, line string, stream curve or complex chain of arcs. There are many options for the conversion, including the number of segments generated.

The gray curves are the original B-splines. In the top pair, the B-spline curve has been dropped to a 20-segment *line string*. The lower example shows the same curve dropped to a chain of 20 *equal length arcs*. The number of segments may be set much higher than in these examples, with closer approximations created.

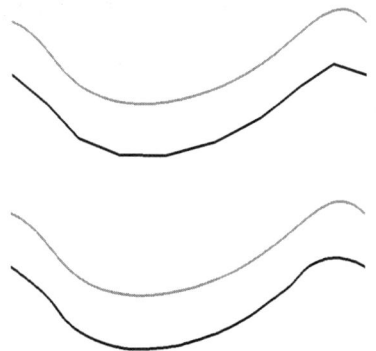

Evaluate Curve

This tool has a range of options for the graphical evaluation of curve data. The top example shows a *Curvature Plot*, where perpendicular lines (gray) are created along the curve with their length proportional to the curvature at that point (the greater the curvature, the longer the line).

The same curve also has *Inversion Points* (gray squares) shown where the curve changes direction.

The evaluation geometry may be saved to the design file as a *Graphic Group*, or only be displayed temporarily.

Sections of the Tool Settings Window

Enter Data Point
Parameter
Node Points
Dist Along Curve
▶ Point Array

Compute Following Attributes:
☐ Points
☐ Tangents
☑ Curvature Plot
☑ Inflection Points
☐ Perpendicular Circles

Options for input of locations

Options for attributes to evaluate

Key-Ins

We can enter instructions and data to control MicroStation from the keyboard. While the Graphical User Interface will provide nearly all the control we are ever likely to need, *Key-ins* still have their occasional uses. They formed an essential part of CADD operations before MicroStation 95 and the *AccuDraw* facility. In this context the term *Key-ins* applies to instructions and data entered from the keyboard into the *Key-in window* only, not keyboard entry to other windows, dialog boxes etc.

The Key-in Window

This window is a utility opened from the Application window menu bar by choosing *Utilities>Key-in*. It can be re-sized to three different formats:

1.   *Minimum*, including the *Entry Field* only;

2.   *Entry Field and Key-in Browser*, which has a four *List Box* panels used to build Key-In instructions;

3.   *Entry Field*, *Key-in Browser* and *History List Box*, with all of the above plus a long list of previous data and instructions keyed in.

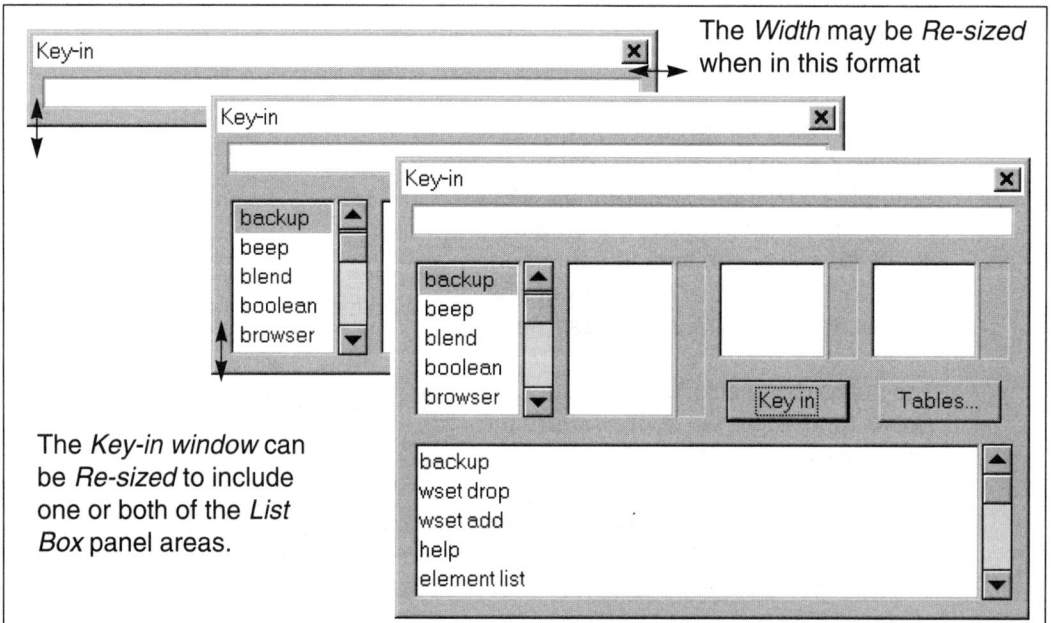

Figure 5.36   Three formats of Key-in Window

The contents of the browser list boxes are keywords of tool names and view controls. There are less-commonly used tools available through the Key-in window browser that are not available from the tool boxes. As well, all of the tools in the tool boxes are also available as Key-Ins, but it is usually more efficient to use the tool buttons.

We can build a tool name (instruction) by progressively selecting keywords from up to four of the browser list boxes using the scroll bars. If we know some of the name, for example the first keyword, we can start by keying the first characters of this into the input field. As the browser finds a match, the first matching word is displayed with highlighting in a list box. Figure 5.37 illustrates an example.

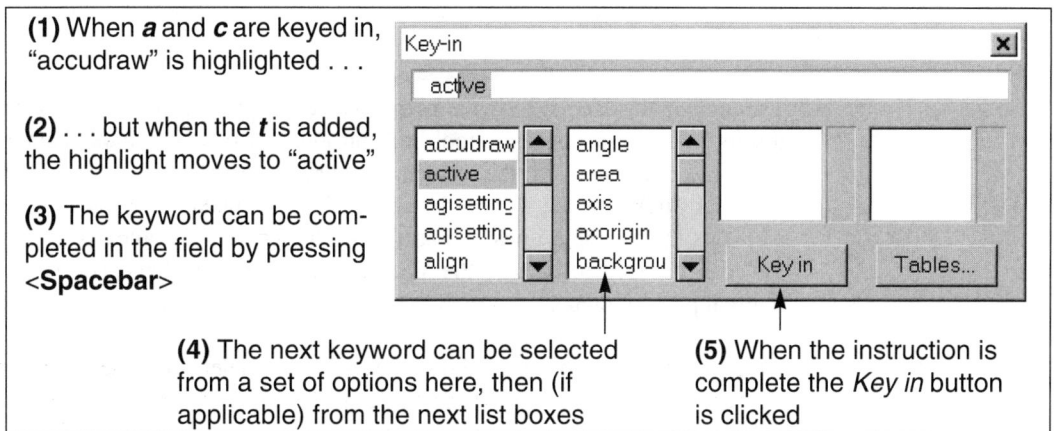

(1) When *a* and *c* are keyed in, "accudraw" is highlighted . . .

(2) . . . but when the *t* is added, the highlight moves to "active"

(3) The keyword can be completed in the field by pressing **<Spacebar>**

(4) The next keyword can be selected from a set of options here, then (if applicable) from the next list boxes

(5) When the instruction is complete the *Key in* button is clicked

Figure 5.37   Building a Key-in

Making a Backup of your design

We will use *Backup* as an example using a *Key-in. The* Backup instruction causes a copy of the active design file to be made in the same directory (in the "as supplied" configuration) with the same file name, except the ".dgn" is replaced by ".bak". Keying in a *path* to the input field after the word "backup" (e.g. "a:\") will save the ".bak" file to the disk and folder specified.

◆ Backup "cells.dgn"

1. Choose *Utiities>Key-in* from the Application window menu, re-size as necessary to display the browser list boxes.

2. With *Input Focus* in the *Key-in* window, press **<b>** ("backup" will highlight), click the *Key in* button or press **<Enter>**.
    The message "Saved to . . .\cells.bak" appears in the Status bar.

Summary

Active Points may be placed individually with data points, or constructed to fall at a specified location or locations. They may be constructed in specified numbers of equally spaced *Active Points* between data points, falling on elements or placed independently. They are often used in the process of construction of a design, where they can be used to *Snap* tentative points to define the location of other elements.

Circular and Elliptical *Arcs* can be placed using tools from the *Arcs* tool box, which also has tools for *Modifying* existing arcs. These modification tools allow us to change the *Radius*, the *Sweep Angle* and the size of an arc along its *Axes*. *Circular Arcs* can be placed about a defined *Center* position or with three data points defining the *Edge*.

The tools in the *Modify* tool box perform a very large number of diverse functions. It differs from the *Manipulate* tool box introduced in the previous chapter in that its tools make alterations to the elements, where the *Manipulate* tools mainly duplicate and reposition elements. The *Modify* tool alone makes a range of alterations to elements from simple lines and arcs to multi-segment complex elements. This one tool can be used to change the size and the shape of elements, operating on the internal parts of elements as well as on endpoints and vertexes.

Other tools in this tool box allow us to partially delete, lengthen, shorten and trim elements using a range of criteria. there are also tools that place new elements in the form of *Fillets* and *Chamfers*, while modifying the geometry they are associated with.

The *Modify* tools from both the tool box of that name and from the *Arcs* tool box may be used to make alterations to existing designs as part of an upgrading or updating process. They are also frequently used as part of the original design process to make elements fit the design. Typical examples of this were practiced while modifying elements associated with the Office Chair project. In this case, they were used to remove unwanted sections of linework to reveal a continuous outline.

The most basic tool to generate curves is the *Place Point or Stream Curve* tool from the *Linear Elements* tool box. The *Curves* tool box provides a wide range of options for placing, modifying and blending more complex curves. It includes a facility for creating our own mathematical curve formulae.

The *Key-in* window is a utility occasionally needed for unusual instructions (tools or viewing controls) and data entry. It has an associated *Key-in Browser* and a *History* list box to help recall instructions.

6 : Cells

We often need to use a drawing over and over again, for example chairs in office layouts, hexagonal bolt heads in an engineering drawing, monument points on a map. There is no need to repeatedly create identical drawings, nor do we have to make multiple copies of groups of components.

We can create frequently used drawings and store them as *Cells* in *Cell Libraries*. From then on it is simply a matter of accessing the appropriate *Cell Library* and we can place as many *Instances* of a drawing as we like. MicroStation comes supplied with libraries of cells, but you will almost certainly need to create your own as well. This chapter contains some examples of creating both a *Cell Library* and examples of *Cells* to be stored in it.

When you have completed this chapter, you will be able to:

- *Attach* and *Browse* an existing *Cell Library*;
- Create a new *Cell Library*;
- Create *Cells* and store them in our own *Cell Library*;
- *Place* cells as *Shared* and individual cells;
- Change the status of a cell placement from *Shared* to *Ordinary*;
- *Drop* a cell to ordinary geometry;
- Use the *Cell Selector* utility to efficiently select and place cells.

Cells

A *Cell* is a permanent group of elements making up a small drawing, which is intended for frequent use. Examples of cells can range from a couple of elements that form a symbol or pattern element, to detail drawings of standard fixtures or furniture for large building projects. Once a *Cell* is created, it may be used in any number of individual designs.

Collections of cell drawings are stored in a MicroStation file called a *Cell Library*. The collection in any one *Cell Library* can be quite large. For easy accessibility, separate libraries will usually hold logical groupings of cells. For example, architectural furniture may be held in one library, mapping symbols in another, civil engineering patterning elements in yet another.

MicroStation is already supplied with large collections of cells for various disciplines, but in many cases we will need to create our own *Cells* stored in our own *Cell Libraries*.

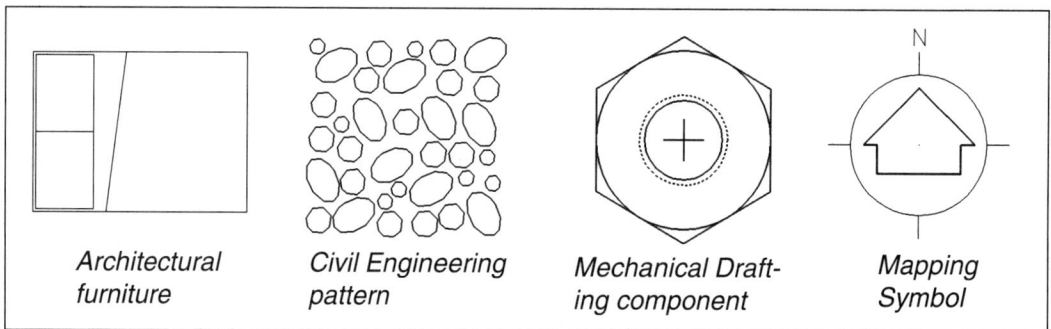

Figure 6.1   Examples of cells supplied with MicroStation

Each of the examples shown above in Figure 6.1 are from separate *Cell Libraries*. There are hundreds of cells supplied, held in a variety of cell libraries, which in turn are supplied in a number of *Directories* or *Folders*. We will locate at least some of these libraries as we work through the next exercise.

In the following exercises, we will *Attach* some of the supplied cell libraries and browse through their contents. *Attachment* of a library allows us access to its cells via the *Cell Library* settings box while working on a design. We attach libraries one at a time, as each time we *Attach* a library the previous one is automatically *Detached*.

Attaching and Browsing a Cell Library

A *Cell Library* is a computer file (usually with the filename extension ".cel") which is placed in a *Directory* or *Folder*. The actual folder used will depend on your particular installation, but for now we will assume that MicroStation has been installed with all of the standard folder structures intact. We will start our browsing in the ". . . *Workspace\projects\examples\arch\cell*" folder.

◆ **Attach and browse an existing cell library**

1. Open (if necessary) "cells.dgn".

2. Choose *Element>Cells* from the Application window menu (the *Cell Library* settings box opens).

3. Choose *File>Attach* from the *Cell Library* settings box menu (the *Attach Cell Library* dialog box opens).

4. Set the folder to **. . . Workspace\projects\examples\arch\cell**, either in the *Directories* panel (or from the *Directory* menu if it is in the "History" of directories used).

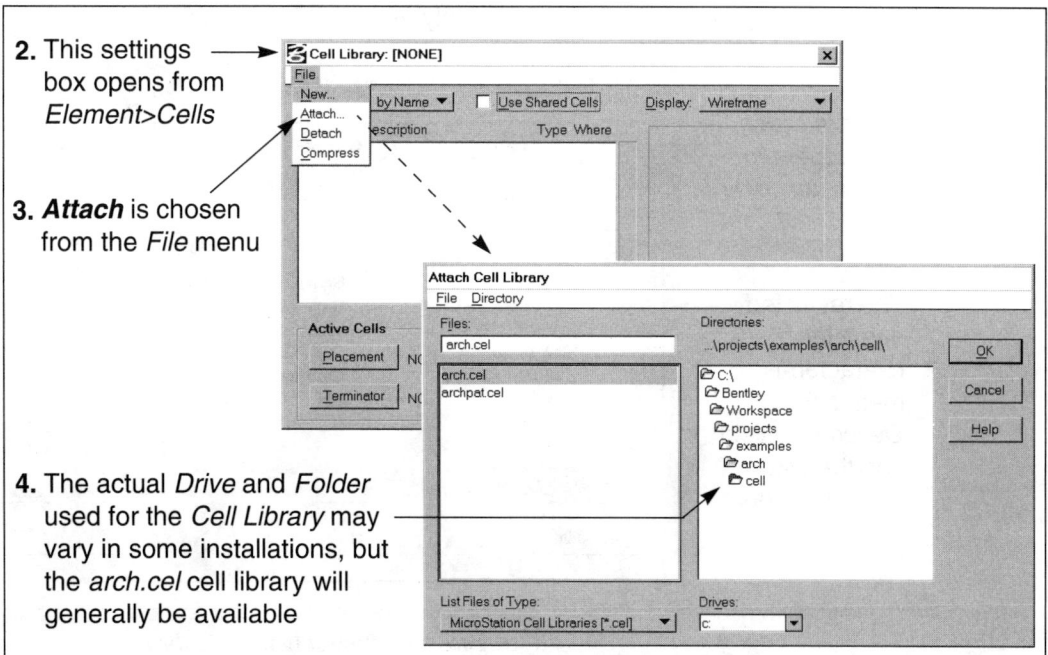

Figure 6.2   Attaching an existing Cell Library

5. Select **arch.cel** from the *Files:* panel, click the **OK** button (or double-click the file name).

The *Attach Cell Library* dialog box will close and the Title bar of the Cell Library settings box will now display "Cell Library: arch.cel", indicating that this is the *Attached Cell Library*. This fact is also reported in right side of the Status bar, where the full path is displayed as well as the ".cel" file name.

As shown in Figure 6.3, the names, descriptions, types and whereabouts of the available cells will now be displayed in the list box on the left.

6. Click on a cell in the list box (an image of the cell appears to the right of the list box).

7. Browse through some of the other cells (using the scroll bar where necessary) to become familiar with the use of the settings box. Try attaching other cell libraries and browse through these as well.

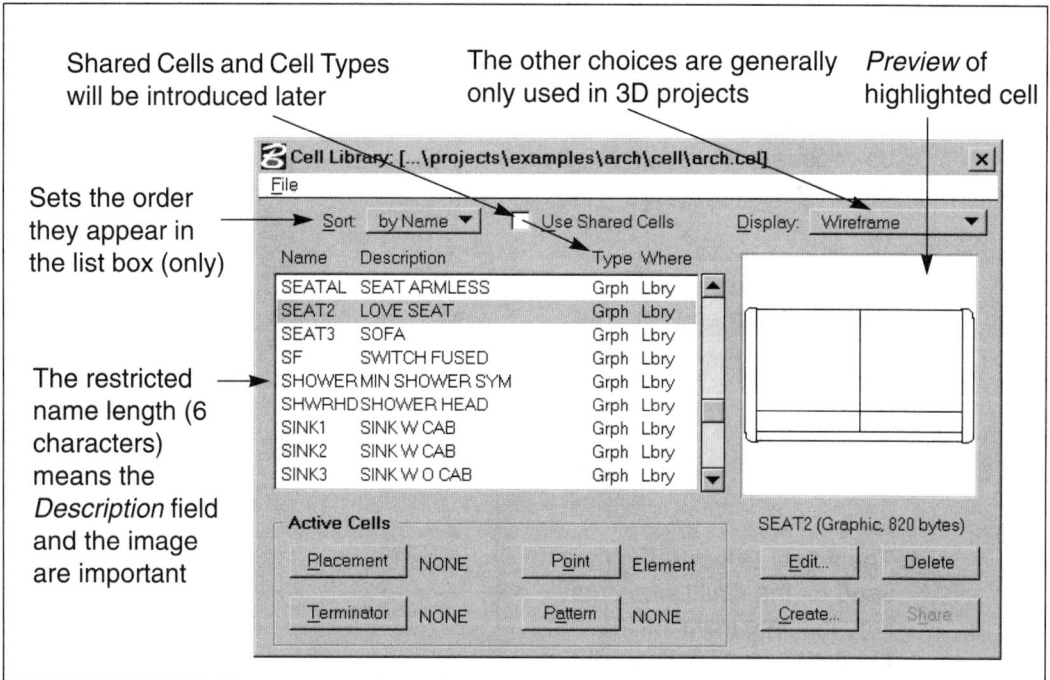

Figure 6.3 Browsing a Cell Library

Creating a Cell Library

The process of creating a new *Cell Library* is not much different from attaching an existing one, although it is a process you will only need to use on occasions. For the next exercise we are again assuming that MicroStation has been installed with all of the standard folder structures intact. We will place our new cell library in the ". . . Workspace\system\cell\" folder if it is available, if not place it in another appropriate folder.

◆ **Create the new cell library "examples.cel"**

1. If the *Cell Library* settings box is not already open, choose *Element>Cells* from the Application window menu.

2. Choose *File>New* from the *Cell Library* settings box menu (the *Create Cell Library* dialog box opens).

3. Set the folder to *. . . Workspace\system\cell*, either in the *Directories* panel (or from the *Directory* menu if it is in the "History").

4. Check that the *Seed File* is *Seed2d.cel* in the *Seed File* panel, if not, click the *Seed* button and select this file to base our library file on.

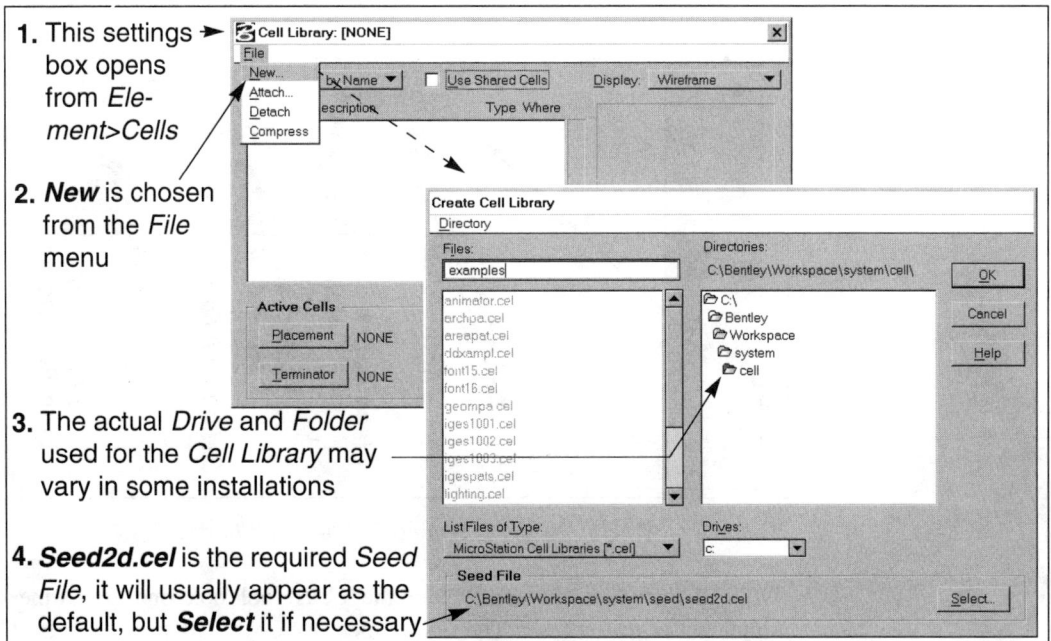

1. This settings box opens from *Element>Cells*

2. *New* is chosen from the *File* menu

3. The actual *Drive* and *Folder* used for the *Cell Library* may vary in some installations

4. *Seed2d.cel* is the required *Seed File*, it will usually appear as the default, but *Select* it if necessary

Figure 6.4 Preparations for creating a new Cell Library

5. Enter the name **examples** to the *Files:* data field, click *OK* or press <**Enter**>

    The default filename extension for cell library files (usually ".cel") is automatically appended. Creating a new cell library automatically attaches it to the design file we are working in (the *Active Design*) and detaches the previous one.

6. Save the attachment setting with *File>Save Settings* (from the Application window menu).

7. Close the *Cell Library* settings box (for now).

This new *Cell Library* file may now be accessed from any design file on the same computer or computer network. The *Cell List box* was empty, but we are about to create some cells of our own and store them in it. The first of these cells will be a practical example, the top view of an office chair. This could be used when designing an office layout in an architectural project.

The Cells Tool Box

The tools in this tool box are used for *Placing* and *Replacing* cells, for *Identifying* cells and for defining the *Origin* of a new cell being created.

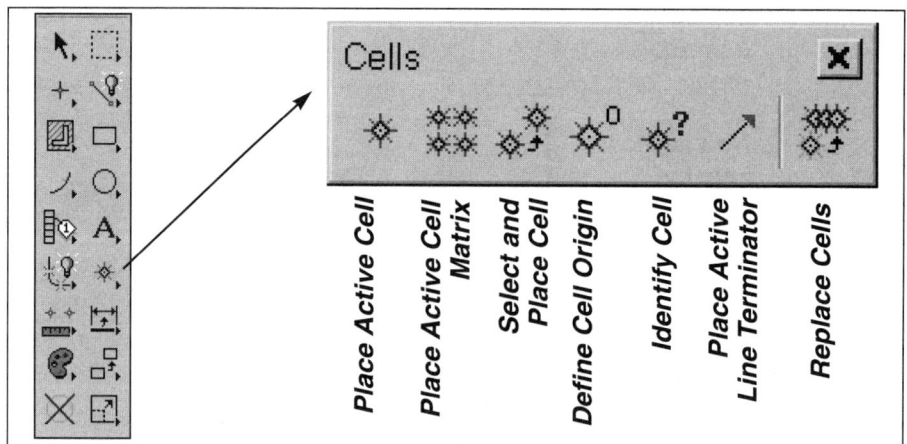

Figure 6.5   The Cells Tool Box

We will introduce the tools from the *Cells* tool box one at a time during the remainder of this chapter. The first of these tools we will apply is *Place Cell Origin*, the only one used from this box during the cell creation process.

Creating Cells

The process of creating a cell consists of:

1.   Create the drawing for the new cell, or decide on the parts of an existing design to be included;

2.   Temporarily group the elements to form the cell, either with a *Fence* or by multiple selection;

3.   Define an *Origin* for the cell (the point by which the position of the cell is defined when it is placed);

4.   Work through the *Create* process in the *Cell Library* settings box to store the new cell in the *Attached* cell library.

Creating the Drawing

There is nothing unusual about creating a drawing for a cell. Any type of design element can be included and the full choice of element attributes can be used, including placing the elements on various levels. We will start by creating a *Cell* from the drawing of the swivel-base office chair we completed in chapter 5.

Grouping the Elements

We will use all of the Office Chair design, so we need to *Temporarily Group* all of the elements to include them as part of the new *Cell*. If we use the *Fence* to group the elements, we need to take note of the *Fence (Selection) Mode* (see page 4-31). We will generally use *Inside* mode, but the other modes are allowed. If we are using the *Element Selection* tool, the quickest way to *Select* all the elements required is to drag a rectangle around them (see page 4-26).

The Define Cell Origin Tool

The *Origin* we put in place is the point on or near the cell drawing where the screen pointer will appear when the cell is being placed. When the origin is first placed, its position is marked by a slightly offset "**o**" symbol. This symbol only remains until the screen is updated. The last *Origin* placed is the one taken by a cell being created, regardless of where it is. If, during the cell creation process we need to place an origin a second time, we just do it. The previous one is overwritten, even though its "**o**" symbol may stay in place until the next screen update.

Creating a Cell - Stage 1

In this stage we will prepare the Office Chair for its continuing existence as a *Cell* by temporarily grouping its elements and defining an *Origin* for it.

◆ Prepare the drawing for cell creation

1. ***Either*** select the *Place Fence* tool, *Fence Type* **Circle** or **Block**, *Fence Mode* **Inside**, place a fence about the Office Chair;
   Or

   Select the *Element Selection* tool, drag a rectangle to surround **All** of the Office Chair.

2. Select the *Define Cell Origin* tool, snap (tentative) to the *Active Point* at the center of the chair, *Accept*, *Reset*.
   An "**o**" appears next to the center point, indicating the origin has been placed.

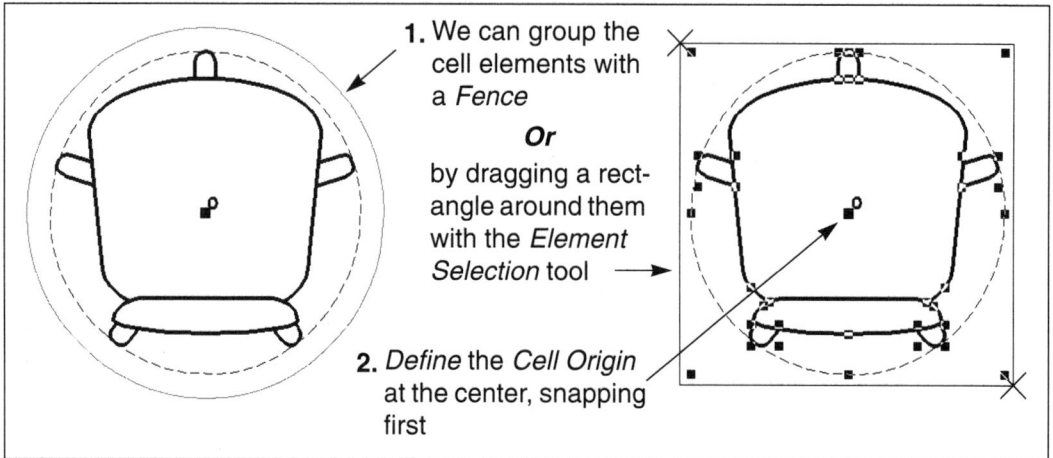

1. We can group the cell elements with a *Fence*

   Or

   by dragging a rectangle around them with the *Element Selection* tool →

2. Define the *Cell Origin* at the center, snapping first

Figure 6.6   Preparing the chair for creation into a cell

The Create New Cell Option

The *Create...* button is found in the lower right corner of the *Cell Library* settings box, accessed via *Element>Cells*. The button will be available (not *Grayed out*) if:

- There is a *Cell Library Attached*;
- There are elements *Fenced* or *Selected*;

• There is a *Cell Origin* placed.

Assuming that the above criteria are met, clicking this button opens the *Create New Cell* dialog box.

Creating a Cell - Stage 2

Now we will *Create* two types of cells form the one drawing, giving them *Names* and *Descriptions*, then storing them in the *Attached Cell Library*, "Examples.cel".

◆ Create the Office Chair cell

1. Check that the Office Chair elements are still *Fenced* or *Selected* and that there is still a *Cell Origin* placed at their center.
Redo **Stage 1** (page 6-8) if necessary.

2. Select *Element>Cells* (for the *Cell Library* settings box), check that "examples.cel" appears in the Title bar as the *Attached Cell Library*.
If not, select the *File>Attach* option and select it from its folder, see the exercise on page 6-5.

3. Click the *Create* button, key in **chair1** to the *Name* field of the *Create New Cell* dialog box.

4. Press <**Tab**>, key in **office chair no arms** to *Description*.
There is an *Cell Type* option menu in the *Create New Cell* dialog box, below the *Description* field. It will be set to ***Graphic*** by default, which is the required setting for now. There is a list describing the cell *Types* on page 6-11.

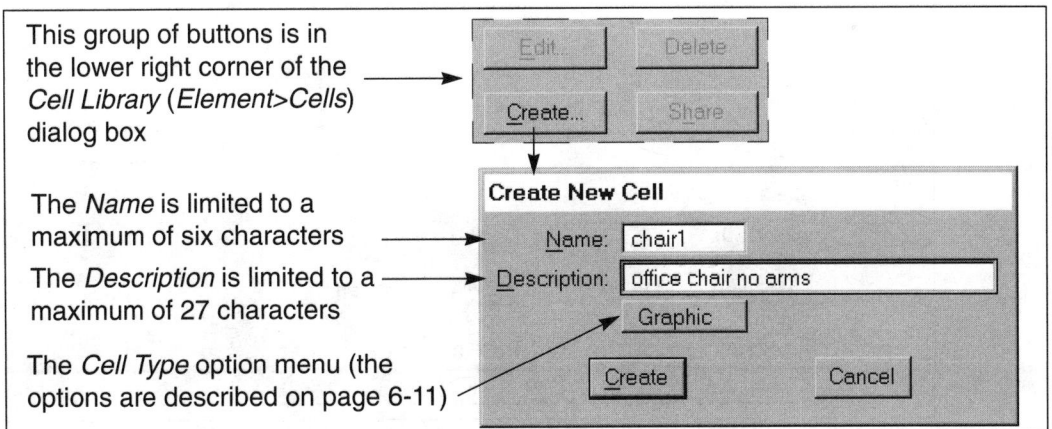

Figure 6.7   Creating Cells

5. Press <**Enter**> or click the *Create* button in the *Create New Cell* dialog box.

   The name and description will appear in the *Cell Library* settings box.

6. Click on the cell name to highlight it (an image of the cell appears in the panel at the left).

   Now we will use the same group of elements, with the same *Cell Origin* to create a *Point Type Cell* for our experiments.

7. Click the *Create* button, key in **Cpoint** to the *Name* field of the *Create New Cell* dialog box.

8. Press <**Tab**>, key in **Office Chair Point** to the *Description* field.

9. Select *Point* from the *Cell Type* option menu.

10. Press <**Enter**> or click the *Create* button in the *Create New Cell* dialog box.

    The name and description will again appear in the *Cell Library* settings box.

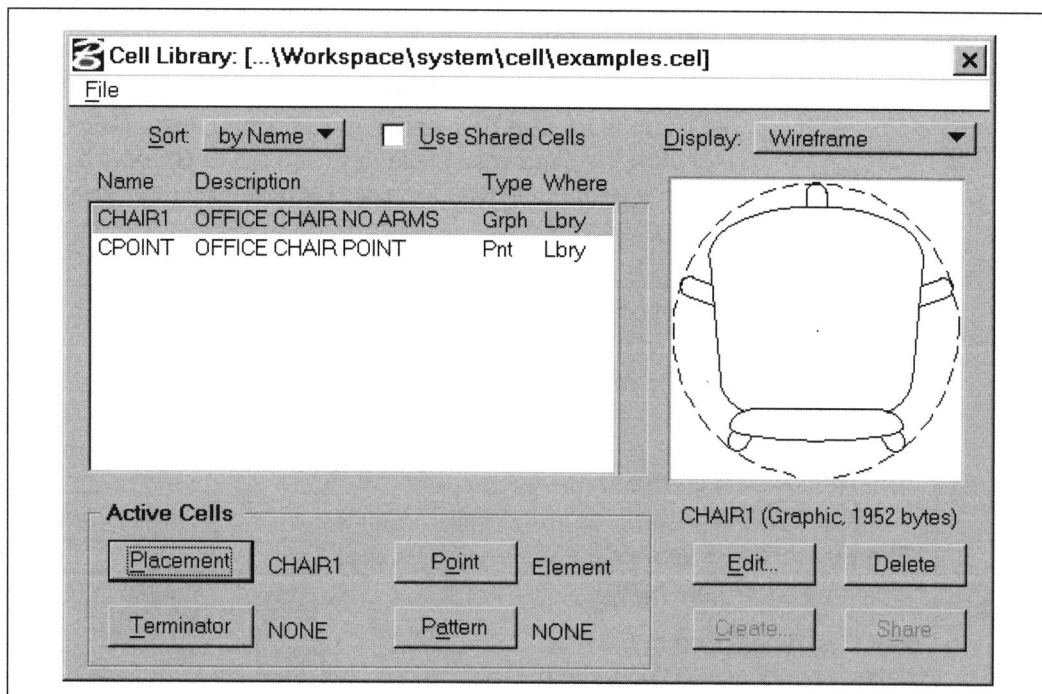

Figure 6.8   The Office Chair cell shown in the library settings box

Cell Types

In the last exercise we created a *Graphic* and a *Point* type cell from the same original geometry - what is the difference? There are actually four *Types* of cells that may be defined at the time of creation:

1. *Graphic*, cells that are *Level Independent*, that is the level(s) they are *Placed* on depends on the level(s) they were *Created* on. They are placed with the *Symbology* they were created with and their keypoints can be snapped to. This type rotates with the view like other elements.

2. *Point* (not to be confused with *Active Point Cell* introduced on page 5-2), which takes the *Attributes* that are *Active* when it is *Placed*. It does not rotate with the view and its only keypoint (for snapping) is at its *Origin*.

3. & 4. *Menu* and *Tutorial* type cells are not commonly used and will not be covered in this book. They relate more to earlier versions of MicroStation.

The Edit Cell Information Option

We can change the name and the description of a *Cell* after it has been created.

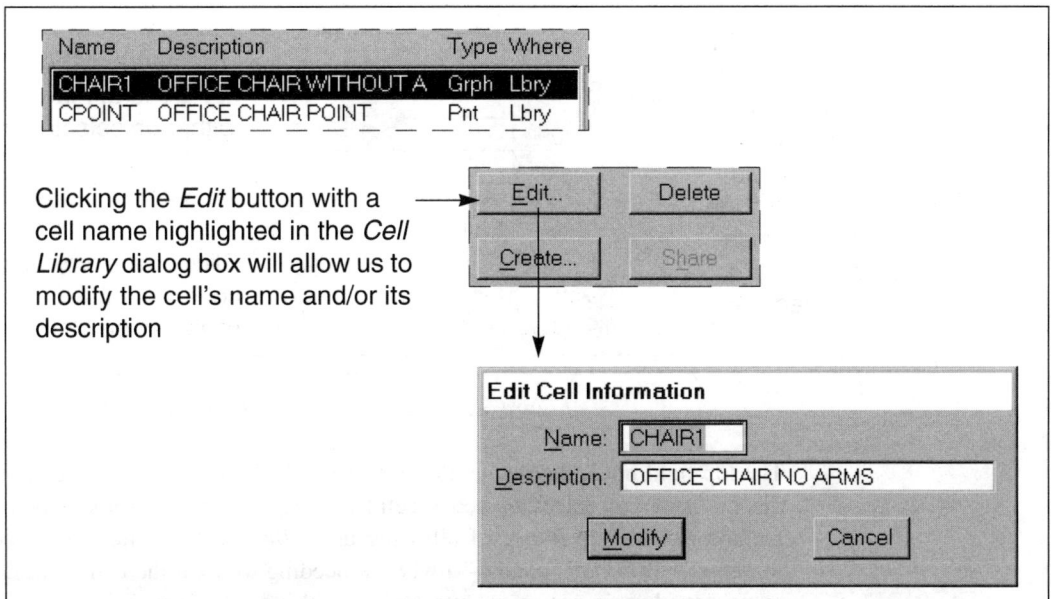

Figure 6.9   Editing cell information

General Placement of Cells

Now we have two of our own cells stored in our own *Cell Library*. We will designate each of them in turn for general *Placement* and use the *Place Active Cell* tool to place them in the design. The cells will be placed in the design where they were created in these examples, but in practice this would seldom be the case.

If we are only likely to use a particular group of components in the one drawing, we do not have to use *Cells* and a *Cell Library*. We could use various techniques for temporarily or permanently grouping of elements, enabling us to copy a whole group at once. We have already worked with some of these in this chapter and in chapter 4, *Multiple Element Selection* and the *Fence*.

The Place Active Cell Tool

This is the tool used for placement of individual cells. Its associated *Tool Settings* window is shown in Figure 6.11. With the settings as shown (the *Relative* and the *Interactive* check boxes are *Off*), the cell is placed independently of the currently active *Element Attributes*. It is placed on the levels it was created on, with its own colors, line styles and line weights (its *Symbology*). This is known as *Absolute* cell placement.

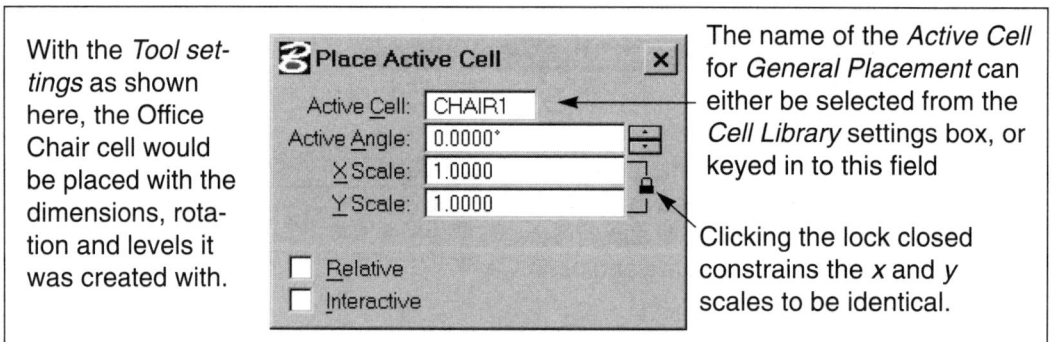

With the *Tool settings* as shown here, the Office Chair cell would be placed with the dimensions, rotation and levels it was created with.

Place Active Cell   [x]

Active Cell: CHAIR1
Active Angle: 0.0000°
X Scale: 1.0000
Y Scale: 1.0000

☐ Relative
☐ Interactive

The name of the *Active Cell* for *General Placement* can either be selected from the *Cell Library* settings box, or keyed in to this field

Clicking the lock closed constrains the *x* and *y* scales to be identical.

Figure 6.10   Tool Settings for Place Active Cell

The top field holds the *Name* of the *Active Cell* for general placement. We can key this in, or we can select the active cell from the *Cell Library* settings box. The latter method has the advantage of allowing us to *Browse* the collection of cells in the *Attached* cell library (page 6-3) without needing to learn the cell names. If the cell name keyed in is not in an attached cell library, the libraries in the directorie(s) defined under *Workspace>Configuration>Cells>Cell Library Directories* are searched. The first cell with the keyed-in name found is becomes the *Active Cell*.

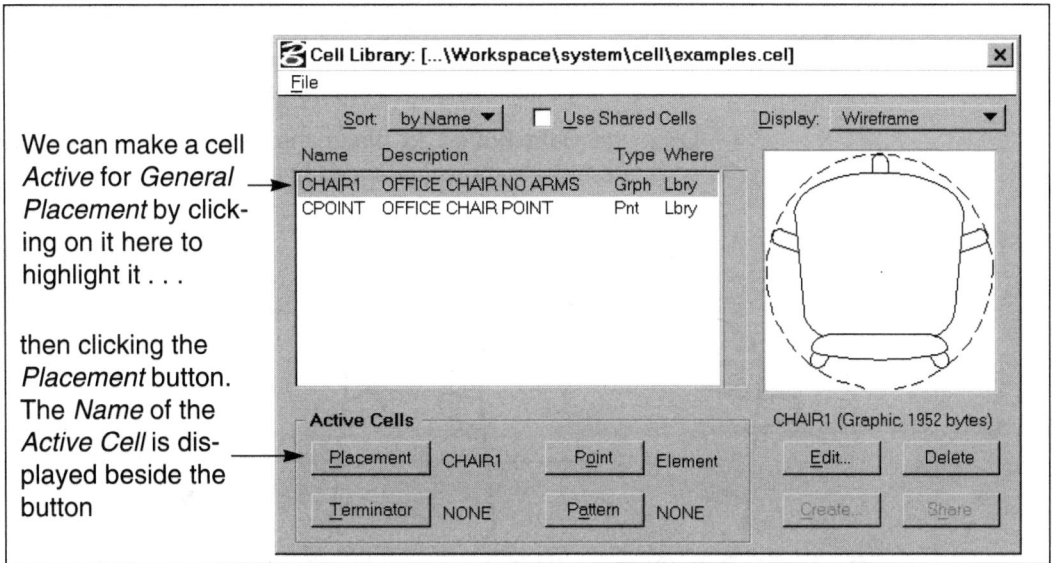

We can make a cell *Active* for *General Placement* by clicking on it here to highlight it . . .

then clicking the *Placement* button. The *Name* of the *Active Cell* is displayed beside the button

Figure 6.11   Using the Cell Library settings box for selection of Placement Cell

The *Active Angle* affects the orientation of the cell as it is placed. The cell is placed with its original orientation when the active angle is set to the positive *x* axis direction (**0°** in *Conventional Angle Mode*). The *Active Angle* may be set from within the *Place Active Cell* tool settings window.

The *Scale* of the cell can be changed as it is placed. The *x* and *y* scale factor fields of the Tool Settings window are set at **1.0** by default. New values may be keyed into both fields simultaneously when they are linked by the closed padlock symbol, or set independently with the padlock open. The padlock is *Toggled* open and closed by clicking it.

We will place a cell with the settings as shown first, then experiment with the *Relative* and the *Interactive* check boxes.

◆ **Placing a cell with the default settings (Absolute)**

1. Choose *Element>Cells* (the *Cell Library* settings box opens), check that "examples.cel" appears in the Title bar as the *Attached Cell Library.*

2. Click on "CHAIR1" to highlight it, click the *Placement* button to make it the general placement cell.

3. Select the *Place Active Cell* tool, check that the *Tool Settings* are as shown in Figure 6.10, move the pointer to a clear space in the design. The cell drawing will appear with the pointer at its center, where we defined the *Origin* when we created the cell.

4. Click the data button to place the cell, *Reset* unless we want to continue placing more *Instances* of the cell.

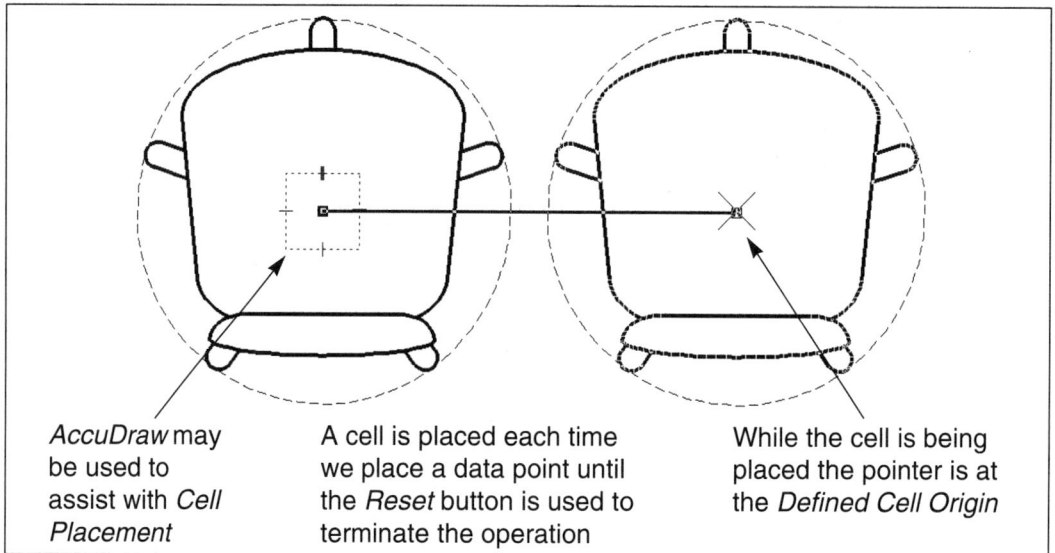

| AccuDraw may be used to assist with Cell Placement | A cell is placed each time we place a data point until the Reset button is used to terminate the operation | While the cell is being placed the pointer is at the Defined Cell Origin |

Figure 6.12   Placing cells using the default settings

The Identify Cell Tool

This tool is used to find the name of a cell that has already been placed and the level or levels that it is placed on. The information is displayed in the *Status Bar*. The same information may be obtained with the *Analyze Element* tool (see "Element Information" on page 3-24), but not as quickly and conveniently. With that tool we need to step through each element in turn (using the *Next* button) to find the levels.

◆ **Display the name and levels of the cell just placed**

1. Select the *Identify Cell* tool, identify any part of the cell with a data point (the whole cell will highlight).

2. Read the information on the left of the Status bar.

3. *Accept* or *Reset* to complete the operation.

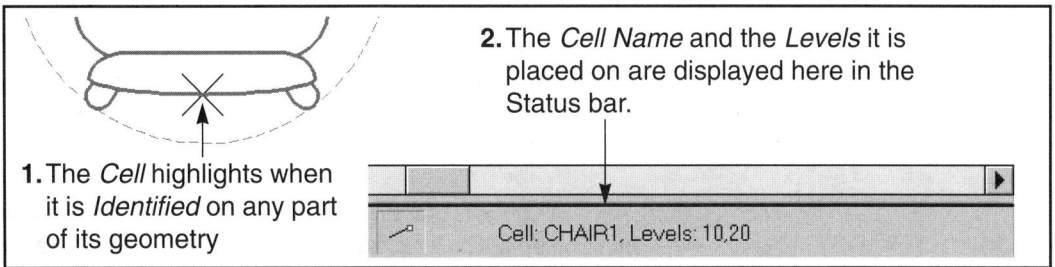

Figure 6.13 Displaying the name and levels of a cell instance

Relative Cell Placement

In this context, the word *Relative* is associated with the level structure. When the *Relative* check box is *On,* the elements on the lowest numbered level used in the cell will be placed on the level that was *Active* when it was placed. Higher cell levels will be placed on relatively higher design file levels.

For example, our Office Chair cell was created on levels 10 and 20. If level 5 was *Active* when the cell was placed, the elements from level 10 (the lowest numbered) will be placed on this level. The elements on level 20 of the cell will now be placed on level 15, the same *Relative* level spacing as the original. We will try this for ourselves.

◆ Placing a cell with Relative *On*

1. Set the *Active Level* to *5*.

2. Select the *Place Active Cell* tool, click the *Relative* check box *On*, move the pointer to a clear space in the design.

3. Place another instance of the "CHAIR1" cell.

4. Display the name and levels of new cell instance with the *Identify Cell* tool, as in the last exercise.

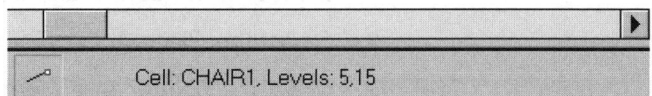

Figure 6.14 The effect of Relative Cell Placement

Interactive Cell Placement

The cells placed so far have been set in their *x* and *y* scales and in their rotation by the tool settings. With the *Interactive* check box *On* in the tool settings window the scales and orientation of the cell are set graphically by the placement of additional data points, or by *Key-ins*.

The first thing we will notice is that the cell does not appear about the pointer as it is being moved into position. The first data point to be placed sets the position of the cell *Origin*, the second data point defines both the *x* and the *y Scales* and the third the *Rotation*.

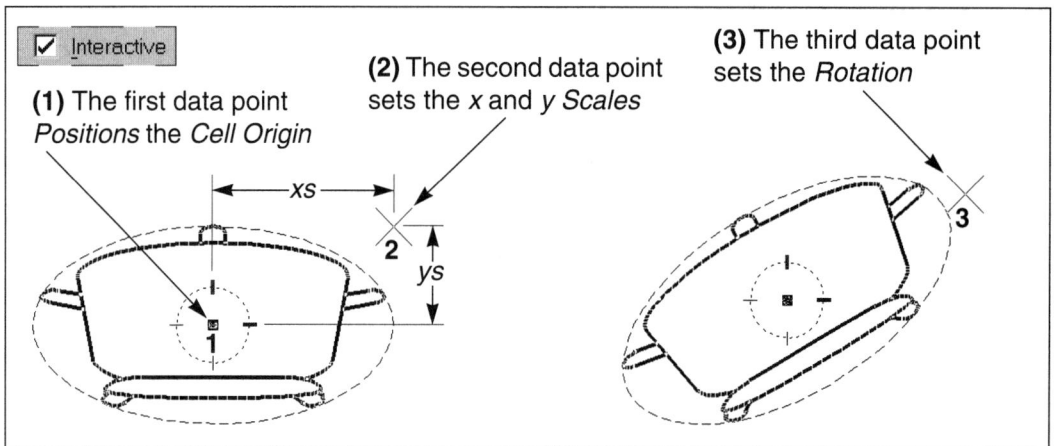

Figure 6.15   Interactive Cell Placement, Graphical method

We can also use the *Interactive* method in conjunction with *Key-Ins* (to the *Key-In* window, see "Key-Ins" on page 5-40). This technique gives us the ability to mix keyboard entry with graphical input. One common application for this is the setting of the *Scales* from the keyboard (usually scales of **1**) and the *Rotation* graphically.

◆ **Place a Chair cell with scales of 1 and freehand rotation**

1. Choose *Utilities>Key-In* from the Application window menu, re-size the *Key-In window* to display the data entry field only.

2. Select the *Place Active Cell* tool, click the *Interactive* check box **On**.

3. Move the pointer to a clear section of the design, position the *Cell Origin* with a data point.
   The text "**XSCALE (1.0):**" appears in the *Key-In* window.

4. Re-direct *Input Focus* to the *Key-In* window, press <**Enter**> to accept an *x* scale of **1.0** as shown in brackets (we had the option of keying in a different scale).

The text "**YSCALE (1.0):**" appears in the *Key-In* window.

5. Press <**Enter**> to accept a *y* scale of **1.**

The text "**ROTATION (0):**" appears in the *Key-In* window and the cell displays at full size, with its rotation under the control of the pointer. Do not enter anything from the keyboard.

6. Move the pointer around the *Origin* of the cell until the desired orientation is found.

7. Enter the rotation with a data point, *Reset*.

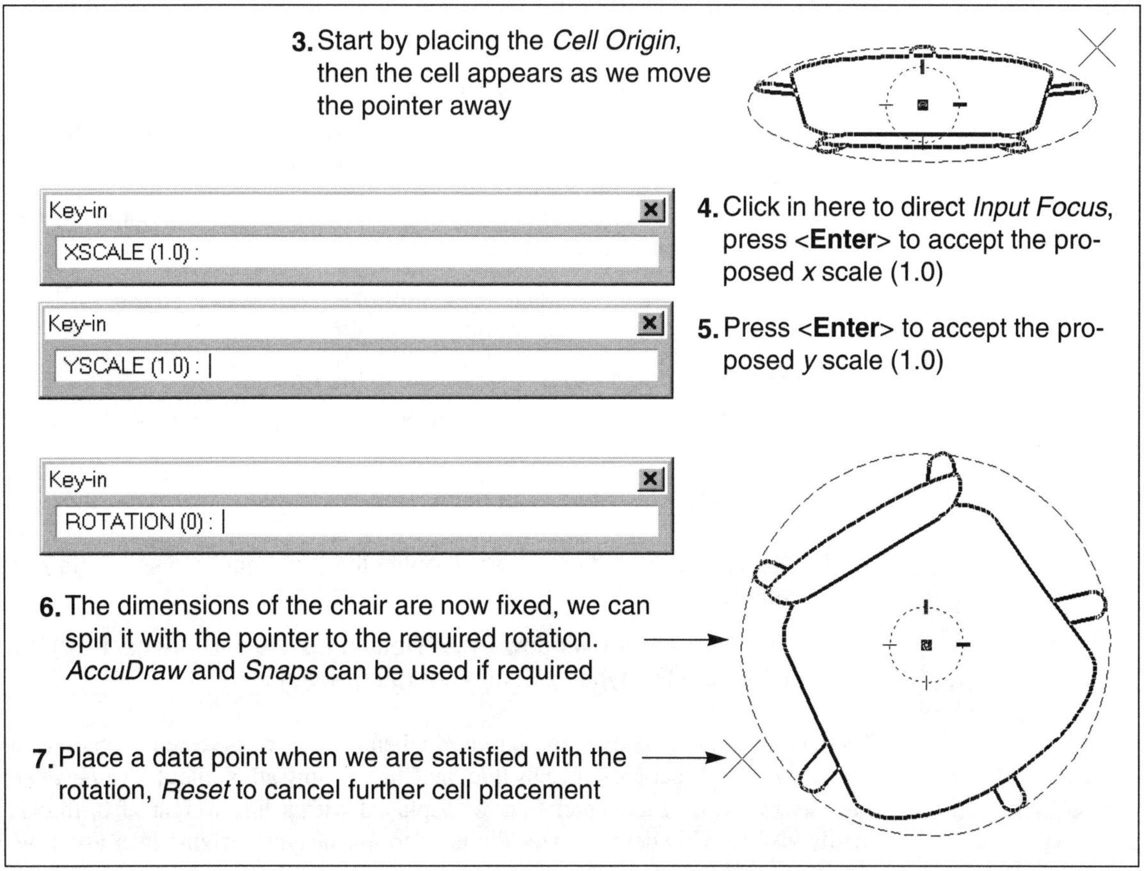

3. Start by placing the *Cell Origin*, then the cell appears as we move the pointer away

4. Click in here to direct *Input Focus*, press <**Enter**> to accept the proposed *x* scale (1.0)

Key-in   ✕
XSCALE (1.0) :

Key-in   ✕
YSCALE (1.0) : |

5. Press <**Enter**> to accept the proposed *y* scale (1.0)

Key-in   ✕
ROTATION (0) : |

6. The dimensions of the chair are now fixed, we can spin it with the pointer to the required rotation. *AccuDraw* and *Snaps* can be used if required

7. Place a data point when we are satisfied with the rotation, *Reset* to cancel further cell placement

Figure 6.16 Interactive cell placement using the Key-In window

When we created the drawing for the "CHAIR1" cell, we placed the *Active Point* and the floor area circle on level 20, the main linework on level 10. Try turning *Off* level 20, then the circle and point should disappear from the cells placed with *Absolute* (non-relative) levels.

Tip!   Use <**Ctrl+E**> to display the *View Levels* settings box, it is quicker than choosing *Settings>Level>Display*.

Placing Point Type Cells

We created two cells from the Office Chair drawing, a *Graphic* type named "CHAIR1" and a *Point* type named "CPOINT" (see "Cell Types" on page 6-11). We will experiment with the second of these cells in the next exercise.

◆ **Place a Point type cell**

1. Set the *Element Attributes* to a *Color* of **5**, a *Line Style* and *Weight* of **0**, with **15** as the *Active Level*.

2. Select *Element>Cells* (the *Cell Library* settings box should show that "examples.cel" as the *Attached Cell Library*).

3. Click on "CPOINT" to highlight it, click the *Placement* button to make it the general placement cell.

4. Select the *Place Active Cell* tool, set the *Active Angle* to **0°**, the *Scales* to **1.0** and both check boxes **Off**.

5. Move the pointer to a clear space in the design.
   The cell drawing will appear with the symbology of the current *Element Attributes*.

6. Place the cell with a data point, *Reset*.

7. Select the *Identify Cell* tool, identify the point cell to display the name and levels.

8. *Rotate* the View window (see "Rotating a View" on page 1-18), note that the *Point* type cell does not rotate with it.

The change in symbology from that used when the cell was created is obvious, and the *Identify Cell* operation reveals that the Chair is now all on the *Active Level* (15). The *Active Point* at its center is now displayed with a line weight of 0, thus it is hardly visible. This demonstrates the need to use heavier weights than usual when placing *Active Points*.

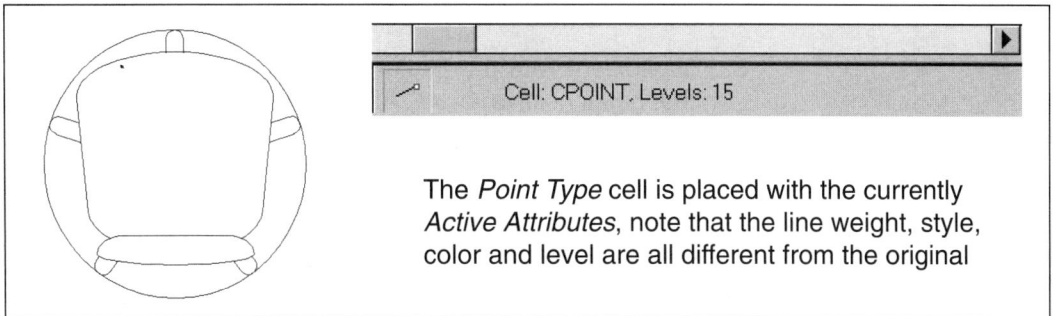

Figure 6.17   Office Chair placed as a Point type cell.

The Place Active Cell Matrix Tool

A *Matrix* of cells, either *Graphic* or *Point* type, is placed with the number of rows and columns and their spacing definable in the Tool Settings window (see Figure 6.18). There are no Relative and Interactive options, the *Matrix* is always placed with Graphic type cells on the same levels as the original definition.

Active Scale and *Active Angle* affect the individual cells in the same way as with the *Place Active Cell* tool, but they do not affect the rows and columns. The *Active Scale* and *Active Angle* may be set under *Settings>Design File*, or we can select the *Place Active Cell* tool initially to set these parameters before selecting the *Place Active Cell Matrix* tool.

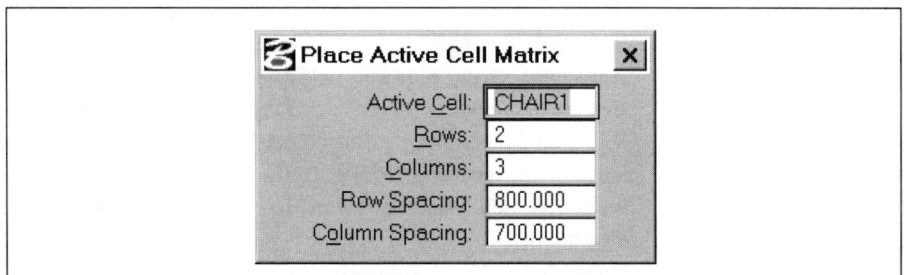

Figure 6.18   The Place Active Cell Tool Settings window

◆ **Place a two by three Matrix of Cells**

1. Select the *Place Active Cell Matrix* tool, set the *Active Cell* to **CHAIR1**, *Rows*: **2**, *Columns*: **3**, *Row Spacing*: **800**, *Column Spacing*: **700**.

2. Place a data point to define the position of the *Origin* of the *Lower Left Cell* of the matrix.

3. Experiment with the placement of matrices of the *Active Cell*, with changes to *Active Angle*, *Active x* and *y Scales*, number and spacing of *Rows* and Columns.

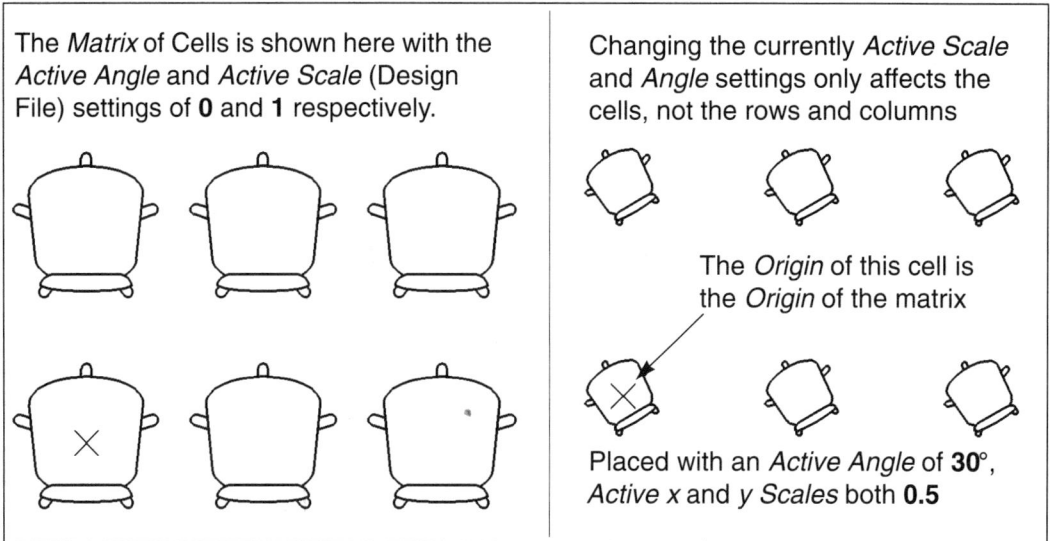

Figure 6.19   *Placing a Matrix of the Active Cell*

The Select and Place Cell Tool

We do not need to key in a cell name, or select it from the *Cell Library* settings box if an instance of the required cell already exists in the design. With this tool, we can click on the existing instance and the identified cell is automatically made the *Active Cell*, then the next data point *Places* an instance of this Cell. The tool settings for this tool are similar to the *Place Active Cell* tool, except it does not have the option of *Interactive* cell placement. For *Select and Place* to work, the following conditions must be met:

The *Cell Library* holding the particular cell selected must be attached;

The *Cell Library* holding the cell selected must be in the *Cell Library List*;

The selected cell instance must have been placed as a *Shared* cell.

The *Cell Library List* is definable by editing the *Cell List* configuration variable under *Workspace>Configuration>Cells*, usually in the form [drive]:\[path]*.cel.

Shared Cells

☑ Use Shared Cells

This check box is in the *Cell Library* settings box, in the center just below the title bar. When it is checked *On*, all cells placed are placed as *Shared Cells*.

When we place a particular cell in the design as a *Shared* cell for the first time, a single *Cell Definition* (defining all the elements of the cell) is stored in the design file. From then on, only a set of position coordinates and a cross-reference to the original *Cell Definition* are stored each time the same cell is placed.

Using *Unshared* cells results in a complete *Cell Definition* being stored each time a cell is placed. It follows that the design file will be larger when there are many instances of the same cell. This is not the only advantage of using *Shared Cells*:

- The *Cell Library* need only be attached while the first instance of a particular cell is placed. From then on further placements use the same cell definition, thus the particular library is not referred to. We can therefore have a different library attached, or no library at all.

- *Updating* any instance of a *Shared* cell (using the *Replace Cells* tool, see page 6-22) will replace *all* shared instances of this cell in the design file.

✔ Association

- A *Shared* cell may be *Associated* with a point on another element. If we have *Association lock On* in the *Locks* settings menu and we *Snap* to the other element before clicking the data button to place the cell, this association is established. If the original element (not a copy) is moved or mirrored, the cell moves with it.

If required, we have the option of keeping a shared instance of the old cell intact while replacing the rest. The particular cell can be *Dropped* from being a shared cell to either an ordinary cell, or to non-cell geometry. To do this we use a multi-function tool from the *Groups* tool box (in the *Main* tool frame) called *Drop Element*.

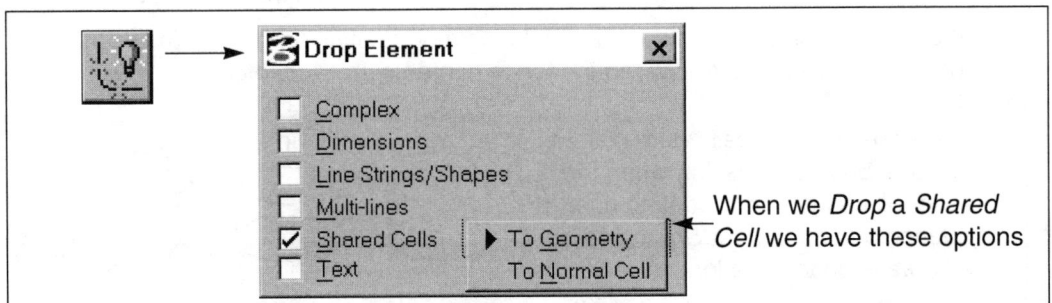

Figure 6.20 Dropping the Shared status of a cell

Replacing Cells

Cells already in place in a design may be changed at any time. They may be *updated* to a new version of the cell (created with the same name as the original), or *replaced* by another cell with a different name.

The Replace Cells Tool

This is the tool used for *Updating* or *Replacing* cells. It has options to replace cells individually, as a group, or all instances of the identified cell in the design file.

Updating Cells to a Revised Definition

When using the *Update* method option, it simply replaces the existing cell instance(s) with one of the same name from the attached cell library. When a *Shared* cell (see "Shared Cells" on page 6-21) instance is updated, it replaces the only definition of that particular cell in the design file. Since all the instances of a particular cell placed as *Shared* use the same definition, all of them will be updated at once.

Unwanted updating of a shared cell instance can be avoided by *Dropping* it, see "Dropping the Shared status of a cell" on page 6-21.

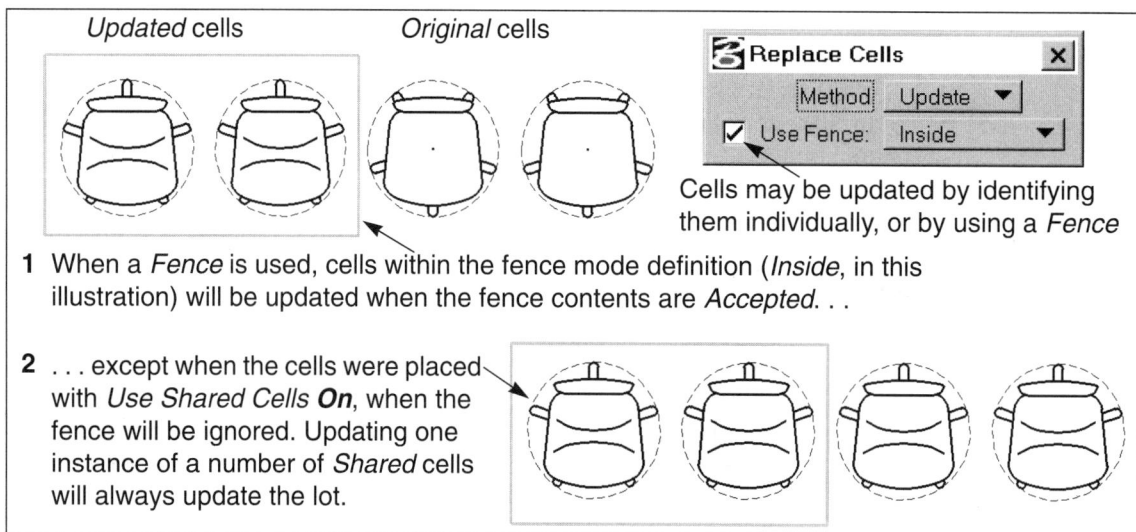

Updated cells   *Original* cells

Replace Cells
Method Update
☑ Use Fence: Inside

Cells may be updated by identifying them individually, or by using a *Fence*

1 When a *Fence* is used, cells within the fence mode definition (*Inside*, in this illustration) will be updated when the fence contents are *Accepted*. . .

2 . . . except when the cells were placed with *Use Shared Cells **On***, when the fence will be ignored. Updating one instance of a number of *Shared* cells will always update the lot.

Figure 6.21   Updating Cells

Replacing Cells

The *Replace* method enables us to replace individual cells, a group of cells, or all of the instances of a particular cell, with any other cell. This is the case regardless of whether the cell(s) were shared or unshared.

This method also allows us to optionally replace any "Attributes" associated with the cell. These attributes may be *Tags* (see "Element Tags" on page 12-24), external database attributes or some other form of *user data*. User data is sometimes generated by other applications running in conjunction with MicroStation.

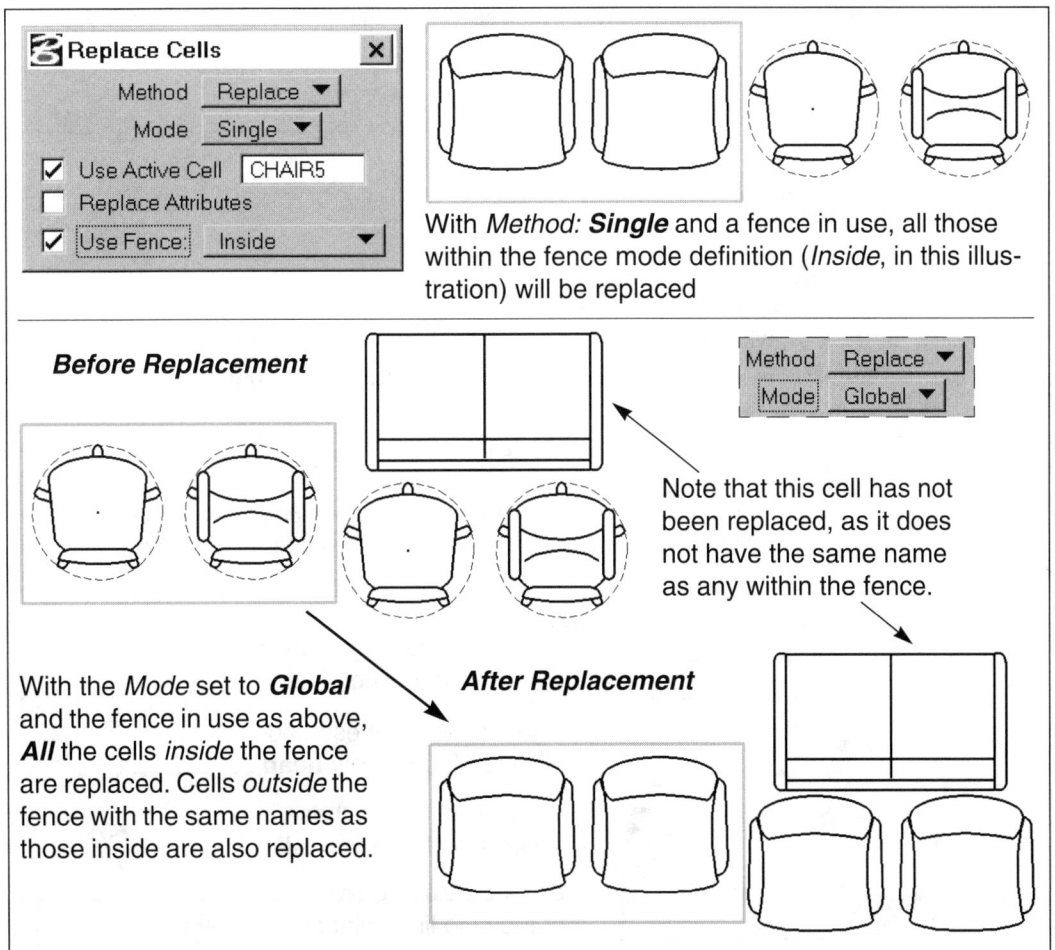

With *Method: Single* and a fence in use, all those within the fence mode definition (*Inside*, in this illustration) will be replaced

Before Replacement

Note that this cell has not been replaced, as it does not have the same name as any within the fence.

With the *Mode* set to *Global* and the fence in use as above, *All* the cells *inside* the fence are replaced. Cells *outside* the fence with the same names as those inside are also replaced.

After Replacement

Figure 6.22   Cell Replacement Using the Fence

Cells as Line Terminators

Cells can be used to terminate a line, for example as arrowheads and arrow tails to indicate direction. Once we have suitable drawings stored as cells, we could use general placement techniques such as *Interactive* to align the cell to the line, but there is a much easier way.

The Place Active Terminator Tool

This tool places a cell on the end of an identified line, line string, curve or arc. The x axis of the cell geometry (when it was created) is aligned to be a straight continuation of the element, regardless of the element's orientation. The cell is attached to the identified element at its *Origin*.

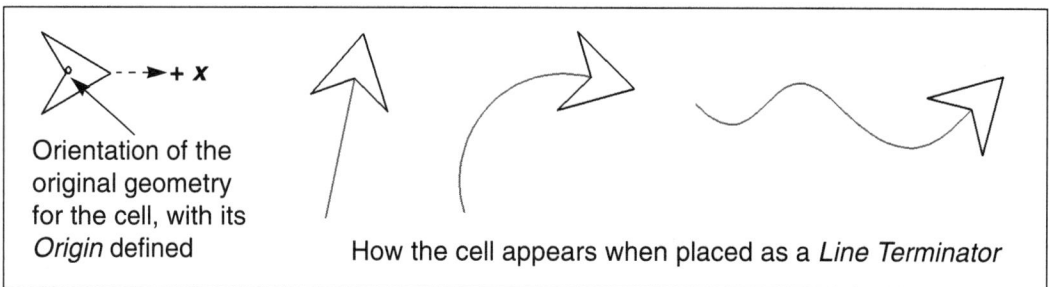

Figure 6.23   Examples of the use of a cell as a Line Terminator

We will create two cells for use as *Line Terminators*, an arrowhead and an arrow tail as shown in Figure 6.24. They are for use as ends of a direction indicator.

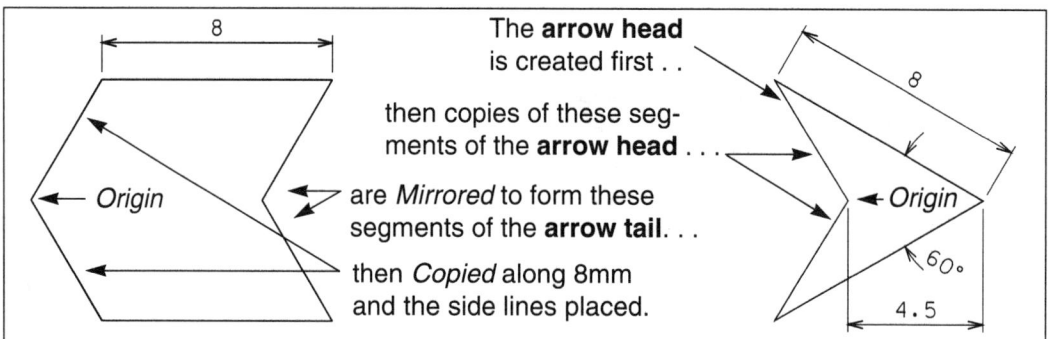

Figure 6.24   The drawings for line terminator cells

◆ **Create the Arrowhead drawing**

1. In "cells.dgn", set the *Active Level* to *1*, *Line Style* and *Color* to *0*, *Line weight* to *1*. Start *AccuDraw* if necessary.

2. Select the *Place Smartline* tool, set the *Segment Type* to **Lines**, click *Join Elements* **Off**, *Vertex Type* to **Sharp**.

3. Place a data point to define the lower left vertex of the arrowhead.

4. With AccuDraw in *Polar* coordinate mode, move the pointer in the direction of the apex, key in an *Angle* of *30°* and a *Distance* of *8*, *Accept*.

   Do not *Reset*, we will keep the tool placing line segments end-to-end.

5. Use the view control tools to adjust the View window as necessary, *Reset* to return to the *Place Smartline* operation.

6. Move the pointer back towards the top vertex, key in an *Angle* of *120°* and *Accept* the *Previous Distance* (the line indexed to **8** with the T stop displayed).

7. Snap to the apex (tentative only), Press <**O**> to move the Origin, press <**T**> (the *AccuDraw Shortcut* to rotate the drawing plane to standard Top view rotation)

8. Move the pointer to the left, while indexed to the *-x* axis key in *4.5* to the *Distance* field, *Accept*.

9. Move the pointer back over the starting point, snap a tentative point to the first line, *Accept*, *Reset*.

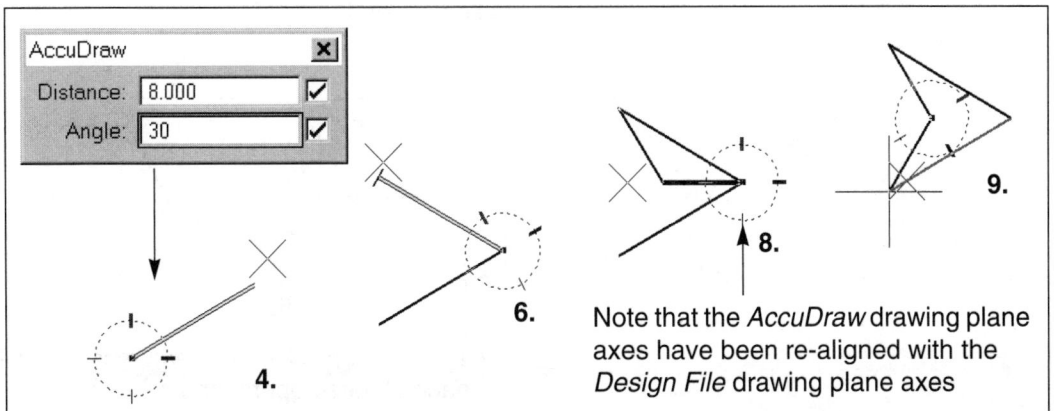

Figure 6.25   Creating the Arrowhead

We will create the other end of the arrow next, then use both drawings to create cells. In step **2.** of the arrowhead drawing exercise we turned *Join Elements Off*, so each of the segments are individual *line* elements. We will copy the two lines forming the back of the arrowhead to form the basis of the arrow tail.

◆ **Create the Arrow tail drawing**

1. Leave the element attributes and the Smartline tool settings as set for the arrowhead.

2. Place a *Block* type *Fence* about the two back lines of the arrowhead created in the last exercise (make sure they are fully inside the fence block).

3. Select the *Manipulate Fence Contents* tool from the *Fence* tool box, set the *Operation* to **Mirror**, *Fence Mode* to **Inside**, *Make Copy* checked **On**, *Mirror About* **Vertical**.

4. Move the pointer to the left to position the fence image to clear the arrowhead geometry, *Accept*, but do not *Reset*.

   We now have one end of the tail drawn, we will copy it along by **8mm** to draw the other end, using the tool that is still running and fence that is still in place.

5. Set the *Operation* to **Copy**, place a data point, move the pointer along the *x* axis by **8**, *Accept*, *Reset*. Click the *Place Fence* tool to remove the fence.

6. Use the *Place Smartline* tool to place the top and bottom segments, snapping tentative points to position the first data points each time.

   The *Previous Distance* of **8** will still be in effect, so we do not need to snap to locate the second end.

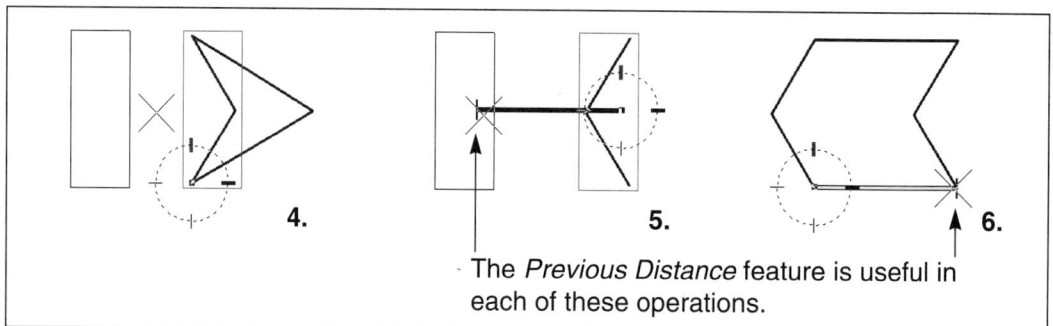

Figure 6.26 Drawing the Arrow tail

Now we will make each of the *Terminator* drawings into ordinary *Graphic* type *Cells*. Since we will be using them as terminators on an element, we would always want them to rotate with the element they are terminating when we rotate a view, so *Point* type would not be appropriate.

We will use the same process that we used to create the cell "AIR1" on page 6-8 and page 6-9, refer back to there if you would like more detail than is provided in the following exercises. Each drawing must be processed separately, only one *Cell Origin* can be in place at one time.

◆ Create cells from the Arrowhead and Arrow Tail drawings

1. Temporarily group the arrowhead elements using the *Fence* or by multiple element selection.

2. Select the *Define Cell Origin* tool, snap (tentative) to the vertex in the middle of the back (see Figure 6.24), *Accept*.

3. Select *Element>Cells*, ensure that "examples.cel" appears in the Title bar as *Attached Cell Library*.

4. Click the *Create* button, key in **ARRHD** to the *Name* field of the *Create New Cell* dialog box.

5. Press <**Tab**>, key in **ARROWHEAD TERMINATOR** to *Description*, the *Type* set to *Graphic*, press the ***Create*** button or the <**Enter**> key.

6. Repeat the above steps, except this time group the tail drawing, placing the *Origin* at the left vertex (see Figure 6.24). The name will be **ARRTL** and the description **ARROW TAIL TERMINATOR**.

Place some linear elements 20mm or more long (to suit the dimensions of the terminators at 1 : 1 scale). Use the *Place Active Terminator* tool (page 6-24) to place ARRHD and ARRTL terminators by data pointing near the ends of the lines, arcs etc. The cell names can be keyed in to the tool settings window, or the *Terminator* highlighted and selected (**1**) in the Cell Library (*Element>Cells*) box.

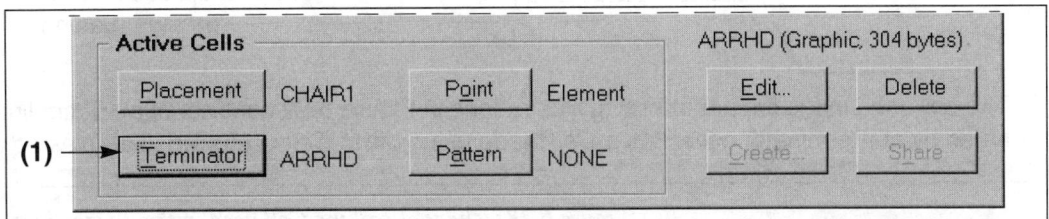

Figure 6.27   Lower section of Cell Library box, showing Terminator selection

Linear Patterning

Linear elements can be replaced by a linear pattern of *Cells*. Figure 6.29 illustrates the effect, where a pattern of cells is placed along linear element, in this case a complex chain consisting of an *Arc* and a *Line* segment.

A similar effect can be achieved (generally more efficiently) by using *Symbols* as a component of a *Custom Line Style*. These are to be introduced in Chapter 11.

The Linear Pattern Tool

The *Linear Pattern* tool's settings window (see Figure 6.28) has options for the type of cycle of pattern cell repetition. The effect of each option is illustrated in Figure 6.29. The other settings are the *Pattern Cell* name, the *Scale* and *Tolerance*. The tolerance relates to patterning along a curved element, where the curve is approximated for the patterning process by a set of straight line segments. The tolerance is expressed in the working units of the design file (mm in this case) and is the maximum deviation from the curve by the approximating segments.

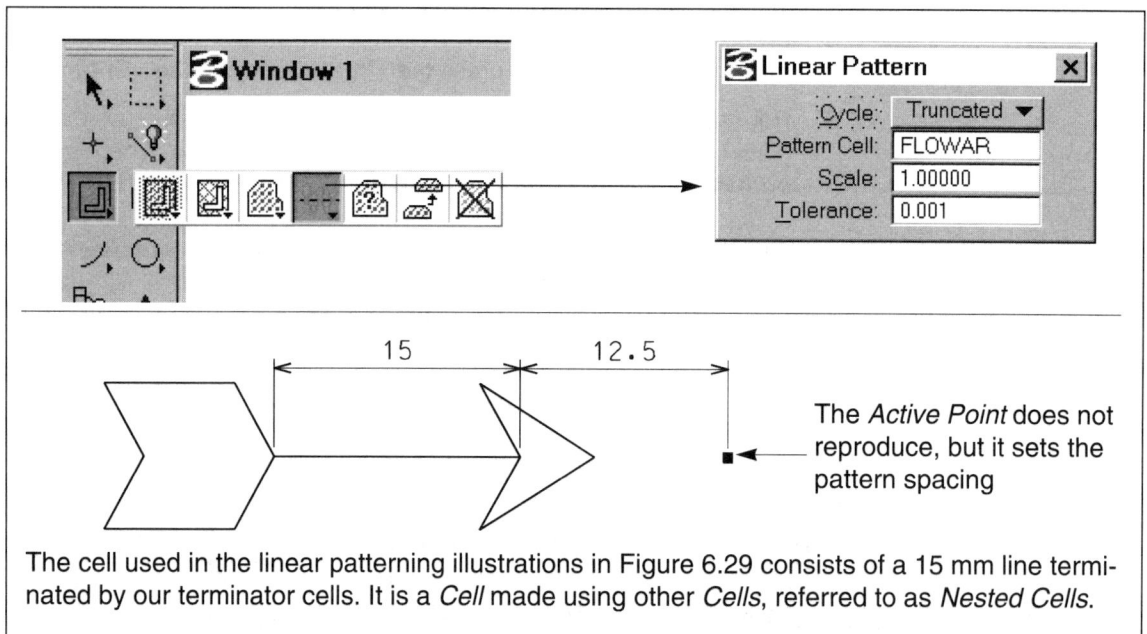

The cell used in the linear patterning illustrations in Figure 6.29 consists of a 15 mm line terminated by our terminator cells. It is a *Cell* made using other *Cells*, referred to as *Nested Cells*.

Figure 6.28   The tool and the Cell used in the illustrations

Truncated

Complete

The complex chain linear element used here consists of an 40mm radius arc and a 40mm line segment

1

2

The first data point identifies the linear element, the second defines the direction.

Linear element before patterning

Single

Multiple

Tolerance: 1.000

Tolerance: 0.001

Examples of a *Tolerance* setting of **1.0** (mm) and of **0.001**.
The original element is shown as a medium dash line

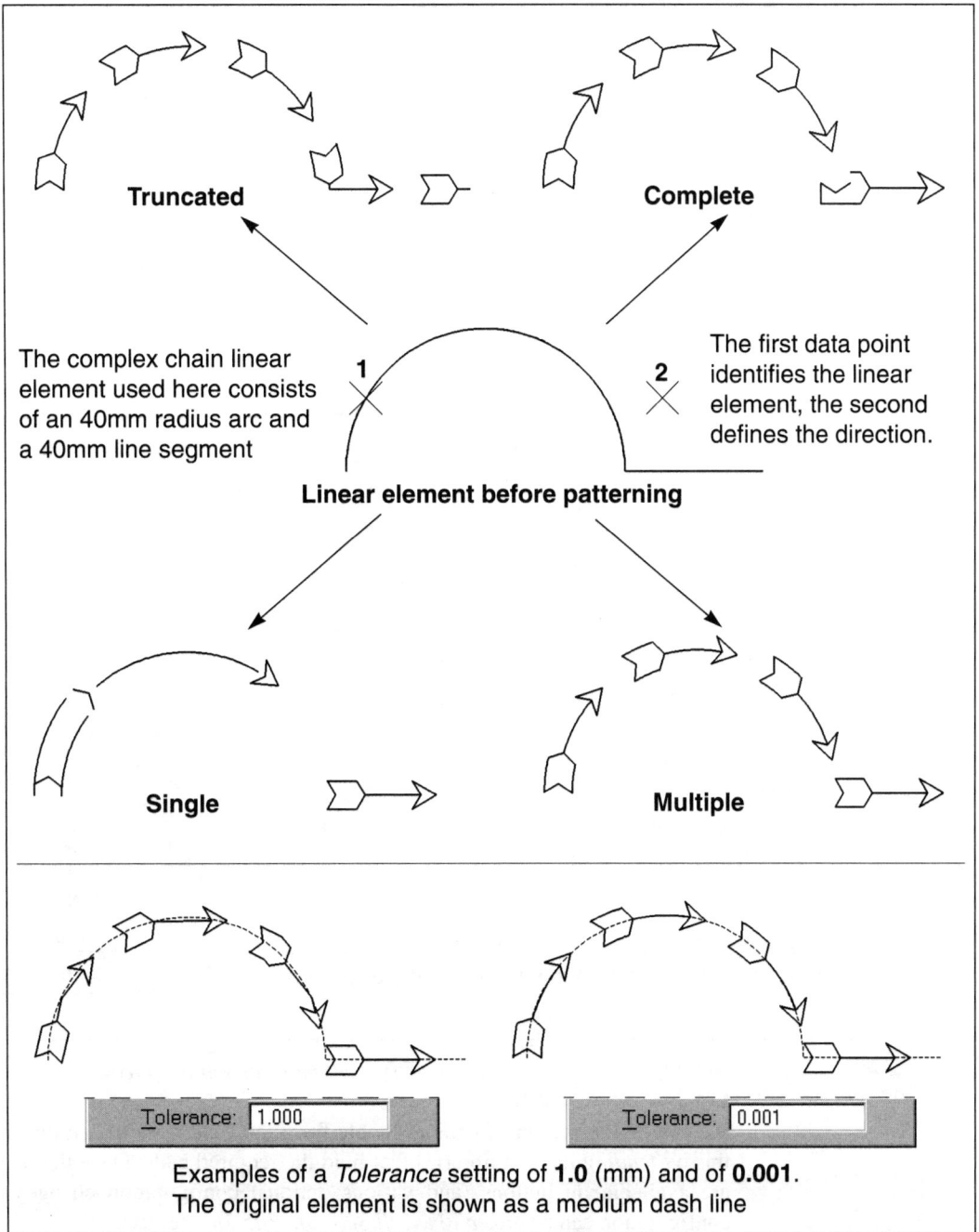

Figure 6.29   Examples of linear patterning options

The Cell Selector Utility

This utility makes the selection and placement of cells easier and faster, displaying the cells as buttons in a settings box. Clicking one of these buttons not only finds and selects the cell to be placed, it activates the appropriate tool to place it with.

The Cell Selector Settings Box

This is accessed via the Application window menu, as *Utilities>Cell Selector.*

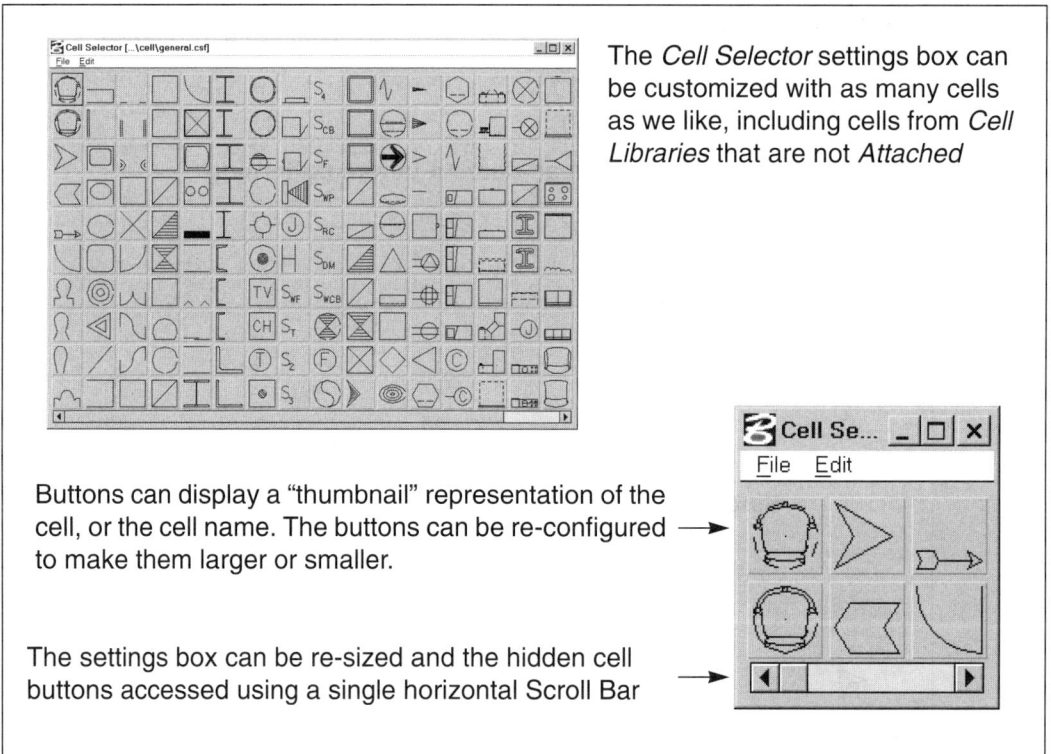

The *Cell Selector* settings box can be customized with as many cells as we like, including cells from *Cell Libraries* that are not *Attached*

Buttons can display a "thumbnail" representation of the cell, or the cell name. The buttons can be re-configured to make them larger or smaller.

The settings box can be re-sized and the hidden cell buttons accessed using a single horizontal Scroll Bar

Figure 6.30   Cell Selector settings boxes

We can define the set of cells available from the *Cell Selector* settings box. We do this by *loading* the cell libraries that hold the required cells. Once the required cells are available on buttons (and various optional configuration changes made) the configuration can be *Saved* to a *Cell Selector File* for later use.

Choosing *Utilities>Cell Selector* has a different result at different stages of configuration of our particular MicroStation installation. In some cases the first dialog box to open will be titled *Select Cell Library to Load.*

If there has previously been a cell library loaded, the *Select Cell Selector File* box may open. If a cell selector file has been included in the *Workspace* configuration, a ready-configured Cell selector settings box opens immediately.

*Choosing **Utilities>Cell Selector** may open a variety of dialog or settings boxes . . .*

*. . . Including an already config-
ured Cell Selector settings box*

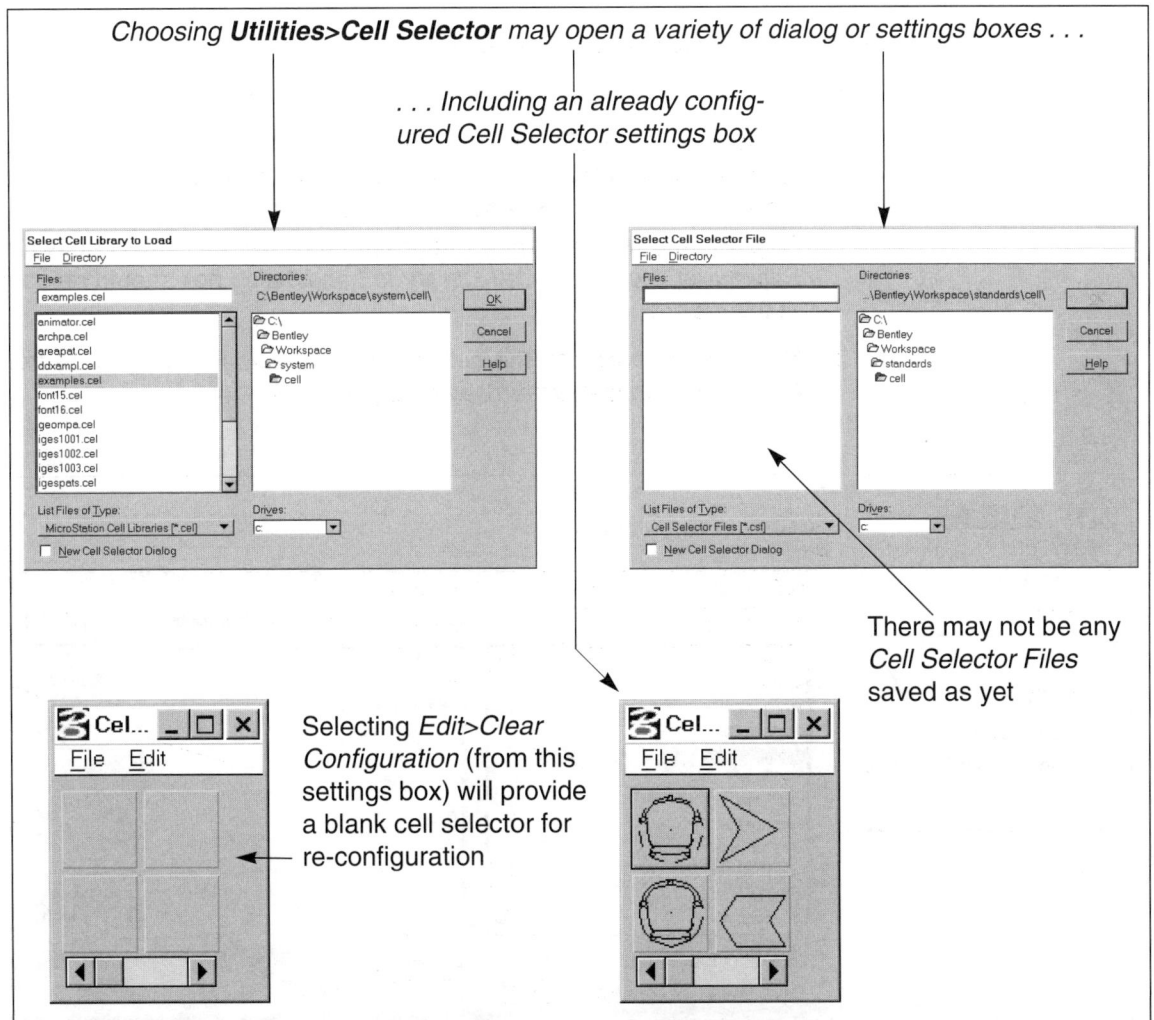

Select Cell Library to Load
File   Directory

Files:
examples.cel

animator.cel
archpa.cel
areapat.cel
ddxampl.cel
examples.cel
font15.cel
font16.cel
geompa.cel
iges1001.cel
iges1002.cel
iges1003.cel
igespats.cel

Directories:
C:\Bentley\Workspace\system\cell\

C:\
  Bentley
    Workspace
      system
        cell

OK
Cancel
Help

List Files of Type:
MicroStation Cell Libraries [*.cel]

Drives:
c:

☐ New Cell Selector Dialog

Select Cell Selector File
File   Directory

Files:

Directories:
..\Bentley\Workspace\standards\cell\

C:\
  Bentley
    Workspace
      standards
        cell

Cancel
Help

List Files of Type:
Cell Selector Files [*.csf]

Drives:
c:

☐ New Cell Selector Dialog

There may not be any *Cell Selector Files* saved as yet

Selecting *Edit>Clear Configuration* (from this settings box) will provide a blank cell selector for re-configuration

Figure 6.31   Preparing to configure the Cell Selector

Cell Selector Files

A *Cell Selector* settings box button configuration can be saved to a file for continuing use. We can store a variety of these configurations and select the one appropriate for our current project. We will configure our own *Cell Selector* in the next exercises, saving the configuration to a *Cell Selector file* named "general.csf". ".csf" is the default file extension for this type of file. To observe the operation of the Cell Selector without any confusion between it and *Attached* cell libraries, start by *Detaching* any cell library by choosing *Element>Cell Library>File>Detach*.

◆ **Create a customized cell selector - stage 1**

1. Choose *Utilities>Cell Selector* from the Application window menu.

2. If necessary, click *Cancel* in the *Select Cell Selector File* dialog box to open a blank *Cell Selector* settings box, choose *File>Load Cell Library* from the *Cell Selector* settings box menu.

    Step **2.** may not have been necessary on newly installed software. Either way, the *Select Cell Library to Load* dialog box should be open at this stage.

3. Select ***Examples.cel*** (the cell library we created on page 6-5) from the *. . .Workspace\system\cell* folder, click *OK*.

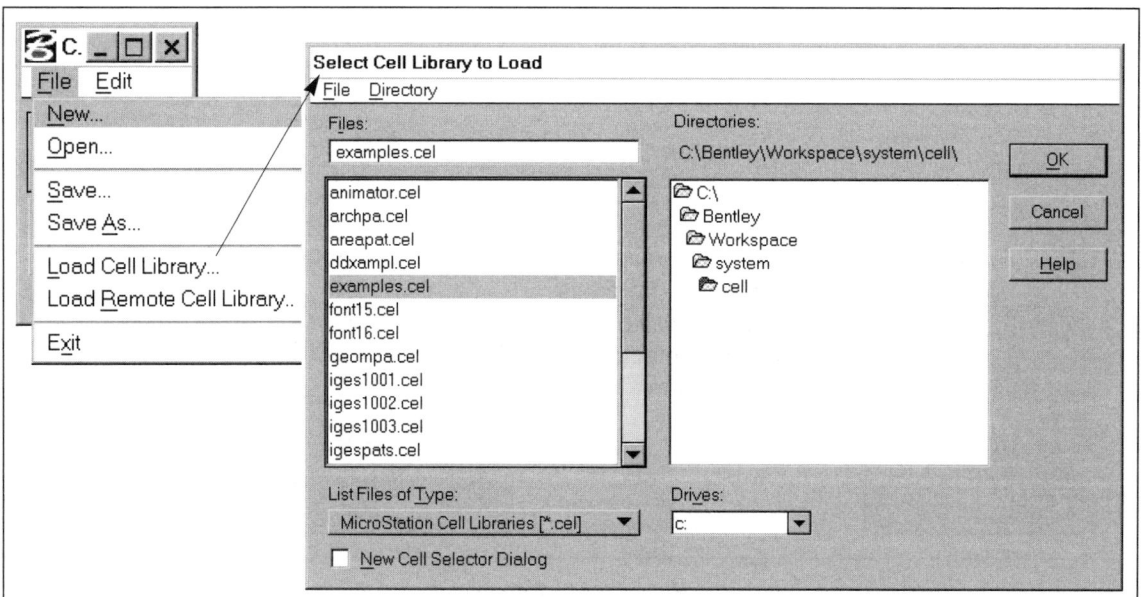

Figure 6.32   Loading a Cell Library to the Cell Selector

At this stage we have our own cell library loaded on to the cell selector, so all of our cells are available on the buttons. Experiment with placing cells, you will find it is only necessary to click a cell selector button and the *Place Active Cell* tool is operational with the loaded cell *Active*.

You will also find that the cells we created specifically as *Line Terminators* are actually being placed as *General Placement* cells. We can change this so that the appropriate tool for placing terminators is activated. This will be introduced shortly, for now we will continue with the basic *Cell Selector*.

◆ Create a customized cell selector - stage 2

1. Choose *File>Load Cell Library* again from the *Cell Selector* settings box menu.

2. (Optional) Set the folder to *. . . Workspace\projects\examples\arch\ cell*, select *arch.cel* from the *Files:* panel.

   This will load the cells from another library on to buttons in our *Cell Selector*, while the previously loaded cells remain.

3. Choose *File>Save As* from the *Cell Selector* settings box menu (the *Define Cell Selector File* dialog box will open).

4. Enter **general** to the *Files:* field (the extension ".csf" will be appended), click *OK*.

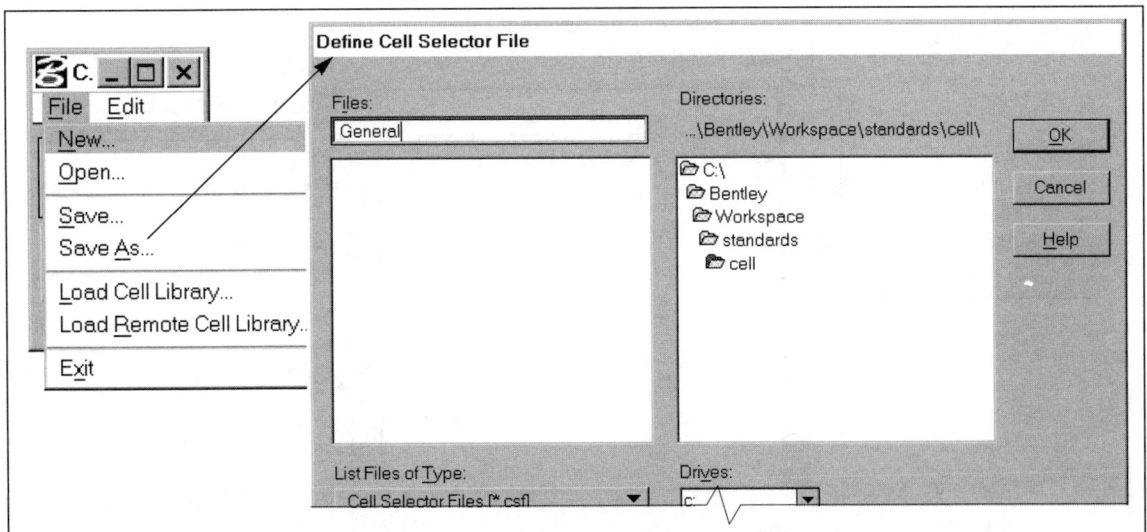

Figure 6.33   Saving the customized Cell Selector

The cell selector file was saved to the default folder, "...Workspace\standards\cell\" in the last exercise. It is possible to save it to a different folder and configure MicroStation to automatically search this folder for *Cell Selector* files. We can configure the current workspace for this directory by selecting it under *Workspace> Configuration>Cells>Cell Selector Directory* (see Figure 6.34).

Now that we have defined a *Cell Selector File* and the cell selector configuration has been saved, it can be recalled at any time from within any design file. We can configure MicroStation to make this the default cell selector by selecting it under *Workspace> Configuration>Cells>Cell Selector File*, as illustrated in Figure 6.34.

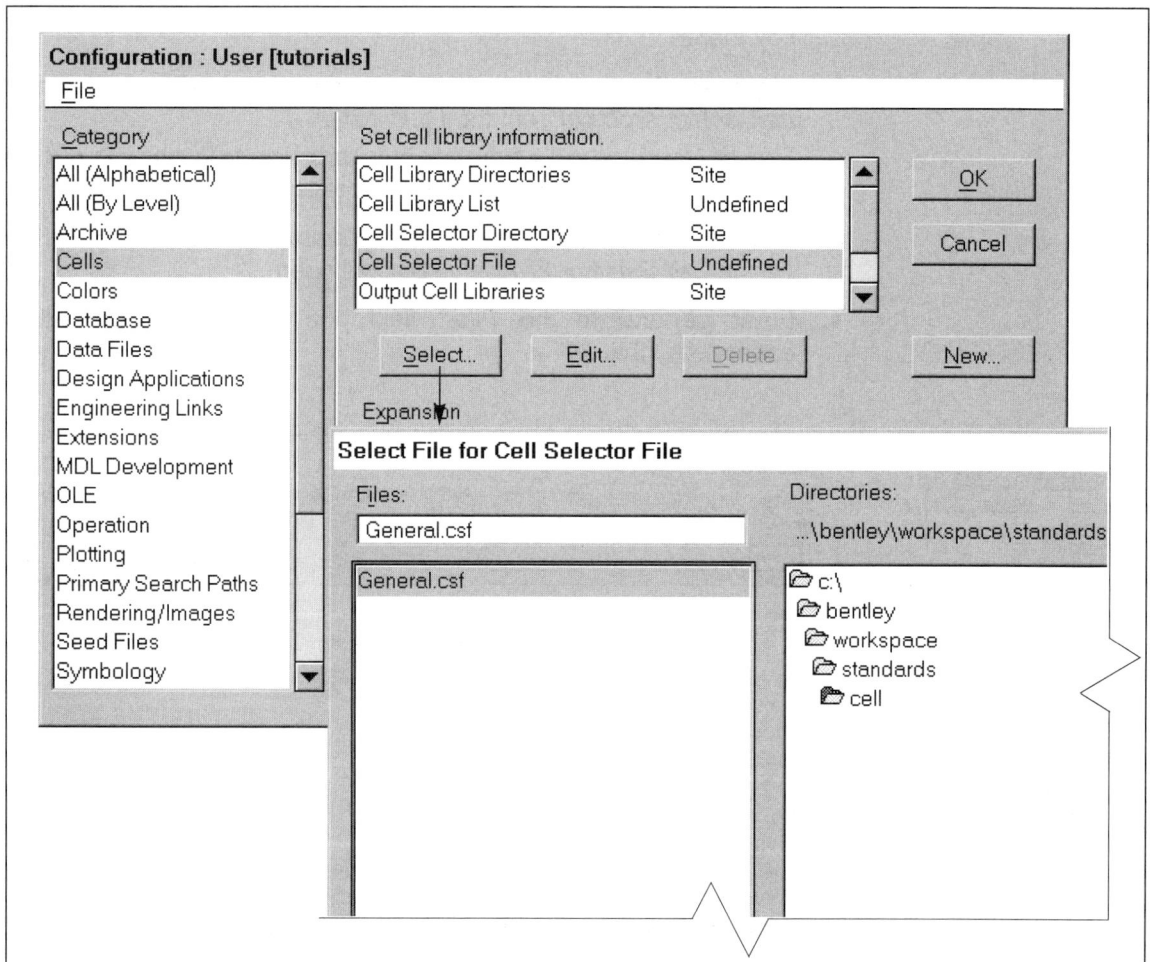

Figure 6.34   Configuring a MicroStation Workspace for a Cell Selector File

Editing Cell Selector Buttons

The cell selector button settings may be individually edited. The cell can be changed, as can the commands for its placement, its presentation on the button etc. The options available under *Edit>Button* are illustrated in Figure 6.35.

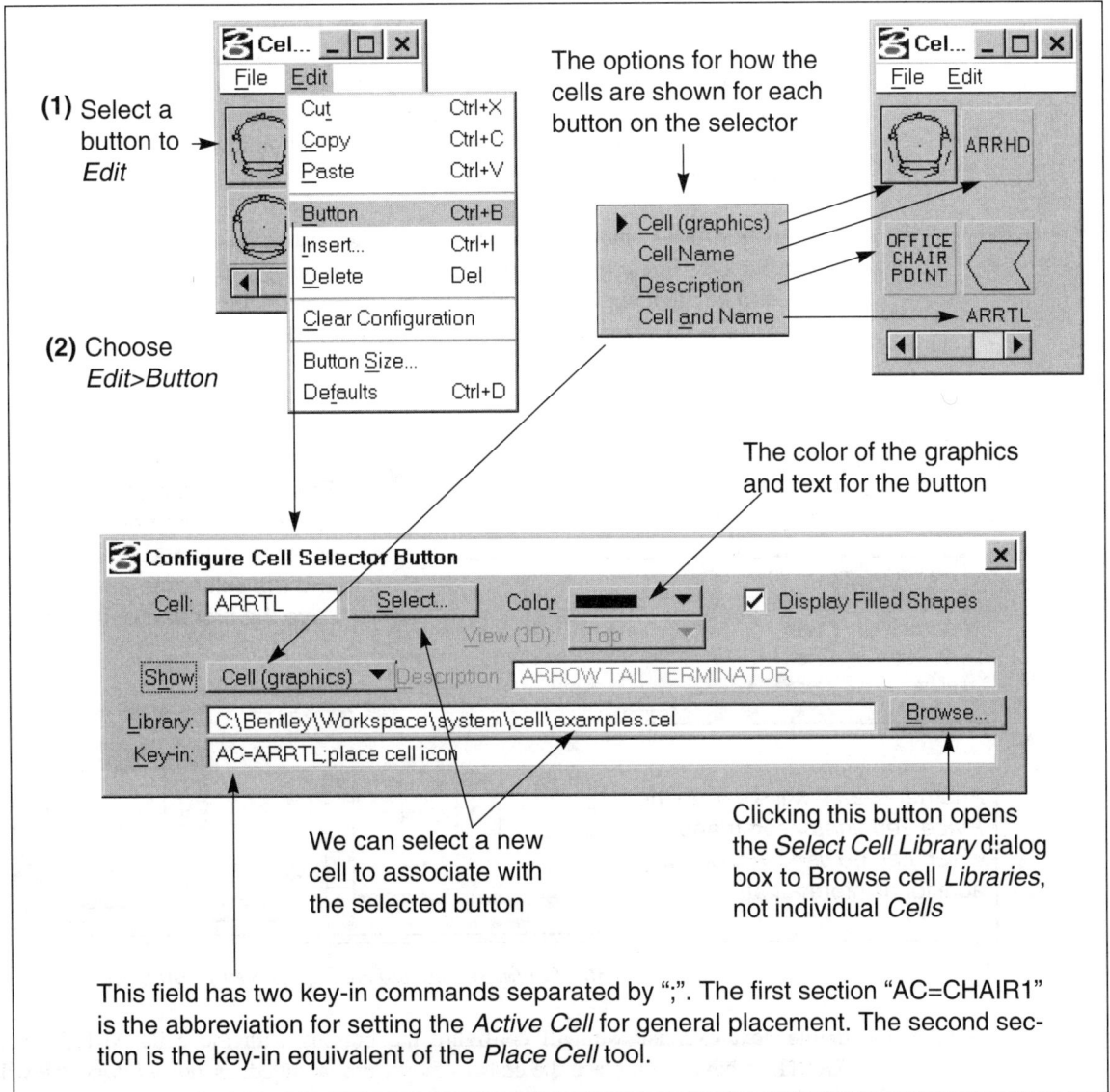

Figure 6.35 Editing options for an individual button

Associated Key-ins

The *Key-in:* field of the *Configure Cell Selector Button* settings box is used to program in the commands for selecting and placing the cell associated with the button being edited.

In their standard format, these commands are closely related to the tool names and the names of associated settings fields. There are abbreviated formats for some of them and this format is often used in default set-ups. Figure 6.35 shows the default contents of the key-in field. The "**AC=<cell_name>**" is the abbreviated form of the command "**ACTIVE CELL = <cell_name>**. The command **place cell icon** has the same effect as clicking the *Place Active Cell* tool button/icon. The two commands are separated by a semicolon (";"). They are not case-sensitive.

The *Key-in Browser* shown in Figure 6.36 can help us with some prompts (see "The Key-in Window" on page 5-40 for more details). Having established the commands, we need to key them into the *Configure Cell Selector Button* settings box manually. The software documentation has complete information on all of the key-ins, including abbreviations.

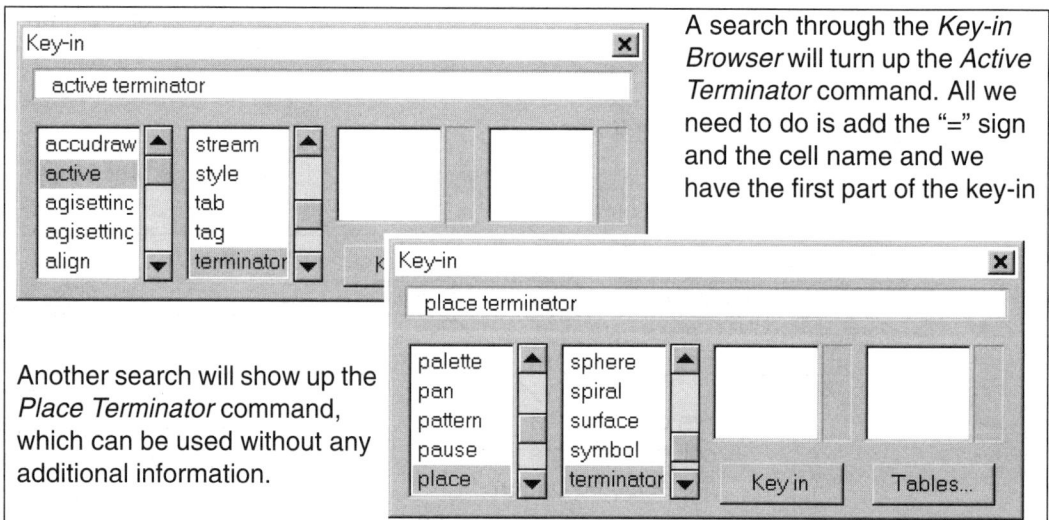

Figure 6.36   Finding commands using the Key-in Browser

In the next exercise we will configure the buttons with the cells ARRHD and ARRTL to have them place the cells as they were intended, as *Terminators*. We will start by establishing the necessary key-in string, using the default string for clues.

◆ **Edit the key-in string for placing a cell as a terminator**

1. Select the Arrowhead button (ARRHD) from the "general" cell selector settings box, choose *Edit>Button* from its menu.

2. Edit the *Key-in:* field, replacing the "AC" with "**active terminator"**, "place cell icon" with "**place terminator**".

   Note that the cell name will already have been entered with the default button configuration.

3. Select the Arrow tail button (ARRTL), repeat step **2.**

   The button to be edited can be selected before or after choosing *Edit* from the option menu.

4. Close the *Configure Cell Selector Button* dialog box, choose *File>Save* from the Cell Selector settings box menu to save the changes to the Cell Selector file "general.csf".

   If we neglect to save the changes now, we will be prompted to do so when we close the settings box.

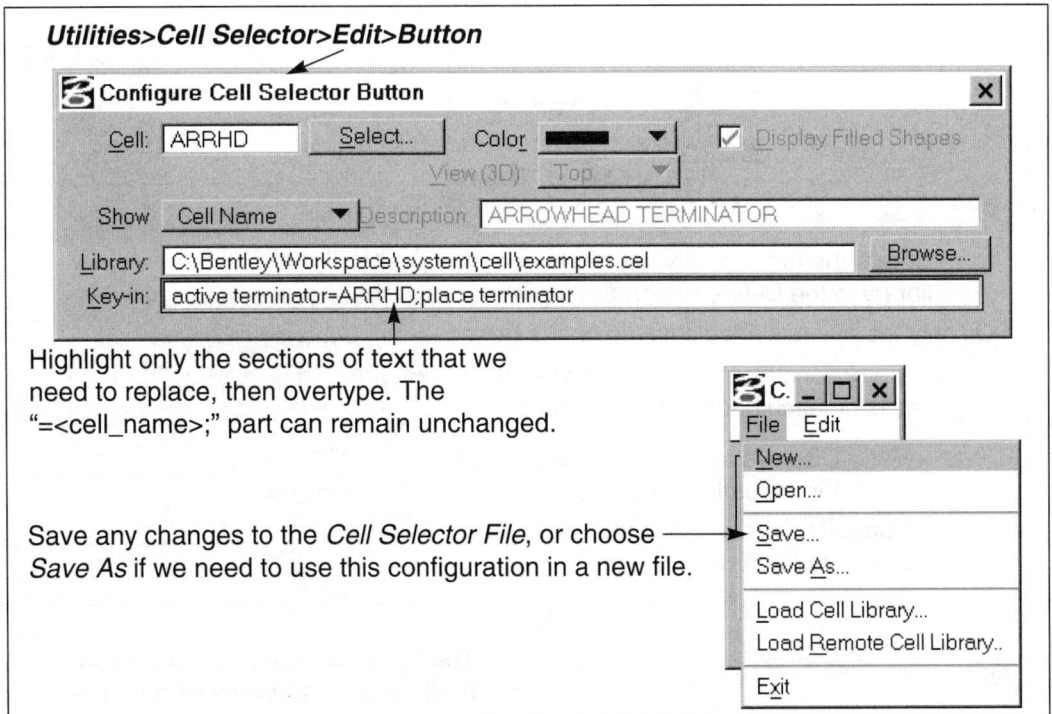

Figure 6.37   Editing the Key-in string

Defining the Default Settings for New Buttons

When we edited a button configuration (see "Editing Cell Selector Buttons" on page 6-35), we found a complete button configuration already in place. This was the *Default* configuration, which we can choose to change before loading or inserting new buttons.

Consider a case where we need to insert some new buttons, all with cells intended to be used as *Line Terminators* rather than as *General Placement* cells. Before inserting the cells, we can select *Edit>Defaults* and define all the configurations for the new cells at once.

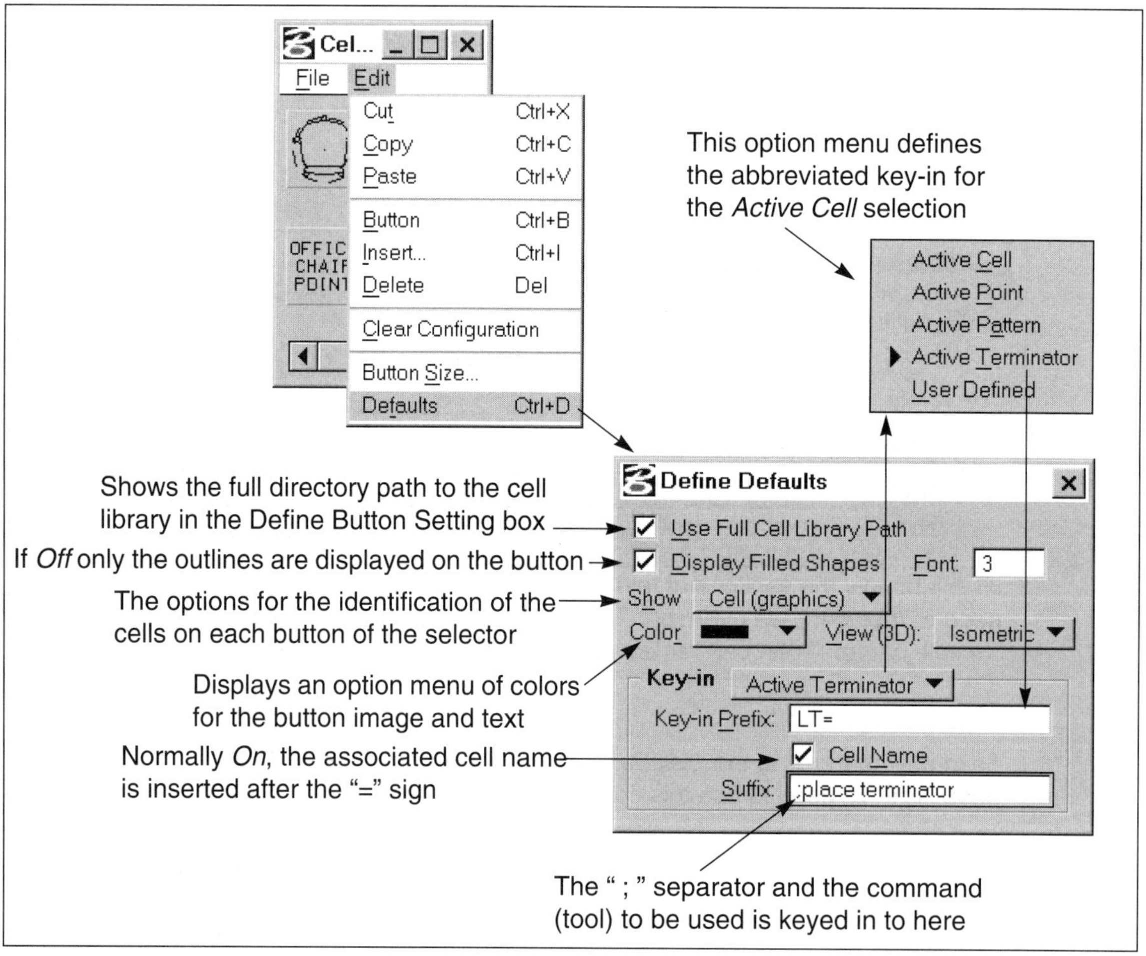

Figure 6.38 Pre-defining cell selector defaults

Inserting and Deleting Individual Cells

As well as loading complete cell libraries, we can insert individual cells into a Cell Selector. A button is selected in the position on the selector where we want to insert the new button. The *Edit>Insert* option opens the *Define Button* dialog box, where the new button configuration can be fully defined. Clicking OK inserts the new button *after* the selected one.

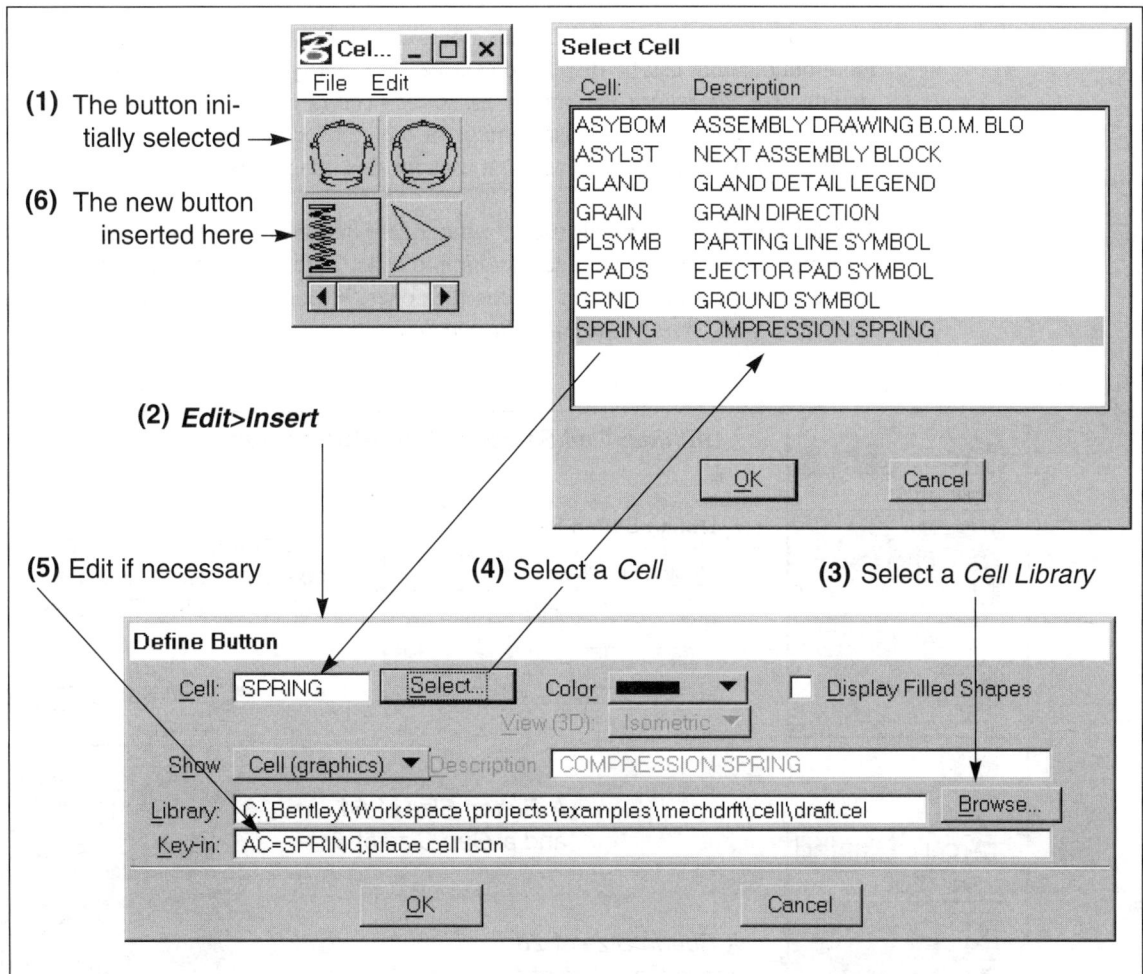

Figure 6.39   Inserting an individual cell

Choosing *Edit>Delete* removes the pre-selected button configuration, but the associated cell remains intact in its library.

Clearing a Cell Selector Configuration

Choosing *Edit>Clear Configuration* clears all of the buttons on the Cell Selector. The cell selector file is only cleared if we save the changes to it. If we make this choice in error, we only need to close the Cell Selector without saving the changes, then re-open it.

Defining the Size of the Selector Buttons

The smaller we make the Cell Selector buttons, the less screen area they cover, or the more buttons that can be displayed at once. The clarity of the cell images limits the size that we can reduce the buttons to, so we need to make a compromise. The cell selector software creates a raster image of the cell for inclusion on the button. The number of *pixels* (picture elements) it uses for this image sets the size of the button.

The default number of pixels used for the square buttons is 48 per side, or 2304 total. This may be more than we need for simple cells, or less than we need to recognize subtle differences between similar complex ones. We can change the button size (and the gap between them) with *Edit>Button Size*.

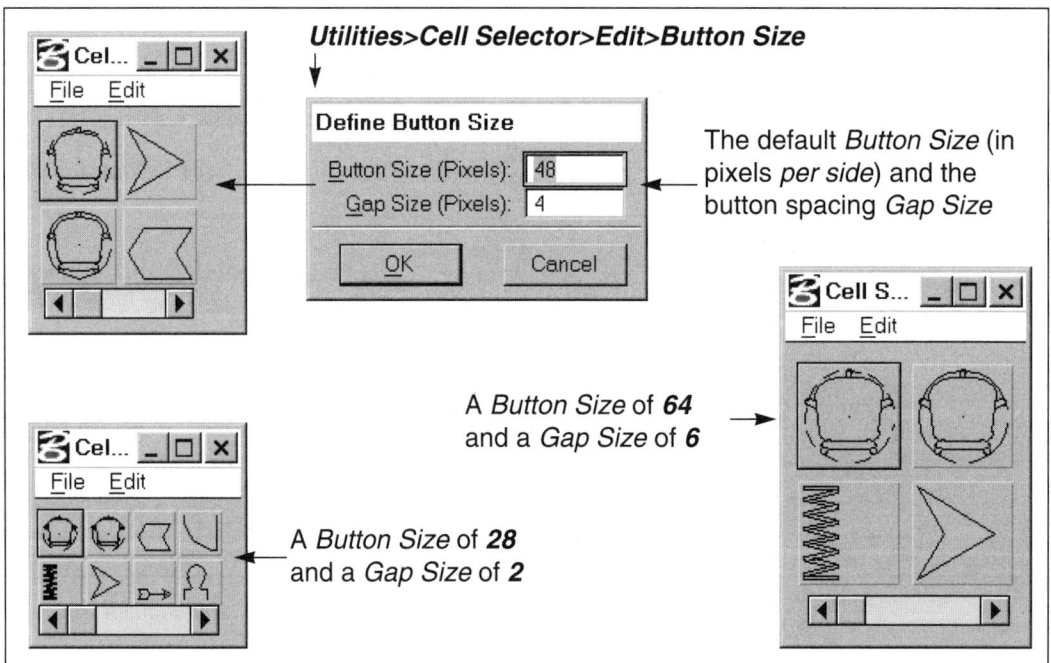

Figure 6.40   Button Size and Gap settings

Summary

Using *Cells* reduces the amount of repetitive work in the design documentation process. MicroStation has many *Cells* delivered with the package, others can be purchased from developers, but almost invariably we will need to make our own as well.

Cells are stored in *Cell Libraries*, which are files of graphics data, similar in many ways to a design file. They are created from a special *Seed File* in a similar way to a design file. A cell library can store a large number of individual cells, but it is usual to have a series of libraries, each holding a logical grouping of cells.

A drawing or section of a drawing to be created into a cell must first have all of its elements grouped together, either by enclosing them in a *Fence* or by multiple element selection. The point by which the position of the cell will be defined when it is being placed is called the *Cell Origin*. This must be defined before the cell can be created.

The Cell Library to hold the new cell must be *Attached* to the current design file. Only one Cell Library can be attached at any one time. Cells can be created as *Graphic* type, where its attributes are set at time of creation, or *Point* type, where the element attributes active at the time of placement apply. *Point* type cells do not rotate when the view is rotated, whereas *Graphic* cells do. *Point* type cells are not to be confused with cells used as *Active Points*.

Cells may be placed individually or in multiples as a *Matrix*. They may be placed on the same levels they were created on, or *Relatively*, where the elements on the lowest numbered level of the cell are placed on the level *Active* at the time of placement. Other levels are placed on level numbers displaced by the same number. For example, a cell with elements on levels one and two would be placed on levels ten and eleven if level ten was active at the time.

It is not always necessary to have the Cell Library *Attached* that holds the cell we need to place. Search paths for cell libraries can be configured into MicroStation as *Cell Lists*, so that a cell not found in any *Attached* cell library will be searched out using this list. Cells placed with the help of the Cell Selector utility also do not need to be in an attached Cell Library.

Cells may be designated for use in *General Placement*, as *Line Terminators*, as *Pattern* elements and as *Active Points*. Different tools are used for their placement in each case. The *Place Cell* tool is the one used for general placement. This tool has settings for *x* and *y* scale, rotation, relative placement and *Interactive* placement, where the scales and rotation may be set graphically or constrained to entered settings as required.

Placement of cells as *Line Terminators* automatically aligns what was the *x* axis of the cell at time of creation with the direction of the line. This feature makes it ideal for the creation of custom North pointing arrows etc. Cells may be placed as *Pattern* elements, either along a line (not often used in later versions of MicroStation) in as an *Area Pattern*, to be introduced in the next chapter. When cells are used to denote *Active Points* it is usual to have a recognizable point on the drawing to designate the precise point it is defining. This could be the intersection of lines forming a cross or some similar arrangement, normally at the *Cell Origin*.

Using *Shared* cell placement saves design file space when multiple copies of the one cell are used in the one design. Only one complete definition of the cell is saved with the design file and all other *Instances* of the cell refer back to this. Each time the same cell is placed, only positional information is added to the file, whereas ordinary placement adds a complete definition for each placement.

The *Cell Selector* utility speeds up the process of finding and placing cells. It presents each of a set of cells as buttons with images of the cells on them, similar to tool buttons. Clicking one of these buttons not only selects the cell for placement, it selects the appropriate tool to place it with as well. The configuration of the Cell Selector can be varied to suit the application, with cells from a number of libraries. Each of the configurations can be saved to *Cell Selector Files* and the configuration recalled as required. A Cell Selector file can be designated as the default in a MicroStation configuration file.

7 : Areas

Until now we have treated our designs as linework, a set of straight and curved lines. In many cases these lines may define an *Area*, such as a section of floor in a building or a panel on an item of mechanical plant. These *Areas* may be *Filled* with a solid patch of color, *Hatched*, *Crosshatched*, or *Patterned* with cells. They may also be *Measured* and even have their mass, perimeter and centroid position computed for a given mass per unit area.

This chapter will introduce the various operations related to areas and the relevant tools provided. We will find that the set of tools for working with areas have much in common.

When you have completed this chapter, you will be able to:

- Discern between a *Closed* and an *Open* element;
- *Drop* a closed element to its component open elements;
- Create a closed element from a set of line segments;
- Temporarily define areas with the *Fence* and with a set of data points:
- Apply *Fill Attributes* and *Background Fills* to *Closed Elements*;
- *Hatch*, *Crosshatch* and *Pattern* areas defined by individual and multiple elements;
- Generate and work with *Associative* and *Non-Associative* patterns;
- Create new closed elements from various combinations of existing closed elements;
- *Measure* areas and perform calculations on them.

Open and Closed Elements

A *Closed* element is one that encloses an *Area* within its *Boundary*. An *Open* element is one with ends that do not join, thus it cannot enclose an area by itself. We have already created closed elements in earlier exercises in the form of complex shapes, simple shapes and ellipses (including circles).

Closed elements are not the only way of defining an *Area*, a set of open elements that abut or cross over can enclose an area as well. However, *Open* and *Closed* status is not always obvious when we visually examine a section of a drawing. The *Analyze Element* tool (page 3-24) is needed to reliably provide this information, but *Snapping* to the element can give an indication.

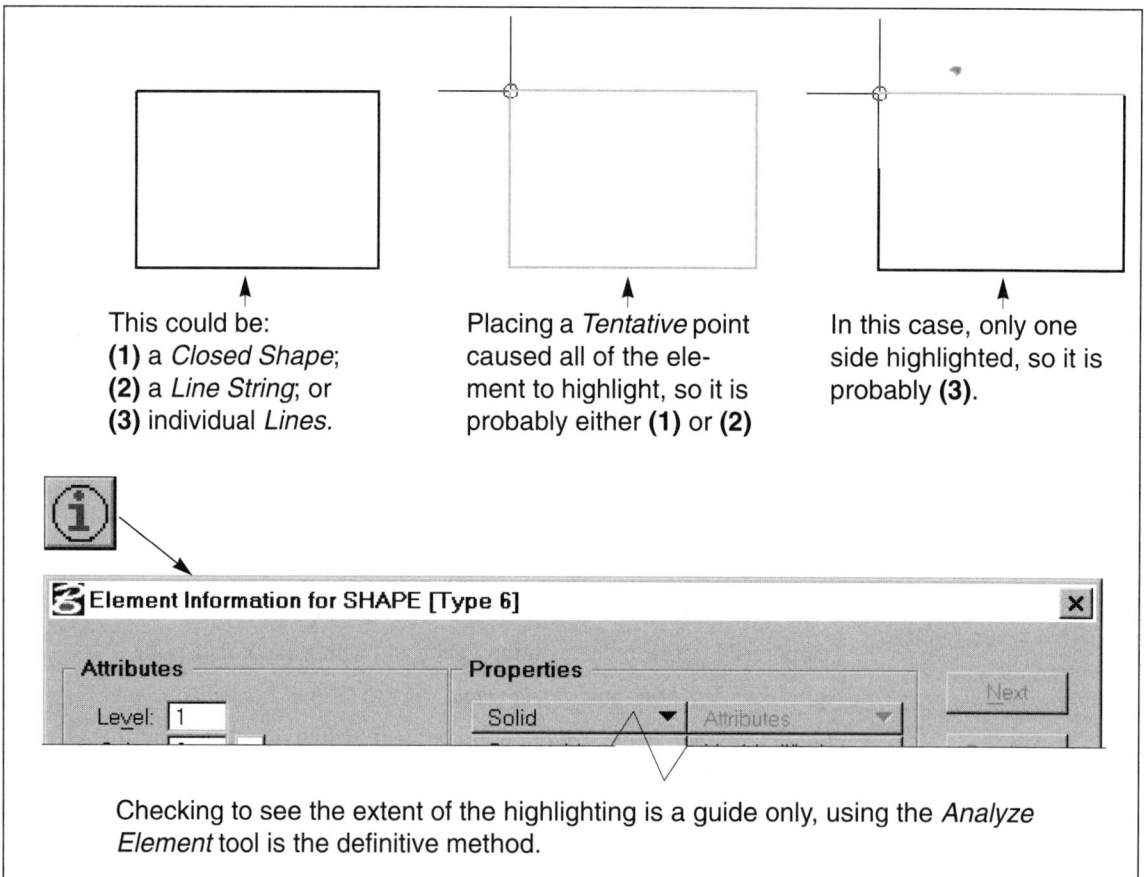

This could be:
(1) a *Closed Shape*;
(2) a *Line String*; or
(3) individual *Lines*.

Placing a *Tentative* point caused all of the element to highlight, so it is probably either **(1)** or **(2)**

In this case, only one side highlighted, so it is probably **(3)**.

Element Information for SHAPE [Type 6]   **✕**

Attributes

Le̲vel: 1

Properties

Solid   ▼   Attributes   ▼

Next

Checking to see the extent of the highlighting is a guide only, using the *Analyze Element* tool is the definitive method.

Figure 7.1   Testing for a closed element

Filling Closed Elements

The *Tool Settings* window usually provides *Fill Attribute* options when we are using tools that create closed elements. These options are additional *Element Attributes* that only apply to *Closed* elements.

In the case of the *Place Smartline* tool, the options only appear when the start and end points of line segments of the element coincide, until then the tool has no indication that we may be creating a closed element. All the other closed element tools, such as *Place Block*, *Place Circle* display the options on selection of the tool.

A closed element can optionally be *Filled* with solid color. This is the case regardless of its *Area* (solid or hole) status, which applies to *Hatching* and *Patterning*, to be introduced shortly. How this appears on paper documents will depend on the type of printer we use, most will reproduce the fill in color or monochrome. Older devices (typically pen type plotters) may not reproduce filled areas.

Elements may not appear filled in a view window even when we have chosen a fill option. The *Fill* attribute must be checked *On* in the *View Attributes* settings box (see "Attributes of the View Window" on page 3-3).

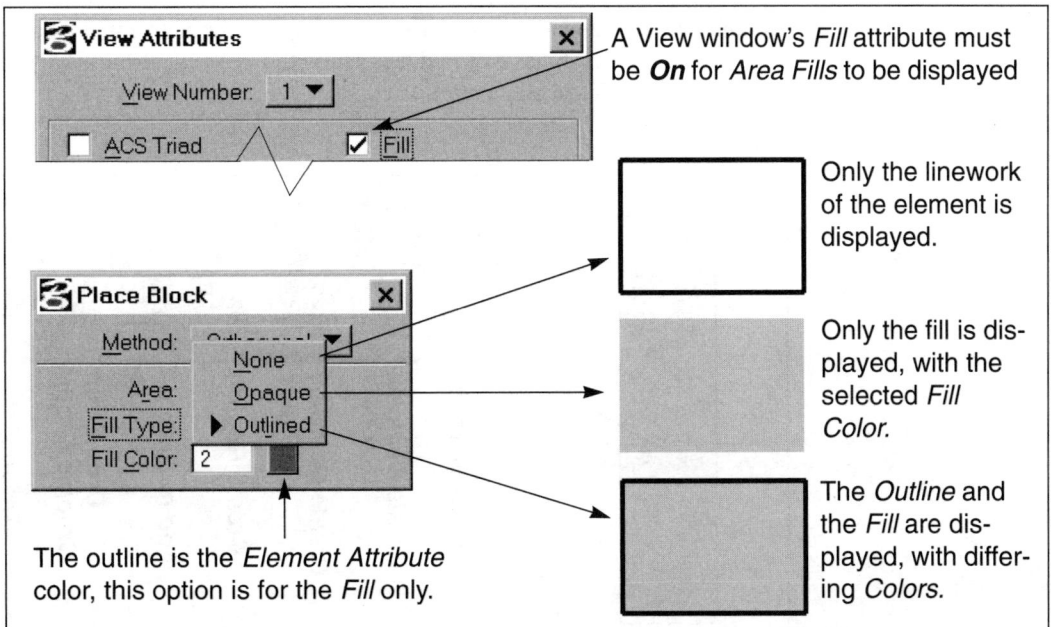

Figure 7.2   Fill Options

Permanent Groups

Permanent groups of elements can take various forms. One form is simply called *Group* or *Orphan Cell*. This one may be created by making a multiple selection of the elements to be grouped (with the *Element Selection* tool), then choosing *Edit>Group*.

Groups of elements that define *Areas* are the ones we are working with in this chapter, so we will concentrate on these for now. *Orphan Cells* are one of these forms of groups.

The Groups Tool Box

The names of the tools we will be using in this chapter are shown in bold in Figure 7.3. The first of these to be used will be the *Drop Element* tool, which actually destroys closed elements as such. We have already used this tool in another mode, when we *Dropped* the shared status of a cell in chapter 6. The *Create Complex Shape* tool does the opposite to *Dropping*, it groups individual elements to form a closed element.

Create Region creates a single closed element from a specified form of combination of other closed elements. *Group Holes* provides an alternative method of creating an *Orphan Cell*. It combines a closed element with the *Solid* attribute with one or more *Hole* attributed closed elements.

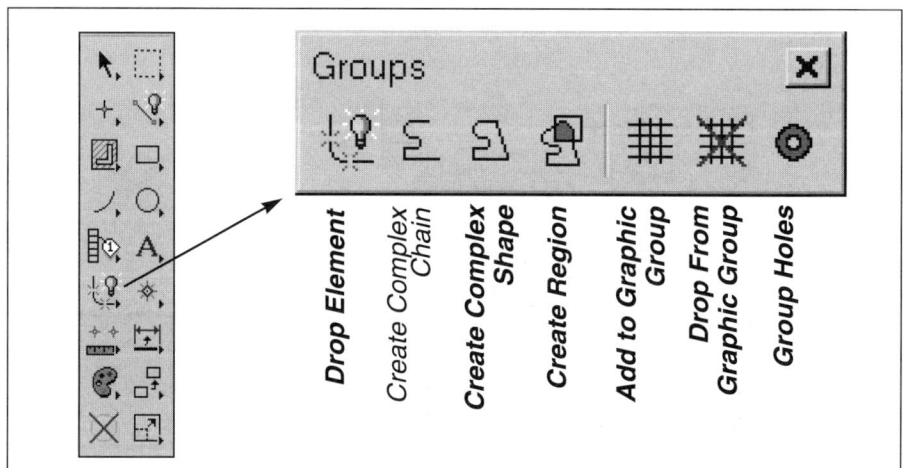

Figure 7.3   The Groups Tool Box

Dropping a Closed Element to its Components

We can convert simple and complex shapes to a set of individual line elements. This may be necessary to allow for some changes to be made to part of the linework, without affecting the remainder. We can use the *Drop Element* tool from the *Groups* tool box to provide this function. *Drop Element* is a "general Purpose" tool for reducing the complexity of a variety of element types. There are also two individual tools, *Drop Line String/Shape Status* and *Drop Complex Status*, found in the *Drop* tool box. This tool box is not in the Main tool frame, it is opened from *Tools>Drop*.

The outline of the Stay Plate we created back in chapter 3 was a *Complex Shape* (see "Analyzing Complex Shapes" on page 3-25). We will use this to experiment on in the next exercises. The experiments will be non-destructive, we need the plate for more exercises later on. A *Backup* copy of the file may be made by keying **backup** into the Key-in window (*Utilities>Key-in*).

◆ **Dropping a Complex Element**

1. Open "second.dgn" and arrange a View window about the Stay Plate.

2. Use the *Analyze Element* tool to check that the outline is still a *Complex Shape*.

3. Select the *Drop Element* tool (from the *Groups* tool box), set *Complex On* in its Tool Settings, place a data point anywhere on the outline of the plate (it will Highlight), *Accept*.

4. Use the *Analyze Element* tool to check some component elements.

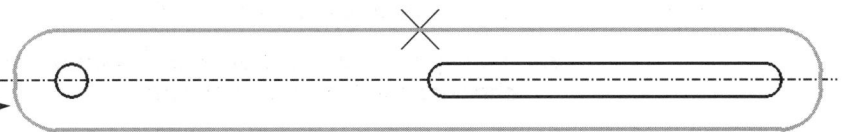

3. It is still a single complex shape when we select it to be *Dropped* →

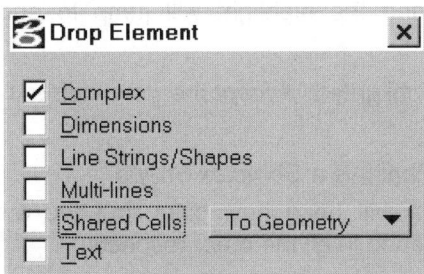

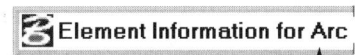

4. Each component is an individual element once the outline's *Complex Status* is *Dropped*

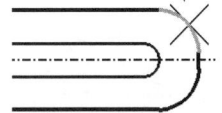

Figure 7.4 Dropping the Complex status of the Stay Plate outline

Creating a Complex Shape from Individual Elements

The Stay Plate outline is now four lines and four arcs, just as it would have been had we drawn it using different tools. If this had been the case, we could still group the individual elements to create a *Complex Shape* after they had been placed. The ends of the elements would need to abut, or at least be very close to it.

In the next exercise we will make believe we had created the outline as separate lines and arcs. We will group them back into a Complex Shape using the *Create Complex Shape* tool. This tool (and its companion *Create Complex Chain* tool) effectively creates a new element, which will take on the currently active *Element Attributes* at the time it is created, regardless of the attributes of the component elements.

Manual Method

There are two *Methods* of adding elements to the new complex shape, *Manual* and *Automatic*. Each element is identified in turn with the former method, then the shape *Accepted* with another data point when the end elements connect. We will experiment with the *Manual* method first.

◆ **Manually create a complex shape**

1. Mark the current position (*Edit>Set Mark*), set the *Element Attributes* to a *Color* of *3* (red), *Level 1*, line style *0*, *Line Weight 2*.
   The originals were specified as color=2 and the level=10.

2. Select the *Create Complex Shape* tool, choose *Method: **Manual**, Area: **Solid**, Fill: **None*** (the *Max. Gap* does not apply in this case, as the elements are already abutting).

3. Identify each of the elements in turn either way around the outline, checking the highlight each time.

4. If the wrong element highlights (such as the centerline in this example) **(a)** press *Reset* and the highlight will jump to another nearby element **(b)**.

5. When the entire outline is highlighted, *Accept* the new element with another data point.

6. *Analyze* the outline to check that it is a *Complex Shape*.
   The complex shape element will be a new color, but the outline should be identical in appearance in all the other respects.

7. *Undo* the operation to restore the individual elements when the new element has been examined. Re-set the *Mark* if you *Undo* to it.

Create Complex Shape [X]

Method: Manual ▼
Max Gap: 0.010

Area: Solid ▼
Fill Type: None ▼
Fill Color: 0

3. Always use data points to identify each of the elements in order around the outline

4.(a) Make sure that the correct element highlights each time. In this case, the *Centerline* has highlighted . . .

4.(b) ... so we press *Reset* and the only other close-by element highlights instead, this time the correct one.

If we continue to press *Reset* after all the close-by elements have highlighted, the operation will be finished by automatically placing a line back to the first element

5. A final data point completes the *Complex Shape* and "Shape Closed" appears in the message area of the Status bar

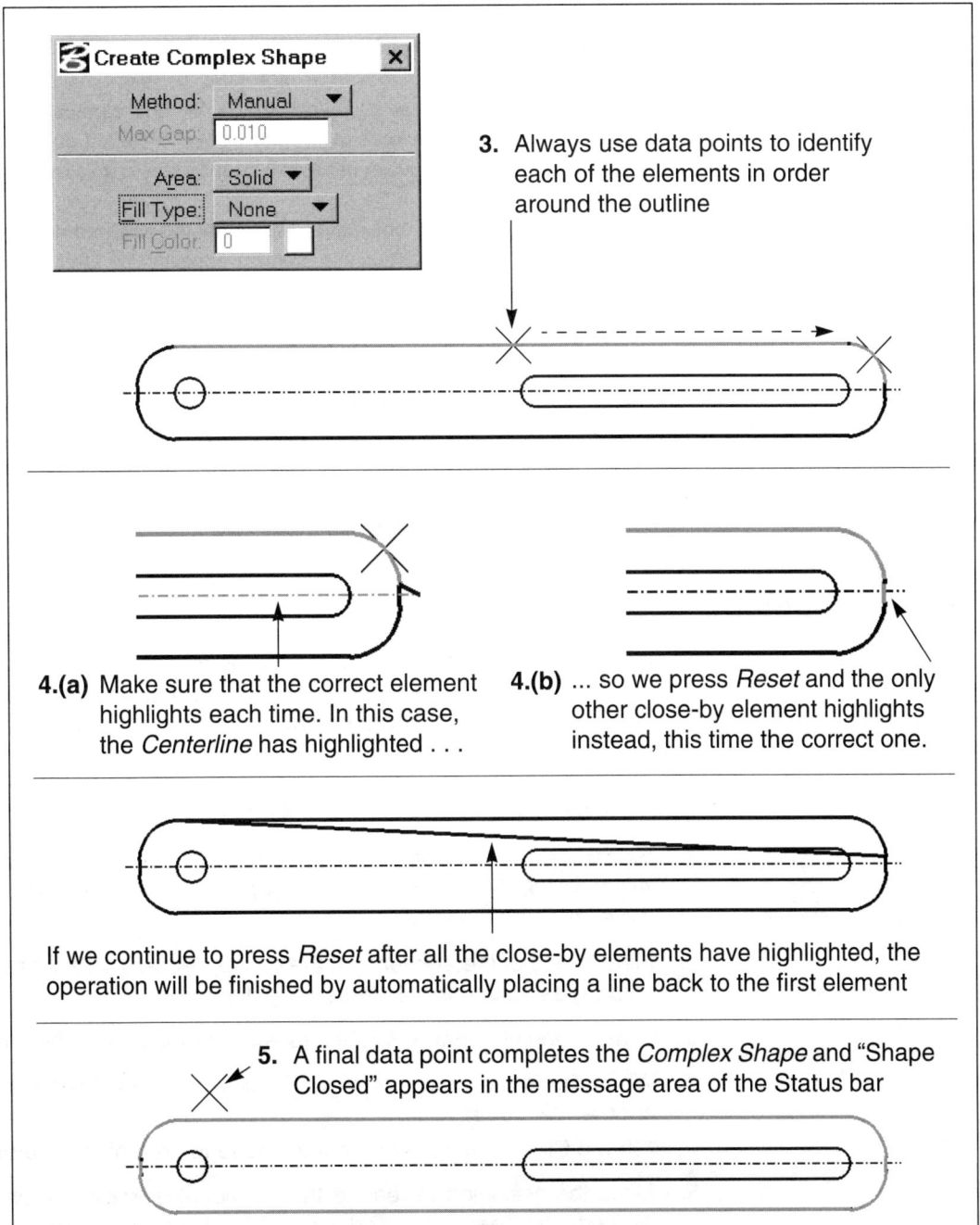

Figure 7.5 Manually creating a Complex Shape

Interruptions to the Process

Once the second element is identified in the process of creating a complex shape, pressing *Reset* a number of times will not take us back to the start point. MicroStation will place a line of its own back to the first element and create an abbreviated *Complex Shape*, without incorporating the bypassed components. This shown in Figure 7.5 as an illustration of the effect of too many *Resets*.

If the complex shape created is not incorporating all the required components, use *Undo* immediately. It is possible that the element appears OK after an early *Reset*, but there may actually be a "shape" created with zero width, or a "line on a line". *Analyze Element* will show this up by informing us that the component appearing to be an individual line is actually a complex shape.

If this is discovered too late to be *Undone*, we can *Drop* its *Complex Status* and delete any spare components. If we need to restore the originals completely, take care that the *Level* has not been changed. Remember, the individual elements from a *Dropped Complex Shape* will be on the level that the shape was created on, which may have been different to that of the originals.

Automatic Method

Using the *Automatic* method to create a complex shape involves identifying one of the component elements with the first data point, then continuing to *Accept* (or *Reset* to reject) other elements as they highlight. Once the first and last elements connect, a final *Accept* closes the *Complex Shape*.

◆ **Create a complex shape using the Automatic option**

1. Select the *Create Complex Shape* tool, choose *Method:* **Automatic**, *Area:* **Solid**, *Fill:* **None** (the *Max. Gap* does not apply in this case, as the elements are already abutting).

2. Identify one of the elements of the outline, *Accept* (without moving the pointer) as each correct element highlights.

3. If the wrong element highlights, reject it with the *Reset* button.

4. When the entire outline is highlighted, *Accept* the new element with another data point.
   "Shape Closed" will appear in the message area of the Status bar.

5. *Undo* the operation to restore the individual elements when the new element has been examined. Re-set the *Mark* if you *Undo* to it.

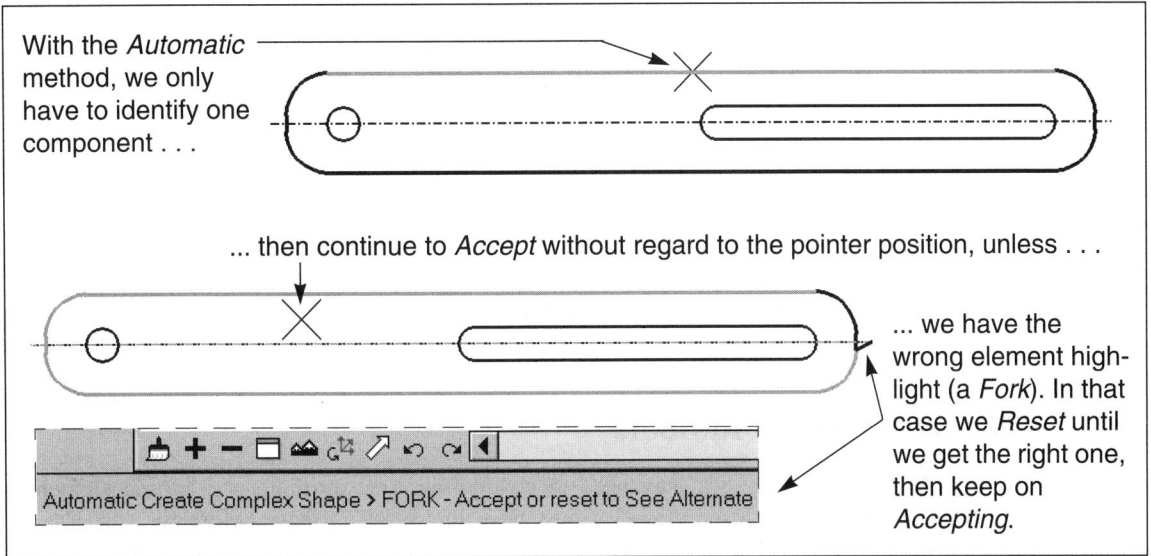

With the *Automatic* method, we only have to identify one component . . .

. . . then continue to *Accept* without regard to the pointer position, unless . . .

. . . we have the wrong element highlight (a *Fork*). In that case we *Reset* until we get the right one, then keep on *Accepting*.

Automatic Create Complex Shape > FORK - Accept or reset to See Alternate

Figure 7.6   Using the Automatic method to create a Complex Shape

Filling Gaps

There are no gaps between the elements of our stay plate outline, so the *Gap* setting did not matter. However, the *Create Complex Shape* tool will tolerate gaps between component elements, with the tolerance set as a *Max(imum) Gap*. If the *Max Gap* is set to zero, only connecting elements will be added to the shape when we use the *Automatic* method. Too large a gap setting may result in the tool attempting to draw its own lines to add distant elements to its shape. We can experiment with this setting by deleting one of the end lines of the stay plate outline and repeating the last exercise. Try *Max. Gap* settings of 4mm and less (the line is 4mm long).

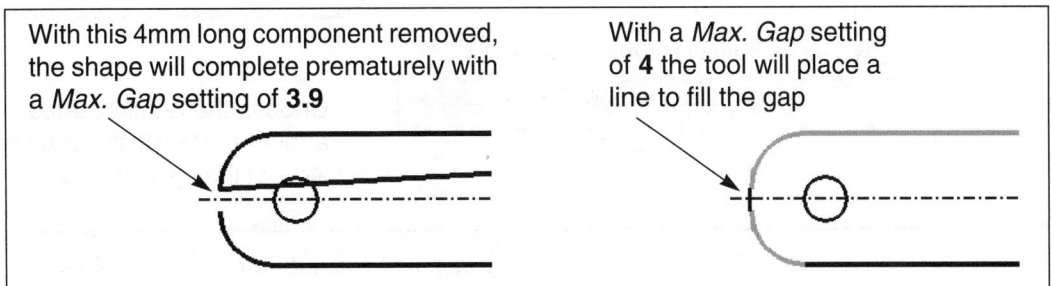

With this 4mm long component removed, the shape will complete prematurely with a *Max. Gap* setting of **3.9**

With a *Max. Gap* setting of **4** the tool will place a line to fill the gap

Figure 7.7   Effect of gaps between components for a Complex Shape

Solid and Hole Areas

Closed elements can enclose two types of *Area*, **Solid** or **Hole**. A *Solid* area is in concept a surface that may support a *Hatching* or an *Area Pattern*. A *Hole* encloses a void, which can not be *Hatched* or *Patterned*. Elements with either of the two *Area* types will look identical when only lines are displayed, we may need to employ the *Analyze Element* tool to ascertain a closed element's *Area Attribute*.

When an element enclosing a *Hole* area is itself enclosed by a larger *Solid* area and the two *Permanently Grouped*, the inner element will appear as a hole in any patterning or hatching of the outer element. We will work with these concepts in more detail shortly.

Changing the Area Attribute

Occasionally, we may need to change the *Area* attribute of a closed element. In general, a closed element must have the *Solid* attribute before we can *Hatch* or *Pattern* it. If it happened to have been created as a *Hole*, it can easily be changed. There is a *Change Element to Active Area* tool available in the *Change* tool box, its application is shown in Figure 7.8.

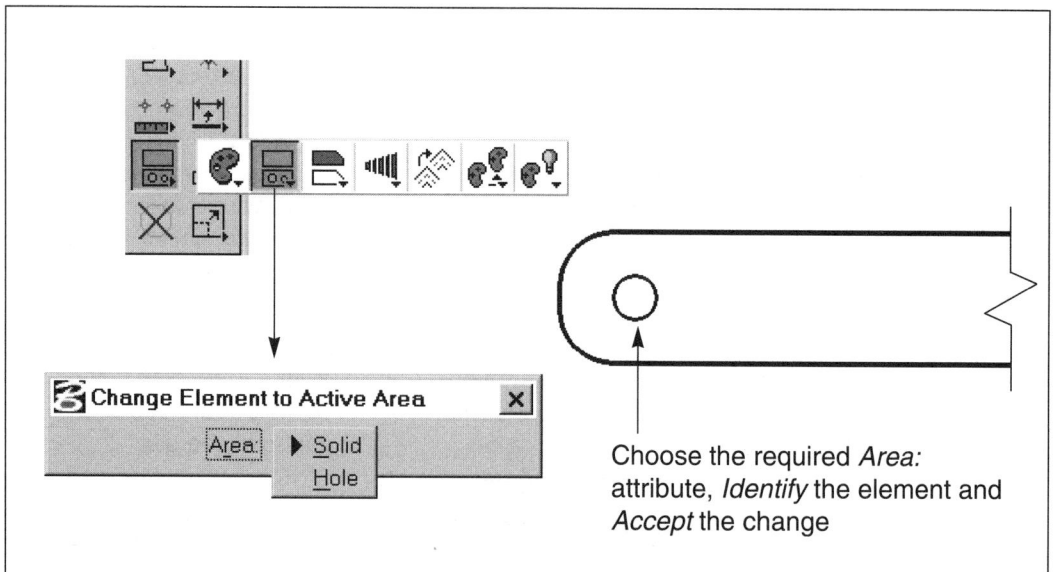

Figure 7.8 Using the Change Element to Active Area tool

Hatching and Patterning

Areas may be automatically *Hatched* or *Cross-Hatched* with parallel lines at a defined spacing and angle(s). The lines will have the element attributes active at the time the operation takes place. Areas can also be *Patterned* with *Cells*.

The Patterns Tool Box

We have already been briefly introduced to one of the tools from this tool box, see "The Linear Pattern Tool" on page 6-28. The tools we are interested in this chapter are the ones relating to *Areas*.

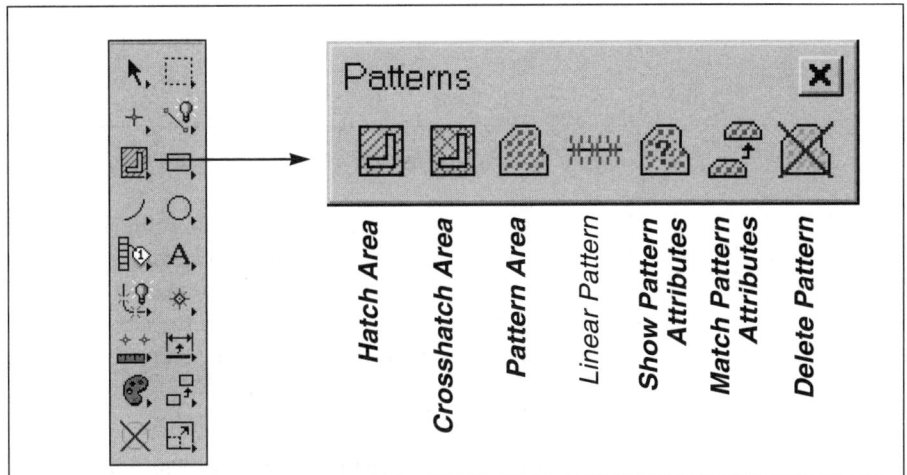

Figure 7.9 The Patterns Tool Box

The Hatch Area and Crosshatch Area Tools

These tools do not only generate a hatching pattern within solid closed elements, they will hatch areas defined by a variety of other methods. The hatching lines are generated with the currently *Active Element Attributes*. The keyed-in settings for the tool are the *Spacing,* the *Angle* and the curve fitting *Tolerance* of the hatching lines. The Settings windows for these tools are illustrated in Figure 7.10.

The *Spacing* is the perpendicular distance between the hatching lines and the *Angle* is the angle of the lines relative to the *View* (not the design plane) x axis. The *Crosshatch Area* tool has two sets of these data entry fields.

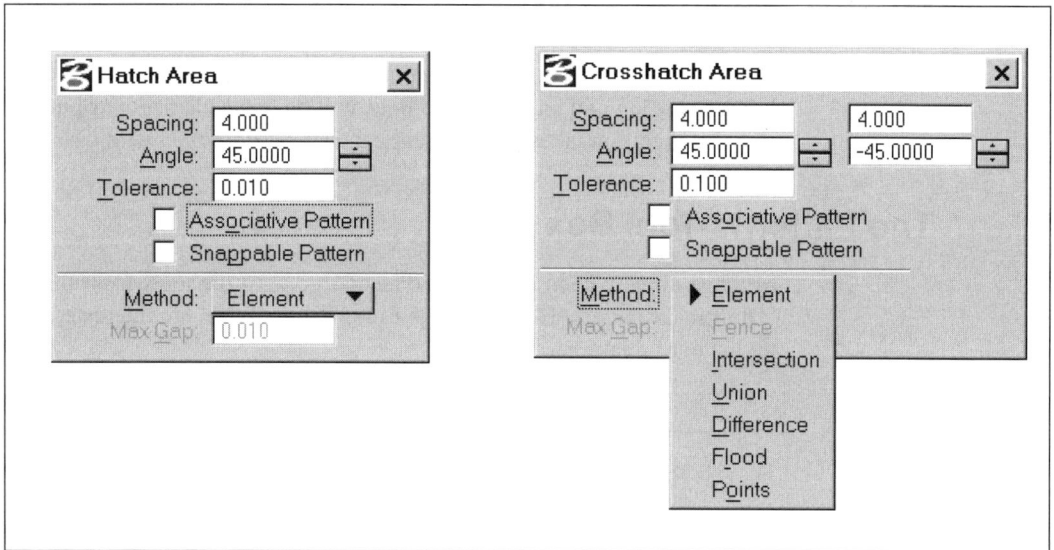

Figure 7.10   Hatching and Crosshatching settings

The *Tolerance* relates to the method of patterning (including hatching) within curves. The curve is approximated for the patterning process by a set of straight line segments and the patterning is actually trimmed by these lines. The dimension of the tolerance is the maximum deviation from the curve by the approximating segments, in the same way as in "Linear Patterning" on page 6-28.

◆ Hatching the Stay Plate outline area

1. *Analyze* the outline of the Stay Plate to ensure it is a *Complex Shape* and has the *Solid* area attribute.

    If necessary *Create* it as a *Complex Shape* (page 7-8) and/or change it to *Solid* status (Figure 7.8).

2. Set the element *Color* to *0*, *Level* to *30*, *Line Style* and *Weight* to *0*.

3. Turn *Off* level **11** to hide the centerline.

4. Select the *Hatch Area* tool, set *Spacing: 4*, *Angle: 45*, *Tolerance: 0.1*, *Associative* and *Snappable Off*, *Method: Element*.

5. Identify the outline, *Accept* with another data point (this point will position the hatching by defining a point that a line must pass through), *Reset* the tool.

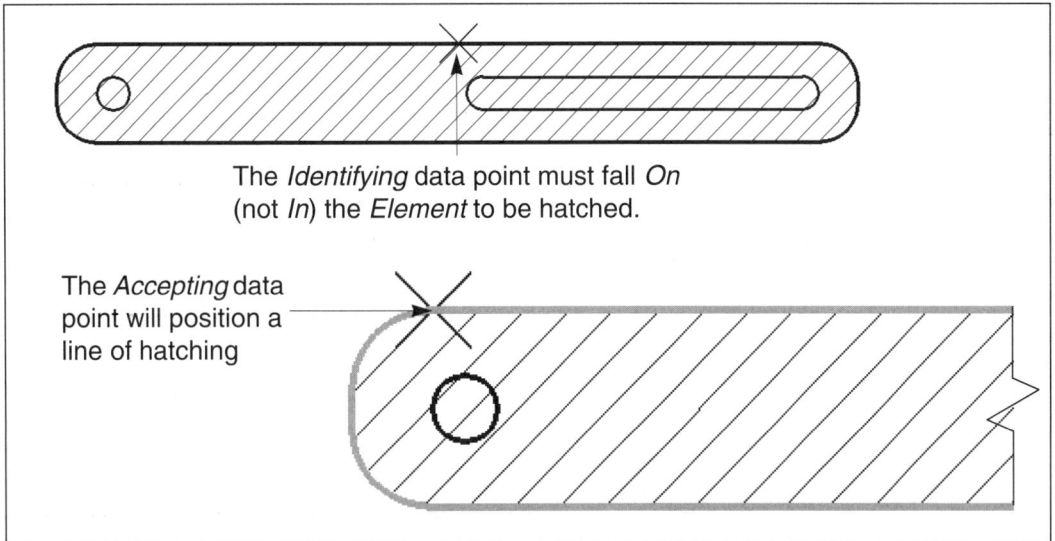

The *Identifying* data point must fall *On*
(not *In*) the *Element* to be hatched.

The *Accepting* data
point will position a
line of hatching

Figure 7.11   Hatching using the Element Method

The hatching has ignored the holes and filled the whole outline. We will repeat the
hatching shortly without covering the round and slotted holes. Before we do that, we
will experiment with *Moving* the hatched outline.

Graphic Group

✓ Graphic Group

A *Graphic Group* (not to be confused with an "ordinary" *Group*) is a permanent
grouping of elements that can be manipulated as one, but only when the *Graphic
Group Lock* is invoked. Elements can be added to a Graphic Group with the *Add To
Graphic Group* tool from the *Groups* tool box (page 7-4). With this tool selected,
elements can be added to the Graphic Group by first identifying an element in the
group, then any others we want to add. If the first element identified is not already
part of a Graphic Group, a new group is created.

We can drop individual elements from membership of the group by identifying them
with the *Drop From Graphic Group* tool and the *Graphic Group Lock Off*. The entire
group can be broken up by identifying an element with the *Drop From Graphic
Group* tool selected and the *Graphic Group Lock On*.

All elements of a pattern (including *Hatching* and *Crosshatching*) are automatically
created as a *Graphic Group*, so we already have an example to experiment with. The
hatching from the last exercise can be manipulated as shown in Figure 7.12.

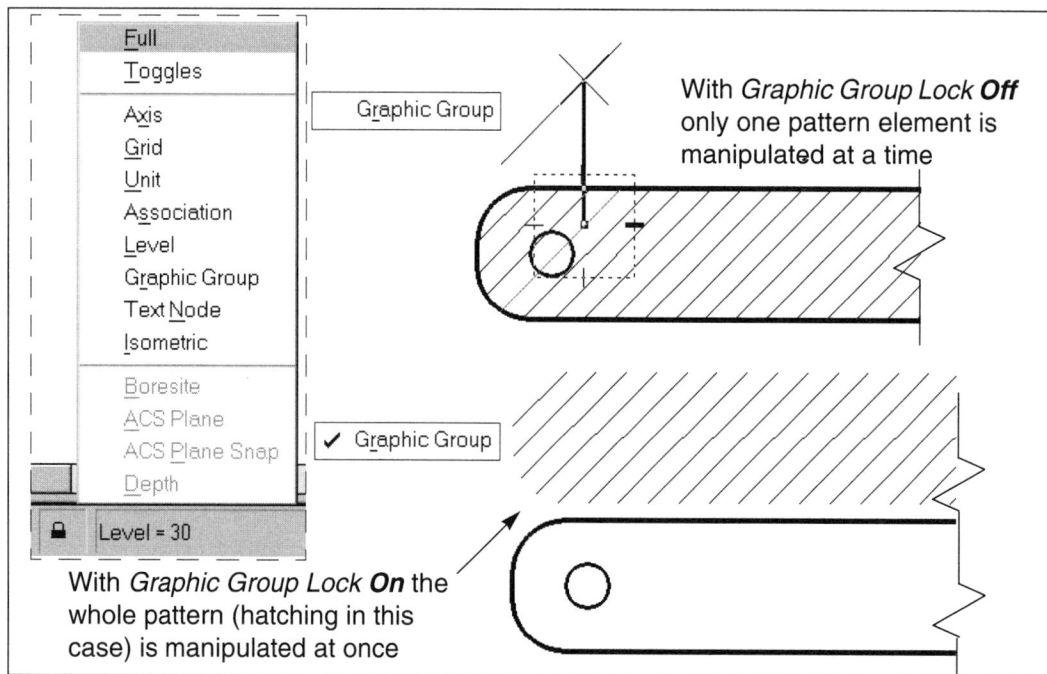

Figure 7.12   The Pattern as a Graphic Group

Deleting Patterns

Pattern elements may be deleted with the usual Delete tool, but the specialized *Delete Pattern* tool is optimized for the job. A pattern such as the hatching just generated can be deleted one element at a time with the regular *Delete Element* tool, or the whole pattern can be deleted if we turn the *Graphic Group* lock **On**.

The Delete Pattern Tool

The *Delete Pattern* tool will delete the entire pattern without the need to turn on the lock, but its main advantage is when we need to delete *Associative patterns* (to be introduced next). With these patterns, using the regular *Delete Element* tool will delete the outline element as well as the entire pattern.

We will use the *Delete Pattern* tool to delete the non-associative hatching generated in the last exercise at the start of the next one. With this type of patterning, we data point a *Pattern Element* to identify the pattern for deletion, then *Accept*. The outline element needs to be identified to delete *Associative* patterns.

Associative Patterns

We turned *Associative Pattern **Off*** in the last exercise, which made the hatching pattern take the shape of the outline, but be independent of it. The pattern was able to be moved outside the outline in Figure 7.12. With *Associative Patterns **On*** the pattern is automatically manipulated or modified with the outline element. The patterned element can be moved, scaled, re-sized with the *Modify* tool etc. and the pattern will be altered with it.

◆ **Experiment with Associative Patterning**

1. Select the *Delete Pattern* tool, identify one of the hatching lines, *Accept.*

2. *Edit>Set Mark*, select the *Hatch Area* tool, check *Associative Pattern **On***, leave the other tool settings as they were set for the last exercise.

3. Identify the outline, *Accept* with another data point defining a *Pattern Intersection.*

4. Try manipulating and modifying the outline in various ways, noting the effect on the pattern.

5. *Edit>Undo Other>To Mark* to restore the outline to its original non-patterned form.

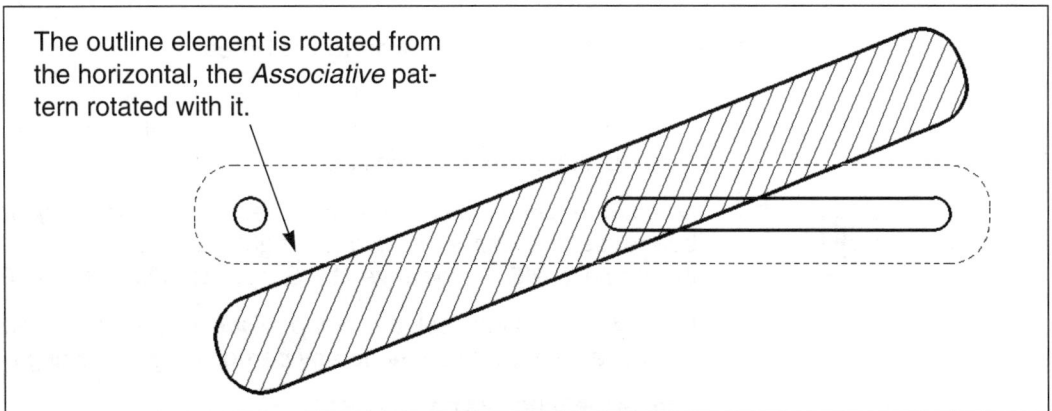

The outline element is rotated from the horizontal, the *Associative* pattern rotated with it.

Figure 7.13   Manipulating an element with Associative Patterning

Patterning Around Holes

Our first hatching has covered over the two elements on the stay plate that would be expected to be holes (see Figure 7.11). Even if the circle and the slot have the *Hole* Area attribute, this may still happen with *Associative patterns.*

Note: With *Associative Patterns On,* the *Hole* elements must be *Grouped* with the *Outline* to prevent them being patterned over. The *Group* is the ordinary type, as may be formed with multiple element selection followed by *Edit>Group.*

Before the group was formed, it would be necessary to make sure that the intended holes actually were created with the *Hole* Area attribute. In practice there is a special tool that takes care of this form of grouping.

The Group Holes Tool

This tool is found in the *Groups* tool box (page 7-4). While forming a group this tool ensures that the outline (which is identified first) has the *Solid* attribution and the subsequently identified elements are *Hole(s).* It changes the *Area* attributes as necessary.

If it is necessary to *Ungroup* the elements, we select the group by identifying one element, then choose *Edit>Ungroup.* Select a blank area of the View window to remove the selection "handles".

◆ Crosshatch the stay plate around the holes

1. Select the *Group Holes* tool, identify the outline as the *Solid Element,* then each of the *Hole Elements. Accept* with another data point, *Reset* to complete the definition.

2. Select the *Crosshatch Area* tool, leave the *Hatching* settings as before, set the *Crosshatching* (the right side fields) line *Spacing* to *4,* the *Angle* to *-45, Associative On, Snappable Off, Method: Element.*

3. Identify the outline, set the *Snap Mode Override* to *Center,* place *Tentative* point by snapping to any part of the group being patterned.

4. *Accept* the tentative point, *Reset.*
    Locating the data point defining a *Pattern Intersection* with the help of a *Center* snap places a symmetrical crosshatching pattern, as shown in Figure 7.14.

The *Holes* have been *Grouped* with the outline, thus they have not been hatched over

3.&4. The pattern can be positioned symmetrically within the outline by preceding the *Accepting* data point with a *Center Snap* to one of the elements

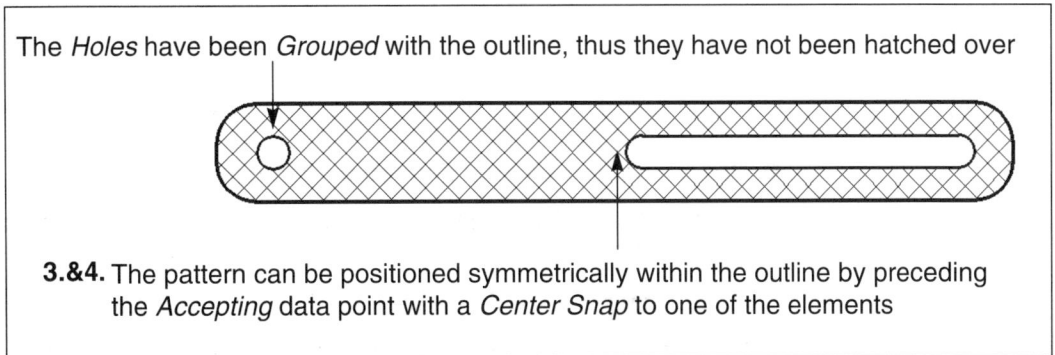

Figure 7.14   The Stay Plate crosshatched around the holes

Defining an Area

In our hatching exercises so far the *Area* to be patterned has been defined by a *Closed Element*, or by a group of closed elements. There are six other *Methods* of defining an area in MicroStation:

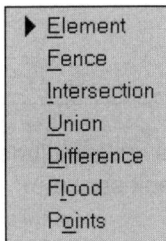

▶ Element
Fence
Intersection
Union
Difference
Flood
Points

- *Fence* - The area inside a fence;

- *Intersection*- The Intersection of two or more closed elements;

- *Union* - The Union of two or more closed elements;

- *Difference* - The Difference between two or more closed elements;

- *Flood* - The minimum area enclosed by a set of intersecting or abutting elements;

- *Points* - The area inside an imaginary shape defined by data points at its vertices.

Areas may be defined by any of the above methods for *Patterning* and *Measuring*.

Areas Not Enclosed by Elements

We may define an area without elements, allowing floating patterned areas to be created. This can sometimes be useful where only fragments of pattern are needed, where the pattern may otherwise hide details in a drawing.

Fence Method

The active *Fence Mode* is ignored when we define an area with this method, the area defined is always *Inside* the fence. A fence of any *Type* may be placed, although *Shape, Circle* and *Block* would probably be the only types used in practice.

◆ **Crosshatching an area defined by a Fence**

1. Use the *Delete Pattern* tool to remove the existing pattern from the Stay Plate, leave the outline and holes *Grouped*.

2. Select the *Place Fence* tool, set the *Type* to **Circle**.

3. Set the *Snap Mode Override* to **Center**, snap a tentative to the outline, *Accept* to start placing the fence.

4. Complete the fence with a data point, making the radius of the fence similar to the width of the plate, as shown in Figure 7.15.

5. Select the *Crosshatch Area* tool, choose *Method:* **Fence**, *Associative Pattern:***Off**, leave the remaining settings the same as the last exercise.

6. *Accept* the fence contents for patterning, select *Place Fence* again (to remove the fence).
   Note the effect of the *Hole* element on the area.

The *Fence Area* overlapping the closed element with the *Hole* attribute is not included in the total *Defined Area*, which takes in the *Solid* element and the blank space.

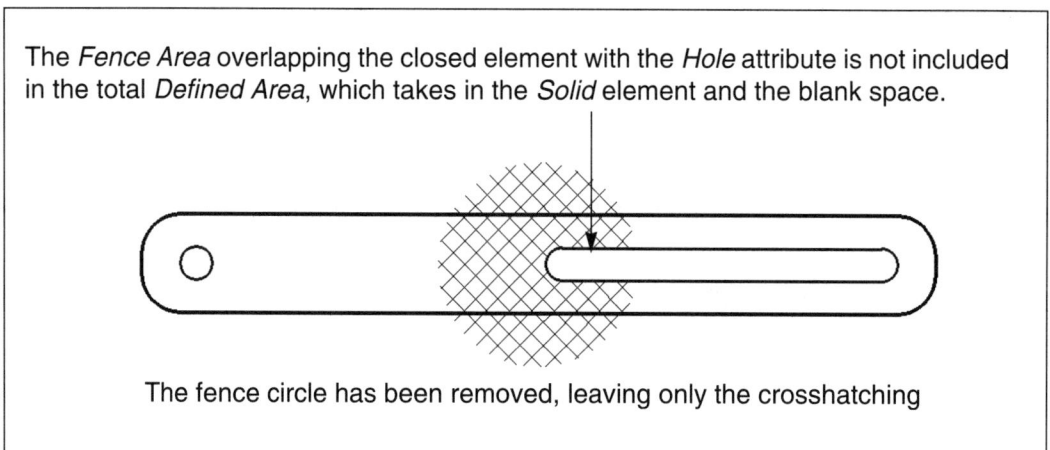

The fence circle has been removed, leaving only the crosshatching

Figure 7.15 The Fence method of defining an Area

Points Method

This method is often used to pattern part only of an area in a design, with data *Points* defining the vertices of the area for patterning. If necessary, we can locate these data points by snapping to any number of existing elements.

◆ Crosshatching an area defined by Points

1. Use the *Delete Pattern* tool to remove the *Fence* pattern.

2. Select the *Crosshatch Area* tool, choose *Method: **Points***, leave the remaining settings as before.

3. *Snap* (Keypoint) to the top of the round hole in the Plate, *Accept.*

4. Snap the next point to the top-left of the slot **(a)**, *Accept, Snap* and *Accept* to the two lower keypoints of the holes **(b)** and **(c)** in circular order.

   Note that a (temporary) closed shape dynamically updates as the pointer is moved and the data points placed.

5. *Reset* to complete the area definition.

   The patterned area appears, without the dynamic shape. The *Hole* elements are ignored, the area is defined entirely by the data points.

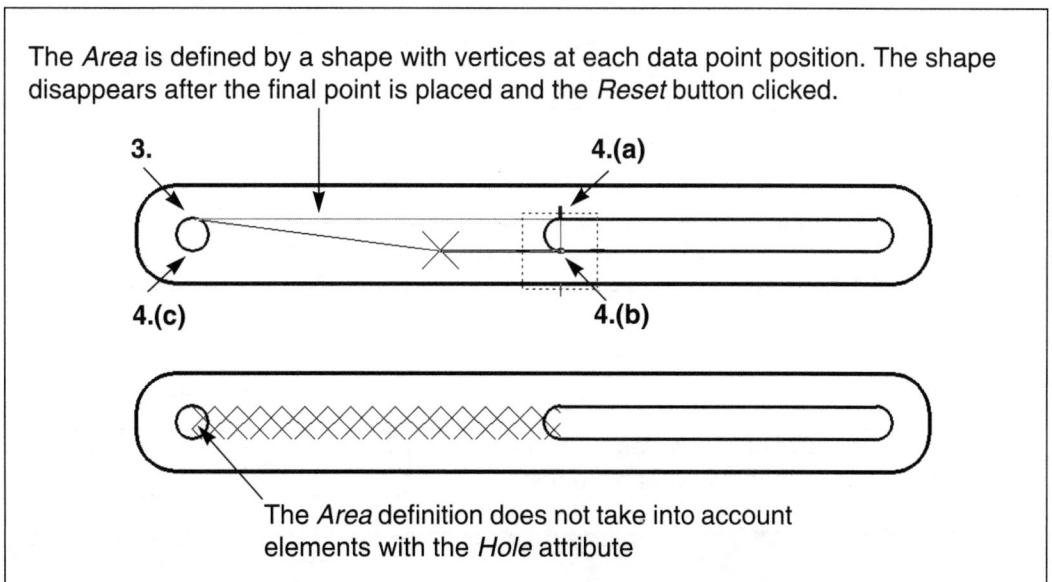

Figure 7.16 The Points method of defining an Area

Areas Defined by Combinations of Closed Elements

Multiple closed elements can be combined to define an area using the *Intersection*, *Union* and *Difference* Boolean operations. We will use crosshatching again to demonstrate the extent of the *Area* defined by each operation. We will start by adding two temporary circles to our Stay Plate drawing.

◆ **Add temporary closed elements for Area experiments**

1. Set the *Active Level* to **25** (to allow us to hide the circles later, rather than Delete them). AccuDraw should be running.

2. Select the *Place Circle* tool, settings *Method:* **Center**, *Area:* **Solid**, *Fill Type:* **None**, *Diameter/Radius* constraint **Off**.

3. Set the *Snap Override* to **Center**, snap to a plate element, *Accept* to define the center of the first circle.

4. Move the pointer to the left, key in **25**, *Accept*.

5. Move the pointer further directly left, key in **50** as the position for the second circle center, *Accept*.

6. Move the pointer to the left again, key in **35**, *Accept*, *Reset*.

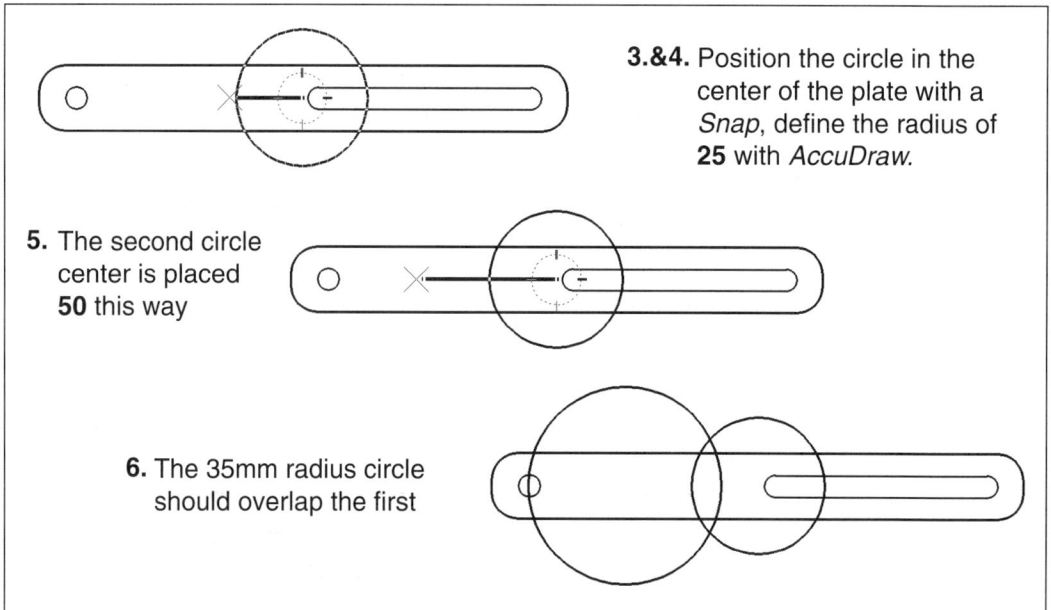

Figure 7.17 Preparing the drawing for Boolean area experiments

Intersection Method

This method defines a single area shared by all the identified closed elements. The area of an identified element that does not intersect with *All* the other identified elements is not included. The message "Element does not intersect" will be returned.

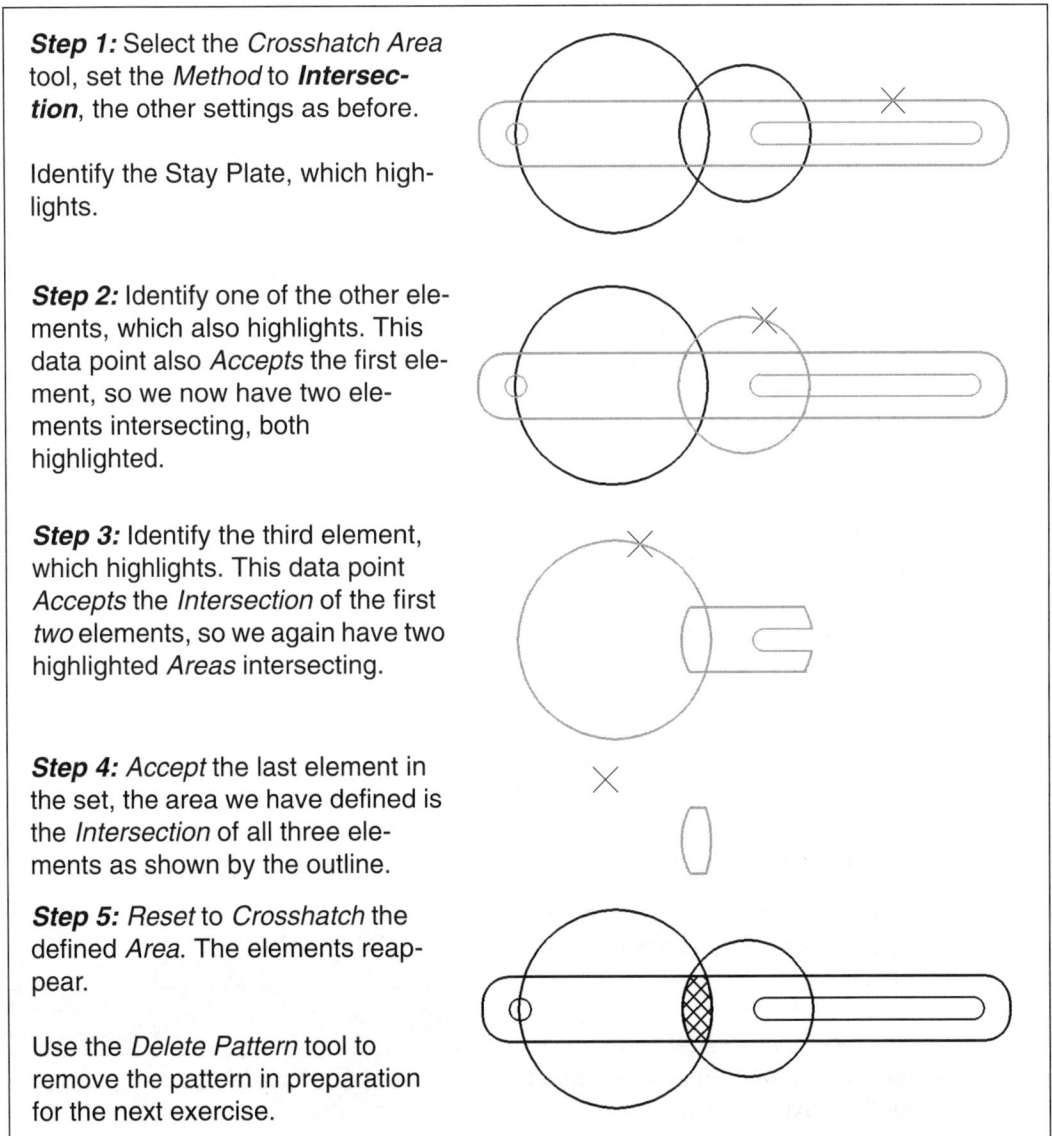

Step 1: Select the *Crosshatch Area* tool, set the *Method* to **Intersection**, the other settings as before.

Identify the Stay Plate, which highlights.

Step 2: Identify one of the other elements, which also highlights. This data point also *Accepts* the first element, so we now have two elements intersecting, both highlighted.

Step 3: Identify the third element, which highlights. This data point *Accepts* the *Intersection* of the first *two* elements, so we again have two highlighted *Areas* intersecting.

Step 4: *Accept* the last element in the set, the area we have defined is the *Intersection* of all three elements as shown by the outline.

Step 5: *Reset* to *Crosshatch* the defined *Area*. The elements reappear.

Use the *Delete Pattern* tool to remove the pattern in preparation for the next exercise.

Figure 7.18   Creating an Area by Intersection of three closed elements

Union Method

This method defines a single area bounded by the outer sections of the element outlines. The elements do not have to intersect as they do in Figure 7.19, the area may consist of two or more unconnected parts.

Step 1: Select the *Crosshatch Area* tool, set the *Method* to **Union**, the other settings as before.

Identify the Stay Plate, which highlights.

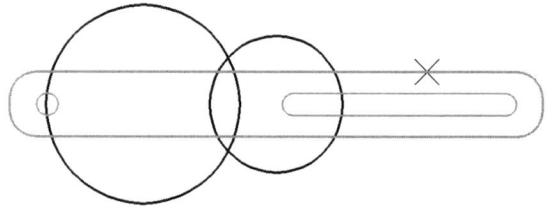

Step 2: Identify one of the other elements, which also highlights. This data point also *Accepts* the first element, so we now have two elements highlighted.

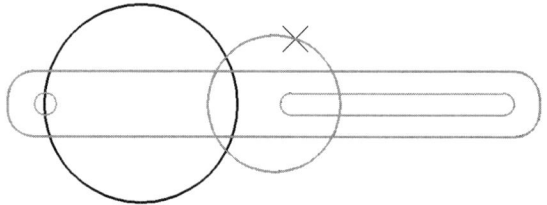

Step 3: Identify the third element, which highlights. This data point *Accepts* the *Union* of the first *two* elements, so we again have two highlighted *Areas*.

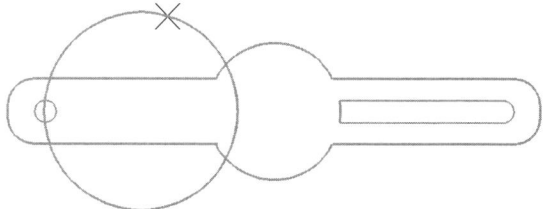

Step 4: *Accept* the last element in the set, the area we have defined is the *Union* of all three elements as shown by the highlight.

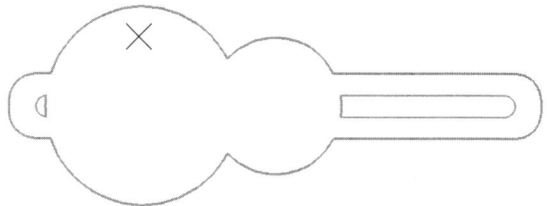

Step 5: *Reset* to *Crosshatch* the defined *Area*. The elements reappear.

Use the *Delete Pattern* tool again to remove the pattern in preparation for the next exercise.

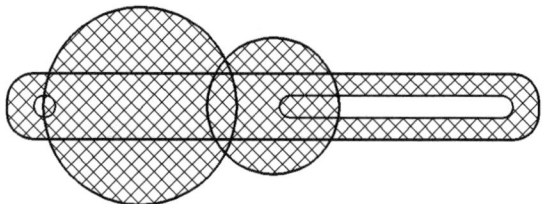

Figure 7.19   Creating an Area by Union of three closed elements

Difference Method

This method defines a single area which is the area remaining from the *First* element identified, after the areas covered by the subsequently identified closed elements are subtracted.

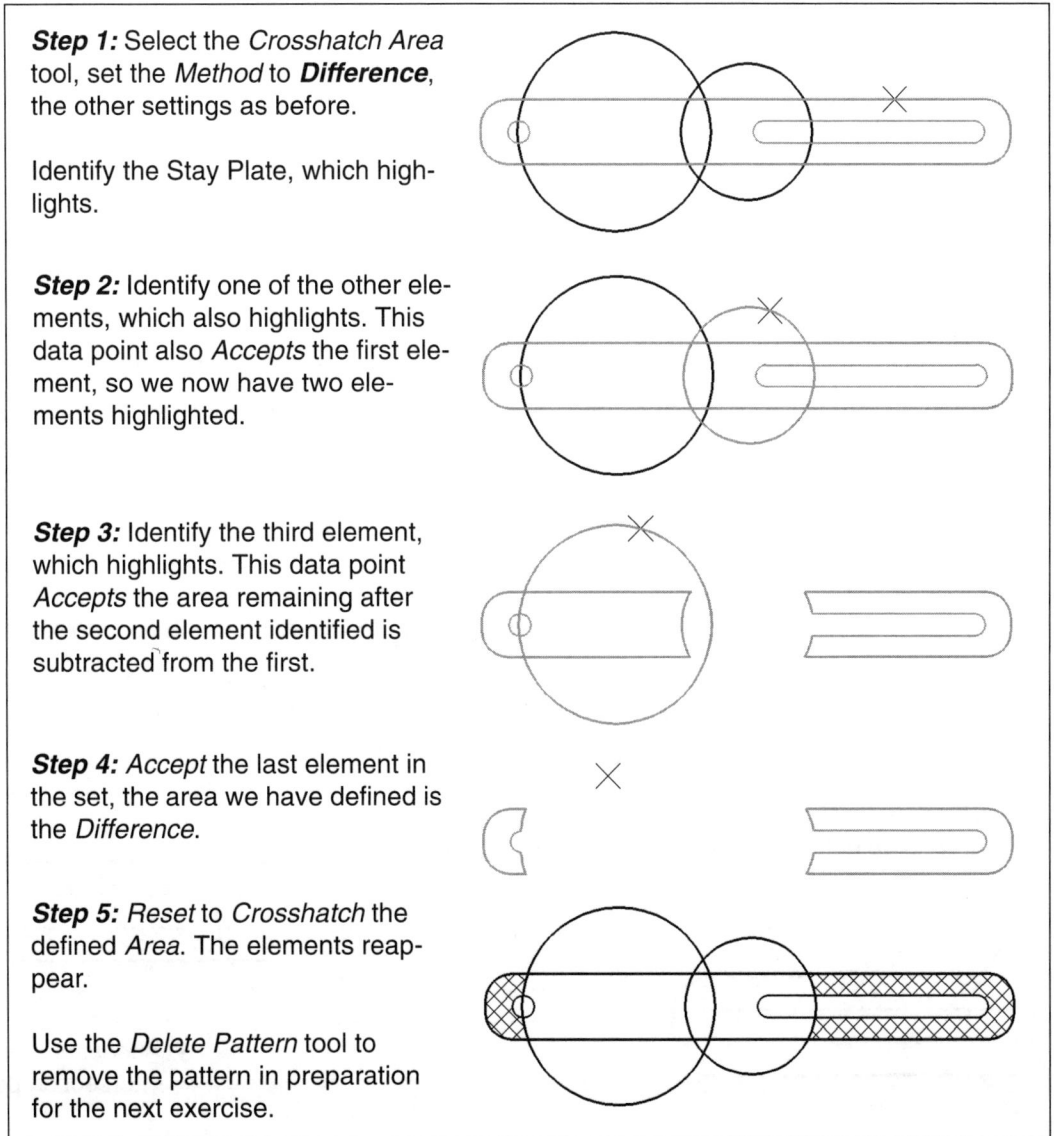

Step 1: Select the *Crosshatch Area* tool, set the *Method* to **Difference**, the other settings as before.

Identify the Stay Plate, which high-lights.

Step 2: Identify one of the other ele-ments, which also highlights. This data point also *Accepts* the first ele-ment, so we now have two ele-ments highlighted.

Step 3: Identify the third element, which highlights. This data point *Accepts* the area remaining after the second element identified is subtracted from the first.

Step 4: *Accept* the last element in the set, the area we have defined is the *Difference*.

Step 5: *Reset* to *Crosshatch* the defined *Area*. The elements reap-pear.

Use the *Delete Pattern* tool to remove the pattern in preparation for the next exercise.

Figure 7.20 Creating an Area by Difference of three closed elements

Areas Defined by Enclosing Elements

Multiple elements, open or closed, may be placed in such a way that they enclose an area. All or part of any type of displayed MicroStation element can be used as part of a "dam" surrounding an area. The area is defined by conceptually *"Flooding"* outwards from a data point placed within the area enclosed by the "dam" elements. If there are any gaps between the elements, they must be less than the *Max. Gap* setting for the tool in use.

Flood Method (Non-Associative Pattern)

We will use our Stay Plate outline and circles once more, this time to define an *Area* and crosshatch it using the *Flood* method. The elements in this drawing are all closed, but this fact it irrelevant to the operation of the *Area* tools when they are using this method. The *Hole* or *Solid* status of the elements has no effect on the operation, nor does their *Grouping*.

◆ **Define and crosshatch Areas using the Flood method.**

1. Select the *Crosshatch Area* tool, set the *Method* to ***Flood***, *Associative Pattern **Off***, the other settings as before (page 7-12).

2. Place a data point inside one of the enclosed areas formed by the Stay Plate and circles.

   Note that sections of elements highlight as the area definition is calculated. *Reset* halts the operation in the event that a "leak" occurs through a gap greater than (or equal to) the *Max. Gap* setting.

3. *Accept* at a point where the pattern is to intersect when the intended area outline is highlighted, repeat for other areas as desired, *Reset*.

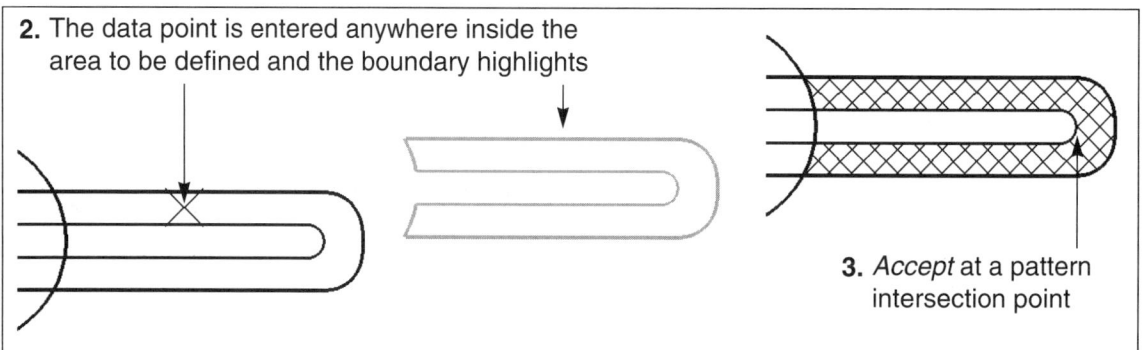

2. The data point is entered anywhere inside the area to be defined and the boundary highlights

3. *Accept* at a pattern intersection point

Figure 7.21   Creating an Area by the Flood method

Flood Method (Associative Pattern)

When we check the *Associative Pattern* box, the hatching or patterning tool creates a new closed element for the pattern to associate with. This element takes the attributes (color etc.) of one of the defining "dam" elements, but there is no association with any of these.

◆ **Associatively Crosshatch an area using the Flood method**

1. Select the *Crosshatch Area* tool, set *Associative Pattern **On***, the other settings as for the last exercise.

2. Place a data point inside one of the enclosed areas formed by the Stay Plate and circles.

3. *Accept* at a point where the pattern is to intersect when the intended area outline is highlighted, *Reset*.

4. Select the *Move Element* tool, identify the outline of the pattern area. (an entire original element will probably highlight with the initial data point, *Reset* until only the pattern highlights).

5. Move the boundary away from the original position, *Accept*, *Reset*.

   The pattern and its boundary element will now be independent of the original elements that they were formed within. The originals will prove to be intact when we *Update* the view.

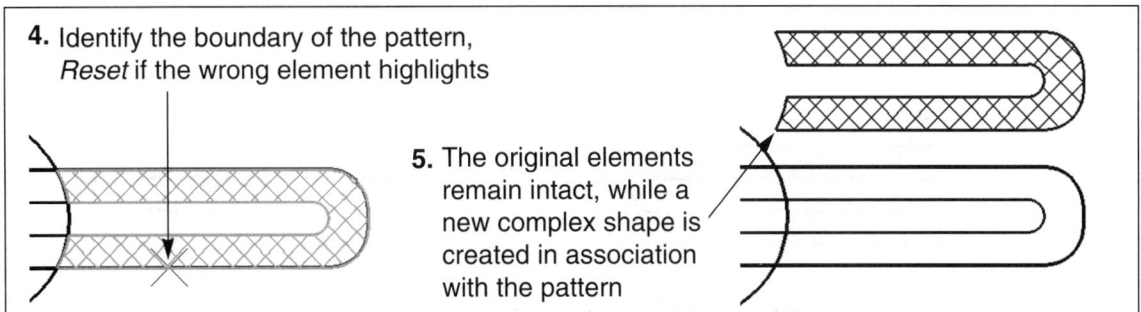

4. Identify the boundary of the pattern, *Reset* if the wrong element highlights

5. The original elements remain intact, while a new complex shape is created in association with the pattern

Figure 7.22   An Associative Pattern created using Flood.

Separating the pattern outline from the pattern

The *new* boundary or outline element created with *Associative Pattern **On*** may be manipulated without manipulating the pattern. To do this if we need disassociate the pattern and boundary shape using the *Drop Associative Pattern* tool, found in the specialized *Drop* tool box from *Tools>Drop* under the Application window menu.

◆ **Drop the Associative Pattern and move its outline**

1. *Undo* the last move (or delete the moved part and crosshatch an area again with *Associative Pattern On*).

2. Select the *Drop Associative Pattern* tool from the *Tools>Drop* tool box (**Not** on the *Main* tool frame).

    If the pattern was not created as *Associative*, there would not be an outline.

3. Identify the crosshatch pattern to be dropped with a data point on its outline, *Accept* when it highlights.

4. Select the *Move Element* tool, identify the outline of the pattern area. (*Reset* as before until only the required pattern boundary highlights).

5. Move the boundary away from the original position, *Accept*, *Reset*.

    The pattern boundary element only will now be independent of the original elements, which remain intact.

6. Use the *Delete Pattern* and the *Delete* tools to remove the crosshatching and the moved boundary element.

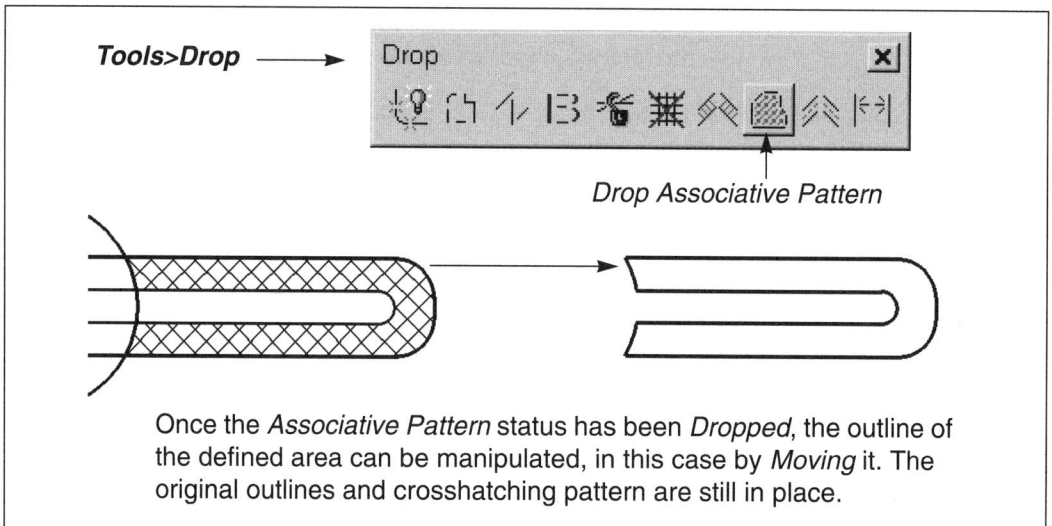

Once the *Associative Pattern* status has been *Dropped*, the outline of the defined area can be manipulated, in this case by *Moving* it. The original outlines and crosshatching pattern are still in place.

Figure 7.23   Manipulating an outline element created by Associative Patterning

The process illustrated in Figure 7.23 could possibly be used when creating detail drawings etc., but it is not the only way of obtaining an outline of a region of a drawing. There is a special tool for this job.

Creating a Region

In this context the *Region* is an area formed by a set of enclosing elements, outlined by a *Complex Shape*. These shapes are created using identical methods to those already introduced for defining areas to be crosshatched.

The Create Region Tool

This tool is in the *Groups* tool box (see Figure 7.3), it creates a *Complex Shape* using the specified *Method* with the currently active *Element Attributes*. The same *Fill* options available in its Tool Settings window as all the other tools that create closed elements. The same Boolean and Flood *Method* options are available as with the hatching tools already introduced. The *Max. Gap* field is also available when the *Flood* method is chosen.

The Complex Shape is normally created with the *Solid* attribute, regardless of the attributes of the original elements. This attribute can be changed to *Hole* with the *Change Element to Active Area* tool (page 7-10). There is a check box option to keep the original elements, or remove them.

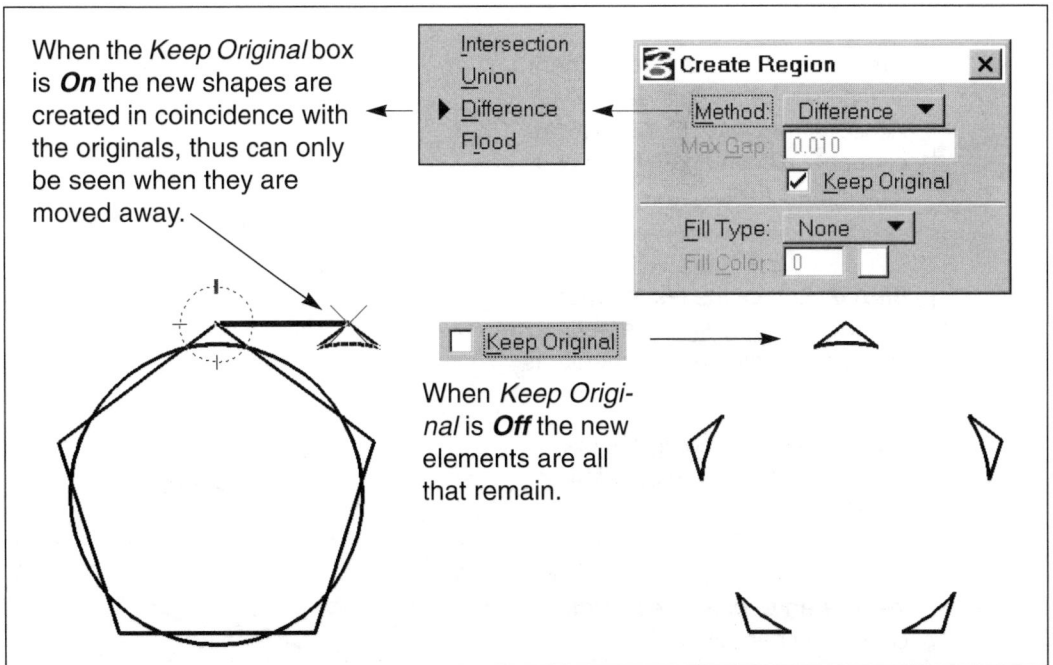

When the *Keep Original* box is **On** the new shapes are created in coincidence with the originals, thus can only be seen when they are moved away.

Intersection
Union
▶ Difference
Flood

Create Region
Method: Difference ▼
Max Gap: 0.010
☑ Keep Original
Fill Type: None ▼
Fill Color: 0

☐ Keep Original

When *Keep Original* is **Off** the new elements are all that remain.

Figure 7.24 The Tool Settings for the Create Region tool and their effect

Union Method Example

This method creates a *Complex Shape* defined by the outer sections of the original element outlines. In this case, the original elements are part of a *Group* from the *Group Holes* example on page 7-16, thus the new elements will also be part of a group, or *Orphan Cell*.

Step 1: Select the *Create Region* tool, set the *Method* to **Union**, *Keep Original* **Off**, *Fill Type:* **None**.

Identify the Stay Plate, which high-lights.

Step 2: Identify one of the other ele-ments, which also highlights. This data point also *Accepts* the first ele-ment, so we now have two ele-ments highlighted.

Step 3: Identify the third element, which highlights. This data point *Accepts* the *Union* of the first *two* elements, so we again have two highlighted *Areas*.

Step 4: *Accept* the last element in the set, the area we have defined is the *Union* of all three elements as shown by the highlight.

Step 5: *Reset* to complete the grouped complex shapes defining the *Region*.

Analyze the region geometry, note that it is an *Orphan Cell* (Group), *Undo* the changes.

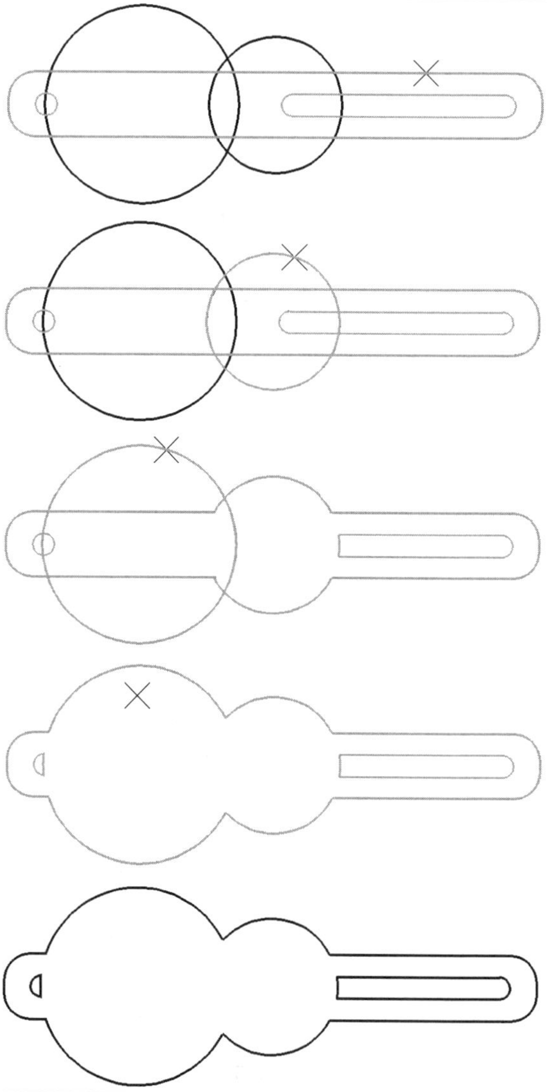

Figure 7.25   Creating a Region by the Union of three closed elements

We can see from the last example that the *Create Region* tool operates in exactly the same way as the other *Area* related tools, such as the patterning tools. The example used the *Union* method, but we can refer back to the *Boolean* and *Flood* examples of crosshatching for the other operations.

Measuring Areas

We have the facility to measure areas defined by any of the methods used so far. MicroStation will also calculate the mass of an area (given a *Mass per Unit Area* for the material). The *Perimeter* length and the position of the *Centroid* of the area may be established with the same operation.

The Measure Area Tool

This tool is found in the *Measure* tool box from the *Main* tool frame. It is one five measuring tools related to 2D, the others are used for linear measurements and angles. The tool settings include the same *Method* options as the hatching tools, along with check boxes for *Mass Parameter* calculation and *Centroid* display.

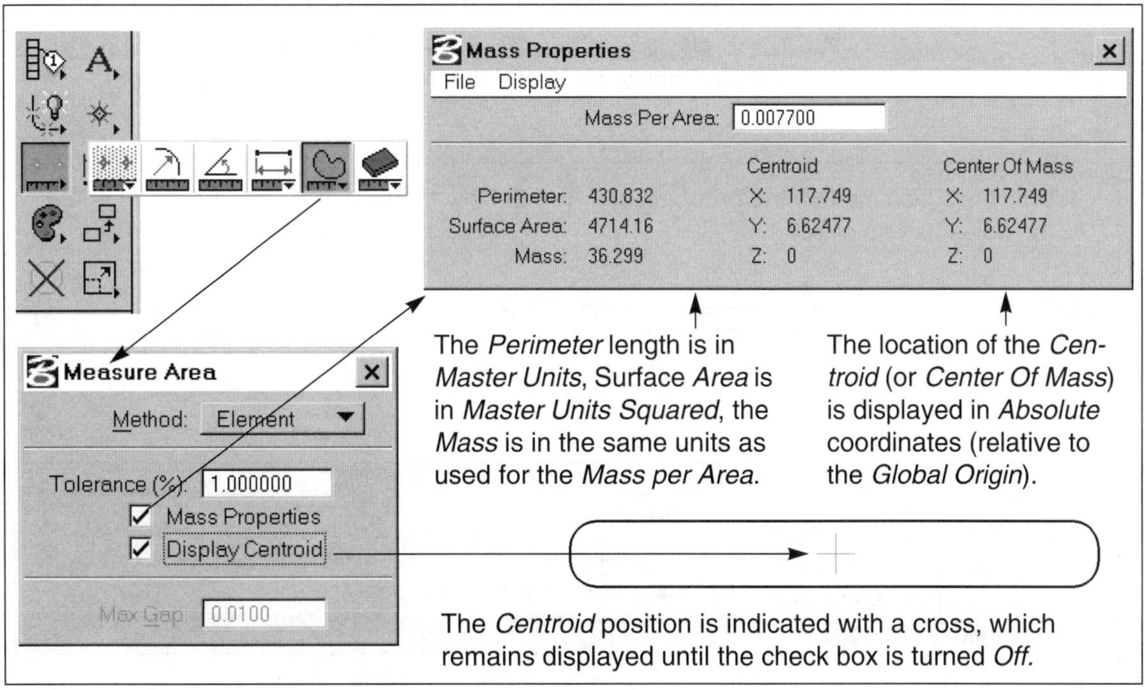

The *Perimeter* length is in *Master Units*, Surface *Area* is in *Master Units Squared*, the *Mass* is in the same units as used for the *Mass per Area*.

The location of the *Centroid* (or *Center Of Mass*) is displayed in *Absolute* coordinates (relative to the *Global Origin*).

The *Centroid* position is indicated with a cross, which remains displayed until the check box is turned *Off*.

Figure 7.26 Measuring Area

In the next exercises we will measure the *Area* and the *Mass* of the stay plate, assuming it is made of steel 1mm thick. We will measure it twice, the first time ignoring the holes, then taking the holes into account.

◆ **Measure the area and mass of the Stay Plate outline**

1. Make level **1** *Active*, turn the display of level **25** *Off* (to hide the circles).

2. Select the *Measure Area* tool, set the *Method* to **Flood**, check the *Mass Properties* and *Display Centroid* both **On**, *Tolerance%:***1.0**.

3. Key in **.0077** to the *Mass Per Area* field of the *Mass Properties* window.

   This figure represents an average figure for the area density of 1mm thick steel.

4. Place a data point inside the plate area (not inside one of the holes).

5. *Accept* the highlighted area, note the *Mass Properties* and the location of the *Centroid* marker.

6. Try changing the *Mass Per Area* figure, note that the calculated information changes without any need to re-identify the area.

7. Turn *Display Centroid* back **Off** and *Reset* when all the measurements are completed (the highlighting is removed).

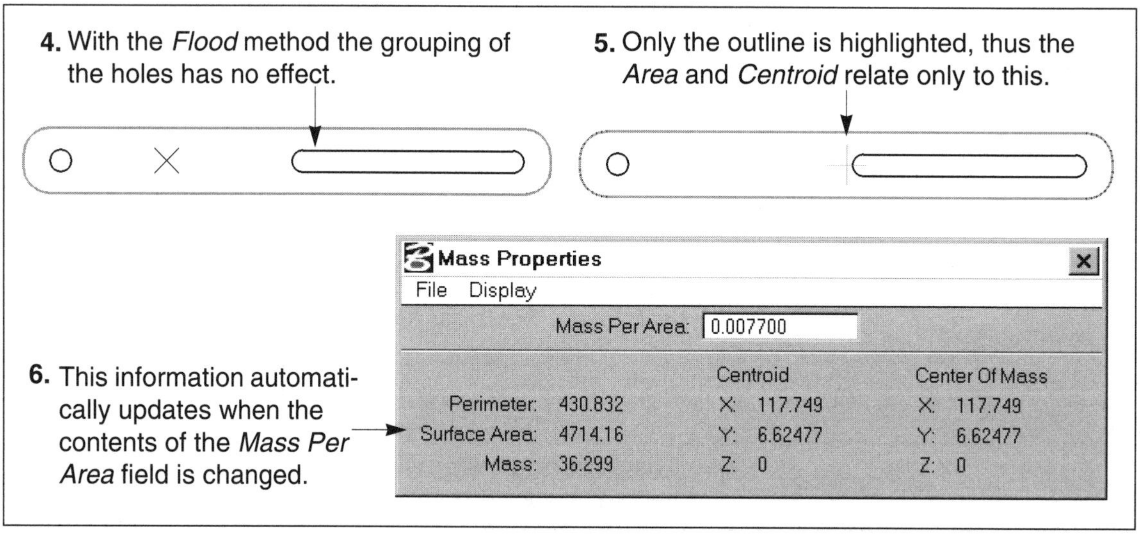

---

4. With the *Flood* method the grouping of the holes has no effect.

5. Only the outline is highlighted, thus the *Area* and *Centroid* relate only to this.

6. This information automatically updates when the contents of the *Mass Per Area* field is changed.

Mass Properties

File   Display

Mass Per Area: 0.007700

		Centroid	Center Of Mass
Perimeter:	430.832	X: 117.749	X: 117.749
Surface Area:	4714.16	Y: 6.62477	Y: 6.62477
Mass:	36.299	Z: 0	Z: 0

Figure 7.27 Measuring an Area using Flood

◆ **Measure the area and mass of the complete Stay Plate**

1. Select the *Measure Area* tool, set the *Method* to **Element**, leave the remaining settings as for the last exercise.

2. Identify the Stay Plate anywhere on its geometry.

3. *Accept* the highlighted area, note the *Grouped Holes* now highlight as part of the area definition.

4. Note the changes in the *Mass Properties* and the location of the *Centroid* marker, showing that the center of mass is now further to the left due to the lightening effect of the slot.

5. *Reset* when all the measurements are completed (the highlighting is removed).

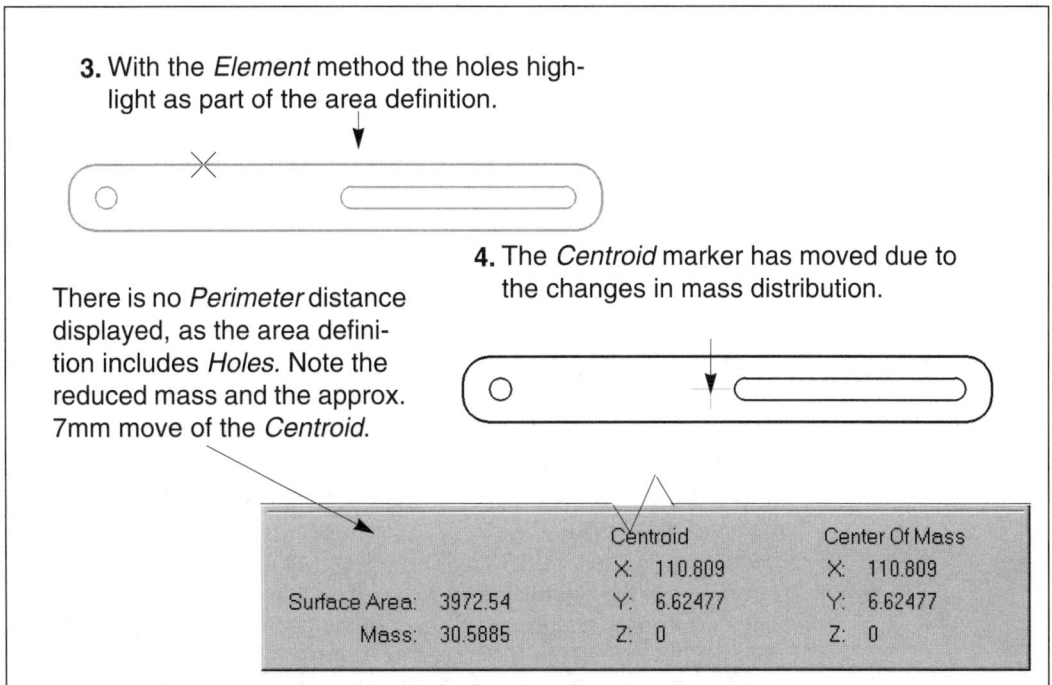

Figure 7.28   Measuring an area including holes

All of the *Methods* of defining an area available with the *Measure Area* tool operate in basically the same manner as the *Crosshatching* tool. Refer back to those exercises if you need to experiment further.

Patterning with Cells

Multiple copies of cells may be used to pattern areas. The cells used will usually be specially created for use in a pattern, with their geometry arranged to suitably orient each instance of the cell to the neighboring instances. An example of the use of a standard patterning cell is illustrated in Figure 7.29. The checkerboard effect has been added show the individual cell instances in this illustration, but normally all the cells would be the same color.

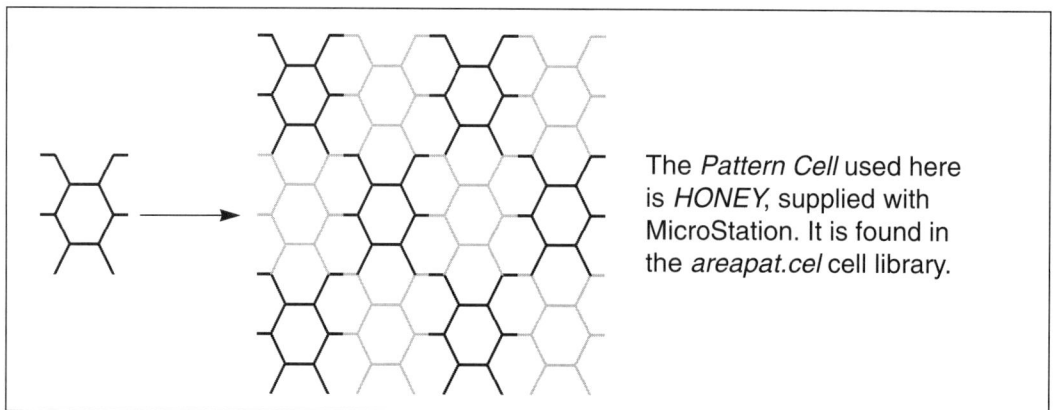

The *Pattern Cell* used here is *HONEY,* supplied with MicroStation. It is found in the *areapat.cel* cell library.

Figure 7.29   Multiple instances of a Cell forming a Pattern

Creating a Patterning Cell

The process of creating a cell for use in patterns is the same as for creating any other cell (see "Creating Cells" on page 6-7). The drawing used for the cell requires careful design, however, as each cell instance will generally need to link with adjoining instances.

The *Range* of the cell (that is the range of coordinates between its extremities in the x and y directions) sets the matrix size of the pattern. The position of the *Cell Origin* does not have an effect. If we need to incorporate blank space between instances we must increase the *Range* occupied by the cell with the addition of an *Active Point* (zero length line) spaced away from the main geometry. This element does not reproduce in the pattern.

Pattern cells may be created as either *Point* type or *Graphic* type. If *Point* type cells are used the pattern is generated with the currently active symbology.

Graphic type pattern cells generate a pattern with the original symbology of their components, but both types take the *Level* attribute of the element (if any) being patterned. Cells placed as a pattern differ from the same cells placed using any of the *Place Cell* tools. The most important differences are:

• Patterns of *Point* type cells are *View Dependent* (they rotate with the view);

• Patterns of *Graphic* type cells are not placed on the same *Levels* as the cell's original components when patterning an *Element*.

In the next exercise we will create a very basic patterning cell to generate a simple 240 X 86 brick pattern. We will create the elements for the minimum *Cycle* for the particular pattern, but in practice we may speed up the patterning process by including more than one cycle in the cell definition. The original drawing for the cell will be created in "cells.dgn" and the cells stored in the cell library "examples.cel".

◆ **Create a Brick pattern cell**

1. Open "cells.dgn", window a clear area about 300 X 200 for the drawing.

   One method of sizing and positioning a View window is to zoom well out and place a 300 X 200 *Block* using AccuDraw. We can then *Window Area* about the block, then delete it.

2. Set the element *Color* to *3* (Red), *Level* to *10*, *Line Style* to *0* and the *Weight* to *1*.

3. Place a *Line String* and a *Line* using the *Place Smartline* tool with *AccuDraw*, *Smart Lock*, *Keypoint* and *Midpoint* snap modes as shown in Figure 7.30.

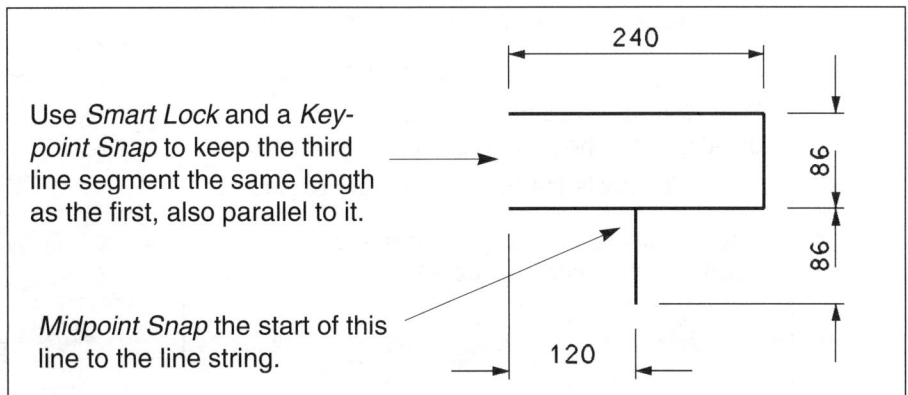

Figure 7.30 Drawing for a brick pattern cell

4. Select the *Define Cell Origin* tool, place the origin with a data point anywhere within the drawing, place a *Fence* around it.

    The actual position is not critical, but an origin must be in place before we can create a *Cell*.

5. Select *Element>Cells* (the *Cell Library* settings box opens), check that "examples.cel" appears in the Title bar as *Attached Cell Library*.

    If not, select the *File>Attach* option and select it from its folder.

6. Click the *Create* button, key in **Brickg** to the *Name* field of the *Create New Cell* dialog box.

7. Press <**Tab**>, key in **Graphic brick pattern** to *Description*, choose the *Graphic* Cell *Type* option.

    Now we will use the same group of elements, with the same *Cell Origin* to create an additional *Point Type Cell*.

8. Repeat steps **6.** and **7.**, except create a ***Point*** type cell named **Brickp**, described as **Point brick pattern**.

The next exercises will make use of these brick patterning cells.

The Pattern Area Tool

The majority of the settings for this tool (found in the *Patterns* tool box, see Figure 7.9) are the same as those for the *Hatching* and *Crosshatching* tools, except now we have data input fields for *Pattern Cell*, *Scale*, *Row* and *Column Spacing*.

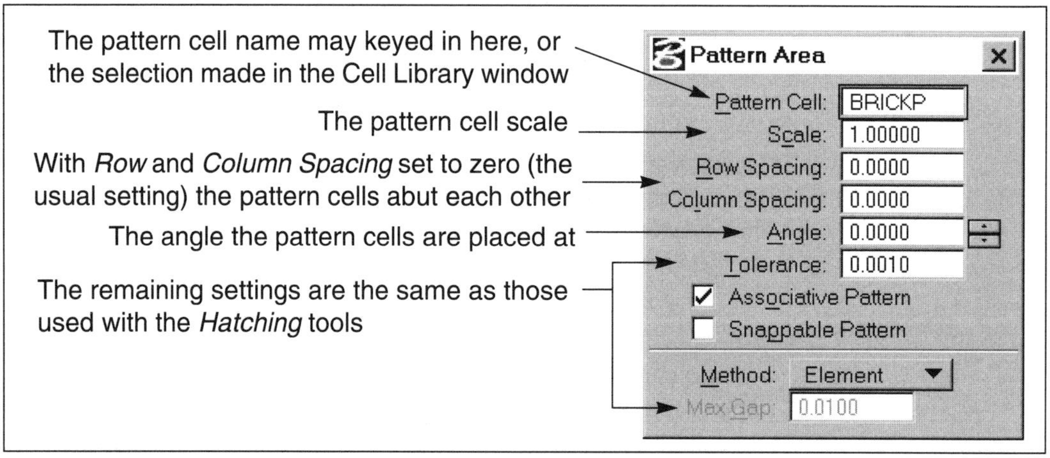

Figure 7.31 Settings for the Pattern Area tool

Point Type Pattern Cells

We will apply the pattern cells just created for some experiments in the next exercises, using "cells.dgn" as the active design file as before. The basic principles of patterning have been demonstrated with *Crosshatching*, so we will only experiment with the unique features of cell patterns. We will start by applying a brick pattern to a 1200 X 860 block.

◆ **Create a block with a Point type brick pattern**

1. Window a clear area about 1300 X 1000 in "cells.dgn".

2. Set the element *Color* to *1*, *Level* to *5*, *Line Style* to *0* and the *Weight* to *1*.

3. Select the *Place Block* tool, use AccuDraw to place a *1200* by *860* block.

4. Change the element *Color* to *2*, *Level* to *10*, *Line Style* to *1* and the *Weight* to *2*.

5. Select the *Pattern Area* tool, key in **BRICKP** as the *Pattern Cell*, set the *Scale* to *1*, the *Spacings* and *Angle* all to *0*, the *Tolerance* does not matter as there are no curves. *Associative* and *Snappable Pattern* can be *Off*, *Method: Element*.

   We could have chosen BRICKP as the *Pattern Cell* from within the *Cell Library* window instead of keying it in.

6. Identify the block, snap to a corner and *Accept* to place the pattern, *Analyze* a component of the pattern and note its *Element Attributes*.

The *Point* type pattern cell BRICKP is placed with the *Active Symbology Attributes* (set in step 4.) but on the same *Level* (5) as the element being patterned.

Align the pattern cycles to the area element by first *Snapping* to a corner to position the "*Accept @pattern intersection*" data point.

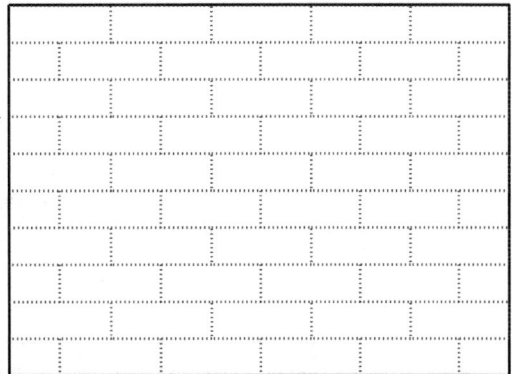

Figure 7.32   A Pattern of Point type cells

Graphic Type Pattern Cells

Next, we will pattern the same block with *Graphic* cells and observe the differences.

◆ Place a Graphic type brick pattern

1. *Undo* or *Delete* (with the *Delete Pattern* tool) the previous point type pattern.

2. Leave the active Element Attributes as before (*Color: 2*, *Level: 10*, *Line Style: 1* and the *Weight: 2*).

3. Select the *Pattern Area* tool, set **BRICKG** as the *Pattern Cell*, leave the rest of the tool settings as arranged in step **5.** of the previous exercise.

4. Identify the block, snap to a corner and *Accept* to place the pattern, *Analyze* a component of the pattern and note its *Element Attributes.*

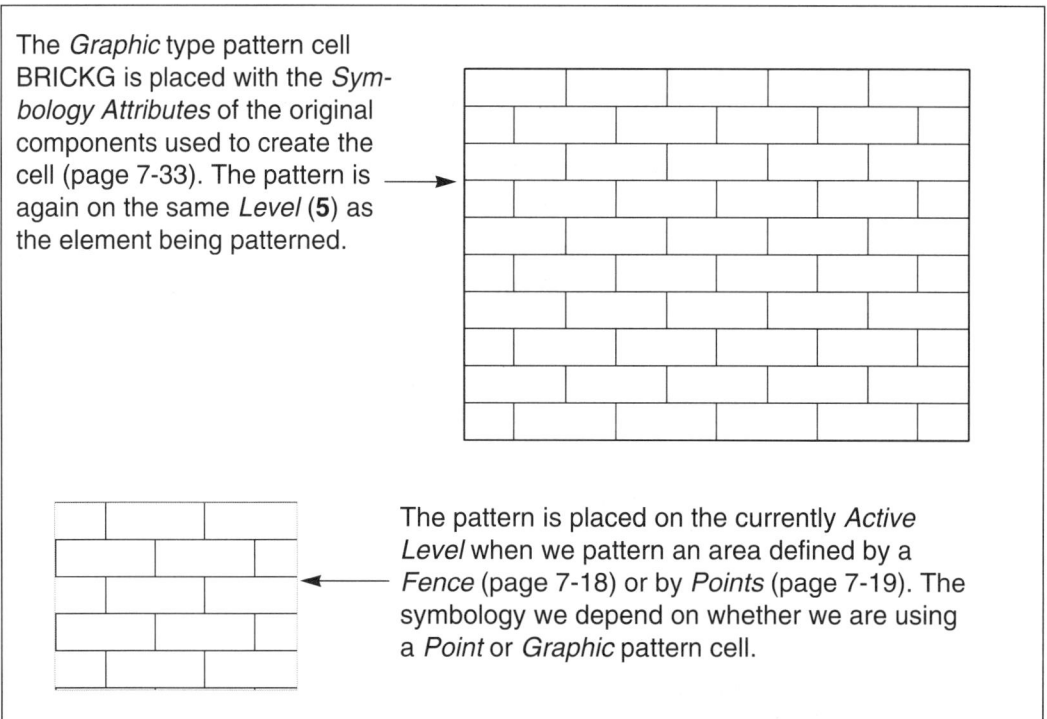

The *Graphic* type pattern cell BRICKG is placed with the *Symbology Attributes* of the original components used to create the cell (page 7-33). The pattern is again on the same *Level* (**5**) as the element being patterned.

The pattern is placed on the currently *Active Level* when we pattern an area defined by a *Fence* (page 7-18) or by *Points* (page 7-19). The symbology we depend on whether we are using a *Point* or *Graphic* pattern cell.

Figure 7.33   Patterns of Graphic type cells

Effect of Spacing and Angle

The *Row Spacing* and *Column Spacing* settings are usually zero, but they may be varied to produce less dense patterning. These *Spacings* are distances between the extremes of the *x* and *y* coordinate *Range* of adjacent cells, not the pattern repetition distance. Where a consistent space between cells is required for a particular pattern, it is more efficient to include an *Active Point* in the cell definition, positioned to increase the *x* and *y* *Range* of the cell (see "Creating a Patterning Cell" on page 7-32).

The *Angle* setting affects the whole pattern, not just the individual cells. The *Rows* and *Columns* remain orthogonal but both rotated by the *Angle*. In the following exercise we will use the "Arrowhead" cell created in the last chapter (see "Create cells from the Arrowhead and Arrow Tail drawings" on page 6-27).

◆ **Place Scaled, Spaced and Angled patterns of Arrowheads**

1. *Undo* or *Delete* the previous graphic type pattern from the block.

2. Select the *Pattern Area* tool, set **ARRHD** as the *Pattern Cell*, the *Scale* to *10*, leave the rest of the tool settings as for the previous exercise.

3. Identify the block, snap to a corner and *Accept* to place the pattern. Note that the arrowhead geometry does not link up in the horizontal direction, but the extremes of the *x* ranges abut one another.

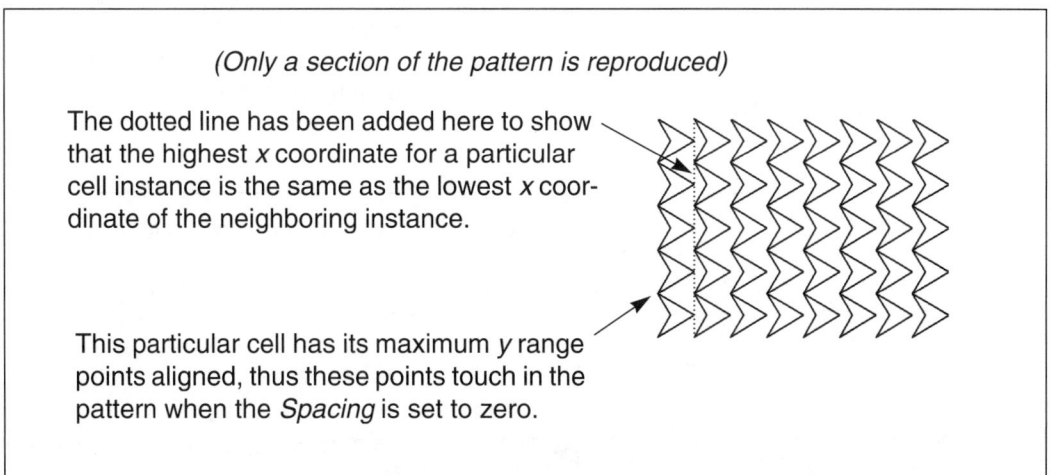

(Only a section of the pattern is reproduced)

The dotted line has been added here to show that the highest *x* coordinate for a particular cell instance is the same as the lowest *x* coordinate of the neighboring instance.

This particular cell has its maximum *y* range points aligned, thus these points touch in the pattern when the *Spacing* is set to zero.

Figure 7.34   Zero Row and Column Spacing pattern

4. *Undo* the pattern, select the *Pattern Area* tool again, this time change the *Row Spacing* and the *Column Spacing* settings to *80*.

5. Identify the block, snap to a corner and *Accept* to place the pattern.

    This time the *Ranges* of the arrowheads are separated by 8mm in each direction.

6. *Undo* the pattern, select the *Pattern Area* once more, now time change the *Angle* to *30°*, leaving *Row Spacing* and the *Column Spacing* settings at *80*.

    The whole pattern will be rotated by 30° in an anti-clockwise direction.

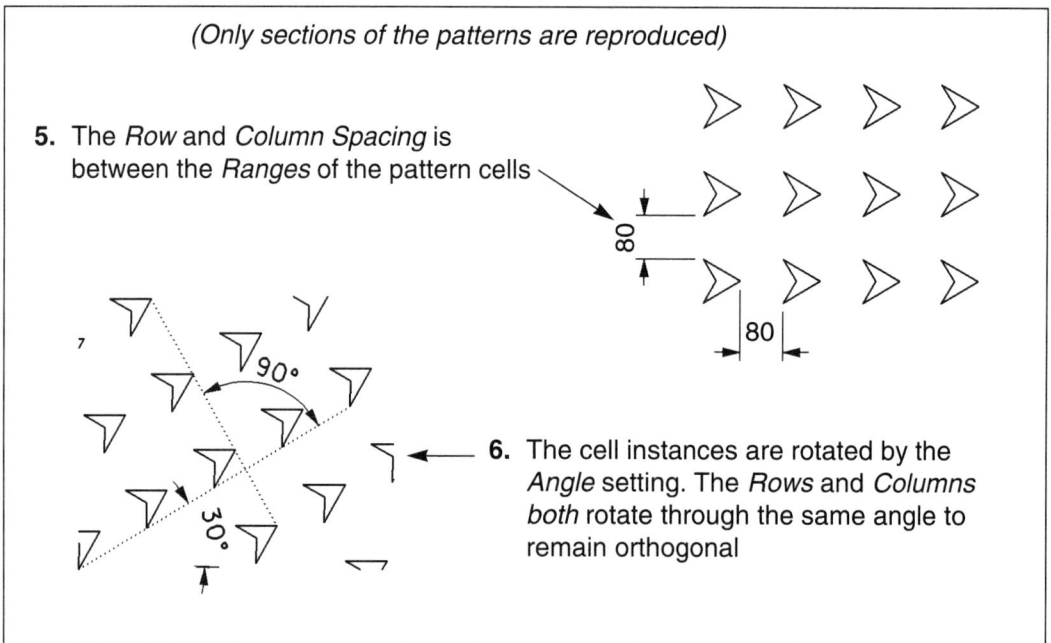

(Only sections of the patterns are reproduced)

5. The *Row* and *Column Spacing* is between the *Ranges* of the pattern cells

80

80

6. The cell instances are rotated by the *Angle* setting. The *Rows* and *Columns* both rotate through the same angle to remain orthogonal

90°

30°

Figure 7.35   Spaced and Angled Patterning

Background Fill

It is sometimes necessary to place a colored fill or "wash" over an area in a drawing, such as in a building plan. Any of the fill types (see "Fill Options" on page 7-3) may be used.

However, the fill may hide any previously placed text or linework, which would generally be unacceptable. To solve this problem, the text and/or linework must be "brought to the front". This requires the elements(s) being re-located further down in the design file, in order that these elements are "read" later and overwrite the fill. The same order of "reading" the elements applies to both the screen display and to printing.

Changing the Fill Type

In the following exercises, we will be working with an existing drawing of a building floor plan. The task is to apply a background fill to areas of the example drawing *igi_flrp.dgn*, with the text inside the deck remaining readable. We will change the fill type of the shape element bounding the deck in the first exercise.

The Change To Active Fill Type tool

This tool is found in the *Change Attributes* tool box from the *Main* tool frame. The fill type currently active is applied to the closed element when it is identified. The active *Fill Type* and *Fill Color* settings may be changed in the Tool Settings window of the tool itself, see Figure 7.36.

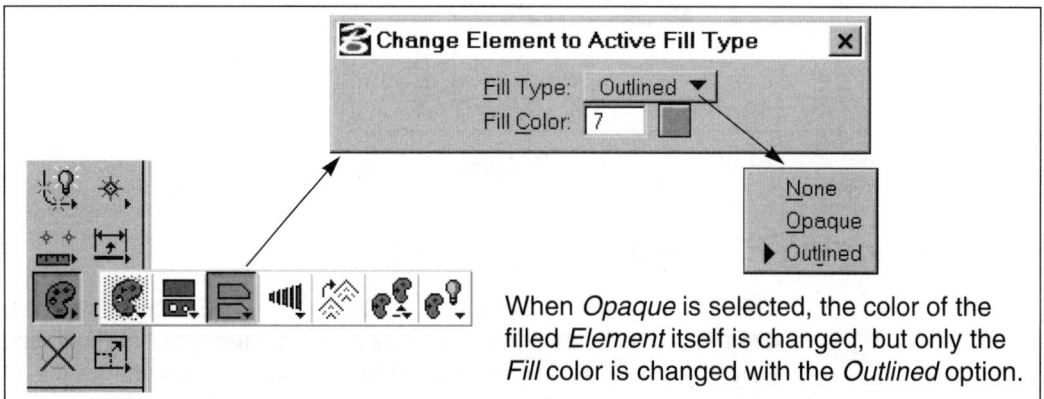

When *Opaque* is selected, the color of the filled *Element* itself is changed, but only the *Fill* color is changed with the *Outlined* option.

Figure 7.36 Changing the Fill Type

◆ **Apply Background Fill to a Floor Plan**

1. Open the example file *igi_flrp.dgn* from the . . . \Workspace\projects \examples\arch\dgn directory.

2. Window the area about the Deck, select the *Change to Active Fill Type* tool, change the *Fill Type* to *Outlined*, select a *Fill Color*. Identify and *Accept* the shape outlining the Deck.

3. Turn *On* the *Fill* view attribute check box in the *View Attributes* settings box (see "Attributes of the View Window" on page 3-3 and "Filling Closed Elements" on page 7-3).

    The Deck area will appear *Filled*, with the text elements hidden.

4. Turn the *Fill* view attribute back *Off*.

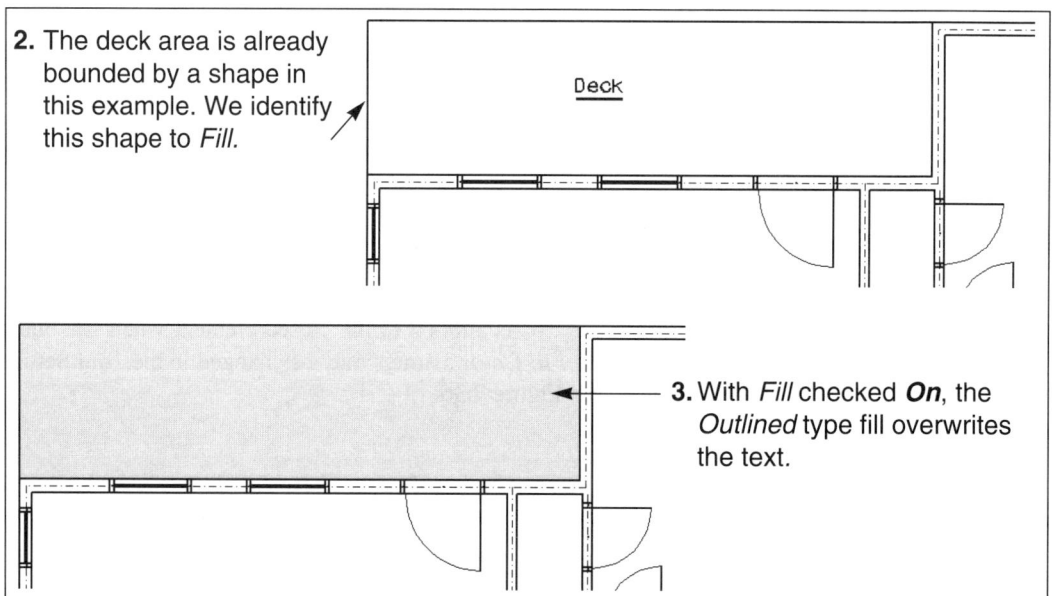

Figure 7.37 Applying a Background Fill

Bringing Elements to the Front

This process involves using two key-ins to the *Key-in* utility, **wset add** and **wset drop**. The original function of these key-ins is for use with "working sets", a concept generally unused in later versions of MicroStation. In this application, elements are added to a working set, then immediately "dropped" from that set, thus re-writing them to the end of the design file.

◆ **Bringing the Text to the Front**

1. With the *Element Selection* tool, select the text "Deck" and the underline (they are separate elements).

2. Open the *Utilities>Key-in* window, use the *Key-in Browser* (see "The Key-in Window" on page 5-40) to key-in **wset add** then **wset drop**.

3. Turn the *Fill* view attribute back *On*.

In the above example, the text was re-written over the top of the fill. In the next example we will use the *Create Region* tool to automatically outline the effective area of an office, creating a background fill at the same time.

◆ **Create a Filled Region**

1. Window the area about the Office, turn the *Fill* view attribute *Off*.

2. Set the *Color* to **0**, *Line Weight* to **1** in the *Primary* tool bar (This sets the attributes for the outline element).

3. Select the *Create Region* tool from the *Groups* tool box, set the *Method* to *Flood*, *Keep Original On*, *Fill Type* to *Outlined*, select a color for the fill.

4. Place a data point inside the office area, *Accept* the region outline created.

5. Use the *PowerSelector* tool to select the text "Office", its underline and the room No., key-in **wset add** then **wset drop**, turn *Fill* back *On*. The final results of the last two exercises are shown in Figure 7.38.

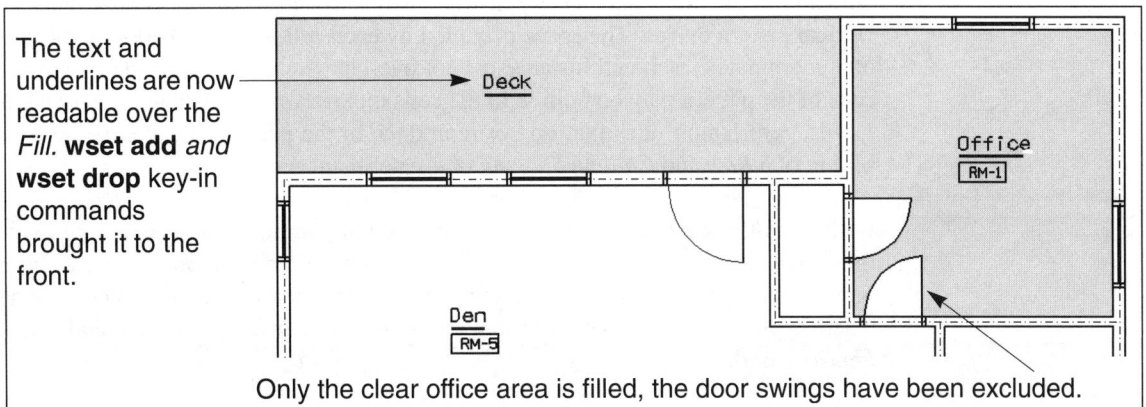

The text and underlines are now readable over the *Fill*. **wset add** *and* **wset drop** key-in commands brought it to the front.

Only the clear office area is filled, the door swings have been excluded.

Figure 7.38 Background Fills

Summary

Areas are defined for the purpose of *Patterning* with hatching or cells, for *Measuring* and *Mass Parameter* calculations, or for creating a shape that outlines a *Region* of a design. *Areas* may be defined by individual *Closed* elements such as simple or complex shapes and ellipses.

A set of open elements that outline an area may be converted into a single *Complex Shape*, thus defining an *Area*. Conversely, *Complex Shapes* may be *Dropped* to the individual lines, curves etc. that formed their component segments. There are a variety of other methods that may be used to define an *Area*, including logical operators. Using these methods, multiple closed elements can be combined in the form of a *Union*, an *Intersection* and a *Difference*.

Areas may also be defined within a set of elements of any type that overlap one another, by using the *Flood* method. For example, elements representing a garden fence, a footpath and a building may define an area of lawn. With this method, MicroStation detects the nearest enclosing elements outside a data point placed within the area. A gap between the elements may be accommodated up to a *Maximum Gap* dimension entered as a tool setting.

The definition of areas in these ways is permanent, or at least it lasts while the component elements remain in the design. Where no suitable elements exist, an area may be defined with a *Fence* or with a series of *Data Points*. This form of definition only exists for the time it takes to complete the particular patterning, measuring or region-defining operation.

Cells that are created specifically for use in patterns differ only at the original drawing production stage. They must be designed with attention to horizontal and vertical pattern cycles. The space occupied by each cell is set by the *Range* of *x* and of *y* coordinates, each cell instance cannot overlap another's range. Spaces between cells of the pattern may be built in to the cells themselves with the addition of *Active Points*, zero length lines that do not reproduce in the pattern. An alternative is the setting of a *Row* and *Column Spacing* of greater than zero.

Both *Graphic* and *Point* type cells may be used in patterns. The former type retains the symbology it was created with, the latter takes on the symbology active at the time the pattern is created. The level attribute is set by the element being patterned where appropriate, or the pattern is placed on the active level where a method such as *Fence* is used.

8 : Adding Text

A design will generally include some text labels, other than the text components of dimensioning. It may be as complex as a comprehensive list of materials, or as simple as the name of a view. It may be input directly from the keyboard into MicroStation's internal text editor, or imported as a file created by another application.

There are a large range of text facilities available in MicroStation. As well as placing text for titles, descriptions etc., text may be placed in the form of notes with leader lines and arrowheads, or as entries to prepared *Enter Data Fields*. Once placed, the text may be edited, with many of the word processor functions such as *Find and Replace* available.

When you have completed this chapter, you will be able to:

- Label a design with text having the desired *Font*, *Size* and *Justification* attributes;
- Place text by a variety of *Methods* to position it as required, with reference to other elements in some cases;
- Place multi-line text, either created in the internal text editor, or imported from another program;
- Utilize the *Text Glossary* to save repetitive keying in of commonly used words and phrases;
- Place *Empty Text Nodes* and *Enter Data Fields* to define the attributes and position of text placed at another time.

Text Facilities

Text is placed as a type of MicroStation *Element*, with some *Attributes* specific to this element type. The ordinary element attributes of *Color*, *Level* and *Line Weight* apply to text elements, along with five additional ones:

- *Font* - the typeface or character design of the text;
- *Text Height* - the height in the design file's units of full height characters;
- *Text Width* - the nominal width of a character and its associated space (the true width will vary above and below this dimension with *Proportionally Spaced* fonts);
- *Justification* - the alignment of the text in relation to the data point used to place it.

Text more than one line long is placed as a *Text Node*, which has the additional attributes of:

- *Line Spacing* - the distance between the bottom of one line of text and the maximum height of the characters on the following line;
- *Line Length* - the maximum number of characters in each line.

After setting the required *Text Attributes*, we can either go ahead and place the text, or we can put "placeholders" in the file. These define the text position and attributes, but not the text itself. We can then fill in the text details at any time in the future without any need to set the attributes again. The placeholders are called *Enter Data Fields* and/or *Empty Text Nodes*. There are tools available for copying, filling and automatically incrementing their contents. The display of text in the design is optional.

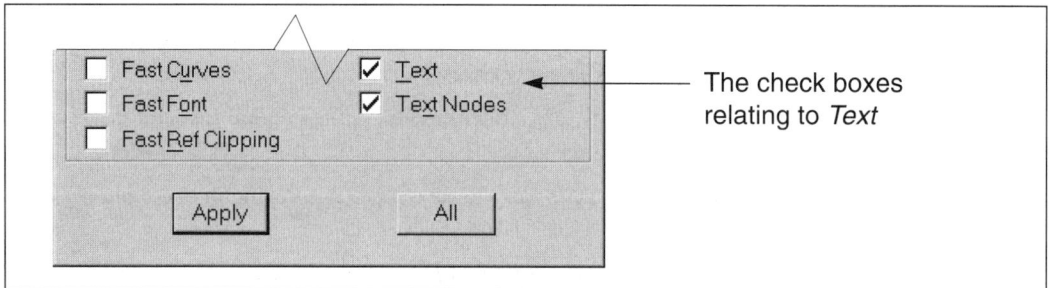

Figure 8.1   The Text part of View Attributes settings box

We can choose to turn Off *Text* in the *View Attributes* settings box (see page 3-3) if we do not need it to be displayed. The display of large quantities of text may slow down screen updates (especially with the more complex font shapes). We may choose to switch the *Text* display Off for other reasons, for example snaps can be attracted incorrectly to the text, or the linework may be partially hidden.

Text Settings

All the attributes and modifiers specific to text elements may be set in the *Text* settings box, found under *Element>Text* from the Application menu. The *Text Settings* box is shown in Figure 8.2. It has input fields, option menus and check boxes that enable us to set all the text-specific attributes and modifiers (e.g. *Underline*). We will work with all the settings in the examples and illustrations in this chapter, experimenting with the font selection methods in the first example.

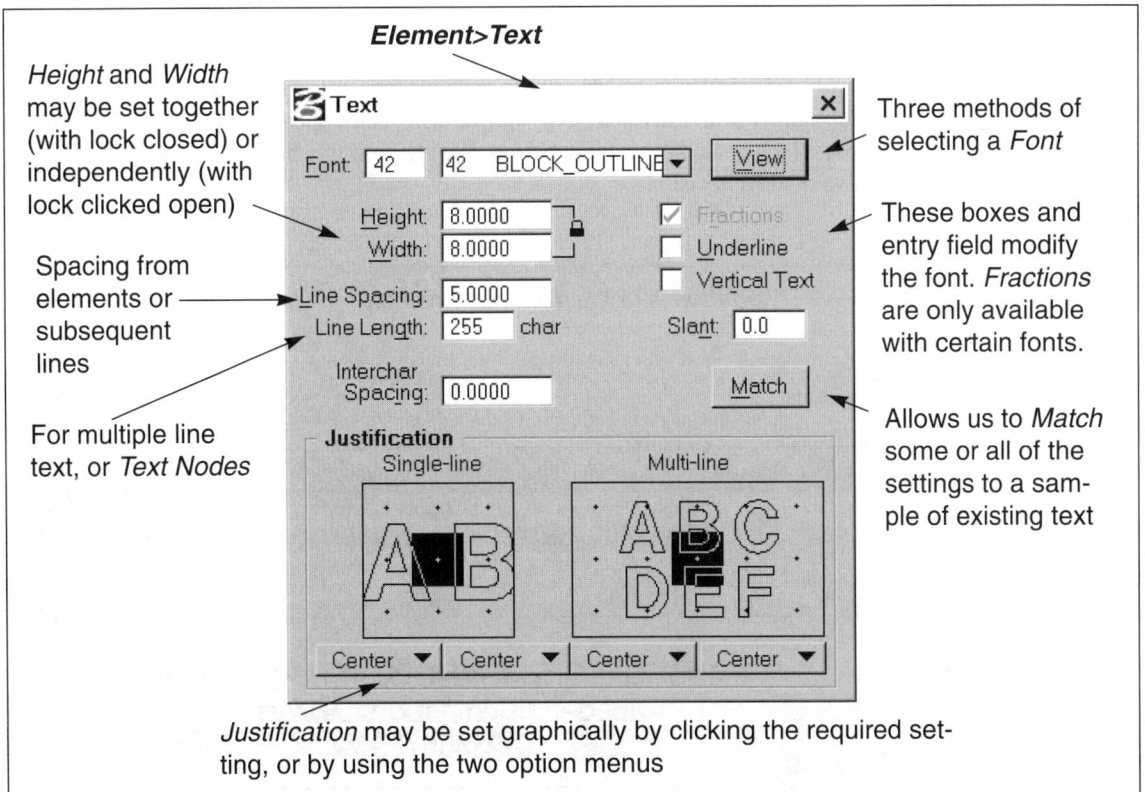

Figure 8.2   The Text settings box

Selecting a Font

There is a good selection of *Fonts* delivered with MicroStation and more can be imported (under *Utilities>Install Fonts*). Imported fonts can come from a variety of sources, including Windows® ".ttf" (True Type Font) files. Each font, original or imported, is identified by a name and number. How we select a font will depend on circumstances, we can browse through the offerings and make a selection by appearance, or we can select them by name. When we become very familiar with the set of fonts we generally use, we will remember enough to select them by number.

Browsing Fonts

When we click the *View button* in the *Text* settings box (Figure 8.2) the *Fonts* settings box opens, with the available selection of fonts displayed in name order. The first three list box columns show the *Number* and *Name*, along with *Type* where appropriate (e.g. Symbol fonts). The other two columns tell us the *Contents*, for example whether it supports lower case or fractions. We can scroll through the rows of the list box to search for a font.

If we wish to view a sample of a particular font, we click on the row for the font to highlight it in the list box. The sample will then appear on the panel below the list box, which is actually a large button. We click on this button to select a font once we have made a decision.

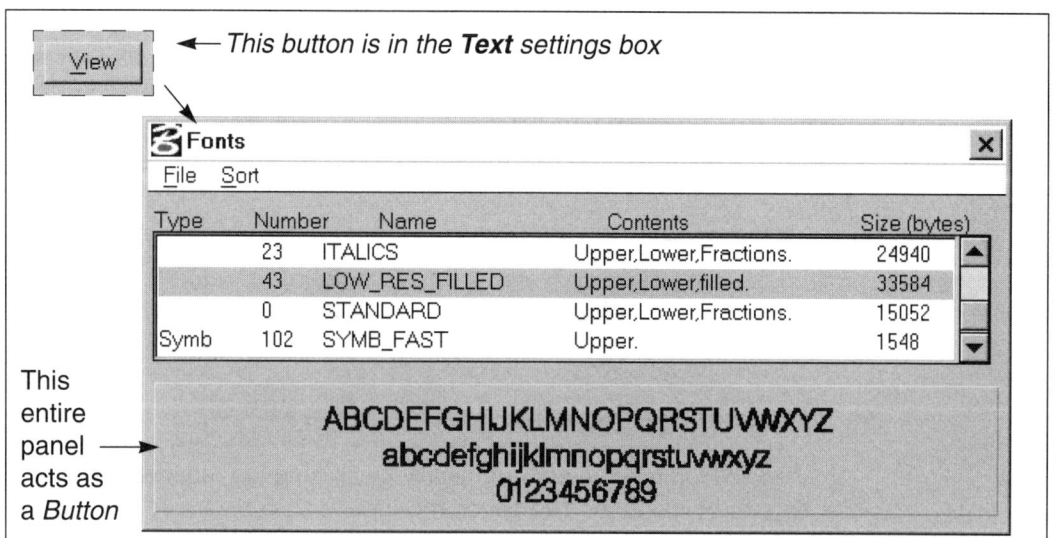

Figure 8.3   The Fonts settings box for browsing

Selecting a Font from the Option Menu

Clicking the *Font* option menu button presents a listing of the available fonts in name order, with the *Font Number* listed for information. This option menu is available in the *Text* settings box and in the Tool Settings window of some text placement tools.

Selecting a Font by Number

Data entry fields for keying in font numbers are available in the *Text* settings box, as well as in various Tool Settings windows.

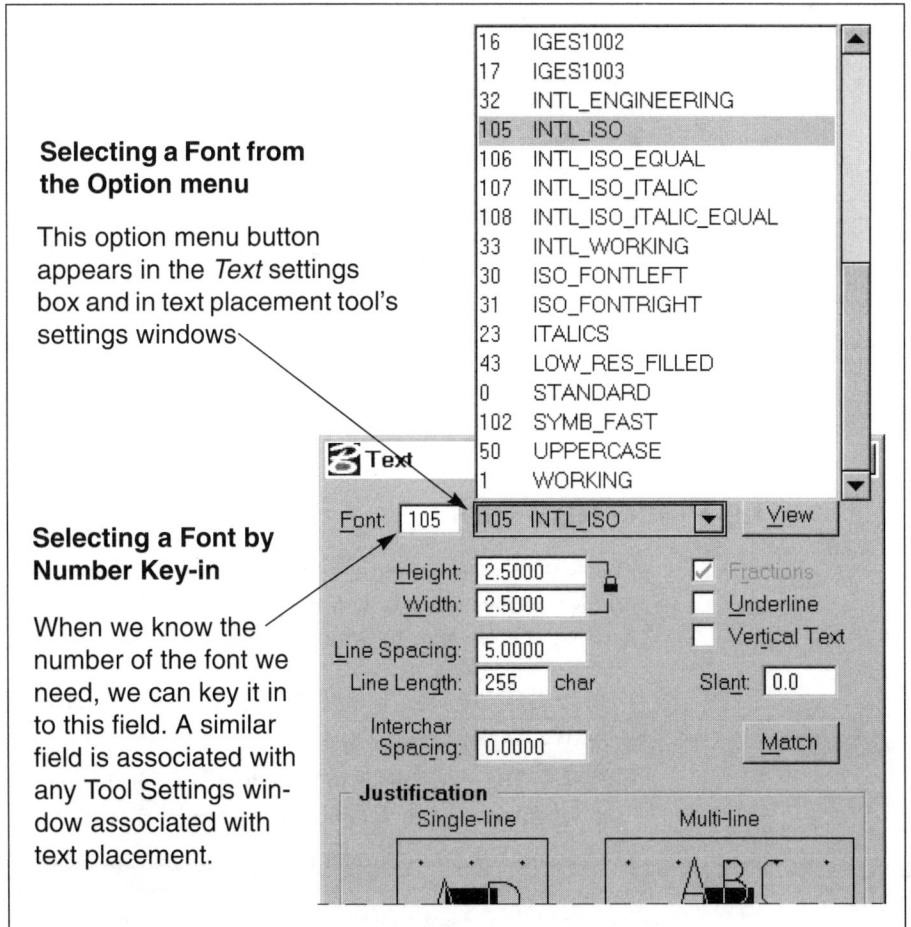

Figure 8.4   The Font Selection Option Menu and Data Entry field

The Text Tool Box

This large tool box is in three sections, separated by gaps in the buttons. The first two buttons are used to place text in the design as we key it in, they are the most commonly used. The middle group is more related to making changes to existing text except for the *Place Text Node* tool, which places a place marker for multiple line text containing all the attributes for the text to be placed in the future. The third group provides the more automated forms of text entry.

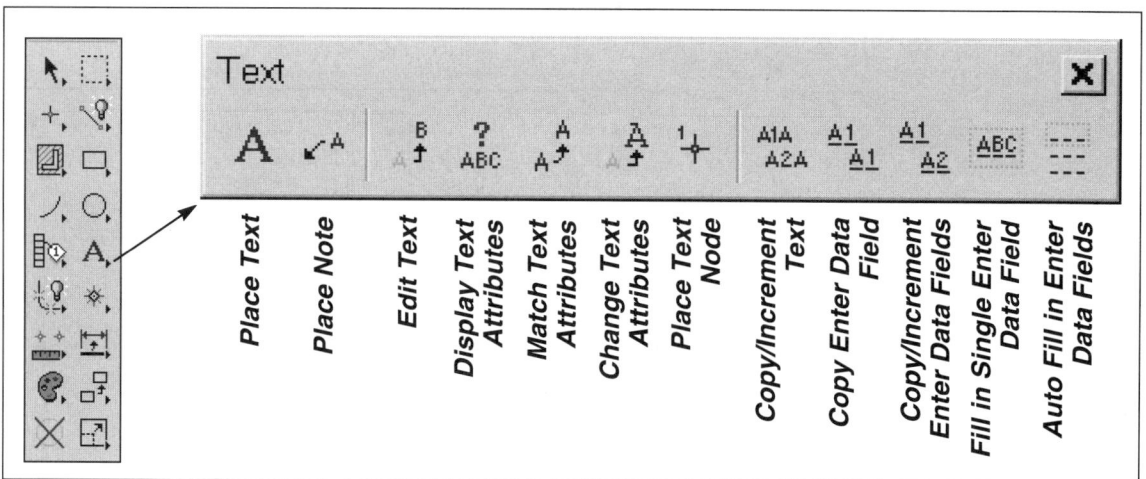

Figure 8.5   The Text Tool Box

The Place Text Tool

This is the general purpose text placement tool. Apart from the basic *Text Attribute* settings options (shared with the text settings box), this tool has a range of *Method* options. The *Methods* by which we place text are:

- *By Origin* - The text is placed with the currently active text settings and at the Active Angle;

- *Fitted* - The text is made to fit between two data points by automatically adjusting its height and width, retaining the set proportions;

- *View Independent* - Similar to *By Origin*, except the text does not rotate with a view rotation;

- *Fitted VI* - A combination of *Fitted* and *View Independent*;

- *Above Element* - Placed with the active text settings above (and parallel with) a line or line segment, spaced away from it by the *Line Spacing* setting;

- *Below Element* - Placed with the active text settings below (and parallel with) a line or line segment, spaced away from it by the *Line Spacing* setting;

- *On Element* - Replaces part of an element (including curved elements) with text placed at the angle of the element at the point it is identified;

- *Along Element* - Above or below an element (including curved elements) with each character of the text placed individually and parallel to the element. Placement above or below is determined by the position of a second data point.

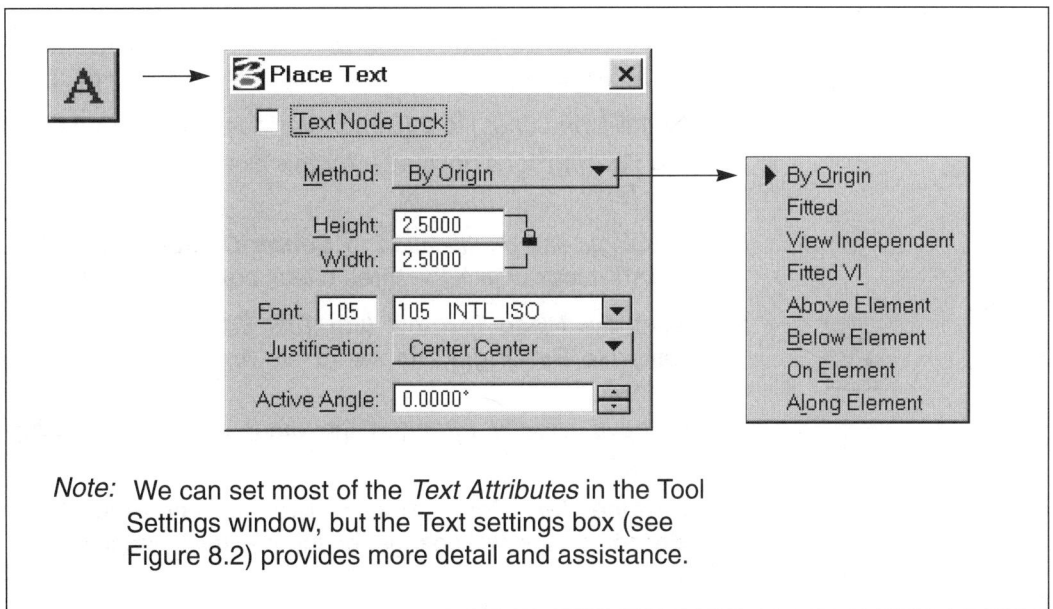

Figure 8.6   The Place Text Tool Settings window

We will use "second.dgn" for our next examples, including the circles we placed for the "Areas" chapter. Some of the labelling will become a permanent part of the design. Other times we will be placing elements, noting the result and *Undoing* the changes. The original design must stay intact for dimensioning etc.

Placing Text by Origin Method

The first exercise with text will demonstrate the most common method of placement. We will experiment with *Font Selection*, *Height*, *Width* and *Justification*.

◆ **Label the Stay Plate**

1. Open "second.dgn", window the area about the Stay Plate, with the plate in the upper part of the View window. Switch level **25 *Off***, make **12 *Active***.

Hint!   Apart from the *Settings* menu, the *Level Display* settings box can be opened from the View window control icon (or button), or by using the keyboard shortcut **<Ctrl+E>**.

2. Choose *Element>Text* (The *Text* settings box opens), click the *View* button, select a *Font* by browsing (see "Selecting a Font" on page 8-4).

   Remember, the panel displaying the highlighted font is the button to make that font *Active*.

3. Click the lock between *Height* and *Width* closed (if necessary), set the text *Size* (height and width combined) to **6**.

4. Set the *Line Length* to **255** and *Interchar Spacing* to **0** (the defaults).

   Line Spacing does not matter for this exercise, as we are using *Single Line Text*.

5. Set *Single-line Justification* to **Center-Center** (click in the center of the "AB" block). Click the three check boxes **Off**, set the *Slant* to **0**.

6. Select the *Place Text* tool (the *Text Editor* window opens), set the *Method* to **By Origin** and the *Active Angle* to **0** in the *Tool Settings* window.

   We have already arranged the other tool settings using the *Text* settings box.

7. Click the *Text Editor* window, key in **Stay Plate** (do **not** press **<Enter>**, as this will change the input to multi-line text).

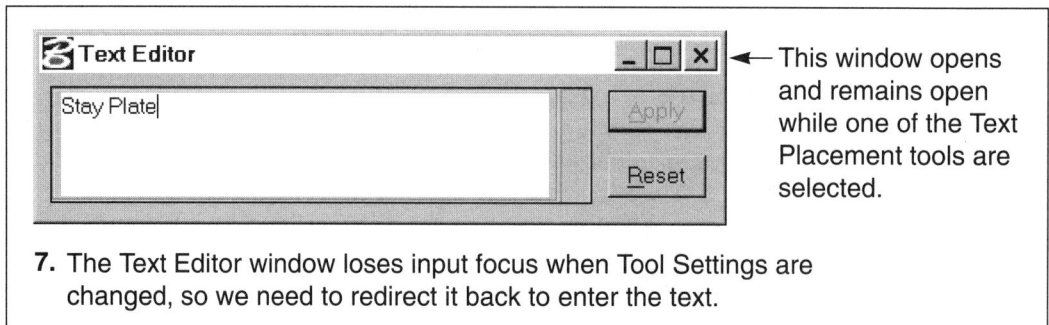

Text Editor   _ □ ✕

Stay Plate| Apply

                                   Reset

◄— This window opens and remains open while one of the Text Placement tools are selected.

7. The Text Editor window loses input focus when Tool Settings are changed, so we need to redirect it back to enter the text.

Figure 8.7   The Text Editor window

8. Start AccuDraw, or click in its window to give it input focus if it is already running. Move the pointer over the lower side of the plate outline, *Midpoint* snap a tentative point to this segment.

9. Move the AccuDraw *Origin* (*<O>*) down by **25**, *Accept* the placement.

10. After *Accepting* the label, the text remains attached to the pointer ready for further placements.

    We can continue to place the same text, change it in the *Text Editor* window before placing more labels, or *Reset* to cancel the process.

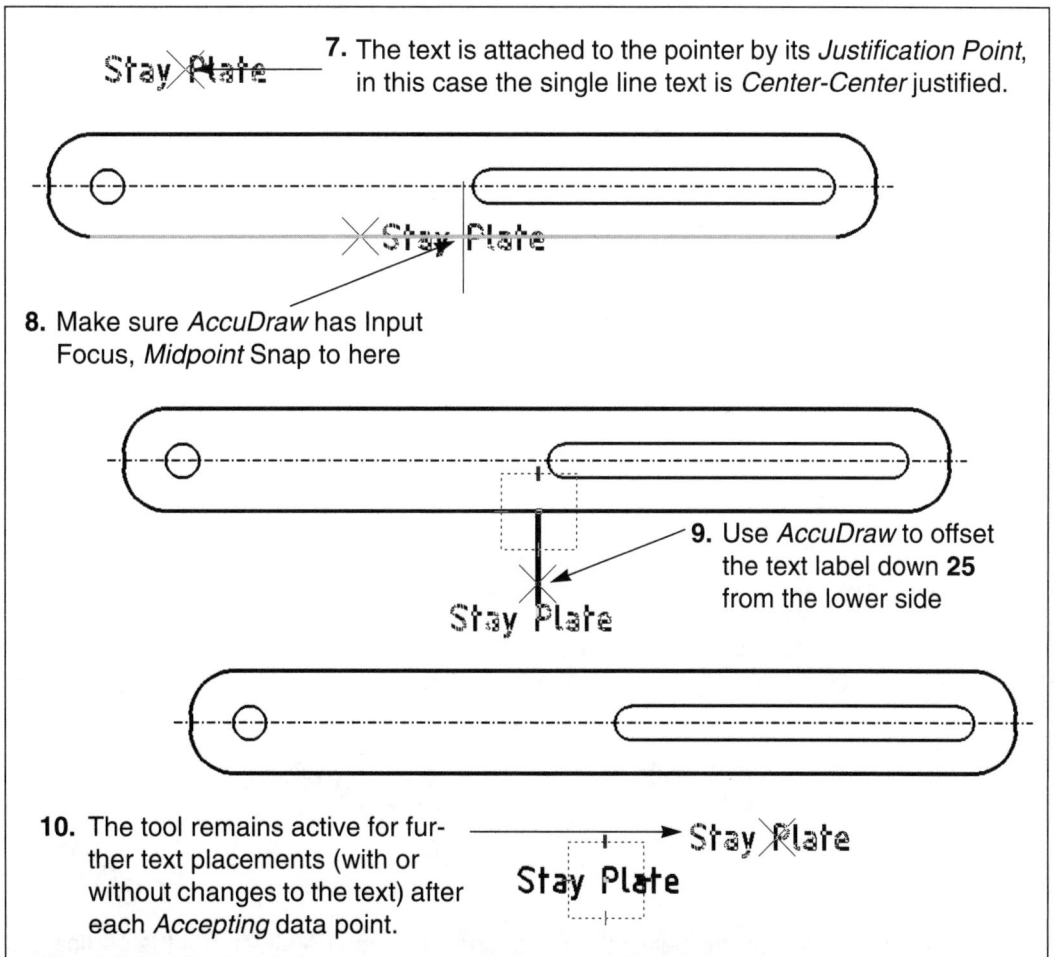

Figure 8.8 Placing a text label by Origin using AccuDraw

Fitted Text

There are occasions where the size of the text needs to be set graphically. This may be to fit it to an available space, or to adjust its size and angle "by eye" to suit the situation. The *Fitted* method is useful in these situations.

◆ Place Fitted Text

1. Select the *Place Text* tool, change the *Method* tool setting to **Fitted**, leave the other settings as arranged for the last exercise.

2. Key in a single line of text to the Text Editor window (remember, do not press <**Enter**>), move the pointer to a clear space in the design. Note that the text does not appear at this stage, unlike the *By Origin* method.

3. Place a data point **(a)**, move the pointer away from it in any direction **(b)**, noting the dynamic updating of the text.

4. *Accept* the text with a second data point.

5. Repeat steps **3.** and **4.** with different *Justification* settings. Remove the *fitted* text, but leave the *Stay Plate* label placed in the preceding exercise.

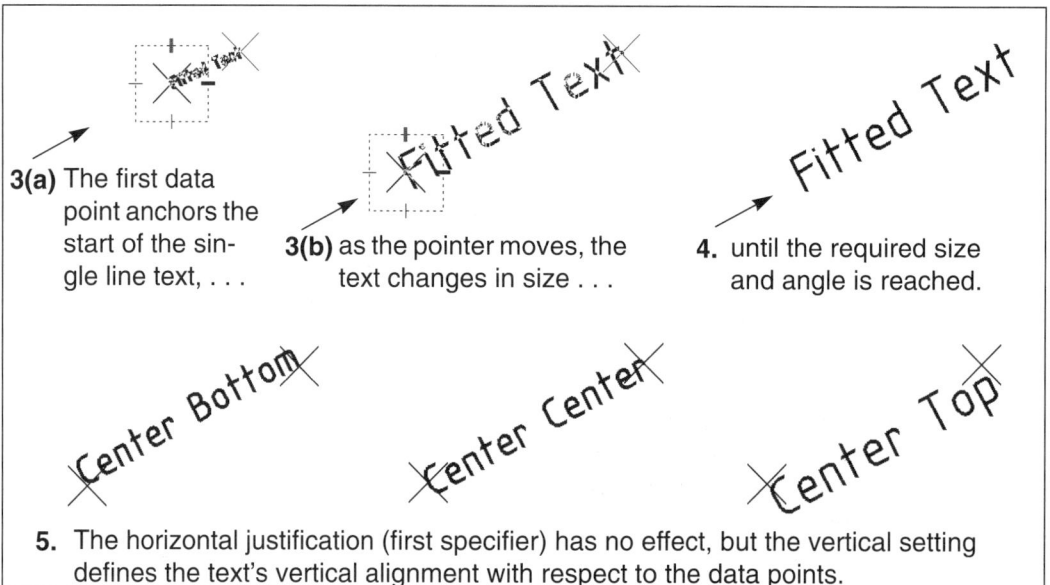

3(a) The first data point anchors the start of the single line text, . . .

3(b) as the pointer moves, the text changes in size . . .

4. until the required size and angle is reached.

5. The horizontal justification (first specifier) has no effect, but the vertical setting defines the text's vertical alignment with respect to the data points.

Figure 8.9 Placing Fitted Text

View Independent Text

View Independent text remains at the same angle when a view window is rotated. This feature can be useful when we need to keep text horizontal when multiple presentations of the graphics are required, each one at a different angle. View independent text may be by origin with the *View Independent* method option, or fitted with the *Fitted VI* option.

Text Placed Above and Below Elements

These methods space the text a fixed distance from an identified element, rotated to be parallel with it at the point at which it was identified. The space between the closest part of the text and the element is controlled by the *Line Spacing* setting in the Text settings box. This spacing is independent of the vertical justification setting. The horizontal justification point (*left*, *Center* or *Right*) of the text will be on a perpendicular to the element from the point it was identified.

◆ **Place text relative to an Element**

1. Set the Text horizontal *Justification* to **Left** (vertical does not matter), the *Line Spacing* to **3**, leave the size as used in the last exercise.

2. Select the *Place Text* tool, set the *Method* to **Above Element** and the *Justification* to **Center-Center**, key in a few characters.

3. Identify a point on the stay plate outline element and *Accept* the placement (do not *Reset*). Try placing the same text on straight and curved segments.

4. Change the *Method* to **Below Element** and repeat **3**.

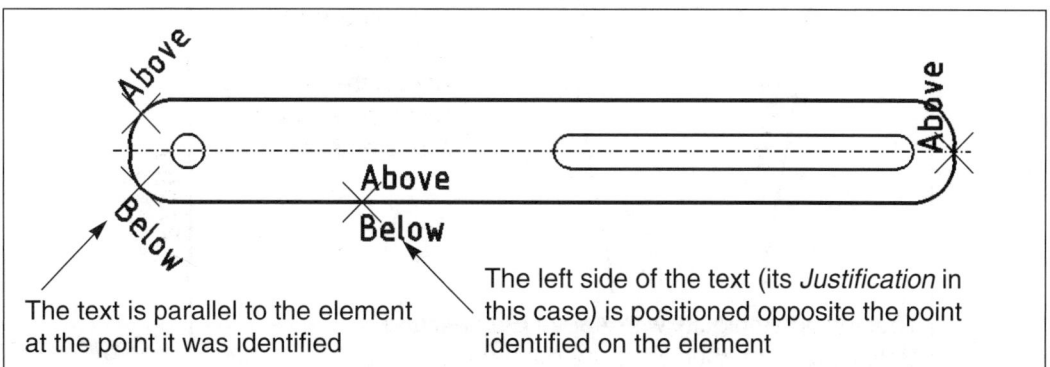

Figure 8.10 Placing text above and below elements

Text Placed Above and Below Vertical Elements

The text "Above" beside the right hand end segment in Figure 8.10 is placed in relation to a vertical line. When an element is anything other than vertical, there is no doubt as to where the text be placed if we use *Above Element* or *Below Element*. However, when the element or segment *is* vertical, how can we predict the orientation of the text placed with those methods? The answer is that the text will be placed with the *Origin* of the segment on its left.

◆ **Place text in relation to vertical lines**

1. Use *Place Smartline* with *AccuDraw* to place a **100** long line indexed to the +*y* axis of the Accudraw compass (start the line from the lower end).

2. Place a second **100** long vertical line, this time indexed to the -*y* axis.

3. Use the *Place Text* tool as in the last exercise to place single line text above both lines, note the difference.

If we find that text placed above or below an element is not running the way we need it, it can be changed. We can substitute *Above* or *Below* with *By Origin*, using an *Active Angle* setting of 90° or 270° (conventional). The text may be spaced away from the element by the equivalent of the *Line Spacing* distance with the AccuDraw *Move Origin* (**O**) facility.

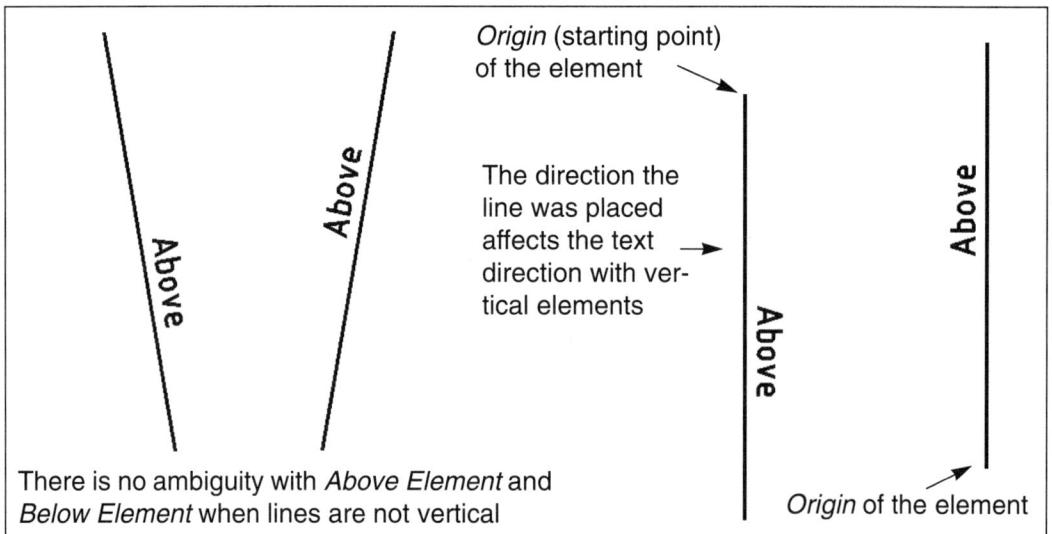

Figure 8.11   Text above and below vertical lines

Text Placed On Elements

With this method we replace a section of the element with text. If the element is a line, placing text *On* it away from an end will convert it into two separate lines. Closed elements will be broken and become open elements, but not if they are part of a group, such as our Stay Plate with its *Grouped Holes*. Text can not be placed *On* any elements that form part of a *Group* (see "Permanent Groups" on page 7-4).

◆ **Place text on elements**

1. Delete the text placed "above" the vertical lines placed in the last exercise.

2. Select the *Place Text* tool, set the *Method* to **On Element**, key in a few characters to the Text Editor window.

3. Identify a point on one of the lines and *Accept* the placement (do not *Reset*). Place the same text on the other vertical line.

We can delete text placed *On* a vertical line and replace it with text placed *By Origin* as we did with text placed *Above* or *Below* verticals. Again, we use an *Active Angle* setting of 90° or 270° (conventional). The text may be centered in the gap left by the deleted text using the AccuDraw *Move Origin* (**O**) facility.

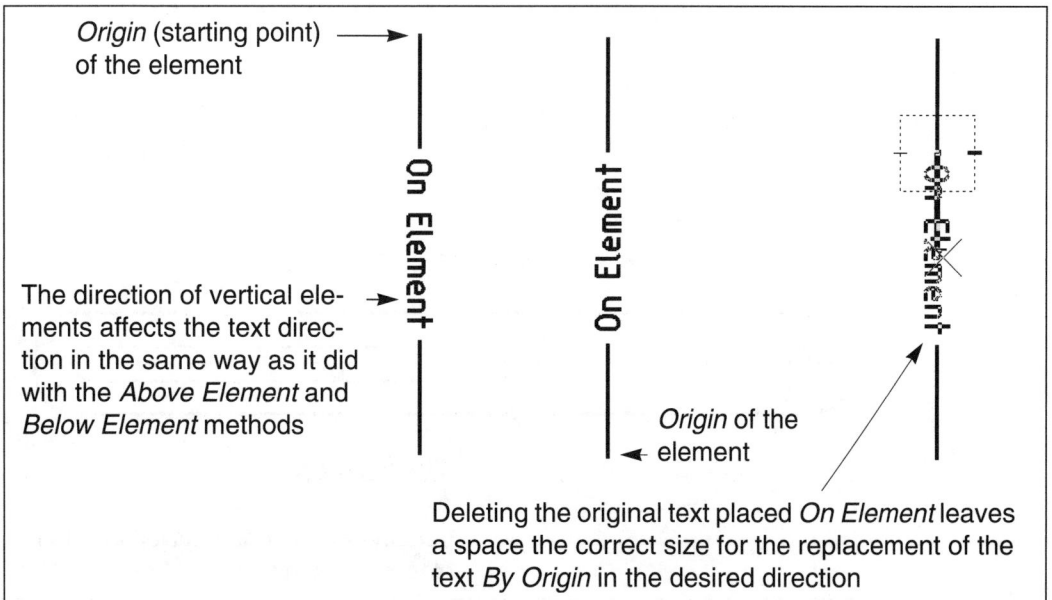

Origin (starting point) of the element

The direction of vertical elements affects the text direction in the same way as it did with the *Above Element* and *Below Element* methods

Origin of the element

Deleting the original text placed *On Element* leaves a space the correct size for the replacement of the text *By Origin* in the desired direction

Figure 8.12   Text placed On vertical lines

If the element is not part of a *Group*, we have the option of changing its direction so that any text placed *Above*, *Below* or *On* the element is in the desired direction. We can swap the *Origin* to the opposite end of the element with the *Change Element Direction* tool from the *Modify Curves* tool box, which is not in the Main tool frame. We access this tool box from the Application window *Tools* menu (see "The Modify Curves Tool Box" on page 5-37).

◆ Placing text on curved elements

1. Turn level **25 *On*** to display the circles previously used in the patterning examples.

2. Select the *Place Text* tool, set the *Method* to ***On Element***, key in a short single line of text.

3. Midpoint snap to the highest keypoint on the smaller circle, *Accept* the tentative, *Accept* the text.

4. Repeat step **3.,** this time at the lowest keypoint with a different horizontal *Justification* setting (the vertical setting has no effect with this method).

5. Identify a point on the Stay Plate outline to check if text can be placed on it, *Reset.*

   If the outline is still grouped with its holes (as it should be), *Element not found* will be returned in the message field.

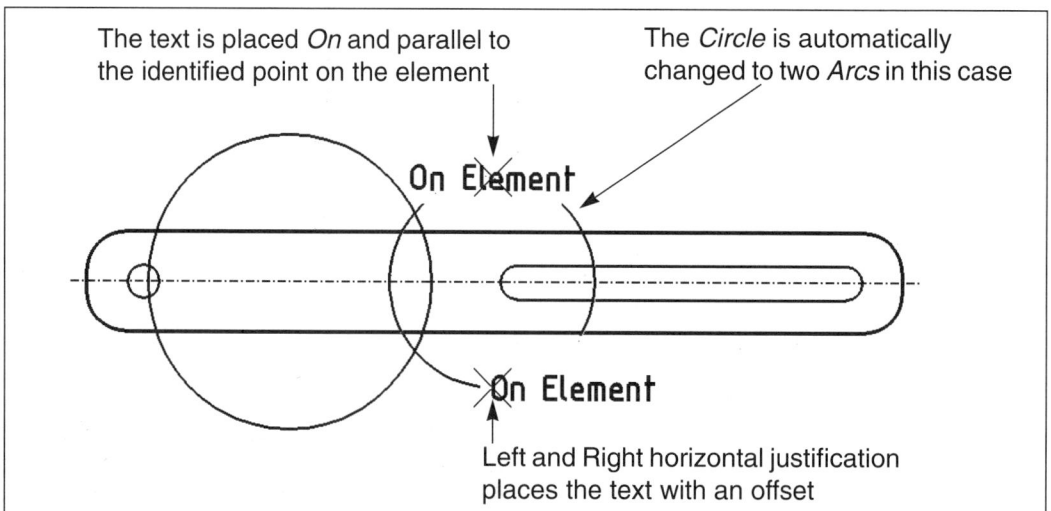

Figure 8.13 Placing text on (initially) closed curved elements

Text Placed Along Elements

Text placed *Along Elements* is able to follow along curves, with each individual character being rotated to remain parallel to the part of the element closest to it. Since the orientation of each character is individually calculated, the line of text keyed in is broken up into individual text elements. The spacing of the text from the element is set by *Line Spacing*, the same as for *Above* and *Below Element*.

However, the entire line of individual characters are included in a specially created *Graphic Group*, in a similar way to individual pattern elements (see "Graphic Group" on page 7-13). Since it is a graphic group, we can manipulate the entire line in as if it were an individual element when the *Graphic Group* lock is *On*.

◆ **Place text along an element**

1. Select the *Place Text* tool, set the *Method* to **Along Element**, key in a short line of text to the Text Editor window.

2. **(a)** Identify a point on the larger circle, move the pointer outside the circle and **(b)** *Accept* the placement.

3. Repeat step **2.**, this time *Accept* the text placement Inside the circle.

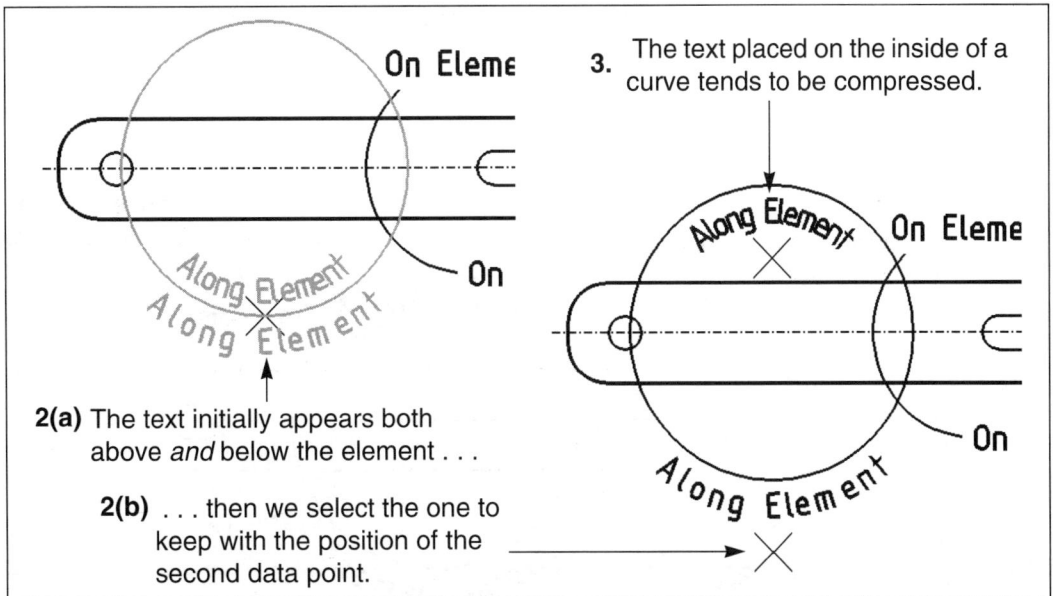

On Eleme

3. The text placed on the inside of a curve tends to be compressed.

On Eleme

On

On

2(a) The text initially appears both above *and* below the element . . .

2(b) . . . then we select the one to keep with the position of the second data point.

Figure 8.14 Text placed along an element

If we examine the text placed in step **3.** of the last exercise, we will see that the characters are too closely spaced, in fact they overlap in some cases. This is due to the spacing of the individual characters being determined on the element, with the characters themselves centered on perpendiculars from it. The compression is greater with small radii curved elements and with greater *Line Spacing* settings. There is a similar increase in intercharacter spacing with the text placed outside a curve.

Intercharacter Spacing

The *Interchar(acter) Spacing* setting for text defines an additional space placed between characters for placing text *Along* the inside of curves. *Along Element* is the only method that has this setting available.

◆ **Place spaced text inside a circle**

1. Delete the existing text inside the larger circle.
    With *Graphic Group* lock **On** the entire line can be deleted at once.

2. Select the *Place Text* tool, set the *Method* to **Along Element**, *Interchar. Spacing* to **1**. Key in a short line of text.

3. Identify a point on the larger circle, move the pointer inside the circle and *Accept* the placement.
    Note that the text is now more acceptably spaced, but it is no longer centered about the identifying data point with *Center* horizontal justification.

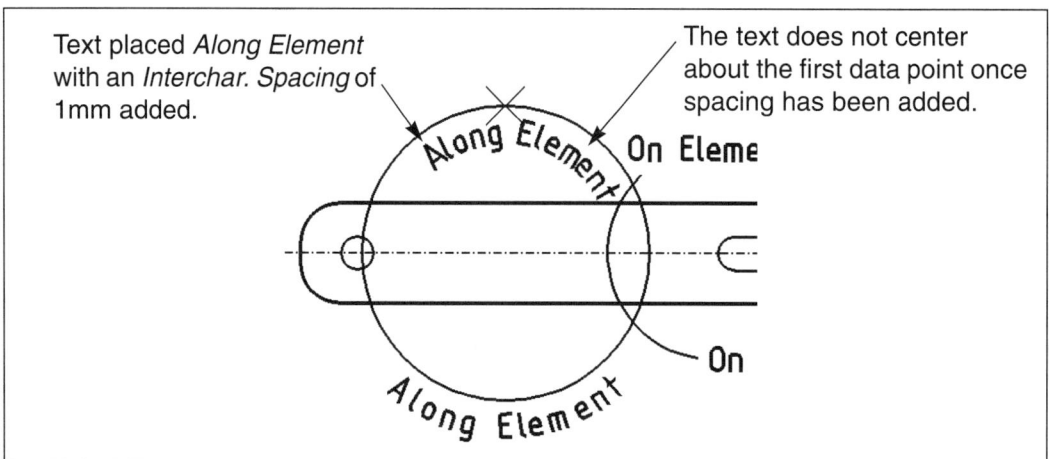

Figure 8.15   Adding Intercharacter Spacing to text placed Along Element

Fractions

Not all fonts support *Fractions*, so this setting may be grayed out in the *Element>Text* settings box. When the active font does include fractions, checking this box causes characters separated by a forward slash (/) to be placed as a single character fraction, as illustrated in Figure 8.16. In general, only the commonly used denominators are available (2, 4, 8, 16, 32), although some fonts provide more. The *View* option will display the range of denominators available for each font. The numerator must not be greater than the denominator.

Underlined Text

Checking the *Underline* box in the Text settings box causes *All* the text element being placed to be underlined.

Vertical Text

When we check the *Vertical Text* the text will be placed top-down, with the spacing set in the *Interchar. Spacing* field. The entire text element may be rotated away from the vertical by the *Active Angle* setting.

Slanted Text

Text may be slanted by a maximum of +/- 89° by entering the angle into the *Slant* field.

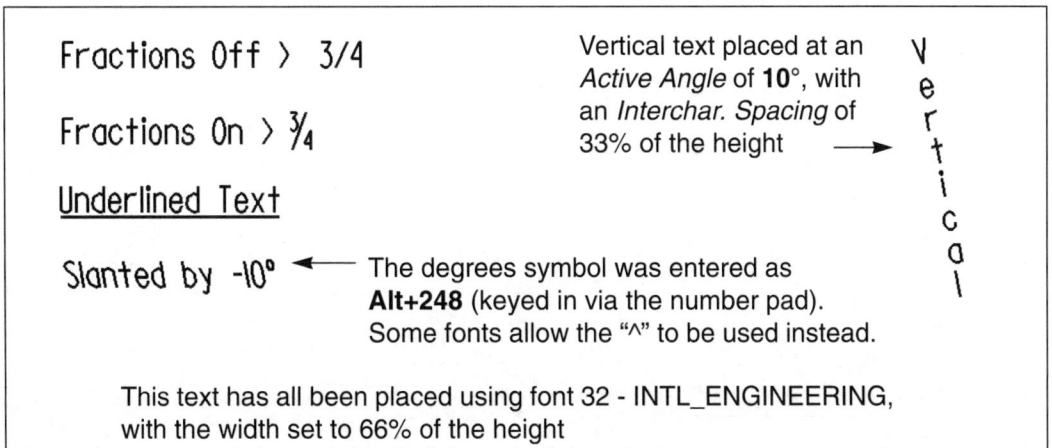

Fractions Off ⟩ 3/4

Fractions On ⟩ ¾

Underlined Text

Slanted by -10° ← The degrees symbol was entered as **Alt+248** (keyed in via the number pad). Some fonts allow the "^" to be used instead.

Vertical text placed at an *Active Angle* of **10°**, with an *Interchar. Spacing* of 33% of the height →

V e r t i c a l

This text has all been placed using font 32 - INTL_ENGINEERING, with the width set to 66% of the height

Figure 8.16   Examples of text placed with modifiers

Text Within Patterns

Text occupies a defined area in a design and thus it has an *Area Attribute* or *Area Property*. While there is not an *Area* setting in the text Tool Settings windows, text is in practice placed with the currently *Active Area Attribute*. In most situations we would not know the difference, *Solid* and *Hole* text looks the same. The difference shows up when we are working with patterns, including hatching and crosshatching.

◆ **Analyze an area of text**

1. Delete all the text placed so far *except* the **Stay Plate** label, also delete the two arcs that remain from the smaller circle.

2. Make level *25 Active*, turn *Off* all the rest.
   This will only leave the larger circle displayed.

3. Place the text "**Text Area**" *By Origin* (with the same size etc. settings as used in the earlier exercises) in the center of the circle.

4. Select the *Analyze Element* tool from the *Primary* tool bar, identify the text just placed.

5. Note the *Area* setting displayed. If it shows *Solid* change it to *Hole* and *Apply* the change to the element, confirming it in the Alert box.

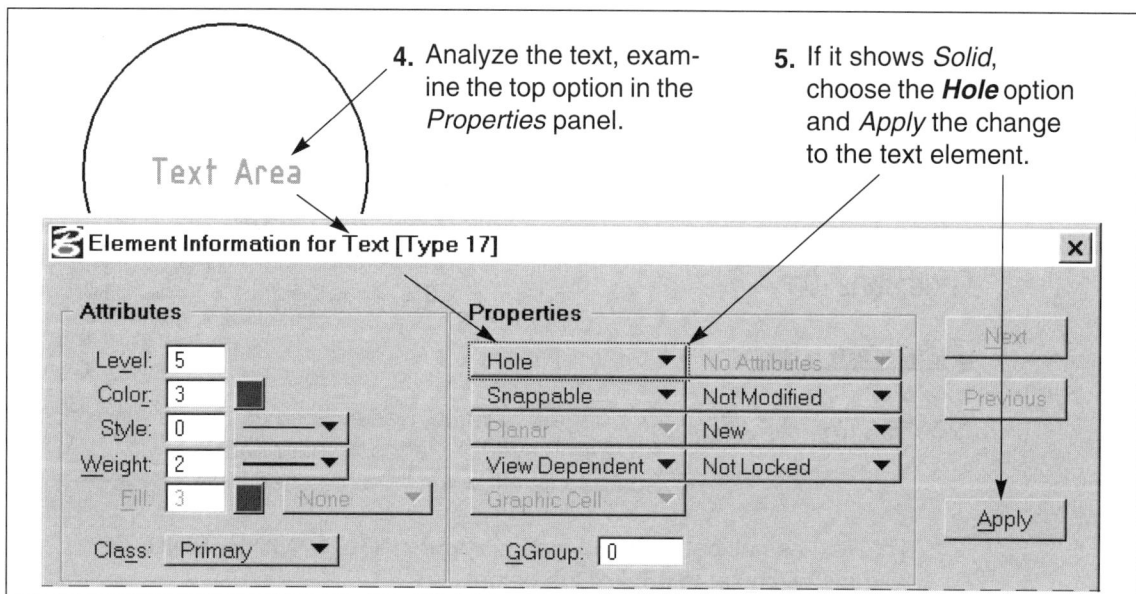

Figure 8.17   Checking and changing the Area Attribute of text

Now we have a circle with the *Solid* area attribute, surrounding some text with the *Hole* attribute. While text has an area attribute, it is not a true closed element and the *Group Holes* operation can not be used with it. This means that we can not use *Associative* patterns if we need to leave the text area clear. The *Text* and the *Closed Element* must also be on the same *Level*.

◆ Pattern the Circle around Text

1. Set the element *Color* to **0**, *Line Style* and *Weight* to **0**.

2. Select the *Crosshatch Area* tool (page 7-12), set the line *Spacings* both to **2**, the *Angles* to **+** and **- 45°**, *Associative* and *Snappable Off*, *Method:* **Element**.

3. Identify the circle, *Accept* it with a data point where the pattern lines will intersect (this data point may be positioned with a *Center* snap to the circle), *Reset*.

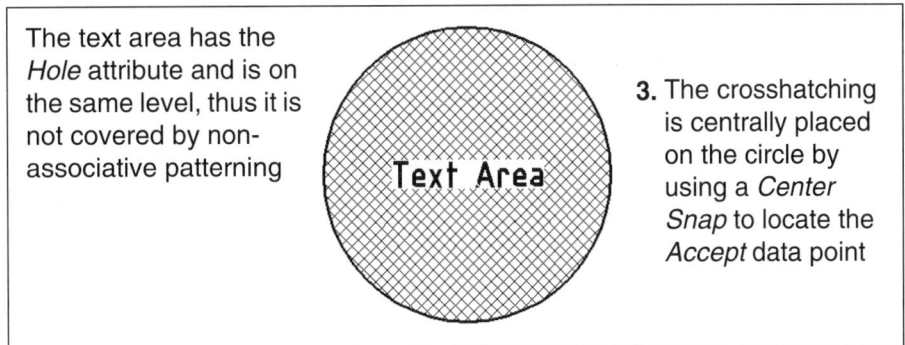

The text area has the *Hole* attribute and is on the same level, thus it is not covered by non-associative patterning

3. The crosshatching is centrally placed on the circle by using a *Center Snap* to locate the *Accept* data point

Text Area

Figure 8.18   Patterning around text

Placing Text as a Hole

We *Analyzed* the text element in the above exercise, making the change between *Solid* and *Hole* in the *Element Information* dialog box. An alternative method is to use the *Change Element to Active Area* tool from the *Change* tool box, see "Changing the Area Attribute" on page 7-10.

If the *Active Area* is already set to *Hole* when the text is placed, there will not be any need to make changes. We can select a tool that has an *Area* option menu and use its Tool Settings window to set the *Solid/Hole* attribute, then select *Place Text* for the rest of the operation. The *Change Element to Active Area* tool has an *Area* option, along with all the tools used for placing *Closed* elements, such as *Place Block* etc.

Multiple Line Text

All the text so far placed has not included a *Carriage Return*, thus it has been *Single Line* text. The inclusion of a carriage return (the **<Enter>** key) defines the text as *Multi-line*.

Text Nodes

All multi-line text is placed as a *Text Node*, which is a complex element consisting of more than one line of text. A text node symbol appears (when it is displayed) as cross hairs with a serial number superimposed, indicating the position of the text justification point. This number increments each time a *Text Node* is placed. The display of *Text Node* indicators is controlled from the *View Attributes* settings box.

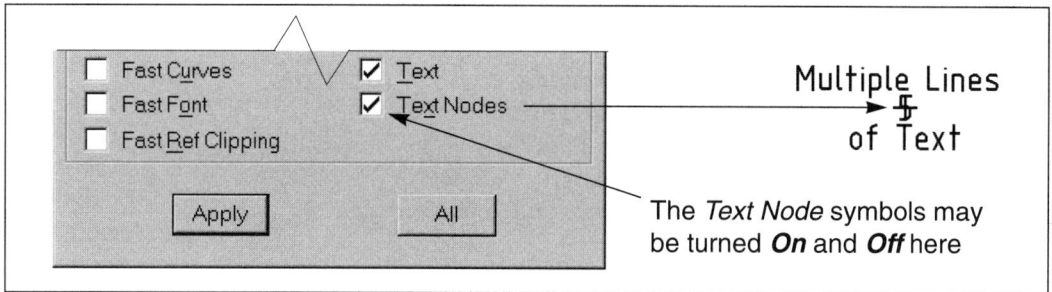

Figure 8.19   Text Node View Attribute

Text entered with a single carriage return (defining it as a *Text Node*) will automatically format into lines not exceeding the *Line Length* setting. These lines will be spaced by the *Line Spacing* and justified as specified for *Multi-line* text.

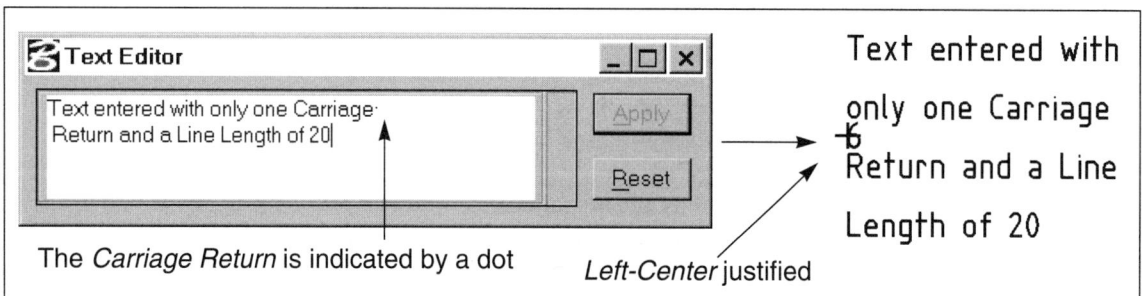

Figure 8.20   Effect of Line Length setting on a Text Node

Using Empty Text Nodes

Empty *Text Nodes* are place markers in the design where text is to be placed later on. The text node is placed with all the text settings and element attributes that are active at the time it is placed. When displayed, the empty node is the ordinary symbol and serial number, the same as is placed with multi-line text.

To place text on these nodes with the *Place Text* tool, we set the *Text Node Lock **On***. This is one of the lock settings that can be made in a number of places, including in the *Place Text* Tool Settings window. With this lock ***On***, text can not be placed other than on an empty text node. The text settings and element attributes active at the time of entering the text have no effect. The *Line Length* required is normally set at the time that we place the text node, so we key in the text without using the <**Enter**> key. Empty text nodes can also be filled by text imported from word processors etc., a concept to be covered shortly.

Tip!   The command to re-set the serial number of *Text Nodes* is **NN=[new number]**, entered via the key-in utility.

The Place Text Node Tool

This tool is found at the end of the second section of the *Text* tool box. It has only two settings, a check box for *View Independent* placement (see "View Independent Text" on page 8-11) and the usual *Active Angle* field.

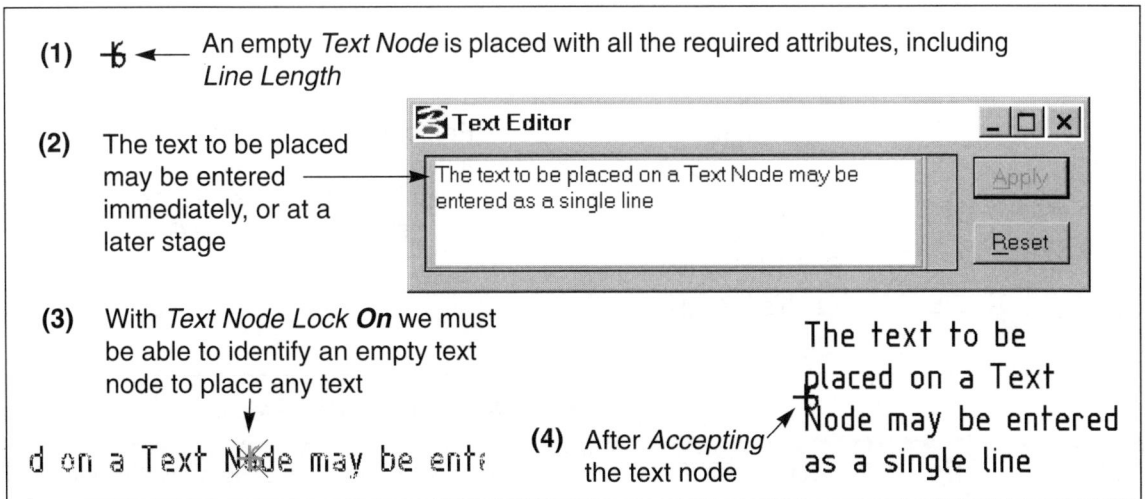

Figure 8.21   *Placing text on an Empty Text Node*

Justification of Multi-line Text

The justification settings for text nodes differ slightly from the single line text equivalents. The vertical justification settings now relate to the entire text element, as illustrated in Figure 8.20. That text is *Left-Center* justified, with the text node symbol indicating the location of the justification point. There are extra horizontal justification settings available for text nodes, *Left Margin* and *Right Margin*. Examples of margin horizontal justification are shown in Figure 8.22.

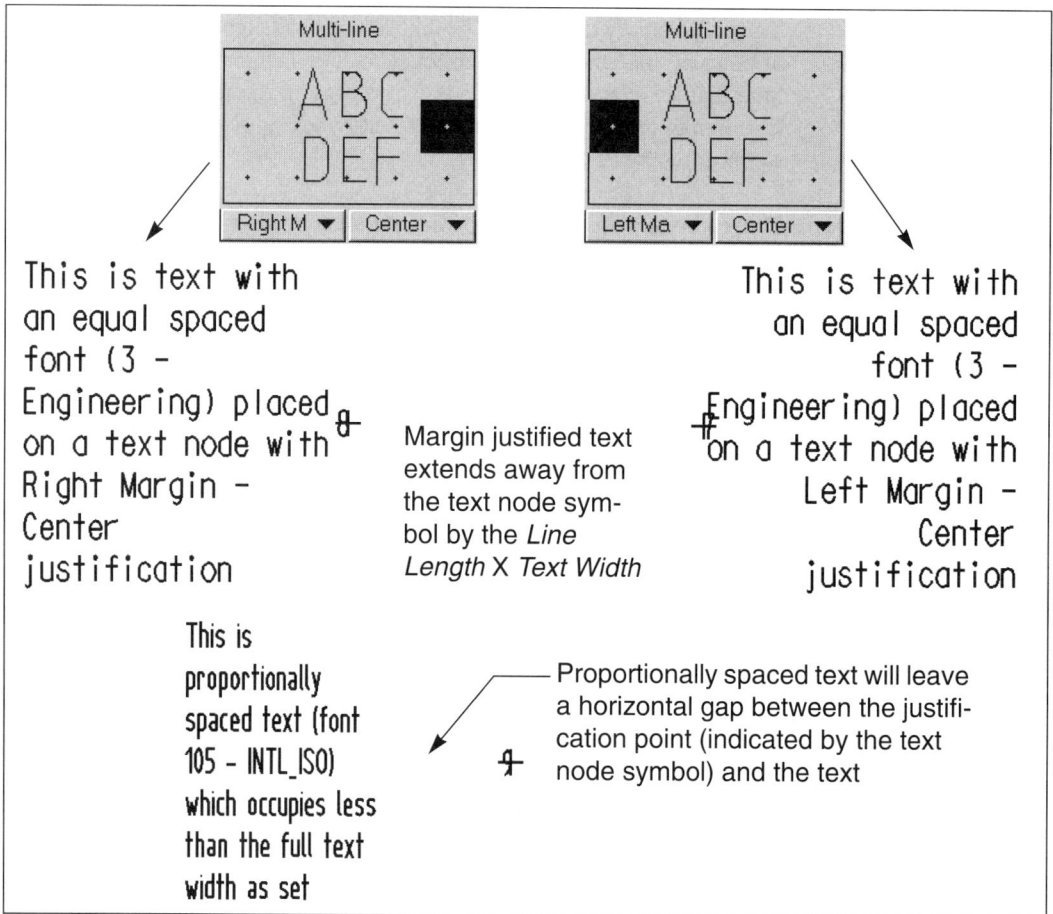

This is text with an equal spaced font (3 – Engineering) placed on a text node with Right Margin – Center justification

Margin justified text extends away from the text node symbol by the *Line Length* X *Text Width*

This is text with an equal spaced font (3 – Engineering) placed on a text node with Left Margin – Center justification

This is proportionally spaced text (font 105 – INTL_ISO) which occupies less than the full text width as set

Proportionally spaced text will leave a horizontal gap between the justification point (indicated by the text node symbol) and the text

Figure 8.22   Margin justification of text nodes

Tip!   Take care when placing multi-line text with right or left margin justification - if the line length is left at the default value (255) the text will appear a long way away from the node symbol!

Importing Text Files

It may be necessary to incorporate text into a design that has been generated elsewhere using another application, such as a text editor, a word processor, a spreadsheet etc. This will normally be a "Text only", "MSDOS Text" or ASCII file. If the text is saved without line breaks, MicroStation will do all of the formatting when we attach it to an empty *Text Node*.

If we need to retain the line breaks from the word processor text, save it *with* line breaks. If we are placing it on an empty text node, place the node with a very long line length (say 255), or there may be line breaks included from both the text node and the original text. Do not use Margin horizontal justification. With *Text Node Lock Off*, the imported text will take on the currently *Active* text attributes at the time we place it.

◆ Place Imported Text on an empty Text Node

1. Using the *Text* settings box, choose a *Font*, *Line Height: 6*, *Line Width: 6*, *Line Spacing: 4*, *Line Length: 30*, *Multi-line justification: Left-Top*.

2. Use the Status bar *Locks* menu to make sure that *Text Node Lock* is *On*, window an area in "second.dgn" with enough space for some lines of text with the above settings.

3. Select the *Place Text Node* tool, place the node at the top left of the View window.

4. Create and save a few lines of text in a word processing application, or find some existing text on your system.

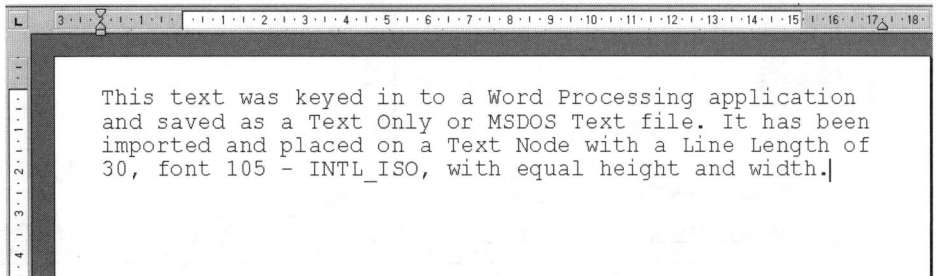

The settings in the external application of font, margins, text size etc. have no effect on files saved as *Text Only*

```
This text was keyed in to a Word Processing application
and saved as a Text Only or MSDOS Text file. It has been
imported and placed on a Text Node with a Line Length of
30, font 105 - INTL_ISO, with equal height and width.
```

Figure 8.23   Preparing text in another application for import into MicroStation

5. Choose *File>Import>Text* (the *Include Text File* dialog box opens), select the required directory and text file in the usual way.

6. Identify the text node placed in step **3.** with a data point, *Accept*, *Reset*.

7. Turn *Text Nodes **Off*** in the *View Attributes* settings box.

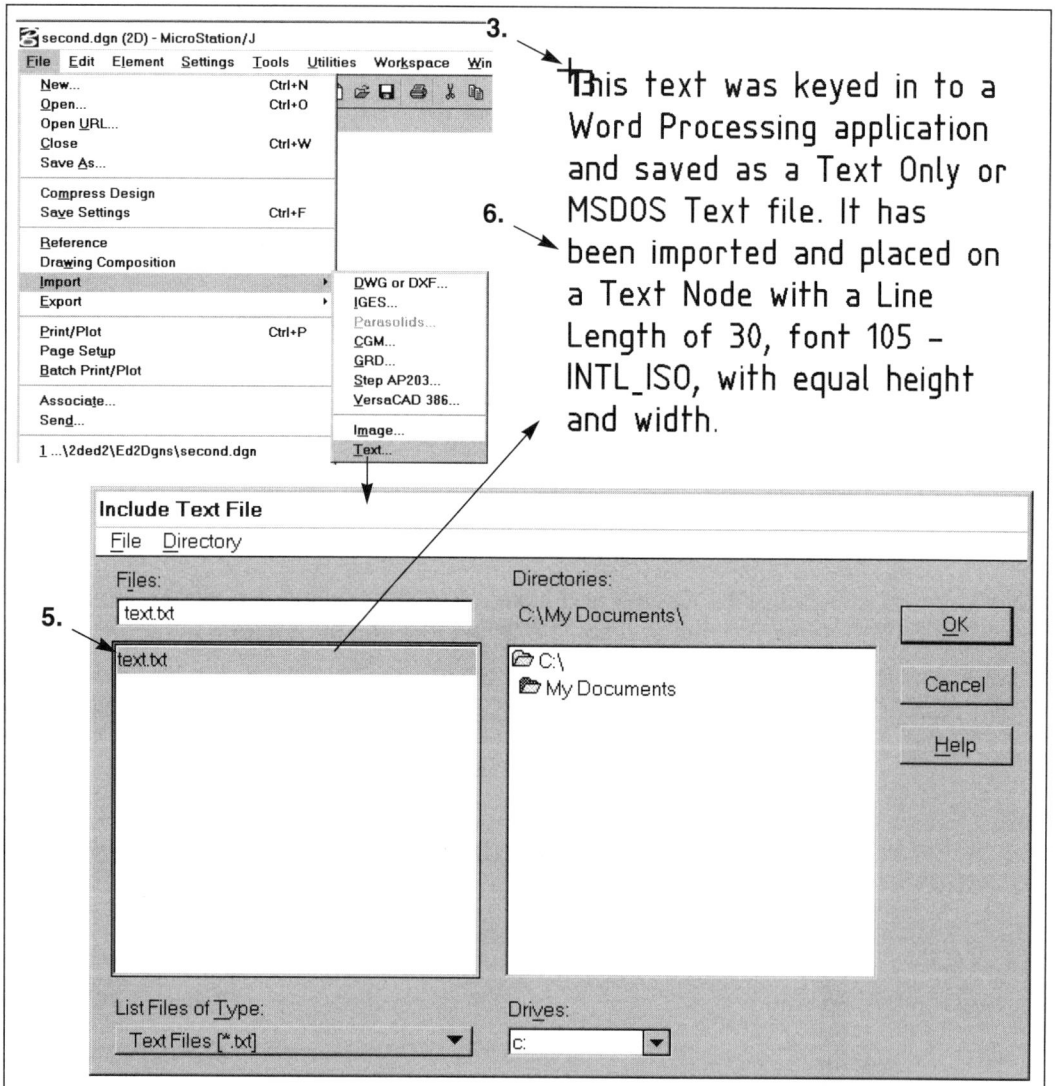

Figure 8.24 Placing imported text on a Text Node

The Place Note Tool

This tool has much in common with the dimensioning tools to be introduced in the next chapter. It places both *Text* and an arrowline. The geometry of the leader line is set as a *Dimension* and active text settings may be overridden by settings in the *Element>Dimension>Text*. For now, we will assume that all the dimension settings are in their default state. The other possibilities will be introduced in detail next chapter. If *Association Lock* is **On** and an element is *Snapped* to when positioning the arrowhead, the arrowline will move with the element when it is manipulated.

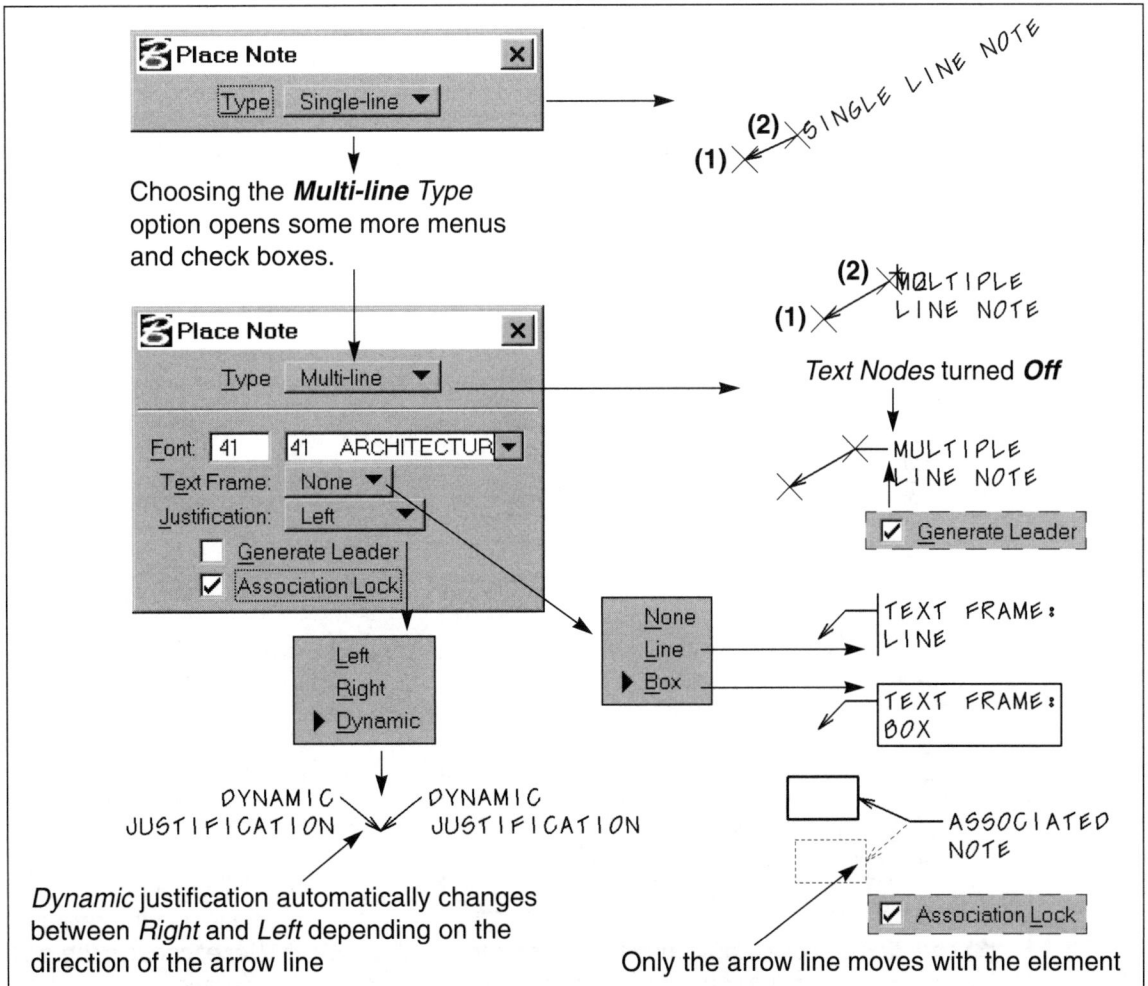

Figure 8.25   Options for Placing Notes

Editing Existing Text

Once the text has been placed, it can be manipulated (*Move*, *Copy* etc.) like other elements. We can also use the common editing techniques to change its content, re-format it, replace words, copy or delete it. The Application *window* Edit menu has the usual editing functions such as *Copy*, *Cut and Paste* and the same *Text Editor* used to input the text may be used to change it.

The Edit Text Tool

This tool (from the *Text* tool box) is used to change text placed with any of the text placement tools, imported text and dimension text. It displays the text in the same *Text Editor* window used when keying in text for placement. It can then be highlighted and edited using the common editing keys (**<Delete>**, **<Backspace>**, **<Ctrl+X>**, **<Ctrl+V>**etc.). The *Carriage Return* dots can be deleted and replaced (with the **<Enter>** key) as needed to reformat the text.

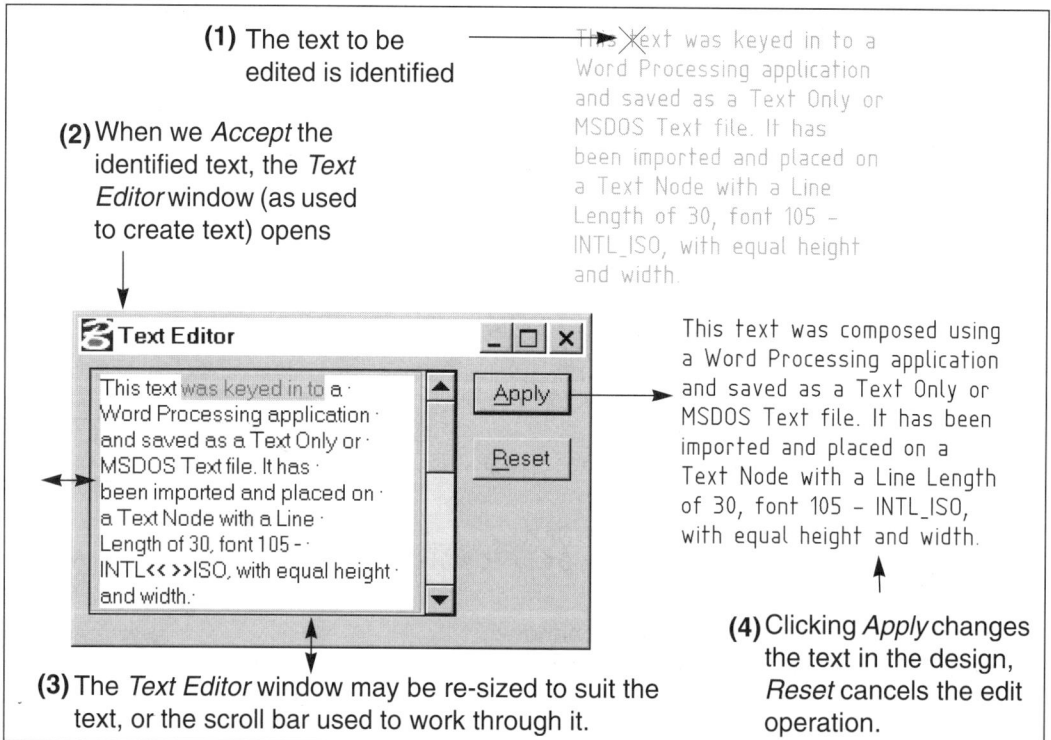

(1) The text to be edited is identified

This text was keyed in to a Word Processing application and saved as a Text Only or MSDOS Text file. It has been imported and placed on a Text Node with a Line Length of 30, font 105 – INTL_ISO, with equal height and width.

(2) When we *Accept* the identified text, the *Text Editor* window (as used to create text) opens

Text Editor _ □ ×

This text was keyed in to a ·
Word Processing application ·
and saved as a Text Only or ·
MSDOS Text file. It has ·
been imported and placed on ·
a Text Node with a Line ·
Length of 30, font 105 - ·
INTL<< >>ISO, with equal height ·
and width.·

Apply

Reset

This text was composed using a Word Processing application and saved as a Text Only or MSDOS Text file. It has been imported and placed on a Text Node with a Line Length of 30, font 105 – INTL_ISO, with equal height and width.

(4) Clicking *Apply* changes the text in the design, *Reset* cancels the edit operation.

(3) The *Text Editor* window may be re-sized to suit the text, or the scroll bar used to work through it.

Figure 8.26   Using the Text Editor

The Application Window Menu Edit Options

Text elements may be selected with the *Element Selection* tool for *Copying* and *Cutting* like any other type of element. These *Edit* menu functions use the computer industry standards for operation, including shortcut keys such as **<Ctrl+C>** for *Copy*. The *Paste* function (**<Ctrl+V>**) has a *Scale* setting not usually found in other applications.

The *Find/Replace Text* option from the *Edit* menu has much in common with word processing applications, but with some added settings applying to MicroStation. The *Fence* may be used to limit the search range, text in *Cells* may be included or excluded. Its settings box is illustrated in Figure 8.27.

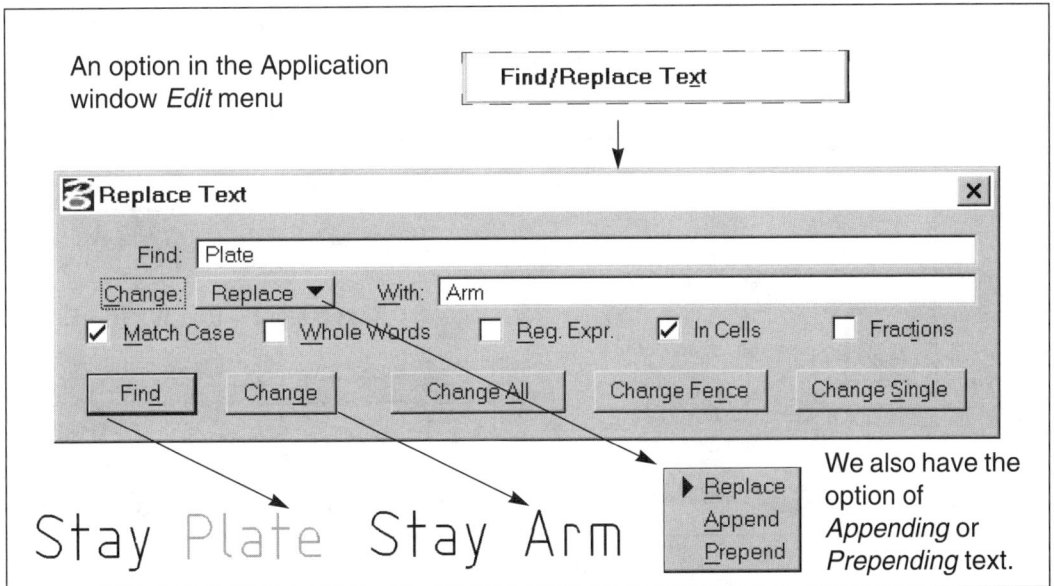

Figure 8.27 Find and Replace Text

Using An External Editing Application

In Windows® or similar operating systems, we can use a more specialized application to edit the text. Text *Selected* with the *Element Selection* tool may be *Cut* or *Copied* to the *Clipboard*. After swapping applications to the other editor, we *Paste* and edit the text as required. It can then be saved as text only and re-imported to a new empty text node (see "Importing Text Files" on page 8-23), or the text can be *Cut and Pasted* back via the clipboard with the currently active text attributes.

Ascertaining and Matching Text Attributes

When we are working on an existing design, it is often necessary to *Match* the text we place to some *Existing* text, i.e. the new text will have the attributes of the existing text. We may also need to establish the *Attributes* of the existing text for general information, or for checking on adherence to standards.

The Display Text Attributes Tool

This tool gives us an instant readout of the *Text* attributes (not the *Symbology* attributes, e.g. line weight) of an identified text element. With the *Display Text Attributes* tool, the basic information on *Font*, *Level*, *Height* and *Width* are presented in the Prompt field of the Status bar for single line text. When multi-line text or an empty text node is identified, the *Node Number*, *Line Length*, *Line Spacing* is displayed, but not the height and width.

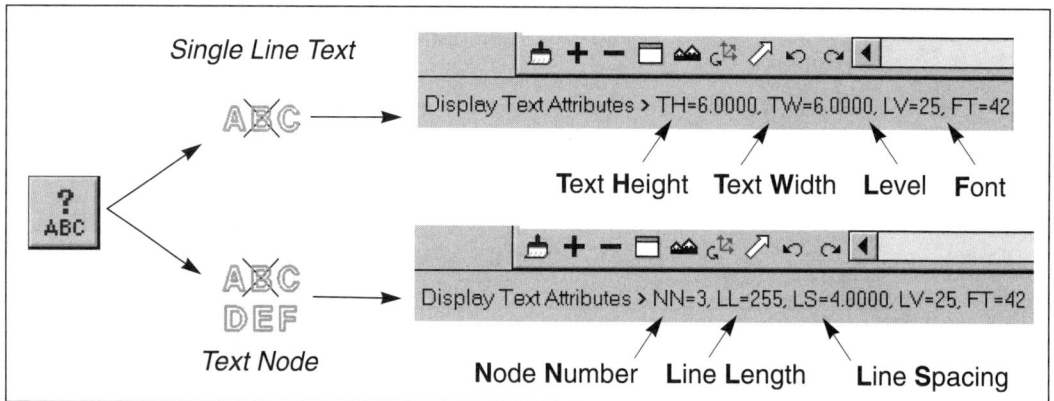

Figure 8.28   Displaying the Attributes of both types of text

The Match All Element Settings Tool

Also called *SmartMatch*, this is the general purpose tool used for setting the *Active Attributes* of all types from an existing element. Its location is shown in Figure 8.30. When a text element is identified when using this tool, both the *Text Attributes* and the *Element Attributes* of the text become the currently *Active* settings.

Identifying a single line text element will set single line justification, without affecting multi-line text settings. When we identify a text node, (including an *empty* one) all the settings for this type of text are matched.

This tool sets the *All* the *Active Attributes* to those contained in an existing element, including both *Element* and *Text* attributes when a text element is identified.

Match All Element Settings

Match Multi-line Caps

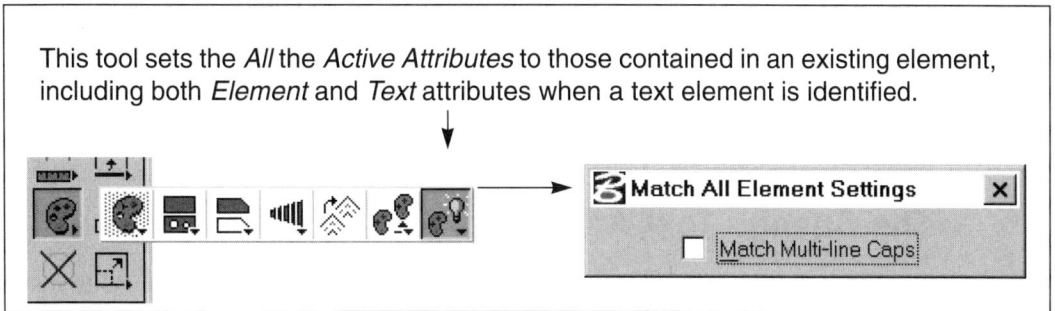

Figure 8.29   Matching all of the Active Attributes to an existing element

The Match Text Tool

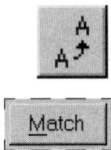

This tool is accessible via the *Text* tool box and as the *Match* button in the *Element>Text* settings box. It only matches the *Text* attributes and the *Element* attributes, including the *Level*, are not affected. It would generally only be used when we need to match selected attributes to the identified text, when it may be used in conjunction with the *Match Element Attributes* tool, as illustrated in Figure 8.30.

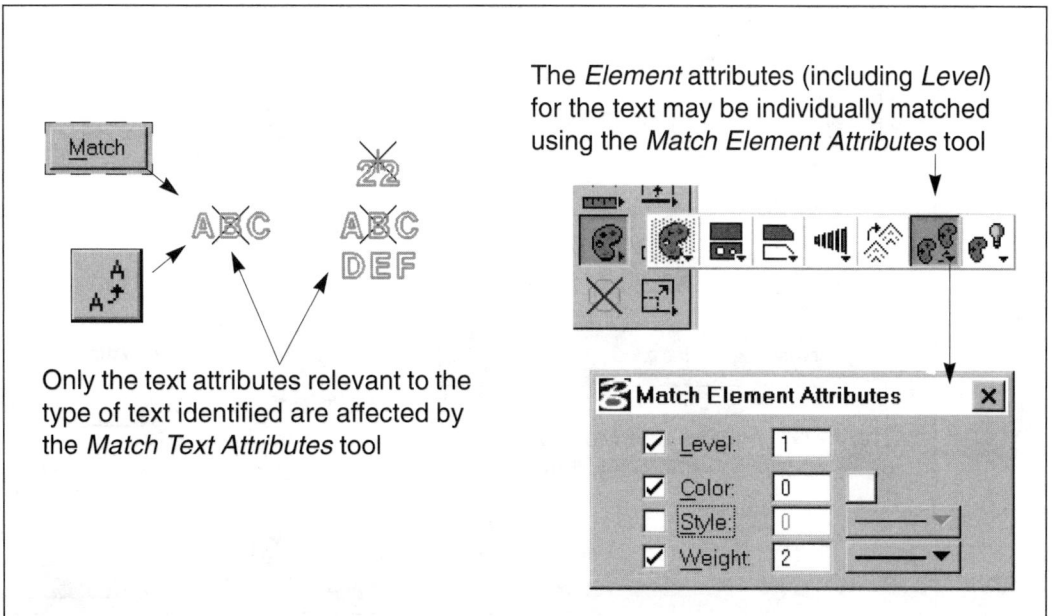

The *Element* attributes (including *Level*) for the text may be individually matched using the *Match Element Attributes* tool

Match

ABC   ABC
       DEF

Only the text attributes relevant to the type of text identified are affected by the *Match Text Attributes* tool

Match Element Attributes

✔ Level: 1
✔ Color: 0
☐ Style: 0
✔ Weight: 2

Figure 8.30   Setting Active Attributes from existing text

Changing the Appearance of Existing Text

Text has two sets of *Attributes*, *Text Attributes* (e.g. *Font*, *Height & Width*) and *Element Attributes* (e.g. *Level* and *Line Weight*). The former may be changed with the *Change Text Attributes* tool, the latter with the *Change Element Attributes* tool.

The Change Text Attributes Tool

We use this tool to update existing text to any or all of the currently active attributes. Like the *Match Text* tool, it causes only the *Text Attributes* to update. Like the *Change Element Attributes* tool, the attributes checked *On* in the Tool Settings window may be overwritten before applying the changes to an element.

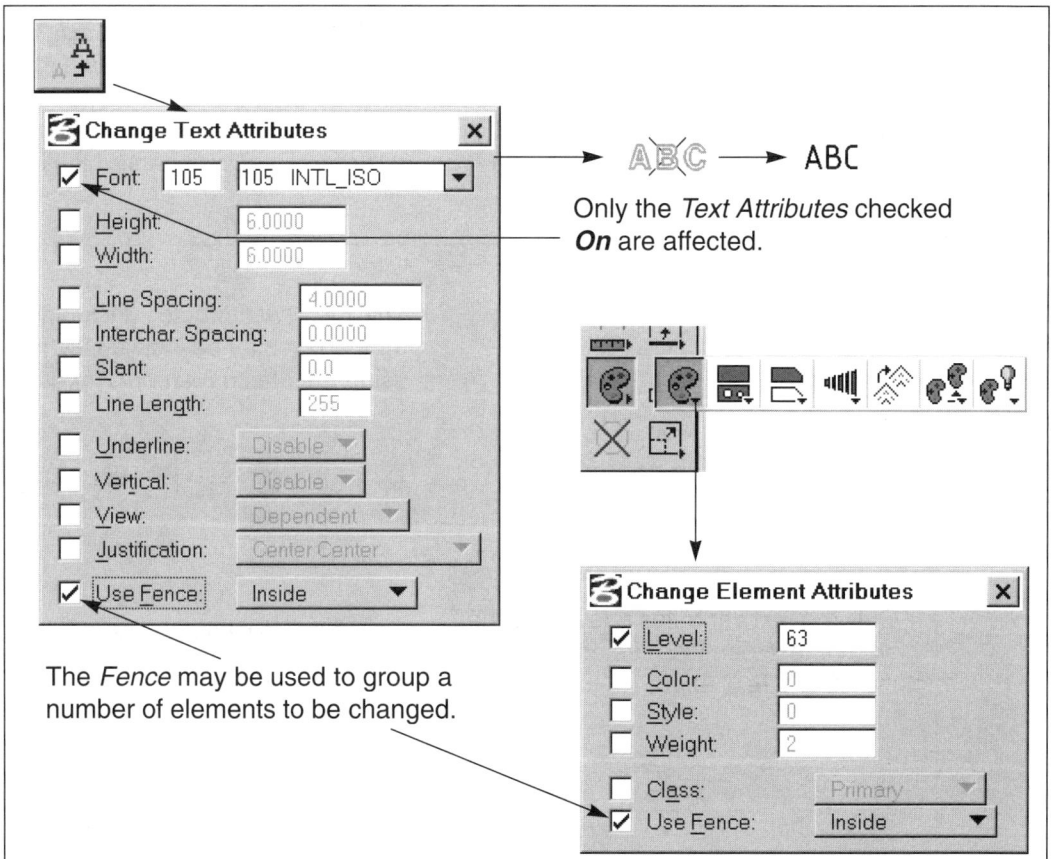

Figure 8.31   Changing Text Elements to the Active Attribute settings

Copying and Incrementing Text

Single line text elements containing numbers may be copied and the numeric part of the copy incremented by a specified value. Any number of copies may be placed, with each one incremented from the last. If there are more than one group of numbers in the text, only the number furthest to the right will be incremented.

The Copy and Increment Text Tool

The only setting for this tool is the *Tag Increment*, the number that the copied text will be incremented by. This must be an integer between 1 and 32767, generally positive, but a "negative increment" can be used while the numbers are zero or greater (see Figure 8.32).

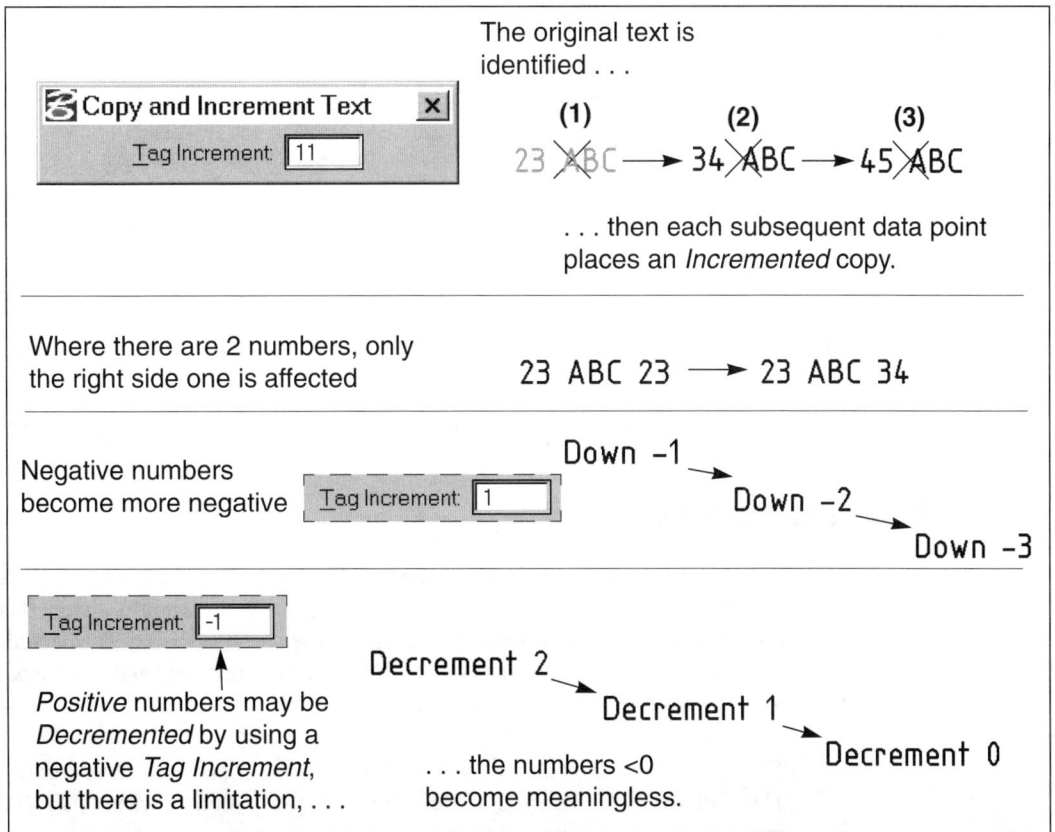

Figure 8.32   Copying text with automatic incrementation

Using a Glossary for Fast Text Entry

MicroStation has the facility to use *Glossary Files* to make the process of entering commonly used words and phrases more efficient. A *Glossary File* may be created with any editor capable of creating a plain text file. This file will contain a set of the commonly used words and phrases, each associated with an abbreviation called an *Alias*. Each Phrase/Alias pair is called a *Glossary Entry*. A sample *Glossary File* called "example.gls" is included with MicroStation in the ...*Workspace\system\data* folder. The first part of the file has an explanation of the structure to use when creating your own file. This is shown in Figure 8.33.

```
#---------------------------------------------------------------------
#
#   Example Glossary Data File.
#
#   $Workfile:    example.gls   $
#   $Revision:    1.1   $ $Date:    13 Feb 1995 15:16:06   $
#
#   This file has the following format:
#   1) The first line is the abbreviation displayed in list
#   2) The second line is the expansion to be placed in design file
#   3) A '#' character in column 1 starts a comment
#
#---------------------------------------------------------------------
ab
anchor bolt
abs
absolute
abv
```

Figure 8.33   The sample "plain text" Glossary File delivered with MicroStation

The Text Glossary Utility

We can retrieve phrases from a Glossary File and place them as text elements using this utility, found under *Utilities* from the Application window menu. The example file illustrated above is opened by default when *Text Glossary* is selected. Selecting *Utilities>Text Glossary* opens the *Glossary* settings box and an associated Tool Settings window, as shown in Figure 8.34.

The *Glossary* list box allows us to select the word or phrase by highlighting its *Alias*. The full text is displayed underneath the list panel. Clicking the *Build* button transfers the text to the field at the bottom of the box and moving the pointer out on to the view will allow us to place this text without any further tool selection.

We can immediately place a single entry, or edit the text within this field and add as many other entries as we require, by continuing to highlight entries and clicking the *Build* button. The case (*Upper* or *Lower*) may be changed as it is placed under the settings box *Options* menu. The *File* menu is for the selection of another *Glossary File*, such as one we have created with words and phrases for our own particular usage.

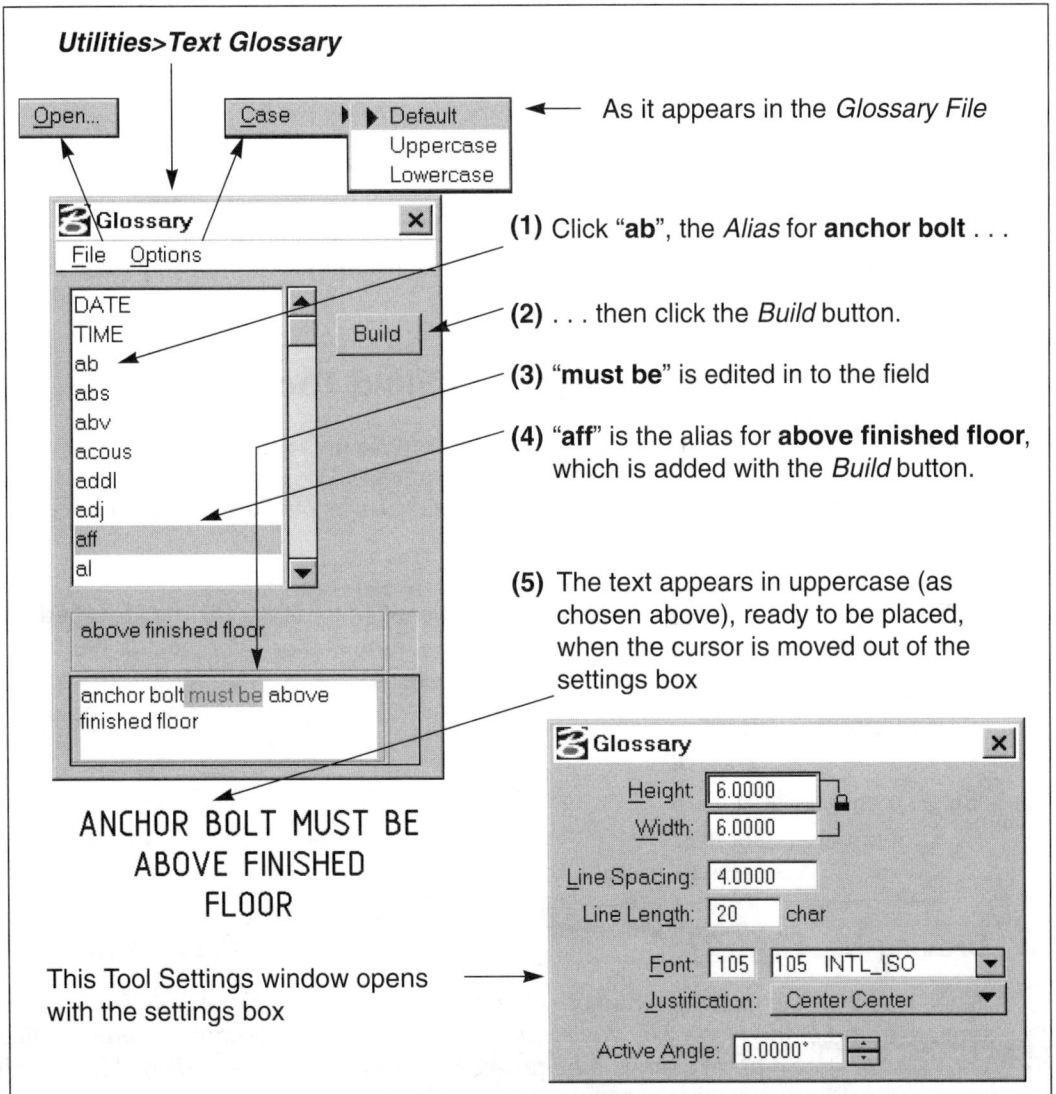

Figure 8.34 Using the Text Glossary

Enter Data Fields

These are single line text placeholders placed in a design, for a character or characters to be entered in the future. One typical example for the use of *Enter Data Fields* is in the title blocks of drawing sheets. In this case, such detail as the variable part of the drawing number could be an *Enter Data Fields*. The drawing sheet design file could then be copied for use with every drawing and the details filled in. The main advantages of *Enter Data Fields* over ordinary text placement is that the position, the text attributes and the maximum permissible number of characters are defined when the fields are originally placed. Excess characters are truncated.

To create an *Enter Data Field* we place a reserved character using the ordinary *Place Text* tool. This character is the underline ("_") in the default MicroStation configuration, but it may be re-configured if necessary. These fields can be combined with other text in the same text element, as is illustrated in Figure 8.35. *Enter Data Fields* may be filled in singly, automatically, or by copying using the related tools from the *Text* tool box.

The Fill In Single Enter Data Field Tool

This is used to fill in or change *Enter Data Fields*. When we select this tool the *Text Editor* window opens and we are prompted to identify the enter data field component of the text element. The text is entered, then placed with a carriage return (<**Enter**>).

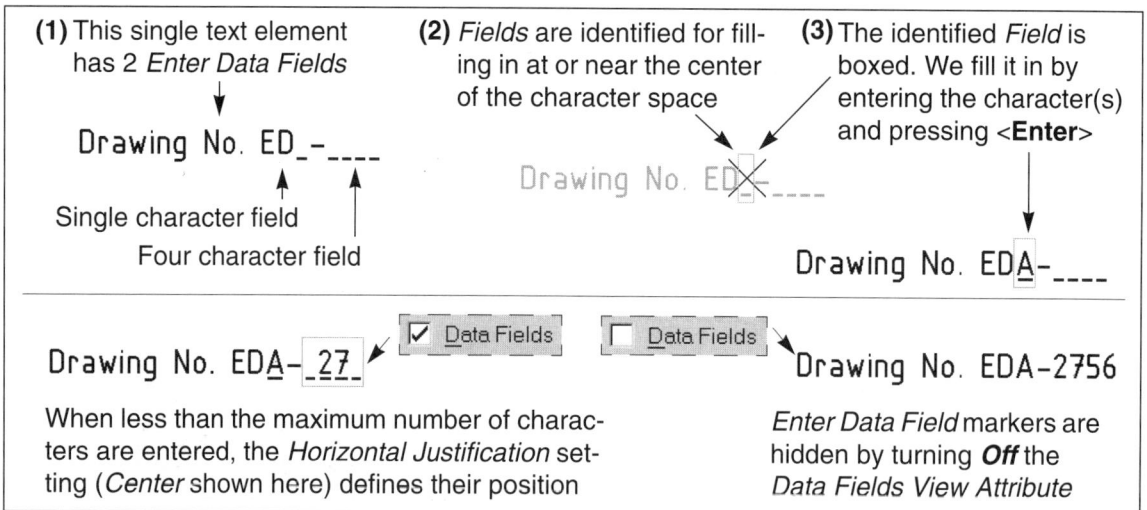

---

(1) This single text element has 2 *Enter Data Fields*

Drawing No. ED_-____

Single character field
Four character field

(2) *Fields* are identified for filling in at or near the center of the character space

Drawing No. ED_-____

(3) The identified *Field* is boxed. We fill it in by entering the character(s) and pressing <**Enter**>

Drawing No. EDA-____

Drawing No. EDA-_27_

☑ Data Fields

When less than the maximum number of characters are entered, the *Horizontal Justification* setting (*Center* shown here) defines their position

☐ Data Fields

Drawing No. EDA-2756

Enter Data Field markers are hidden by turning **Off** the *Data Fields View Attribute*

Figure 8.35   Enter Data Fields

The Automatic Fill In Enter Data Fields Tool

The operation of this tool is comparable to the *Fill In Single Enter Data Field* (page 8-34). The main difference is that *Blank* Enter Data fields displayed in a *Selected View Window* are automatically identified in the order they were placed. The first field within the area of the selected view is identified when a data point is placed anywhere in the view. Text entered in the Text Editor window is placed in this field when the **<Enter>** key is pressed and the next field within the view window is automatically identified.

Each time a carriage return is entered (i.e. each time **<Enter>** is pressed) to fill in a field, another field is identified in the placement order. This process will continue until all of the *Blank* fields *Within The View Window* are filled in, when the prompt *"Element Not Found"* is displayed in the status bar. The numbers in the parenthesized *Enter Data* fields of Figure 8.36 are the order they were filled in.

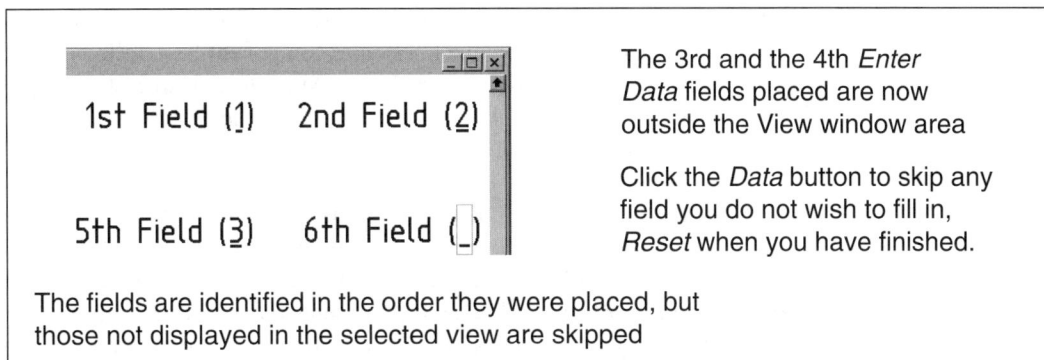

1st Field (1)   2nd Field (2)

5th Field (3)   6th Field (_)

The fields are identified in the order they were placed, but those not displayed in the selected view are skipped

The 3rd and the 4th *Enter Data* fields placed are now outside the View window area

Click the *Data* button to skip any field you do not wish to fill in, *Reset* when you have finished.

Figure 8.36 Automatic identification of Enter Data Fields

The Copy Enter Data Field Tool

This tool is used to copy the data contained in one Enter Data field into other Enter Data field(s). It copies the data only from the identified field, not the entire text element.

The Copy and Increment Enter Data Field Tool

Similar in operation to *Copy Enter Data Field*, but a number included in the field is incremented by the *Tag Increment* setting. The incrementation works in a similar way to the *Copy and Increment Text Tool* (see "The Copy and Increment Text Tool" on page 8-31), but this tool will only copy from and to existing Enter Data fields.

Summary

The *Attributes* specific to all text are the *Font*, the *Text Height*, the *Text Width* and the *Justification*. Text more than one line long is placed as a *Text Node*, which has *Line Spacing* and *Line Length* attributes. All of these attributes may be set in the *Element>Text* settings box, or some may be set in the Tool Settings window of the tools used for text placement.

The *Font* attribute has the largest range of options, with many fonts supplied, together with the option of installing more. Font selection may be by *Viewing* samples, *Choosing* one by name from an option menu, or by keying in its number. *Text Height* and *Width* may be locked together to allow simultaneous setting of both to the same value. This is the arrangement generally in use, but some of the older style fonts may be improved by setting the width to about 70% of the height.

The *Justification* is set separately for single line and multi-line text. It may be set graphically or with an option menu appearing in text placement tool setting windows. The options show the horizontal component first, followed by the vertical component, e.g. *Right-Center*. Text Node (Multi-line) justification settings have an additional *Left* and *Right Margin* setting, where the text is spaced away from the locating data point by the *Line Length* setting.

The general purpose tool to use with text is *Place Text*. The text is entered in a *Text Editor* window and placed with a data point (or points) *By Origin*, *Fitted*, *View Independent*, *Fitted View Independent*, *Above Element*, *Below Element*, *On Element*, or *Along Element*. The other text placement tool is *Place Note*, where the text is accompanied by an arrowline to draw attention to a design feature. There is tool to place *Empty Text Nodes*, which are placeholders for multi-line text placed later with the *Text Node* lock **On**. There are special tools to *Copy* text, with or without incrementation of a number in the text element.

Placeholders for single line text for later filling in are called *Enter Data Fields*. These can be filled in individually, automatically selected as a series, or their contents *Copied* with or without incrementing a numeric component.

The *Text Glossary* is a utility designed to make the entry of frequently used text more efficient. To use this utility we select a word or phrase from a list by its *Alias*, an abbreviation of the full entry. *Glossary Files* can be created with any plain text editor by defining the aliases and the phrases on subsequent lines. These files may be selected and accessed as an option under *Utilities>Text Glossary*.

9 : Dimensioning a Design

Dimensions are labels combining geometry and text into one *Dimension Element*, automatically generated by MicroStation. We can create linear, angular and radial dimensions for any element or combinations of elements. There are many types of dimensioning, with a large number of individual tools to enable us to create each type. A dimension label may optionally be *Associated* with the element or points being dimensioned. Dimensions automatically update to remain accurate after elements have been manipulated if this *Association* is established.

Dimensioning styles vary from country to country, with the particular discipline we work in, even with our personal preferences. Every component of the *Dimension Element* can be customized to suit the local needs.

When you have completed this chapter, you will be able to:

- Recognize the components of a *Dimension Element*;
- Use the *Linear* dimensioning tools to dimension elements and between points;
- Use the *Radial* dimensioning tools to place dimensions on arcs and circles;
- Configure the style of the various dimension element types to comply with any dimensioning standard.

The Dimension Element

A *Dimension Element* is made up from a set of components, which may include:

- *Extension Lines* - lines extended from the dimensioned points;
- *Dimension Line* - a line the same length as the dimension, usually parallel to it;
- *Dimension Line Terminators* - symbols such as arrowheads helping to define the ends of the dimension line;
- *Dimension Text* - the dimension in the chosen units of the design file;
- *Prefix or Suffix* - may be used to indicate that the dimension is of a diameter, radius etc.

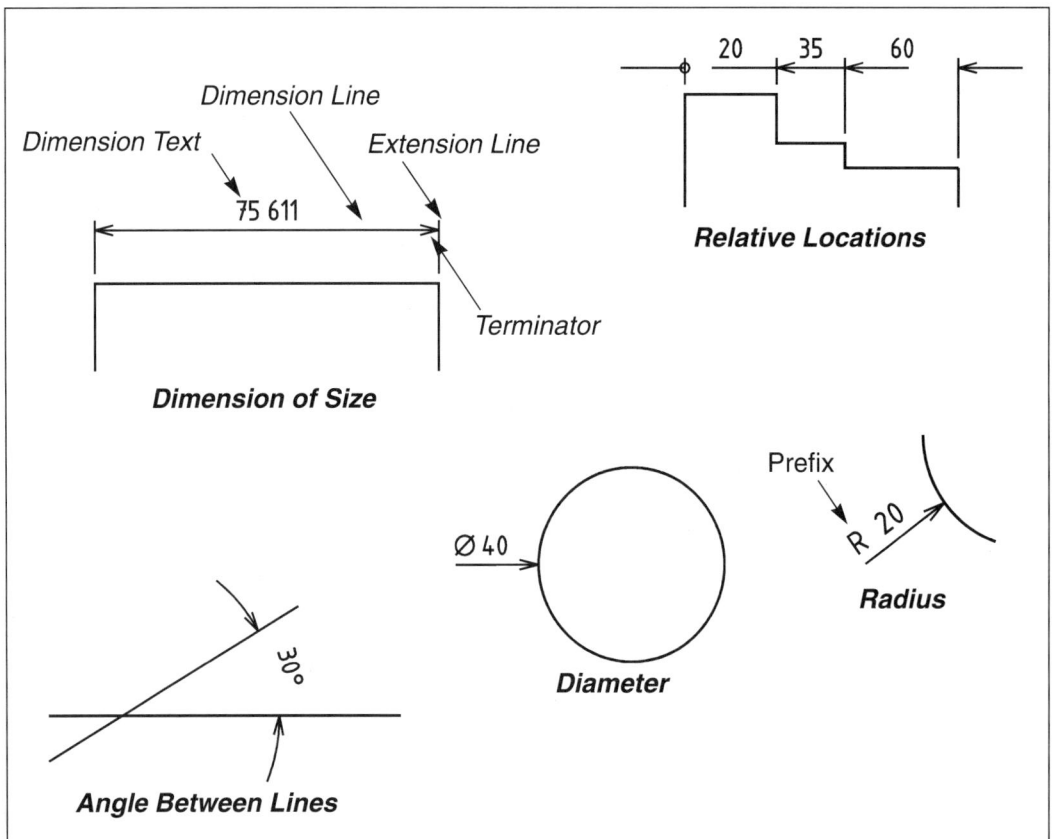

Figure 9.1 Some samples of dimensioning

The Dimension Tool Box - Basic Linear Tools

The whole *Dimension* Tool Box has 16 tool buttons, but we will introduce only the eight mainly involved with *Linear* dimensioning at this stage.

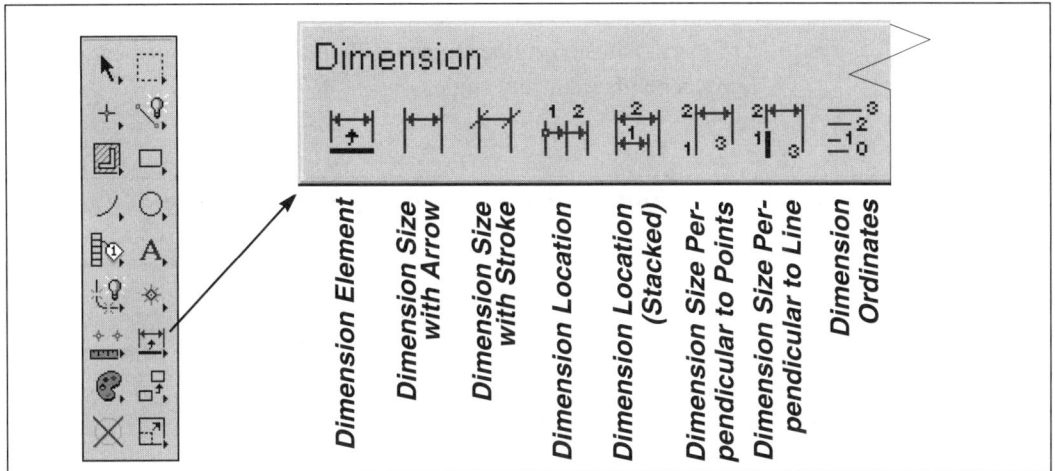

Figure 9.2   The Dimension Tool Box, Element and Linear Dimensioning tools

The Dimension Element Tool

This is the most automated of the dimensioning tools. It may be used to place different types of dimensions, depending on our requirements and the type of element identified. It will place a variety of types of both *Linear* (distance in a straight line) and *Radial* (radius and diameter) dimensions.

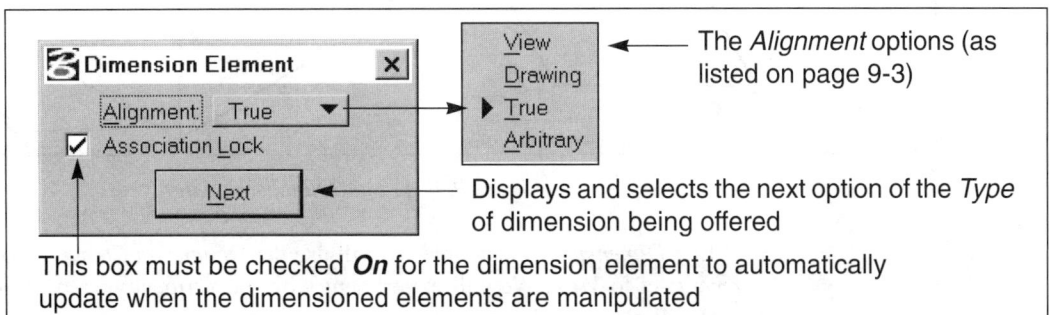

Figure 9.3   Dimension Element tool settings

Alignment of Linear Dimensions

Linear dimensions can be placed with a choice of the following *Alignments*:

- *View* - aligned with the *x* or *y* axis of the View window;
- *Drawing* - aligned with the *x* or *y* axis of the Design Plane (see page 2-14);
- *True* - aligned to be parallel with the dimension being labelled;
- *Arbitrary* - dimension line aligned with the element or segment, but the extension line can be placed at any angle.

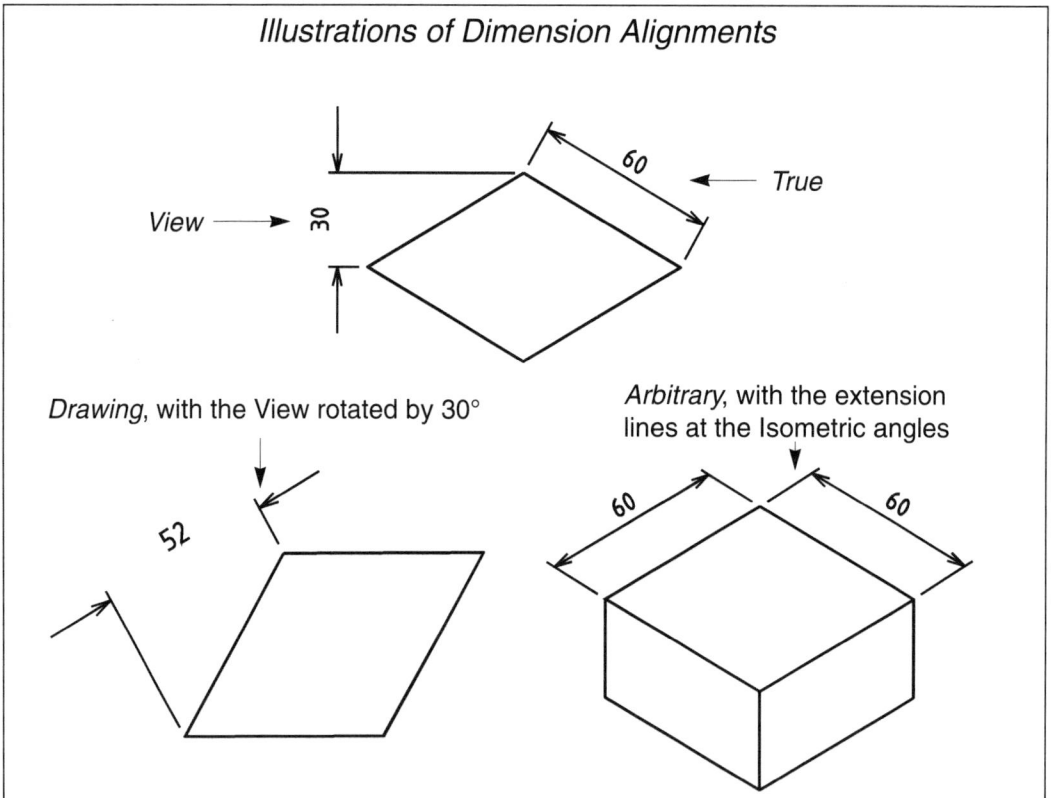

Figure 9.4   Linear Dimension Alignments

In our first *Dimensioning* example we will use the *Dimension Element* tool, with the *Alignment* set to **View**. We will experiment with the various types of dimensioning this tool will place to label a circle.

◆ **Dimension a Circle**

1. With "second.dgn" open, make *Level **25** Active*, turn all the other levels *Off*, *Window Area* about the circle.

2. Select a font and set the *Text Height* and *Width* to ***6*** (as before) in the *Text* settings box (*Element>Text*).

3. Select the *Dimension Element* tool (page 9-3), set the *Alignment* to *View*, the *Association Lock* either way.

4. Identify the circle, then move the pointer above or below it. Press the <**Enter**> key until the diameter of the circle is offered as a *Linear Dimension* aligned with the *x* axis of the *View*.

    We could *Accept* this dimension in this position with a data point, but leave it floating for now.

5. Move the pointer to a side of the circle.

    The diameter is now offered with *View y* axis alignment.

6. Press the <**Enter**> key (this has the same effect as pressing the **Next** button in the Tool settings window when this window has *Input Focus*, but without moving the pointer).

    Now the *Radius* is offered as a *Radial Dimension*. All Radial dimensions can be moved all around the circle, inside and out.

7. Press the <**Enter**> key again.

    This time we will be offered the *Radius* again, but in the *Extended* form with an extension line from the center to the circumference.

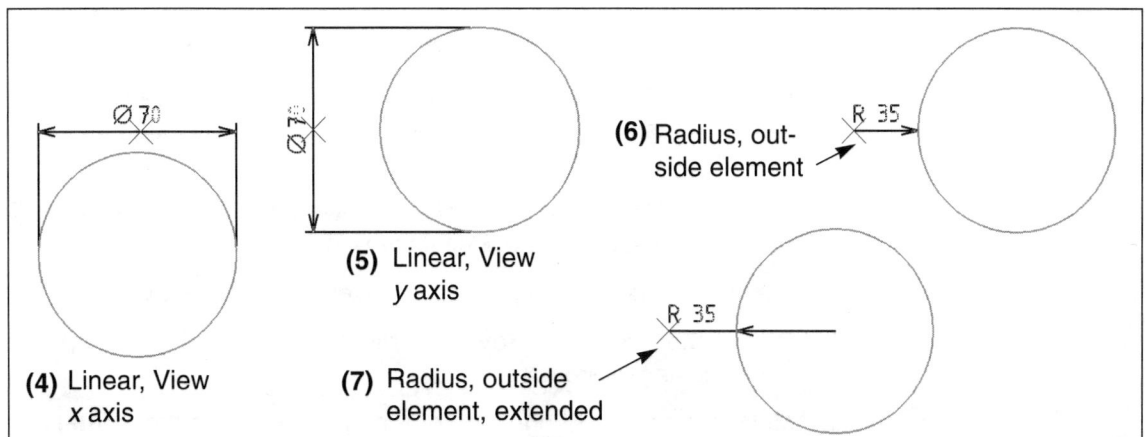

Figure 9.5   Dimensioning of a circle with the Dimension Element tool

8. Press the <**Enter**> key again.

This time we will be offered a *Diameter* once more, this time as a *Radial Dimension*.

9. Press the <**Enter**> key again.

The *Radial* presentation of the *Diameter* will now be in the *Extended* form.

10. Another press of the <**Enter**> key will return us to the first offering and the cycle will start again.

(8) Diameter, outside element   **(9)** Diameter, outside element, extended

Figure 9.6   Dimensioning of a circle with the Dimension Element tool

Some of the possibilities of *Linear* and *Radial* dimensioning using the *Dimension Element* tool are illustrated in Figure 9.5. The linear dimensioning is in *View* alignment, but this setting does not have any effect on radial dimensioning, e.g. *Radius* or *Diameter*. In the exercise that follows we will experiment with the options offered by this tool when dimensioning a line, this time using the other alignments.

◆ **Dimensioning a line segment with the Dimension Element tool**

1. Leave the element and text settings as for the last exercise. Still on level *25* of "second.dgn", place a line of a length similar to the circle's diameter, at any angle.

2. Select the *Dimension Element* tool, leave the *Alignment* as **View** (for now), the *Association Lock* either way.

3. Identify the line with a data point, move the pointer above it.

4. Press the <**Enter**> key several times, noting the types of dimensioning offered.

5. Move the pointer to one side of the element, press the <**Enter**> key some more times, again noting the types of dimensioning offered.

The results may look like those illustrated in Figure 9.7. Note that the set of options of dimension types has changed with the different element. The first dimension type offered will not always be the same, it depends on the type that was last used.

6. Change the *Alignment* setting to **True**, repeat steps **4.** and **5.**

7. Change the *Alignment* setting to **Arbitrary**, try placing a *"Size"* dimension (see Figure 9.7) with the extension lines angled.

Hint!

☒ **Isometric**

Turning the **Isometric** lock **On** (from the Status bar *Locks* menu) will constrain the extension lines to the appropriate angles for dimensioning any isometric views in a design. There is an illustration of this in Figure 9.4 on page 9-4.

*Dimensioning options for a Line using the Dimension Element tool, **View** alignment setting*

| Size with arrows, View *x* aligned | Size with arrows, View *y* aligned | Size with strokes, View *x* aligned | Labelled with length & angle | Perpendicular offset |

*Differing options, **True** alignment setting*

Arbitrary alignment setting

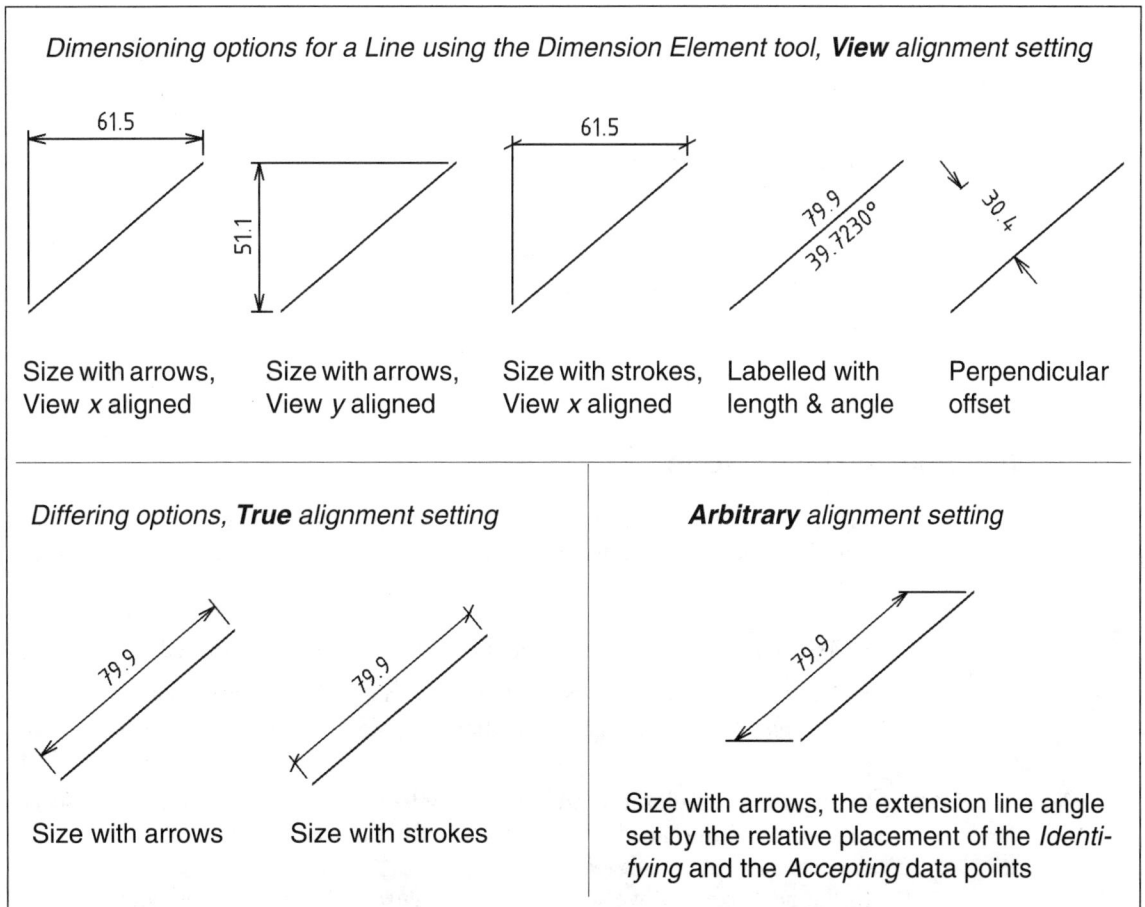

| Size with arrows | Size with strokes |

Size with arrows, the extension line angle set by the relative placement of the *Identifying* and the *Accepting* data points

Figure 9.7 Some samples of dimensions on a line segment

The Dimension Size Tools

These two tools, *Dimension Size with Arrow* and *Dimension Size with Stroke* operate identically, the only difference being the *Terminators* used. The main difference between these tools and the Dimension Element tool is that they are able to dimension between *any* points, they are not restricted to a single element. These are specialized tools for *Linear* dimensioning, they have no facility to cycle through types of dimensioning like the Dimension Element tool.

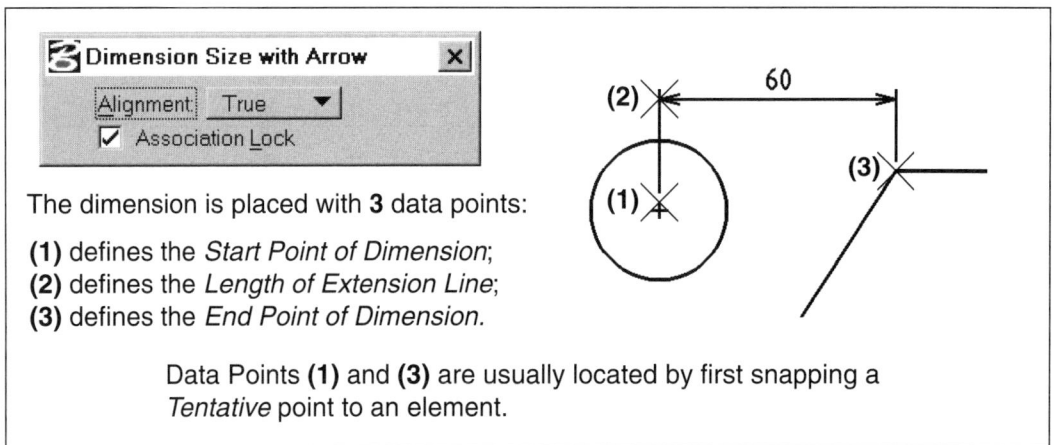

Dimension Size with Arrow

Alignment: True

☑ Association Lock

The dimension is placed with **3** data points:

(1) defines the *Start Point of Dimension*;
(2) defines the *Length of Extension Line*;
(3) defines the *End Point of Dimension*.

Data Points **(1)** and **(3)** are usually located by first snapping a *Tentative* point to an element.

Figure 9.8　General procedure for the Dimension Size operation

Associated Dimensions

An *Associated* dimension updates automatically when the element it is associated with is modified. For a dimension to be created as *Associated*, two criteria must be met:

* *Association Lock* must be *On* at the time the dimension is placed;

* The element being dimensioned must be *Snapped to* and the tentative point *Accepted* to establish the start and/or end point as an *Association Point*.

Note:　Snapping to an element and *Accepting* to identify it will establish *Association* of a dimension placed using the *Dimension Element* tool.

In the next exercise we will use the *Dimension Size with Arrow* tool to create an *Associated Dimension*.

◆ **Create an Associated dimension between two points**

1. Place a line near the circle on level **25** of "second.dgn", similar to the illustration in Figure. 9.9.

2. Select the *Dimension Size Arrow* tool, set the *Alignment* to **View**, *Association Lock* **On**.

3. *Center* snap to the circle, *Accept* to select the *Start Of Dimension.*

4. Move the pointer to just above the circle, place a data point to define the length of the *Extension Line.*

5. *Keypoint* snap to the upper end of the line and *Accept* as the *Dimension Endpoint.*

    We now have the option of continuing straight along, defining more dimension endpoints in a *Chain* of dimensions.

6. Press *Reset* to terminate this *Chain.*

    The tool is still active, now we have the option of continuing "around the corner" to dimension down the side (watch the prompts).

7. Press *Reset* to terminate the *Dimension Size* operation.

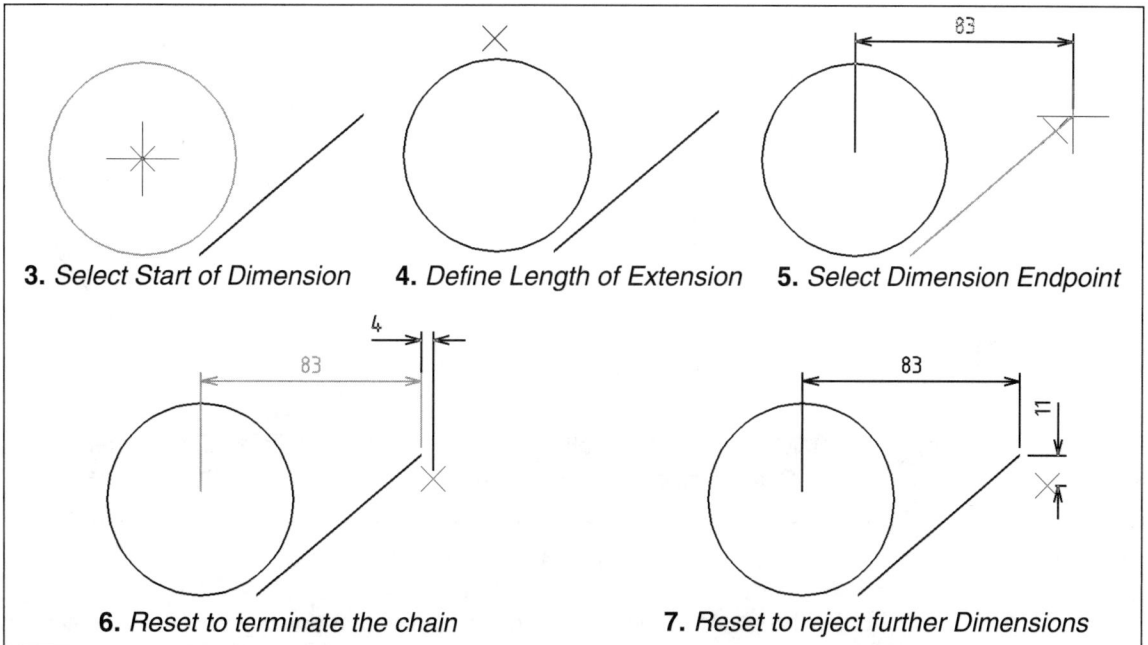

3. *Select Start of Dimension*   4. *Define Length of Extension*   5. *Select Dimension Endpoint*

6. *Reset to terminate the chain*   7. *Reset to reject further Dimensions*

Figure 9.9 Using the Dimension Size tools

◆ **Modify and Manipulate the elements to prove Association**

1. Select the *Modify Element* tool (see "The Modify Element Tool" on page 5-15), identify the upper end of the line and move it.

2. *Accept* its new position, *Reset* the tool.
   Note that the dimensioning updates.

3. Select the *Move* tool (see "The Move Element Tool" on page 4-2), identify the circle and move it.

4. *Accept, Reset.*
   Again, the dimensioning will update to remain accurate.

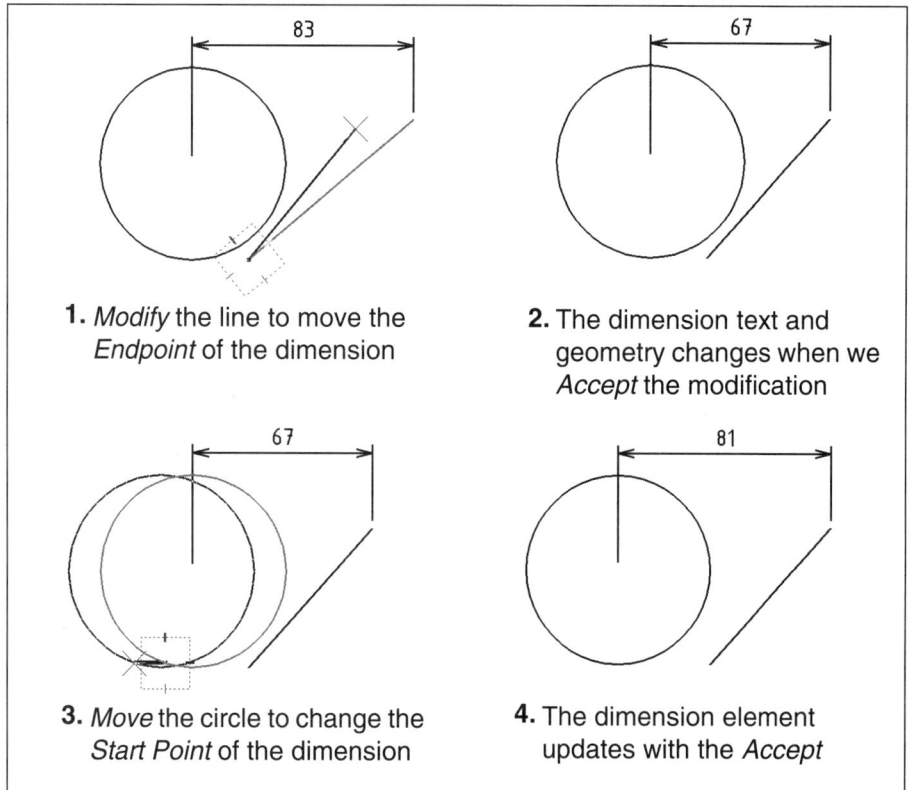

1. *Modify* the line to move the *Endpoint* of the dimension

2. The dimension text and geometry changes when we *Accept* the modification

3. *Move* the circle to change the *Start Point* of the dimension

4. The dimension element updates with the *Accept*

Figure 9.10 Associated Dimensions

If you happened to move either of the association points vertically, you may have noticed that the extension lines and dimension line are no longer in the appropriate relationship. We will introduce a *Dimension Setting* shortly that will fix this problem.

Dimension Settings

In our first dimensioning examples we set the text size in the *Text* settings box and the dimension alignment in the *Dimension Element* tool settings box. The dimensions were placed with the currently active element attributes. We accepted the default settings for the dimensioning elements.

There are a huge number of options available for placing dimensioning in MicroStation. The *Dimension Settings* box (Figure 9.11, opened from the Application menu bar under *Element>Dimensions*) lists the categories of settings that can be made. The category illustrated is *Text*.

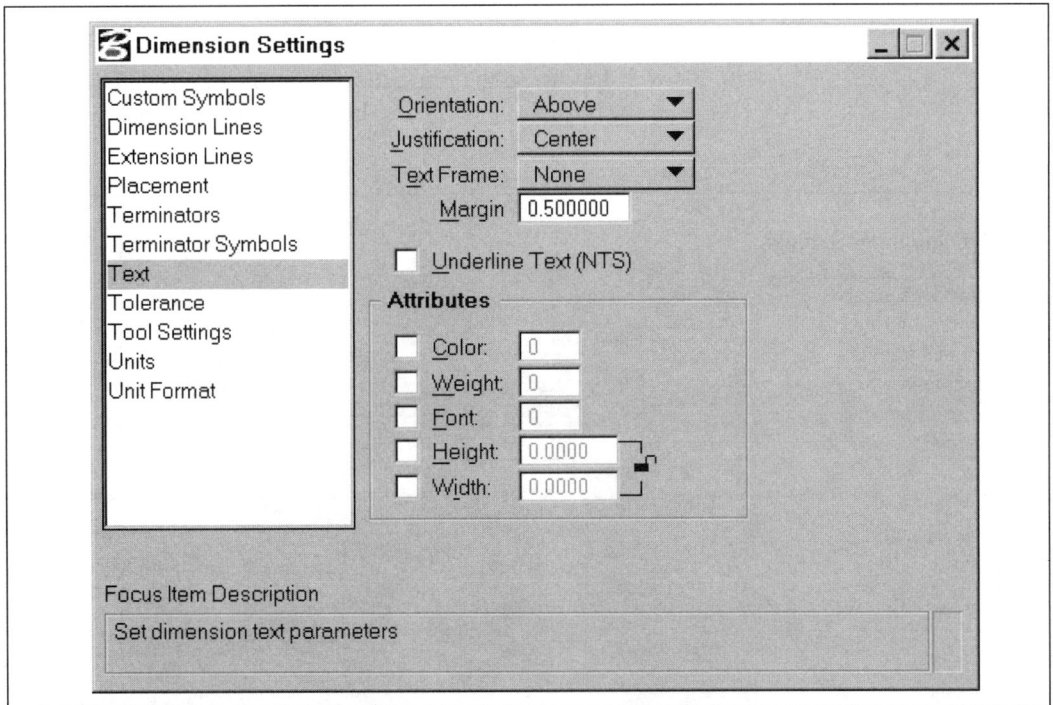

Figure 9.11   The Dimension Settings box, Text settings

There are a series of check boxes in the *Attributes* panel of the *Element>Dimensions>Text* settings illustrated above. Checking these *On* causes the particular *Dimension Setting* to override the *Active Attributes* current at the time a dimension is being placed. Any of the categories of settings where attributes are involved has comparable *Override* options.

The *Attribute* settings for the text component of the dimension element include both *Element Attributes* and *Text Attributes*. You may note from Figure 9.11 the lack of a *Level* setting under *Text*. This override setting is only found under *Dimension Lines*, but it applies to the entire dimension element.

The dimension settings chosen will depend largely on national standards, the particular discipline, company standards and the project being undertaken. In practice, it is unlikely that the default settings will be entirely suitable, so we will look briefly at the options available. There are so many that we will only illustrate a representative few, starting with the *Custom Symbols* category. This category sets the custom symbols (if any) used as a component of the dimension element.

Custom Symbols

When we choose a category such as this from the list in the left panel of the box, a description of it appears in the *Focus Item Description* panel. This panel, located at the bottom of the box, changes to describe every item in the box with *Input Focus*.

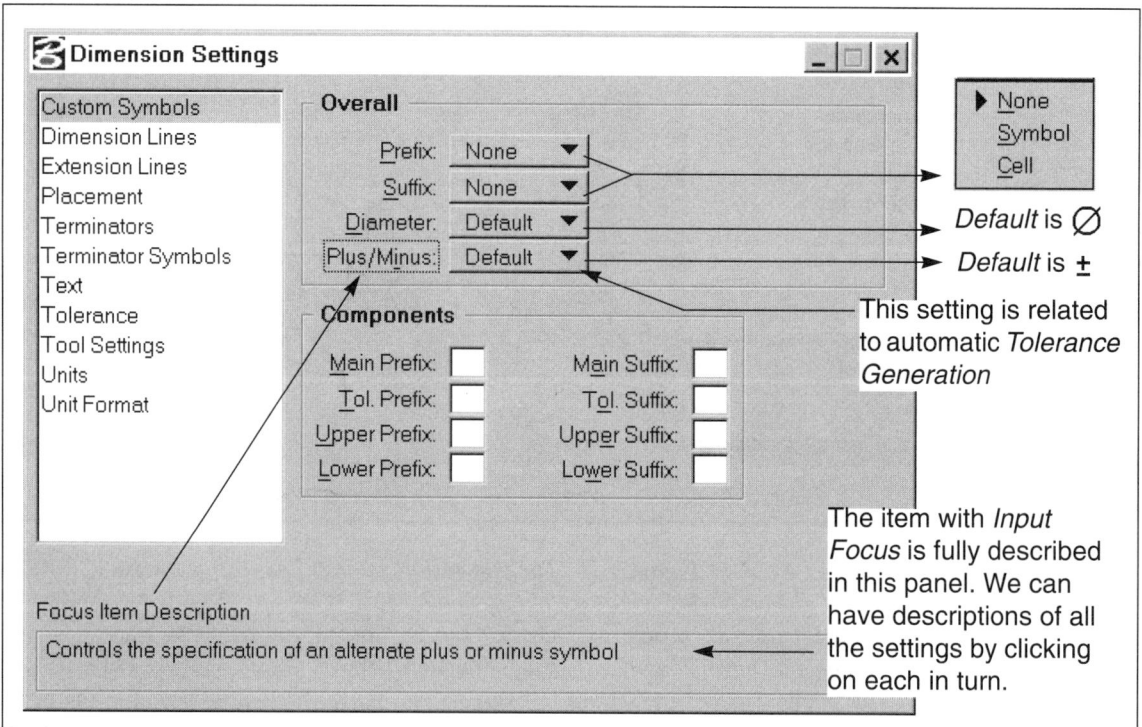

Figure 9.12   Using a Dimension Settings box

Dimension Lines

This category of settings may have effect on all of the dimension element, not just the *Dimension Line*. The *Level* override applies to all of the components of the dimension element. The *Attributes* override will apply to all the components as well, unless the attributes of individual components (such as *Text*) are further overridden under their own category.

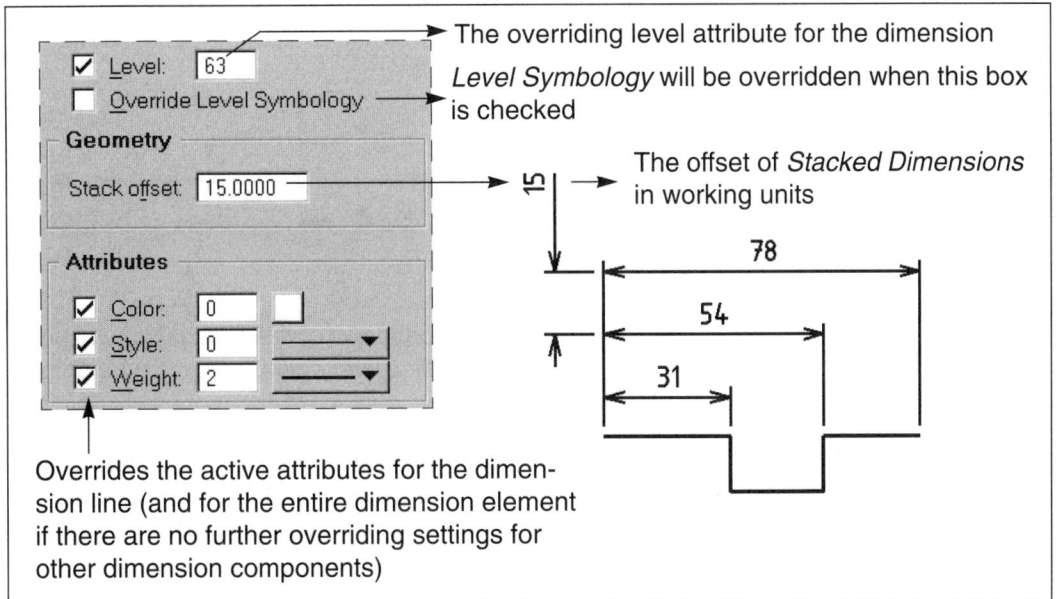

Figure 9.13   Dimension Line settings (part only of settings box shown)

Extension Lines

The symbology attributes of the extension lines will be defined by the *Attribute* settings of this settings box when the override boxes are checked *On*. If these boxes are *Off*, the symbology will be the same as for the *Dimension Lines*.

We can turn extension lines *Off* altogether in the *Extension Lines* check box. The *Join When Text Outside* setting defines whether a line is to be placed linking the dimension lines when they fall outside the extension lines. This is illustrated in Figure 9.14, as is the meaning of *Offset* and *Extension* distances, which are both are entered in terms of *Text Heights*.

Fixed Length Extension Lines

In some cases it is not desirable to have extension lines running all the way into a drawing to the dimensioned point. We have the option of using a *Negative Offset* extension line, which is fixed at the length (in text heights) keyed in to the *Offset* field preceded by a minus sign.

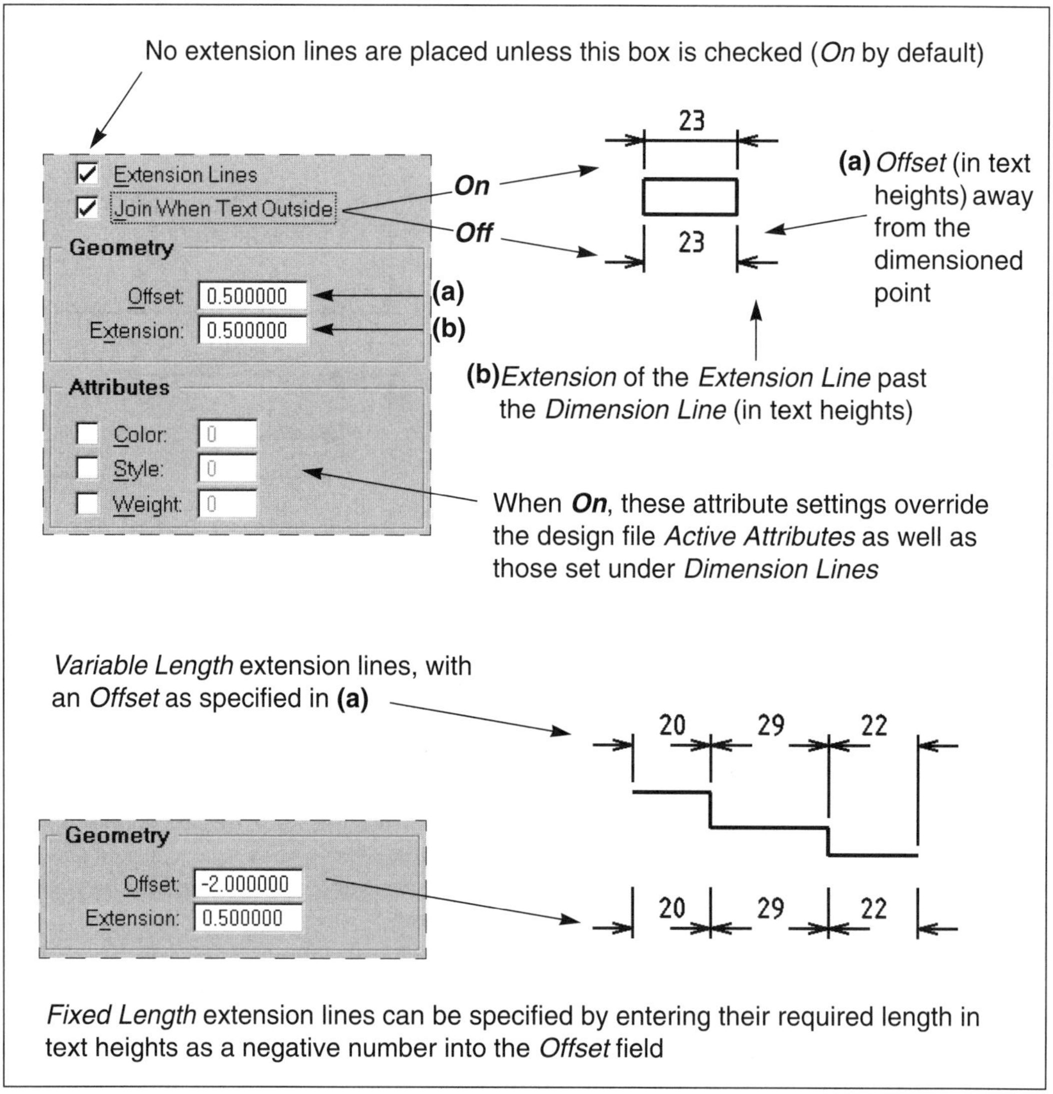

No extension lines are placed unless this box is checked (*On* by default)

☑ Extension Lines
☑ Join When Text Outside

On
Off

(a) *Offset* (in text heights) away from the dimensioned point

Geometry

Offset: 0.500000 **(a)**
Extension: 0.500000 **(b)**

(b) *Extension* of the *Extension Line* past the *Dimension Line* (in text heights)

Attributes

☐ Color: 0
☐ Style: 0
☐ Weight: 0

When **On**, these attribute settings override the design file *Active Attributes* as well as those set under *Dimension Lines*

Variable Length extension lines, with an *Offset* as specified in **(a)**

Geometry

Offset: -2.000000
Extension: 0.500000

Fixed Length extension lines can be specified by entering their required length in text heights as a negative number into the *Offset* field

Figure 9.14   Extension Line settings

Placement

These settings define the parameters for the placement of the *Dimension Lines* and *Dimension Text*, as described in Figure 9.15. The *Reference File Units* setting (**a**) will be introduced with Reference Files later on. Placed with *Relative Dimension Line* (**b**) is *On*, an *Associated* dimension line will move to remain a constant distance from the *Start of Dimension* point when that point is moved (see page 9-16).

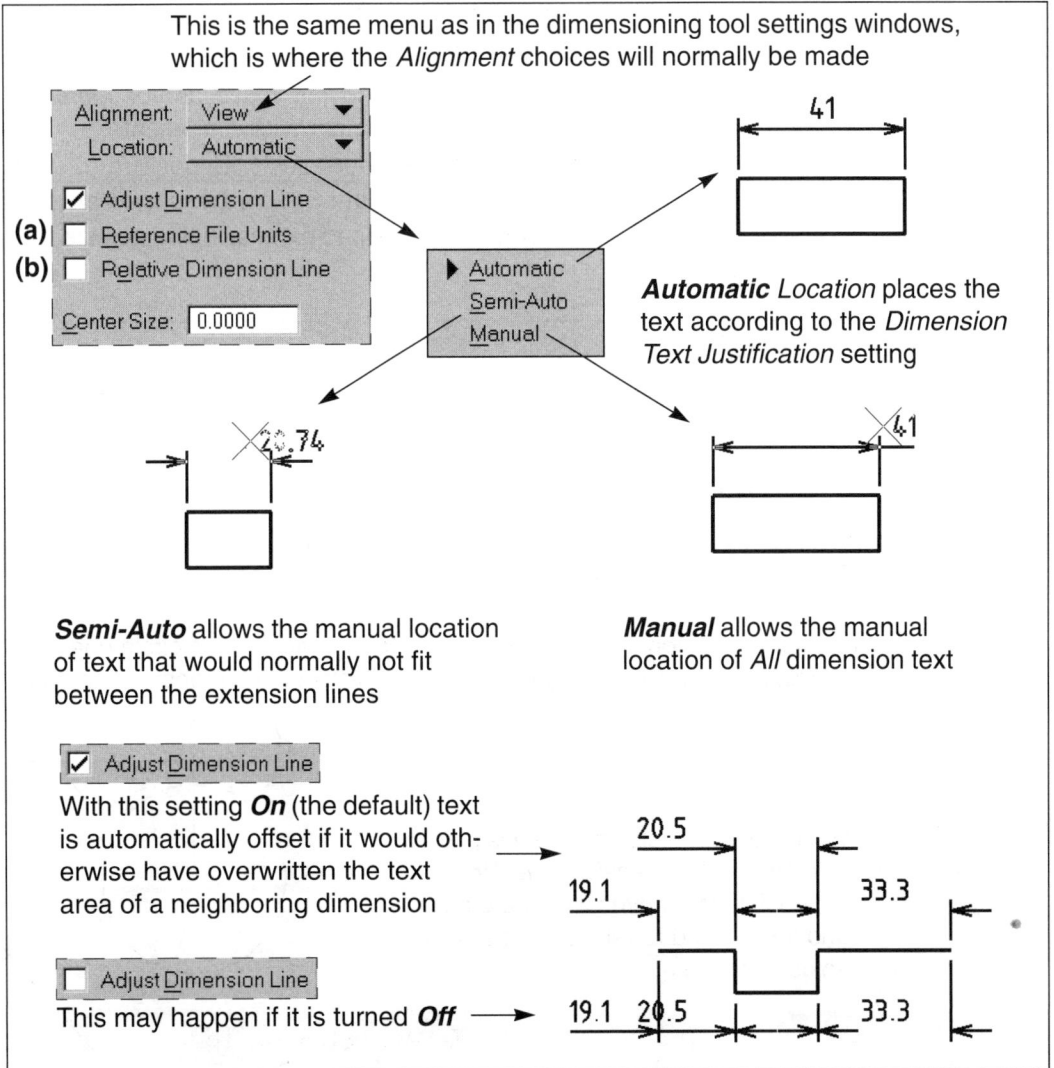

Figure 9.15   Placement settings

◆ **Relative Dimension Lines**

1. Make sure that *Relative Dimension Line* is **Off** (the default setting) in the *Element>Dimensions>Placement* settings box, delete and replace the *Size* dimension between the circle center and the line.

2. Use the *Move* tool to move the circle vertically upwards.

   Note that the dimension line does not move and the extension line from the circle center adjusts in length.

3. *Undo* the both the move and the dimension, check the *Relative Dimension Line* box **On**.

4. Repeat the dimensioning and the *Move* and/or *Modify* operations, note the different effect on the dimension element.

   This time the *Dimension Line* adjusts its position to keep the *First Extension Line* (placed from the *Start of Dimension* association point) at its original length. The second extension line adjusts.

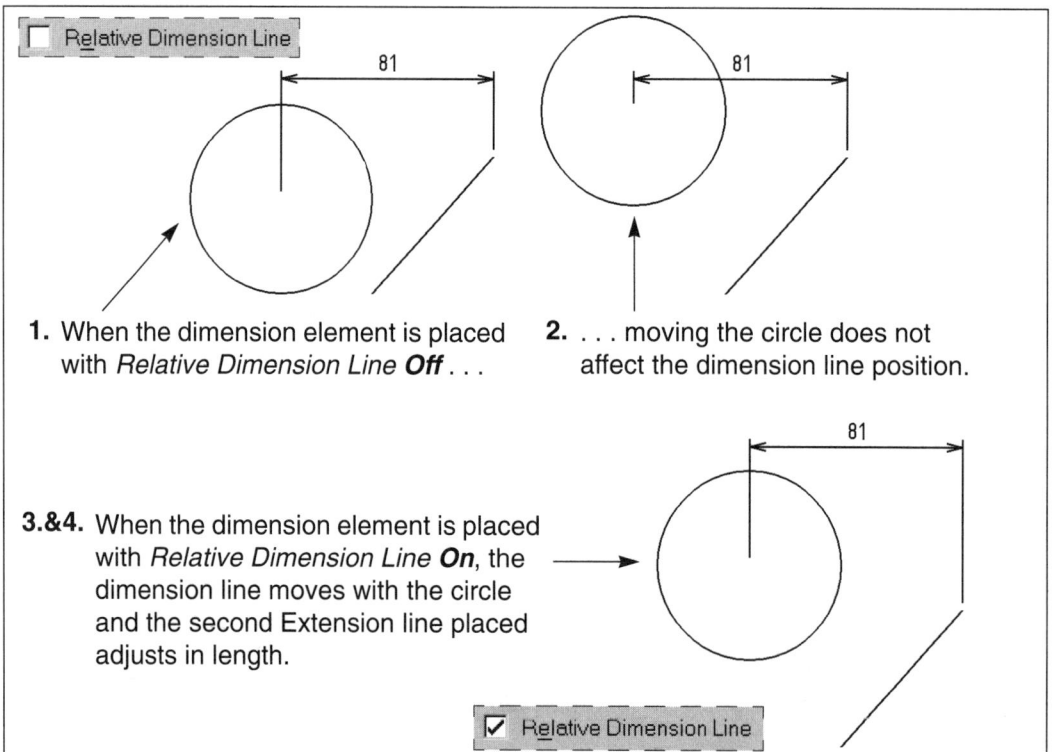

1. When the dimension element is placed with *Relative Dimension Line* **Off** . . .

2. . . . moving the circle does not affect the dimension line position.

3.&4. When the dimension element is placed with *Relative Dimension Line* **On**, the dimension line moves with the circle and the second Extension line placed adjusts in length.

Figure 9.16 The effect of the Relative Dimension Line setting

Terminators

The terminators will almost invariably be arrowheads or strokes. Except for the *Arrowhead* options, the settings in this category relate to both types and to *Custom Terminators* as well. The first of the two settings in the *Orientation* panel, *Terminators*, relates to linear dimensions. The other *Orientation* setting is for the appearance of the arrowhead, whether it is *Open*, *Closed*, or *Filled* with the terminator color.

The *Geometry* settings are for the height and width of the terminator and for the *Minimum Leader* size. The *Leader* is the space between the text and the extension lines. All of these sizes are in text heights.

The *Attribute* overrides enable us to give the terminators a different color, line style and line weight to the other dimension geometry.

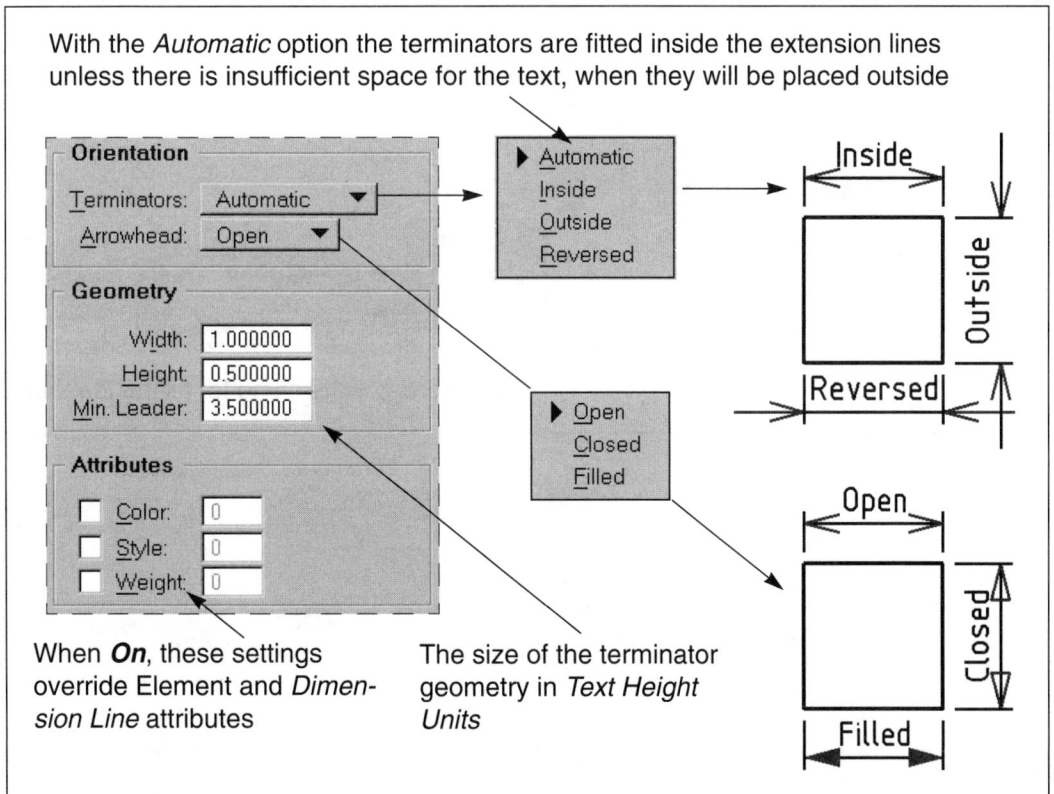

Figure 9.17   The Terminators settings

Terminator Symbols

If we need to create customized forms of dimension line terminators, this is the category we use to select them. The default Arrowhead and Stroke terminators used on both ends of the dimension line, the circle for a dimension *Origin*, or the dot for a dimension joint may all be replaced. The same three options are available for all four terminators, *Default*, *Symbol* and *Cell*.

When *Symbol* is chosen, two fields appear. The *Char.* (character) field is for the keyboard equivalent of the symbol from the symbol type font specified in the *Font* field. The field will display the ordinary text character of the key (a, b, c), not the symbol "mapped" to it.

Choosing *Cell* displays a field for the cell *Name*, which must be available in a cell library accessible from the design file, meeting the same conditions as needed for "The Select and Place Cell Tool" on page 6-20. Regardless of the dimensions of the cell as it was created, its size will be set by the terminator *Geometry* settings.

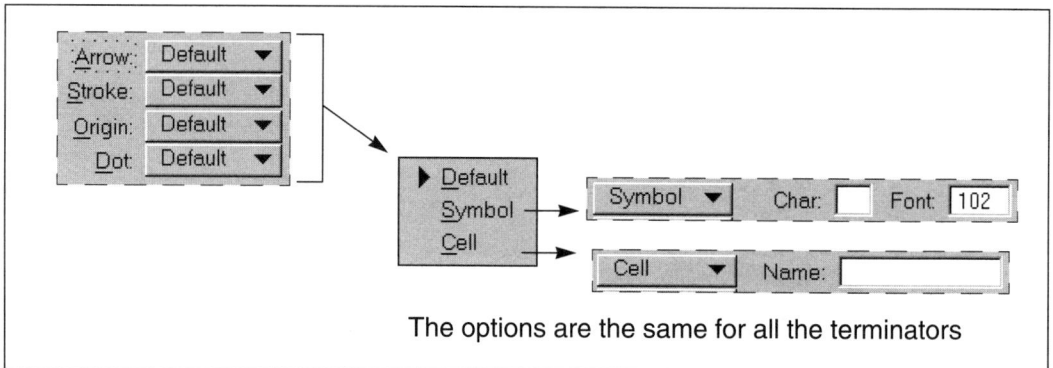

Figure 9.18   Terminator Symbol settings

Text

The settings in the *Attributes* panel of this dimension setting category has already been introduced, see "Dimension Settings" on page 9-11. The other *Dimension Text* options are illustrated in Figure 9.19.

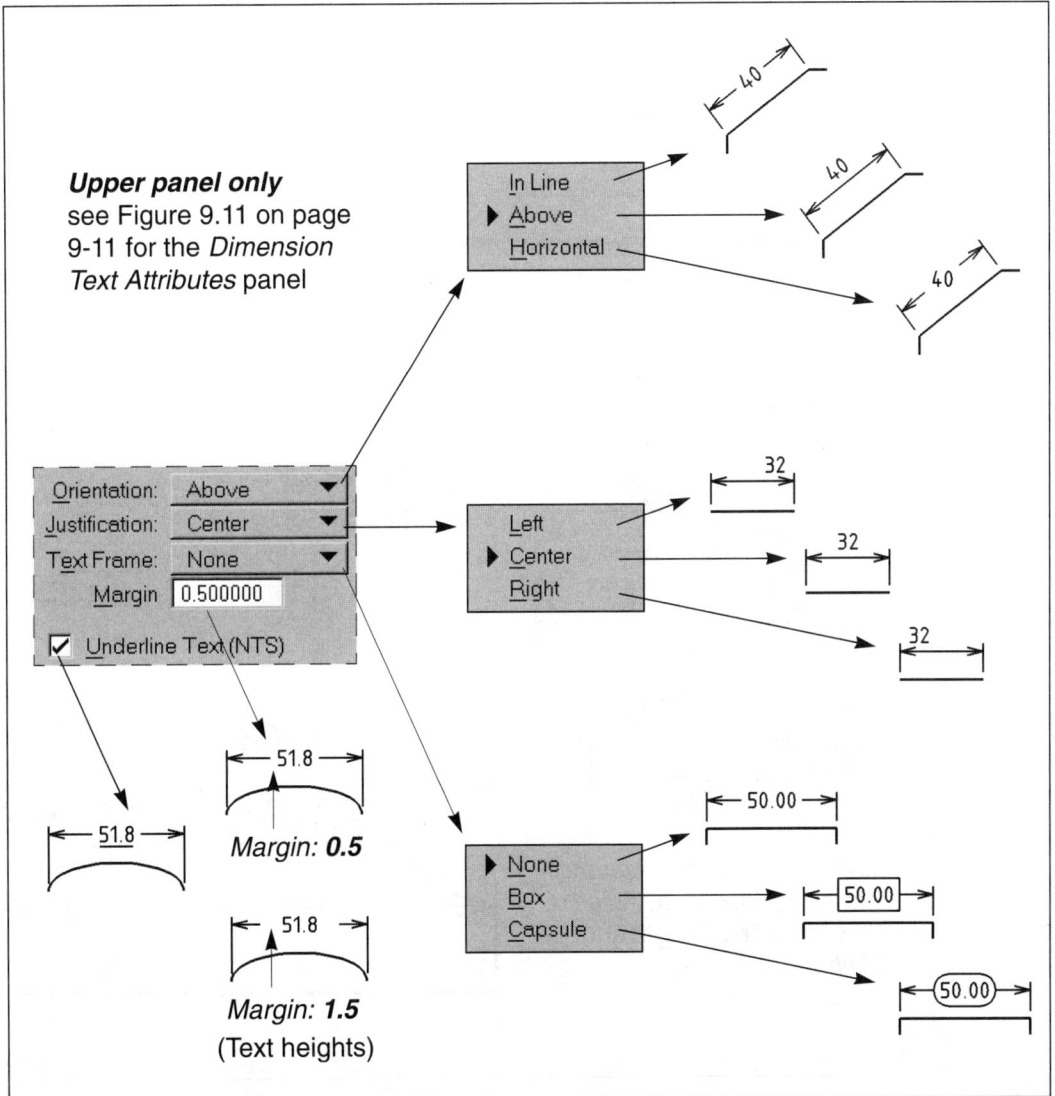

Figure 9.19   Dimension Text options (excluding Dimension Text Attributes)

Tolerance

Dimensioning may have a *Tolerance* component automatically appended. The tolerance range may be specified as *Dimension Limits* (maximum and minimum sizes) or as *Maximum Deviations* (+ and - deviations). The size and spacing of the tolerance text may be set in *Dimension* text heights.

The number of decimal places shown in the *Upper* and *Lower* fields is set by the design file *Coordinate Readout* setting (*Settings>Design File>Coordinate Readout*). The tolerance component generated will have the number of decimal places specified in the *Dimension Units* setting, to be introduced shortly.

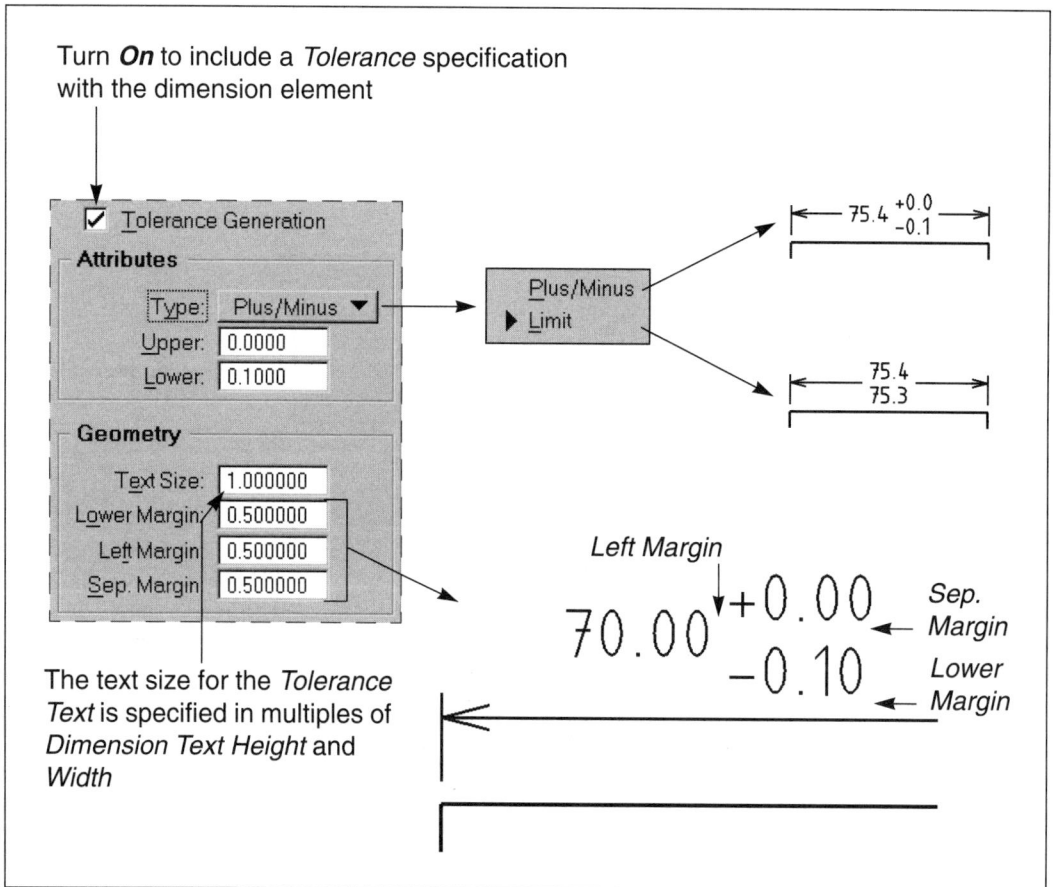

Figure 9.20 Tolerance Settings

Tool Settings

This settings box enables modifications to be made to an *Individual Tool*, whereas the other dimension settings generally apply to *All* the dimensioning tools. Most of the settings in this category are dependent on other settings. For example, when an *Arrowhead* is specified for the left terminator of a dimension, it will be the *Arrow* defined under *Terminators* (page 9-17) and *Terminator Symbols* (page 9-18).

There are more tools shown in Figure 9.21 than appear in the *Dimension* tool box. Some of these tools are actually options offered while using other tools, such as the one we first worked with, *Dimension Element*. They can also be accessed by *Key-in Commands* (see "Key-Ins" on page 5-40).

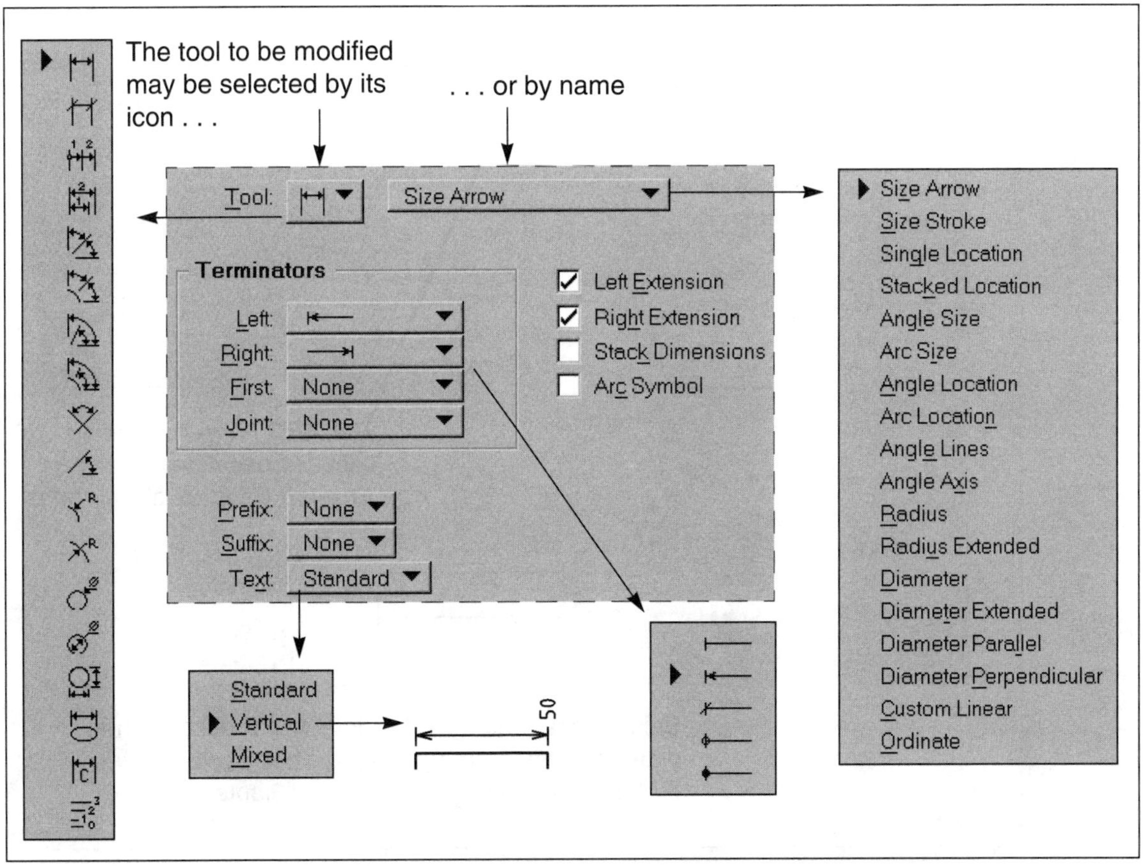

Figure 9.21   Typical Dimension Tool Settings

Units

The type of *Units* to be used in the dimension element may be **Metric** and/or **English**. When working with one standard as our **Primary** units, we have the option of including the other standard as **Secondary** units, as illustrated in Figure 9.22.

For the text to appear as it does in that illustration, we would need to choose the double-quote (") as a *Lower Suffix* from the **Components** panel of the *Custom Symbols* category of *Dimension Settings* (page 9-12). We would also need to be using a *Font* that supports *Fractions* (32 - INTL_ENGINEERING in this illustration) and *Fractions* would need to be **On** in the *Element>Text* settings box.

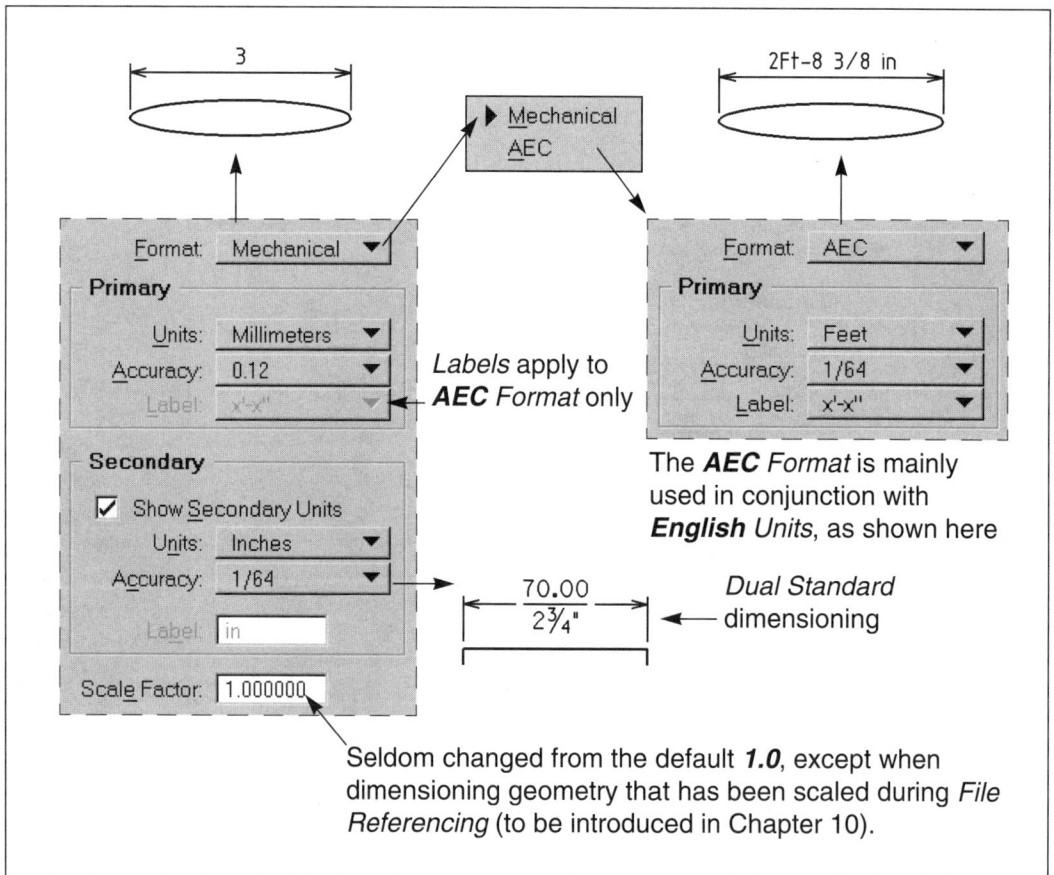

Figure 9.22 Dimensioning Units settings

Unit Format

The top panel in the settings box for this category is used to select and format the *Angle* units. The **Metric Format**, **Primary** and **Secondary** panels are used to format the other units as selected under the *Units* category (page 9-22).

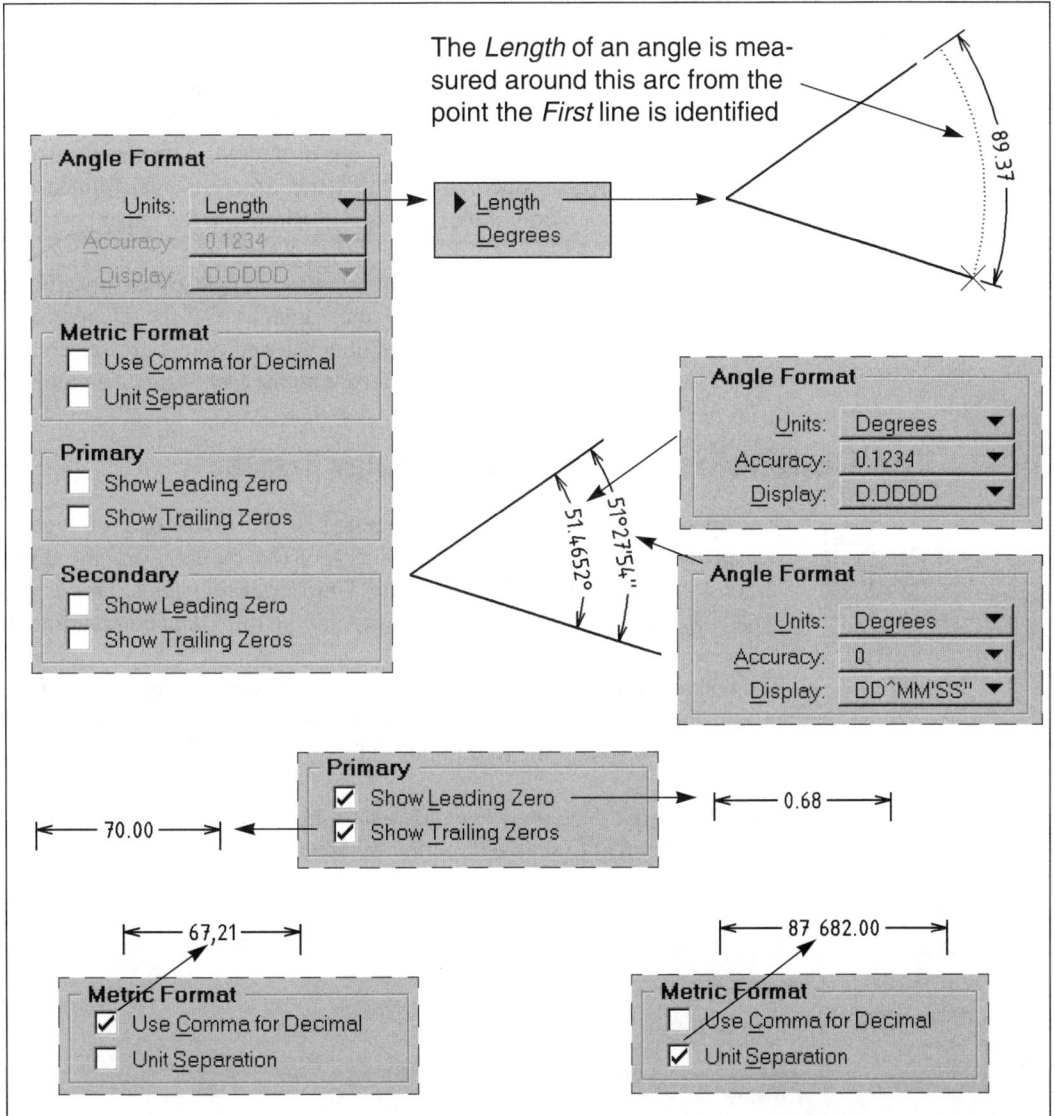

Figure 9.23 Dimension Unit Formatting

The Dimension Tool Box - Other Linear Tools

Now that we have been introduced to the range of settings available to us for the dimensioning process, we will introduce the remaining linear tools. Using these tools will generally require more changes to dimension settings than the basic ones.

The Dimension Location Tools

These two tools dimension distances from a common datum or *Origin*. The left side one is called *Dimension Location*, the other is *Dimension Location (Stacked)*. They differ only in the way the dimensions are presented, with the former created in a *Chained* format (in a single line), the latter *Stacked* (each dimension vertically separated). The operation of these tools is illustrated in the upper part of Figure 9.24.

The dimensioning of all the points is placed as a single *Dimension Element* by both tools. The tool settings options are the same as for the *Dimension Size* tools, *Alignment* and *Association Lock*. The dimensioned points are selected in the same way as for a *Chain* of dimensions created with the *Dimension Size* tools (page 9-9).

The Dimension Size Perpendicular Tools

The operation of these tools is illustrated in the lower part of Figure 9.24. The *Dimension Size Perpendicular to Points* tool (on the left) sets the direction of the dimension to be *Perpendicular* to the *First Extension Line*. This is placed in the usual way with the first two data points, with the third data point defining the end.

The operation of this tool differs from the *Dimension Size* tools with *True* alignment in that the direction is set by the relative position of the *First Two* data points, whereas the *Start* and the *End* points define the direction with *Dimension Size*.

The *Dimension Size Perpendicular to Line* tool uses a perpendicular from an identified element to set the direction of the dimension.

This is the *Origin Symbol* as set under *Element>Dimensions>Terminator Symbols>Origin* (see "Terminator Symbols" on page 9-18)

The dimension element is placed with a series of data points:

      (1) defines the *Start Point of Dimension*;
      (2) defines the *Length of Extension Line*;
      (3), **(4)** and **(5)** define the *End Points* of each dimension.

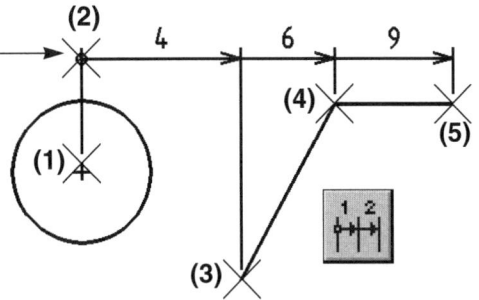

The separation of the stacked dimension lines is set in working units under *Element>Dimensions>Dimension Lines>Stack Offset* (see Figure 9.13 on page 9-13).

Data Points except **(2)** are usually located by first snapping a *Tentative* point to an element.

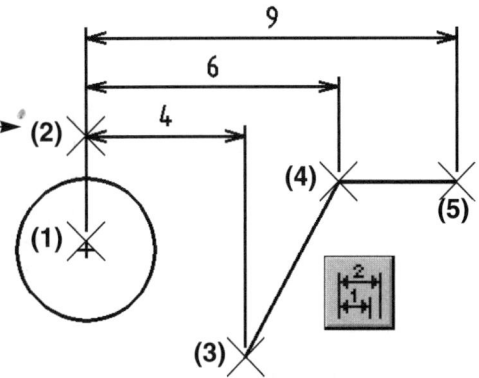

The distance dimensioned is *Perpendicular* to the first *Extension Line*

The dimension element is placed with three data points:

      (1) defines the *Start Point of Dimension*;
      (2) defines both the *Length of Extension Line* and the orientation of the *y* axis of the dimension;
      (3) defines the *End Point* of the dimension.

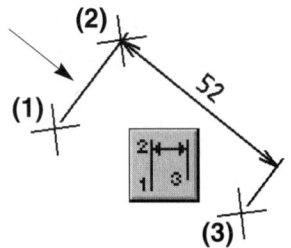

The distance dimensioned is *Perpendicular* to the element identified with the first data point

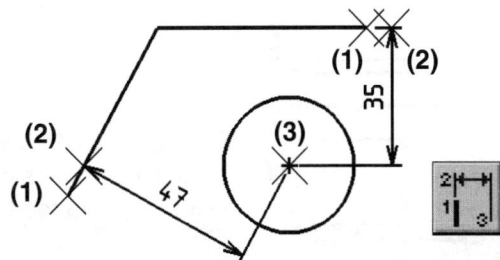

Figure 9.24   Dimensioning Locations and along Perpendiculars

The Dimension Ordinates Tool

This tool is used to label distances along a defined axis from a datum or *Origin*. As can be seen in Figure 9.25, the labels are placed with extension lines, but without dimension lines. The *Alignment* choices are the same as those found in the Tool Settings windows of the other *Linear Dimensioning* tools. The illustration is using the *View* alignment option, with examples of both *x* and *y* axis alignments.

There are two sets of ordinate dimensioning shown here. The dimensioned points were at the intersections of the curve with a grid of equally spaced vertical lines. The construction grid was hidden after the dimensioning was placed.

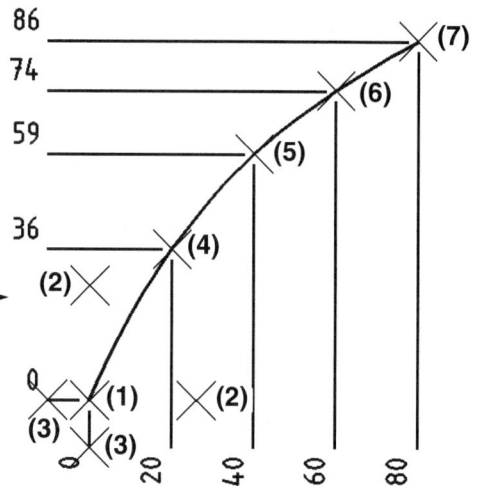

The Data Points:

(1) defines the *Origin of Dimension*;
(2) defines the *Axis* for the ordinates;
(3) defines the *Length* of the *Extension Line* and places the zero label;
(4) to **(7)** dimension the other ordinates.

This check box is found under *Element> Dimensions>Tool Settings*, the *Ordinates* tool (see "Tool Settings" on page 9-21)

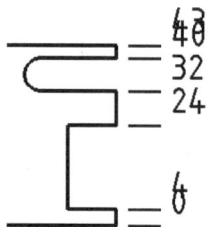

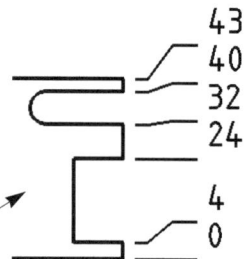

Turning *Stack Dimension On* for this tool causes the dimension lines to "jog" where necessary and the text does not overlap

Figure 9.25 Dimensioning Ordinates

That completes our introduction to the tools from the *Linear Dimensioning* part of the tool box. The number of combinations of tools and settings is huge, but only a limited number will be used on any one project. Later in the book (Chapter 11) we will work with *Settings Files* that enable us to save a particular combination of dimension settings as a *Dimensioning Style*.

We will now go on with the remaining tools from the Dimensions tool box, the *Angle* and *Radial* dimensioning tools are next.

The Dimension Tool Box - Angle and Radial

This section of the tool box has five tools for dimensioning angles. Two dimension angles that are defined by data points, three dimension angles of lines. The lines may have angle dimensions created between two lines, or between a line and an *x* or *y* *Axis*.

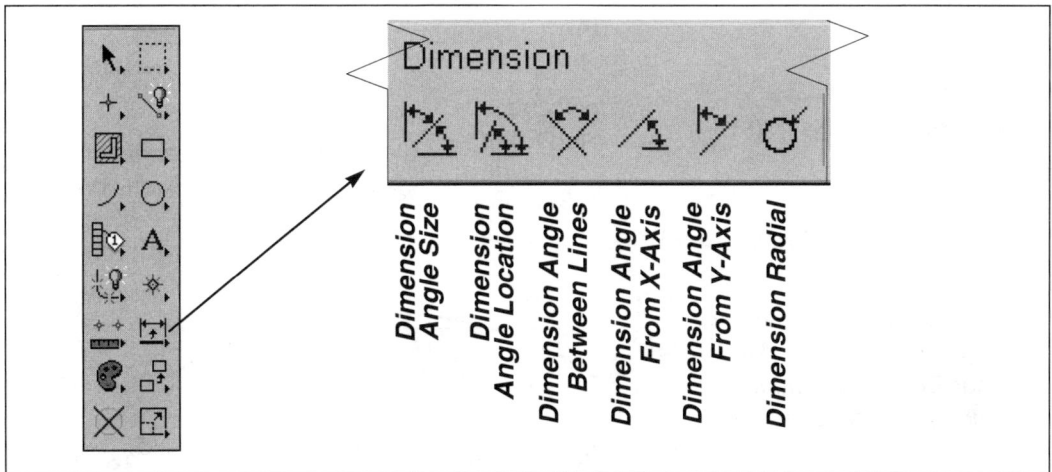

Figure 9.26   The Dimension Tool Box, Angle and Radial Dimensioning tools

The Dimension Angle (Points) Tools

We use these tools, *Dimension Angle Size* and *Dimension Angle Location* to dimension angles formed by three points. The angles are dimensioned in an anticlockwise direction about a *Vertex* point, between an *Origin* point and an *Endpoint*.

With the *Size* tool, multiple adjoining angles about a single vertex may be dimensioned like a *Chain* in the linear size dimensioning tool. The *Endpoint* of one angle defines the *Start* point of the next angle, continuing in the anticlockwise direction. The *Location* tool dimensions the angles in an anticlockwise direction from a common *Origin*.

If *Association Lock* is **On**, positioning the data points by first *Snapping* to elements will *Associate* the angular dimension with that element (page 9-10). The *Association Lock* check box is the only setting in the Settings windows of these tools.

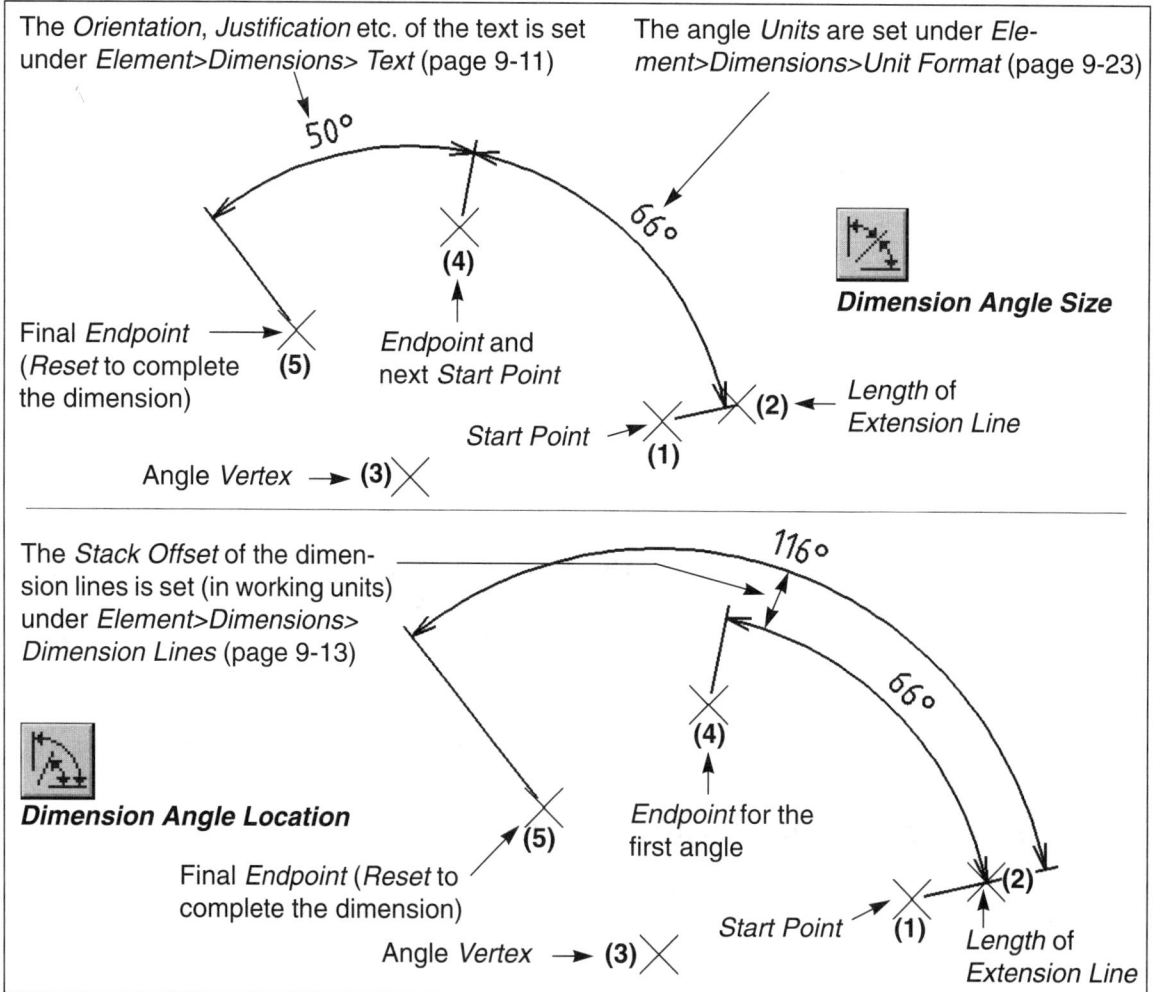

The *Orientation, Justification* etc. of the text is set under *Element>Dimensions> Text* (page 9-11)

The angle *Units* are set under *Element>Dimensions>Unit Format* (page 9-23)

50°

66°

Dimension Angle Size

(4)

Final *Endpoint* (*Reset* to complete the dimension) **(5)**

Endpoint and next *Start Point*

Length of Extension Line **(2)**

Start Point **(1)**

Angle *Vertex* ➤ **(3)**

The *Stack Offset* of the dimension lines is set (in working units) under *Element>Dimensions> Dimension Lines* (page 9-13)

116°

66°

Dimension Angle Location

(4)

Final *Endpoint* (*Reset* to complete the dimension) **(5)**

Endpoint for the first angle

Angle *Vertex* ➤ **(3)**

Start Point **(1)**

Length of Extension Line **(2)**

Figure 9.27 Dimensioning Angles defined by points

The Dimension Angle Between Lines Tool

This tool differs from the *Angle Size* and *Location* dimensioning tools in that we do not need to identify a vertex, the angle is taken from the difference in direction of the two lines. The angle is always dimensioned in the anticlockwise direction, so the order in which the lines are identified is critical (see Figure 9.28).

The Dimension Angle from View Axes Tools

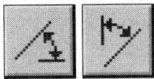

The *Dimension Angle from X-Axis* and the *Dimension Angle from Y-Axis* tools need only two data points to dimension the angle of a line or (line segment) from the screen horizontal or vertical. Unlike the other *Dimension Angle* tools, these will dimension in a clockwise as well as in an anticlockwise direction.

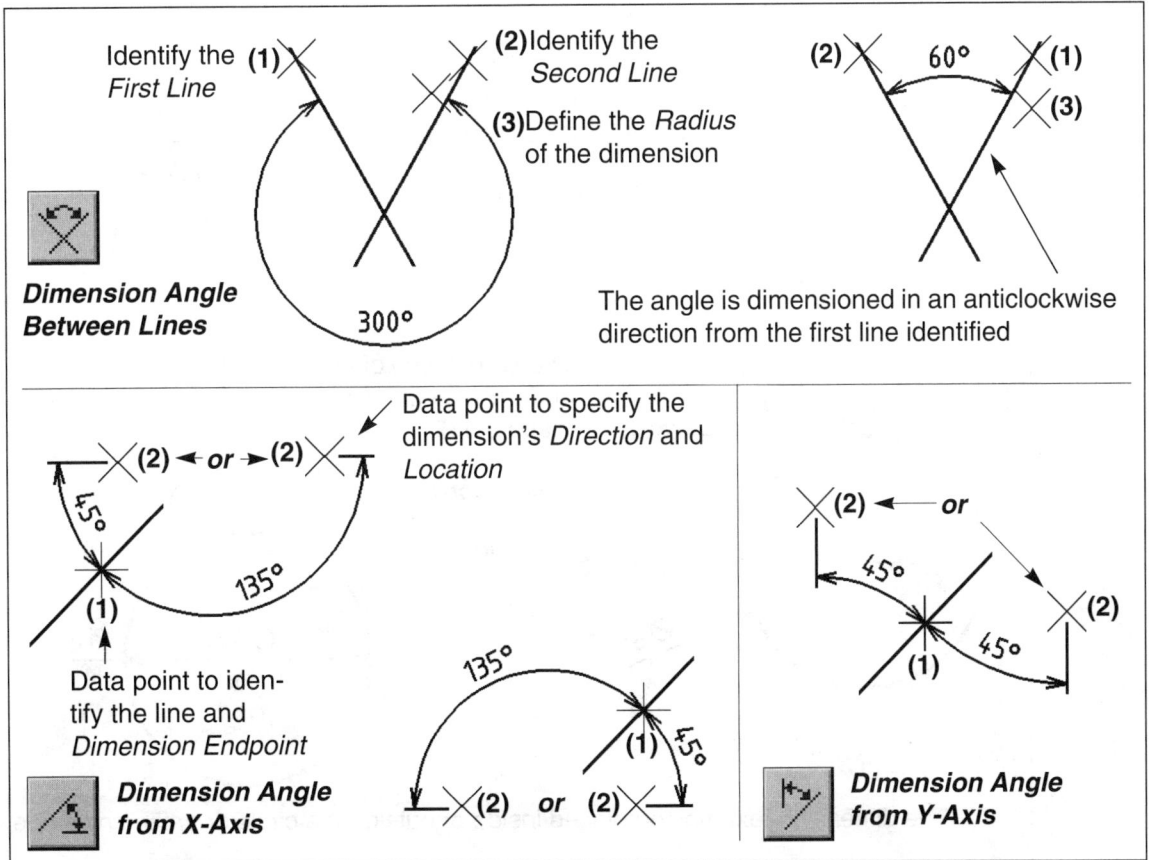

Figure 9.28   Dimensioning the Angles of Lines

The Dimension Radial Tool

This tool may operate in five different *Modes*. It is used for dimensioning the *Radius* or the *Diameter* of circles or circular arcs, and for placing *Center Marks*. There are two modes of *Radius* and two modes of *Diameter* dimensioning, together with the *Center Mark* option. The *View* options and the *Association Lock* check box are the same as found with the linear dimensioning tools.

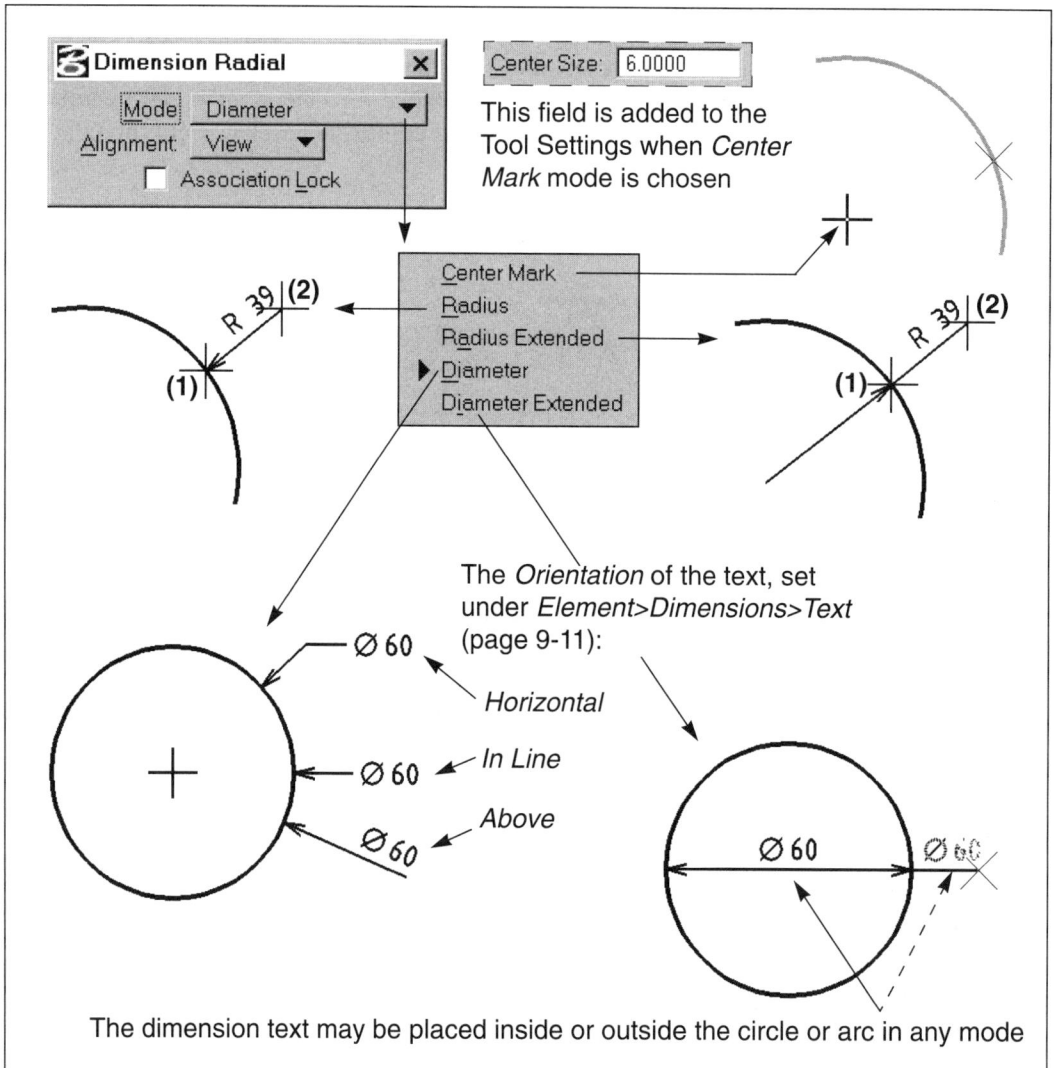

Figure 9.29   Modes of Radial Dimensioning

Dimension Tool Box - Change and Tolerance

This last section of the tool box has two tools with totally different applications. One is used to update the style of dimensions already placed, the other to build a *Feature Control Frame* containing the symbols for use in indicating *Geometric Tolerancing*.

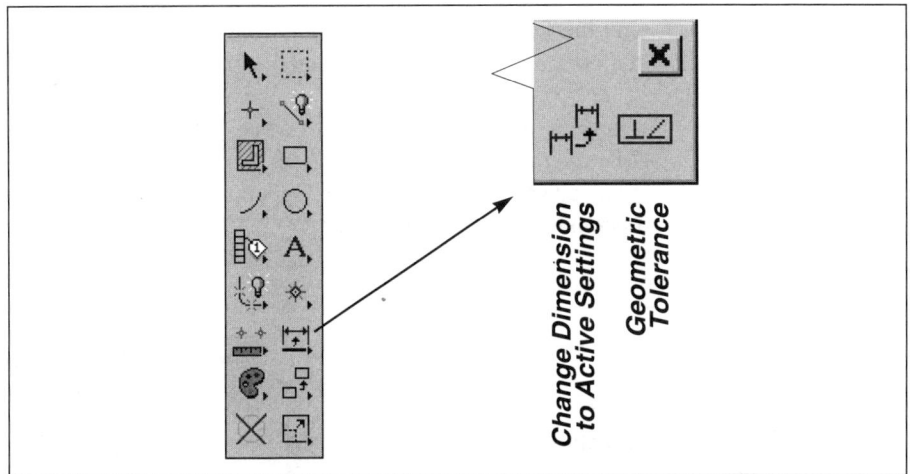

Figure 9.30   The Dimension Tool Box, the miscellaneous tools

The Change Dimension to Active Attributes Tool

The active dimension settings can be imposed on existing dimension elements by identifying the dimension with this tool. It can be used in conjunction with *Match All Element Settings* (the *"SmartMatch"* tool, see page 8-28) to change one existing dimension element to match another.

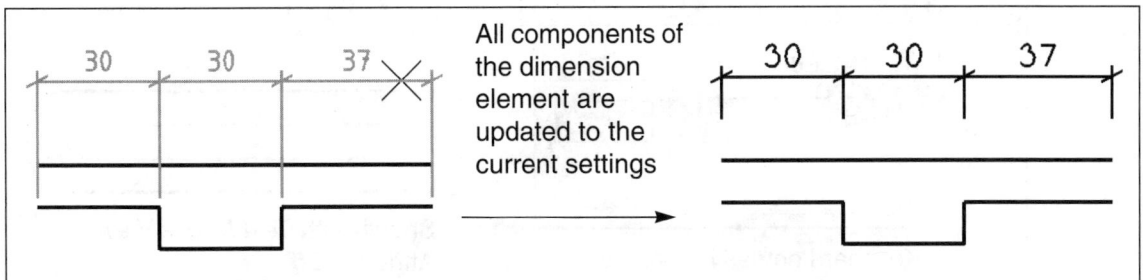

Figure 9.31   Changing style of existing Dimension Elements

The Geometric Tolerance Tool

We can use this tool to specify permissible deviations of a manufactured item from the design geometry. It generates a *Feature Control Frame* using a combination of standard symbols and ordinary uppercase text.

When we select the tool, the *Geometric Tolerance* settings box opens (see Figure 9.32). It has a *Font* menu, usually with two options, the ANSI Symbols font (100) and the Feature Control Symbols font (101, the default). The active text font will temporarily change to the chosen one of these while the settings box remains open.

The *Text Editor* window also opens. When one of the buttons in the *Geometric Tolerance* settings box are pressed, its equivalent character (usually lower case) will be displayed in the *Text Editor.* Upper case characters may be keyed in to the window to complete the specification.

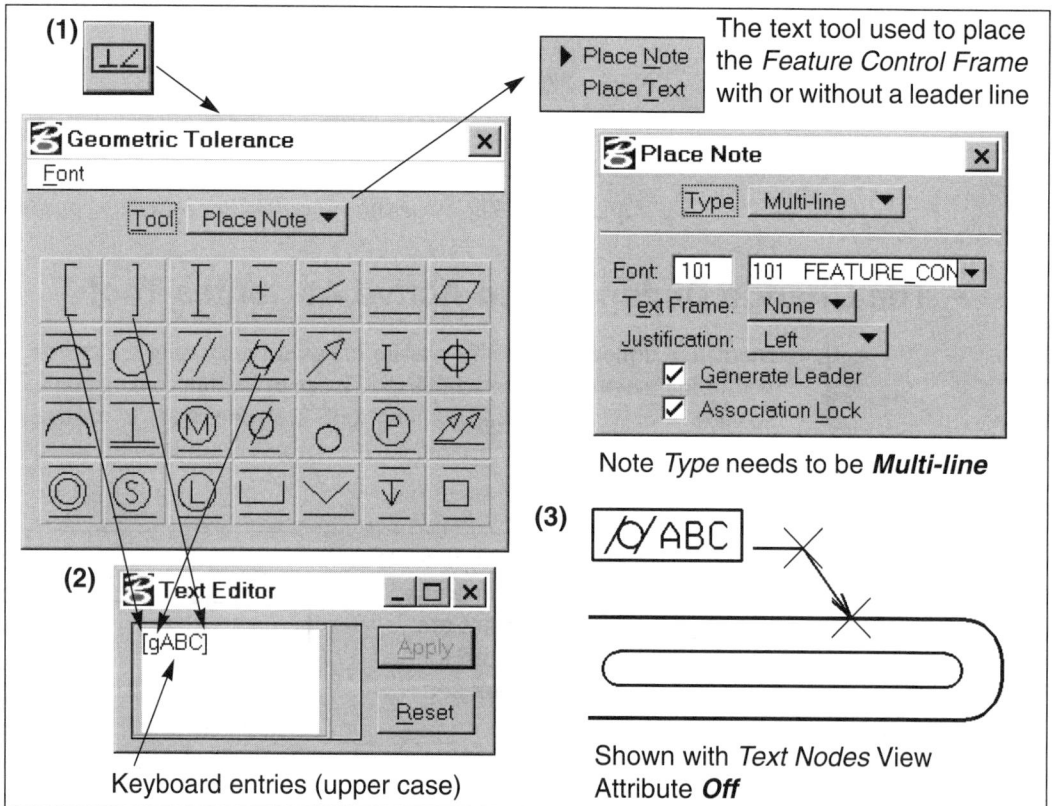

Figure 9.32 Placing a Feature Control Frame

Dimensioning Practice

We have been introduced to the tools and settings associated with the dimensioning process, now it is time for a practical exercise. We will dimension the Stay Plate created in "second.dgn", using a style that best suits your own needs. Leave the dimensioning of the Pivot Pin for now. The style of dimensioning on the Stay Plate as shown in Figure 9.33 is one example only. The standards you apply in the following exercise, including dimension text size, will be your own.

◆ Dimension the Stay Plate and Pivot Pin

1. Open "second.dgn", keep the original stay plate and pivot pin and "Stay Plate" text, delete all other unrelated elements on all levels.

2. Decide on a dimension text size, constrain it to these settings under *Element>Dimensions>Text* (see "Dimension Settings" on page 9-11).

3. Constrain the dimension elements to fall on level **63** under *Element>Dimensions>Dimension Lines* (page 9-13).

4. Work through the other dimension settings as required, making any changes needed to suit your particular standard style.

5. Place Dimensions using the tools introduced earlier, snapping to the geometry as and where required.

6. Experiment with different settings, use the *Change Dimension to Active Attributes tool* to update existing dimensioning.

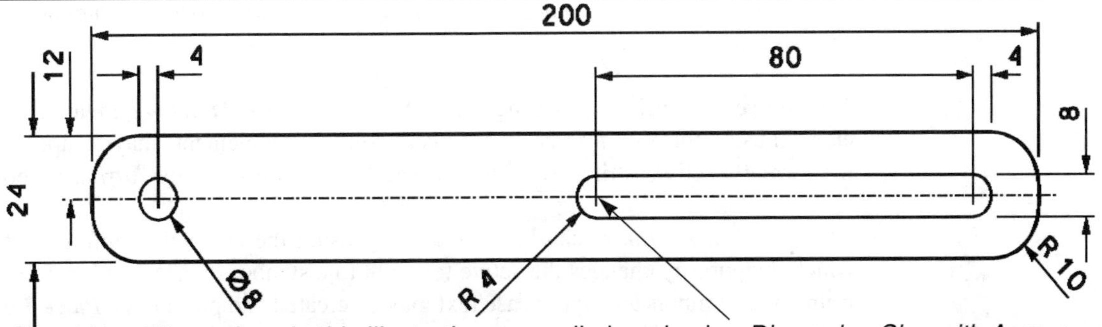

The *Linear* dimensions in this illustration were all placed using *Dimension Size with Arrows*. The dimension points at the center of the circle and arcs were located with *Center* snaps to the element, thus the extension lines overlap the *Center Marks*. An alternative is to place center marks first, then *Keypoint* snap to these.

Figure 9.33 The Stay Plate with Dimensioning

Summary

The *Dimension Element* is a complex element made up from lines, arcs, text and in some cases, cells. The components of the element are *Dimension Text*, *Dimension Lines*, *Extension Lines*, *Terminators* and *Symbols*.

The *Attributes* of the various component parts of the complex element can be set independently of one another, or overall default settings used. There are a number of categories of setting used to define the dimension style. These settings are accessed via *Element>Dimensions* from the Application window menu. As well as overall settings, there are individually configurations possible for each of the dimensioning tools, under the *Tool Settings* category.

Dimensions may be placed with a "general purpose" tool titled *Dimension Element*, or with a variety of more specialized tools. Regardless of the tool used to place them, dimensions may be made *Associative*. When a dimension is *Associated* with a point on an element, it automatically updates if the point is moved by an element manipulation or modification. These associations are made when *Association Lock* is **On** by preceding the data point defining a dimensioned point with a *Snap* to the element.

The dimension line may optionally be made *Relative* to the first dimension point placed. When this is the case, it will move to maintain the length of the first extension line if the dimensioned point is moved.

The units and the unit format for dimensioning is partially independent from the design file coordinate readout settings. The accuracy (decimal places) settings, angle format etc. are set under the *Units* and *Unit Format* categories of *Element>Dimensions*.

The *Active* dimensioning settings may be changed by *Matching* to an existing element using the *SmartMatch* tool. Existing dimension elements may be updated to the currently active settings with the *Change Dimensions to Active Attributes* tool.

Feature Control Frames can be generated by using the *Geometric Tolerance* tool, which temporarily changes the active text font to a symbol font. A combination of a frame with symbols and upper case text may be created and placed as a *Place Text* or a *Place Note* operation.

10 : Reference Files

Reference files are not special files, they are ordinary MicroStation design files or raster image files. What *is* special is the way we can combine large numbers of individual files to produce a single drawing, using the file *Referencing* technique. A *Reference* file is a file that is *Attached* to the *Active* design file. The active design file is the one we are working on at the time, the only design file that we can actually modify.

A *Reference Design* file that is *Attached* can be displayed and printed in part or full, it can optionally be snapped to and copied from, but it cannot be modified in any way. A *Reference Raster* file may be modified by the referencing process, thus it is usually a duplicate file that is attached.

When you have completed this chapter, you will be aware of the benefits of *File Referencing* to the design production process. You will be able to:

- Attach Reference Design Files and Reference Raster Files, using *Coincident* and *Saved View* attachment modes;

- Manipulate both *Design* and *Raster* format reference file attachments;

- Control the display of reference design files with the individual *Level* and *Level Symbology* settings;

- Integrate *Design* and *Raster* reference file geometry with the active design for document production.

Creating a Workspace User Configuration

When we start working with *Reference Files* we will need to configure MicroStation to be able to find a path to these files. The most efficient way to store a definition of these paths is in a *Workspace*.

When MicroStation is installed on a network, the Network Administrator may make configuration arrangements (such as directory paths to certain files) part of a particular *Project* or *Interface* workspace component. These components are selectable directly from the bottom panel options of *MicroStation Manager*. However, as individual users, we are able to make all of the configuration settings we are likely to need under *Workspace>Configuration* from the Application Menu.

We can change the *Workspace Components* in the bottom panel menus of *MicroStation Manager*. However, since the existing components (including the ones we are currently using) may be used as a basis for other workspaces, they are best left unchanged. In order to keep the supplied *User* components intact, we will create our very own workspace *User Configuration File* and modify this. We do this from MicroStation Manager.

◆ **Create a new Workspace**

1. Close any open design file, select **New** from the *User* options in the *Workspace* panel of the *MicroStation Manager* dialog box.
   The *Create User Configuration File* dialog box opens.

2. Name your new *User Configuration File*. The file extension ".ucf" will automatically be appended.
   The new user configuration (".ucf") and preference (".upf") files will be in the "Bentley \Workspace\users\" directory by default, but this path may be re-configured.

3. Click **OK** and the second *Create User Configuration File* dialog box opens, with your workspace name in the title bar. Key in a description.

4. Select . . .***Workspace\projects\tutorials\intro.pcf*** for the *Project* component and **Default** for the *User Interface* component.

5. Click **OK** to return to MicroStation Manager, where your new workspace will already be chosen.

Tip! If we need to rename or delete a workspace, it can be done from within MicroStation Manager (or Windows Explorer etc.) by renaming or deleting the ".ucf" and the ".upf" files. It is essential that we have another workspace selected before we do this.

User: [New...   ▼] ───► **Create User Configuration File**

1. This option is in the *User* menu of the   Name: [My Training]   [OK]
MicroStation Manager dialog box
                                                         Files: [examples.ucf ▲]   [Cancel]
                                                                 [mech2d.ucf]

Create User Configuration File [My training]
                                                                            ▼

Workspace

   Description: [Training User Configuration   ]   ...uration file.

   User Configuration: ...\Workspace\users\My training.ucf

Components   New *Project* and
                                                                            User Interface com-
   Project: intro   [Select...]   ponents may be
     ...\Workspace\projects\tutorials\intro.pcf   created, but the
                                                                            supplied ones are
   User Interface: default   [Select...]   generally OK for
     ...\interfaces\MicroStation\default\   trainee users

       [OK]   [Cancel]

Select Project Configuration File

Files: Directories:
[intro.pcf   ]   ...\Workspace\projects\tutorials\   [OK]

[intro.pcf   ]   📂 C:\   [Cancel]
[visualization.pcf   ]   📂 Bentley
                                        📂 Workspace   [Help]
                                          📂 projects
                                            📂 tutorials
                                              📁 intro
                                              📁 visualization

List Files of Type: Drives:
[*.pcf   ▼]   [c: ▼]

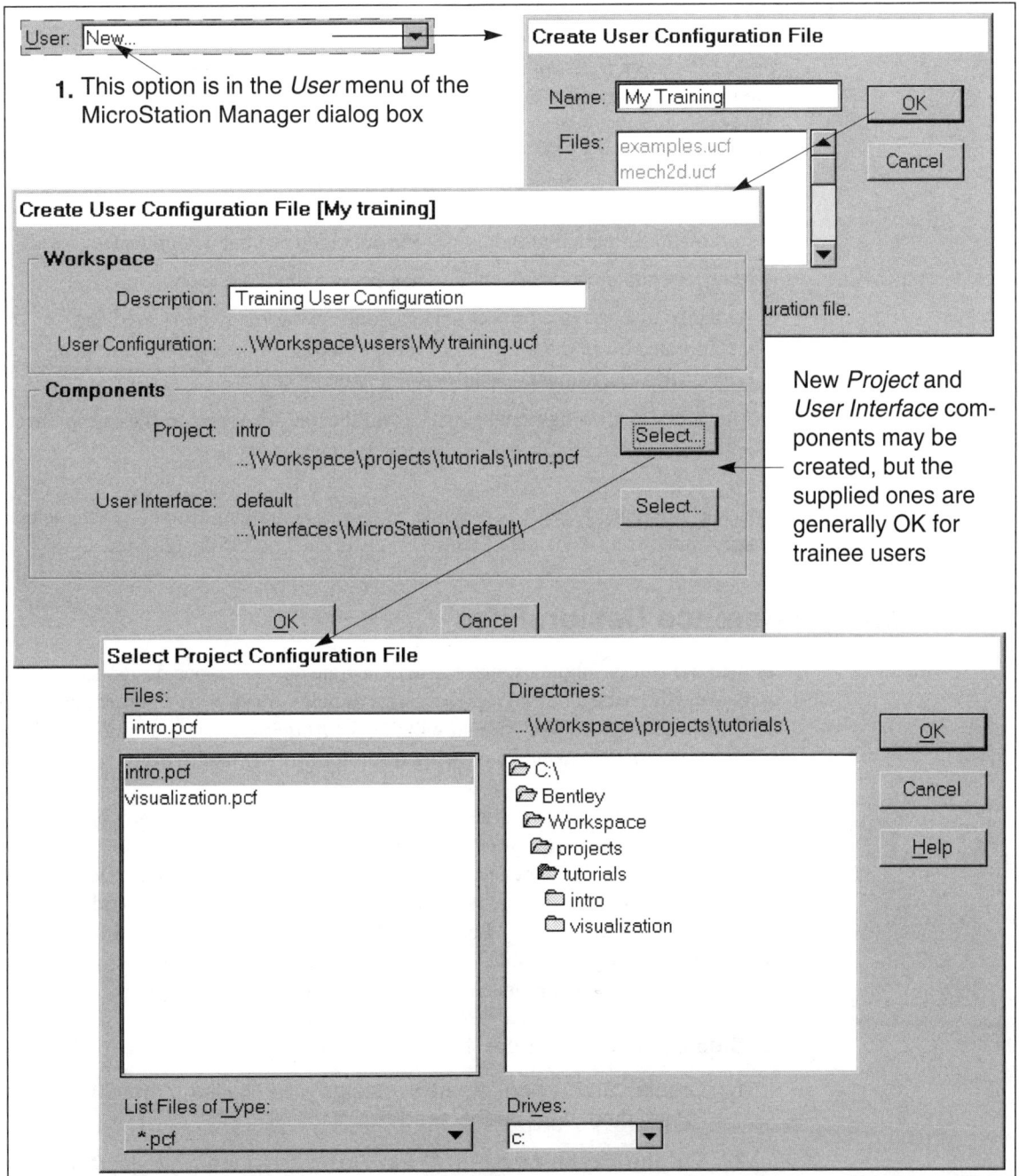

Figure 10.1   Creating our own Workspace User Configuration

Reference Design Files

Up to 255 design files can be attached as reference files to a single design, the actual maximum number for a particular MicroStation configuration is set under *Workspace>Preferences>Reference File*. There are many advantages to be gained from using reference files, when compared to the inclusion of all of the information in the one design file. Some of these advantages are:

- Information common to more than one drawing need not be duplicated;
- Many operators may work on the same project simultaneously;
- A change to a part of a project made by one operator may be viewed and incorporated by an other operators while working on their parts of the same project (this can happen instantly over a network);
- An variety of drawings can be made from the one set of design files, each one optimized with the information required by a particular user.

By using reference files, it is possible for a single drawing to incorporate selected design components from any of the 63 levels in each of 255 design files.

Using Reference Design Files

We will use a very simple example to demonstrate how reference design files may be used. We will create a design representing a drawing sheet, with a border and a basic title block. The "Stay Plate" design will then be *Attached* to the drawing sheet file as a *Reference File*, to make up a drawing ready for printing and issue.

The intention of the following exercise is to produce a sheet that may be used with the printer associated with your hardware arrangements. It will be saved as a *Seed File* to allow other files to be created as similar "drawing sheets". The sizes of border indicated are to fit within "A4" (297 X 210), with allowance for the margins required. If your printer uses "Letter" (279 X 216) or another size, or if the margins do not suit, modify the border size accordingly. Figure 10.2 shows one possible design, but the one you produce may be entirely of your own design.

◆ Create a Drawing Sheet

1. Create and open a new design file called "me0001", using "seed2dmm.dgn" as the seed file.

2. Set the *Active Level* to *1*, the *Color* and *Line Style* to *0*, the *Line Weight* to *3*.

3. Use the *Place Block* tool to place a border rectangle to suit the size of paper used by your printer, allowing for margins. The lower-left corner should be placed at the *Global Origin.*

Hint!   277(*x*) X 190(*y*) is usually printable on A4 size paper, 260 X 196 on Letter size.

4. Reduce the *Line Weight* to **2**, select the *Place SmartLine* tool to place a line string for the title block. Start from a tentative point at the lower-right vertex, offset the AccuDraw origin from this point for the start.

5. Place text and *Enter Data Fields* (see "Enter Data Fields" on page 8-34) as required.

6. Use *File>Save As* to save this design for later use as a *Seed File* with a name such as "a4sheet.dgn" (see "Creating a New Seed File" on page 3-36). Re-open "me0001.dgn".

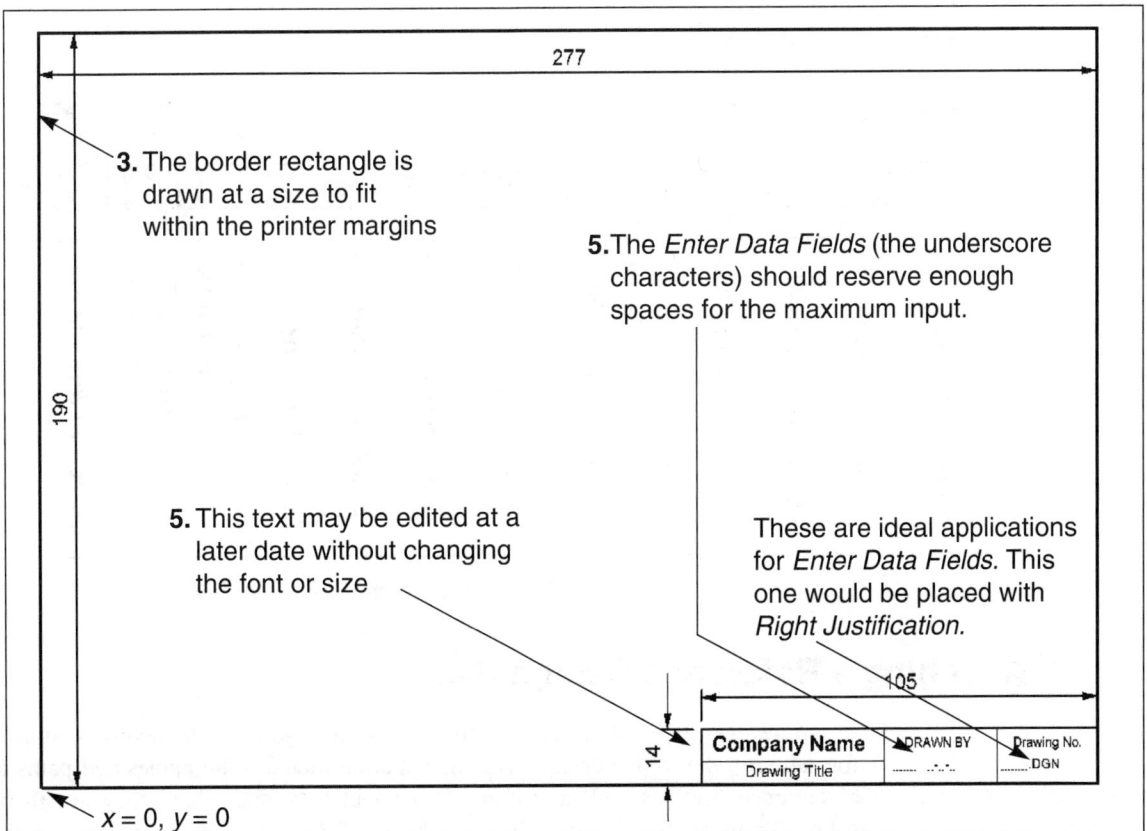

Figure 10.2   A design for a simplified A4 size drawing sheet

The Reference Files Tools

The tools we use to work with *Reference Files* may be accessed two ways:

- From the *Reference Files* tool box, opened under *Tools>Reference Files*, see Figure 10.3.
- From the *Tools* options menu in the *Reference Files* settings box, opened under *File>Reference*, see Figure 10.4;

We will be using the settings box for the following exercises, as more information is available and more settings can be made from within this box. However, the tool box has the advantage of single-click selection and it occupies less screen space. Figure 10.3 shows the tools that are available from the tool box, but all of these are also available from the *Reference Files* settings box *Tools* menu.

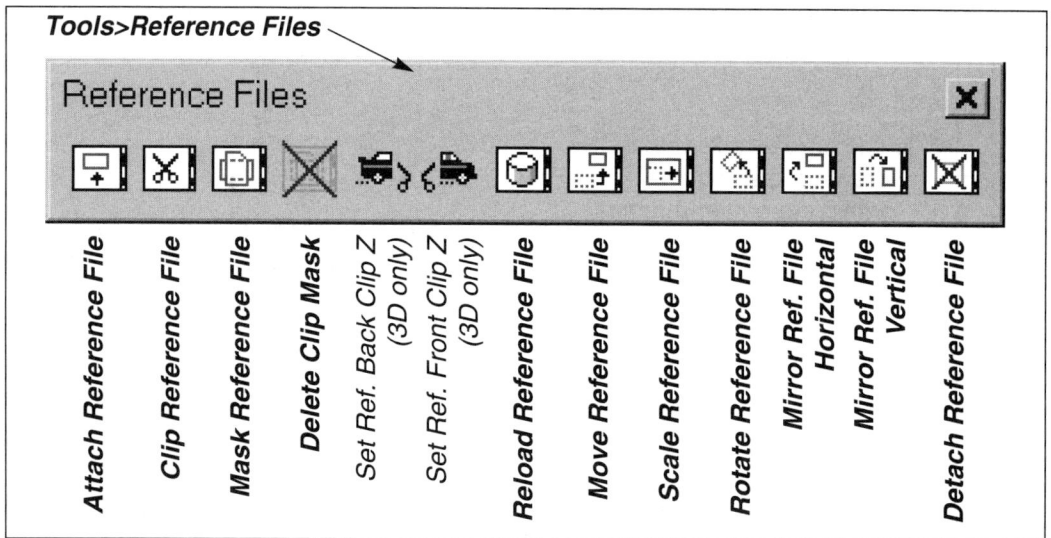

Figure 10.3   The Reference Files tool box

Attaching a Reference Design File

The *Attachment* of each reference file to another design file involves storing information in the *Active* design. This information includes the names and paths to the reference files, as well as information about how and where they are to be displayed, how much will be visible etc. None of this information is stored in the reference files, these files are not altered in any way.

◆ **Attaching "second.dgn" as a Reference File**

1. With "me0001.dgn" reopened, choose *File>Reference.*

    The *Reference Files* settings box opens, by default it will have *Design Files (0)* showing in its Title bar. If it shows *Raster Files (0)*, change to *Design* under the settings box *Display* menu.

2. Choose *Attach* from the settings box *Tools* menu.

    The first of two dialog boxes opens, this one titled *Preview Reference.*

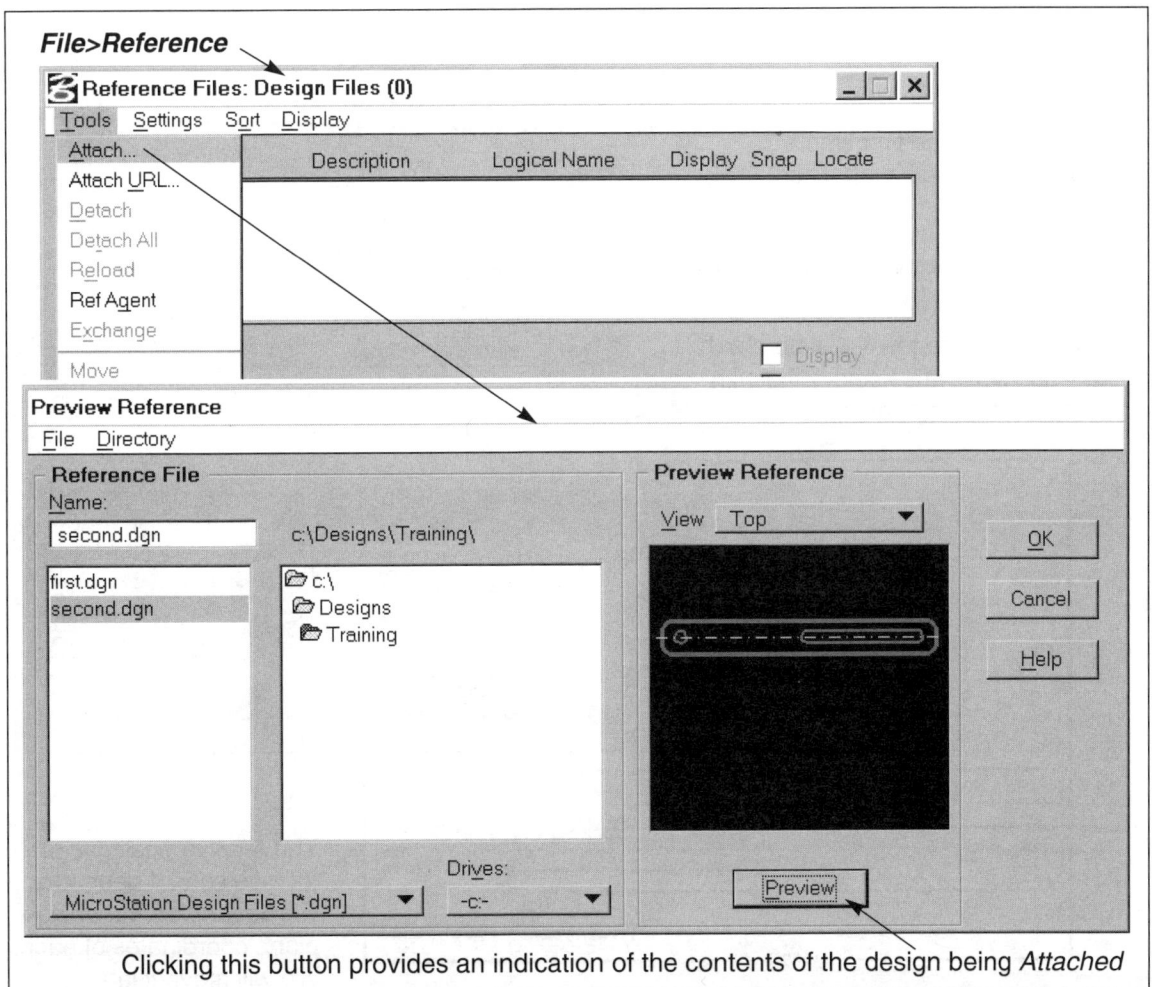

Figure 10.4   Opening the Preview Reference File dialog box

3. Select "second.dgn" (the file with the Stay Plate and Pivot Pin design) from the *Preview Reference* dialog box, click **OK** and the *Attach Reference File* dialog box opens.

We select *Which File to Attach* in the *Preview Reference* dialog box. We define *How to Attach it* in the *Attach Reference File* dialog box.

4. Fill in the attachment details as shown in Figure 10.5, click **OK** and the stay plate will appear as a *Reference File* to "me0001.dgn".

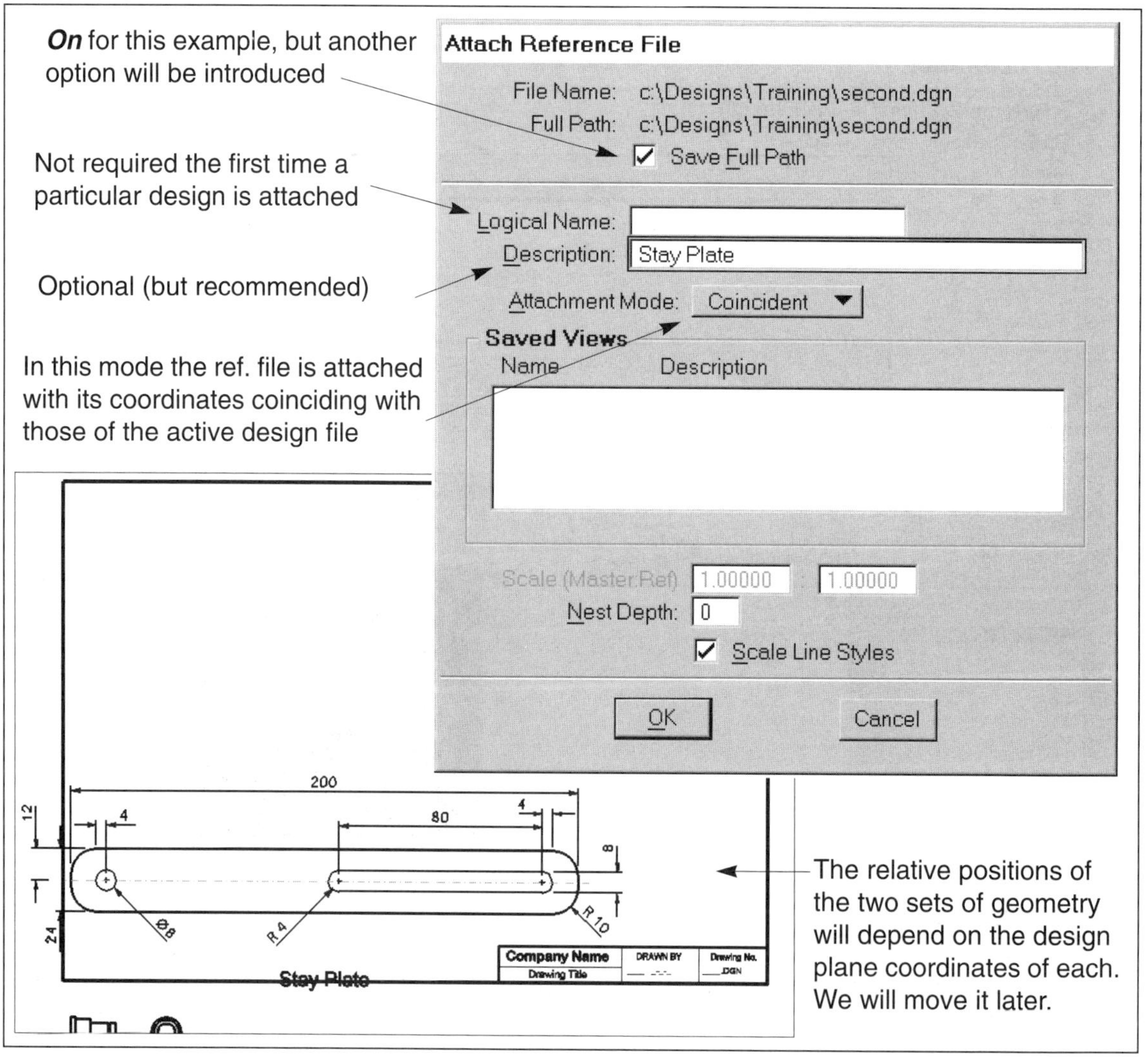

On for this example, but another option will be introduced

Not required the first time a particular design is attached

Optional (but recommended)

In this mode the ref. file is attached with its coordinates coinciding with those of the active design file

Attach Reference File

| File Name: | c:\Designs\Training\second.dgn |
| Full Path: | c:\Designs\Training\second.dgn |

☑ Save Full Path

Logical Name:
Description: Stay Plate

Attachment Mode: Coincident ▼

Saved Views
Name   Description

Scale (Master:Ref)   1.00000 : 1.00000
Nest Depth: 0

☑ Scale Line Styles

OK   Cancel

The relative positions of the two sets of geometry will depend on the design plane coordinates of each. We will move it later.

200
80
4
12 4 8
24 ∅8 R 4 R 10

Company Name | DRAWN BY | Drawing No.
Drawing Title | | .DGN

Stay Plate

Figure 10.5   Coincident attachment of a Reference File

Moving the Referenced Geometry

Designs are sometimes created with their elements placed in their "real world" positions using a standard coordinate system, such as a mapping grid. When these design file are attached to one another in *Coincident* mode, their coordinate systems will coincide. This means that two maps, created this way and referenced together, will display their individual features in the correct positions in relation to one another.

Drawings such as the Stay Plate and the Drawing Sheet do not have designated positions in the "real world". When the Stay Plate was attached to the Drawing Sheet in the last exercise, the geometry did not appear where we will finally need it (see Figure 10.5). In the next exercise, we will move the *Reference File* (the Stay Plate) into position on the *Active File* (the drawing sheet), using AccuDraw to place it precisely. It may also be placed freehand, but AccuDraw provides more control.

The Move Reference File Tool

We can select this tool from the *Reference Files* tool box, or choose it from the *Tools* menu of the *Reference Files* settings box. We will use the latter method at this stage. We place two data points to move a reference file with this tool, the first one represents a *Point To Move From*, the second is the *Point To Move To*. It does not really matter where these points are placed with respect to the reference file geometry. The move is defined by the distance and direction between the two points.

It is usual to define the *Point To Move From* by snapping a tentative point to a particular feature on the reference geometry and *Accepting*. The new position of this feature may then be defined by snapping to another location, probably using an offset from this tentative point to complete the move. The distances in the following exercises are designed to position the reference file in an A4 sized sheet. The distances may need to be changed, or the moves made freehand if your version of "me0001.dgn" is designed for a different paper size.

◆ Move the first Reference File

1. Make sure that the *Display*, *Snap* and *Locate* check boxes are *On* in the *Reference Files* settings box, choose **Move** from the settings box *Tools* menu.

2. *Keypoint* snap to the *Center* of the circular hole on the left end of the plate, *Accept* to "Enter the point to move from".

3. *Keypoint* snap to the top-left corner of the border, offset (<**O**>) the AccuDraw origin **50** to the right and **60** down from this point, *Accept*.

The View window should now show the Stay Plate in a suitable position on the drawing sheet file (see Figure 10.6). We will not need the Pivot Pin for now as we will reference that in separately later on, so we will *Clip* this off in the next exercise.

The Define Reference File Clipping Boundary Tool

This is the full name of the tool, but it is abbreviated to "Clip Boundary" in the *Reference Files* settings box *Tools* menu. The same tool displays the tool tip "Clip Reference File" in the tool box. With it we can clip off the display of any reference geometry falling outside a *Fence* placed before the tool is activated.

The *Clip* may be redefined by placing a new fence and choosing the tool again. We may place the fence about the entirety of the reference geometry (even though it is not all displayed) to fully restore it. The *Clip Boundary* does not rotate when a View window is rotated.

◆ **Clip the reference file to remove Pivot Pin component**

1. Place a fence about the Stay Plate, its text and dimensioning.

2. Choose **Clip Boundary** from the settings box *Tools* menu.
   The clip takes place and the tool cancelled without any further actions.

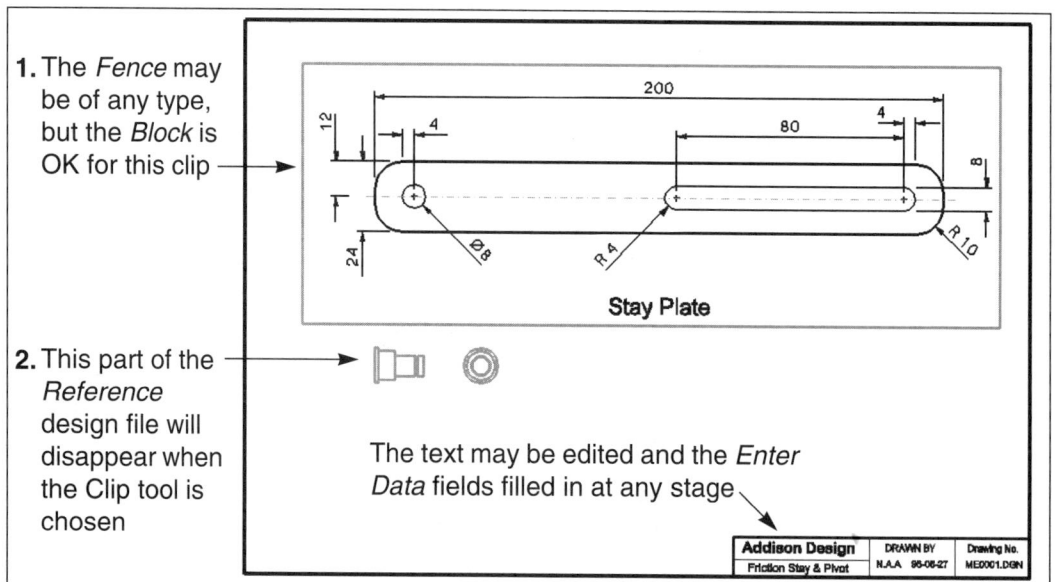

Figure 10.6 Using a fence as a Clip Boundary with a reference attachment

Reference Design File Attachment Options

The reference attachment of "second.dgn" to "me0001.dgn" was made using mostly default settings. We will now introduce more of the detail related to each of the options available in the second *Attach Reference File* dialog box.

Directory Path

We checked *Save Full Path **On*** in the last exercise to provide a path for MicroStation to find the reference file the next time "me0001.dgn" is opened. This method, however, is not always the most efficient for setting the path to a reference file. The preferred method is to define paths to where reference files may be found, in the *Configuration* of MicroStation. There may be a number of these paths defined, to allow for design files to be kept in a variety of directories.

As stated above, if the reference file is not in one of the defined directories and the full path is not saved, it will not display the next time the active file is opened. The path to your files may not be defined as a *Primary Search Path* for reference files in your configuration, that is why we opted for the *Save Full Path* option. The disadvantage of taking this option is that the reference files are not "portable", that is they cannot be moved to another directory without re-defining their attachments.

If we do not check the *Save Full Path* box, the file can be moved to any directory in the set of *reference file paths* without having any effect on referencing. In the next exercise we will include your file path (for example "...\projects\tutorials\intro\dgn") in the *Primary Search Path* for reference files. We will set the path as a *User Level* workspace configuration in this case, but the administrator on a network installation may set this at a different level.

We created our own workspace on page 10-2, now we will make the first change to the "inherited" default user configuration.

◆ **Define a Path to Reference Files**

1. With "me0001.dgn" open, choose *Workspace>Configuration*.
    The *Configuration : User* dialog box for your workspace opens.

2. Choose *Primary Search Paths* from the *Category* panel, *Reference Files* from the *Set Paths* panel.

The current settings for the paths are shown in Figure 10.7, the "as delivered" configuration of MicroStation for the workspace components currently in use. We will leave these paths intact and add another.

3. Click the **Select** button and the *Select Path For Reference Files* dialog box opens.

4. Select the new path to your design files being attached as reference files (i.e. "...\projects\tutorials\intro\dgn"), click the **Add** button.

   This step may be repeated for additional paths, any unwanted paths may be deleted with the **Remove** button.

5. Click the **Done** button when the selection of path(s) is completed.

6. Click **OK** in the *Configuration* dialog box and again in the *Alert* box to write the change to your *User Configuration File*.

Note: Clicking the **Edit** button (instead of **Select**) allows more advanced editing of the paths, including *Prepending* and *Appending* search paths to change the search order. If two designs with the same name exist in different folders, the first to be found is the one that is attached.

From now on any files in the selected directories may be used as reference files without checking the *Save Full Path* box. If we move these files into a different directory at a later date, we only need to change the *Reference File Primary Search Path* in our workspace configuration. If we use the *Save Full Path* option, it would be necessary to change every reference file attachment in the event of the reference files being moved to another directory.

Defining Individual Attachments

After the decision of *Which* design file to attach has been made using the *Preview Reference* dialog box, we must define *How* it is to be attached. We do this in the *Attach Reference File* dialog box (see Figure 10.8), which is opened by *Preview*.

Logical Name

A logical name is necessary when a particular file is attached more than once, but it is optional in other circumstances. The logical name may be up to 20 characters long, but it is usually much shorter. MicroStation must have a logical name for each attachment of a particular file in order to identify the individual attachments. The ordinary file name is used when there is only one attachment.

When we are using tools from the Reference Files tool box we may need to key in (to the *Key-in window* utility) the name of a reference file for the tool to operate on. Under these circumstances we may key-in the *Logical* or the *File* name for single attachments, but we must use the *Logical* name when the same file is attached more than once.

Workspace>Configuration

Configuration : User [My training]

File

Set default search paths for locating files.

Category				
All (Alphabetical)	Design Files	User		OK
All (By Level)	Reference Files	System		
Archive	Visible MDL Applications	System		Cancel
Cells	MDL Applications	System		
Colors	Macros	System		
Database				

Select...   Edit...   Delete   New...

Expansion

C:\Bentley\Workspace\projects\tutorials\intro\dgn\
c:\bentley\workspace\standards\dgn\
c:\designs\training\

Description

Search path for reference files. (MS_RFDIR)

Category list:
Data Files
Design Applications
Engineering Links
Extensions
MDL Development
OLE
Operation
Plotting
Primary Search Paths
Rendering/Images
Seed Files
Sy...

Select Path for Reference Files

Directory

c:\Designs\Training\

🗁 c:\
  🗁 Designs
    🗁 Training

Done

Cancel

Help

Directory List

c:\bentley\workspace\projects\tutorials\intro\dgn\
c:\bentley\workspace\standards\dgn\
c:\designs\training\

Add

Remove

4. The new path to your reference files is selected in the upper panel, then clicking the **Add** button appends it after the existing path or paths.

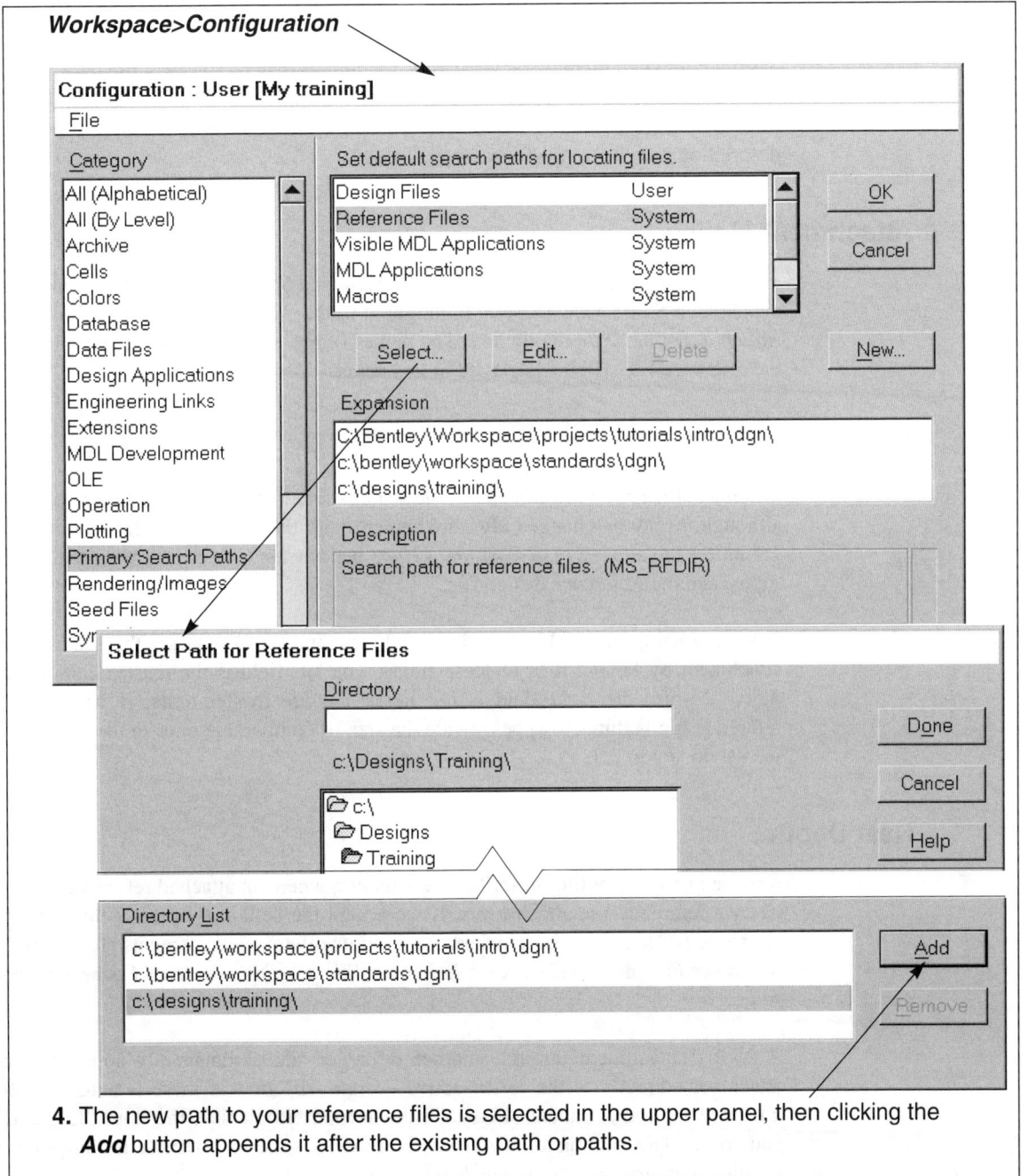

Figure 10.7   Choosing the Reference Files primary search path for configuration

Description

A description for a reference file attachment is optional, but it is generally worthwhile when there are several attachments. This is particularly the case when a file is attached more than once. The description displays in the lower panel *Reference Files* settings box when a particular attachment is highlighted in the upper panel. The description may be up to 40 characters long.

Attachment Modes

There are two modes of attachment, *Coincident* and *Saved View*. For this option to be available, a *Saved View* must be highlighted in the *Saved Views* panel of the second *Attach Reference File* dialog box. The names of any saved views (see page 1-27) in the reference file will be displayed in this panel.

Scale

When an attachment is *Coincident*, the scale is fixed during the attachment process, although it may be changed after attachment with the *Scale* tool. The scale will be *1:1* unless the allocation of *Positional Units* per *Master Unit* is different between the *Active* and the *Reference* design file.

If we are using *Saved View* as the attachment mode, we can set the scale of the attachment by keying it in to these fields. The left field is the master units of the *Active* design, the right field is the *Reference file* master units. If we want an reference file features to appear twice the size of comparable ones in the active file, we would key in *2:1*.

Nest Depth

Nesting of reference files describes the situation where an attached reference file has its own reference file attachments. If we accept the default *0* in this field, only the reference file itself will be attached, ignoring its reference attachments. To attach the *Reference File* along with its own *Reference File*, a nesting depth of *1* is needed, and so on.

A *Nested* attachment through another reference file automatically appears as an attachment directly to the to the active design. The first of these is automatically allocated the logical name "Logical", the second "Logical0", the third "Logical1" and so on. The automatic attachment is initially made to resemble the original in position, clipping etc., but it may be changed.

Scale Line Style

Unlike standard line styles, *Custom Line Styles* (to be introduced in Chapter 11) have patterns of line strokes and gaps that have actual dimensions in the design. The scaling of these dimensions with the rest of the geometry is optional.

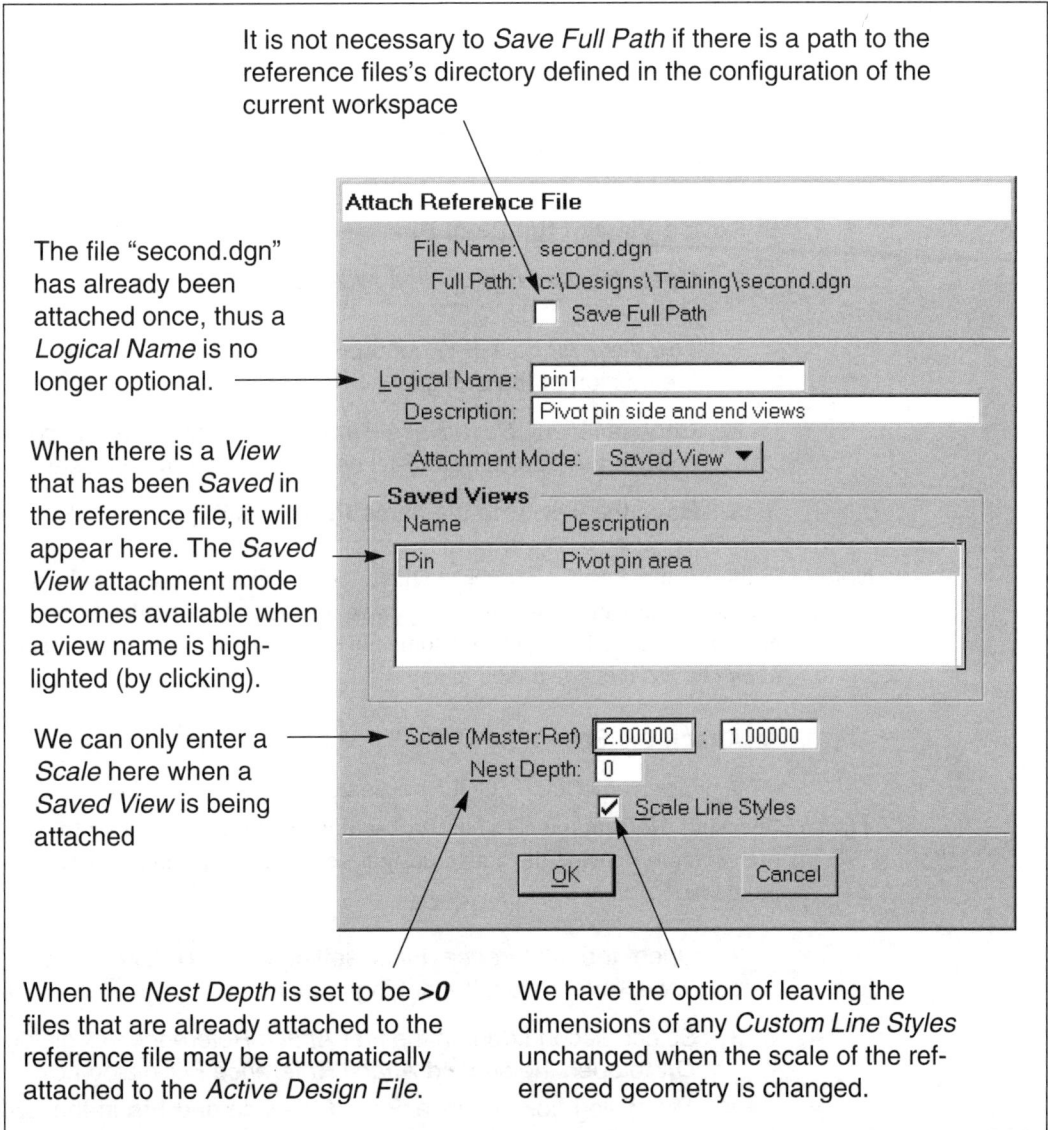

It is not necessary to *Save Full Path* if there is a path to the reference files's directory defined in the configuration of the current workspace

The file "second.dgn" has already been attached once, thus a *Logical Name* is no longer optional.

When there is a *View* that has been *Saved* in the reference file, it will appear here. The *Saved View* attachment mode becomes available when a view name is high-lighted (by clicking).

We can only enter a *Scale* here when a *Saved View* is being attached

Attach Reference File

File Name: second.dgn
Full Path: c:\Designs\Training\second.dgn
☐ Save Full Path

Logical Name: pin1
Description: Pivot pin side and end views

Attachment Mode: Saved View ▼

Saved Views

Name	Description
Pin	Pivot pin area

Scale (Master:Ref) 2.00000 : 1.00000
Nest Depth: 0
☑ Scale Line Styles

OK   Cancel

When the *Nest Depth* is set to be *>0* files that are already attached to the reference file may be automatically attached to the *Active Design File*.

We have the option of leaving the dimensions of any *Custom Line Styles* unchanged when the scale of the ref-erenced geometry is changed.

Figure 10.8   Attachment options in the Attach Reference File dialog box

Using the Saved View Attachment Mode

We can attach the same file as often as we like (up to the *Maximum Reference Files* configuration setting, see page 10-4). In the next example we will attach "second.dgn" once more, but this time using a *Saved View* of the *Pivot Pin* geometry.

Preparing the Reference File

The design file "second.dgn" probably does not have any *Saved Views* (page 1-27) at this stage, so we will start by re-opening the design and naming a view containing the Pivot Pin only. The view does not have to include all of the dimensioning, as this will be hidden after the file has been referenced.

◆ Save a View of the Pivot Pin

1. Open "second.dgn", *Window Area* about the two views of the Pivot Pin.

   The View window may optionally be re-sized to suit the proportions of the section of the design.

2. Choose *View Save/Recall* from the *View window control* menu, choose the appropriate *Source* view number if necessary.

3. **Save** the view with the name **Pin** and with your own description.

Note: In this example we have access to the reference file for changes to be made. In some networking situations we may only have access to a particular file on a *Read Only* basis, thus we would depend on someone else's *Saved Views*. A reference file may be *Read Only* as it is not altered in any way.

◆ Attach the Saved View "Pin"

1. Open "me0001", fit *All* the design.

Tip! Choosing *All* from the *Fit View* Tool settings window will ensure that any reference file geometry outside the active design area will be displayed, as well as the active design itself.

2. Open the *Reference Files* settings box (*File>Reference*), choose *Tools>Attach* from the settings box menu.

3. Select "second.dgn" in the first *Attach Reference File* dialog box, click **OK** to open the second *Attach Reference File* dialog box.

   The dialog box shows a *Saved View* named **Pin** in the *Saved Views* panel. The following settings are illustrated in Figure 10.8.

4. Set the *Save Full Path* check box *Off*, key in **Pin1** as the *Logical Name*, key in your *Description*.

5. Click the *Pin* row in the *Saved Views* panel.

    It will highlight and the *Attachment Mode* will automatically change to *Saved View*.

6. Enter *2* in the left *Scale* field, leave *Nest Depth* at zero, *Scale Line Styles* does not matter. Click *OK* and a dotted *Boundary* representing the area of the reference file geometry appears under the pointer.

7. Position this boundary in the lower-left area of the drawing sheet, *Accept* the attachment with a data point.

Tip!   Boundaries may be displayed permanently by checking *Ref. Boundaries* *On* in the *View Attributes* settings box, otherwise they disappear when the attachment is accepted.

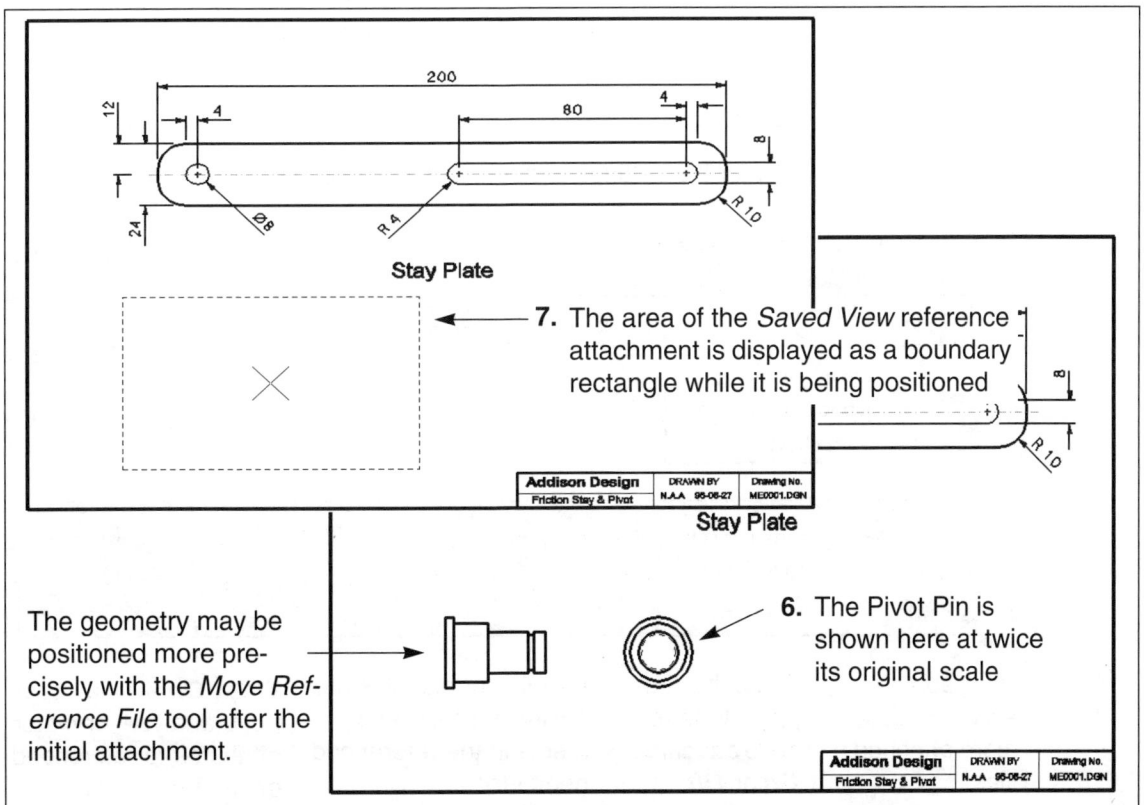

Figure 10.9 Attaching part of "second.dgn" using a Saved View

The Reference Files Settings Box Options

We have used some of the *Tools* options from this settings box, now we will work with the *Settings* options. There are check boxes for *Display*, *Snap* and *Locate* in the settings box itself. These settings define how a reference attachment may be used.

There is also a *Settings* option menu, with options for:

- *Attachment* - this option allows us to change the reference file used for a particular attachment, as well as the logical name and description;

- *Levels* - opens the *Reference Levels* settings box for the highlighted attachment, allowing the display of individual levels *On* and *Off*;

- *Level Symbology* - we may define individual level symbology settings for each attachment in exactly the same way as for the active design (page 3-22);

- *Update Sequence* - the sequence of "reading" files when a view is updated;

- *View Reference* - Displays an image of the highlighted reference file.

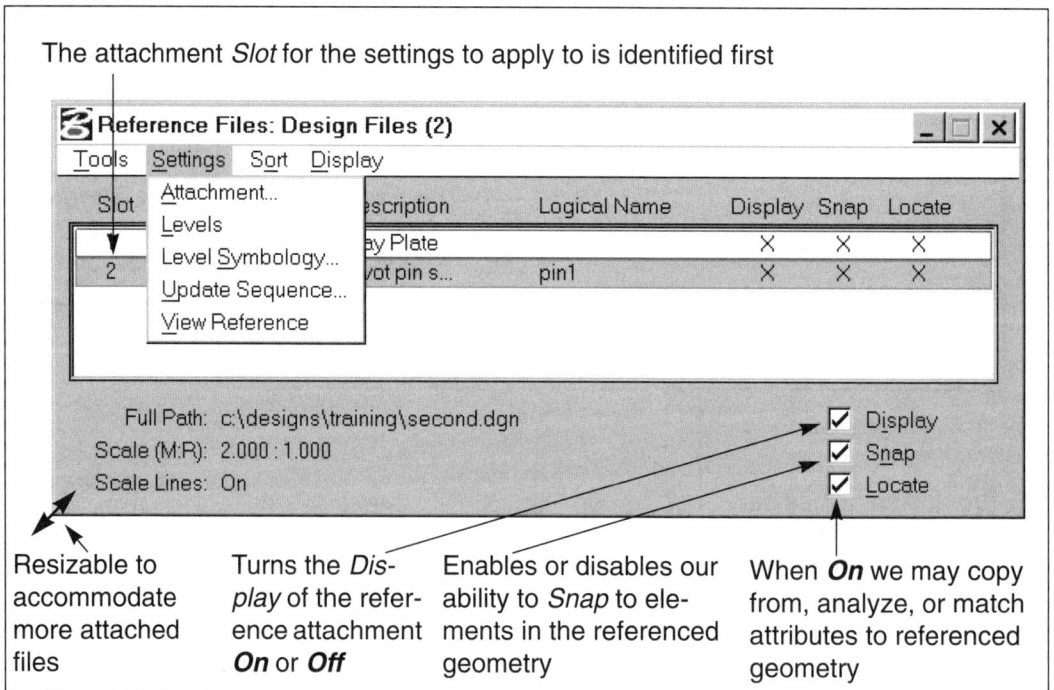

Figure 10.10   Reference File settings

Settings Menu Options

These settings apply to one reference attachment only. Each reference attachment made to our active design is allocated a *Slot Number* in the settings box, when there is only one attachment, the single slot is always highlighted. When we have multiple attachments we need to select the slot to be changed, then make the settings changes.

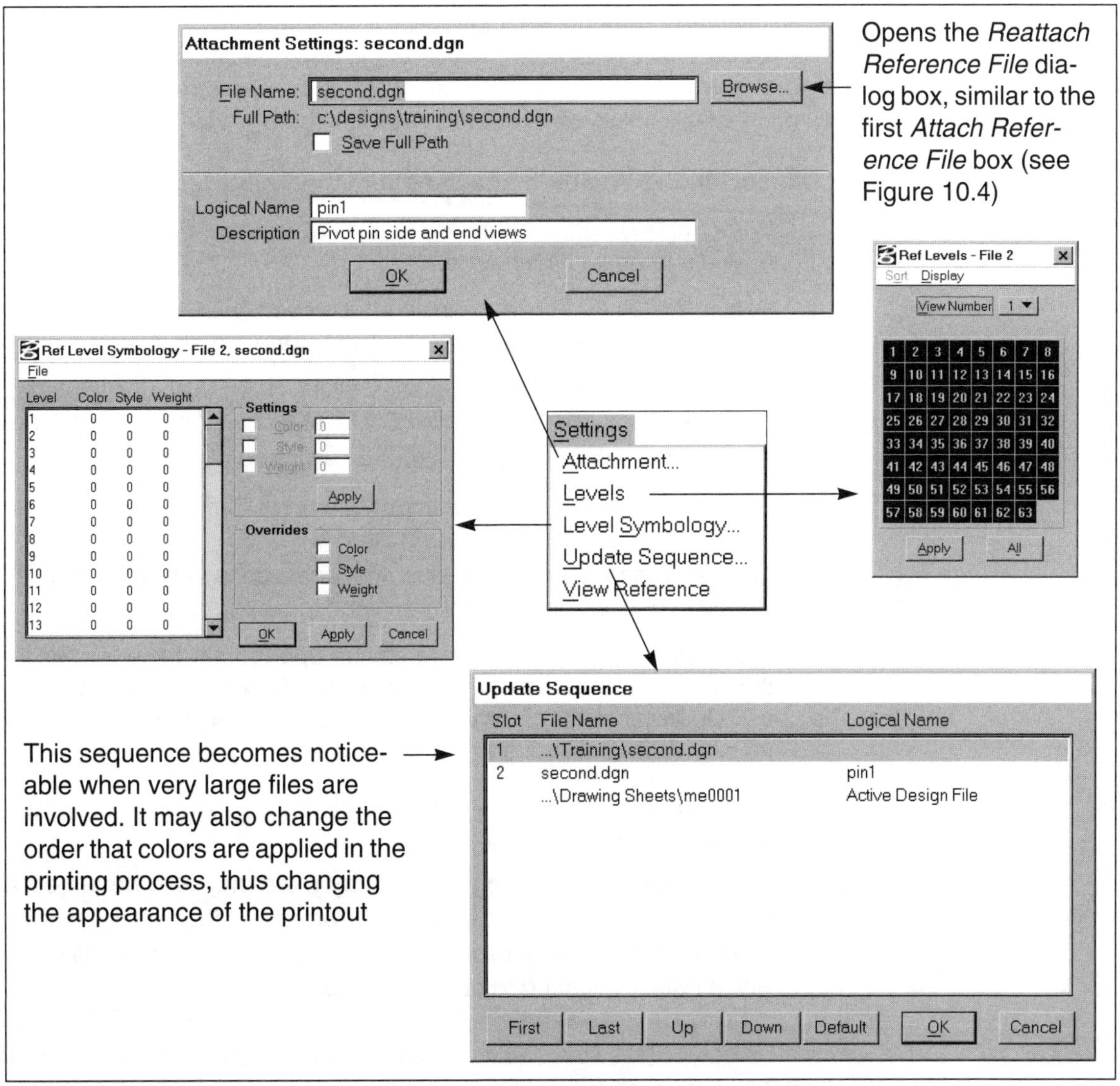

Figure 10.11   The Settings options

The fact that we have separate control on the level display of each of the reference attachments (as well as the active file) can be very useful. As an example, let us consider that the dimensioning in "second.dgn" is inappropriate in some way, perhaps the text size does not suit the scale we will use when it is printed. We will hide the existing dimensioning by turning *Off* the display of the level with the original dimensioning, then dimension the Pivot Pin in the *Active* file, "me0001.dgn".

With *Snap* turned *On* for the Pivot Pin attachment, we can snap our dimensioning to the referenced geometry as if it were part of the active design. In this example, we will make use of the *Scale Factor* setting in *Element>Dimensions* to place correct dimensions on the pin, despite the fact is now shown at twice full size.

◆ **Dimension the Pivot Pin attachment in the Active file**

1. With "me0001.dgn" open, open the *Reference Files* settings box (*File>Reference*) if necessary.

2. Select the Pivot Pin reference attachment (with the logical name "pin1"), ensure that *Display*, *Snap* and Locate are all *On*.

3. Choose **Levels** under the *Settings* dialog box menu (the *Reference Levels* settings box opens), turn **Off** level **63** and *Apply* the change.
   The dimensioning will now disappear, as it was placed on level 63.

4. Set the *Scale Factor* to **0.5** under *Element>Dimensions>Units* (see "Dimensioning Units settings" on page 9-22).
   The reference attachment was made at twice full size, thus this setting is necessary for the dimensions to be correct.

5. Make the other dimensioning settings appropriate to your style and the size that the sheet would print out. A *Text Size* of **2.5** to **3** is usually acceptable on small sheets, such as A4. Larger sheets are usually viewed from a greater distance and may need larger text.

6. Make (design file) level **63** *Active*, place dimensioning on the Pivot Pin as desired (see Figure 10.12).
   The existing dimensioning on the Stay Plate may also be turned **Off** as in steps **2.** and **3.** and replaced. Remember that this geometry is attached with a scale of **1 : 1**, so the *Element>Dimensions>Units> Scale Factor* will need to be set back to **1**.

We will make use of the *Locate* setting in the next exercise, where we will *Match* the text settings of the *Active* design to the text in a *Reference* Attachment. We will go on to use the *Analyze Element* tool to find information about the reference files.

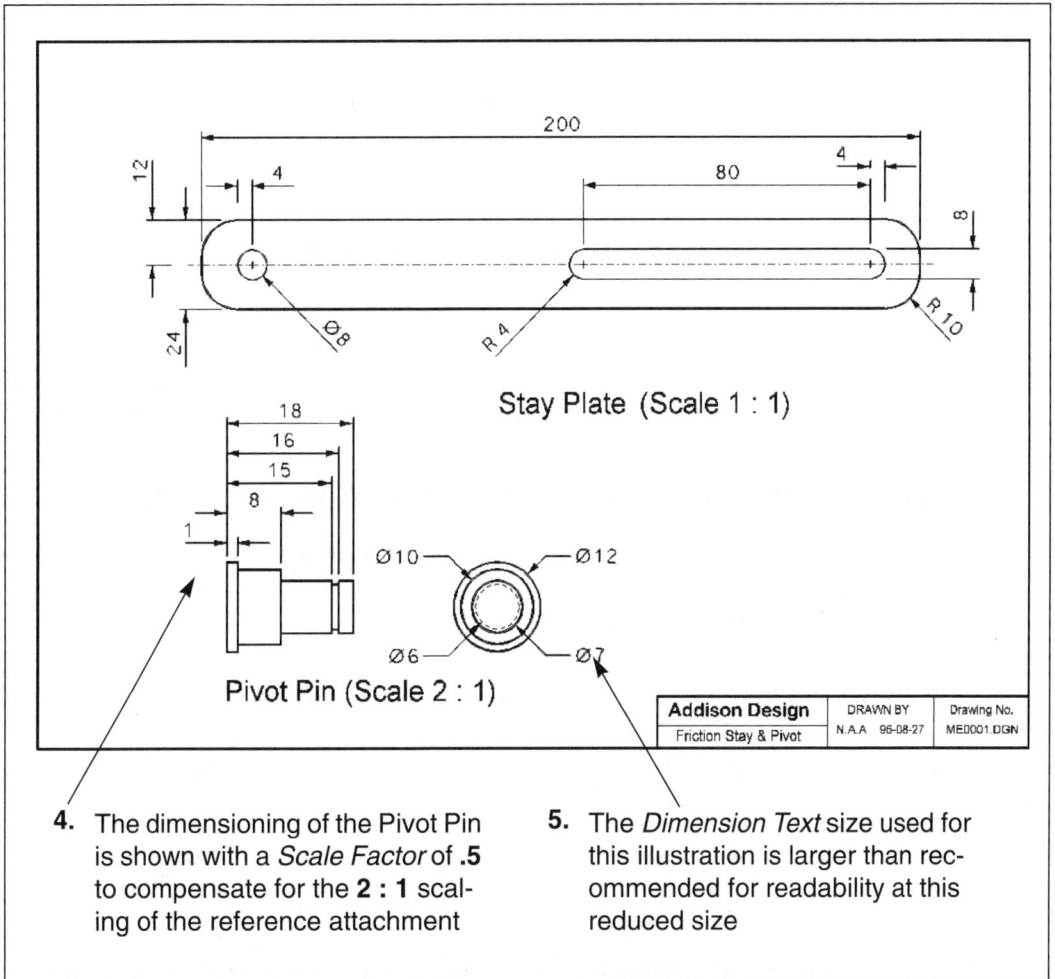

Figure 10.12   The completed drawing, "me0001.dgn" and Reference Files

◆ **Add matching text**

1. Open the *Match* tool box, select the *SmartMatch* tool (page 8-28), identify the text "**Stay Plate**" in the first attachment of the reference file, *Accept* to set the text and element attributes.

2. Use the *Place Text* tool to label the Pivot Pin views (see "The Place Text Tool" on page 8-6).

3. Add the **Scale** to the *Stay Plate* label. Use an AccuDraw *Offset* from the existing (referenced) text to align the new text.

More Reference File Tools

We have been able to create a drawing presentation using only the *Attach*, *Move* and *Clip Reference File* tools. We will now introduce the remaining tools for *Reference File* manipulation, most of which have *Active Design* equivalents in the *Manipulate* tool box.

The Mask Reference File or Clip Mask Tool

This tool is a reverse of the *Clip Boundary* (*Clip Reference File* in the tool box) tool already used on our first attachment of "second.dgn". A fence (any type) is used to mask out a section of the reference file. The fence is placed *before* selecting the tool, as we did when we used Clip Boundary. Multiple clip masks may be defined.

The Delete Clip Mask or Clip Mask Delete Tool

When this tool is selected, a *Clipping Mask* highlights. If this is the mask we wish to delete, we *Accept* with the data button, otherwise we *Reset* until the required mask highlights before *Accepting*.

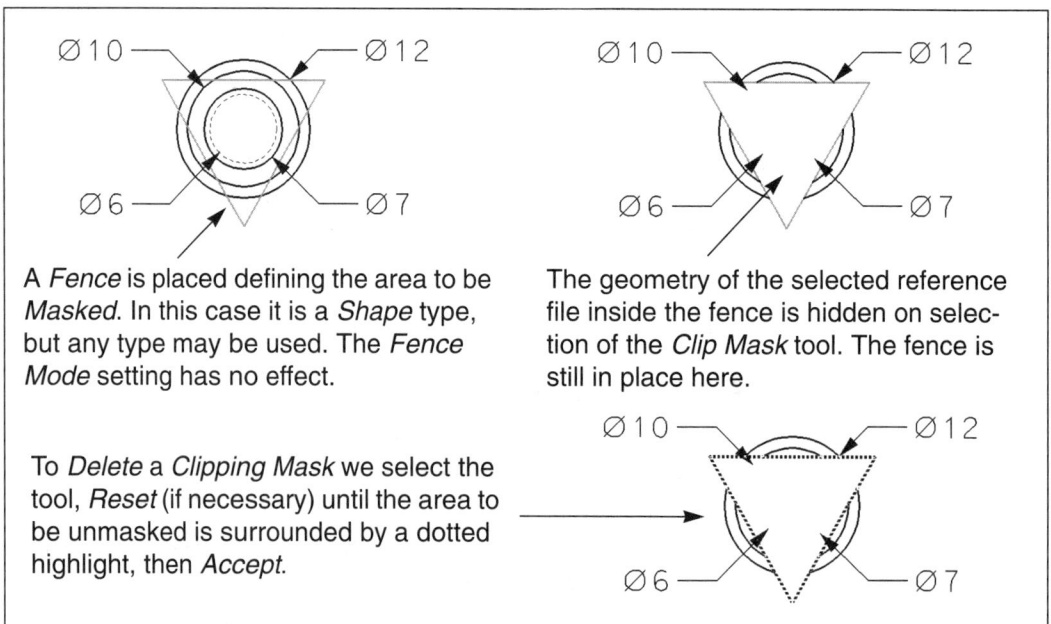

A *Fence* is placed defining the area to be *Masked*. In this case it is a *Shape* type, but any type may be used. The *Fence Mode* setting has no effect.

The geometry of the selected reference file inside the fence is hidden on selection of the *Clip Mask* tool. The fence is still in place here.

To *Delete* a *Clipping Mask* we select the tool, *Reset* (if necessary) until the area to be unmasked is surrounded by a dotted highlight, then *Accept*.

Figure 10.13   Masking and Deleting a Mask

The Reload Reference File Tool

When we first *Attach* a reference file or re-open a file with a reference file already attached, the attached file is loaded into a memory cache and displayed from there. If the file changes after attachment, the changes will not be reflected in the display until the file is *Reloaded* into memory. We use this tool in a network environment when we are using reference files that are subject to change.

The Scale Reference File Tool

We have already scaled a file as part of the *Saved View* attachment process. We can scale a file *after* it has been attached by using this tool. Files attached as *Coincident* may be scaled with it, whereas they could not be scaled in the process of their attachment.

This tool is similar in operation to its *Active Design* equivalent *Scale* tool, in that the features of the geometry are scaled about a point defined by the position of the screen pointer. It is probable that a *Scale* operation will need to be followed by a *Move* (page 10-9) operation to correctly position the scaled geometry.

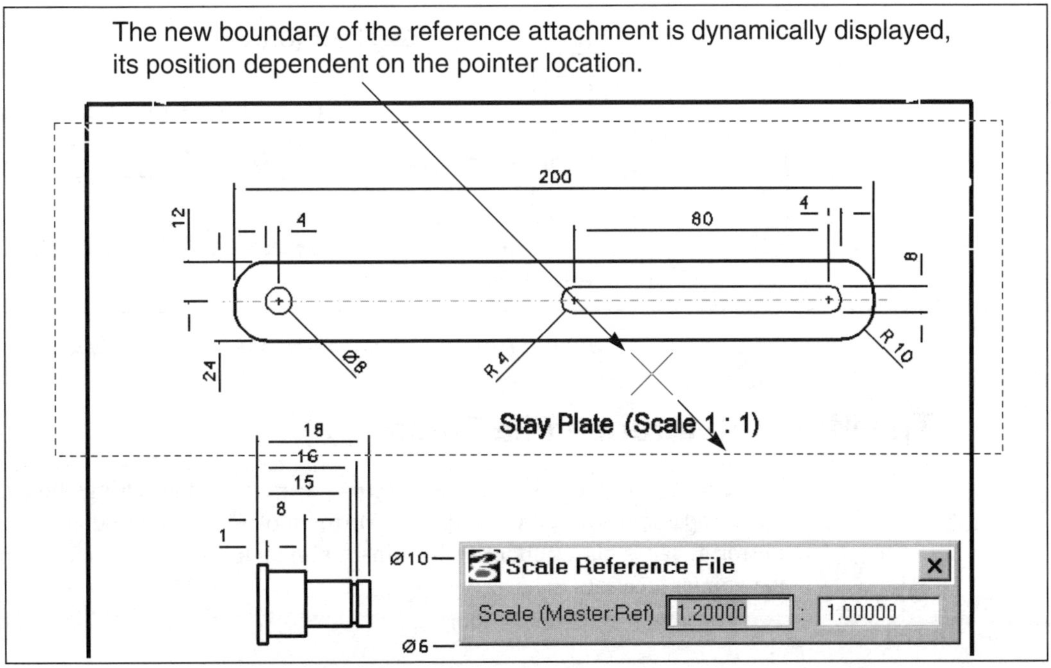

Figure 10.14 Scaling a reference file after attachment

The Rotate Reference File Tool

The rotation we apply to a reference attachment with this tool is by an angle keyed into the Z field of the tool's Settings window. The rotation is about a point defined by the location of the pointer, which may be snapped to an element to define the axis if necessary. The axis may also be defined by a keyed in absolute coordinate using the AccuDraw "**P**" shortcut.

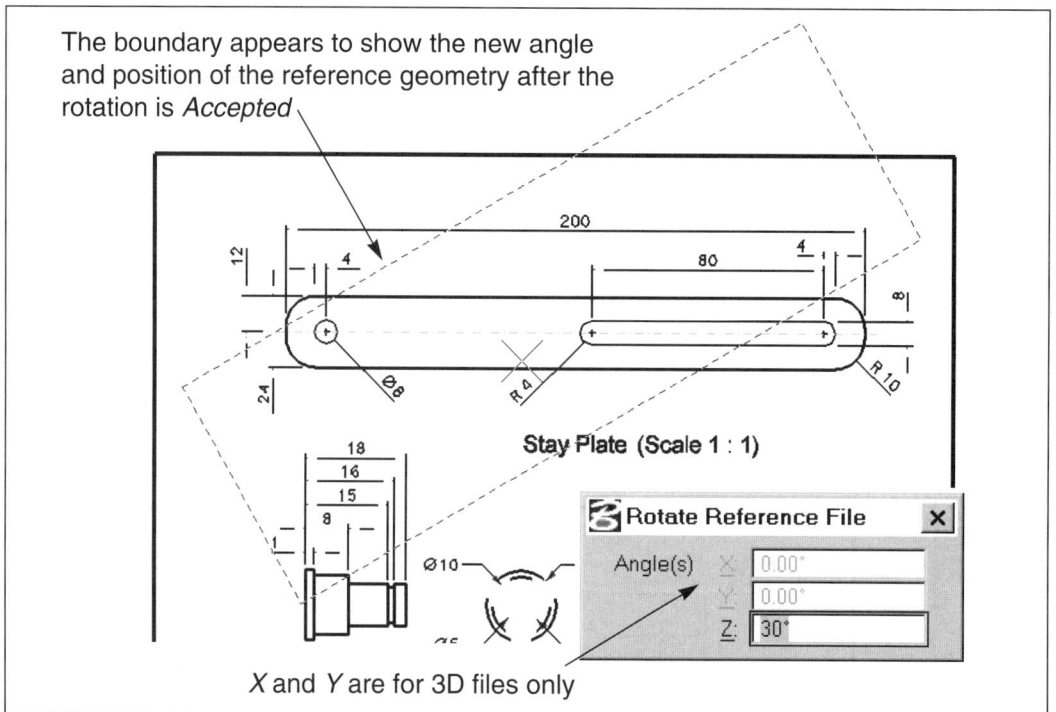

The boundary appears to show the new angle and position of the reference geometry after the rotation is *Accepted*

Stay Plate (Scale 1 : 1)

X and Y are for 3D files only

Figure 10.15   Rotating a Reference File attachment

The Mirror Reference File Tools

These tools, *Mirror Horizontal* and *Mirror Vertical* in the settings box *Tools* menu are comparable to the active design Mirror tool in the Manipulate tool box. The mirroring takes places about an imaginary horizontal or vertical line extending from the pointer location.

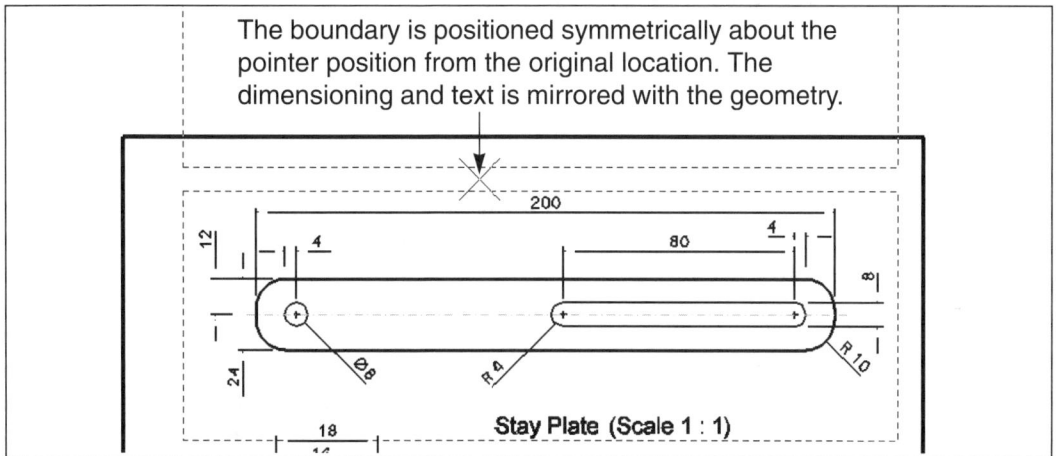

The boundary is positioned symmetrically about the
pointer position from the original location. The
dimensioning and text is mirrored with the geometry.

200

12   4   80   4

8

24   R 10

R 4

8

18   Stay Plate (Scale 1 : 1)

Figure 10.16   Mirroring a Reference File attachment about a Horizontal

The Detach Reference File Tools

There are two of these tools available from the settings box *Tools* menu, *Detach All*
and *Detach*. Only the latter tool is to be found in the tool box. The *Detach* tool
removes the identified reference attachment(s) only, the *Detach All* removes all
reference file attachments.

Note: Multiple attachments may be identified to be *Detached* by selecting the required
rows in the *Reference Files* settings box while holding down the <**Ctrl**> key. A range
may be identified by clicking one end, then clicking the other end of the range with
the <**Shift**> key held.

The Analyze Element Tool

This tool was originally introduced on page 3-24, but it behaves slightly differently
when we seek *Element Information* from a *Reference Design File*. For a start, for the
tool to analyze an element in any reference design file attachment, its *Locate* setting
must be *On* (see "Reference File settings" on page 10-18). We can not *Apply* any
changes, so this button is grayed out. The Reference file (slot) number will appear at
the bottom of the information panel as "*File=*". *File=0* indicates the element is in the
active design file.

Tip!   When we *Identify* an element in a reference file with a tool such as *Analyze Element*
(remember, *Locate* must be *On*), the *Reference Number* or the *Logical Name* of the
attachment appears in the Status bar.

Reference Raster Files

MicroStation Design files are a type of *Vector file*, where the graphical information is stored in a data base in the form of start points, distances, directions, end points, symbology definitions etc. *Raster* files are image files made up of finite size dots, called **Pixels** (short for *Picture Elements*). All of the images in this book have been made into *Raster* files for reproduction. *Raster* files may be attached as reference files to *Design* files using similar techniques to those used earlier with reference Design files.

The usual source of raster files for referencing is *Scanning*. Existing documents from the days of the drawing board are often electronically scanned to create raster files in a variety of standard formats, both color and monochrome (black and white). There is a large variety of *File Formats*. These formats vary not only between monochrome, grey scale and full color, but in the data compression techniques used. MicroStation supports virtually all of the formats in common use.

Using Reference Raster Files

Reference attachment of raster files can be useful in many ways. Images (including photographs) may be used to provide additional information with a design. Old line drawings may be used as a background for tracing, or included in a new design with new *Vector* information added.

One of the fundamental differences between using *Raster* reference files (as compared to design files) is that the reference file may be altered in some cases. For example, when a raster attachment is *clipped*, the image itself has pixels removed. This does not present a problem, however, as we are prompted to save a copy of the file when alterations are to take place. It is the copy that is manipulated when we accept this option, thus our original images may be kept intact.

We will attach a color image supplied with MicroStation in our first Raster Reference file exercise.

◆ Attaching the Global Map image

1. With "me0001.dgn" open, window the area of the title block, leaving some room to place an image on the left end of the block.

2. Open the *Reference Files* settings box (*File>Reference*), choose **Raster** from its *Display* menu.

3. Choose *Attach>Interactive* from the settings box *Tools* menu.
   Note that the tools menu has changed slightly for *Raster Display*.

4. Select the image file "glbworld.jpg" from the ". . . \image\" directory of the *Attach Raster Reference File* dialog box.

   The ".jpg" indicates that the image is in the "JPEG" raster format.

5. Click the **Preview** button (the image is *Stretched* rather than *Clipped* to fit the square format of the preview panel).

6. (Optional) Give the file a *Logical Name* and a *Description*, click **OK.**

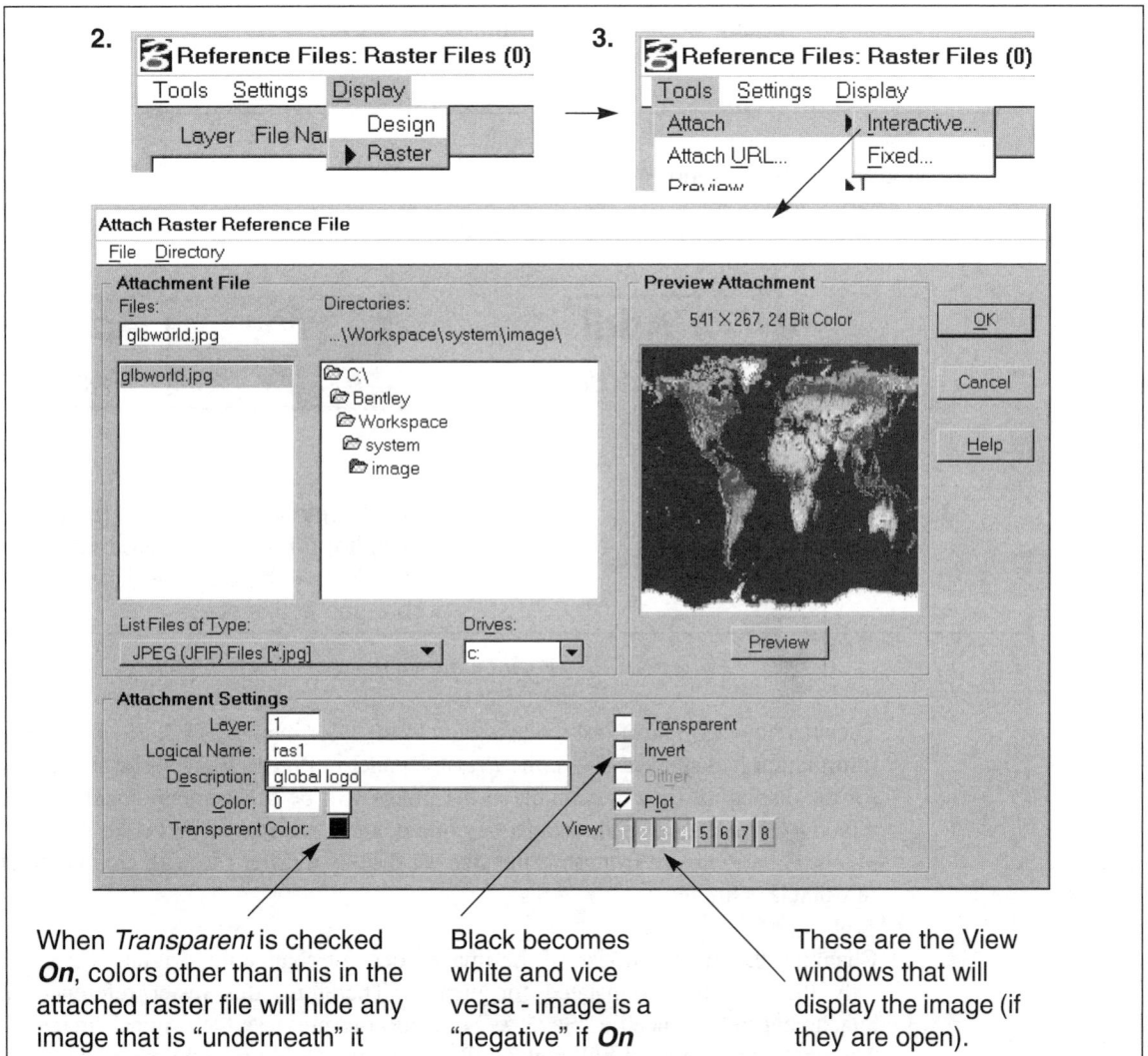

Figure 10.17   The Attach Raster Reference File dialog box

At this stage the *Attach Raster Reference File* dialog box closes and we are prompted to "Enter Reference Origin".

7. *Keypoint* snap to the top-left corner of the title block, *Accept* this as the *Reference Origin.*

    A boundary rectangle dynamically displays as we move the pointer.

8. *Nearest* snap to the bottom border, to the left of the title block, *Accept* to define the other reference corner.

    The map of the world appears beside our title block. You may like to modify the block to incorporate it as a logo.

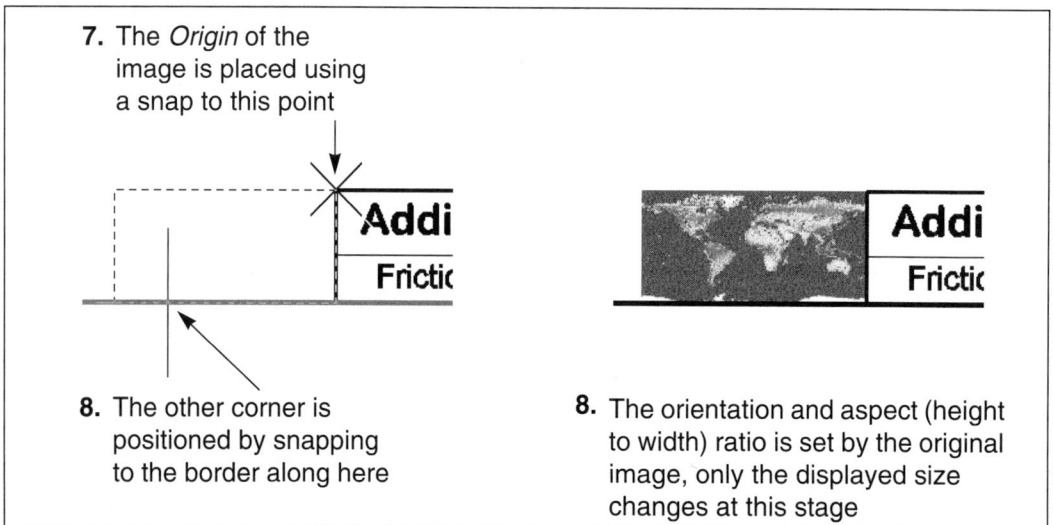

Figure 10.18   Positioning the reference raster file image

The attachment we have just made is of a 24 bit color image, 541 X 267 pixels (this information is displayed above the *Preview* panel in Figure 10.17). The size chosen for the display of the quite small, so the image will be of acceptable quality. If we window a small area of the image, say one country, we may observe the individual pixels. As we can see from this, the size we display a raster file with comparatively few pixels is limited.

Changing the displayed size of the image does not change the original image file, only the way it is translated for display. Therefore, this raster reference file attachment did not need a "Save As" operation to preserve the original image file. The next attachment we will make will involve image file manipulation, so we will be prompted to "Save As" at the appropriate time.

There is more information about the image attachment to be found in the *Reference Files* settings box. The information displayed is for the file highlighted in the settings box, see Figure 10.19. Note that the file highlighted by name in the settings box is also highlighted by a boundary on the image in the View window. This *Element Highlight* colored boundary appears regardless of the *Reference Boundaries* view attribute.

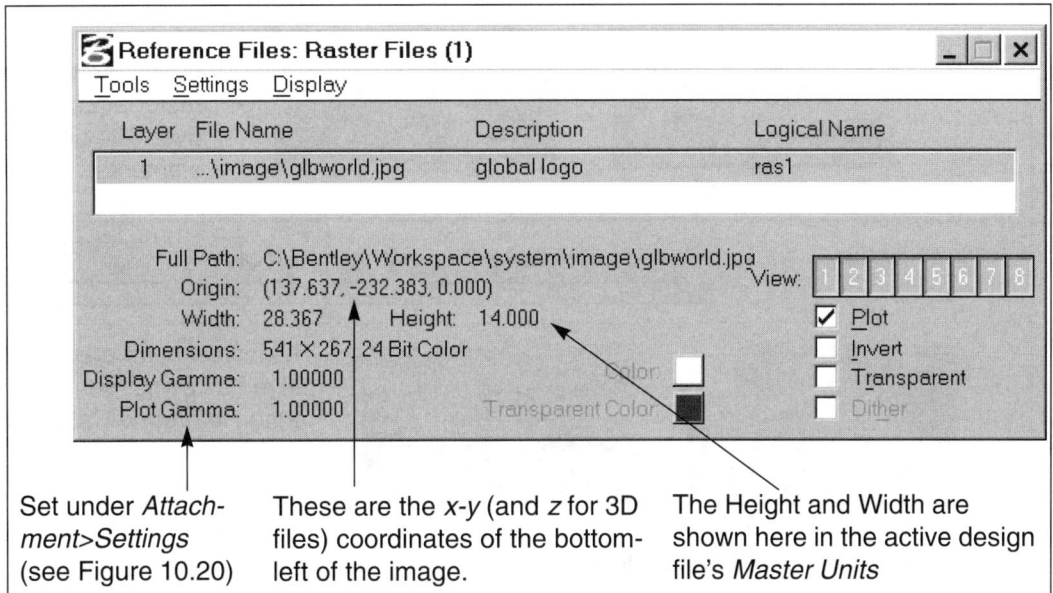

Figure 10.19   The Reference Files:Raster Files settings box

The Settings Options for Raster Reference Files

The *Settings menu* of the *Reference Files:Raster Files* dialog has two options, *Attachment* and *Update Sequence*. The latter option opens the same settings box as used for reference *Design* files (see "The Settings options" on page 10-19). If we open this settings box now, "Raster Reference Files (All)" will be found to occupy first place, which is the default arrangement.

Unlike design files, raster files are not displayed with *Levels*. Multiple raster images are attached in *Layers*, the higher numbered layer obscuring any other image attachments it overlaps. By default, the layer of each new attachment is one higher than the preceding one, but we can override this. This setting may be made in the *Attach Raster Reference File* dialog box, or, more usually, in the *Attachment Settings* dialog box.

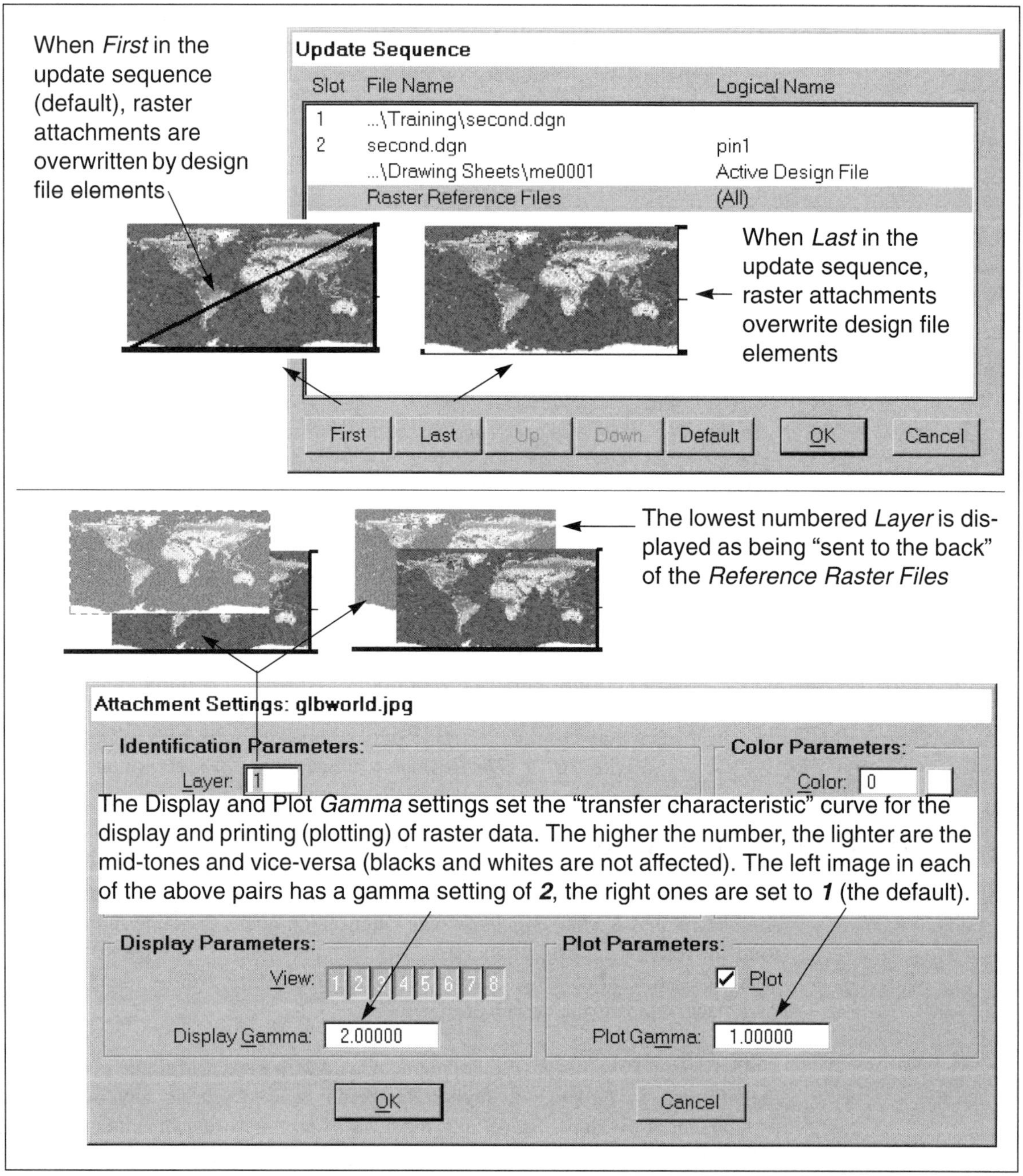

When *First* in the update sequence (default), raster attachments are overwritten by design file elements

Update Sequence

Slot	File Name	Logical Name
1	...\Training\second.dgn	
2	second.dgn	pin1
	...\Drawing Sheets\me0001	Active Design File
	Raster Reference Files	(All)

When *Last* in the update sequence, raster attachments overwrite design file elements

| First | Last | Up | Down | Default | OK | Cancel |

The lowest numbered *Layer* is displayed as being "sent to the back" of the *Reference Raster Files*

Attachment Settings: glbworld.jpg

Identification Parameters:

Layer: 1

Color Parameters:

Color: 0

The Display and Plot *Gamma* settings set the "transfer characteristic" curve for the display and printing (plotting) of raster data. The higher the number, the lighter are the mid-tones and vice-versa (blacks and whites are not affected). The left image in each of the above pairs has a gamma setting of *2*, the right ones are set to *1* (the default).

Display Parameters:

View: 1 2 3 4 5 6 7 8

Display Gamma: 2.00000

Plot Parameters:

☑ Plot

Plot Gamma: 1.00000

| OK | Cancel |

Figure 10.20   Some Raster Reference file Settings options

Reference Raster Line Drawings

The color image used in the last examples is only one form of Raster Reference File. One of the most valuable uses for the reference raster file facility is to integrate electronically scanned line drawings with design files, thus producing a *Hybrid* design.

The original paper drawings may be distorted in various ways, they may include unwanted material, or even have parts missing. The scanning process itself may also add some distortions, so there are tools available to make corrections and integrate the *Raster* linework into a *Design File*.

We will make use of the *Save Image* utility to generate a raster file from the contents of a View window in the next exercise. This image is intended to be used for some raster file manipulations, but another file may be substituted for it in later exercises. If you have the facilities of a scanner, or some suitable image files of scanned line drawings, you may choose to skip to the exercise on page 10-33.

◆ **Create an Image file**

1. Window the area about the stay plate (reference file) in "me0001.dgn, turn **Off** *Reference File* level **63** (see "Settings Menu Options" on page 10-19) for the attachment (to hide the dimensioning).

2. Re-size the View window by reducing its height to closely fit the stay plate outline (see Figure 10.21).

   The image size will be set by the View window area. Making the window fit the area of interest will produce an image with the least number of redundant pixels.

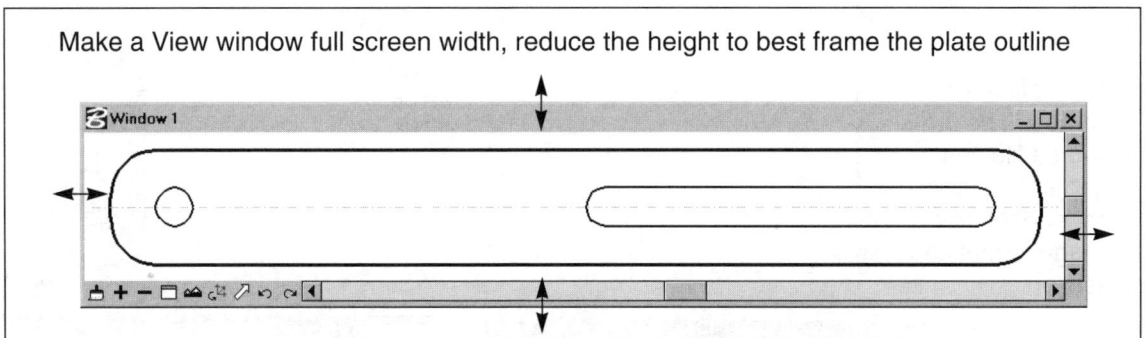

Figure 10.21 Preparing the View window for Saving the Stay Plate image

3. Choose *Utilities>Image>Save*, choose the *Save Image* options as illustrated in Figure 10.22, click **Save**.

4. The *Save Image As* settings box opens, click **OK** to accept the default file name and directory, or choose new settings.

   We now have an image file of the Stay Plate in *Raster* format.

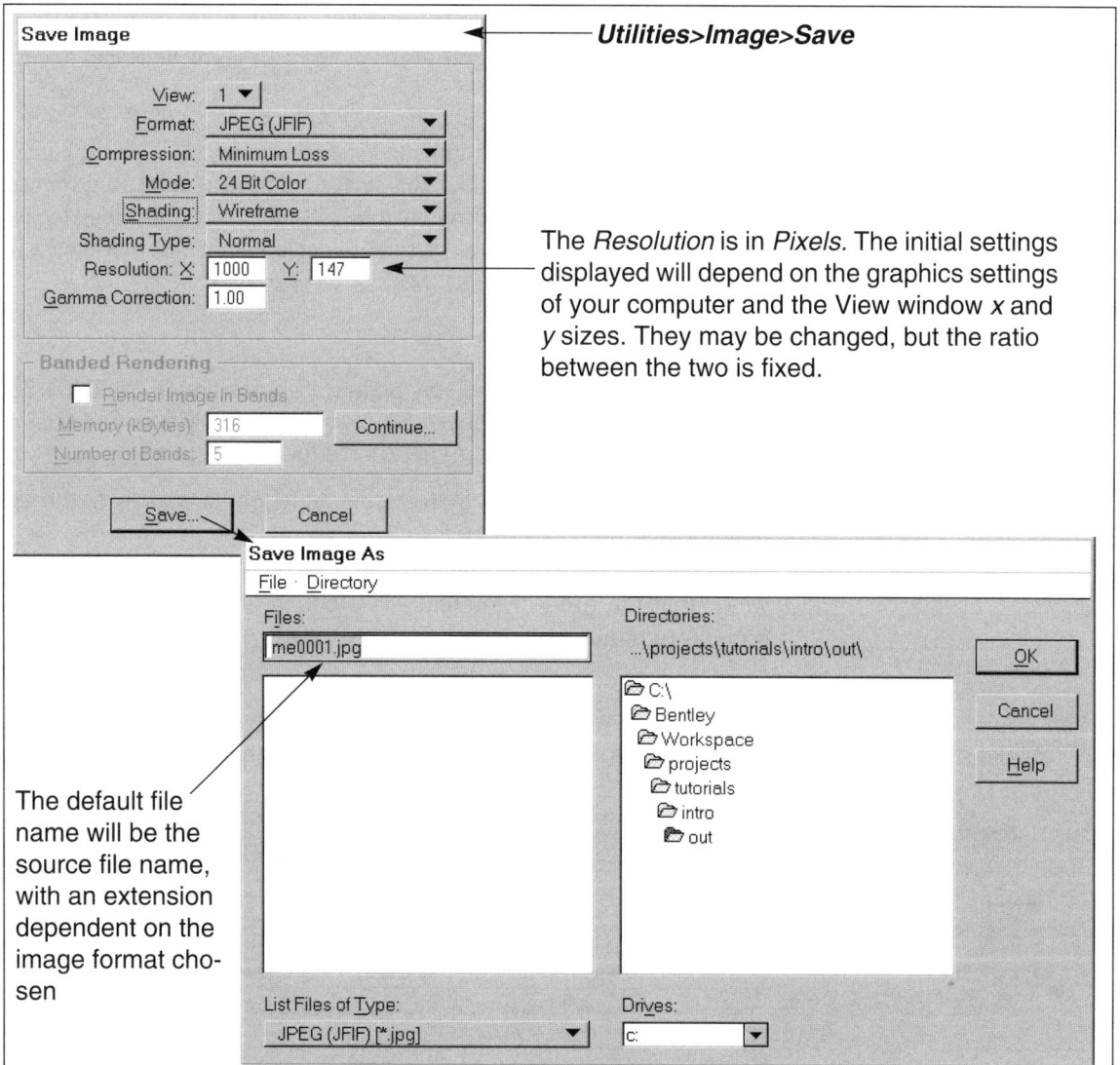

The *Resolution* is in *Pixels.* The initial settings displayed will depend on the graphics settings of your computer and the View window *x* and *y* sizes. They may be changed, but the ratio between the two is fixed.

The default file name will be the source file name, with an extension dependent on the image format chosen

Figure 10.22   Saving View window contents as a Raster Image file

We will now attach our new raster format linework as a reference file to "me0001.dgn". We will position and modify the image to fit to lines placed in the *Active* design file, to help match the scale of the image to the design geometry.

◆ Attach the Raster Line Drawing image

1. In "me0001.dgn", place two **24** long vertical lines, vertically aligned and **180** apart (the length and spacing of the stay plate sides).

2. Open the *Reference Files* settings box, if necessary set the *Display* option to ***Raster***.

3. Choose *Attach>Interactive* from the settings box *Tools* menu, select the new raster file created in the last exercise.

4. Check *Transparent **On***, optionally allocate a *Logical Name*. Position the attachment between the parallel lines.

5. Use the **(a)** *Move* and **(b)** *Modify reference file* tools to align the ends of the straight sections of the stay plate sides with the vertical lines as shown in Figure 10.23.

6. Turn *Transparency **Off*** under *Settings>Attachment* (the guide lines placed in step **1.** will be hidden).

These illustrations were produced using a white background and black outlines for print reproduction purposes. The procedures explained here will be correct when using the usual black background.

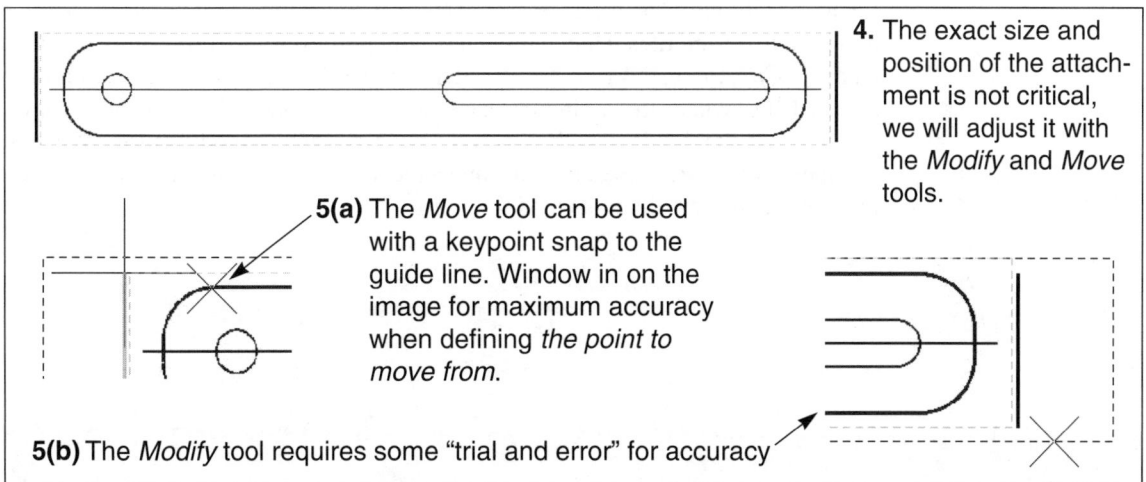

4. The exact size and position of the attachment is not critical, we will adjust it with the *Modify* and *Move* tools.

5(a) The *Move* tool can be used with a keypoint snap to the guide line. Window in on the image for maximum accuracy when defining *the point to move from.*

5(b) The *Modify* tool requires some "trial and error" for accuracy

Figure 10.23   Attaching and scaling the line drawing raster reference file

Summary

The examples of the use of *Reference Files* in this chapter were very simple, but they embodied most of the principles of this production technique. Using reference files to combine design data and presentation geometry in the *Drawing Sheet* examples is only one of many applications. Reference files are used any time a design project can be broken down into sections. One type of project where file referencing is used widely is in the design of large buildings.

The components of the design may be divided between work groups and individuals, each one working within their area of specialization. The results may be hundreds of individual design files and images. Various combinations of files from this pool of data may be created using reference file techniques to produce documentation optimized to suit the user. This optimization will often extend to differing choices of levels from the reference design files. The same design data may be used many times over, thus eliminating duplication of effort. It is feasible for the number of individual output documents to exceed the number of design files.

When a *Reference Design File* is attached to an *Active Design File*, it is fully protected from being changed, either deliberately or accidentally. This allows for the control to be maintained over each part of the design process by the responsible person or group. In one person or other small operations, control of the reference files may be in the same hands as the output document production. In these cases the use of reference files still provide all the reductions in duplication of effort.

Raster reference files may be used as illustrations, company logos, as a pictorial base for a new design. They are also frequently used to integrate *Scanned* electronic images into design files. Unlike reference *Design* files, some forms of manipulation (such as *Clipping* and *Masking*) of raster files necessitates the modification of the attached file. Under these circumstances we are automatically prompted to save a duplicate of the original with a new name, prior to its modification. When we complete this *Save As* operation, the attachment details are automatically updated to incorporate the new file in its modified form.

11 : Increasing Efficiency

By now we have worked with a good many of the tools from the MicroStation tool boxes. The examples have been used to introduce the most representative tools, the rest operate in a manner you will find familiar. We could confidently take on any design project within our general capability, using MicroStation all the way.

Of course, to be able to complete a design project quickly and efficiently will take time and practice. The facilities about to be introduced will increase our efficiency by reducing the need for repetition.

We will learn about managing settings, to be able to recall a whole range of settings used in the past with a minimum number of actions. We will also learn to create large parts of a design with very few data points. The *Multi-line* facilities enable us to place numerous lines at once, even when they have different attributes.

Custom Line Styles provide the means to create a linear element that may be made up of many *Strokes* and *Symbols*. This is more efficient than using linear patterning in most cases. It is faster to produce and display and it does not add the patterning elements to the design file, thus making smaller files.

When you have completed this chapter, you will be able to:

- Use *Settings Files* and *Settings Groups* to save complex combinations of settings;
- Create *Custom Line Styles* with *Stroke* and *Symbol* components;
- Use *Multi-lines* to place numbers of differing lines simultaneously.

Managing Settings

When we invest our time in arranging settings to complete a task, it makes sense to *Save* our investment. Using dimension settings as an example, it is most likely that we will be using the same settings over and over again. If we save them in a *Settings File*, we can set up our dimensioning *Style* with a single action the next time we are performing a similar task.

Settings Files

A *Settings File* is a data file used to save *Styles* and *Settings Groups*. The structure of these *Settings Groups* is very flexible, in that they may include many *Components* of differing types in each one. For example, a particular dimensioning *Style* may be made a *Component* of a *Settings Group*.

Figure 11.1 represents part of a hypothetical settings management structure, with the *Settings Files* shown with their default ".stg" filename extensions. These files are placed by default in a directory under ". . . Workspace\system\data\".

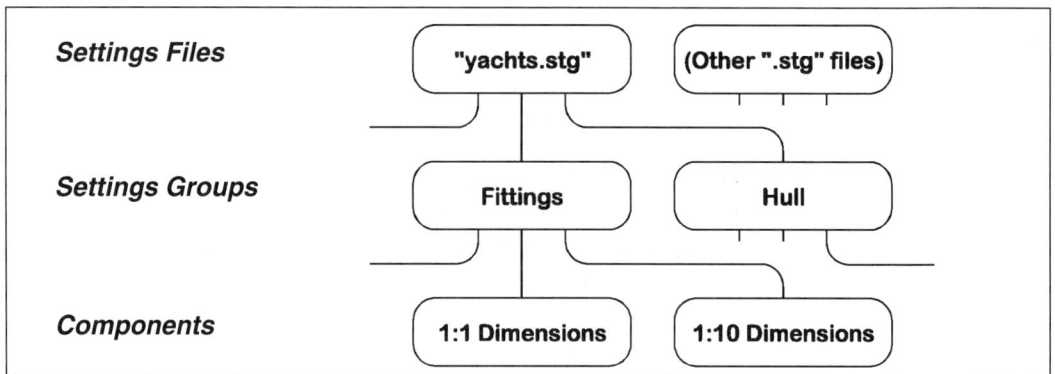

Figure 11.1   A Settings Group structure

A *Settings File* may be part of a "module" of files to do with a particular workspace *Project* component. The creation of projects for groups of users is generally a system administrator's responsibility, but we can (and will) create our settings files as individual users. In practice it is not critical where the files are placed, but for the purposes of this example, we will place our file under ". . . Workspace\system\data\".

In the next exercises, we will create a new *Settings File*, then create a dimension *Style*. Later on, we will create a *Settings Group* in that file. The first *Component* of the new *Settings Group* will be the dimension *Style* created earlier. The settings file will be named "yachts.stg", the settings group "Fittings" and the component "1:1 Dimensions", as shown diagrammatically in part of Figure 11.1.

◆ **Create the Settings file "yachts.stg"**

1. Choose *Manage* from the Application window *Settings* menu (the *Select Settings* window opens).

2. Choose *File>Edit* from the *Select Settings* window menu (the *Edit Settings* settings box opens).

3. Choose *New* from the *File* menu of the *Edit Settings* settings box menu (the *Create New Settings File* dialog box opens.

4. Check that ". . . \Workspace\system\data\ is the directory path, enter **Yachts** into the *Files:* field, click **OK**.

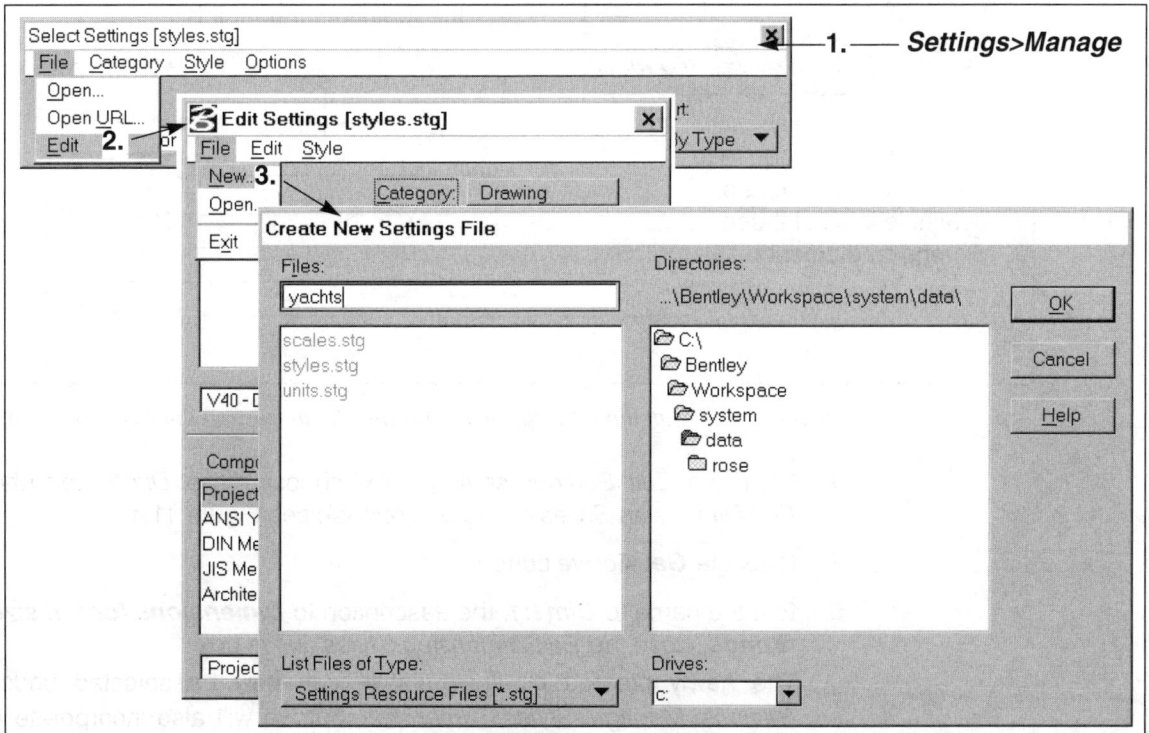

Figure 11.2   Creating a new Settings File

Creating a Dimension Style

We will save the dimension settings that we used to dimension the Stay Plate. It is to be saved as a dimension *Style* for dimensioning a drawing that will be printed out at 1:1 scale.

◆ **Create the dimension style "Dim1:1"**

1. With "me0001.dgn" open, turn the display of level **63 *On*** in the first reference *Design* file attachment (*File>Reference>Settings>Levels*).

2. Open the *Match* tool box (*Tools>Match*), select the *Match Dimension Settings* tool.

3. Identify one of the dimension elements on the Stay Plate, *Accept*.
   The dimension settings that were *Active* at the time the identified dimension was placed, are now *Active* again.

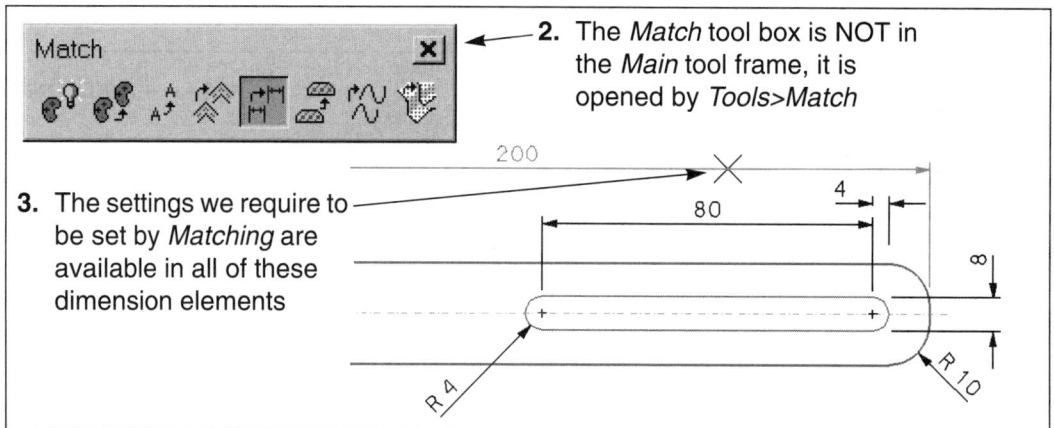

Figure 11.3   Matching the dimension settings to an existing dimension element

4. From the *Edit Settings* settings box, choose *Style>Dimension* (the *Edit Dimension Styles* dialog box opens), see Figure 11.4.

5. Click the ***Get Active*** button.

6. Edit the name to ***Dim1:1***, the description to ***Dimensions for full size fittings***, close the *Edit Dimension Styles* dialog box.
   The newly created dimension style can now be selected under *Settings>Manage>Styles>Dimension*, but we will also incorporate it into a *Settings Group Component*.

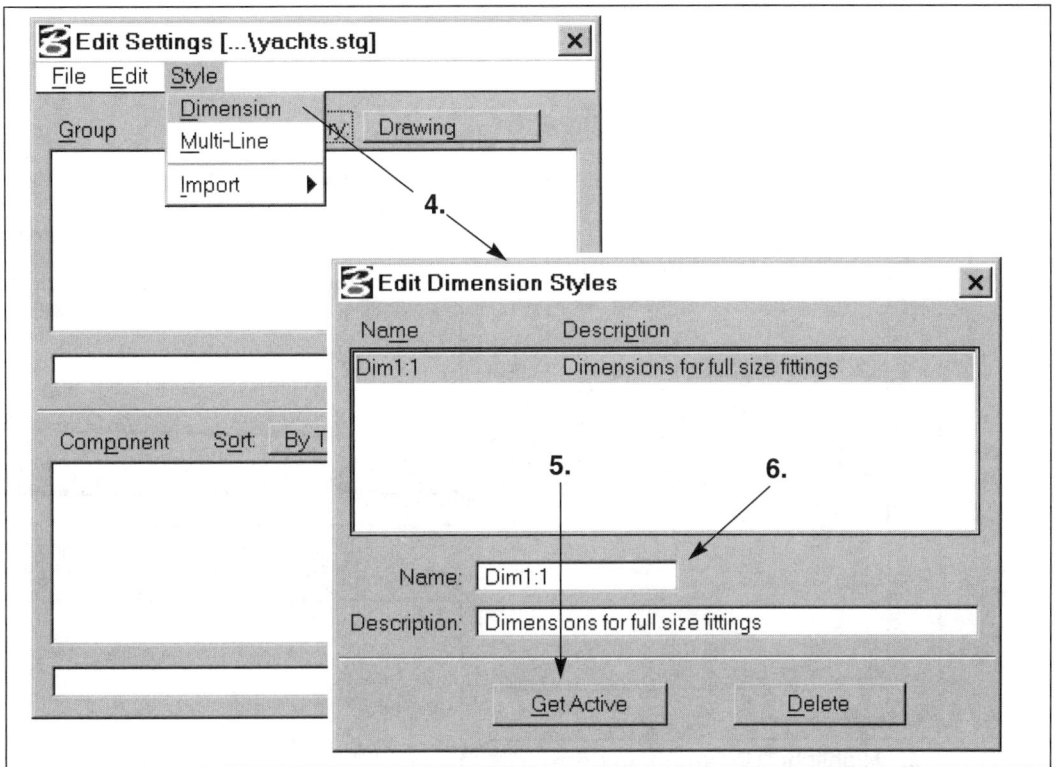

Figure 11.4   Getting and Naming the Dimension Style

Settings Groups

When we closed the *Edit Dimension Styles* settings box in step **6.** of the last exercise, the *Edit Settings* settings box regained input focus. This will now be used to create a new *Drawing* settings group.

◆ Create a Settings Group

1. Open the *Edit Settings* box (*Settings>Manage>File>Edit*).

2. From the *Edit Settings* box *Edit* menu, choose *Create>Group* (*Unnamed* appears in the *Group* panel and in the data input field immediately below it), see Figure 11.5.

3. Change *Unnamed* in the data input field to **Fittings**, press <**Enter**>. We now have a new *Settings Group* (currently empty of components). You may choose to add more groups now, or leave just the one.

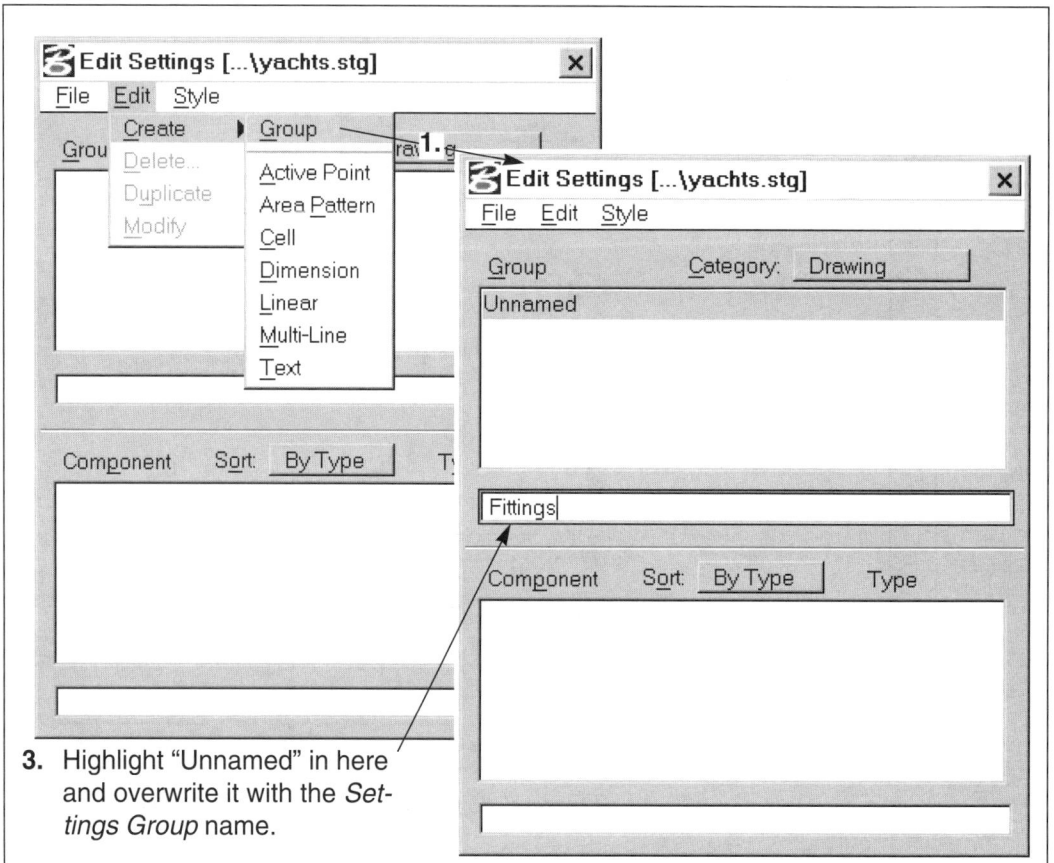

Figure 11.5   Creating a new Settings Group

Settings Group Components

The *Edit Settings* settings box still has input focus after creating our new settings group. If this is not the case, re-open it. This time we will use it to create a new *Dimension* type *Component* within the *Fittings* settings group.

◆ **Create a Settings Group Dimension Component**

1. With the settings group *Fittings* selected, choose *Edit>Create> Dimension* (*Unnamed* appears in the *Components* panel and in the data input field immediately below it).

2. Change *Unnamed* in the *Component* data input field to *1:1 Dimensions*, press <**Enter**>.

This has named the component, now we have to define the dimension *Style* (combination of dimension settings) to go with it. We will use the style made active by *Matching* on page 11-4.

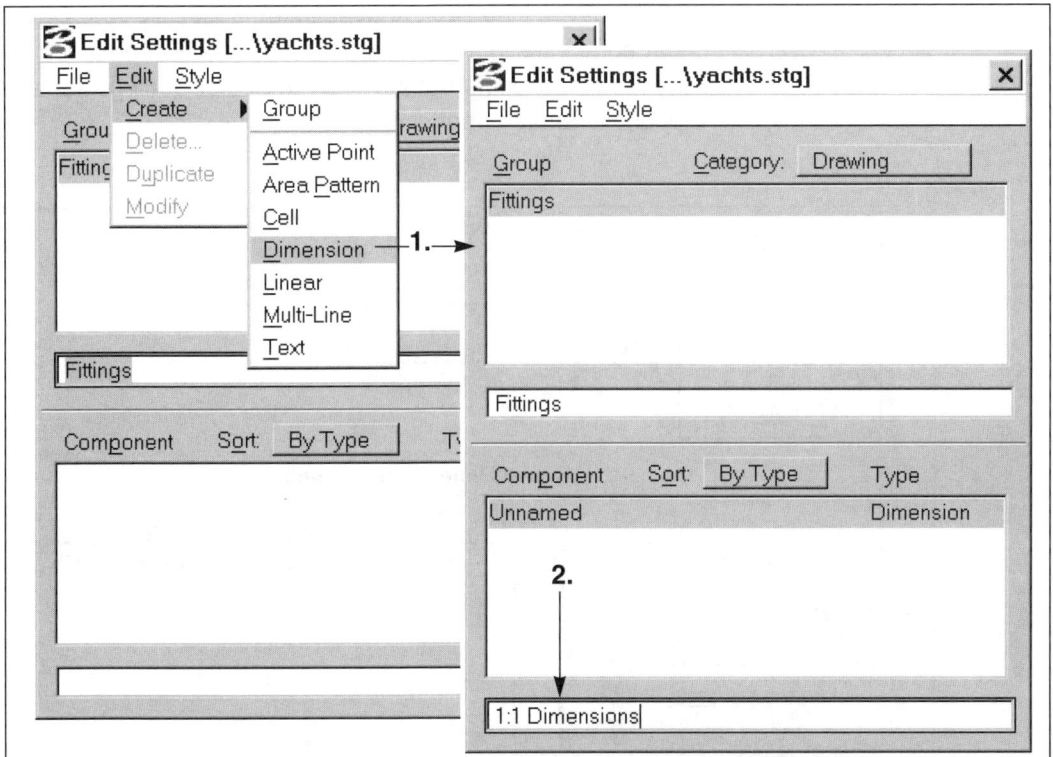

Figure 11.6   Naming a Component

3. Click on the new *1:1 Dimensions* component in the lower panel of the *Edit Settings* settings box.

This identifies the particular component we intend to modify. In the future we may have several to choose from, but for now there is only the one.

4. Choose *Edit>Modify* from the *Edit Settings* settings box (the *Modify 1:1 Dimensions* dialog box opens).

5. Click the **Select** button (the *Select Dimension Definition* dialog opens), select *Dim1:1*, click **OK**.

We now have selected the *Dimension Style* as defined on page 11-4, to be incorporated into the component.

6. The *Modify* settings box regains input focus, click the **Save** button.

That completes the defining process. The *Edit Settings* settings box may now be closed, but the original *Select Settings* settings box may optionally remain open.

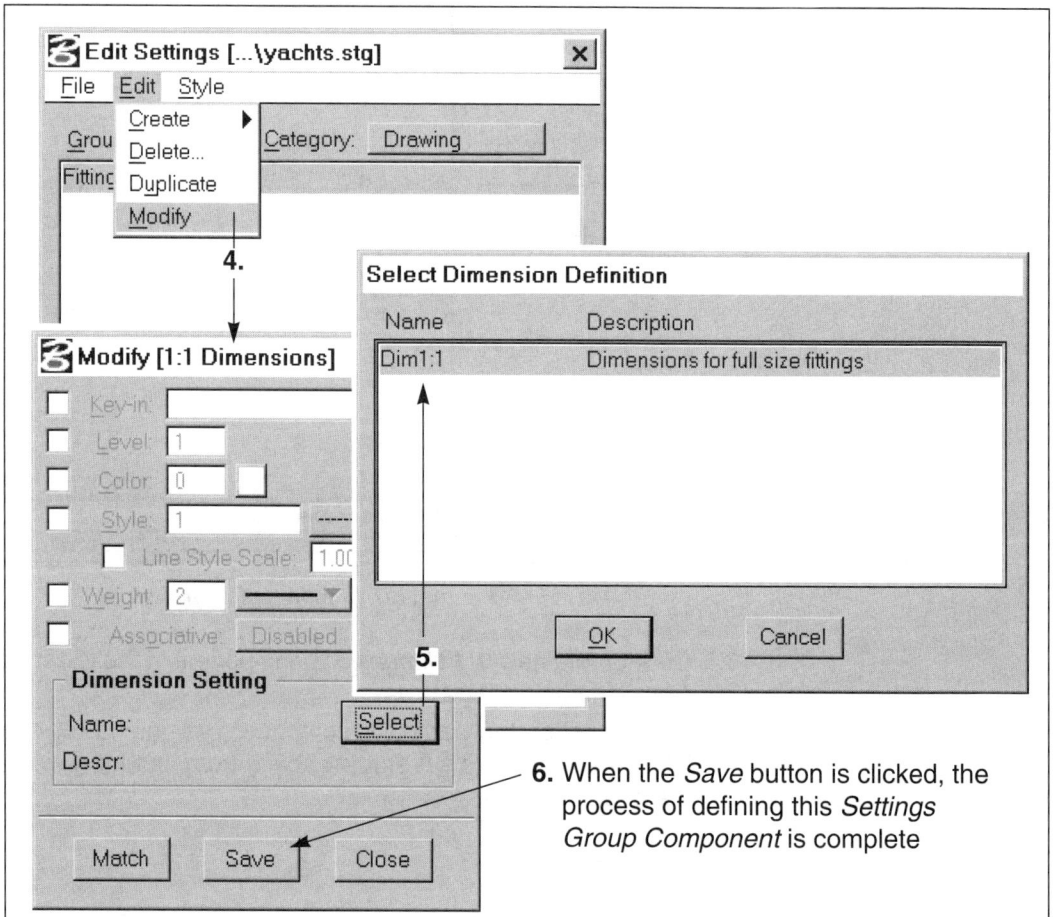

Figure 11.7 Selecting and saving the Dimension Style

Using the Settings Files

The *Settings File* we created in the last set of exercises is very basic so far, it has only one *Settings Group*. This settings group may only have the one component.

To help us with our experiments with our settings file, we will produce another dimension style. We will save this as another *Component* of the *Fittings* settings group within the *Yachts* settings file. This new style will be set up for the dimensioning of drawings that we intend to print out at a scale of **1 : 10**, thus its text etc. will be ten times larger than the one we used for **1 : 1**. The actual sizes stated in the next exercise are suggestions only.

◆ **Create a second Dimension Component**

1. With "me0001.dgn" open, make sure the dimension style is the one used on the Stay Plate, *Match* again (page 11-4) if you are not sure.

2. Under *Element>Dimensions* set the *Text* size to **70** (see "The Dimension Settings box, Text settings" on page 9-11).

3. Choose *Dimension Lines* from the same settings box, change the *Stack offset* to **70** (see "Dimension Lines" on page 9-13).

   These are all the changes we will need to make, the remaining geometry sizes are defined in *Text Height* units, so they will change automatically.

4. If necessary, open the *Select Settings* window (*Settings>Manage*), Check that "yachts.stg" is still the *Settings File* listed in the Title bar, re-open it if necessary (*File>Open*).

5. From the *Edit Settings* settings box, choose *Style>Dimension* (the *Edit Dimension Styles* dialog box opens), click the **Get Active** button.

6. Edit the name to **Dim1:10**, the description to **Dimensions 1:10 scale fittings**, close the *Edit Dimension Styles* dialog box.

7. Work through the same process as we used to create the *1:1 Dimensions* component (starting on page 11-6), using appropriate names and descriptions.

8. With the *Select Settings* window open, try clicking each component in turn, placing a temporary dimension each time to check the operation of our settings management initiative.

Tip!   The *Select Settings* window is intended to be left open while we are working with it. It works just as well when it is *Re-sized* down to its minimum width, while it takes up a lot less screen real estate.

Custom Line Styles

We may create our own *Custom Line Styles*. They may be used to improve the presentation of a design, while speeding up the design process. A custom line style is made up from *Components*, which may include:

- *Stroke Patterns* of dashes and gaps;
- *Point Symbols* (similar to cells);
- *Compound*, combinations of the above.

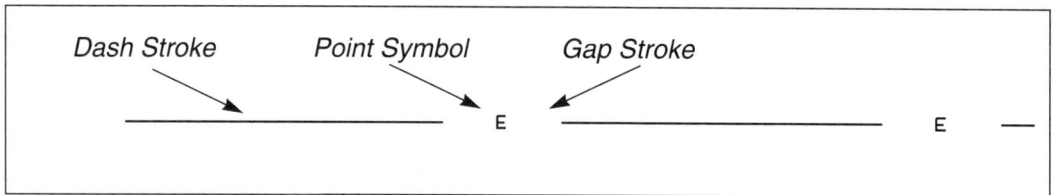

Figure 11.8 A simple Compound Custom Line Style

Line Style Libraries

A *Line Style Library* is a special file, comparable to a *Cell Library* or a *Settings File*, containing a set of custom line style definitions. Line style library files have the filename extension ".rsc", which stands for *Resource* file. MicroStation is supplied with some sample custom line style libraries, which are the first ones we will use.

In the *Default* workspace, these files are stored in the ". . . Workspace\system\symb\" directory. We do not need to select any particular line style library, as all of the styles from all of the library files in the project's directory are available from a single menu.

Using Supplied Custom Line Styles

We will start by experimenting with line styles from the sample *Line Style Libraries* in the next exercise.

◆ Place lines with an existing Custom Line Style

1. Create and open a *New* design file named "linestyl.dgn", using the Drawing Sheet seed file we saved in Chapter 10 (see "Create a Drawing Sheet" on page 10-4).

We will use the border rectangle to provide an indication of the *Scale* of the line styles.

2. Choose **Custom** from the *Style* options of the *Primary* tool bar.

    The *Line Styles* settings box opens, displaying the styles available from the current workspace.

3. Click the *Show Details* check box.

    The settings box expands to display more information, including a panel displaying the highlighted style. This panel is a large button to *Activate* the displayed style, like selecting a text *Font* using the *View* facility.

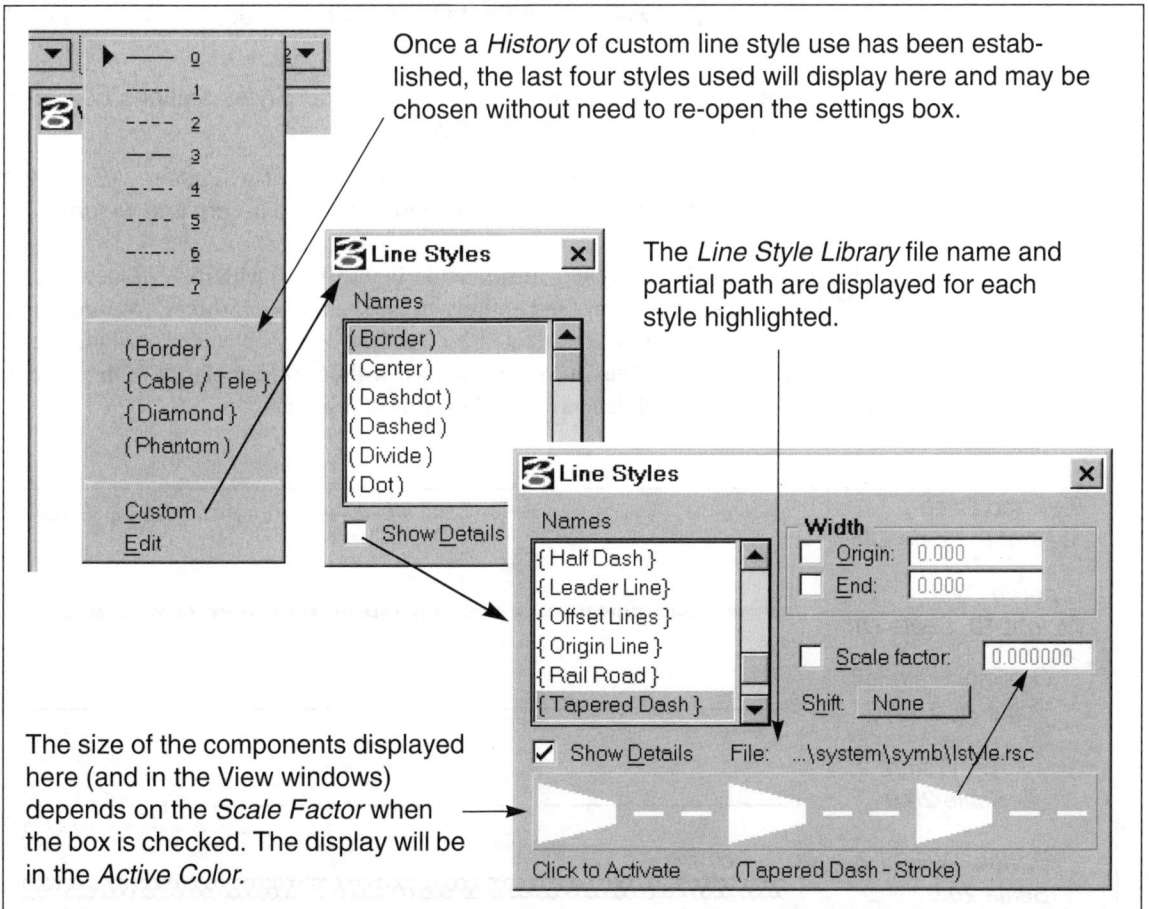

Once a *History* of custom line style use has been established, the last four styles used will display here and may be chosen without need to re-open the settings box.

The *Line Style Library* file name and partial path are displayed for each style highlighted.

The size of the components displayed here (and in the View windows) depends on the *Scale Factor* when the box is checked. The display will be in the *Active Color.*

Figure 11.9   The Line Styles settings box configurations

4. Choose **Tapered Dash** from the *Names* panel by either double-clicking it or by clicking it once and clicking the style display panel. Leave the *Scale Factor* box **Off**.

   Double-clicking is the only method used when the *Show Details* box is not checked.

5. With the *Line Weight* element attribute set to **0**, place a line across the width of the border rectangle.

   Note the results with *Fill* **Off** in the *View Attributes* (the tapered elements will appear as outlines), then again with *Fill* **On**.

6. With the *Line Weight* set to **10**, place another line across the width of the border rectangle.

   Again, note the results with *Fill* **Off** (the dash strokes will have changed in weight, but the tapered elements outlines will remain the same).

7. Set the *Scale* check box **On** in the *Line Styles* settings box (*Show Details* **On**), enter a scale of **20**.

8. Place elements at the above scale using the *Gasline*, *-E-* and the *Batten* custom line styles. Experiment with different line weights.

The *Tapered Dash* line style is illustrated in Figure 11.10 with the *Fill* view attribute *Off*. This line style is composed entirely of *Dash* and *Gap Strokes*. You may notice that the ordinary dashes are affected by the *Line Weight* element attribute, but the tapered ones are not. They have been shown without fill for clarity in this case, but this view attribute will generally be **On** for most printouts.

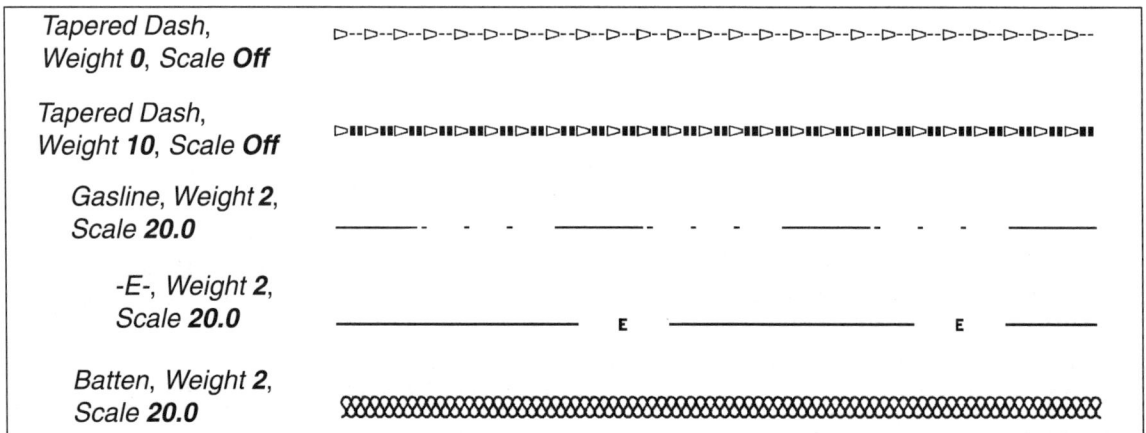

Figure 11.10   Sample printouts of some Custom Line Styles as supplied

The *Stroke Pattern* of a "Standard" line style with gaps does not have actual dimensions until it is printed out. They always look the same on the screen, regardless of magnification. *Custom* line styles ***do*** have defined dimensions, therefore their *Scale* needs to be taken into account, as shown by the different scales used in Figure 11.10. Unlike a standard line style, it is possible to zoom out on a custom line style and have it appear solid, or zoom in on a gap and have it disappear.

Line Style Modifiers

Some details of a custom line style definition may be modified as we use it. We have already used one *Line Style Modifier*, the *Scale* factor activated in the last exercise. We find the modifiers in the "show details" version of the *Line Styles* settings box.

Scale Factor

A custom line style is defined with specified dimensions and by default it will be placed with these dimensions. The default *Scale Factor* of **1.0** may be overridden by setting its check box ***On*** and keying in a scale factor to the associated field.

Width

Dash strokes of a style that are defined as having *Width* may have this width modified. Taking the *Tapered Dash* style as an example, the tapered component of the style has *Start* and *End* widths, but the other two dash strokes have none. Where a dash has "*None*" as its width, it takes the *Active Line Weight* (see Figure 11.10).

The widths at the *Origin* of the line (or other element) and at the *End* may be separately overridden, with new dimensions keyed in to the *Width* data entry fields. These widths apply along the length of the element, not to individual strokes.

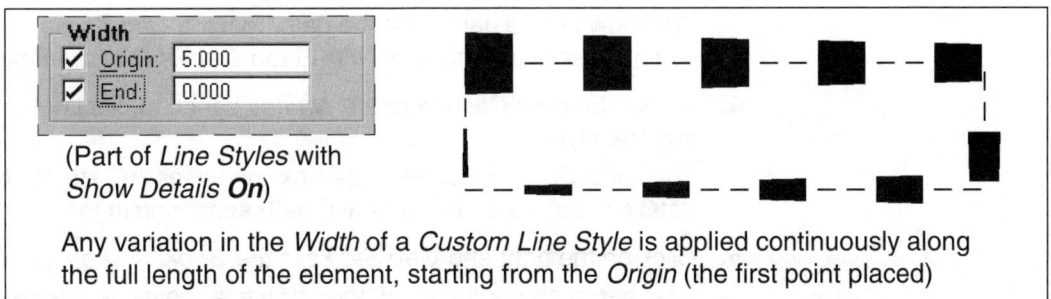

Width
☑ Origin: 5.000
☑ End: 0.000

(Part of *Line Styles* with *Show Details **On***)

Any variation in the *Width* of a *Custom Line Style* is applied continuously along the full length of the element, starting from the *Origin* (the first point placed)

Figure 11.11   Using the Width Line Style Modifier

Shift

When the *Shift* is set to *None*, the element starts with the start of the first stroke in the definition. If a shift *Distance* is keyed in, the line style starts that distance "in" from its origin as originally defined.

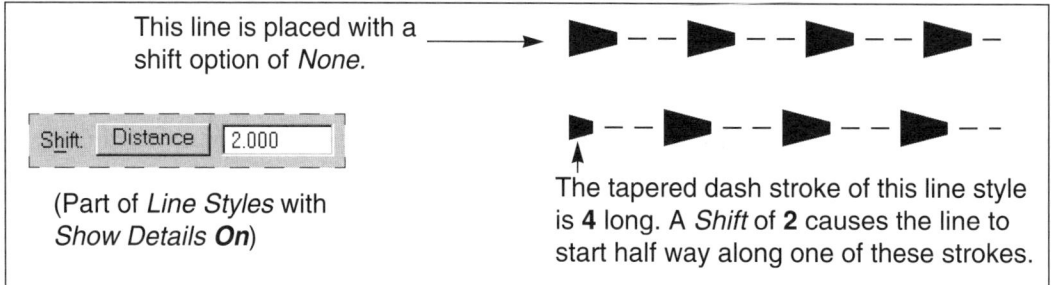

This line is placed with a ——————→ shift option of *None*.

Shift: Distance 2.000

(Part of *Line Styles* with *Show Details On*)

The tapered dash stroke of this line style is **4** long. A *Shift* of **2** causes the line to start half way along one of these strokes.

Figure 11.12   The effect of defining a Shift Distance

The Line Style Editor

This settings box is normally used to *Edit* existing custom line styles or to *Create* new ones. In the next exercise, however, we will not do either, only observe the construction of an existing *Custom Line Style*.

◆ **Investigate the Tapered Dash Line Style**

1. Choose *Edit* from the *Line Style* options of the *Primary* tool bar.
    The *Line Style Editor* settings box opens.

2. Choose *File>Open* from the settings box menu (the *Open Line Style Library* dialog box opens).

3. Select *lstyle.rsc* from the "*. . . \Workspace\system\symb*" directory.
    We know the file name and the path from the *Line Styles* settings box, when we selected this style with *Show Details On* (see Figure 11.9).

4. Select *Tapered Dash* from the *Names* panel, to display the details of this line style.
    The *Line Style Editor* settings box increases in size to display the details of the style, its name and path appearing in the Title bar.

5. Click on the right end *Gap Stroke* in the *Stroke Pattern* panel.
    The bar representation of this stroke appears to depress and its details are displayed, note the *Length* of the end *Gap* stroke (**1.0**).

Line Style Editor

File Edit Sort

New...
Open...
Close
Manage...
Save
Save As...
Exit

Open Line Style Library

File Directory

Files:

lstyle.rsc

acadlsty.rsc
font.rsc
internat.rsc
lstyle.rsc

Directories:

...\Bentley\Workspace\system\symb\

C:\
Bentley
Workspace
system
symb

OK

Cancel

Help

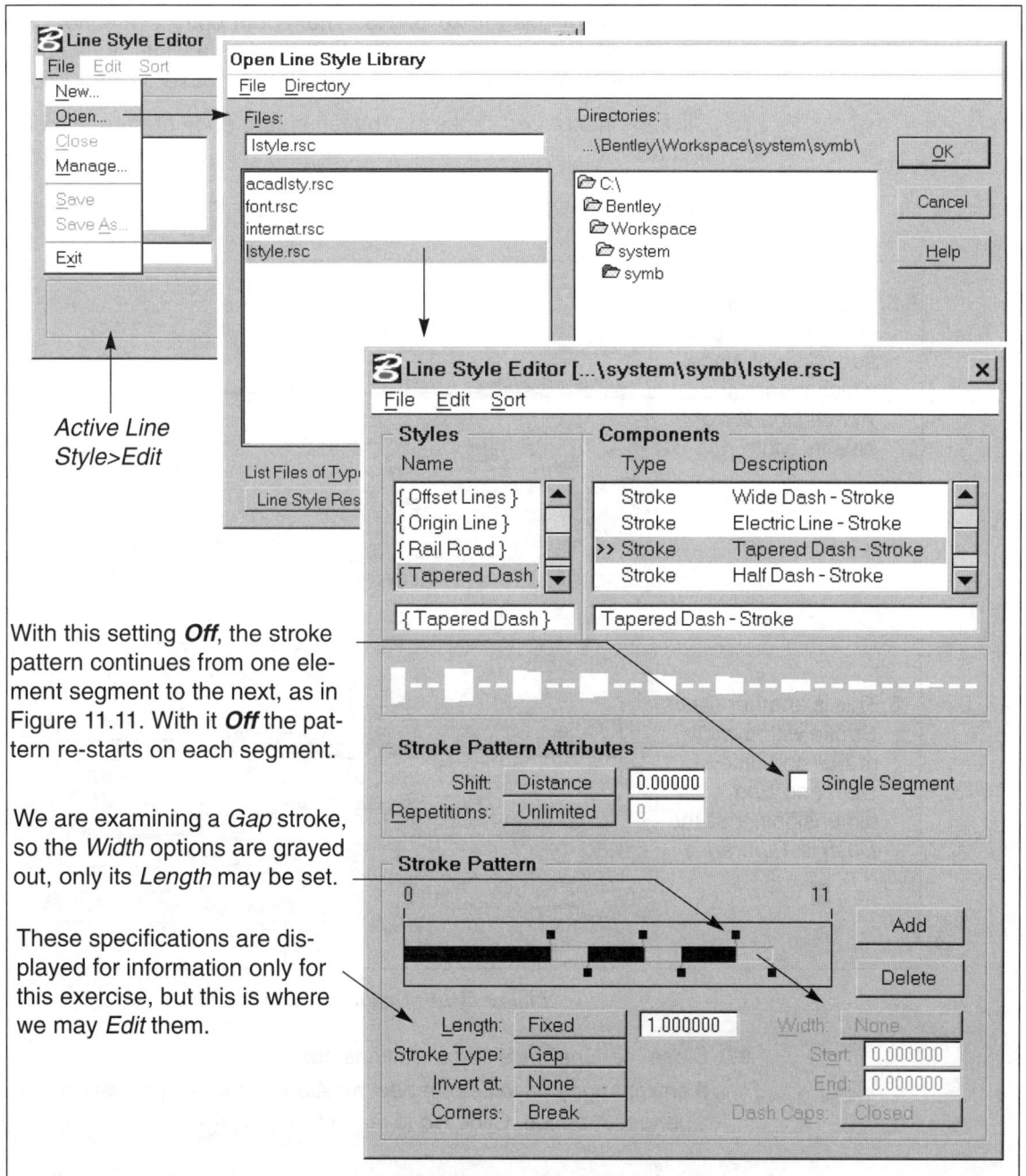

*Active Line
Style>Edit*

List Files of Type

Line Style Res

Line Style Editor [...\system\symb\lstyle.rsc]   ✕

File Edit Sort

Styles

Name

{ Offset Lines }
{ Origin Line }
{ Rail Road }
{ Tapered Dash }

{ Tapered Dash }

Components

Type	Description
Stroke	Wide Dash - Stroke
Stroke	Electric Line - Stroke
>> Stroke	Tapered Dash - Stroke
Stroke	Half Dash - Stroke

Tapered Dash - Stroke

With this setting *Off*, the stroke pattern continues from one element segment to the next, as in Figure 11.11. With it *Off* the pattern re-starts on each segment.

We are examining a *Gap* stroke, so the *Width* options are grayed out, only its *Length* may be set.

These specifications are displayed for information only for this exercise, but this is where we may *Edit* them.

Stroke Pattern Attributes

Shift: Distance 0.00000

Repetitions: Unlimited 0

☐ Single Segment

Stroke Pattern

0   11

Add

Delete

Length: Fixed 1.000000   Width: None
Stroke Type: Gap   Start: 0.000000
Invert at: None   End: 0.000000
Corners: Break   Dash Caps: Closed

Figure 11.13 Opening the Line Style Library file

6. Click on the next stroke to the left, a *Dash* stroke.

The length of this stroke is **1.5**. The *Width* options are no longer grayed out, but this particular *Dash Stroke* has a width of *None*. The *Dash Caps* options only apply to dash strokes with a defined *Width*.

7. Click the next three strokes to the left in turn (they are repeats of the first two).

8. Click the left side *Dash* stroke, note the *Width*, *Start* and *End* settings.

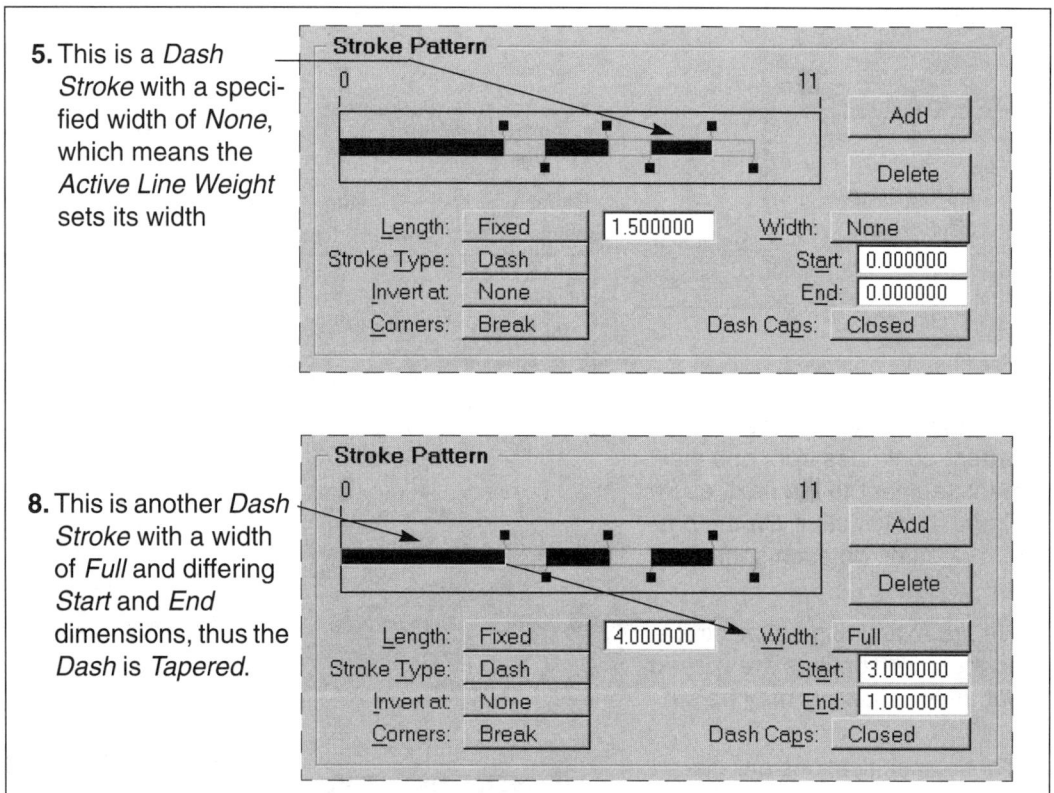

5. This is a *Dash Stroke* with a specified width of *None*, which means the *Active Line Weight* sets its width

Stroke Pattern
0   11
Add
Delete

Length: Fixed   1.500000   Width: None
Stroke Type: Dash   Start: 0.000000
Invert at: None   End: 0.000000
Corners: Break   Dash Caps: Closed

8. This is another *Dash Stroke* with a width of *Full* and differing *Start* and *End* dimensions, thus the *Dash* is *Tapered*.

Stroke Pattern
0   11
Add
Delete

Length: Fixed   4.000000   Width: Full
Stroke Type: Dash   Start: 3.000000
Invert at: None   End: 1.000000
Corners: Break   Dash Caps: Closed

Figure 11.14   Details of Dash Strokes

9. Close the *Line Style Editor* settings box.

If any changes have been made, an *Alert* box will display with a "*Save Changes?*" option. Click **No** to leave this line style intact.

Now that we have seen some details of an existing *Custom Line Style*, we will create our own *Line Style Library* file, then a couple of our own *Line Styles*.

Creating a New Line Style Library

We will use a new library file for the *Custom Line Styles* we will create shortly. This file will be in the same directory as the one we have looked at already. By placing it in ". . . Workspace\system\symb\", our line styles will appear in the menu along with the others. It is often worthwhile to copy these files into another directory outside the MicroStation path, to avoid accidental loss when the software is upgraded.

◆ **Create the Line Style Library "training.rsc"**

1. Choose *Edit* from the Primary tool bar, choose *File>New* from the *Line Style Editor* settings box.

   The *Create Line Style Library* dialog box opens, with the directory already set to suit the workspace component.

2. Key in **training** to the *Files:* field (".rsc" will be appended), click **OK**.

   The dialog box will close and focus will now pass back to the *Line Style Editor* settings box, which will now have the name of our new file in its Title bar.

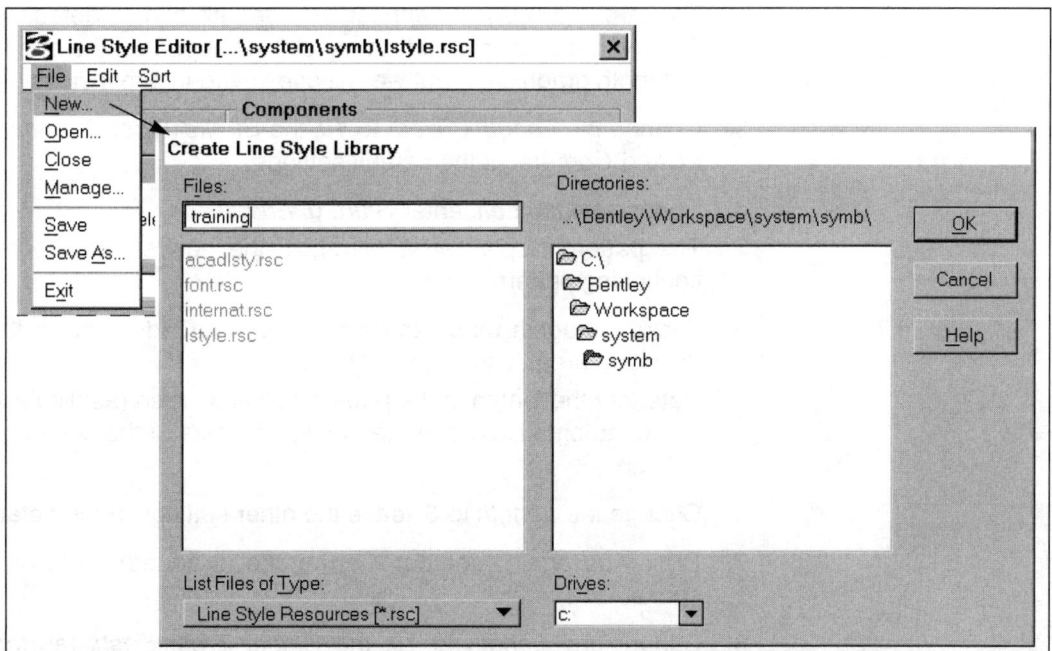

Figure 11.15   Creating a new Line Style Library file

Creating a Stroke Type Custom Line Style

Having opened a new Line Style *Library* or *Resource* file, we may now proceed to create the first of the custom line styles to be saved to it. This first one will be a *Stroke* type, in other words it will be lines only, no *Symbols*. The process of defining a line style of this type involves defining each stroke component individually. The basic settings for each component are whether it is a *Dash* or a *Gap*, its *Length* and (optionally) its *Width*. In practice, it may save time to *Duplicate* an existing style and modify this to create a new one, but this time we will start "from scratch".

◆ **Create a "sawtooth" Line Style**

1. Choose *Edit>Create>Stroke Pattern* from the *Line Style Editor* settings box.

    At this stage the lower part of the *Line Style Editor* opens. In the upper part, the *Styles* panel will be blank (at this stage there are no styles defined in the new file). *Stroke - new stroke component* will be highlighted in the *Components* panel.

2. Click *Add* in the *Stroke Pattern* panel (a *Gap* stroke is added to the formerly blank pattern definition area), click on this stroke.

    The stroke display will appear "pressed in" and its default length will display in the *Length* field. A handle will appear at the end for setting its length graphically, but we will use keyed-in dimensions.

3. Change the *Length* (*Fixed*) to **10**, the *Stroke Type: Dash*, leave *Invert at:* and *Corners:* at the default settings.

4. Choose *Width: Left*, enter *Start: 0*, *End: 8*.

    The pattern display area will show the new stroke repeating as a continuing pattern.

5. Click *Add* again (another *Gap* stroke is added to the to the pattern definition area), click on this stroke.

    Note that the length of the pattern definition area (as displayed above it) has automatically changed to suit the size of the component being built up.

6. Change the *Length* to **3**, leave the other settings at the defaults.

7. Click *Add* again (another *Gap* stroke is added), click on the new stroke.

8. Change the *Length* to **10**, the *Stroke Type: Dash*, (as for the first stroke), Choose *Width: Right*, enter *Start: 0*, *End: 8*.

9. *Add* another **3** long *Gap* to the end, as in steps **5.** and **6.** above.

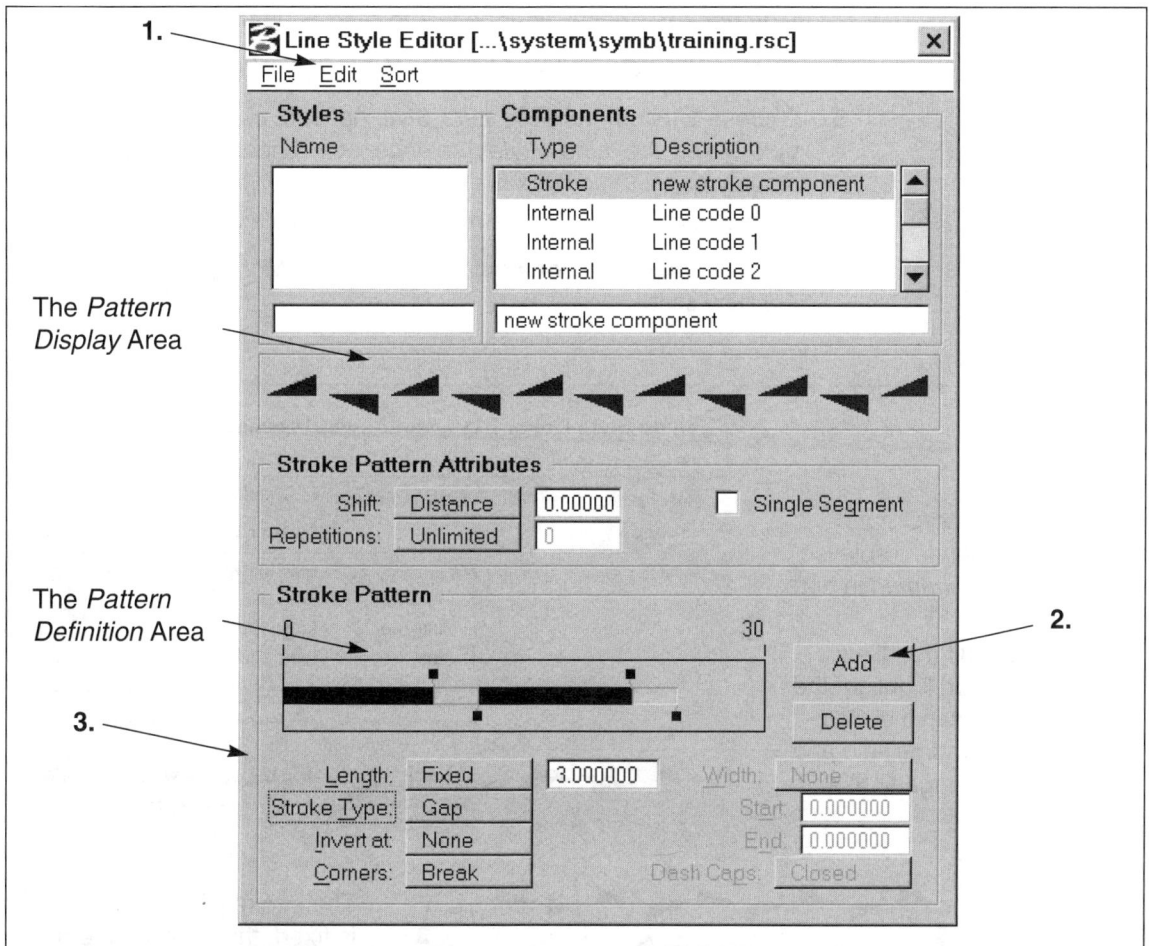

Figure 11.16   Using the Line Style Editor

We have defined a *Custom Line Style*, now we will *Name*, *Describe* and *Save* it to our *Line Style Library*.

◆ Name and Save the Line Style Definition

1. Choose *Edit>Create>Name* from the *Line Style Editor* menu. *Unnamed* appears in the *Style* panel and the field below it.

2. Change *Unnamed* in the data entry field to read **Saw**.

3. Highlight the text "new stroke component" in the field under the *Component* window, change this to read ***Bilateral Sawtooth***.

4. Choose *File>Save*, then close the *Line Style Editor* settings box.

5. Choose *Custom* from the *Line Style* options, check the *Show Details* box ***On*** in the *Line Styles* settings box, choose *Saw,* click on the display panel to activate it.
   With *Show Details **Off***, we may select the style by double-clicking.

6. Place elements, experiment with *Line Style Modifiers* (page 11-13) on the new style.

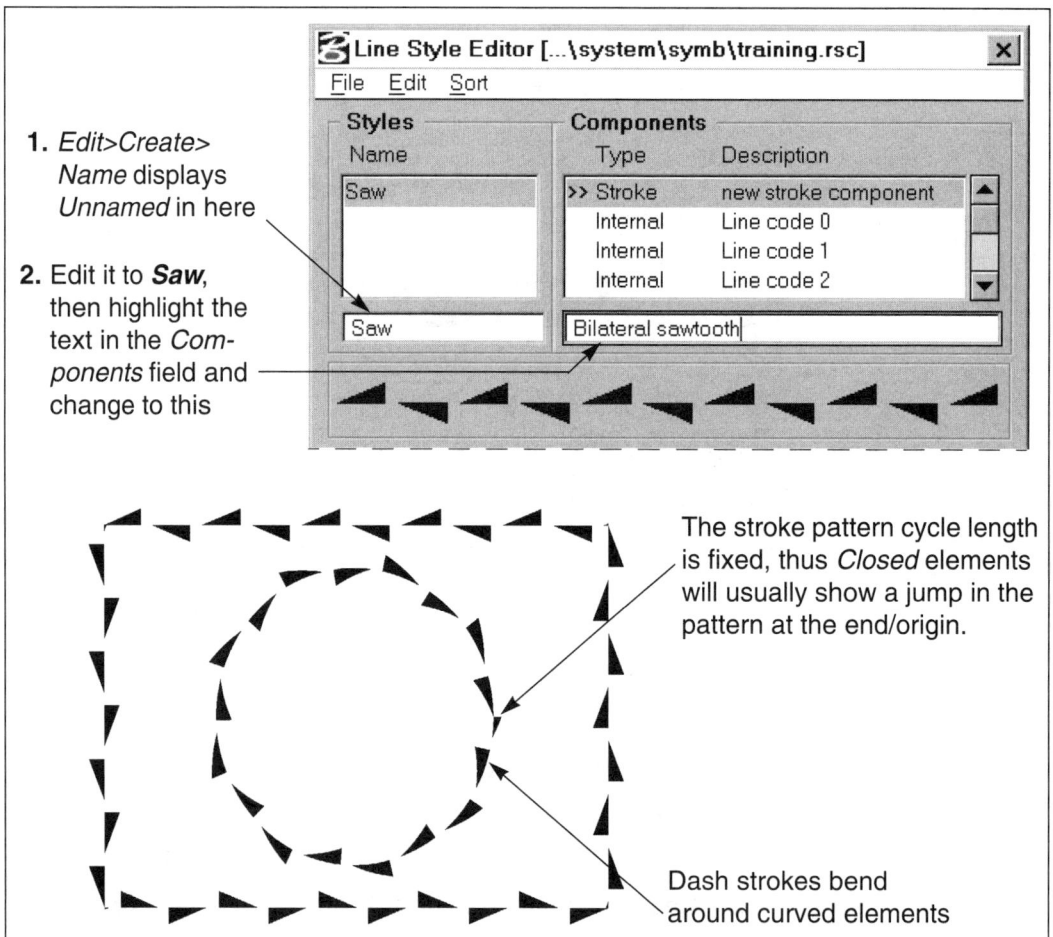

Figure 11.17   Naming and using the new Custom Line Style

Transporting Design Files with Custom Line Styles

Each time an element is displayed with a *Custom Line Style,* the *Line Style Library* is accessed to get the style definition, it is not stored in the design file itself. It follows that any time such a design file is to be displayed, MicroStation must have the appropriate line style library available. If we are sending a design file to another computer or computer network, it may be necessary to send a copy of your line style library to be installed on the receiving system.

There is another option, we may *Drop* the *Line Style* using the *Drop Line Style* tool from the *Drop* tool box from the *Tools* Application window menu. When we use this tool, an element created using a custom line style is changed to a group of elements (shapes etc.) with the same appearance.

The advantage of *Dropping* an element with a custom line style is that the design will now display (and print out) correctly on any system with MicroStation. It removes the need to install the appropriate line style library. A disadvantage is that the design file size increases with the larger number of elements. Another disadvantage is that what was a single element for manipulation, change or modification, is now a number of elements.

Editing Existing Custom Line Styles

The procedure used for *Editing* a line style is very much the same as creating a new one, except we choose a style to edit from the *Styles* panel of the *Line Style Editor.* When we have made the required changes, they need to be saved, just as we did when we created our new one.

Note: When a particular *Custom Line Style* is edited (re-defined), *All* lines placed in *All* design files on the system using this style will be displayed with the new definition.

Once a document has been issued using a particular custom line style, the style will seldom be edited. If some changes are required, it is usual to *Duplicate* the style, make the changes to the duplicate, then save it with a new name. This way the original line style definition is retained for existing designs, but the modified form is available for new ones.

◆ Edit a Duplicate of the Saw line style

1. Click on *Line Style>Edit*, choose *File>Open* and open (if necessary) *training.rsc.*

2. Click on *Saw*, then choose *Edit>Duplicate* in the *Line Style Editor* settings box.

A new *Stroke* component will appear in the *Components* panel, with the same description as the original. This component will be highlighted, indicating that it is the one we are working on.

3. Turn *Single Element **On*** in the *Stroke Pattern Attributes* panel.

4. Change the two *Dash Strokes* to ***Full*** width (instead of *Left* and *Right*).

5. Change the *Component* description to ***Full width sawtooth***

6. Choose *Edit>Create>Name* from the *Line Style Editor* menu.

   Unnamed appears in the *Style* panel and the field below it. The *Component* just re-described has ">>" beside it, indicating that this *Stroke Pattern Component* is *Linked* to the new name.

7. Change *Unnamed* in the data entry field to read ***Sawf***.

8. Choose *File>Save* to save the new line style definition, close the *Line Style Editor* settings box.

9. Choose the new line style from the *Line Style* menu, experiment with placing multi-segment elements. Compare the symbology with *Saw.*

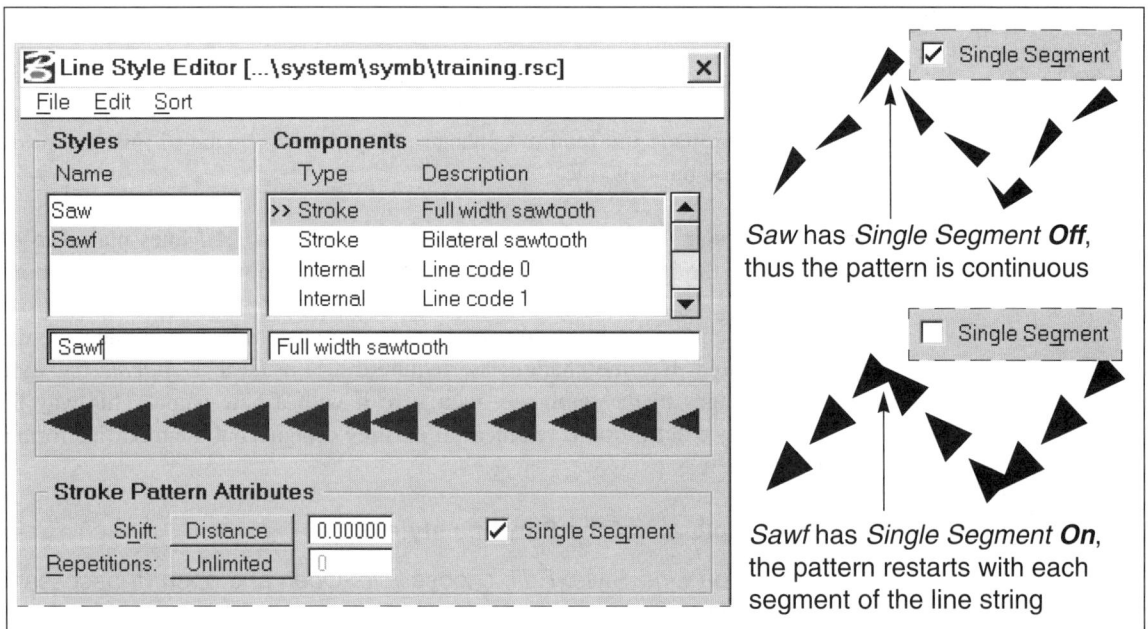

Saw has *Single Segment **Off***, thus the pattern is continuous

Sawf has *Single Segment **On***, the pattern restarts with each segment of the line string

Figure 11.18   Creating a Line Style by Editing a Duplicate

Creating a Compound Custom Line Style

A *Compound* line style has two types of *Components*:

- A *Stroke* component, usually with one or more *Gap* strokes to receive one or more *Point Symbols*;

- A *Point Symbol* component, with one or more symbols, usually positioned by an offset to fit into a *Gap* stroke component.

In the next exercise we will create one of these line styles, with one *Point Symbol* positioned in the gap between two *Dash Strokes*. When it is placed, it will look like the one illustrated in Figure 11.19.

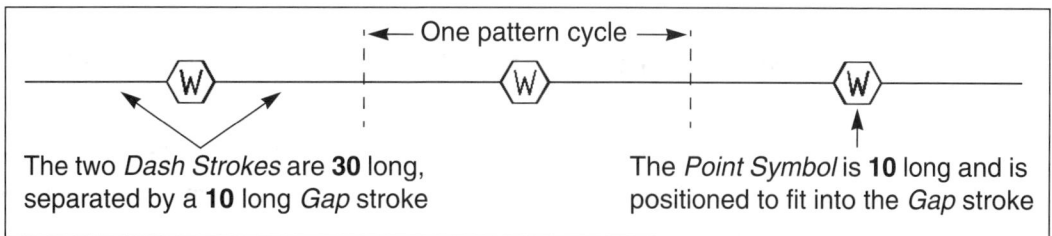

Figure 11.19   The Compound Line Style "HexW"

The Symbol Drawing

A *Point Symbol* is similar to a cell, it is a group of elements named and filed away for future use. It may take on the element attributes that are active when it is placed as part of a custom line style, or the original symbology as created. As in cell creation, the elements are temporarily grouped with a fence (or by multiple element selection) for the *Symbol* creation process. It is usual to define an *Origin* for the symbol at this stage as well, but this is not mandatory, as it may be defined later on.

◆ Draw the Point Symbol

1. Use the *Place Regular Polygon* tool (from the same tool box as the *Place Block* tool) to place an *Inscribed* hexagon with a radius (half-width) of **5**.

   Leave the *Radius* tool setting at **0** and use AccuDraw to place a vertex **5** along the x axis from the center.

2. Open the Text settings box, select a font, **Center-Center** *Justification*, *Text Height* and *Width* of **5**.

3. Place an upper case "**W**" in the center of the hexagon using a *Center* snap to position it.

4. Place a fence about the hexagon, select the *Define Cell Origin* tool (page 6-7), snap a *Tentative* point to position the origin in the center of the hexagon, *Accept.*

The Stroke Pattern

Now we have a symbol drawing complete, we will create the *Stroke Pattern* to go with it. As shown in Figure 11.19, the stroke pattern consists of two *30* long *Dashes*, separated by a *10* long *Gap*. The process is similar to the one used to create the stroke pattern components for the Sawtooth line styles. This stroke pattern will only be created to the *Component* stage, it will not be linked to a name as a line style in its own right.

◆ Create the Base Stroke Pattern for a Compound Line Style

1. Open the *Line Style Editor* settings box, open the "training.rsc" *Line Style Library* file if this does not already appear in the Title bar.

2. Choose *Edit>Create>Stroke Pattern* from the *Line Style Editor.*

3. Click *Add* in the *Stroke Pattern* panel to add a *Gap* stroke pattern definition area, click on this stroke.

4. Change the *Length* (*Fixed*) to *30*, the *Stroke Type: Dash*, leave the *Width* set to **None**, the other settings at the default values.

5. Click *Add* again, click on this stroke, change the *Length* to *10*, leave it as a *Gap*, leave the other settings at the defaults.

6. Click *Add* again (another *Gap* stroke is added), click on the new stroke.

7. Change the *Length* to *30*, the *Stroke Type:* **Dash**, *Width* **None** (as for the first stroke).

8. *Replace* 'new stroke component" in the *Components* field with the description **Stroke pattern for Hexline** (remember to **<Tab>**).

9. With *Input Focus* still in the *Components* panel, choose *File>Save* to save the stroke component.

The settings are illustrated in Figure 11.20, at the stage of entering the stroke pattern description (step **8.**). At this stage we have the *Stroke Pattern* component for our *Compound* line style. It does not matter which existing style is highlighted.

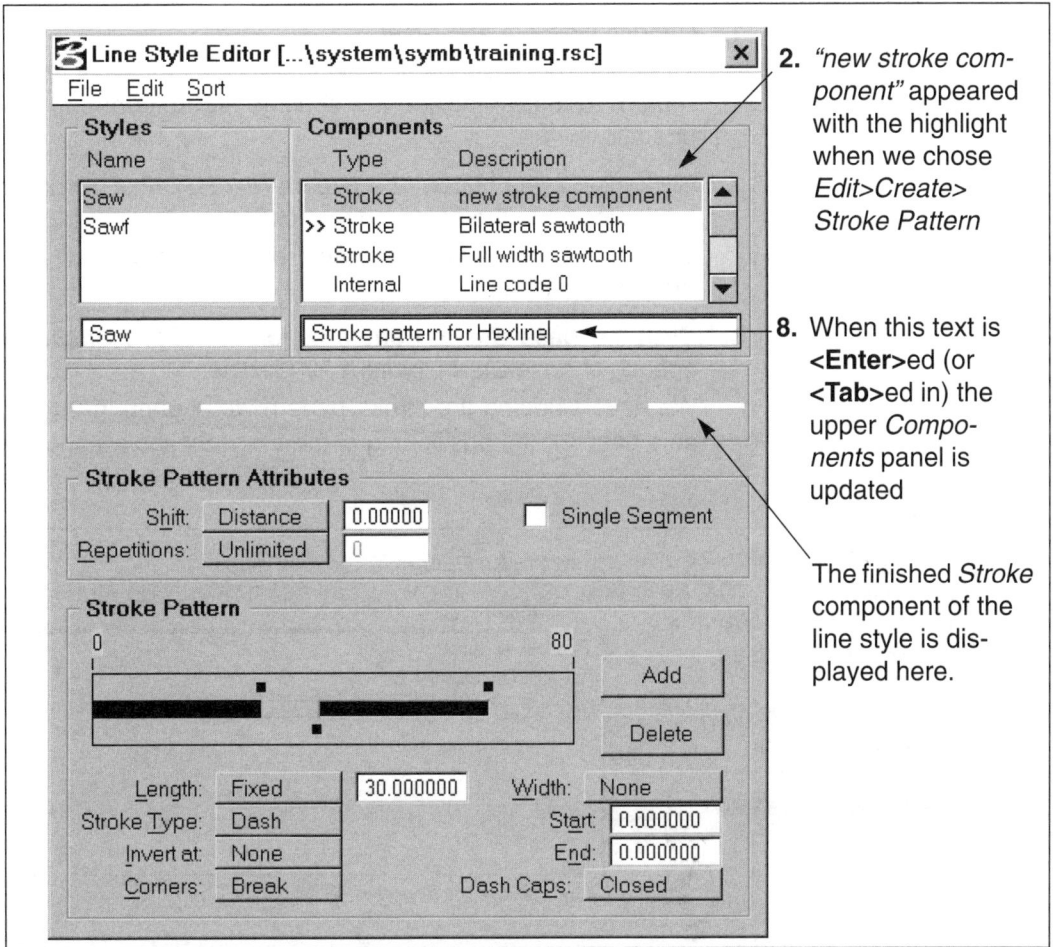

Figure 11.20   Settings for the Stroke Pattern Component

The Point Symbol Component

At this stage we have a *Drawing* prepared from the previous exercise, with the elements fenced and an *Origin* defined. As yet, it has not been saved as a *Symbol* to our ".rsc" file. That will be the first action in the next exercise. We will then use the *Symbol* in to create a *Point Symbol Component*. This component will have the offsets for spacing the symbol to fit the *Stroke Pattern Component* defined in it, as well as the name of symbol itself.

◆ **Create a Symbol and Point Symbol Component**

1. Choose *Edit>Create>Point*.

   The lower part of the *Line Style Editor* changes away from the *Stroke Pattern* format to include the settings and buttons for *Point Symbol* operations.

2. Click the *Create* button (the *Create Point Symbol* dialog box opens), enter **Hex1** into the *Name* field, click **OK**.

   The *Create* button will be grayed out if there are not any elements fenced or selected.

3. Click the *Base Stroke Pattern* button (the *Base Stroke Pattern* box opens), choose *Stroke pattern for Hexline*.

   We have selected the stroke pattern we created in the last exercise as a base for the positioning of the *Point Symbols* along the line.

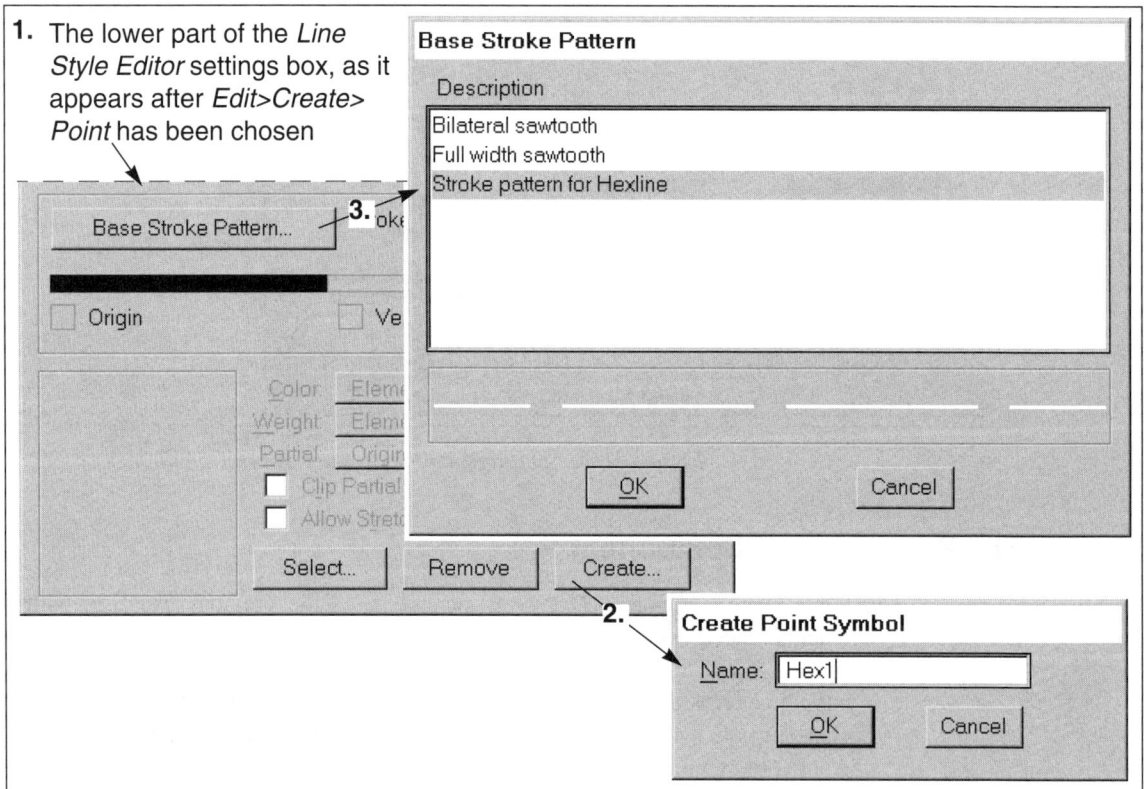

1. The lower part of the *Line Style Editor* settings box, as it appears after *Edit>Create>Point* has been chosen

Base Stroke Pattern... ⌐3. oke

☐ Origin   ☐ Ve

Color Elem
Weight Elem
Partial Origin
☐ Clip Partial
☐ Allow Stret

Select...   Remove   Create...

Base Stroke Pattern

Description

Bilateral sawtooth
Full width sawtooth
Stroke pattern for Hexline

OK   Cancel

2.

Create Point Symbol

Name: Hex1

OK   Cancel

Figure 11.21   Creating the Symbol and selecting the Base Stroke Pattern

◆ **Positioning the Point Symbol**

1. Click the *Gap* in the *Base Stroke Pattern* bar display, check that the *Justify* setting is *Center*.

    This identifies the position that the *Origin* of the *Point Symbol* will take with respect to the *Stroke Pattern*.

2. Click the *Select* button to open the *Select Point Symbol* dialog box.

3. Select *Hex1*, click **OK**.

    The point symbol will display in the left side panel and in the line style display above the *Base Stroke Pattern* button.

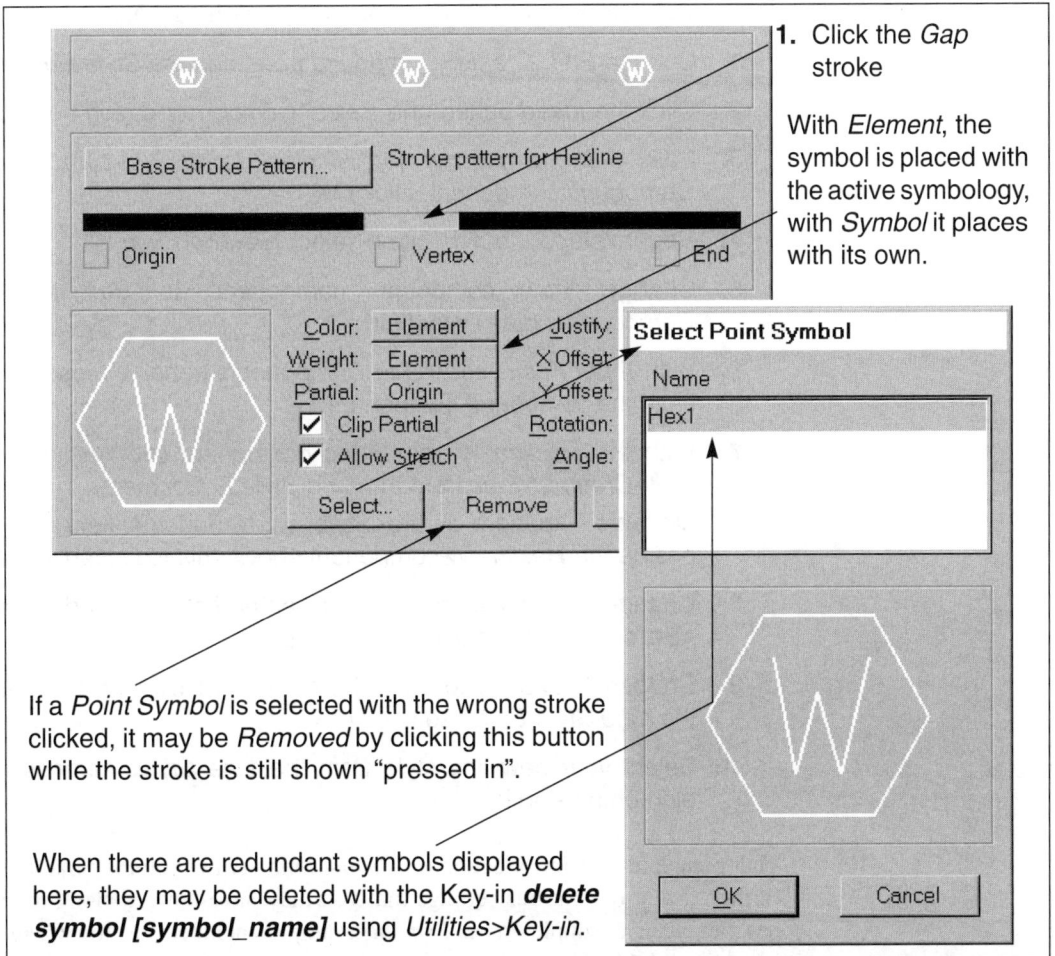

Figure 11.22   Positioning and Selecting the Point Symbol

4. Change "new point component" to **Hexagon with W** in the *Components* data entry field.

5. With *Input Focus* still in the *Components* panel, choose *File>Save* to save the point component.

Putting It Together

We now have the two components we require for our *Compound* custom line style, the *Stroke* component and the *Point Symbol* component. It only remains to combine these in a *Compound* component and allocate a *Name*.

◆ Create a Compound Component and link it to a Name

1. Choose *Edit>Create>Compound* from the *Line Style Editor*.

2. Click the *Insert* button (the *Select Component* dialog box opens).

3. Select *Stroke pattern for Hexline* as a *Sub-component* of the *Compound* component, click **OK**.

4. Repeat step **2.**, but this time select *Hexagon with W*.

5. Change "new compound component" to *Hexline W* in the *Components* data entry field.

6. With *Input Focus* still in the *Components* panel, choose *File>Save* to save the compound component.

7. With the *Hexline W* compound component still highlighted, choose *Edit>Create>Name* from the *Line Style Editor* menu.
   Unnamed appears in the *Style* panel and the field below it, ">>" beside the *Hexline W* component shows this is *Linked* to the name.

8. Change *Unnamed* in the data entry field to read **HexW**, press **<Enter>** to change it in the *Styles* panel.

9. Choose *File>Save* to save the completed *Custom Line Style*, close the *Line Style Editor* settings box.

10. Select your new line style from the *Line Styles* settings box, place elements using it.

That completes our introduction to *Custom Line Styles*. You may like to experiment further, trying out various settings that you may have noticed along the way. There has not been a simple *Point Symbol* example included, as the *Compound* style incorporated this. However, this is one area you may like to try for yourself, perhaps starting by editing a duplicate of the *Batten* style.

The settings box is shown here with the *Compound Component* being described, before a new *Name* for the *Style* has been created.

5.

2. Insert the two *Sub-components*, one at a time. If an incorrect sub-component is inserted, highlight it and click the **Remove** button.

4. *Insert* this *Point Symbol* . . .

3. **after** selecting this *Stroke Pattern.*

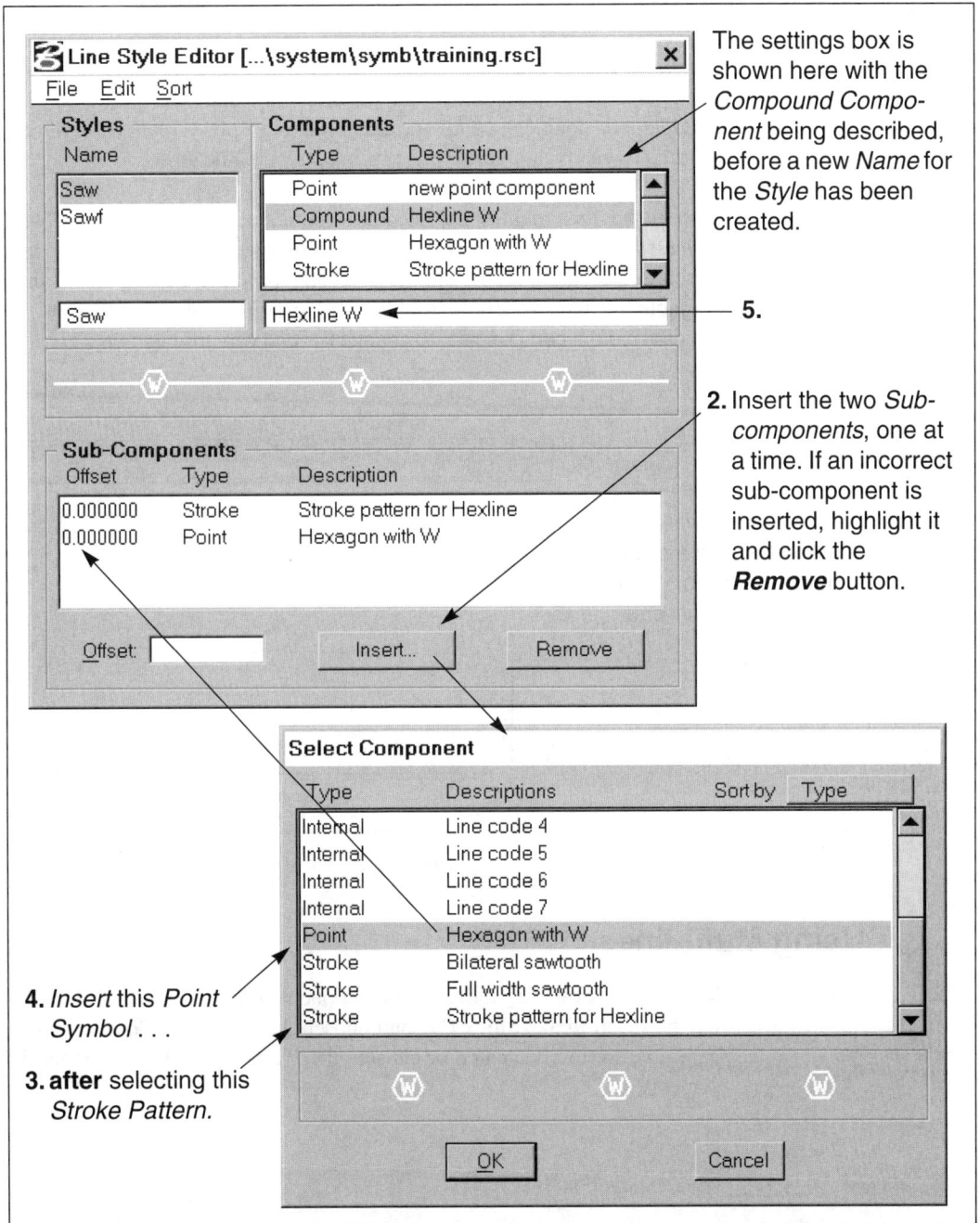

Figure 11.23 Assembling the Compound Custom Line Style

Multi-Lines

The Multi-line facility allows us to place elements consisting of up to 16 parallel lines, with or without end caps, placing only one data point per vertex. As an example, we could place all the lines making up the plan view of the walls of a building as easily and quickly as placing a single line string.

Each of the lines making up the multi-line element may be defined with individual attributes (including *Custom* line styles). The spacing of these component lines from a theoretical base line is also individually defined. Once placed, there are tools available from the *Multi-line* tool box to create joins of various forms, to cut gaps in any or all of the components, to change the end cap arrangements etc.

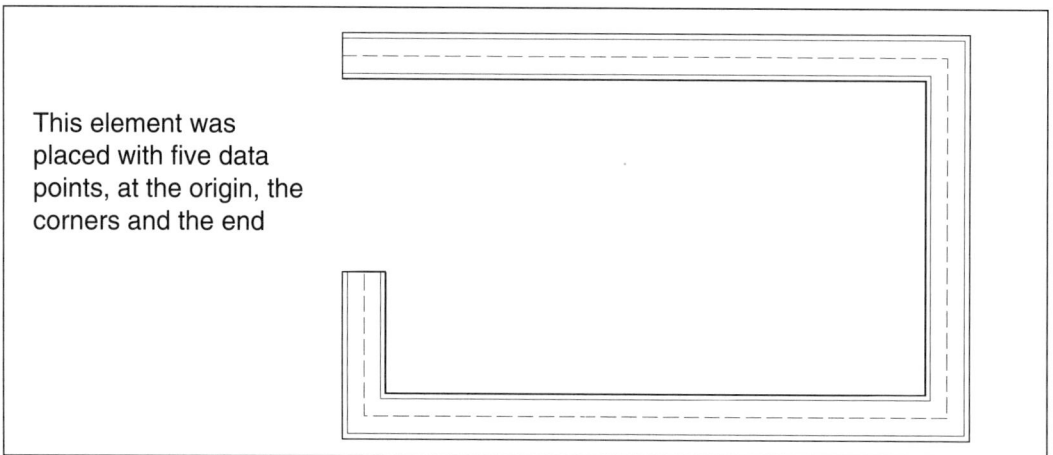

This element was placed with five data points, at the origin, the corners and the end

Figure 11.24   A Multi-line element

Using Multi-lines

We need to define the individual component lines of a multi-line first. Definitions may be saved to a *Settings File* and chosen from there, or defined as we need them. Once a definition is created or chosen, the *Place Multi-line* tool is used to place the elements.

Defining a Multi-line

A multi-line is made up of *Line* and *Cap* components. Each individual component can have its own *Element Attributes* (level, color, line style and line weight). *Line* components also have a distance from a datum line, thus defining their distance apart.

Any of the components can be defined as taking on any or all of the element attributes active at time of placement of the multi-line. The more generally used alternative is to override the active element attributes, with settings that form part of the *Multi-line Definition*. The definition is created in the *Multi-lines* settings box.

The Multi-lines Settings Box

This settings box opened by choosing *Element>Multi-line* from the Application window menu. It provides the facilities to *Insert*, *Delete* and *Duplicate* lines, individually define the attributes for the components. The line is displayed as it is being defined.

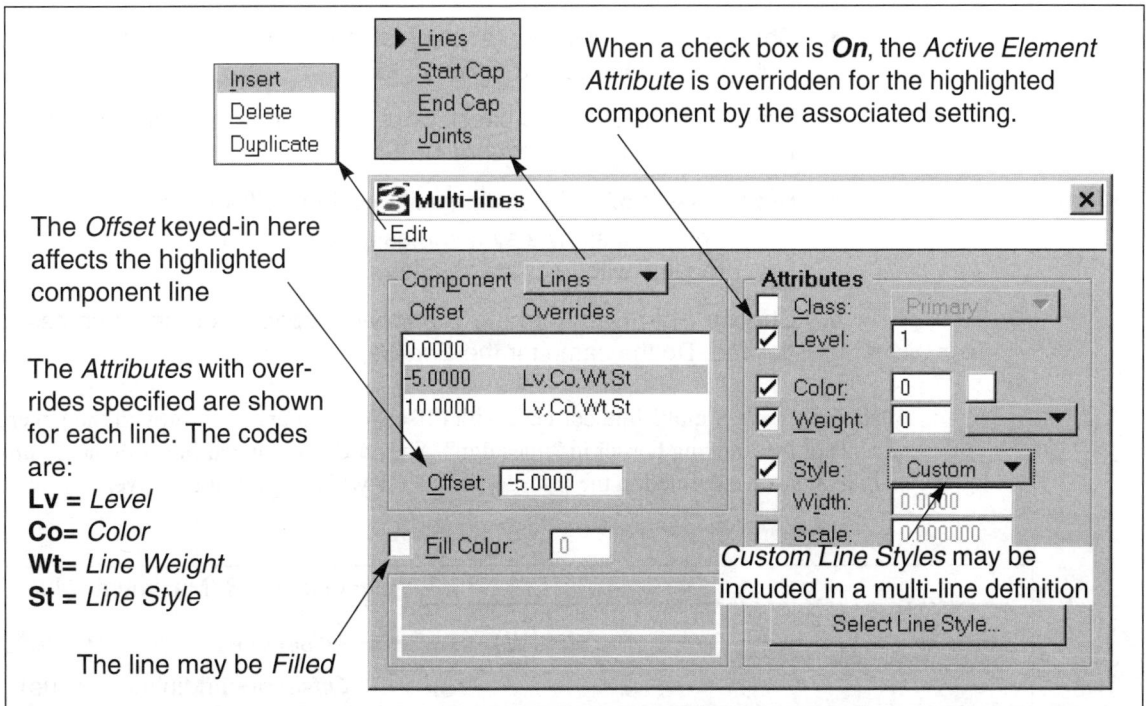

Figure 11.25   The Multi-lines settings box

We will *Define* a simple multi-line and place multi-line elements with it in the next exercises. We will use a similar definition to introduce *Multi-line Joints*.

◆ **Define a Multi-line**

1. Choose *Element>Multi-lines* to open the *Multi-lines* settings box.
   The box will display an existing definition, which we will modify.

2. If necessary, choose *Lines* from the *Components* menu, then choose *Edit>Delete*.
   The previously highlighted line definition will be deleted and the highlight move to another line.

3. Continue deleting lines as above until there is only one left.
   The last line definition will not delete.

4. Overwrite the contents of the *Offset* data entry field with *0*.

5. Turn *Off* all of the constraint check boxes in the *Attributes* panel.
   This component will now take on the element attributes *Active* at the time it is placed, including a custom line style. The display panel will show the currently active symbology.

6. Choose *Edit>Duplicate* (a copy of the previous definition is now highlighted), change the *Offset* to *-5*.

7. Turn all of the *Attribute* check boxes *On*, choose a *Level*, a *Color*, a *Line Weight* and a *Standard Line Style*.

8. Repeat steps *6.* and *7.*, but this time set the *Offset* to *8*.
   The display will show a symmetrically spaced three component multi-line, probably with contrasting caps.

9. Choose *Start Cap* from the *Component* options, set its attributes as desired. Do the same for the *End Cap*.

Now we have a multi-line defined, with offsets chosen are to fit in with the general scale of the drawing border in "lines.dgn". They are also compatible with the *Custom Line Styles* we defined in the last section, *HexW* will appear if it is active.

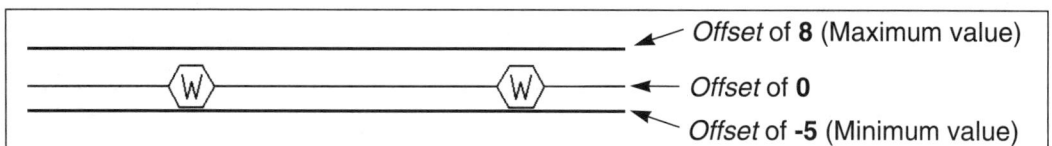

Figure 11.26 A multi-line incorporating the active line style

The Place Multi-line Tool

This tool operates like the *Place Smartline* tool in that it will create a single *Open* or *Closed* element. Its Tool Settings window (illustrated in Figure 11.28) has *Length* and *Angle* constraint settings, together with *Place by* options and an *Association Lock* check box.

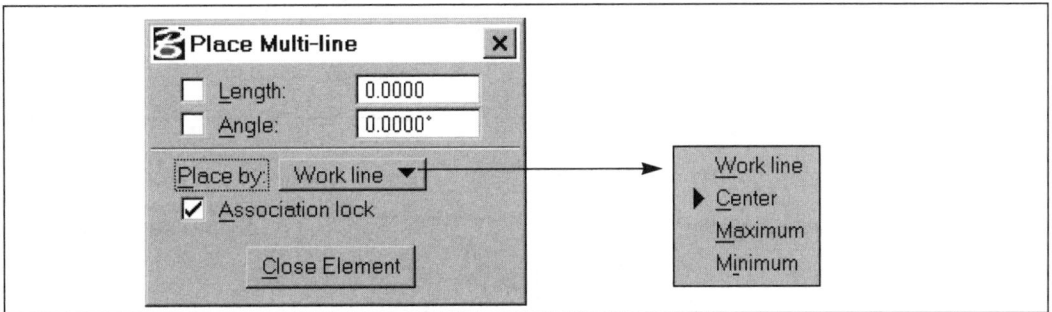

Figure 11.27   The Place Multi-line tool settings

Multi-lines are often placed with the help of tentative points on a setting-out grid or other construction guides, with which they may be *Associated*. We will use a series of square blocks for construction guides in the following exercises.

◆ **Prepare guide blocks for Multi-line exercise**

1. Set the active color to *Yellow*, the *Line Style* to *2* (medium dash) and the *Line Weight* to *0*.

2. Use *AccuDraw,* the *Place Block* and *Copy Element* tools to place five *50* square blocks (anywhere) to use as guides.

Now, to place some multi-line elements, with the origin located with a snap to the top-right corner of one of the guide blocks. The *Place By* options define how the multi-line is positioned with respect to the data points used to place it. Multi-line vertices may be *Associated* with points on another element or elements.

◆ **Placing a Multi-line by Workline**

1. Set the active color to *0*, the *Line Style* to (Custom) *HexW*.

2. Select the *Place Multi-line* tool, found next to the *Place Line* tool in the *Linear Elements* tool box (the one with *Place Smartline* on the left).

3. Leave the tool settings at the defaults (*Length* and *Angle* unconstrained, as shown in Figure 11.27).

4. Place the start point by snapping to the top-right vertex of a guide block, *Accept*, then snap to the bottom-right, *Accept.*

5. Snap to the bottom-left and *Accept.*

We are placing the multi-line around the block in this direction to place the *Maximum* offset value line on the outside, for comparisons with other *Place By:* settings in later exercises.

6. Snap and *Accept* the last point at the top-left, *Reset* to complete the element.

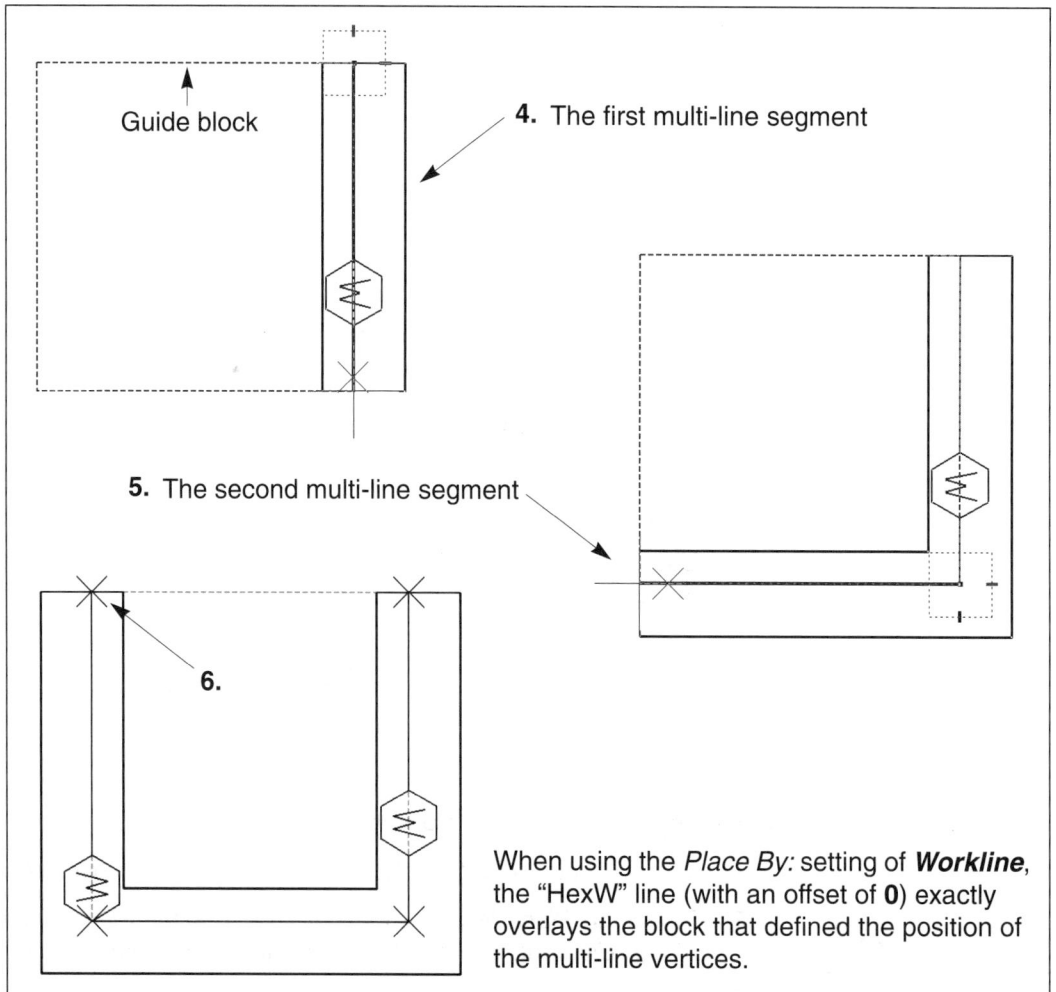

Guide block

4. The first multi-line segment

5. The second multi-line segment

6.

When using the *Place By:* setting of **Workline**, the "HexW" line (with an offset of **0**) exactly overlays the block that defined the position of the multi-line vertices.

Figure 11.28 Placing a Multi-line by Workline

In the last exercise the multi-line was placed with its position defined with respect to a line with *0 Offset*. In our example, there happened to be an actual line with this "lack of" offset, but the line may well be hypothetical. This is not always the most convenient method of positioning a multi-line. For example, consider a case where the *Outside* of all the lines forming the **U** is to have the specified dimensions.

The first point to consider is "which of the lines do we want on the outside?" (for the exercise, we will take it to be the one with the *Maximum Positive Offset*). The next point is "which side of the line is the positive side?" (that is the *Left* side of the line, looking away from its origin). We will try all this out in the next exercise.

◆ Placing a Multi-line by Maximum and Minimum

1. Leave the settings as they were made for the last exercise.

2. Select the *Place Multi-line* tool, change the *Place By:* tool setting to **Maximum**.

3. Place a **U** shaped multi-line in an clockwise direction, positioning the start, end and corner vertices with snaps to another of the blocks.

   Placing it in the clockwise direction puts the *positive* side of the multi-line to the *outside* of the shape or string.

4. Repeat steps **2.** and **3.**, this time with *Place By:* **Minimum**.

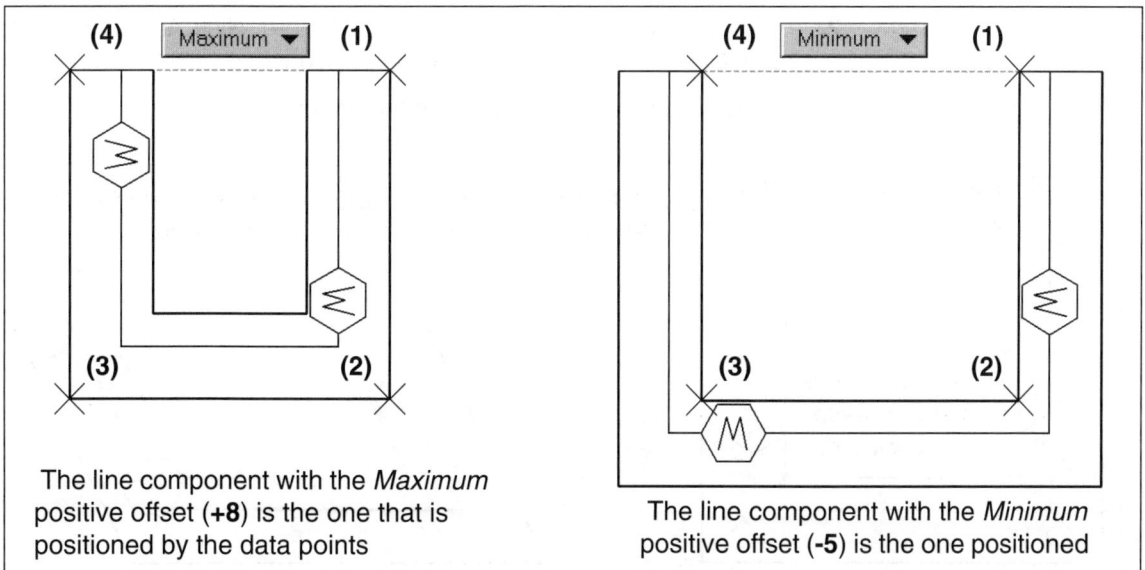

The line component with the *Maximum* positive offset (**+8**) is the one that is positioned by the data points

The line component with the *Minimum* positive offset (**-5**) is the one positioned

Figure 11.29   Placing a Multi-line by Maximum and Minimum

Associating Multi-lines

An *Associated* end or vertex of a multi-line moves automatically when the element it is associated with is modified. For a multi-line vertex to be *Associated*, two criteria must be met:

- *Association Lock* must be *On* at the time the vertex is placed;
- The *Association Point* on the element must be *Snapped to* and the tentative point *Accepted* to establish the multi-line vertex as an *Association Point.*

If these criteria look a little familiar, it is because they are very similar to those for an *Associated* dimension, as introduced in Chapter 9. We placed the multi-lines in the last exercises using snaps, with *Association Lock On*, so they should be associated with the square blocks used as a guides. If you try manipulating or modifying one of the blocks, the associated vertices will move with the point that were snapped to when the multi-line was placed. It is not necessary to make *All* of the vertices of a particular multi-line *Associated*, as they were in the earlier exercises. We will experiment with this in the next exercise.

◆ Placing a Multi-line Partially Associated

1. Select the *Place Multi-line* tool, *Place By: Center*, place the origin of another **U** shaped multi-line using a snap to another of the blocks, click *Association Lock Off After* placing the origin.

2. Place the two corners using snaps as before, click *Association Lock* back *On*, then place the end, again positioning it with a snap.

3. Try *Moving* the guide block, note the effect.

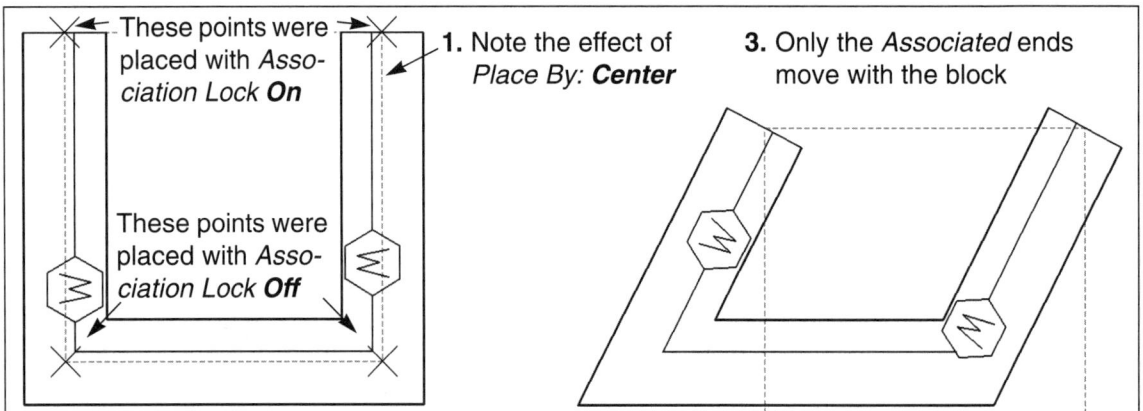

Figure 11.30 Selective Association of a Multi-line element

Closed Multi-line Elements

The *Place Multi-line* tool settings include a *Close Element* button. Clicking this will result in the multi-line extending from the last data point placed back to the origin, in the same way as with tools such as *Place Shape*. All of the component lines are joined and the caps eliminated, making a set of closed shapes.

We will produce a closed multi-line element in the next exercise, trying out some other features at the same time. When we are placing a multi-line in relation to other elements (e.g. a plan grid), it is often necessary to swap between *Place By* settings for each segment. This allows us to place the lines inside the grid for one segment, centered for another, outside for another, and so on.

Another setting we will use this time is *Fill Color*. This is a setting made in the *Multi-lines* settings box when defining the multi-line.

◆ **Place a closed and filled multi-line element**

1. Check *Fill On* in the *Multi-lines* settings box, choose a *Fill Color*.

2. Place a multi-line element as before (using a guide box), except swap between *Place By* tool settings before each segment and DO NOT *Reset* after the fourth data point.

3. Click the *Close Element* button.

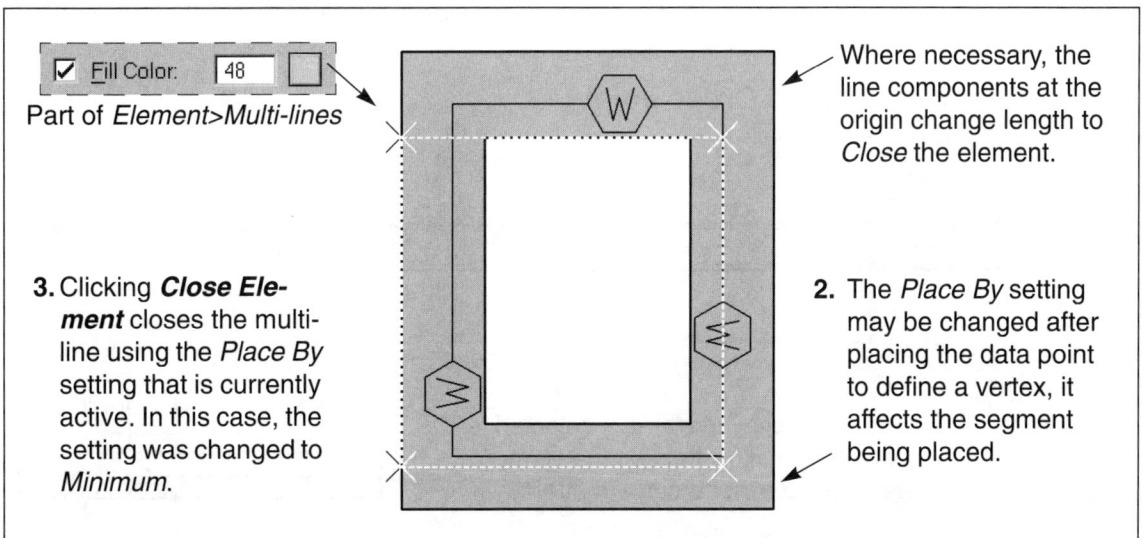

☑ Fill Color: 48 ☐
Part of *Element>Multi-lines*

Where necessary, the line components at the origin change length to *Close* the element.

3. Clicking **Close Element** closes the multi-line using the *Place By* setting that is currently active. In this case, the setting was changed to *Minimum*.

2. The *Place By* setting may be changed after placing the data point to define a vertex, it affects the segment being placed.

Figure 11.31   A Closed, Filled Multi-line element, various Place By settings

The Multi-line Joints Tool Box

This tool box must be opened from the Application window *Tools* menu. The tools operate on multi-lines as single elements. When the Multi-line, or individual component lines are cut, the remaining parts either side of the cut may still be manipulated as a single element. The exception is when the *Multi-line Partial Delete* tool is used on an open multi-line, when two elements are created from the one.

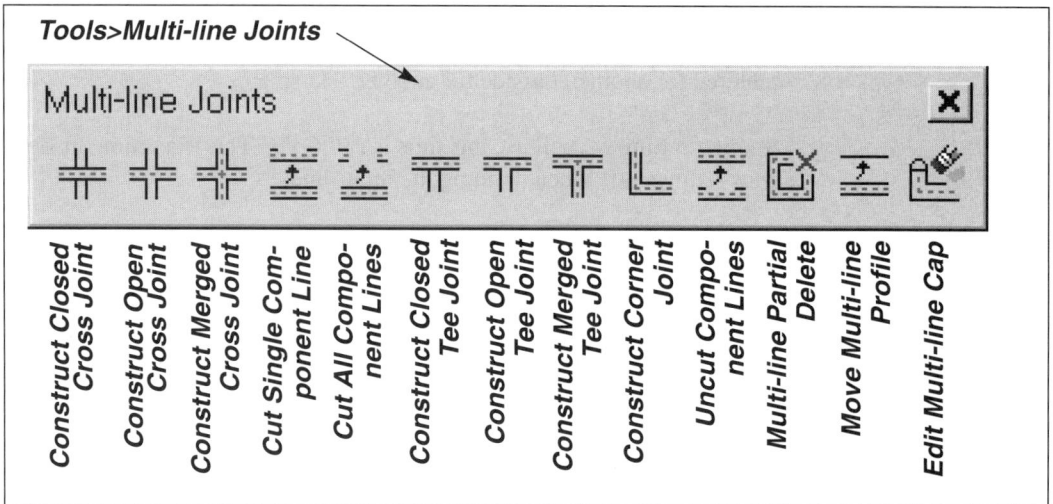

Figure 11.32   The Dimension Tool Box, Angle and Radial Dimensioning tools

Construct Closed Cross Joint

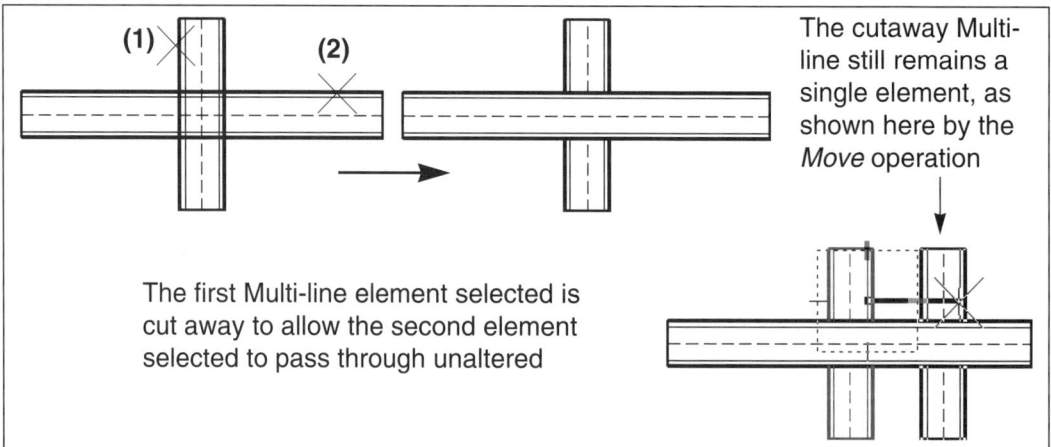

The cutaway Multi-line still remains a single element, as shown here by the *Move* operation

The first Multi-line element selected is cut away to allow the second element selected to pass through unaltered

Construct Open Cross Joint

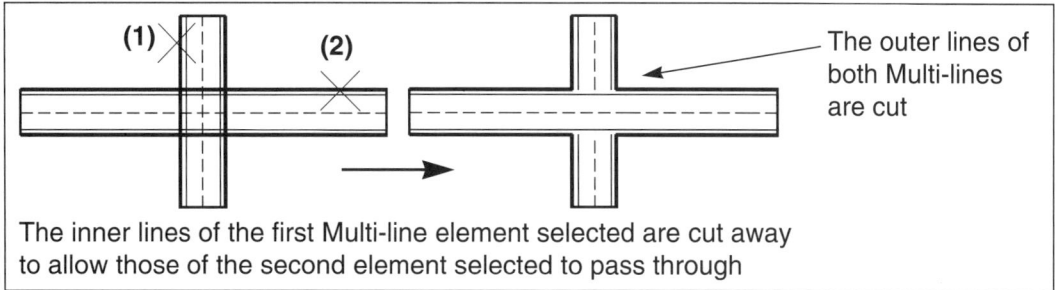

The outer lines of both Multi-lines are cut

The inner lines of the first Multi-line element selected are cut away to allow those of the second element selected to pass through

Construct Merged Cross Joint

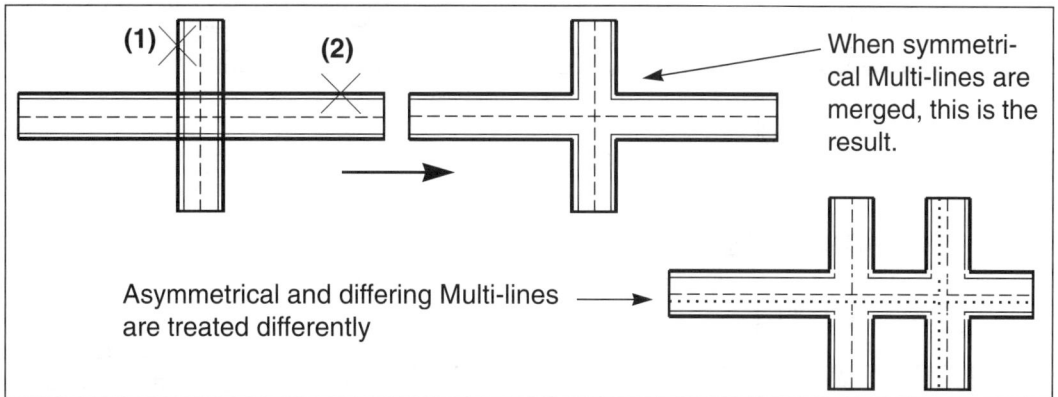

When symmetrical Multi-lines are merged, this is the result.

Asymmetrical and differing Multi-lines are treated differently

Cut Single Component Line

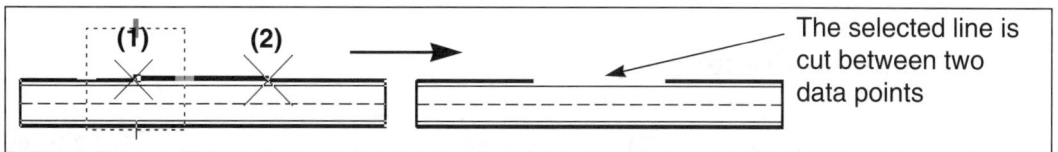

The selected line is cut between two data points

Cut All Component Lines

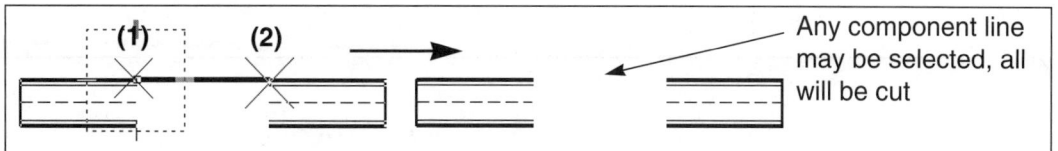

Any component line may be selected, all will be cut

Construct Closed Tee Joint

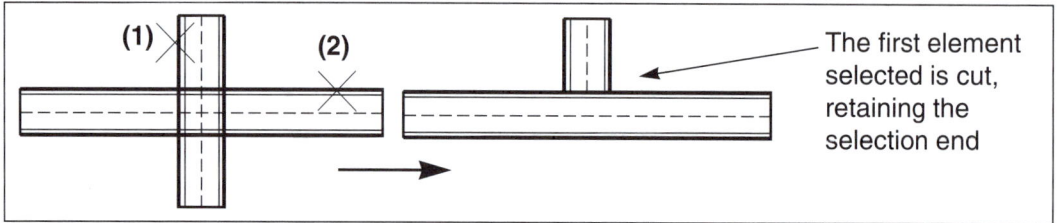

The first element selected is cut, retaining the selection end

Construct Open Tee Joint

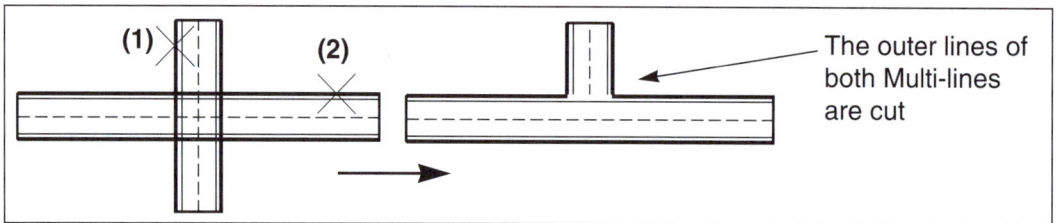

The outer lines of both Multi-lines are cut

Construct Merged Tee Joint

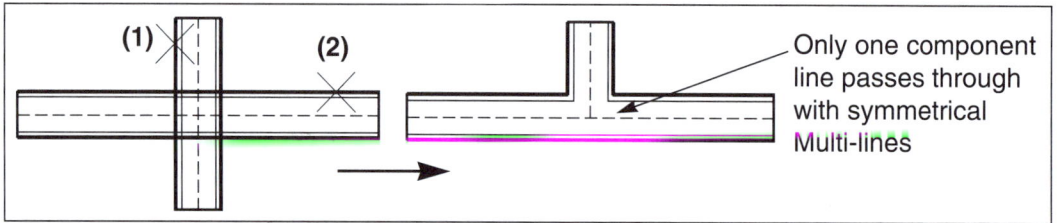

Only one component line passes through with symmetrical Multi-lines

Construct Corner Joint

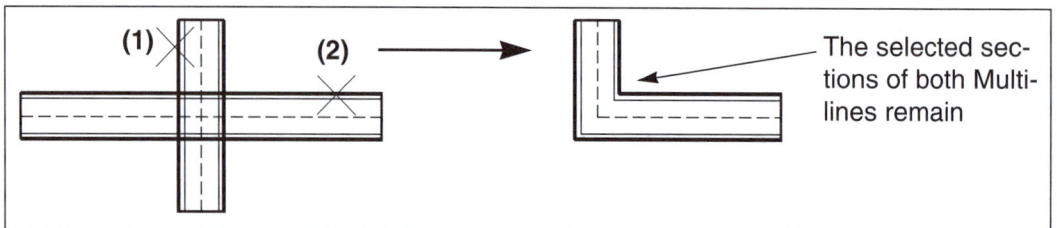

The selected sections of both Multi-lines remain

Uncut Component Lines

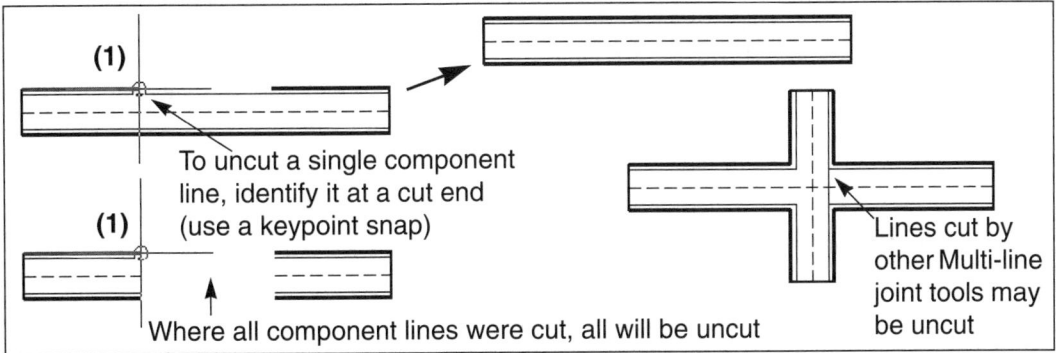

(1)

To uncut a single component line, identify it at a cut end (use a keypoint snap)

(1)

Where all component lines were cut, all will be uncut

Lines cut by other Multi-line joint tools may be uncut

Multi-line Partial Delete

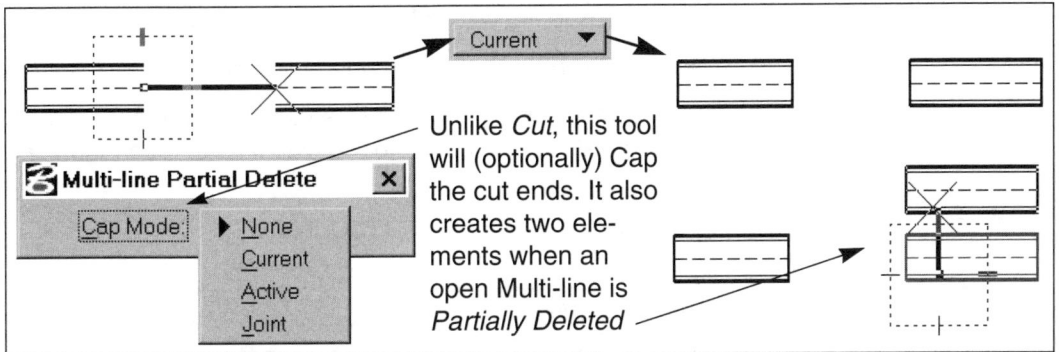

Current

Unlike *Cut*, this tool will (optionally) Cap the cut ends. It also creates two elements when an open Multi-line is *Partially Deleted*

Multi-line Partial Delete ☒

Cap Mode: ▶ None
Current
Active
Joint

Move Multi-line Profile

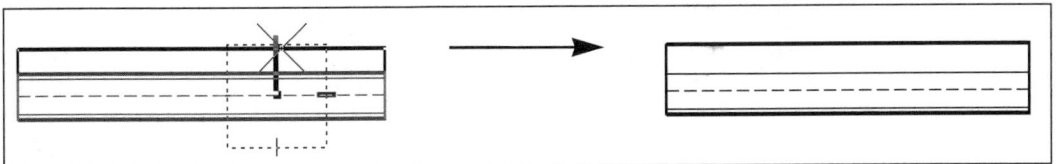

Edit Multi-line Cap

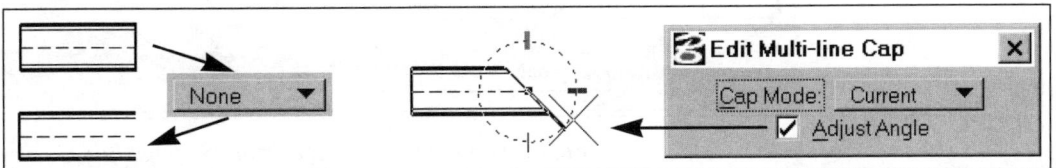

None ▼

Edit Multi-line Cap ☒

Cap Mode: Current ▼
☑ Adjust Angle

Multi-lines in Settings Files

Generally, any Multi-line definition we create will be useful in more than one design file. Likewise, we will probably need more than one multi-line style in a particular design, so we can increase efficiency by *Saving* a set of styles for general use. Multi-line styles may be defined and saved in *Settings Files*, making them permanently available, including across a network.

Saving a Multi-line Definition

We will save our current multi-line definition in our settings file "yachts.stg" (created on page 11-3) in the next exercise.

◆ **Saving the active Multi-line definition**

1. Check that the *Active* multi-line definition in the *Element>Multi-lines* settings box is the one to be saved (re-define it if necessary).

2. Choose *Settings>Manage* to open the *Select Settings* settings box.

3. Choose *File>Open* (from the settings box menu) for the *Open Existing Settings file* box, choose "yachts.stg" (see Figure 11.33).

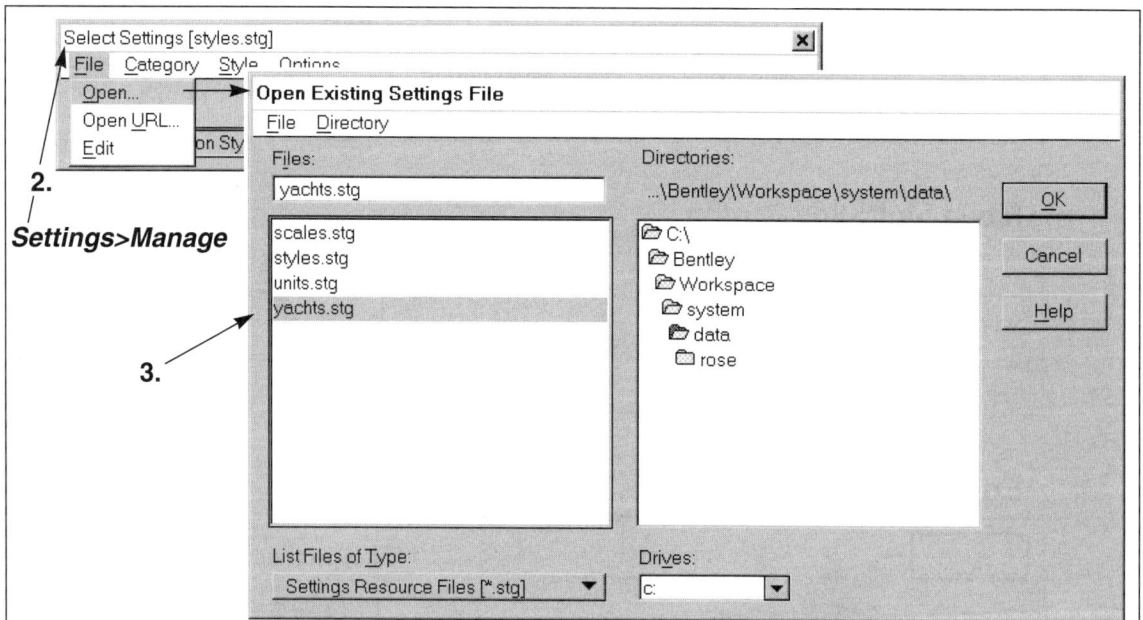

Figure 11.33 Opening an existing Settings File

4. Open the *Edit Settings* settings box (*File>Edit* from the *Select Settings* menu).

5. Choose *Style>Multi-line* from the *Edit Settings* menu (the *Edit Multi-line Styles* dialog box opens), click the *Get Active* button.

6. Overwrite the *Name:* field with **Multi1**, *Description:* with **First training style**.

7. Close the *Edit Multi-line Styles* dialog box and the *Edit Settings* settings box.

   The multi-line *Style* is automatically saved to the open settings file.

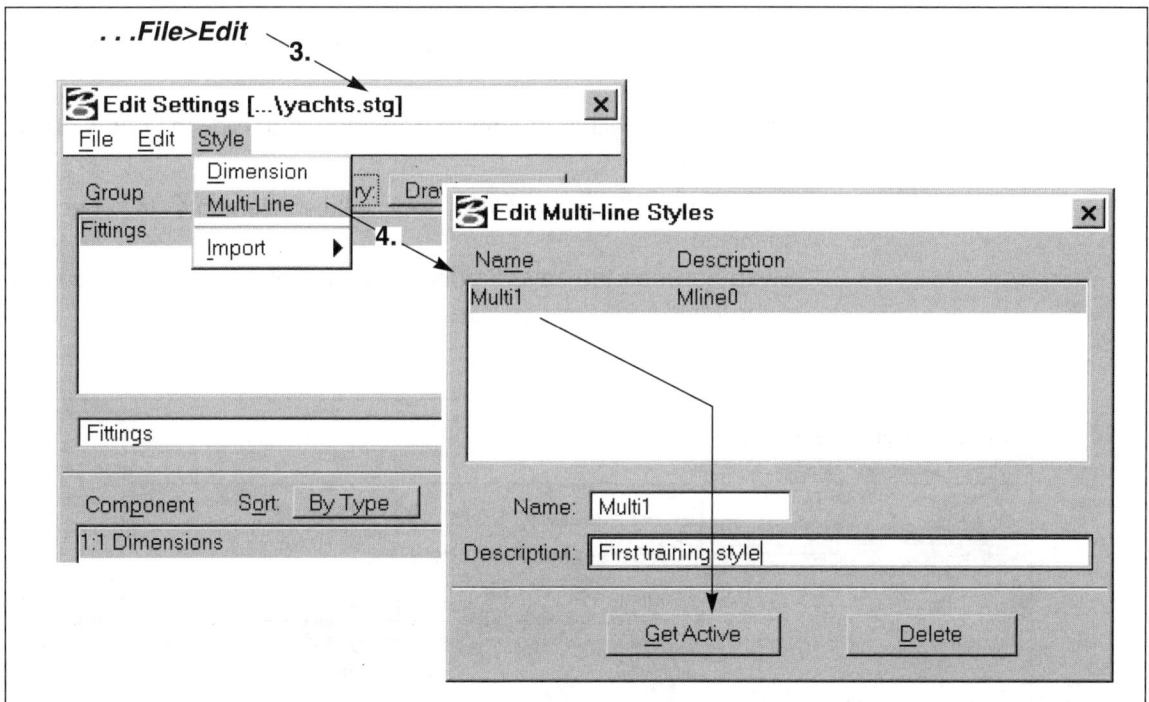

Figure 11.34   Saving the Active Multi-line definition

Styles Vs. Components

Saving multi-line definitions as named *Styles* can be achieved very quickly and easily. We can save as many styles as may be useful, but take care with names and descriptions. Redundant styles can easily be deleted, note the ***Delete*** button in Figure 11.34.

Sometimes the large number of saved *Styles* (which may include *Dimension Styles*), makes selection difficult. This is where we break the styles down into areas of utilization, then making them *Components* of *Settings Groups*. The one *Style* may be used in more than one *Settings Group* where appropriate.

Using Named Multi-line Styles

We were introduced to the concept of settings group components at the start of the chapter. This time we will practice selecting the styles directly from the *Style* menu.

◆ Making a Named Multi-line style active

1. Choose *Settings>Manage* to open the *Select Settings* settings box.

2. Choose *Style>Multi-line* to open the *Select Multi-line Style* settings box.

3. Select a style (either double-click the name, or click the name and the *Load* button).

4. Select the *Place Multi-line* tool, place elements to check the definition.
   Swap between the saved multi-line style and other definitions set up in the *Multi-lines* settings box.

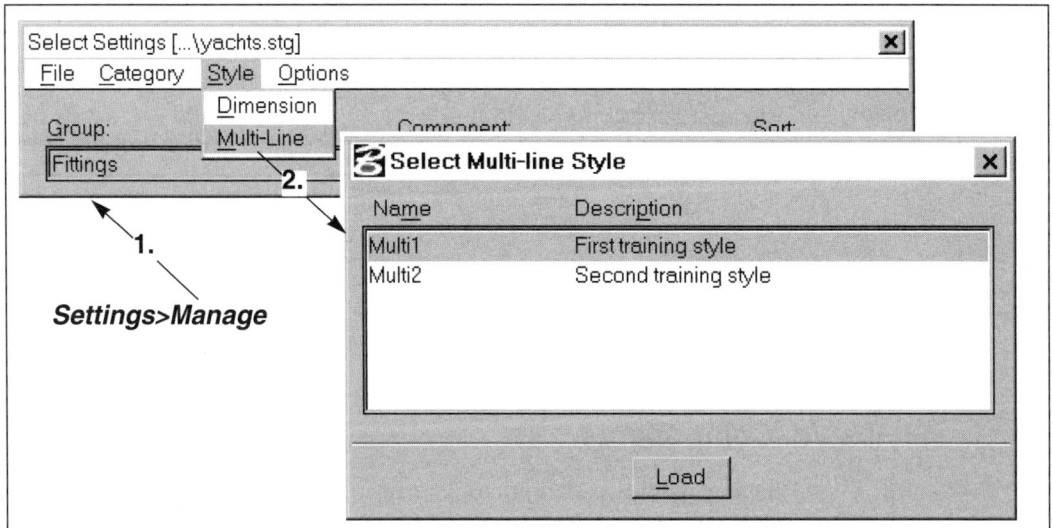

Figure 11.35 Selecting a Named Multi-line style

Summary

The number of combinations of settings we require to complete a design can be quite large. This is especially the case when we are working with dimensions. If we use a *Settings File* we can *Save* a particular dimensioning settings arrangement as a *Dimension Style*. This permits re-using exactly the same settings as often as we need them, even though we have been through many re-arrangements in the meantime.

In the course of completing a variety of designs, we will need to use a large number of *Styles*. It is generally worth naming each combination of dimension settings we use and saving it. Before long, we will have too long a list of styles to search efficiently. We have the option of using *Settings Groups* to solve this problem, by splitting the settings into any logical groupings we care to design. A *Settings Group* may have *Styles* as *Components*.

When compared to the use of the *Linear Pattern* tool (page 6-28), *Custom Line Styles* increase efficiency by permitting linear patterned elements to be placed with a single operation. They make smaller, faster updating design files than would be the case when we create an element, then patterning it. A *Custom Line Style* may consist of *Stroke* components, which in turn may be *Dashes* or *Gaps*, have a defined *Width* or not. It may also include *Point Symbols* or a combination of both. *Point Symbols* are a saved group of elements, similar to a *Cell*.

Dimensions are not the only settings arrangements that may be saved as *Styles*. *Multi-line* definitions are usually saved in a similar way. A *Multi-line* definition includes the number and spacing (offsets) of lines and their individual attributes. Start and end cap attributes, fill (if any), the width of custom line style dash strokes (where applicable) and the scale of any custom line style complete the definition.

Multi-lines may be placed with the *Place Multi-line* tool as single-segment, multi segment or closed elements. There are tool settings options for position of the component lines with relation to the data points used to place them. They may be placed as *Associated* with points on other elements that are *Snapped* to, with *Association Lock* **On**.

<This page has been intentionally left blank>

12 : From Design Files to Documents

"Last, but not least" is probably a good introduction for this chapter. Everything we have worked on to date in this book has been towards this goal, the output product. Two forms of documentation will be introduced. The first form will be the printout or "plot output" of the design graphics and text. The other output will be text information contained in *Tags* attached to design elements.

The preparation of our design files for printout and, to an extent, the structuring of the practical design process as a whole will be introduced in this chapter. We start our preparation for document production from the moment we open the first new design file for a project. A knowledge of the end product requirements will be useful right from the beginning.

When you have completed this chapter, you will be able to:

- Decide on a suitable technique for combining design files into the final drawing;
- Use the system printer to produce small format printouts;
- Create various configurations for the printed output and save these for later use;
- Make text substitutions and re-symbolize geometry at plot time using *Pen Tables*;
- Create *Tag Sets* and attach data to design elements with *Element Tags*;
- Use attached tags to generate reports and as element selection criteria.

Preparing the Design

As we found in Chapter 10, by using *Reference Files*, a complete design may be spread over many design files. Reference files are a central part of most of our techniques for creating the printed documentation of our designs. Even in the situation where all of the actual design geometry is on the one file, what about the title block and border? It would be most inefficient to draw a new one for every document.

Some Options for Document Production

There are a huge number of options available to us, from simply printing out the entire active design file, to sophisticated techniques using combinations of reference file attachments. We will briefly describe three basic techniques.

The Single Design File

A design may be complete in itself, with the title block and border drawn as part of the project. This could be inefficient, as we may be creating the same geometry over and over again.

We may reduce this repetition by having *Seed Files* with the drawing common components, such as the title block, already in place. Using this technique, we start with the drawing sheet in the design, then create the geometry within it.

We have already produced one such seed file, the "drawing sheet" on page 10-4. This design was produced at paper size, which means that only small objects could fit within the boundary. If we had a design (say) 100 times larger, the sheet seed file would also need to be 100 times larger. The drawing would then be printed out at 1:100 scale, which is allowed for in the printing (or plotting) process.

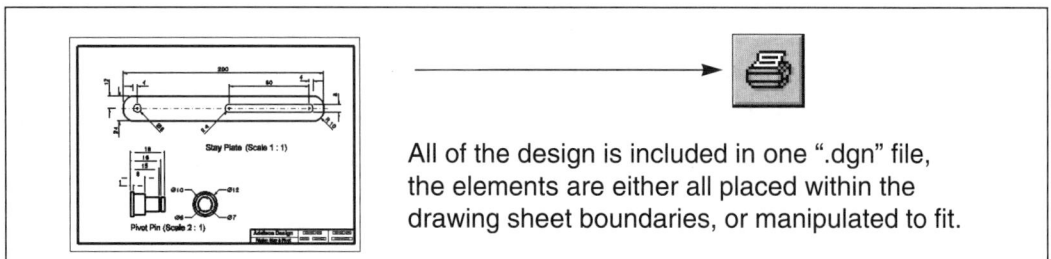

All of the design is included in one ".dgn" file, the elements are either all placed within the drawing sheet boundaries, or manipulated to fit.

Figure 12.1 The Single Design File option

Attaching a Drawing Sheet as a Reference File

We may attach a drawing sheet file that was originally created at "paper size" as a reference file. The *Scale Reference File* tool (page 10-23) may be used to make the border fit the design, by setting a reference scale that complements the intended scale for the document. A disadvantage of this system is that details in the title block cannot be changed, as they are in a reference file. If the attached drawing sheet file is modified at a later date, the changes will appear in the document. This may be either an advantage or a disadvantage, depending on the situation.

Drawing Sheet, with Reference Files

This technique is similar to the *Single Design File*, in that we create the active file with the drawing sheet/border. We then attach the design geometry to the sheet as reference files. An example of this technique was used to introduce reference files in Chapter 10.

Dimensioning and text elements can be placed in any of the files. The title information is in the active design file, thus it may readily be edited, *Enter Data* fields filled in etc. This is the most flexible technique, especially where large numbers of reference files are involved.

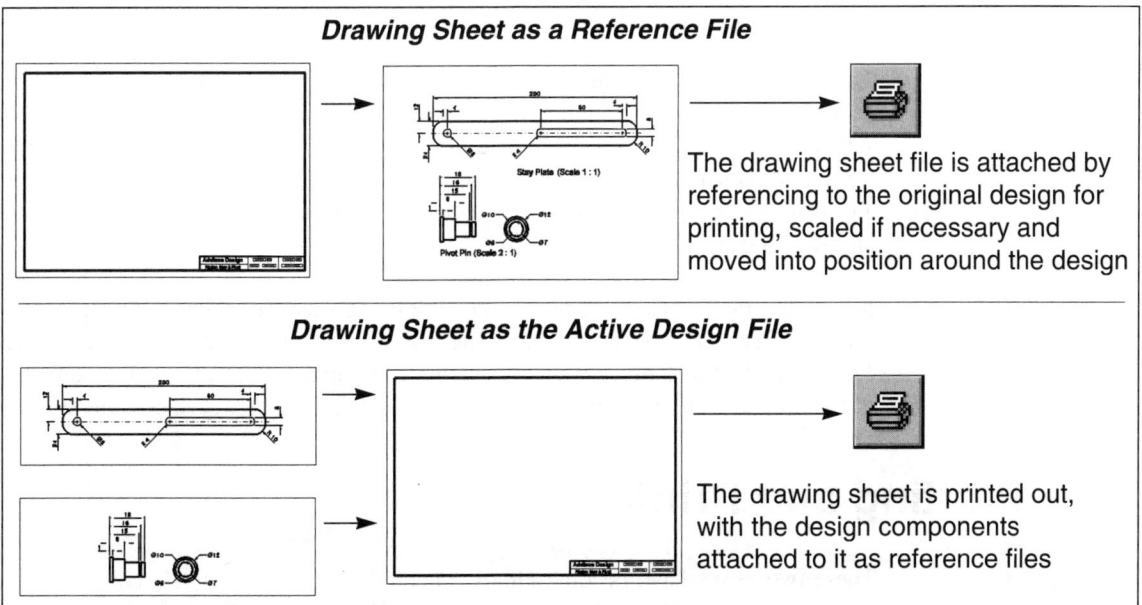

Figure 12.2 Combining files for printout

Drawing Scale

We will by now be used to the fact that we create our designs notionally at full size. Drawing scales are only applied at the time we print the design out, but this does not mean we can forget about them completely during the design process. It is common for one set of geometry to be printed out at a variety of scales, so we will consider that for a start.

As an example, the wall construction of a building may be drawn in plan view with details of wall thickness, lining, cladding and insulation, probably using multi-lines. If a part of the design is printed out as a detail drawing with a scale of 1:10, all of the lines will appear well separated and have meaning. It would seem efficient to print out the same design at a scale of 1:200, as part of a site plan. Without prior planning, the finely detailed linework of the wall would now be compressed into approximately half a millimeter, thus it would appear as a series of lines on top of other lines.

The planning needs to start right back in the early stages of the design process, or even before the design is started. Using the same design at 1:10 and 1:200 is fine, but only if we use a suitable *Level Structure*. This will probably involve *Naming* levels (page 2-40) and may also be worth *Grouping* levels for simultaneous switching (*Settings>Level>Names>Display>Group Operations*). If we have different degrees of detail at different levels, we can simply select the detail we need for the scale of the document being produced.

The size of text and dimensioning must be chosen to reproduce correctly at the printed scale. Again, levels may be useful, as we can place text and dimensioning suited for each of the scales we intend to use on different levels. The other option for text and dimensioning is to place these elements in a *Sheet File*, with the geometry attached as reference files. We have already been introduced to this process, starting on page 10-4.

It is quite practicable to produce a set of drawing sheet files for each scale that we print at. Once the first of the sheet files are created, it involves little more than a *File>Save As* and a *Scale Fence Contents* operation. If we are using a number of paper sizes as well, we will need a drawing sheet seed file for each combination.

Plotting and Printing

These two terms have become almost interchangeable in the CAD context. Either one describes the action of outputting design files to paper. Traditionally, the output device for producing large format documents was a *Plotter.*

It had *Pens* that were moved over the paper or film by a series of distance and direction commands, analogous to a navigator plotting a course on a map or chart. There are still many of these devices in use and MicroStation will produce the necessary "vector" output format to "drive" them.

Using the System Printer

Where our computer system provides this facility, it provides the quickest and easiest way to obtain a paper copy of our work. In the following exercise, "me0001.dgn" will be printed out, complete with its reference file attachments. We will start by quickly skipping through the process, then introduce the details as the chapter progresses.

◆ **Print out "me0001.dgn"**

1. Open "me0001.dgn", check that the file reference attachments within the border are as required.

2. Place a *Fence* (block) closely around the drawing sheet border.

   The area to be printed is to be defined by the fence in this example. If the fence is too big, we may not be able to draw to the required scale.

3. Select the *Print* tool from the *Standard* tool bar.

   The *Plot* settings box opens, with its own menus and *Icon* bar.

4. From the setting box menus, choose *Entity>Fence*.

   If we had not placed a *Fence* in step **2.**, we could have used *Entity>View*.

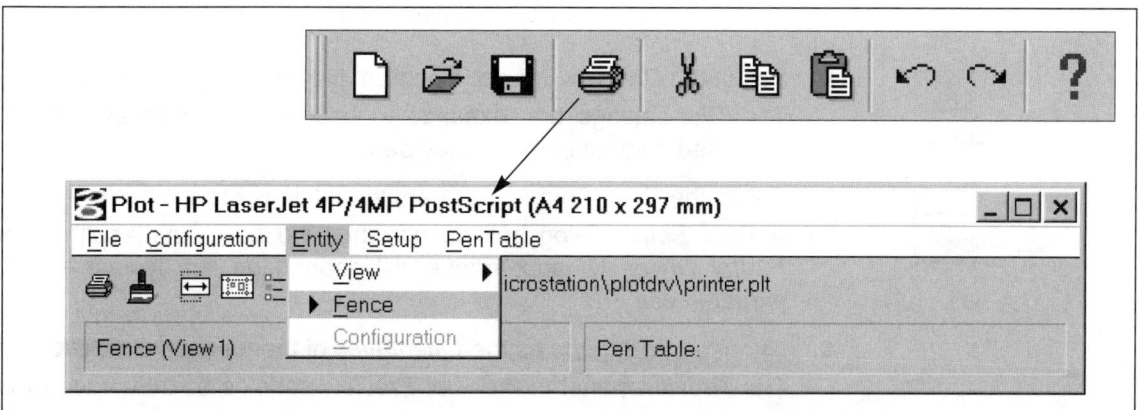

Figure 12.3   Opening the Plot settings box

5. Select the *Plotter Driver* icon from the settings box icon bar, select *printer.plt* from the ". . . \plotdrv\" directory.

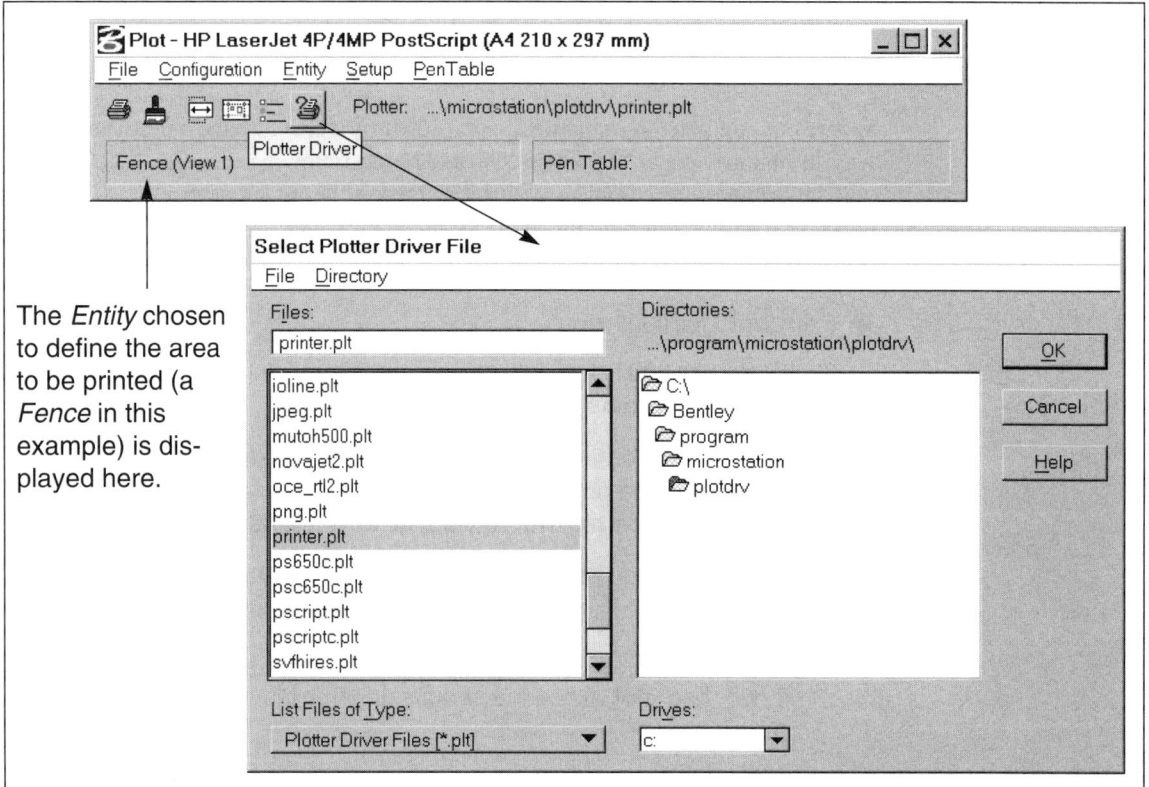

The *Entity* chosen to define the area to be printed (a *Fence* in this example) is displayed here.

Figure 12.4   Selecting a Plotter Driver file

6. Select the *Preview Refresh* icon from the settings box icon bar.

The *Plot* settings box expands to become *Plot Preview,* with the proposed printout in the display panel.

7. Select the *Page Format* icon from the settings box icon bar.

A *Print Setup* dialog box opens when we have "printer.plt" as our *Plotter Driver.* Its appearance will depend on the system and the printer in use.

8. Choose **Landscape** as the *Orientation* of the printout, click **OK**.

The *Preview* panel in the *Plot Preview* settings box changes to the new orientation and the design automatically maximizes to fit it.

6. This is the display panel section of the *Plot Preview* settings box, shown in *Portrait* orientation

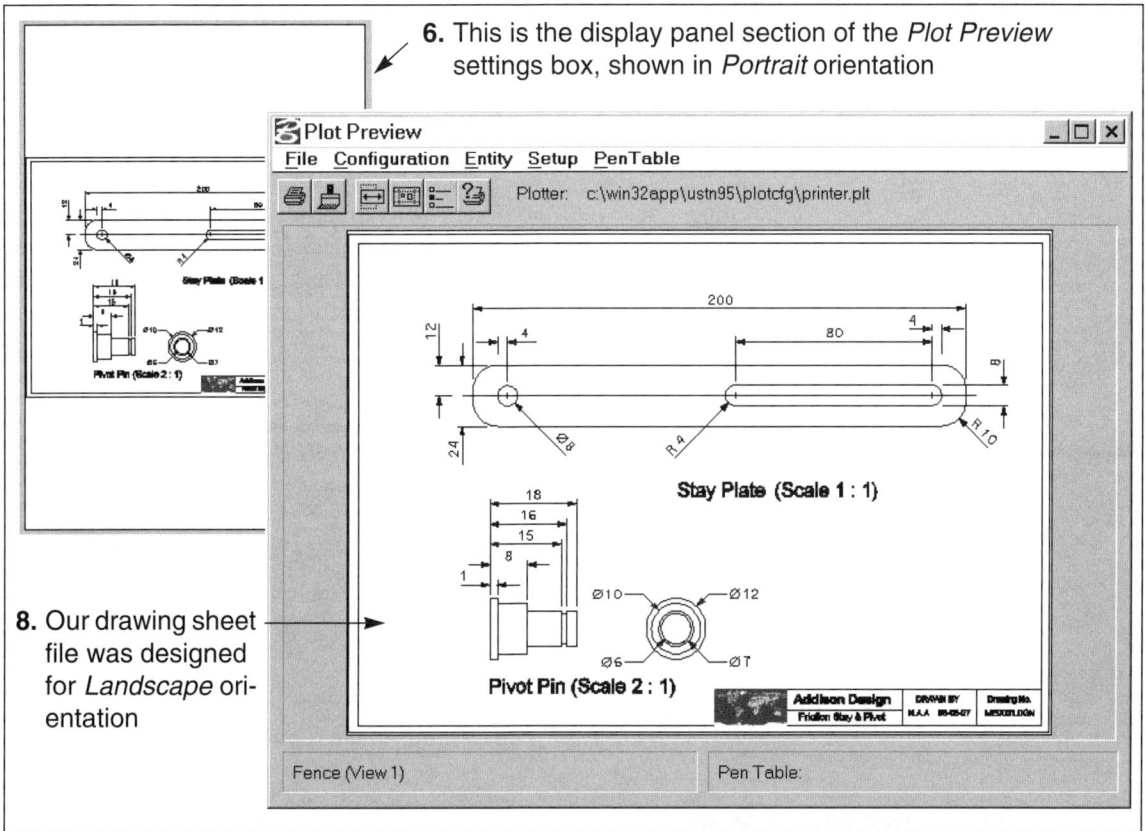

8. Our drawing sheet file was designed for *Landscape* orientation

Figure 12.5 Previewing the printout

9. Make sure that the system printer is ready, select the *Plot* icon from the plot preview settings box.

Check the printout carefully, including the *Scale.*

The printout may have a second border printed outside the one from the file, in the position of the fence. It is probably slightly larger than full size, which was the intended scale. We will look at some other settings that will allow us to fix these problems.

The Plot Icon Bar

The icon buttons in the *Plot* settings box resemble a tool bar, but, unlike *Tools* they generally do not initiate commands, nor do they have associated tool settings windows. They are similar to an options menu, each one opening a dialog box in most circumstances.

The *Plot* settings box is *Non-Modal*, which means other operations can be undertaken while the box remains open. A *Modal* dialog box is one that we must finish with and close before we can do anything else, for example the *Open Design File* dialog box. Clicking some of the icons from the *Plot* icon bar open *Modal* dialog boxes.

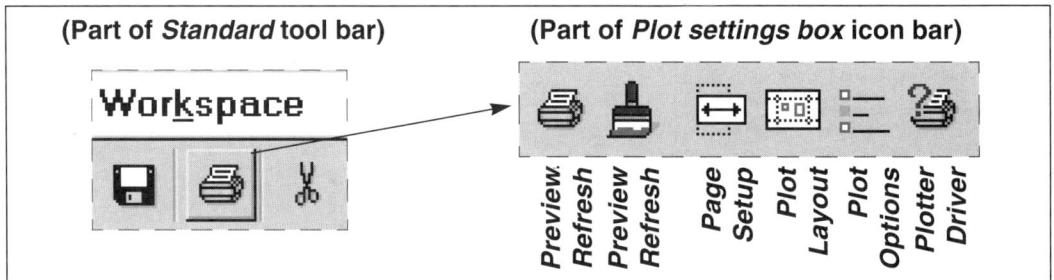

Figure 12.6   The Icon Bar in the Plot Settings Box

The Plotter Driver Icon

Clicking this icon opens the *Select Plotter Driver File* dialog box, as illustrated in Figure 12.4, on page 12-6. There are plotter driver files supplied for most types of printers or plotters. These are a text file with various settings for configuring the plotter to the standards we require. These files may be edited with any text editor. Some of the settings will reflect in the *Page Setup* dialog boxes.

There are two basic types of *Plotter Driver File*, one type produces an output that will drive a particular type of printer to produce a paper document directly. This output may be stored in a file for later output to the printer, or sent directly to the printer as required. The other type produces an *Image File*, a file in a standard image format that may be incorporated into another document, such as a letter or book.

There are *Plotter Driver Files* supplied with MicroStation for most common printers, plus drivers to produce *JPEG* and *TIFF* Image files (*jpeg.plt* and *tiff.plt*). They are supplied in the ". . . \program\microstation\plotdrv" directory, but MicroStation may be re-configured to find them in another directory.

The particular configuration settings available for change will depend on the type of printer/plotter, but typically settings can be made for:

- *Plotter Units*, e.g. inches or millimeters;

- Page *Sizes* and default orientation;

- The line *Widths* associated to each line *Weight* in the design file (optionally, the line width may be associated with the *Color* of the element);

- The *Lengths* of the dashes and gaps of *Standard* line *Styles*.

The finer details on the configuring of the plotter driver files will not be covered here, but the files will generally only need editing when a new device or new software is installed, perhaps not even then. In any case, the files are generally well commented and the settings logical.

Part of a typical plotter driver file is shown in Figure 12.7. There are options built in to simplify changes that are frequently needed, such as changing from *English* to *Metric* units. Note the instructions for "commenting out" (with leading semicolons) and "uncommenting".

```
; To use CMYK output rather than the default RGB output, uncomment the
; following line:
;
;CmdName /appname="pscript" /parsed="colorScheme" /unparsed="CMYK"

communication = (eol1=13,eol2=0)
; communication = (handshake=0,baud=9600,par=none,data=8,stop=1)

;   This configuration file contains the necessary records for English
;   and metric resolutions.  English units are used by default.  To use
;   the metric setting, comment out all lines in the ENGLISH section and
;   uncomment the RESOLUTION and SIZE lines in the METRIC section.  The
;   SIZE records define the plotting area of the page.

; ENGLISH resolution and SIZE records
size=(7.4,10.0)/num=4/off=(.5,.5)/name=letter    ; leave room for border
resolution(IN)=(0.003333333333333333,0.003333333333333333) ;300DPI
; resolution(IN)=(0.001666666666666666,0.001666666666666666) ;600DPI

; Metric resolution and SIZE records
; size=(188,254)/num=4/off=(12,12)/name=letter  ; leave room for border
; resolution(MM)=(0.08466666666666666,0.08466666666666666); 300DPI

; Stroke_tolerance determines tolerance for arcs and circles.  Value is
; between 0 and 10 with 10 being the greater tolerance.  Larger values
; also create larger plot files.
stroke_tolerance=10
```

Figure 12.7 Part of the Plotter Driver File "pscriptc.plt"

The Page Setup Icon

Clicking this icon may open the *Print Setup* or the *Page Setup* dialog boxes. Both of these dialog boxes offer different options, depending on the *Printer Driver* chosen earlier. We were using *Printer.plt* as our *Plotter Driver* in the earlier exercise. In that case the *Print Setup* box was used to change from *Portrait* to *Landscape* paper orientation.

Where there are different page sizes available, they are selectable from an option menu in this dialog box. The paper sizes are in the units of the device, which is often *Inches* by default. Typical *Print Setup* and *Page Setup* dialog boxes are shown in Figure 12.8.

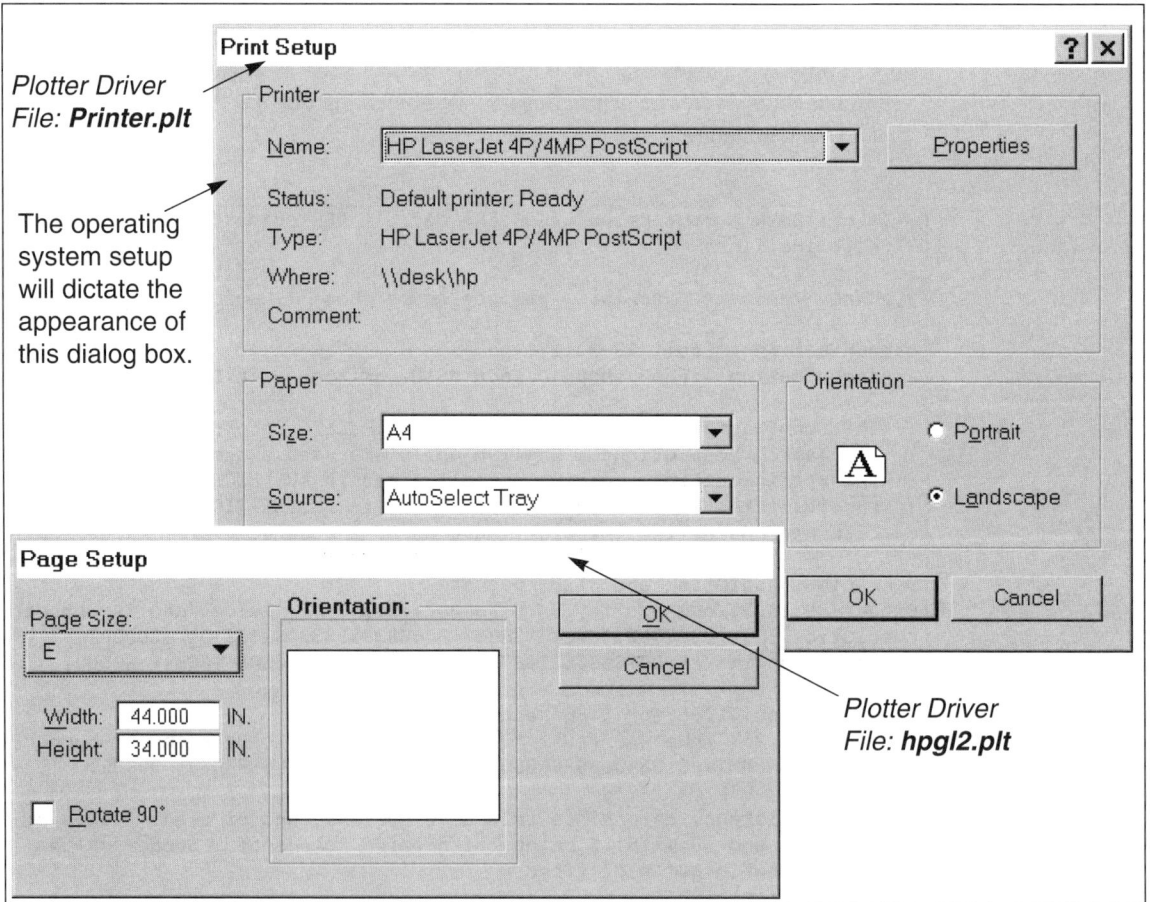

Figure 12.8   Print Setup and Page setup dialog boxes (Only one appears)

The Preview Refresh Icon

When the *Plot* settings box is in its smaller form, clicking this icon increases it in size and displays a representation of how the finished printout will look. When it is already in this larger *Plot Preview* format, clicking this icon updates the display with any changes that may have been made since the last preview.

The settings box may be moved aside or re-sized for changes to be made to the design file to correct problems shown up by the preview. We can reduce it back to the smaller format by resizing it from the bottom.

The Plot Icon

Clicking this icon with "printer.plt" as our plotter driver file sends the design (in the appropriate format) to the system print manager. When we are using other driver files, it may open the *Save Plot As* dialog box (depending on the configuring of the *plotter driver file*), where a file name and directory is allocated to the *Plotfile* that is to be created.

Plotfiles are files with all the necessary data to produce the desired printout when the file is eventually sent to the printer. The format of this file will depend on the *Plotter Driver* selected, which was, in turn, selected to suit the plotter hardware. The file may be in *Raster* or *Vector* format. The techniques for sending these files to the printer will depend on your local setup.

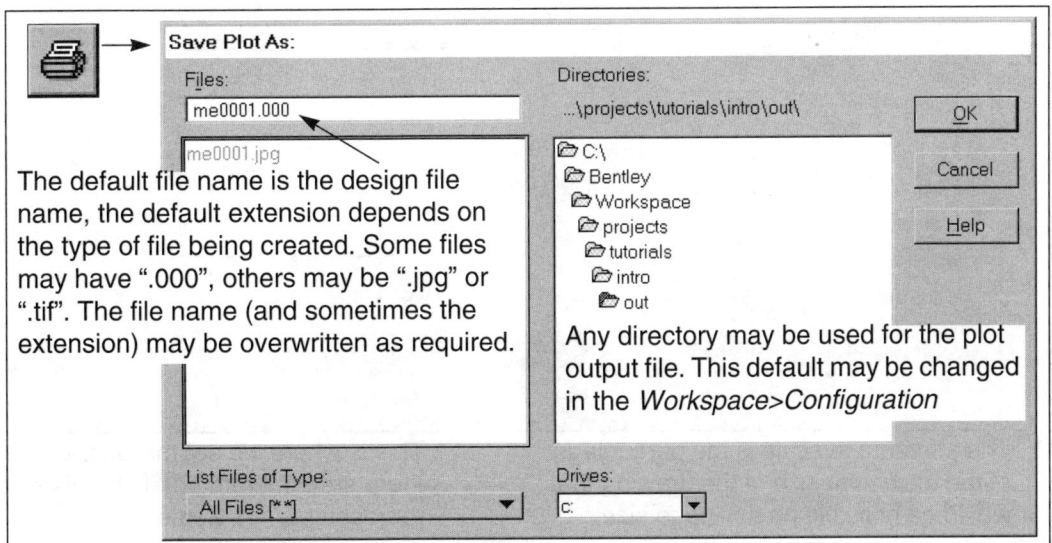

Figure 12.9 Saving a Plotfile for later printout

Tip!   We can send the Plotfile direct to the printer by giving it the *Port Name* of your printer/plotter port (e.g. "*lpt1*"), instead of an ordinary file name. Likewise, in Windows we can send a file to the printer from a DOS prompt with **Copy /b <Plotfile name> <port name>**.

Plotfiles may also be saved to diskettes for transport to other systems for printout, although for very complex designs, the Plotfile may need to be compressed to fit. They may be sent via the "internet" for printing, or transported any other way. We do not need to have MicroStation on the system that is sending them to the printer.

Plot Layout

The settings box opened by this icon is the all-important one where we set the actual scale of the printout. The settings can be made with the priority on margins or on plot size, but generally the *Scale To:* [design file units] / [plotter units] will be used.

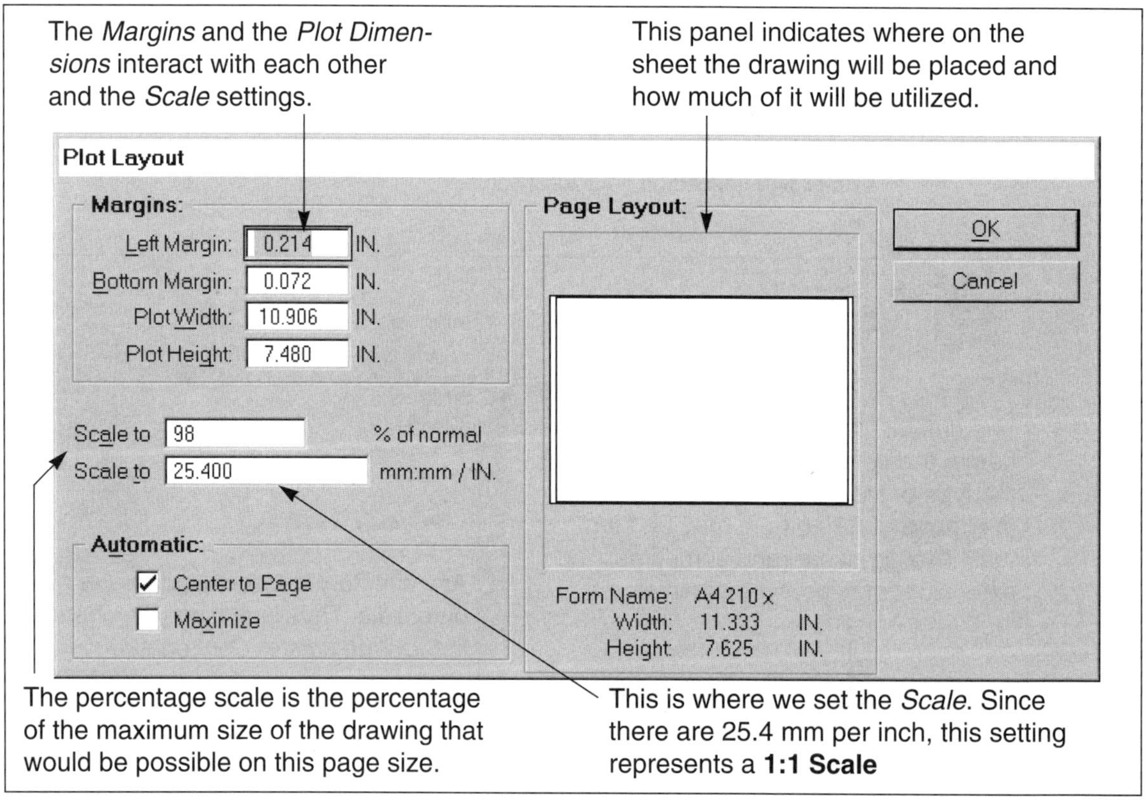

The *Margins* and the *Plot Dimensions* interact with each other and the *Scale* settings.

This panel indicates where on the sheet the drawing will be placed and how much of it will be utilized.

Plot Layout

Margins:

Left Margin:	0.214	IN.
Bottom Margin:	0.072	IN.
Plot Width:	10.906	IN.
Plot Height:	7.480	IN.

Scale to 98   % of normal
Scale to 25.400   mm:mm / IN.

Automatic:
☑ Center to Page
☐ Maximize

Page Layout:

[OK]
[Cancel]

Form Name: A4 210 x
    Width: 11.333   IN.
    Height: 7.625   IN.

The percentage scale is the percentage of the maximum size of the drawing that would be possible on this page size.

This is where we set the *Scale*. Since there are 25.4 mm per inch, this setting represents a **1:1 Scale**

Figure 12.10   The Plot Layout settings

Plot Options

Selecting this icon will open the *Plot Options* dialog box. When we use the fence to define the area to be plotted (as we did in the last exercise), only two settings are available. These are *Fence Boundary* and *Plot Border*, as shown in Figure 12.11. The other options become available when we use a *Configuration* file (see "Plot Configuration Files" on page 12-14), but otherwise they are set by the *View Attributes* of the design file at the time it is being plotted.

The options shown as unavailable are actually *View Attributes* set in the design file before plotting.

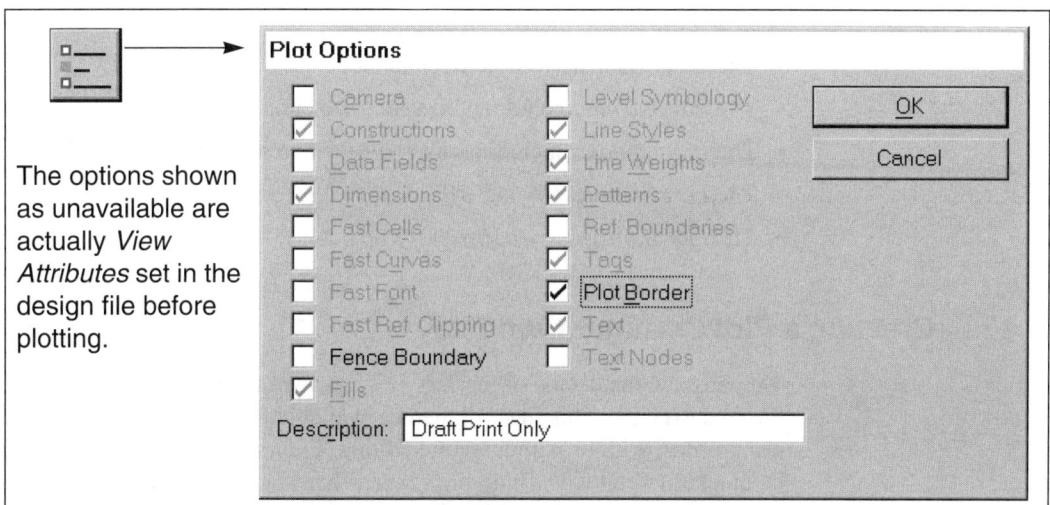

Figure 12.11   Plot Options, when using a fence or view to define the printout

If we enter text to the *Description* field, it is printed out at the bottom-left of the optional border (not a border that may be part of the design). This is only printed if the *Plot Border* option is *On*. If the fence is used, the *Fence Boundary* option plots a rectangle representing the fence, which will overlay the optional border.

◆ **Print "me0001.dgn" with changes to the configuration**

1. Repeat steps **1.** to **4.** of the exercise "Print out "me0001.dgn"" on page 12-5.

2. Select the *Plot Layout* icon, change the *Scale to:* figure to **25.4**, turn *Center to Page On* (Figure 12.10).

3. Select the *Plot Options* icon, turn *Fence Boundary* and *Plot Border* *Off*.

4. Repeat the remaining steps of the previous exercise (page 12-6).

Plot Configuration Files

These files are used to save a configuration used to generate a plot/printout. Do not confuse these with *Plotter Configuration Files*, the predecessor of *Plotter Driver Files* (page 12-9).

A plot configuration file takes only seconds to create, but it can save time and mistakes when we need to generate a similar plot more than once.

The following details are saved with a *Plot Configuration File:*

- The *Area* of the design file to be plotted;
- The *Plot Layout*, including the scale, size etc.;
- The *Plot Options*, including the view attributes set in the design file;
- The *Levels* turned *On* and *Off*;
- The *Pen Table* (if any, see page 12-16).

Creating a Plot Configuration File

We will save the details of our last plotting operation to a *Plot Configuration File* in the next exercise. This file will then be available for later use with this and with other design files, with or without some editing. Even if changes need to be made, it will be quicker to edit a configuration, rather than start again from scratch. For example, we could find it useful with drawings being created from the same drawing sheet seed file used for "me0001.dgn".

◆ Create a Plot Configuration File

1. Examine the printout of the Stay Plate last generated. Open the *Plot* settings box, make any changes to settings necessary in both the *Plot* settings and in the design file itself.

2. Select *Preview Refresh*, check the proposed plot.

3. Choose *New* from the settings box *Configuration* menu.

4. Name the file and choose a directory.
   The default directory is "Workspace\system\data\" from the MicroStation root directory, but it may be created in another directory.

5. Click the *OK* button and the configuration is saved.

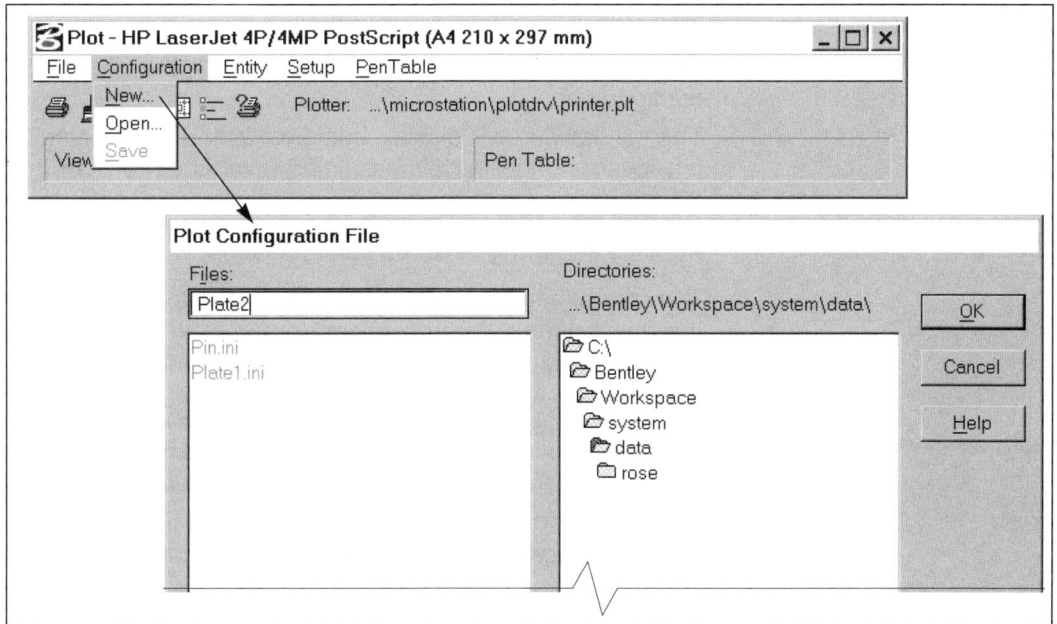

Figure 12.12   Saving a Plot Configuration File

Using a Plot Configuration File

When we intend to use a saved *Configuration* to define a printout, there is no need to place a fence, or even to have the area to be printed out within a view.

We *Open* plot configuration files from the *Configuration* menu in the *Plot* settings box. *Configuration* is also one of the options in this settings box's *Entity* menu. Choosing this defines the plot configuration to be the last such file used or defined.

◆ Experiment with Plot Configuration Files

1.   Place the fence about the Pivot Pin area of "me0001.dgn".

2.   Turn level **63 *Off*** in the design file to hide the pivot pin dimensioning. This level should also be ***Off*** in the reference file settings for the pivot pin attachment, so none of the pin dimensioning should display.

3.   With the *Plot* settings box open, choose *Entity>Fence*, click the *Preview Refresh* icon.

4.   Change other settings until the "dimensionless" pivot pin is displayed as desired.

5. Choose *Configuration>New*, save this configuration with a name of your choice.

6. Choose *Configuration>Open* and select the first (full drawing) configuration.

   The full drawing will display, complete with dimensioning for the pivot pin, even though the dimensioning level is turned **Off** in the design file.

7. Practice swapping between configurations.

8. Turn the dimension level display back **On** in the design file, choose the "pivot pin only" configuration, or *Preview Refresh* if this ".ini" file name already appears at the bottom of the settings box.

   The dimensions will not re-appear in the preview.

9. Move the settings box aside and place an extra element in the pivot pin area, move the box back and *Preview Refresh*.

   The new geometry will appear, thus proving that a *Plot Configuration* saves *Settings* (including level display) but not the actual geometry.

10. Delete the extra element.

Pen Tables

Pen Tables are used for *Text Substitution* and *Plot Resymbolization*. They can:

• Substitute new *Text Strings* for ones existing in the design files.

• Re-define the symbology of selected elements at plot time, overriding the original element or level symbology definitions in the design file.

• Override the *Update Sequence* (page 10-30) to set the order that design file and attached reference file elements are plotted out (the last line placed is on top, thus order affects appearance).

Note: Pen tables are for making limited numbers of specific alterations to a document. The most efficient place to define overall appearance is still in the design file itself.

When a *Pen Table* is used to alter the appearance of the plotted output of a file, a defined set of *Evaluation Criteria* are compared with each element in the design. Each time a match is found, a particular defined set of modifications (*Output Actions*) are made before the element is converted into data for the plotter. Each set of *Evaluation Criteria* has a corresponding set of *Output Actions*, making up a *Section* (see Figure 12.13 on page 12-18).

The parameters that may be included in the evaluation criteria of a section are the:

- Element Type;
- File name (including attached reference files);
- Element attributes;
- Link and entity numbers in any linked external database.

When an element is found that matches a defined combination of these parameters (an *Evaluation Criterion*), an associated *Output Action* is initiated. Pen table data structures are saved to *Pen Table Files*, stored by default in the ". . . \tables\pen\" directory. They have the default filename extension ".tbl".

Preparing to Use Pen Tables

Text string substitution is a *Global Action* in the pen table context. The only criterion searched on in the design is the text, no other parameters are taken into account. However, more parameters need to be included in the criteria when we are selecting elements for resymbolization.

We need to examine the design file before setting up a pen table, to make our decisions on *Selection Criteria*. We may also need to make some additions and/or changes, especially if a *Text Substitution* is intended. With this in mind, we will make some text additions to "me0001.dgn". After this, we will create a pen table to perform a text substitution and the re-symbolization of some of the elements.

◆ **Preparing for the Pen Table Exercise**

1. In "me0001.dgn", use the *Match All Element Settings* and the *Match Text* tools (page 8-29) to match the active element and text attributes to some of the title block text.

2. Select the *Place Text* tool, set the *Justification* to *Right-Center* in the Tool Settings window.

3. Place the text string **Design updated to** above the title block.

4. Change the *Justification* to *Left-Center*, place the text string **$update$** to flow on from the other string (use AccuDraw).
   The dollar signs are not essential, but they are included to reduce the likelihood of the wrong text string being substituted.

Setting up a Pen Table

The *Pen Table* option menu is in the *Plot* settings box. We will use it to create a new file, then set it up to:

1.   Substitute the current date for the text string "$update$

2.   Substitute the text string "Slide Plate" for "Stay Plate"

3.   Change all the ellipses in both reference file attachments to line style *1* (dotted).

◆ Create and modify a new Pen Table File

1. Open the *Plot* settings box, choose "*printer.plt*" as the *Plot Driver*.

2. Choose *Pen Table>New* (the *Create Pen Table* dialog box opens).

3. Name the new file **training**, click **OK** and the *Modify Pen Table* settings box opens.

Element Criteria + Output Actions = Section (page 12-16)

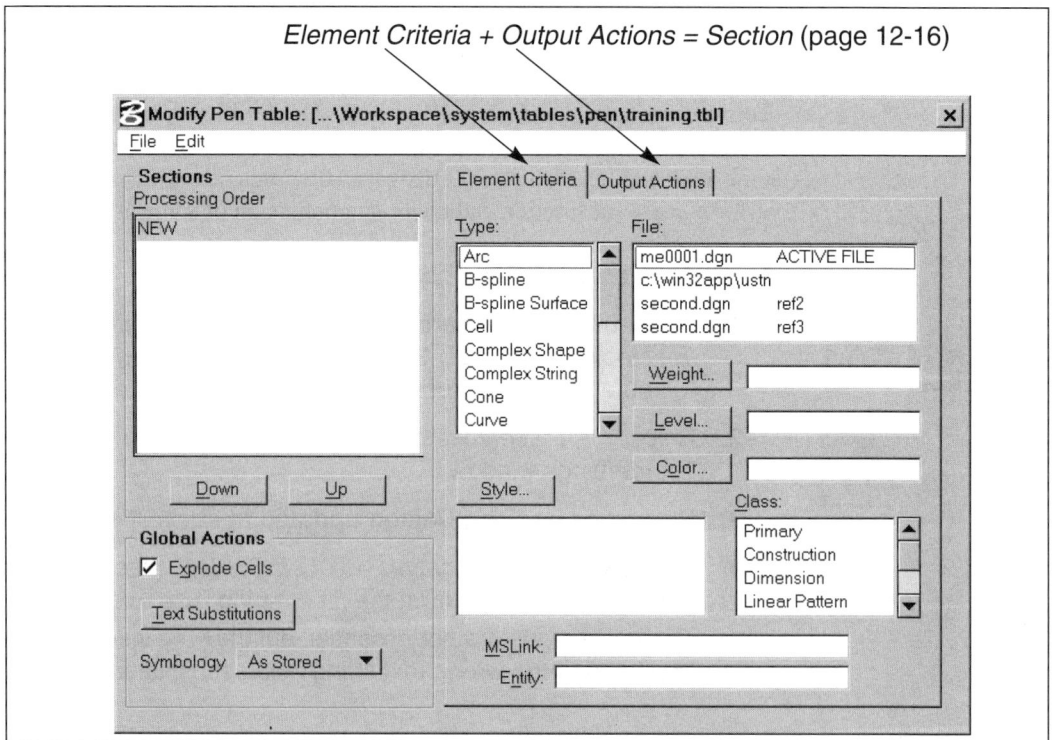

Figure 12.13   The Modify Pen Table settings box

Text Substitutions

We will create our Pen Table in two stages, the first will be the *Text Substitution*, which is a *Global Action* (see page 12-17).

◆ **Set up Text Substitutions**

1. Click the *Text Substitutions* button in the *Global Actions* panel.
   The *Text Substitutions* dialog box opens.

2. Choose *Edit>Insert New* from the box menu (a new line appears in the display panel), change the *Actual* field to **Stay Plate**, the *Replacement* field to **Slide Plate**.
   Make sure the text strings are entered on to the displayed line.

3. Choose *Edit>Insert Date* (another new line appears, this time with $DATE$ and _DATE_ as the *Actual* and the *Replacement* strings).

4. Edit the *Actual* field to read **$update$** (the string in the design file we intend to alter), *Enter* the change, close the dialog box.

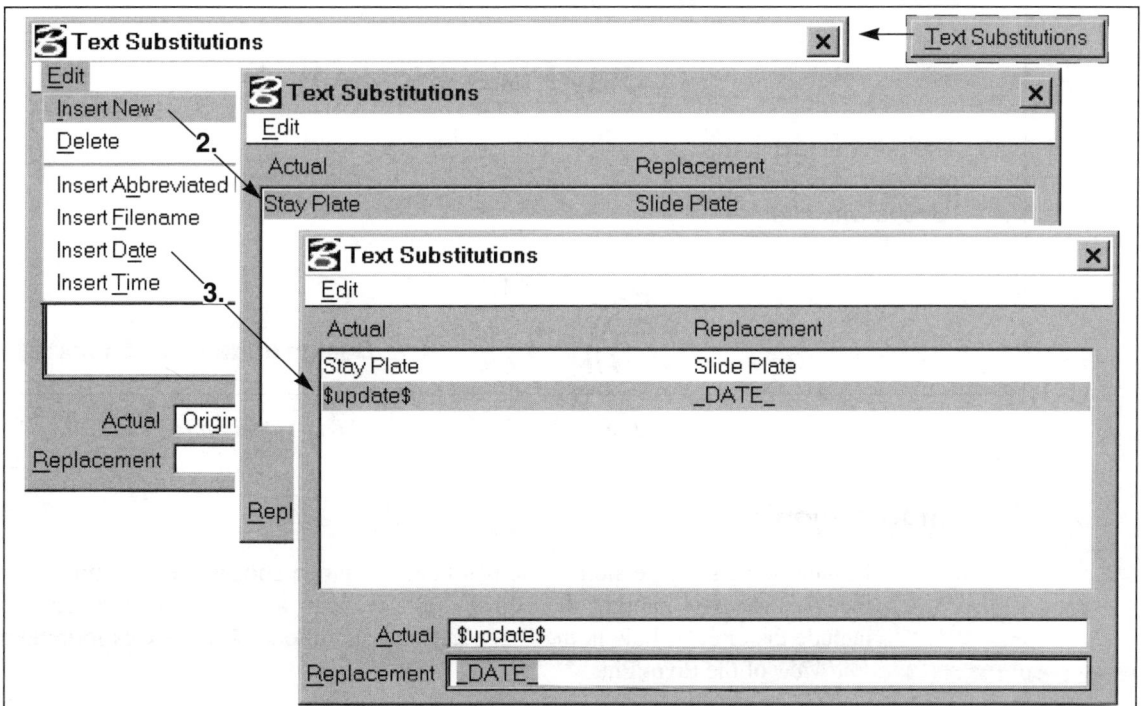

Figure 12.14 Defining Text Substitutions

5. Save the file (*File>Save*), close the *Modify Pen Table* settings box. The pen table just modified is automatically *Loaded*, so it will apply the next time the preview is refreshed.

6. Click the *Preview Refresh* icon, note the changes in the preview display.

7. Choose *Pen Table>Unload*, then *Preview Refresh*, again note the changes in the preview display.

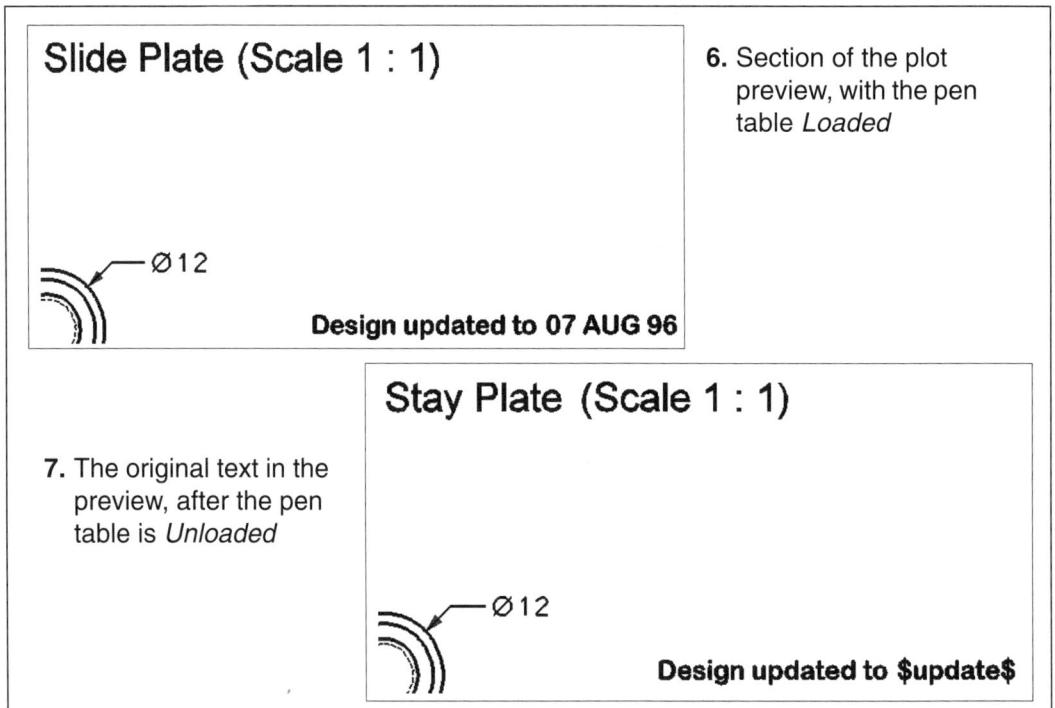

Slide Plate (Scale 1 : 1)

6. Section of the plot preview, with the pen table *Loaded*

⌀12

Design updated to 07 AUG 96

7. The original text in the preview, after the pen table is *Unloaded*

Stay Plate (Scale 1 : 1)

⌀12

Design updated to $update$

Figure 12.15   The effect of Text Substitution

Resymbolization

Having proven this version of the pen table to be operational, we will modify it to include a *Section* altering the ellipses (circles) with a *Line Style* of *0*. This will include the circular hole in the Stay Plate and all but one of the circles forming the *End View* of the Pivot Pin.

◆ **Add a Resymbolization Section to the Pen Table File**

1. Choose *Pen Table>Modify* (the *Select Pen Table* dialog box opens), select "*training.tbl*".
   The *Modify Pen Table* settings box re-opens, with *NEW* highlighted in the processing order list of the *Sections* panel.

2. Choose *Edit>Rename Section* (the *Rename Section* box opens), rename the new section to **circles**, click *OK*.

3. In the *Element Criteria* panels, select *Type:Ellipse*, *File:both reference attachments*.
   Where we need to include more than one selection (or de-select one) in this settings box, <**Ctrl+click**>.

4. Select *All* from the *Weight, Level* and *Color* dialog boxes, as opened by the three buttons.

5. Click the *Style* button, select *0* (only).

6. Select *Primary* as the *Class*.

7. The *Element Criteria* for the *Section* is now defined, the next job will be setting the section's *Output Actions*.

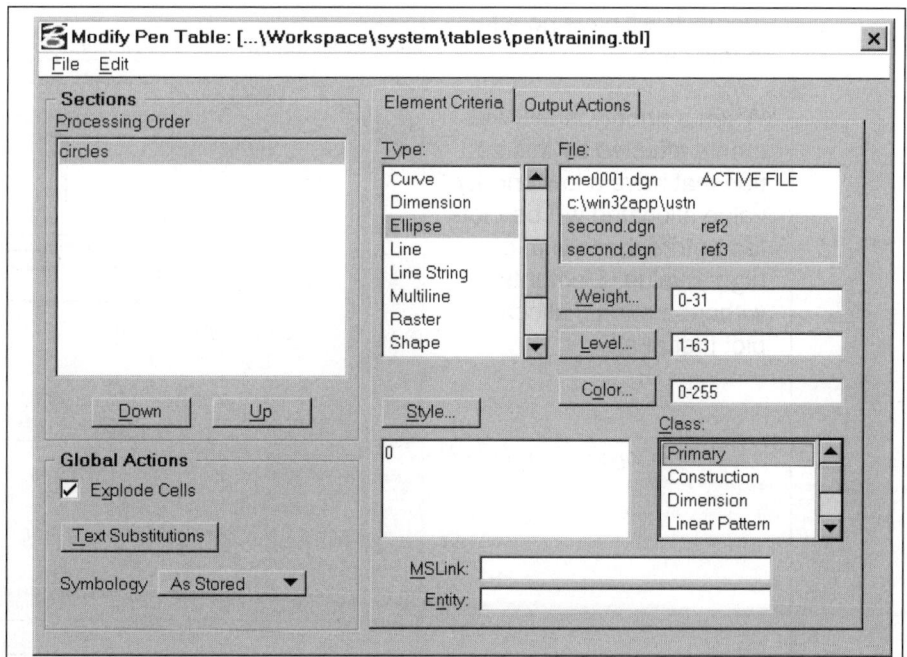

Figure 12.16 The Element Criteria settings for the circles section

Note: By default, *Explode Cells* is **On** in the *Global Actions* section. This means that each component element of any cells will individually be compared to the *Element Criteria* of each section. If it is turned **Off**, the cells are treated as single entities.

8. Click the *Output Actions* tab, click the *Styles* check box **On**, enter **1** (dotted) as the line style.

Change other attributes if you wish.

9. Choose *File>Save* to save the changes.

If we were modifying an existing file as a basis for a new one, use *Save As* and key in a new name.

10. Check the previews with the pen table "training.tbl" *Loaded* and *Unloaded*, note the effect on the circles (the only ellipses in the design, see Figure 12.18).

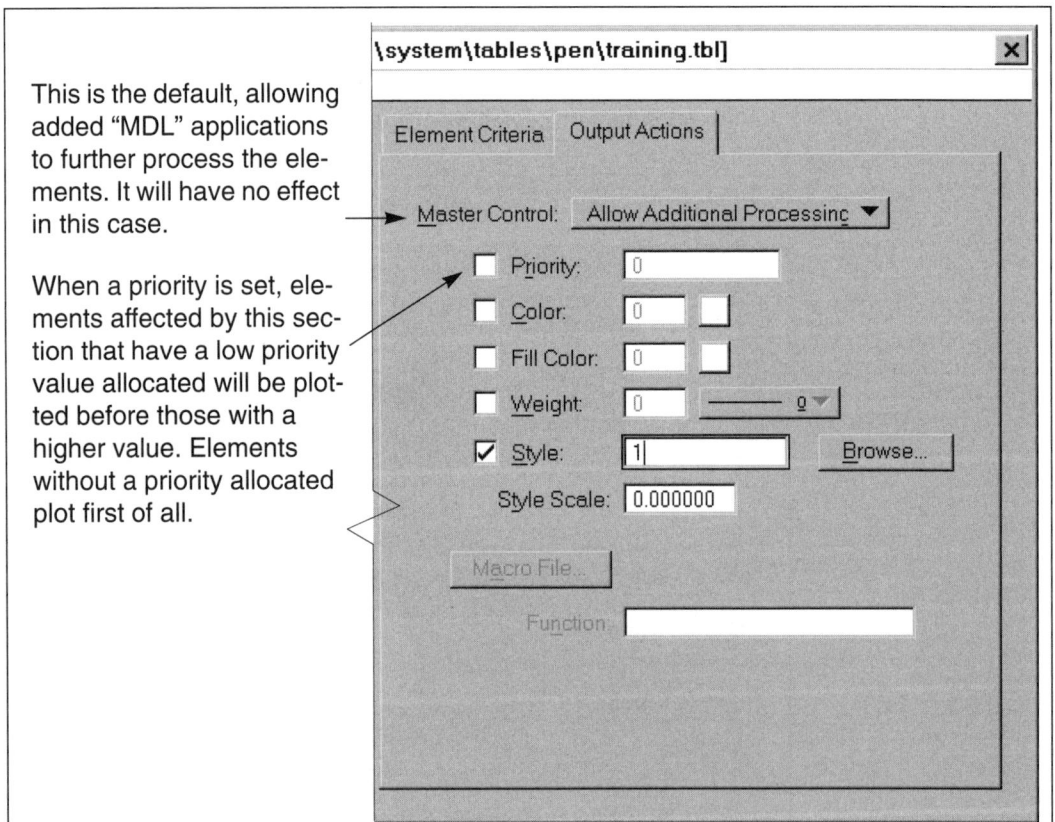

This is the default, allowing added "MDL" applications to further process the elements. It will have no effect in this case.

When a priority is set, elements affected by this section that have a low priority value allocated will be plotted before those with a higher value. Elements without a priority allocated plot first of all.

```
\system\tables\pen\training.tbl]                              ☒

  Element Criteria   Output Actions

     Master Control:   Allow Additional Processing ▼

          ☐ Priority:      [0
          ☐ Color:         [0    ] [ ]
          ☐ Fill Color:    [0    ] [ ]
          ☐ Weight:        [0    ] ——— 0 ▼
          ☑ Style:         [1|        ]        Browse...
          Style Scale:     [0.000000 ]

          Macro File..

              Function  [                    ]
```

Figure 12.17 The Output Actions for the section

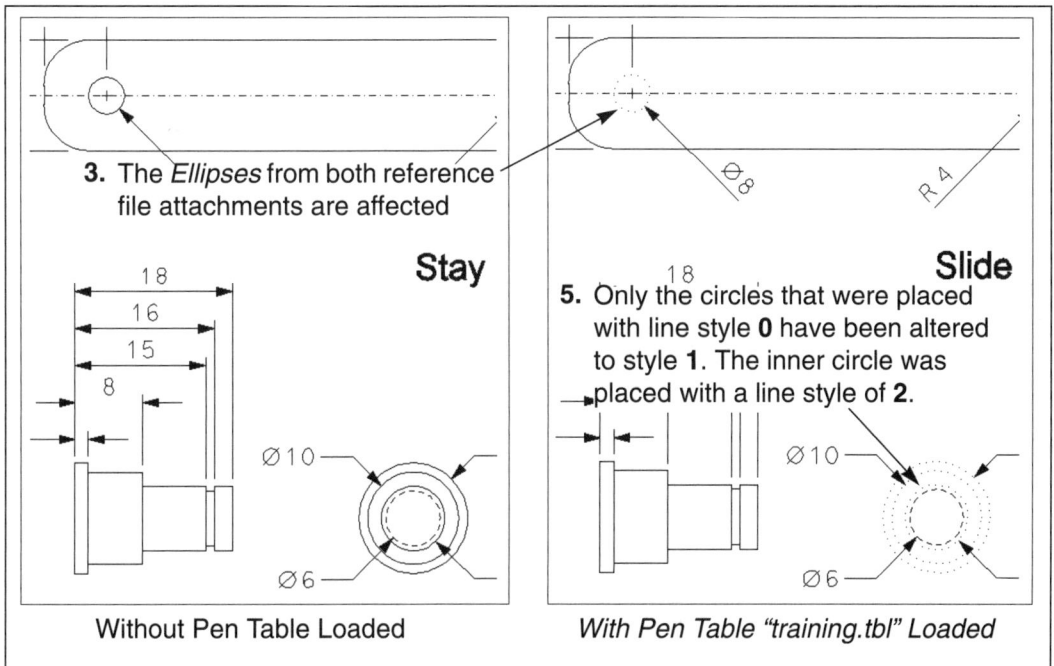

Figure 12.18   The alterations to circles made by the Pen Table

Pen Tables with more than one Section

The process of creating more sections is basically the same as for the first, but the *Order* of the sections should be considered. When we created our first section, we *Renamed* the existing (empty) section. All subsequent sections must be inserted *before* or *after* a highlighted *existing* section, these options are in the *Edit* menu.

The sections are processed in order. When the first section processed finds an element that matches its element criteria, it makes the alterations specified in its output actions. These will be the only alterations made to this element, If a later section in the processing order has an overlapping set of element evaluation criteria, it will not change the element again. Therefore, the *Processing Order* that the sections are placed in is critical.

Including a Pen Table in a Plot Configuration File

All that is necessary is to *Load* the required *Pen Table* while the *Plot Configuration File* is open, then *Save* the plot configuration file.

Element Tags

Documentation of a design is seldom purely graphical. Information such as component specifications for a mechanical services design, materials lists for a building, file information for parcels of land will all be in text form. While we can include text on the graphical design, the amount is limited. External databases of all the common types can be linked to MicroStation with the interfaces supplied, providing the potential for relating large amounts of data with elements of a design file.

Attaching *Tags* to elements does not involve the use of an external database file, but it still allows quite sophisticated linking of graphical elements with text information. Tag information may be used in the following ways:

- Displayed in the design file;
- Available for review on identifying the tagged elements;
- Compiled into reports for use in external applications;
- Provide criteria for element selection.

Defining Tag Sets

A *Tag Set* consists of a number of *Tags*, each containing data related to the element being tagged. Each *Tag* is allocated a unique *Name*, a *Data Type*, a *Display Attribute* and (optionally) a *Default Value*. A *Tag Set Definition* is comparable to a record structure in a data base, each *Tag* is comparable to a data field in that record.

Our example of tags will make use of the supplied design file "office.dgn", the file we started with in chapter 1. We will attach tags to the office plants, with data on their type, identification number, installation date and the date they are due for replacement. We will start by defining a set of tags to accept this data.

◆ Define a Tag Set for Plants

1. Open "office.dgn" from the ". . . \dgn\learning\" directory.

2. From the Application menu, select *Element>Tags>Define*.
   The *Tag Sets* settings box opens, with panels for *Sets* and *Tags*.

3. Click the *Add* button in the *Sets* panel.
   The *Tag Set Name* dialog box opens.

4. Enter the name **Plants**.

Now we have a *Tag Set* named, we will define the individual *Tags* in the set.

5. Click the *Add* button in the *Tags* panel.

   The *Define Tag* dialog box opens. If there had been other tag set names displayed in the *Sets* panel, we would have needed to select the one we wished to *Add* tags to.

6. Key in **variety** to the *Tag Name* field, <**Tab**> to the *Prompt* field, Key in **Plant Variety?**.

   The *Prompt* will display when we are attaching the tag. If we leave this field blank, the default prompt is "Value?".

7. Choose *Character* as the *Type*, *Variable* **On**, *Default* **Off**, *Display Tag* **Off**. Click **OK**.

   The first tag of the set is defined.

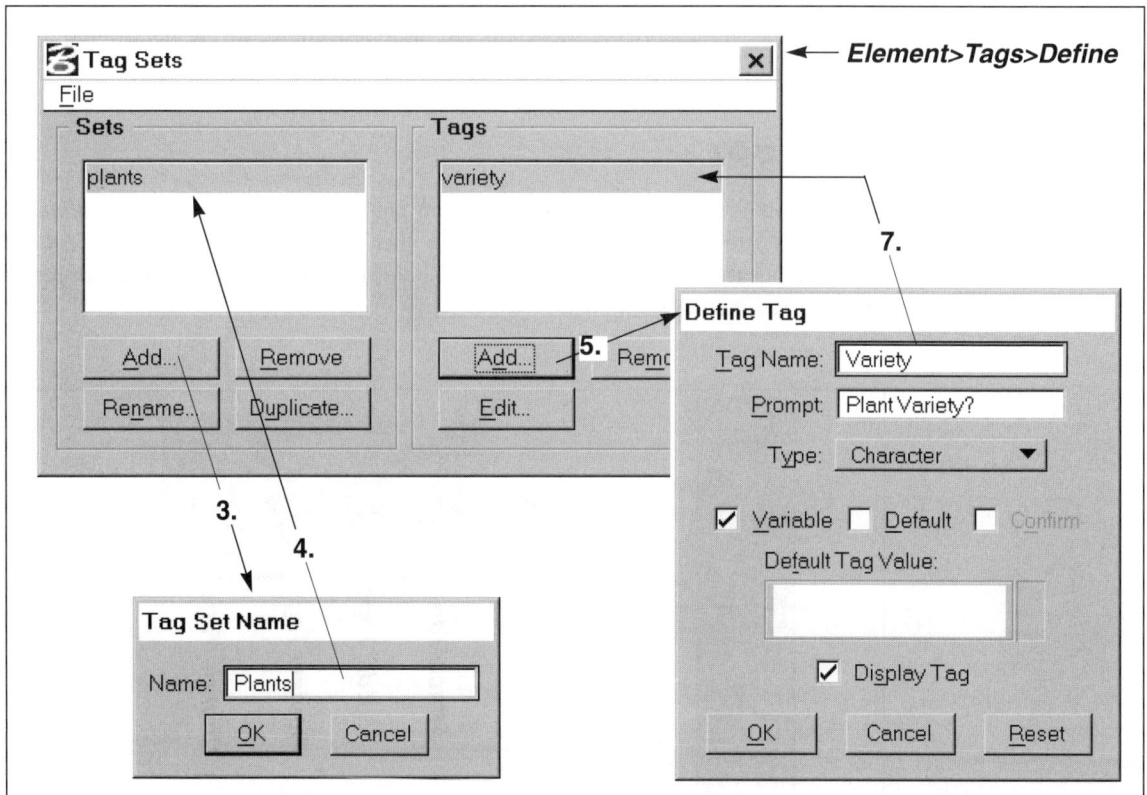

Figure 12.19   Naming a Tag Set and defining Tags

The *Default* check box and the *Default Tag Value* field enable common data values to be automatically entered, with the option of overwriting this value if necessary. This field "word wraps" if the text is too long to fit in one line and it has a scroll bar for multiple line display. Allow the word wrap, do not use the **<Enter>** key during an entry, unless carriage returns are needed in the data.

◆ **Define the other Tags**

1. Repeat steps **5.**, **6.** and **7.** of the previous exercise, except define the *Name* as **indate** and the *Prompt* as **Date installed (Mmm yyyy)?**

2. Repeat steps **5.**, **6.** and **7.** of the previous exercise again, defining the *Name:* **outdate**, the *Prompt:* **Date removal due (Mmm yyyy)?**

3. Repeat the steps again, finally define the *Name* as **ident** and the *Prompt* as **Identification number?**. Check the *Display* check box **On**, close the *Tag Sets* settings box.

We now have four *Tags* in the *Tag Set* for this particular design file. We have the option of defining more tag sets using the same procedure, we are not limited to one. Now we will see how to attach tags to elements using this *Tag Set Definition.*

The Tags Tool Box

These tools are used to work with element tags using existing *Tag Set Definitions.* The tools provide the means to *Attach* the tags to elements and to *Edit* the attachments after they have been made. The third tool provides one means of reading the data attached to an element.

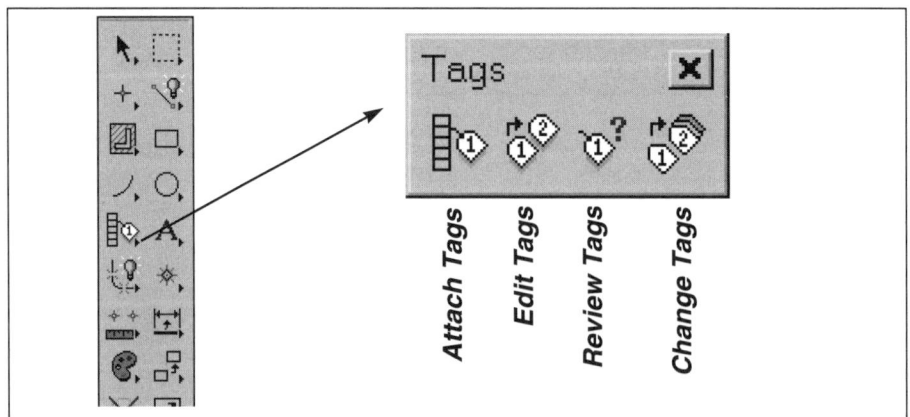

Figure 12.20   The Tags Tool Box

The Attach Tags Tool

Attaching element tags requires a tag set definition to be active. So far, we have defined only one of many tag sets that could potentially apply to this design. For this reason, the tool settings window with this tool consists entirely of a list box of *Tag Sets*. There may only be the one available for the following example, the one we have just defined.

◆ **Attach Tags to Office Plants**

1. Make *33* the *Active Level*, set the *Color* to *Red*, the *Line Weight* to *1*.

2. Open the *Text* settings box (*Element>Text*), set the *Text Height* & *Width* to *30*, *Center-Center* single-line *Justification*, select a font.

3. Select the *Attach Tag* tool, select the *Plants Tag Set* from the tool settings window.

4. Identify one of the plants in "office.dgn" with a data point, *Accept*. The *Attach Tags* dialog box opens, with *Variety* prompted for.

5. Click in the data entry field and key in a plant variety (say, **Dieffenbachia Amoena**), but **do not** press <**Enter**> at this stage (or the dialog box will close).

6. Click on the next tag name (indate), then again in the data entry field, key in a month and year (say, **Jul 1997**).

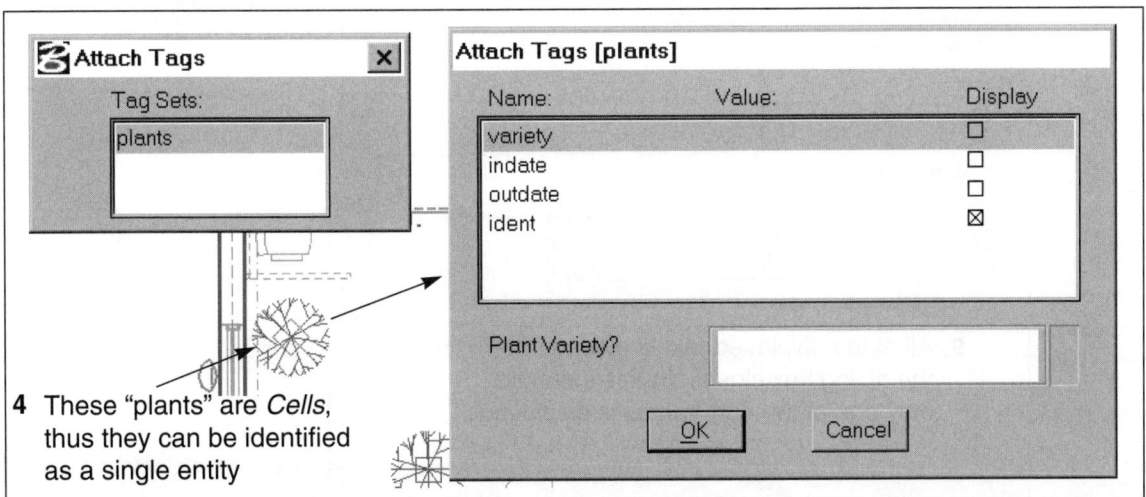

4 These "plants" are *Cells*, thus they can be identified as a single entity

Figure 12.21 The Attach Tags tool settings and dialog box

7. Click on the next tag name (outdate), then in its field, key in a month and year (say, **Jul 1999**).

8. Click on the last tag name (ident), then again in the data entry field, key in an identification number (say, **1**).

    Note that the box in the *Display* column of the list panel is checked.

9. Click **OK** or press <**Enter**> (the dialog box closes), position the displayed text, *Accept*.

The *Ident* text (**1**) will be placed with the currently active element and text attributes. Had the *Display Tag* check box been **On** when the other tags were defined, their text would also be placed now. The display may be switched on and off using the *Tags* check box in the *View Attributes* settings box.

10. Repeat steps **4.** to **9.** to attach tags to some of the other plants.

    Where a whole section highlights, the *Analyze Element* tool will reveal it is a *Nested Cell*. *Reset* and use the *Drop Element* tool (page 7-5) **once** to drop the complex status back one level of nesting.

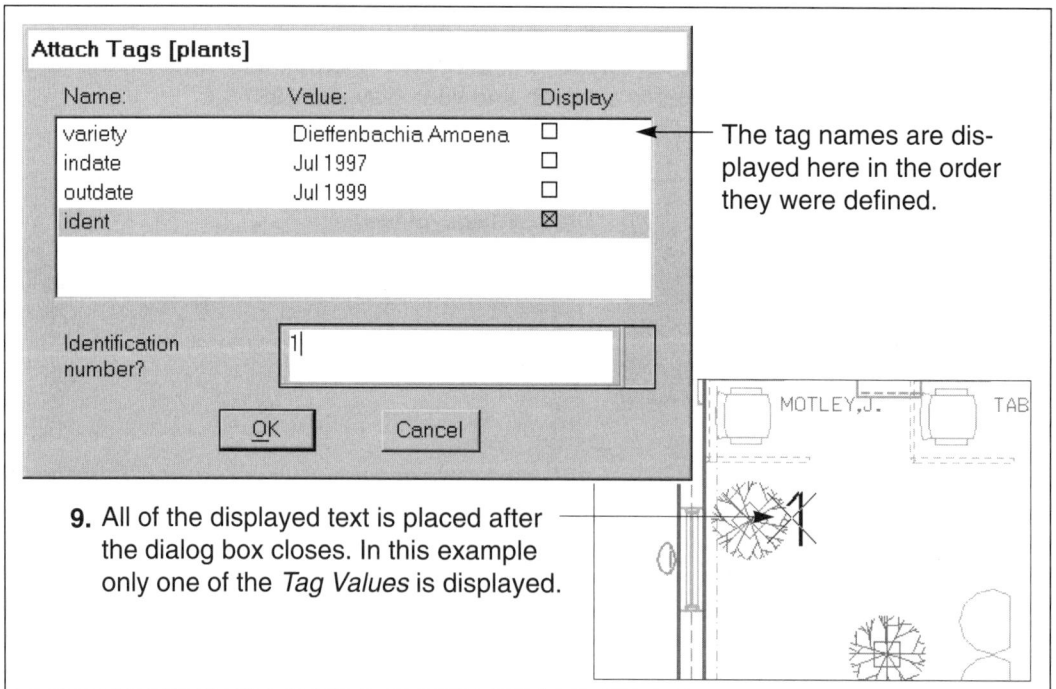

Figure 12.22   Attaching an element tag

The Edit Tags Tool

Any of the tags attached to an element may be edited. With this tool selected, identifying an element with attached tags opens the *Edit Tags* dialog box. Where tags from only one tag set are attached, the box will resemble the *Attach Tags* dialog box, operating in the same way.

Where there are tags from more than one set of tags attached to a particular element, the Edit Tags dialog box opens in two formats, the first one is a list box for selecting the *Tag Set* to edit. When we have selected a tag set from this list, the *Edit Tags* dialog box for the selected tag set opens, as in Figure 12.23.

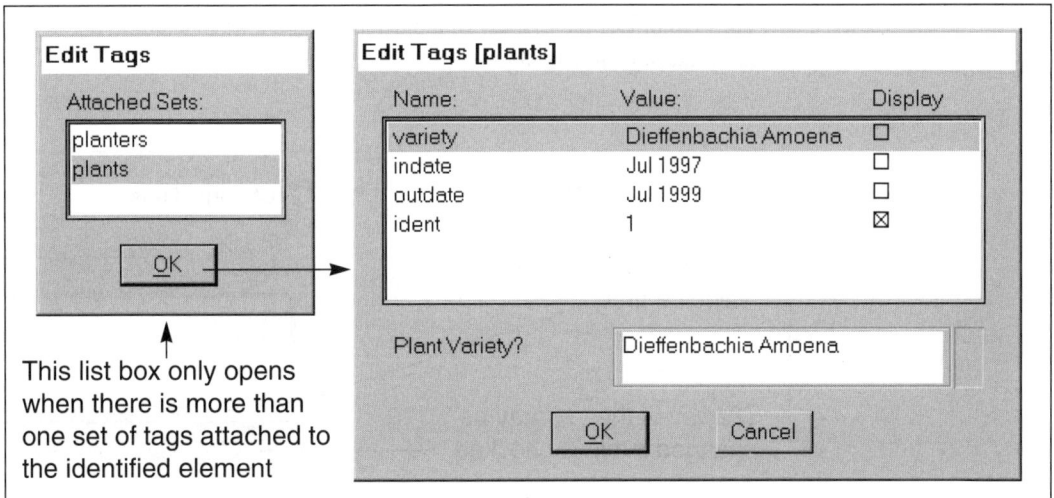

Edit Tags			
Attached Sets:			
planters			
plants			

OK

This list box only opens when there is more than one set of tags attached to the identified element

Edit Tags [plants]			
Name:	Value:		Display
variety	Dieffenbachia Amoena		☐
indate	Jul 1997		☐
outdate	Jul 1999		☐
ident	1		☒

Plant Variety?   Dieffenbachia Amoena

OK   Cancel

Figure 12.23   The Edit Tags dialog boxes

The Review Tags Tool

The only noticeable difference between the *Edit Tags* and the *Review Tags* tools is the option of changing the tag data. With this tool selected, a list box of the tag sets represented opens if the element has tags attached from more than one *Tag Set*. The dialog box that opens for the particular *Tag Set* is similar to its *Edit* equivalent, but without the data entry field and the *Cancel* button.

The Change Tags Tool

This tool is used to manipulate *Tag Values*. It differs from the *Edit Tags* tool in its method of operation. It incorporates a *Find and Replace* facility and it may operate on a *Group* of tags (as defined by a *Fence*), on the *entire Tag Set*, or on individual tags.

It may be used to:

• Search out and substitute a new value for particular tag values in a single tag, a group of tags, or all the tags in a design;

• Replace the tag value in a single tag, a group of tags, or all the tags in a design, regardless of the current value;

• Turn On or Off the display of a particular tag value in a single tag, a group of tags, or all the tags in a design.

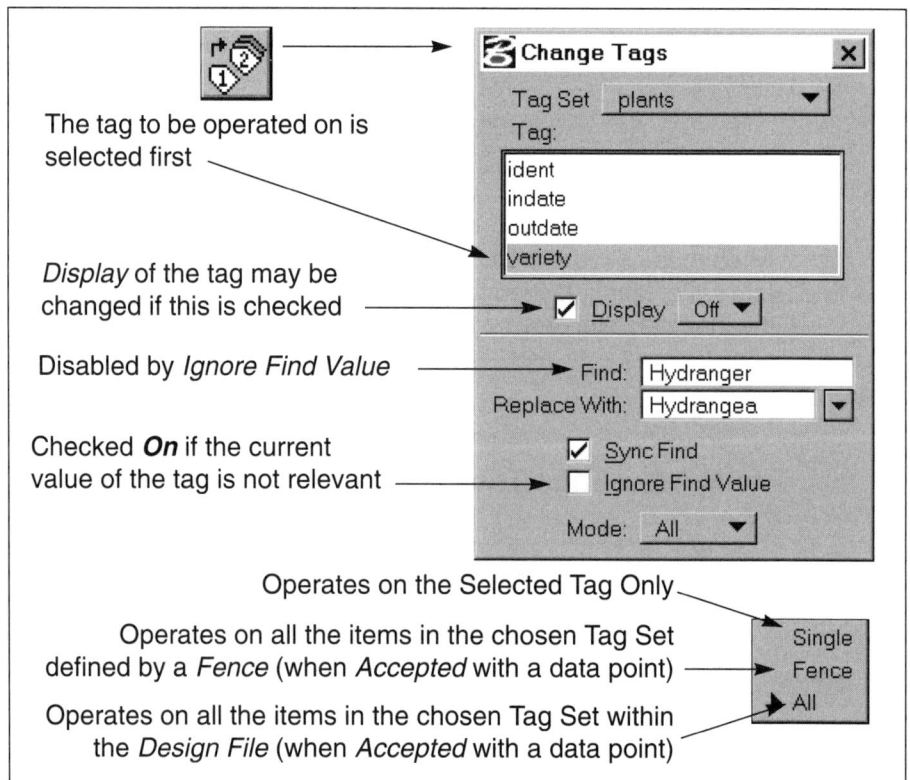

Figure 12.24   The Change Tags settings box

Tag Set Libraries

A *Tag Set Library* is a file of *Tag Set Definitions* for use in more than one design file. The tag sets we defined in "office.dgn" are already saved as part of that design, but they may be useful with other design files. If we save the definition to a library, we can use it other design files, anywhere that plants need to be managed with the help of element tags.

Creating a Tag Set Library

We create a new library file from the *File* menu of the *Tag Sets* settings box, the same settings box used to define our "plants" tag set on page 12-24. A single library file may contain a number of tag definitions. However, it is created with one tag definition to start with, then others may be appended later. The directory is optional, the default is ". . . \out\" and the filename extension is ".tlb", as shown in Figure 12.25.

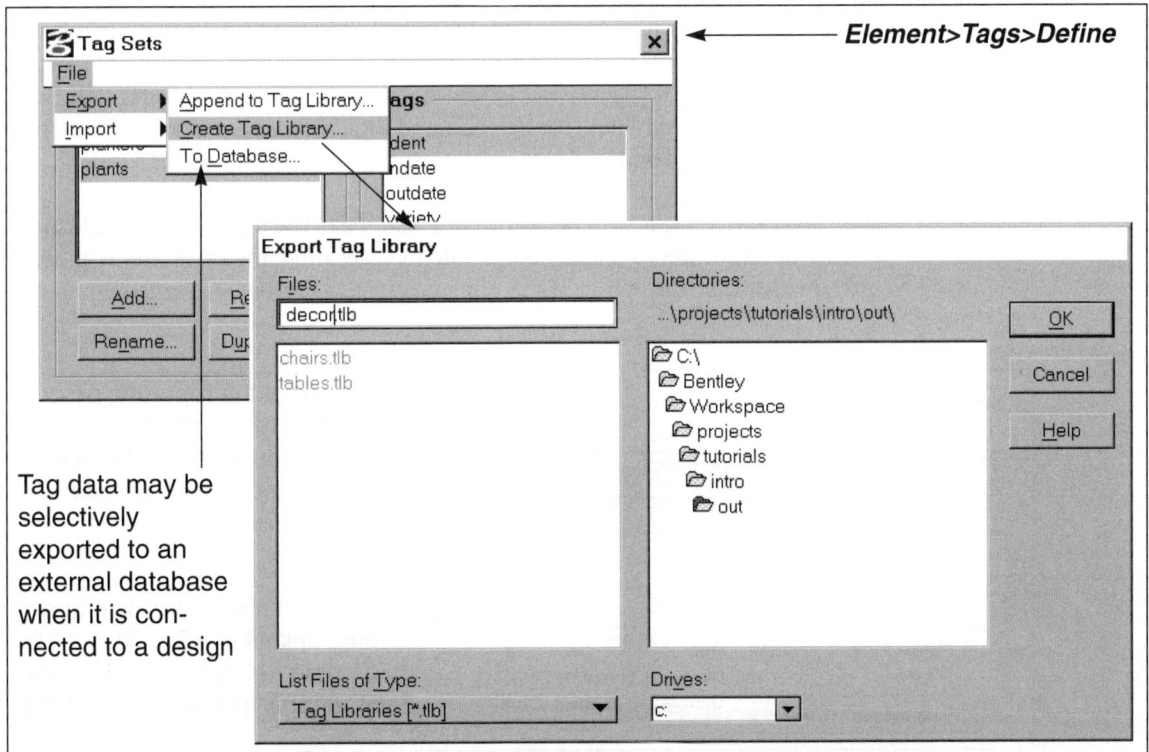

Figure 12.25 Creating a new Tag Set Library

Appending Tag Set Definitions to a Library

The *Tag Set Library* is created with a selected definition already stored in it. The procedure for appending more tag set definitions is basically similar to the *Create* process. The definition to be appended is selected in the *Tag Sets* settings box and the *Export Tag Library* dialog box is opened, this time by choosing *File>Export>Append to Tag Library* from the settings box menu.

Importing a Tag Set Definitions from a Library

To use a previously defined and saved *Tag Set Definition* in a design file, we again open the *Tag Sets* settings box. We then choose *Import* from the settings box *File* menu to open the *Open Tag Library* dialog box. A tag set definition is selected from this box, which resembles the *Export Tag Library* box illustrated in Figure 12.25 in all but the title.

Generating Reports on Tags

Reports on tags are output in the form of comma-delimited ASCII text files. This file format is an industry-wide standard that can be imported directly into external applications such as databases, spreadsheets and word processors. The set of elements reported on may be the entire design file, or a number of elements temporarily grouped with a *Fence* or by multiple *Element Selection*.

The contents of a tag *Report* is defined in a *Template*. The report may include the text of any, or all, of the tags attached to a defined set of elements. Along with the tag text, we also have the option of reporting on element attribute information.

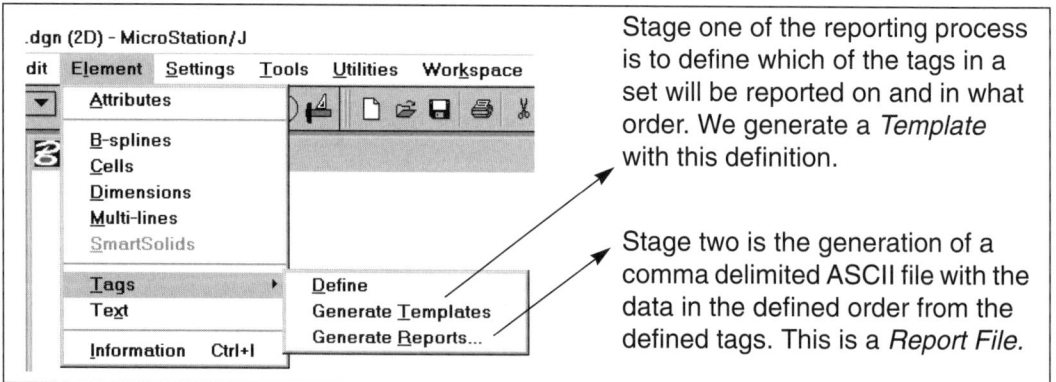

Stage one of the reporting process is to define which of the tags in a set will be reported on and in what order. We generate a *Template* with this definition.

Stage two is the generation of a comma delimited ASCII file with the data in the defined order from the defined tags. This is a *Report File.*

Figure 12.26   The Stages of creating a Tag Report

Tag Report Template Files

We create these files to specify the contents of the reports to be generated. The specification consists of the tag set to be reported on, the tags and any graphical element attributes to be included in the report. These files are created using the *Generate Templates* settings box (see Figure 12.27), opened from the application window *Element* menu by choosing *Tags>Generate Templates*.

The settings box has a *File* menu with the options of opening an existing template that has been saved to a ".tmp" file. The other options are to save a template that has been changed and to *Save As* a new file name for creating a new template. The other menu, *Report On*, has the options of reporting on *All Elements* in the grouping, or only those with tags attached (the default).

◆Generate a Template for a report on tagged plants

1. With "office.dgn" open, choose *Element>Tags>Generate Template* to open the *Generate Templates* dialog box.

2. Select the settings illustrated in Figure 12.27.

3. Choose *Tagged Elements* from the settings box *Report On* menu.

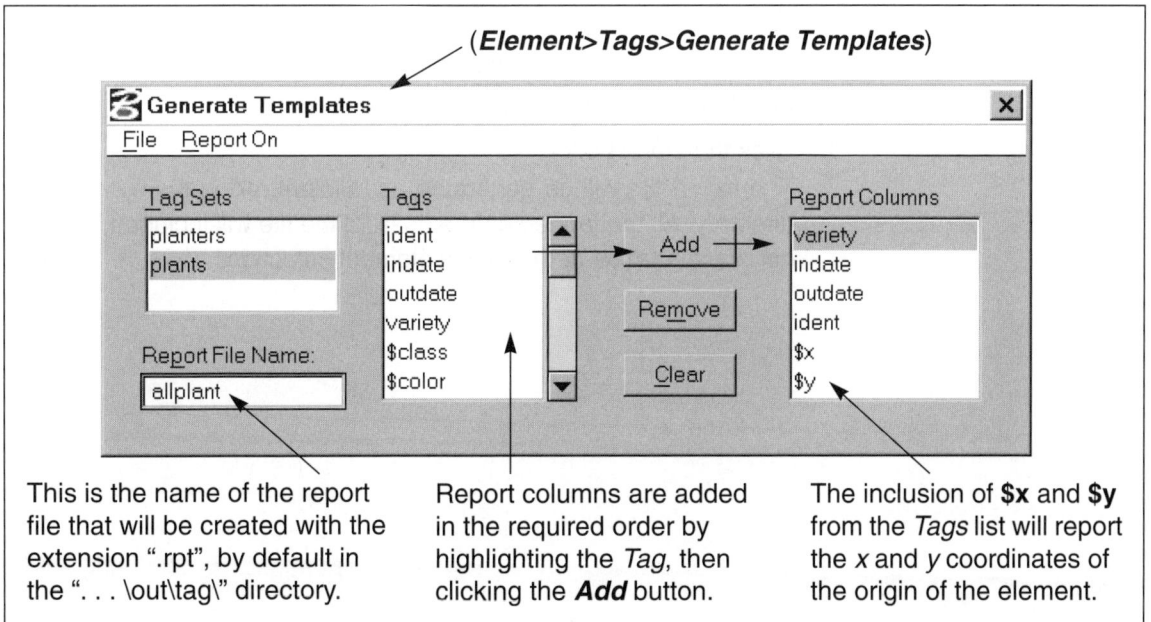

(Element>Tags>Generate Templates)

Generate Templates   ✕

File   Report On

Tag Sets	Tags		Report Columns
planters	ident	Add	variety
plants	indate		indate
	outdate	Remove	outdate
	variety		ident
Report File Name:	$class	Clear	$x
allplant	$color		$y

This is the name of the report file that will be created with the extension ".rpt", by default in the ". . . \out\tag\" directory.

Report columns are added in the required order by highlighting the *Tag*, then clicking the **Add** button.

The inclusion of **$x** and **$y** from the *Tags* list will report the *x* and *y* coordinates of the origin of the element.

Figure 12.27   Generating a Template for a tag report

4. Choose *Save As* from the settings box *File* menu, enter the file name "plantrep" to the *Save Template As* dialog box.

5. Close the *Generate Templates* settings box.

Tag Report Files

Most of the work towards generating report files is completed in the template generation process. To generate the report itself, it only remains to define the set of elements to be reported on and the template to use. The default set of elements is the entire design file. We can limit the extent of the set by placing a *Fence* about the elements we are interested in, or by using the *Element Selection* tool to make multiple selections.

The *Generate Reports* dialog box is opened from the application window *Element* menu by choosing *Tags>Generate Reports*. The only setting to make is the addition of one or more *Template* files to a template list. Each template has its own *Report File Name*, thus there will be multiple report files generated when more than one template is on the list.

◆**Generate a Report File on all the tagged plants in "office.dgn"**

1. Choose *Element>Tags>Generate Reports* to open the *Generate Reports* dialog box.

2. Select "plantrep.tmp" in the *Files* list panel, click the **Add** button to add this to the *Templates for Reports* list panel.

3. Click the *Done* button.
   The report file will be generated as "allplant.rpt" in the ". . . \out\tag\" directory. All the tagged elements from the file will included, as we did not place a fence or make any element selections.

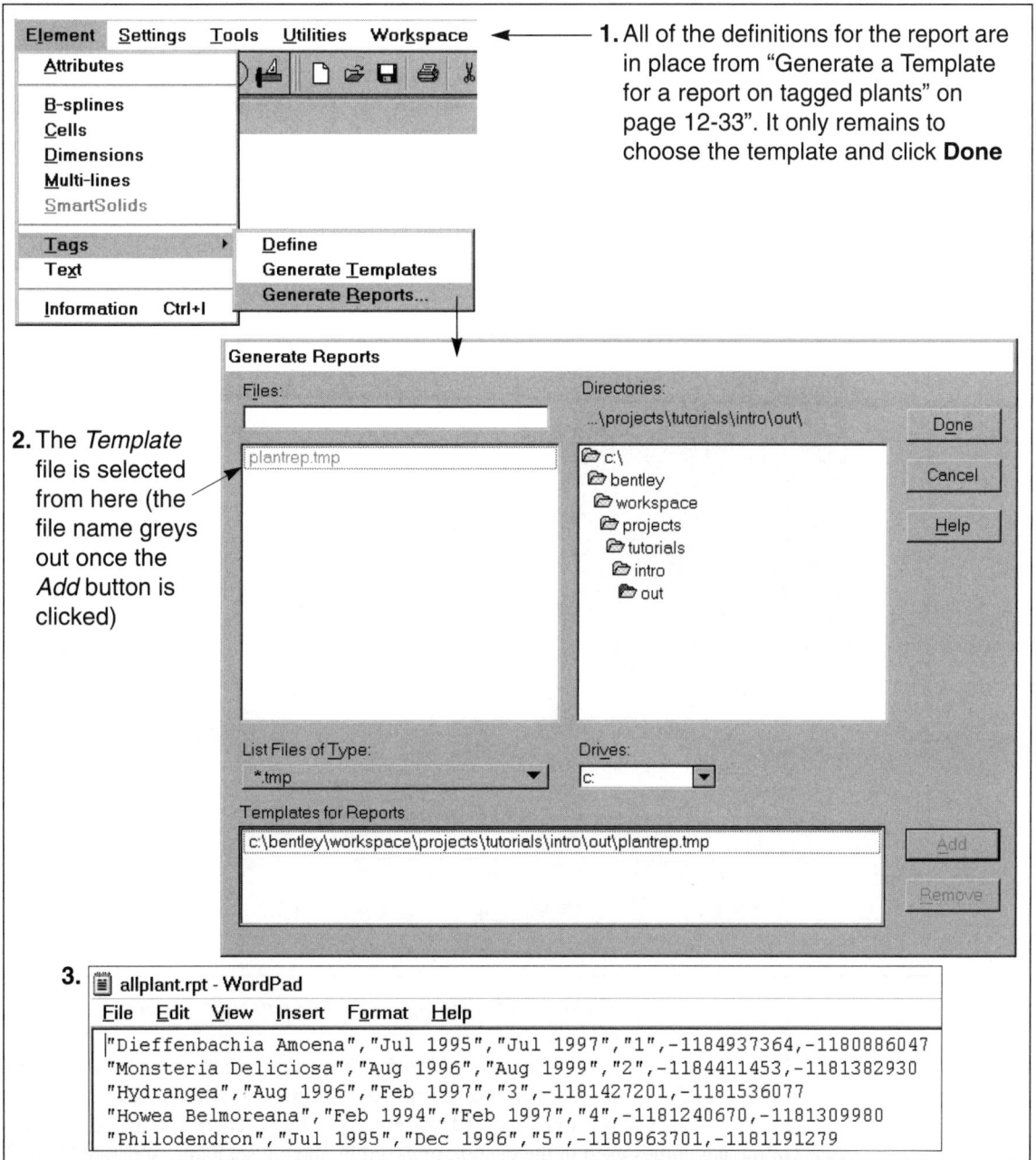

1. All of the definitions for the report are in place from "Generate a Template for a report on tagged plants" on page 12-33". It only remains to choose the template and click **Done**

2. The *Template* file is selected from here (the file name greys out once the *Add* button is clicked)

```
Element   Settings   Tools   Utilities   Workspace
    Attributes
    B-splines
    Cells
    Dimensions
    Multi-lines
    SmartSolids

    Tags              ►    Define
    Text                   Generate Templates
                           Generate Reports...
    Information   Ctrl+I
```

Generate Reports

Files:

Directories:
...\projects\tutorials\intro\out\

plantrep.tmp

```
c:\
  bentley
    workspace
      projects
        tutorials
          intro
            out
```

Done

Cancel

Help

List Files of Type:
*.tmp

Drives:
c:

Templates for Reports
c:\bentley\workspace\projects\tutorials\intro\out\plantrep.tmp

Add

Remove

3. allplant.rpt - WordPad

File   Edit   View   Insert   Format   Help

```
"Dieffenbachia Amoena","Jul 1995","Jul 1997","1",-1184937364,-1180886047
"Monsteria Deliciosa","Aug 1996","Aug 1999","2",-1184411453,-1181382930
"Hydrangea","Aug 1996","Feb 1997","3",-1181427201,-1181536077
"Howea Belmoreana","Feb 1994","Feb 1997","4",-1181240670,-1181309980
"Philodendron","Jul 1995","Dec 1996","5",-1180963701,-1181191279
```

Figure 12.28   The Generate Reports dialog box, with a sample ASCII report file

Selecting Elements by Tag Values

The *Select By Attributes* facility from the Application window *Edit* menu selects elements according to defined selection criteria. *Tag* values may be included in these criteria. The *Select By Attributes* settings box is shown in Figure 12.29. The default settings (as shown) will select elements all types with all symbologies and on any level, but for now we are mainly interested in the *Tags* options.

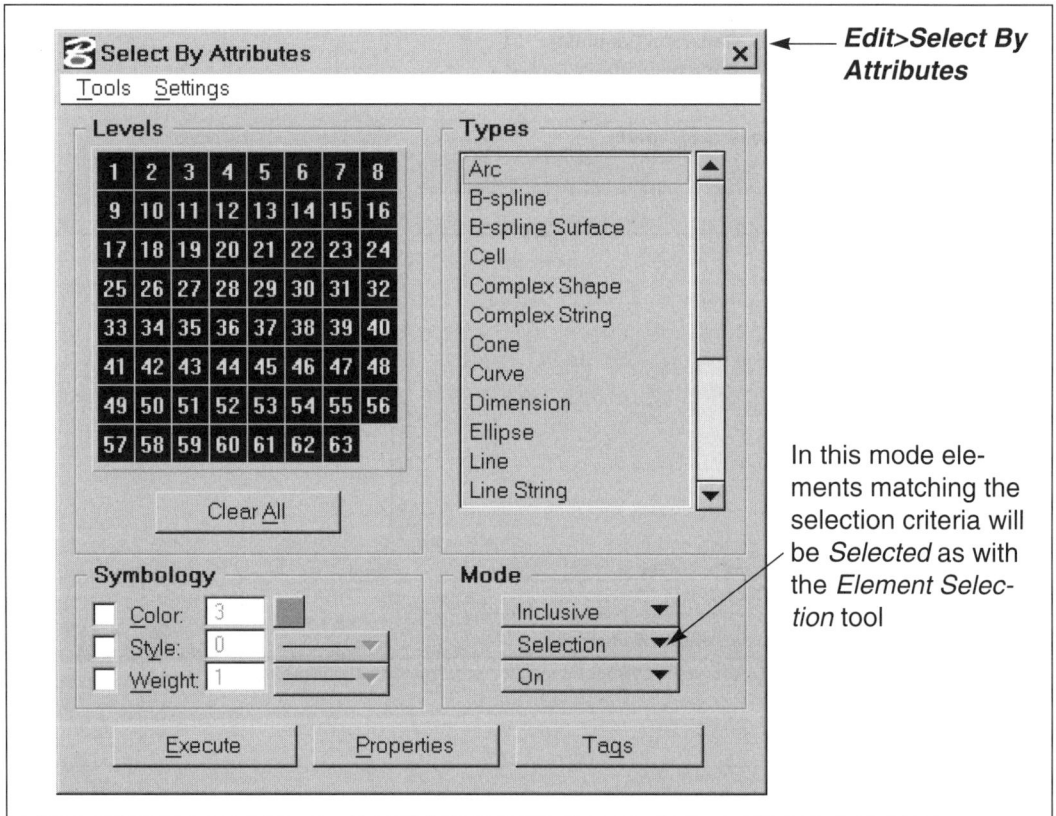

Figure 12.29   The Select By Attributes settings box

When we click the *Tag* button the *Select By Tags* settings box opens, as illustrated in Figure 12.30. This settings box allows the setting of criteria based on logical combinations of tag values, as well as on single values. There is a list panel with all of the tag names used in the design, prefixed by the tag set name, separated by a dot. The other list panel in the top section provides a selection of *Operators* such as "Greater than or equal to", "Equal to" etc.

Still in the top section, there is a data entry field for an expression for the selected tag to be compared to, using the selected operator. In the case of text type values, as in our example, the expression will be a text string that may be found in the tags. The operator will generally be "equal to".

Once we have a *Tag*, an *Operator* and an *Expression*, we click the *Insert* button to include the combination in the *Criteria* list. We can insert more criteria in a similar way, selecting either of the logic operator buttons *And* or *Or* after each one to combine the criteria as required. Clicking the *Execute* button in the *Select By Attributes* settings box will result in all of the tagged elements matching the selection criteria being selected. Once selected, they could be used in any way we like, including generating exclusive tag reports.

Another option is to choose *Display* instead of *Selection* in the *Select By Attributes* settings box. This will turn off the display of all but the selected elements. The display will remain off until the settings box is closed and *Cancel* clicked in the alert box that displays.

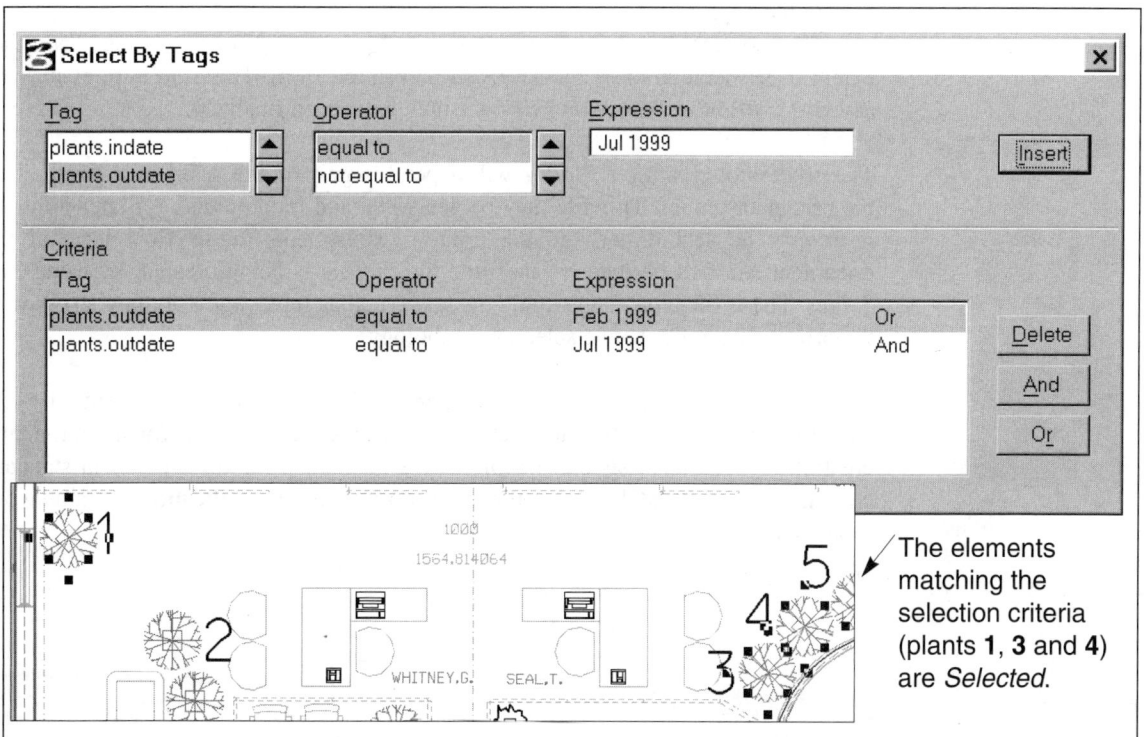

Figure 12.30   Select by Tags criteria

Summary

The preparation of a design for output fall into three main areas, Reference file use, printing scale considerations and the amount of the design file to be printed. Reference files will almost certainly be used in all but the simplest documentation. The decisions about the structure of reference file attachments will need to be based on the requirements of the project and the organization. While the details will vary to a large extent, the basic system of attaching design detail to an "electronic drawing sheet" will usually be the most efficient.

Printing scale considerations are best taken into account from early in the design process. If it is intended that the same basic geometry will be used at different scales, the placing of finer the details on different levels to the broader design may be required. Text and dimensioning element sizes will have to be chosen to suit the final scale, but this may all be done on the "drawing sheet" in some cases. Defining level symbology settings may also be useful (especially for line weights) when producing drawings with different scales from the same design files.

Still in the preparation stages, we need to define the extent of the file to be printed out. The area may be defined by a fence or by a view window outline. The other extent to be decided on is the levels to be printed from. These definitions may be saved as a *Plot Configuration File* once they have been finalized.

The process of creating a *Plotfile* will depend largely on the destination for the file, the printer or plotter. This file may be generated and filed on disk for later printout, or it may be sent directly to the printer. Adjustments to the final form of the document can still be made at the time the Plotfile is being created, by using *Pen Tables*. These files may substitute new text (such as replacing a dummy string with the printout date) or change selected symbology.

Element Tags are a method of attaching non-graphic data to design elements. Typical uses for this data may be for assets and facilities management, for the automatic creation of materials lists etc. *Report* files generated from tag data are in standard comma-delimited ASCII format for inclusion in external applications such as word processors.

Index